CW01019538

CRUISERS, CORSAIRS & SLAVERS

1. The Capture of the slaver *Opposicao* by H.M.S. *Pearl*, commanded by Lord Clarence Paget.

From a painting by W. A. Knell in the National Maritime Museum. [*Frontispiece.*

CRUISERS, CORSAIRS & SLAVERS

An Account of the Suppression of the Picaroon, Pirate & Slaver by the Royal Navy during the 19th Century

By BASIL LUBBOCK

BROWN, SON & FERGUSON, LTD.
4-10 DARNLEY STREET, GLASGOW, G41 2SD
1993

First Edition 1993

ISBN 0 85174 593 8

Made and Printed in Great Britain

By the same author

THE CHINA CLIPPERS
THE COLONIAL CLIPPERS
THE LOG OF THE *CUTTY SARK*
THE LAST OF THE WINDJAMMERS, Vol. I
THE LAST OF THE WINDJAMMERS, Vol. II
THE BLACKWALL FRIGATES
THE DOWN EASTERS
THE OPIUM CLIPPERS
THE NITRATE CLIPPERS
THE ARCTIC WHALERS
COOLIE SHIPS AND OIL SAILERS
THE WESTERN OCEAN PACKETS
ROUND THE HORN BEFORE THE MAST
BULLY HAYES — SOUTH SEA PIRATE

PREFACE

I have compiled this chronology of Naval actions against the picaroon, pirate and slaver of the nineteenth century for three reasons.

In the first place I wish to show the modern generation of sailors how their ancestors carried on their 'lawful occasions'.

In these days of trust in the machine the human element is in some danger of losing its power of initiative, and that spirit of dash and enterprise, which should compose the ground tier of every naval officer.

Admiral of the Fleet, Sir George Keyes tells us in his memoirs that there were two schools of thought in the Royal Navy during the Great War—the 'material' school and what I will call the 'do and dare' school. By the end of the war, officers who had followed out the tenets of the latter school were to be found at the head of things—in every fleet, on every station, through every clime they were the leaders of the King's Navy!

But in peace time the lessons of war tend to be forgotten and specialists in the complicated machinery of the modern war engine gradually slip into all the best jobs, whilst the all round sailor, who may possess the gift of command and that priceless Nelson touch—that spice of nerve and daring, which must be met at the bottom of every successful action, is liable to miss his chance through lack of opportunity.

At the same time, many a clever and promising officer is led away from the executive into the soul-deadening den of the scientific expert, where he loses his individual personality in familiarizing himself with the mathematical symbols of astronomy and physics, the combinations and coefficients of machinery, the abstractions and permutations of the master gunner, the chemical formulae of the gas man and the delicate explosive forces of the mine and torpedo man.

Yet there is nothing in mechanics that the most moderate brain cannot grasp, and only practise is needed to make one perfect in the most complicated engine of destruction, whereas the command of men and of ships needs every virtue of the spirit, every effort of the mind and all the strength of the body, and when these attributes are present, on top of them, full years of rich experience.

In the following pages the reader will find countless examples of superb leadership and, I hope, will gain a very good idea of why the British Navy became such a power in the world.

My second reason for this book is my desire to trace the development of the ship of war, especially in the smaller, more hard-worked, if less spectacular, classes, from the time of Nelson down to the appearance of the first armour-clad battleship.

This takes in a period when ship speed was becoming of the first consideration, when the paddle and the screw were slowly ousting canvas, wire and chain conquering hemp and manila and iron plates and rivets being seriously suggested as a substitute for the frames, beams and planking of oak, teak and pine, which for a thousand years had been the material; composing Britannia's Wooden Walls.

It was also a time of iron discipline and that smartness in sail drill, which produced the most athletic, not to say acrobatic, sailor the world has ever known.

Lastly no attempt has ever been made to drag the gallant record of the Royal Navy, in its hard task of suppressing the pirate and the slaver, from the musty shelves of the Admiralty and the Public Record Office.

This has badly needed doing and I only wish someone with greater skill and knowledge than myself could have been induced to attempt it.

BASIL LUBBOCK

CONTENTS

LIST OF ILLUSTRATIONS

CHAPTER I

INTRODUCTION

"The King's Navy exceeds all others in the world for three things, viz:- beauty, strength, and safety. For Beauty, there are so many Royal Palaces; For Strength, so many moving castles and barbicans: And for Safety they are the most defensive Walls of the realm. Among the ships of other nations, they are like Lion's amongst Silly Beasts, or Falcons amongst Fearful Fowl".
(Lord Coke's Fourth Institute)

Our Sea Heritage

MORE great families in the British Commonwealth of nations have been founded by sailors than by any other profession or calling.

Salt water courses through the veins of all of us. Our whole literature is redolent of the sea. Our whole speech is full of nautical expressions. We have salt water ballads, sea songs and chanties galore; a sailor poet laureate and sailor novelists of world wide fame. And yet the published work of our naval historians has scarce done more than 'holystone the quarterdeck', though the senior service has a record of glorious achievement second to none. Victories are scattered through its pages like plums in a spendthrift's duff and the names of great admirals are familiar to every schoolboy. Yet who remembers the grey-haired, war-worn first lieutenant, the old sea-wise mate or the cut-and-thrust senior mid.

Ships of the Line, too, and cracked frigates have their names emblazoned on England's roll of fame, but who remembers the small fry, the gun brigs, the war schooners and revenue cutters, whose work was often as spectacular, as bravely done, as that of any battle ship or lordly frigate.

For they were the policement of the seas. They hunted the pirate out of his snug anchorage. They chased the smuggler out of the lonely cove. And it was the sloop and gunbrig, which brought the slaver to book.

A Heroic Page of Naval History

There is no more heroic page in the history of the Royal Navy than which tells of its efforts to suppress the horrible traffic in human lives, which was carried on from the surf-swept beaches, pestilential creeks and jungle-banked rivers of the East and West Africa during the greater part of the nineteenth century. Yet, though the literature on the slave trade must run to hundreds of volumes, no attempts, except in a few little-read Naval officers memoirs, have been made to shoe the part played by the Royal Navy in its suppression.

No war lasted as long as this campaign of mercy.
And its casualties were indeed heavy.

"Beware, oh, beware of the Bight of Benin.
Few come out, though many go in!"

If you follow the coast line from Cape Verd to Cape Frio and from Delagoa Bay to Cape Guardafui; amongst the bones of myriads of negroes, which pave the sea floor, your diver would find many a sparkling crown and anchor button. With the microbe undiscovered and the mosquito considered harmless, what wonder if the saviours of the slave paid for his salvation with their own health and even life.

If service on the Coast of Africa brought promotion and prize money in days of piping peace; too often the promotion ended a promising career and the prize money was swallowed up by a doctor's bill.

Great Britain took up the work of emancipating slaves and surpressing the slave trade at a time when she was engaged on every sea on the world war at the end of the eighteenth century and early years of the nineteenth, when she was fighting for the whole of Europe against the Napoleonic Terror; our fleets, our cruisers, even our revenue cutters and the smallest of national ships, were being worked to the bone from Spitzbergen to the Horn, from the Bay of Bengal to the Gulf of Mexico, from the River Plate to the Yellow Sea and were even hiring Newcastle collier brigs and Bristol sugar wagons to act as convoys to merchantmen, yet when the Government approached the Admiralty with the suggestion that a squadron should be sent the coast of Africa for this new task of stopping the conveyance of African negroes to the West Indies and the Americas, the Sea Lords confidently replied:—"Outlaw the brute, give us the right of capture and prize money, and we will soon rid the world of this scourge".

Little did either the British Government or the Admiralty realize the new war in which they were embarking.

At first, in the midst of a stupendous war, the work of a Commodore in a frigate, with a gun brig and a couple of hired schooners, seemed amply sufficient to keep the trade in slaves from the West Coast of Africa in subjection. Whilst our cruisers in the West Indies were only too glad to add slavers to their list of enemy ships, which with the extinguishing of French and Spanish trade to the Caribbees, was almost entirely composed of picaroons and pirates, letters of Marque and privateers.

A Campaign of Over A Hundred Years

The Royal Navy's campaign against slavery, which began in 1807, lasted for well over a hundred years. (Note the last capture of a slave dhow with slaves on board was made by H.M.S. *Cornflower* in June 1922).

On the West Coast of Africa from a frigate, a brig and a couple of Colonial (Sierra Leone) schooners the squadron was gradually increased year by year, until by 1850 it consisted on some thirty vessels, half of them steamers.

But it is only fair to remember that during the war the Bights of Benin and Biafra shipped nearly ninety per cent of the slaves sent across the Atlantic, whereas in 1850 the coast from Cape Verd to twenty degrees South had to be watched and every one of its countless river mouths continually visited and blockaded.

On the East Coast of Africa a flourishing Portuguese slave trade in the Mozambique Channel was supplemented by an equally successful Arab trade, which extended from Quilimane or even as far south as Lorenzo Marquez, right away to the Persian Gulf.

It was not only on the Coast of Africa that British cruisers found need for activity; the length and breadth of the West Indies, from the Great Bahama Bank as far south as the Dutch Islands, had to be watched, not to mention the South American coast from Maranhao to the La Plata.

Tiny war schooners, such as the *Pickle*, the *Nimble*, and the *Monkey*, the *Skipjack* and the *Speedwell*, brought prizes of twice and three times their size into the Havana to the fury of the hostile Cuban population.

At Rio de Janeiro the same thing happened; Brazilian coffee merchants, who depended on slave labour, had the mortification of watching their consignments of slaves taken from them by rakish R.N. brigantines like the *Dolphin* and the *Dart*, or haughty brig-sloops such as the *Frolic*.

It was a war, indeed, not only against the slavers themselves, but against the African chiefs who supplied the barracoons in the slave rivers with negroes; against the powerful slave-merchants such as De Souza of Whydah, Mongo John of Bangalang in the Rio Pongas, Pedro Blanco of the Gallinas, and Theodore Canot of New Florence; and even against Spanish and Portuguese Colonial Governors and officers of authority, who in spite of treaties, were generally heavily interested financially in the trade.

Spithead in War and Peace

When peace came after the long years of naval warfare, the Royal Navy found itself the first object of the British Government's attention, in the sudden pressing need for economy. Half its ships were laid up.

"Portsmouth is a very different place from what it was in the height of the war, and Spithead cuts a very shabby appearance with three colliers, two indiamen, a convict ship, an American packet and two or three yachts riding there in comparison to the spectacle it used to exhibit when twenty or thirty sail of the Line and a dozen frigates, crowded round the buoy of the *Royal George* and emulated each other in the celerity of their movements, the magic of their discipline, the symmetry of their appearance and withal in the matchless efficiency of their power of action at the moment of need".

So wrote the correspondent of the United Service Journal.

By 1817 only twenty-one frigates out of one hundred and six remained in commission; corvettes in commission were cut down to nine and ship-sloops to five; Whilst of that favourite and hard worked class the eighteen gun-brigs, only seventeen remained in Commission out of sixty-seven. Even the little ten-gun brigs, called by their admirers 'the tinnys' and by their detractors 'the coffin-brigs' only had fourteen kept in commission.

In 1816 the Admiralty had two hundred and forty seven ships in Commission and even this was a great drop compared with the Nelson period; a year later there were only one hundred and fourteen.

This meant more than half the commissioned ranks on half pay, and for as the old Nelsonian man of war's man, thousands of these were begging their bread. A few years after the peace, there was a line of beggars, stretching from Liverpool to London. These were all old soldiers and old sailors, selling trifles of curios made with their own skilful hands or singing naval choruses and 'Come all ye's'. Only officers with pull or political influence could obtain employment—promotion was, of course, brought to a full stop; and grey haired midshipmen were to be seen blacking boots on Portsmouth hard.

Many smart lieutenants took service under foreign flags, donned the expensive uniform of the Honourable East India Company, or even took the job of a mate in a West Indiaman.

Their lament for the old days is thus voiced in the Naval Sketch Book:—

'As sure as a gun
We shall all be undone
If longer continue the peace;
A top we shan't know
From a futlock below
Nor a block from a bucket of grease!

When young Dalrymple Hay was about to join his first ship in 1834, Admiral Sir F. Maitland thus addressed him:—

"You are a great fool for going to sea: go home again: There are over four thousand lieutenants and twelve hundred mates and midshipmen, and it is impossible that you can ever hope to be a lieutenant before you are thirty years of age".

It will thus be seen that the coming of peace produced real hardship in the Senior Service.

The Picaroon Turns Pirate and Slaver

Then just when the Royal Navy seemed to be in danger of being forgotten by the British Nation and choleric admirals and stiff-necked post-captains were loudly complaining that the service was going to the dogs—out of the blue came new work with more than a spice of danger and even some hopes of prize money.

For peace brought a tremendous lift up not only top British trade but to all foreign trade. Once more Cuba could sell all the sugar and tobacco she could grow. Once more there was a great demand for the coffee and other products of the Brazil plantations.

Then both Cuba and Brazil called loudly for negro labour—the price of slaves went sky high. Brigs, brigantines, polaccas, two-topsail and fore-top sail schooners, and feluccas, seaworth or otherwise, set off for the African Coast—these were mostly commanded by out of work privateermen, those of them who had not already turned pirate and joined Lafitte or Gasperilla or one of the numerous corsairs who lurked behind the Cuban reefs.

And what with half the French and Spanish privateersmen turned pirate and the other half into Guinea Captains, it was soon found that our West Indian and West African Squadrons needed doubling and trebling. The demand, however, was not for frigates and much less for battle ships; even corvettes and ship-sloops were on the big size for chasing shallow drafts pirates and slavers amongst the coral reefs and shoals of Cuba and the cays of the Bahama Bank.

Again upon the Coast of Africa a frigate's tall spars could be seen like warning towers sticking up above the blue horizon. Nor could any warship of sixteen foot draft and over get across the bars of the African rivers.

The Need for Speedy Small Fry

Thus it came to pass that there was a great need for small fry, brigs and schooners. Curiously enough though we had many fine revenue cutters employed against the smugglers round our coasts, this type of craft was never used against the African slaver, except in one instance, that of the *Windflower*, a cutter designed and built by the West African Commodore himself. In order to supply this need for small craft, the Admiralty began supplementing the old twelve-gun Pelter brigs by larger ten-gun brigs on the lines of the old Rolla. But neither of these classes proved able to overtake the clipper-lined Baltimore built schooners and brigs, which formed the greater number of the vessels employed in the slave trade; and this led to the new interest in ship design from a speed point of view, which was soon animating the British Admiralty.

But before we soon proceed to deal with this fascinating subject of ship design, I will attempt to give a picture of the personnel of the service and to show how the naval type maintained those sea-bred characteristics for which it was famed in spite of changing times and changing materials.

The Mark of the Sea

The naval officer, who fought the pirate and the slaver of the nineteenth century, differed but little from the Nelson type.

In the days of our Wooden Walls the sea laid its mark upon its followers in a very much clearer fashion than it does at the present time, when all men, whether landsmen or sailors, through constant rubbing of shoulders, tend to conform to a general mould.

There was no need to note the epaulets, or the middies' dirk, the boatswain's pipe or the seaman's kerchief, the outward bearing of the seafarer—the 'cut of his jib', to use an old sailorly expression, gave an instant clue to his rank or rating.

By the time the naval officer had reached the top rung of promotion's ladder, his character, if not his appearance, became more or less stereotyped and fixed through long custom to a wide horizon, the heave of the seas and the despotic authority of the quarterdeck.

Bluff, hearty, hard-nerved, loud-voiced, irritable, singularly unable to brook opposition of any sort, yet often amazingly soft-hearted, the Admiral was a person to be treated with a wholesome respect.

Before, however, such dizzy heights as those of post-captain, commodore and admiral were reached, the young officer had usually the chance of developing his bent and taking a definite line in the service.

In the days of masts and yards though breech-lading guns, delay-action fuses, torpedoes, and mines were still in the future there were yet many directions along which the lieutenant could set his course.

Kiddy Blades or Tarpaulin Men

Basil Hall, writing in 1832, has divided the members of the ward-room and gun-room, into 'kiddy blades' or 'tarpaulin-men', 'star-gazers' or 'dictionary-men', and the plain ordinary watch-officers who carried on their duty as efficiently as possible without specializing in anything in particular, being content to rub along to the best of their ability.

As regards the 'tarpaulin-men', here are a few extracts from Basil Hall's "Fragments"— "... their whole soul is wrapped up in the intricate service of cutting out sails, and of rigging the masts and yards. Their dreams are of cringles and reef-tackles, of knots, splices, grummets, and dead-eyes. They can tell the length, to a fathom, of every rope in the boatswain's warrant, from the flying-jib downhaul to the spanker sheet, and the height of every spar from the main-topgallant truck to the heel of the lower mast.

Their delight is in stowing the hold; dragging about kentledge is their joy: and to form a good bend in the cable tier, without calling for a standfast at the capstan is their great pride.

In harbour they are eternally paddling in the boats, rowing, or skulling, or sailing about—and they are always the first in fishing or bathing parties—in short they are for ever at some sailor-kind of work.

"The harder it blows and the faster she goes", the merrier are they: "strong gales and squally" is the item they love best to chalk on the log-board: and even when the oldest top-men begin to hesitate about lying out on the yard to gather in the flapping remnants of the torn canvas, these gallant youngsters glory in the opportunity of setting an example of what a gentleman sailor can perform. So, at it they go, utterly wreckless of consequences: and by sliding down the lift, or scrambling out, monkey fashion; to the yard-arm, where they sit laughing—at the risk of their lives though the spar be more than half sprung through—they accomplish their purpose of shaming the others into greater exertions... These are the dashing boys who cut out privateers, jump overboard after men who cannot swim, and who, when the ship is on fire, care not a farthing for the smoke and heat, but dive below with the engine-pipe in their hands, and either do good service or perish in the flames with a jolly huzza on their lips. Such may fairly be called the muscular parts of our body nautical, for there is no gummy flesh about them: and when handled with skill they form stout instruments which help essentially to win such battles as the Nile and Trafalgar".

It was mostly from this class that the after-guard of the small cruisers were chosen. Their seamanship, like their gallantry, was beyond compare; but their methods of discipline were not to the liking of the taut-handed, kid-gloved, high-caste officer.

From the close association with their men during long commissions in small vessels, they became more like elder brothers than strict superiors: and it was greatly due to this familiarity between officers and men that made the 'briggy' or brig officer looked down upon his smart, severely-correct rival in the crack frigate or lordly line of battleship.

Some of these 'kiddy-blades' ended their days as notorious first-lieutenants—and so wedded to the routine of ship's life did they become, that they could rarely be persuaded to go ashore on any pretext.

Indeed there was no greater fish out of water than the old time seaman ashore.

Of such was Cummins, first lieutenant of the *Lancaster*. After being seven years aboard without stepping off the gangway, he was at last induced to dine ashore at Montevideo—the ship, as if offended at his absence, broke away from her moorings before he had drunk his first glass of wine. He dashed off at once and could never be persuaded to land again.

When the ship was at length paid off, he went to Bedfordshire to take possession of a property to which he had succeeded, but he soon tired of the land, and obtaining a permanent appointment aboard the *Royal Billy* at Portsmouth, remained in her until he died.

The Star-Gazers

The 'star-gazers' were the scientific officers from whose ranks the world navigators, surveyors and Arctic explorers as well as the naval ship designers and gunnery experts were drawn.

Whilst the 'tarpaulin' officers were mostly quite unknown outside the service, the 'star-gazers' often achieved a world-wide renown. Witness the following:—Parry, Franklin, Beechey, Owen, Ross, Kellett, McClure and McClintock.

Besides being the profession par excellence of certain old county families, such as the Hothams, the Parkers, the Seymours, the Otways, the Hoods, etc., the service became very popular during the first half of the nineteenth century with the aristocracy.

Young sprigs of the nobility, as they were called, were to be found mostly in flash frigates, but many of the more enterprising, such as Harry Keppel, were to be found commanding gun brigs and schooner tenders.

The Midshipmite

As regards the mids, boys at sea have always been the same kind of mischievous monkeys, the torment of the duller witted members of the crew, but with a very wholesome dread of the senior executive officer, whether he was the commander of a flag ship, the first lieutenant of a frigate, or the mate of a merchant ship.

"Shivering he treads the quarter-deck
And dreads the First Lieutenant's check,
Who walks the weather side:
With glass and trumpet in his hand
He bellows forth his harsh command,
With insolence and pride".

Apparently they used to differ in quality just as the ships to which they belonged differed in rate. Jonathan Oldjunk makes the following distinctions:—

"Ships of the Line more or less resembled first and second rates in the character of their young gentlemen". (Young gentlemen was the correct service way of referring to midshipmen and cadets).

The Captain, however, seldom or never saw them, except on the quarter-deck, or at his own table, where, of necessity, they were compelled to behave in an officer-like manner. The cockpit was like a sealed sepulchre to the lieutenants, unless occasionally one condescended to stoop from his high station to pass a jovial Saturday night amongst the reefers. The mates were chiefly elderly men, who from some explained cause or other had no chance or prospect of obtaining promotion, or else had been advanced from before the mast for some meritorious action: but I scarcely ever knew one that was not a half-and-man when mixing a tumbler of grog.

The frigates were considered the elite of the service, and the midshipmen were mostly dashing young blades, with plenty of prize money, and many opportunities in port to spend it.

They were the "saucy ones" of the Navy, and prided themselves on the quality and fame of their ship: and as there was a clear unobstructed sight from the taffrail to the figurehead, right fore and aft, so there could be but small chances of escape from the quick eye of the First Lieutenant.

The sloops of war were principally midshipmanned by youths with especial recommendations from persons in authority, who had been instrumental in raising the Commander to his epaulette on the left shoulder, and by young men of little interest, who had, however, been distinguished as smart, active fellows by their captains when only first lieutenants: though it frequently happened that the sloops became a sort of refuge for oldsters of unsteady hands and inflamed eyes—men who were fond of a little water with a great quantity of rum added to it. In latter days of eighteen-gun brigs and dashing corvettes, it must be allowed that this class became greatly improved . . .

The gun-brig and cutter's midshipmen were generally a dirty, groggy, low-class of the Sheerness and Chatham school,—the sons of petty tradesmen, with whom the lieutenant in command had dealings, and exacted long credit for making their boobies officers.

This account, of course, refers to the bad old war days. When peace came there was no room for such officers, and the typical cutter-mud and the oldsters with unsteady hands were speedily relegated to the beach.

Passing Conundrums

Many amusing tales have been told by the old time officer on his examination for entry into the service.

John Morseby, as late as 1842, was asked this question:—"If fifty pounds of salt pork costs two pounds ten, what is the price of one pound?".

Harry Keppel in 1822 after his term at the Royal Naval College, Gossport, had a far stiffer mathematical exam, but he had the misfortune to be caught blowing his nose with a handkerchief on which the map of England was printed.

If the entry into the service was wholly dependant upon the whim of the examiner, so also was that dreaded viva-voce examination in seamanship before the midshipman could receive a commission.

Here is a conundrum prepounded by a captain, who was notorious for failing youngsters:

"You are officer of the watch, sir. It is blowing fresh and you are under double-reefed topsails and topgallant sails—mark that! The Captain comes on deck and asks you how the wind is. You make the proper response. He then puts his hand in his pocket and produces a small leather case—mark that! He opens it and presents you with a cigar. Now, sir—quick!—which end would you put in your mouth? Quick, which end?"

The youngster instantly replied:—"The twisted end if a Havana, sir, and either end if a cheroot!". "Right, by gad, sir! You have passed an excellent examination. You have presence of mind. I have no further questions to ask".

The Decay of Seamanship

It is one of the privileges of the old to hold the belief that his generation was far superior to that of his son or grandson: man, by nature, is conservative, and changes one hundred and fifty years ago were much harder to bring about than in these days: thus the sailor of the American War of Independence was as critical of the Trafalgar tar, as that clean-shaved, pig-tailed salt was of the bushy-whiskered Victorian.

Brenton in his "Life of St. Vincent" wrote:—"The old school of officers, like the old school of ship builders, were very bigoted in their systems. Red muzzles to the guns, white tompions, petticoat trousers for the sailors and long cues tied down their backs had a formidable and war-like appearance".

But it was not until the advent of steam that every single officer with two swabs on his shoulders began to lament the decay of seamanship and to declare with all the emphasis of clenched fists that the service was going utterly to the dogs.

When the captain was lost, according to the finding of the Court Martial:—"By the strength of the wind and heave of the sea". That famous member of the Jockey club, Admiral Roos wrote furiously to the Times:—"It would be more consonant to Common sense to say:—'Lost by the officer of the watch not knowing how to shorten sail or keep his men on deck'. The truth is that the boiler has emasculated seamanship. No man can serve two masters—he will hold to the tea kettle and despise the canvas. You can no more rear a seaman in a steamer than on the Bridgewater Canal, and in ten years time the British seaman will be a rare bird among the sailors in the Royal Navy".

Yet, for all that, the seaman of the early Victorian age and even until well after the Crimean war, was still widely different to the landsmen both in character and physique. At a time when scornful old timers were dubbing the bluejackets of the day 'hot roll and milk every morning sailors', Robert C. Leslie, the artist, painted a picture in order to show what a contrast there was between the small, perky, officious under-developed landsman and the long-limbed, wide-shouldered, narrow-hipped athlete of a jack-tar.

Competitive Sail Drill

The activity of the blue jacket in the last days of masts and yards was almost incredible.

Lord Charles Beresford has immortilised the two crack topmen of the *Marlborough*, George Lewis and Ninepin Jones, in the year 1861. At one time on the command *Awayaloft* the upper yard men used to start from the deck, but the strain in competitive drill became so great that men's hearts and lungs were injured, and so the order went forth, that the upper yard men were to start from the top and not from the deck.

In the *Marlborough* the height from the deck to the maintop was sixty-seven feet, and from the top up the topmast riging and out to the topgallant yardarm sixty-four feet.

George Lewis went out to the main yardarm from the top in thirteen seconds; this record was never beaten though it was equalled by Ninepin Jones at the fore.

A Herculean Seaman

And here is an earlier record, showing a physical strength which would have aroused envy in a mountain-gunner.

"There was a seaman of herculean frame in her (Hun brig W-) whose strength was in proportion to his bulk, and whose mildness was equal in degree to his great muscular power and courage.

His name was Odgen or Ogburn, I forget which: and he alone managed the foremost gun, a carronade upon a carriage: when this gun became heated it repeatedly upset, but was instantly righted by him, apparently without much effort: it was a curious sight to see the earnestness and ease with which this single homo performed his part, loading, priming, firing, sponging and running out his piece, without the slightest assistance from any other person: and all executed in equal time with the others! he performed the feat of lifting up a carronade (I believe a twelve-pounder) from the hold, placing it on his shoulder, and ascending with it to in that position up the ladder to the deck"!

If the sailor surpassed the landsman in his physique, in character the difference between them was even more striking. Cheery, virile, stoical, strong-nerved, generous to a fault, child-like and ever full of fun, the old time bluejacket had one great failing—rum was his ban.

A Day in Jarvis' Fleet

The service was a hard, merciless one. Officers were still martinets, who could watch a delinquent's back cut up by a cat'o'nine tails with calm demeanour and steady pulse, yet their men were always ready to follow them through thick and thin .

In many ways the service has not changed since that Sunday morning in Jarvis' fleet off Cadiz, when Nelson with the inshore squadron was in action with the Spanish gunboats: the main body of the fleet, under the Commander-in-chief were at prayers with their church pendants flying, whilst the outside and windward squadron were busy at that terrible punishment of flogging men round the fleet with, in their very midst, the battleship *St. George* showing four mutineers hanging at her yardarms.

Following the years of ship to ship actions of cutting out affrays, and coastblockades came the days of crack saildrill, smartness in evolution, experimental sailing, and super seamanship.

Naval Classics

Though I fancy they are little read in these days, there are several Naval clasics of this date; notably Captain Frederick Marryat's books. Of these "The Pirate and three Cutters" deals with the exact period of this book. Even still more rich in character and local colour are Michael Scott's two books, "Tom Cringle's Log" and "The Cruise of the Midge".

The Good Old Commodore

In the latter we have the description of the West Coast of Africa Commodore, which must have been taken straight from life, it runs as follows:—

"The Commodore was a red-faced little man with a very irritable cast of countenance, which, however, was by no means a true index to his warm heart, for I verily believe that no commander was ever more beloved by officers and men than he was.

He had seen a great deal of service, and had been several times wounded; once, in particular, very badly by a grape-shot, that had shattered his left thigh and considerably shortened it, thereby giving him a "rick in his gallop", as he himself used to phrase it, until the day of his death. ... The gallant old fellow was dressed in faded nankeen trousers—discoloured cotton stockings—shoes, with cornholes cut in the toes—an ill-washed and rumpled white Marseilles waistcoat—an old blue uniform coat, worn absolutely threadbare, and white and soapy at the seams and elbows: each shoulder being garnished with a faded gold lace strap, to confine the epaulets when mounted, and that was only on a Sunday.

His silk neckcloth had been most probably black once, but now it was a dingy brown: and he wore a most shocking bad hat—an old white beaver, with very broad brims, the snout of it fastened back to the crown with a lanyard of common spunyarn: buttoned up, as it were, like the chapaux in Charles the Second's time, to prevent it flapping down over his eyes".

A Popular First Lieutenant

Probably there is a good deal of caricature in this description; and the officer, with whom he was perambulating, his first lieutenant, is described at even greater length and with still greater discoursiveness, from which one can glean the main characteristics, as follows:— "a tall man, at the very least six feet high and stout in proportion; very square-shouldered ... below these wide-spreading upperworks he tapered away to nothing at the loins ... his thighs were very short, but his legs, from the knee down, were the longest I ever saw in a man ... his head was very large, thatched with a great fell of coarse red hair, hanging down in greasy masses on each side of his pale freckled visage, until it blended in two immense whiskers, which he cultivated under his chin with such care that he appeared to be peeping through a far collar, like a Madagascar ourang-outang".

Michael Scott's careful discription of his dress is again of interest— "... an old fashioned uniform coat, very far through, as we say: long-waisted, with remarkably short skirts, but the strap for the epaulet new and bright as the loop on the hat... a dingy white Kerseymer waistcoat, over which dangles a great horn eye-glass, suspended by a magnificent new broad watered black ribbon;... ancient duck trousers, extending about halfway down the calf of the leg... leaving his pillar-like ankles conspicuously observable".

Next he gives us the character of this queer looking first officer:— "a most excellent warm-hearted person at bottom: straightforward and kind to the men; never blazoning or amplifying their faults, but generally, on the other hand, softening them; and often astonishing the poor fellows by his out-of-the-way and unexpected kindness and civility. Indeed he plumed himself on the general polish of his manners, whether to equals or inferiors, and the Gazelles repaid the compliment by christening him; at one time, "Old Bloody Politeful"... beloved by the men, to his brother-officers he was the most obliging and accommodating creature that ever was invented—Numberless were the petty fueds which he soldered, that, but for his warm-hearted intervention, might have eventuated in pistol-shots and gun-powder; and the mids of the ship actually adored him".

Neither of these pictures show the stern disciplinarian. Of course it must be realised that the Coast of Africa was not like the West Indies or the Mediterranean—discipline had to be relaxed a trifle in that enervating climate. Even with the help of the Kroomen, ships were generally shorthanded with fever filling the sick bays, prize crews denuding the watches and often armed boats away up amongst the mangroves and the crocodiles for days at a time.

The many quotations which I give from official reports and officers' letters will serve to show the present day members of the Royal Navy that in the long weary campaign against the outlaw and the slaver in the nineteenth century a fervent zeal, an unflinching readiness to fight against any odds, a resolute bearing in the face of the utmost danger and a cheerful spirit in standing up to privation, hardship and sickness ever animated the service.

CHAPTER II

THE DESIGNING OF SMALL CRAFT IN THE ROYAL NAVY

"She walks the waters like a thing of life"

IN this chapter I propose to try and trace the development of ship design in the smaller classes of the Royal Navy, from the days of the Napoleonic wars down to the mid Victorian era, when the service was in a state of flux, with the screw replacing the sail and the paddle-wheel, iron and wire being substituted for wood and hemp, and the pivoting battery taking the place of the broad side carriage-gun.

Those who are not interested in the fascinating subject of ship architecture are advised to skip, though I intend to avoid technical details as much as possible and to relegate statistical lists to the appendix.

Misconceptions of Naval Historians

Owing to the fact that so much of our sea history has been written by university professors and not by naval architects, many misconceptions and wrong conclusions have been forced upon students and repeated so often that they are taken as correct, without further examination. Nor have naval officers of the past done anything to disabuse the laymen and dissipate such wrong conceptions.

Indeed where ship design is concerned the sailor generally shows two failings—he is always unduly biassed, from a sense of loyalty, in favour of his own ship; and he is naturally so conservative—or, at any rate the sailor of the sail used to be—that anything novel in design is at once a target for his most severe criticism.

Clever and Seaworthy Designs

In the matter of sea worthiness, ships have been efficient enough in build and design ever since prehistoric times.

We have only to inspect the types of craft which have survived unchanged through the ages, to prove this contention.

Let me instance the Arab's dhow, the Chinese junk, the Esquimaux's kayak, the Malay's prahu, the American Indian's birch-bark, and the war-canoe of the Solomons.

Nor were our direct ancestors lacking in sea sense and technical skill.

Whether Phoenician, Greek, Frank or Norseman, they did not put out into the squally Mediterranean or stormy Atlantic in unseaworthy craft. Nor did the great discoverers, Christopher Columbus, Bartholomew Diaz, Vasco da Gama, Francis Drake, John Hawkins, William Barentz or Henry Hudson tempt the Main in rough built cockle shells.

As a matter of fact the *Santa Maria,* of Columbus, Drake's *Golden Hind,* and Hudson's *Half Moon* were infinitely more safe and seaworthy than the over-rigged, plank-on-edge, one hundred ton yacht with a lead mine on her keel, in which some thirty years ago the writer ventured across the Bay of Biscay, and afterwards weathered out the worst Adriatic bora known in years.

Throughout a long and glorious history of work in every part of the world well and successfully carried out, the ships of the Royal Navy have always come in for adverse criticism from our seamen, from whom landsmen and historians have naturally enough taken their cue.

Superiority of Stuart Ships

It is true that in the stormy days of our Cromwellian and Stuart navies, our first rates and frigates were considered far superior to the Dutch, contemptuously alluded to by our swaggering tarpaulins as 'Flemish butter boxes'. This it must be confessed was solely due to the fact that Dutch men of war could not afford the draft of water owing to the shallows of their home ports. But when Louis XIV built his superb French navy, somehow or other British seamen lost confidence in their own designs, and ever since that date the grumbling naval officer of the Wooden Walls was wont to compare the different British rates unfavourably with those of foreigners, whether French, Spanish or American.

Unfair Criticism of our Designers

Our surveyors and shipwrights were accused of being ignorant and hide-bound, ultra-conservative and unenterprising, wanting in technical skill and artistry.

Criticism of self is healthy—indeed—a very healthy sign in a nation; and from this naval habit of scathing criticism we may conclude that at no time were our shipwrights quite so inefficient and so slack, or the Admiralty quite so corrupt and self-satisfied as history would have us believe.

Publications by the Navy Records Society are tending to prove that even the most abused of First Lords did their duty as well as they were able and that on the whole our sea service was managed just as well as that of any other nation.

Royal Interest in the Naval Service

From the days of the Stuarts the Navy Royal has always had the keen interest of our rulers. Indeed Charles II, James II and Prince Rupert, besides being real seamen, were far from ignorant about shipbuilding and even had small craft built to their own designs.

The set an example which was followed by George III and William IV.

But if professional and royal criticism were not enough, ever since the shipmoney days of Charles I, the Royal Navy has been the stalking horse of politicians; and the Admirlaty of the day constantly had to bear with the really venomous insinuations of an opposition without any scruples whatever. Thus an inefficient administrator, a stupid surveyor or a slack dockyard Admiral had little chance of concealing his delinquencies.

Development Through Practical Experience

It was by the gradual accumulation of experience rather than by any inspired talent that the 'Great ship', the *Garrack* and the *Caravel* became transformed into the 'three-decked first-rate', the Frigate-built line of battle-ship' and the *Indiaman.*

And it was by such slow and sure means that the 'galley-frigate' of the Stuarts became the 'ship-sloop' of the Georges, that the 'brigantine' of Charles II became the 'gun-brig' of George III, and the Ketch of the Dutch wars blossomed into the saucy revenue-cutter of the early nineteenth century.

But all the time whilst our wooden walls were slowly reaching their prime, controversy rages, and neither men nor their work received their just need of praise.

It is only by careful research and a close study of the ship plans in the office of the Admiralty curators that we can gain a just appreciation of the work of our ancestors in this matter of warship development.

Modern Yacht Architects' Opinions

Ask the yacht architect, the only man who still designs sea going vessels of wood construction, what he thinks of the models in the South Kensington museum, at Whitehall and at Greenwich, or of the line, sheer and body plans at the Admiralty Curators, and I venture to prophecy that he will not only voice his admiration for many of the designs but his astonishment at the knowledge and cleverness of the designers. More than once too, he will be brought up all standing by lines which resemble those of a modern yacht.

Our surveyors, right from the days of Sir Thomas Slade and Sir John Williams—aye, and even from Sir Anthony Deane, have always shown themselves capable of designing ships every bit as good as their chief rivals—The trouble, however, has ever been the Admiralty's system of over-gunning—cramming too many guns into a hull of a certain specification, beyond which the surveyor was not allowed to go.

Comparisons of Different Nationalities

Thus it came about that French ships were always bigger than British ships of the same rate, and when the Americans came upon the scene the difference was even more evident.

Our surveyors did their best within the limits set them by the Admiralty and they were always out to learn. This cannot be said to have been the case either with the French, Spanish, or Americans. They stuck strictly to their own recognised types and developed along their own lines without taking heed of the designs of other nations; but, in England, every prize of any reputation, whether she was French, Spanish, American, Dutch or Dane was carefully examined by our surveyors and shipwrights, and every model with a good record had her lines taken off and built upon.

Hard Worked Small Fry in the R.N.

In this book we are not concerned with the line-off-battle ships or even the heavy frigates. It was the dainty flush-decked corvette, the sturdy ship-sloop, the saucy gun-brig, the rakish brigantine and the West Indian and Bermuda Schooner, which fought and overcame the slaver.

It was the sixth rate and the ships below it which were ever the hardest worked in the Royal Navy. They had to do all the convoying, all the scouting and despatch carrying; they were the explorers, they it was who surveyed unknown, often hostile and generally fever stricken shores. They had to keep the seas free of pirates, privateers and contrabandistas. They even had to run the mails and play the part of packet boats. What wonder than an American officer said:—

"The English work their gun-brigs to the bone!"

Though there were hundreds of these small fry at the tail end of the old Navy Lists, there were never enough of them.

Prizes Made Use of

Thus it happened that practically every prize taken, that was in a fit condition, was recommissioned as a British cruiser.

It was all the same whether she was a French naval corvette 'a batterie couverte' or 'a matereau' — a polacre-rigged brick-goelette from Toulon — a 'bombarde' ketch from Marseilles — a Tunisian felucca — Turkish xebec — an Adriatic trabaccole — a Dutch galliot — a St. Malo lugger — a Hamburg pink — a Baltimore clipper — a Chesapeake pilotboat — or a West Indian Ballahou schooner.

The lines of many of these foreign types are to be found at the Admiralty curators, sandwiched in between the plans of Slade, Williams, Henslow, Rule, Peake, Seppings and Symonds. Nor need their British gun-brig and cutter designs fear comparison with any of this motley collection of foreign craft. Sometimes, indeed, the surveyors had rather unexpected successes, as for instance, when a class of fire-ships*.

Brig and Brigantine

The surveyors were particularly happy in their gunbrig (NOTE: There has been a great deal of discussion in nautical circles with references to the terms brig and brigantine).

Falconer in his Marine Dictionary of 1769 makes no distinction between brig and brigantine, hence it has been assumed that brig is simply a contradiction for brigantine. Though Steel in 1794 gives plates of the snow with its trysail mast, the brig with no square mainsail and an early form of two-topsail schooner he makes no mention of the term 'brigantine'. The subject, however, is treated most exhaustively and delightfully in the "Mariner's Mirror", (the journal of the Society for Nautical Research). Sir Alan Moore, also, in his "Last Days of Mast and Sail" traces the descent of the brig and her North country cousin, the snow.) designs or perhaps it would be more correct to say brig-sloop designs.

The first mention of brigantine or brig as a class of naval vessel is given by Derrick as being in 1697, when nine brigantines are listed. These must have been quite small craft, as they only had a complement of from thirty to thirty-five men. By 1702 we find these brigantines dropped to six with a total tonnage of only four hundred and fifty six tons, in 1711 there are only two, and two years later the class no longer exists. However this does not mean that the rig had been dropped by the navy—In 1702 we find, under the heading of sloops, ten vessels totalling six hundred and twenty nine tons and undoubtedly these were mostly brig rigged.

The earliest model that I know of is a very interesting one lent to the South Kensington museum by Captain H. Quill R.N. This dates back to 1810—11, and may be the *Happy,* built by Ackworth at Woolwich. She is very handsome little vessel of one hundred and fourteen tons burthen, with a full poop and topgallent forecastle, her poop break coming just aft of the mainmast and the forecastle break just aft of the foremast, the belfry being on the edge of the forecastle break.

Her dimensions are gundeck sixty two point six feet: Keel fifty point two feet: beam twenty feet seven inches: depth nine feet. She carries fourteen guns, eight being on the main deck. These were four-pounders.

In rig she is shown with fore and main courses, fore and main topgallantsails, big jib, small foretopmast stay sail, two stay sails between the masts, and a fore and aft mainsail without a boom, the mainsheet belaying to the taffrail. She is a smart looking little thing with bright topsides, black stroke and white bottom. Along her rail run two narrow lines of colour, the upper red, and underneath blue. She has a fiddle head and is a handsome, sweet-lined sloop-of-war, which undoubtedly had speed off the wind.

Anson's *Tryall* was a very similar sloop, and we can trace the class right away from the *Happy* down to the training brig *Martin,* which in the eighteen nineties used to run away from some of the smartest yachts in the Solent.

National Types of British Small Craft

There were two types of small craft in the Royal Navy, the brig and the cutter, which have always been considered peculiarly British, just as the lugger was reckoned a French-fied rig and the fore and aft schooner essentially American.

---

* *Incendiary* and her sisters, designed by Williams in 1778. Tons 396. Length gundeck 110′8″. Breadth 29′2″. Depth 12′0½″ Length of Keel 87′4″. They had ten ports aside, and shapely quarter-galleries) showed such weatherly qualities and sea kindliness that they were speedily converted into ship-sloops.

Though so different in rig, the brig and cutter in the second half of the eighteenth century bore a close resemblance to each other in their lines—the brigs too were clench built.

Childers* and *Speedy

Amongst this cutter type of brig were two very famous vessels—the the *Childers,* launched in 1778, and the *Speedy* launched in 1782.

They belonged to a class, which were designed by the surveyor J. Williams, a most talented and efficient naval architect. The first of these brigs was the *Alert,* launched in 1775 of two hundred and two tons: gun deck seventy eight feet, six inches, keel sixty feet, seven inches, beam twenty feet, depth of hold eleven feet.

Following her came the *Childers* (1778), *Lively* (1779) *Scourge* (1779), *Swallow* (1779), *Drake* (1779), *Scout* (1781), *Flirt* (1781), and the *Speedy* (1782). Each succeeding brig was slightly altered in lines and dimensions from her predecessors. For instance there is a plan at the Admiralty Curators showing *Speedy's* bow pencilled onto the lines of *Lively.*

Everyone of them must have been extremely able as well as fast, especially off the wind: and all they needed was a little more dead wood and a slightly deeper keel to have made them very good to windward. At first *Alert* was given ten four pounder broadside guns and sixteen half pounder swivels, but after a few years the swivels were done away with, and the class given fourteen four-pounders.

Childers was the longest lived of the class and captured a tremendous number of enemy ships. Almost as many distinguished officers commanded or served in her as in *Speedy.*

When she was almost falling to pieces in 1808 she had a hot action and saved the Gottenburg trade from the large Danish brig-corvette. *Lougen,* armed with eighteen-pounder carronades. She is chiefly remembered because she was the first British vessel to be in action in the war of 1793; when in the entrance of Brest Harbour, she suddenly found herself under a cross fire from the shore batteries as she was drifted under them in calm weather by the tide. Manning her sweeps she slowly worked out of range, but not before a forty eight pounder round shot had come aboard her.

The *Speedy* is generally associated with that wonderful seaman, Cochrane, in our memories, but practically everyone of her commanders rose to eminence in his profession. One only need mention the following names—George Maude, Charles Cunningham, George Cockburn, George Eyre, Thomas Elphinston, Hugh Dowman, and Jahleel Brenton, to show that Lord Cochrane was not the only one.

Indeed, the little *Speedy* did more damage to the enemy in her time than many a first-class frigate.

In appearance she was a most taking little vessel, closely following the stock cutter lines of these brig-sloops of Williams. She was an improvement of the rest of her class, with a leaner bow, easier bilges and a finer run. Though quite sharp, she was more round in section than a Baltimore clipper.

She had a rockered keel like a cutter and was steered by a long tiller. The head room in the cabin was small enough to prove Cochrane's assertion that he had to put his head throught the skylight in order to shave.

Being only armed with four-pounders, there is no doubt that Cochrane could have walked round the deck with his ship's broadside in his tail-coat pockets.

Nelson's Flying *Badger*

During the seventeen seventies and the American War of Independence, prizes and merchantmen of unusual speed were at once taken into the service and at the first opportunity the lines of such vessels were invariably taken off in the dockyards and closely studied by the English surveyors.

Probably the most interesting and remarkable of all these outside designs was that of Nelson's *Badger,* the first command of that famous hero, a small brig, known throughout the West Indies as the *Flying Badger.*

Whether her lines came from the brain of some Virginia draughtsman of from the Down East shore, or possibly from a clever Nassau or 'Mudian shipwright can now never be known, but at any rate the man who designed her had extraordinary talent for they show a most interesting vessel, very extreme in her sharpness and with a reverse curve in the keel line. She must have been very fast, but ticklish to handle and requiring plenty of ballast to keep her upright.

She was bought into the Royal Navy in 1776, and when she came home from the West Indies in the following year, her lines were at once taken off by the second surveyor, Edward Hunt.

Her armament consisted of twelve four-pounders with a dozen of the usual half-pounder swivels along her rails.

This rakish brig was commanded by Nelson and Collingwood in turn, and in spite of her want of stability, survived two hurricanes, being sold out of the service at Jamaica in June 1783.

In the Royal United Service Museum at Whitehall, there is a piece of keel exhibited, which was taken from a mooring barge in Table Bay in 1895. This bit of wood is credited in the catalogue as coming off Nelson's *Badger:* but it really was a ten-gun brig of that name which was converted into a sheer hulk at the Cape in September 1833. Her commander, Lieutenant Stow, officers and men being brought home in the brigantine *Charybois.*

As showing the variety of build and rig in brigs of this class, here is a table of dimensions for the two surveyor-designed brigs, *Childers* and *Speedy,* and the two bought brigs *Badger* and *Camelion,* a larger fourteen gun brig, bought in 1781.

Name	Length gun deck	Length keel	Beam extreme	Depth of hold	Tons Burthen	Main-mast deck to truck	Main yard	Main boom	Bow-sprit and jib-boom
Badger	68′6″	54′3″	21′10″	9′4″	138′	98′3″	36′6″	50′	71′
Childers	78′11″	60′8″	25′	11′	202	112′	41′6″	45′	62′
Camelion	85′	58′7″	29′3″	12′	268′	130′	46′6″	47′4″	71′
Speedy	78′3″	59′	25′5″	10′10″	207′	112′	41′	45′	62′

In giving the tonnage, I have given to the nearest ton.

In sail plans it must be remembered that flying kites, such as studding-sails, ring-tails, water-sails, etc., nearly doubled the plain-sail area.

Childers and *Speedy* and their class were certainly good lookers as well as fast sailers, even to modern eyes, but the clinker built *Camelion* was certainly a quaint craft in appearance whilst the flying *Badger* had a high pinky stern with four windows under an arched taffrail and a low fiddle-headed bow, which must have made her very wet forward on occasions.

With the outbreak of war with Revolutionary France in 1793, the British seas were speedily infested with the most daring of French privateers and the Admiralty were soon in great want of small craft.

Brig-Sloop Classes

By 1795 brig sloops were being built not only in Royal yards, but in merchants' yards all round the coast. First came the *Harpy* class, consisting of eight brigs of three hundred and eight tons, then came the *Despatch* class of eight brigs, measuring a foot or two larger all round and of three hundred and sixty five tons burthen.

These were speedily put in the shade by the launch of the beautiful brig-sloop *Cruiser* of three hundred and eighty two tons, in 1797. This brig, whose design was signed by both Henslow and Rule, mounted sixteen thirty-two pounder carronades and two six-pounder long guns on a deck one hundred feet long. She turned out to be a great success, able to carry out all the work of a modern destroyer and the equal in sailing of the fastest of the *Mounseers.*

By the end of the Napoleonic wars over eighty of these eighteen-gun brigs had been built; those of them which had short lives, generally had their names revived in a duplicate—thus there were two *Pelicans,* two *Grasshoppers,* two *Kingfishers,* two *Harriers,* etc.

There is a very beautiful model of one of these fine brig-sloops, the *Raleigh,* complete down to the smallest detail, at the Royal United Service Museum, Whitehall.

Some Famous War Brigs

Every officer that served in these brigs gave them unstinted praise. They were considered capable of protecting themselves against ships of double their force; for instance, the *Sylph,* Captain Charles Dashwood, had two long actions in the summer of 1801, with the French forty-gun eighteen-pounder frigate, *Artemise;* and each time the frigate had more than enough of it. French journals stated that the French captain was court-martialled and shot.

In the same way, the *Pelican,* Captain John Clarke Searle in September 1796, fought off the French thirty six-gun frigate *Medee.*

Perhaps a few notes on the work of these celebrated brigs will give an idea of their all round capabilities.

The *Cruiser* herself was by no means the least successful Under Captain Charles Wollaston between 1798 and 1801, she captured six French privateers. Commanded by Captain John Hancock blockading the French coast betwen Ostend and Boulogne she was in action one hundred and four times between 1803 and 1805. During the next three years she did equally good work against the Danes under Captain Pringle Stoddart.

A Trafalgar Tragedy

There have been many *Weasels* (first spelt *Weazle*) in the Royal Navy, the name dating from 1705.

The second *Weazle* a fourteen-gun brig-sloop of 1745 was a very pretty little vessel of the following dimensions.

Length of gun deck	94′5″
Length of keel	76′8″
Breadth extreme	24′3½″
Depth of hold	12′4″
Draught of water at 12′4″	forward
Best sailing trim	11′6″ aft
Burthen in tons	303 43/94

On October eight, 1746, this *Weazle* distinguished herself by capturing the *Jeantie* and the *Fortune.*

The sixth *Weazle* was an eighteen gun brig of the *Cruiser* class, had had the honour of being the foremost scout in Nelson's fleet off Cadiz before the battle of Trafalgar. It was she that made the signal to Blackwood that the Franco-Spanish fleet were coming out. Blackwook promptly hustled her off to Gibraltar for the ships which were revictualling. Young Peter Parker, her commander, was so upset at the prospect of missing the battle, that he wept on his own quarterdeck. She afterwards distinguished herself for several years in the Mediterranean, under John Clavell (Collingwood's favourite protégé), Henry Prescott,

William Andrew and other commanders. Besides spreading havoc amongst the various strangely rigged craft of the Adriatic and Tyrian seas, such as trabacolos, xebecs, misticos, feluccas, scampavias, and settees, she helped to destroy many forts, arsenals, and batteries on the Italian coast. Amongst other famous brigs in the Mediterranean was the *Redwing,* from 1806 to 1814 under Captains Thomas Ussher, E.A. Down and Sir John Sinclair. Once when attacked in line abreast by two schooners, three gunboats, a mistico and a felucca, Ussher loaded each of his broadside guns with one round shot, one of grape, and one of canister, and rammed each home with a bag of five hundred musket balls—When the attackers arrived within pistol shot, he gave the order to fire. The two schooners *(Diligente* and *Boreas)* hit along the water line, gave two or three sickly rolls, the turned over and went down with all on board. This happened off Cape Trafalgar.

Two of the gunboats and four of a convoy of merchantmen drifted into the surf and were wrecked, whilst the mistico and seven traders were captured. Only the felucca, one gunboat and one of their convoy of twelve sail managed to escape.

The *Pilot* under John Toup Nicolas was equally successful cruising in the Adriatic and between Sicily and the African coast; and so was *Cephalus* (Captains Edward Harvey and Sir Augustus Clifford).

The *Scorpion,* when commanded by Philip Cartaret with William Symonds as his first officer, was considered the fastest sailor in the West Indies—Other very successful cruisers in the Caribbean were the *Racoon,* under Austin Bissell and that most popular Officer, afterwards Admiral Sir James A. Gordon, *Reindeer* (Captains John Fyffe and Peter Douglas) and *Kingfisher* (II) under Captain Nat Cochrane.

The *Royalist,* saw such hard service in the Channel we are told she wore out six second lieutenants, but she captured an enormous number of French privateers.

Pheasant saw service at Montevideo, *Busy* did good work in the North Sea. *Thracian* which we shall later hear of capturing West Indian pirates, blockaded the Norwegian coast in 1813.

Mosquito served on the Coast of Africa in the early days under Captain George Brine, who was succeeded in 1819 by the Honourable Henry John Rous, as well known on the turf as on the quarter deck.

Bellette, when sent home with dispatches from Copenhagen, beat off sixteen gun vessels which had been sent out to capture her. In 1818 under G.R. Pechell, she took twenty prizes in the Nova Scotian coast.

Amaranthe was commanded by Captain Brenton, the Naval Historian.

Barracouta distinguished herself in the East, under Commander Charles Rayley. In operations against the Rajah of the Sambar river, Borneo, she received ninety three round shots in her hull and masts from the forts.

Another eighteen-gun brig to make history in Borneo water was the *Procris,* Captain Ben Roberts, who, against the Palambang pirates, took two hundred and forty one cannon including one hundred and forty pieces mounted in the Sultan's palace.

Another vessel out in the Far East was the *Harrier,* Captain Edward Ratsey. She assisted the *Phaeton* frigate in her attack on the French *Semillante.* In January 1807 the *Harrier* sailed from Madras for the cape in Company with the *Blenheim* (Admiral Sir Thomas Troubridge) and the *Java. Harrier* was the only one of the three to fight her way successfully through an Indian Ocean cyclone: however, just two years later, she went missing in another cyclone. This was the first *Harrier,* the second of that name served on the Baltic and Halifax Stations.

Attempts to Improve the Eighteen-Gun Brig

From time to time improvements were made in this favourite class of brig-sloops for instance at the close of 1814 Captain Nicolas applied to the Admiralty for leave to have the *Pilot* altered on a plan by which shot holes could immediately be stopped between wind and water; and we are told that all eighteen-gun brigs under repair at the time were altered to his suggestions.

Other alterations were not always an improvement, for instance, poops fitted as a protection to the men rather spoilt their sailing—the fore and aft mainsail of an eighteen-gun brig contained two thousand, one hundred and fifty square feet of canvas* the eddy wind from this sail (called the boom mainsail) and the square mainsail, rushing along the deep waste of the brig, was forced under this deck and could only be got away by opening the stern and lee ports. The fact was, that these brigs like most sailing vessels required careful trimming. They usually carried a little under fifty tons of iron ballast, and when complete with provisions and water were lively and buoyant: nor were they ever crank, even when their stock was nearly out, they always stood up well to their canvas, carried their guns high and indeed seldom were in trouble. Crack brig officers preferred the foremast to be stayed up-right, but the mainmast with as much rake as possible, without spoiling the set of the square mainsail.

The Famous *Primrose*

In 1809 an improved eighteen-gun brig-sloop was launched at Portsmouth the draft of her lines being signed by Rule and Peake. This was the famous *Primrose,* of three hundred and eighty two tons burthen. Her dimensions were, length gun deck 108 feet: length of keel 87 feet: beam extreme 28′9″; depth of hold 13′6″: draft foreward 7′7″: aft 10′10″.

When the *Cruiser* was designed, her plans showed steps for three masts, with the idea of making these brigs, if they did not succeed into ship-sloops.

Brigs Altered to Ship Rig

In January 1824 the *Primrose* was altered to ship rig, her foremast being moved five feet six inches further forward, and her main eight feet six inches. About the same time several other eighteen-gun brigs were refitted as ships, such as the *Grasshopper,* the *Fly,* which gave Admiral Martin his first nickname, and of course, the *Beagle* of Darwin fame.

In every case the alteration spoilt the ships' sailing, but one of the strange arguments put forward for the change was that a three masted ship obtained more respect, and could put on more 'dog' than a two masted one.

It was soon realised that it was poor policy to spoil a beautiful brig in order to make an indifferent ship, and this practice was soon discontinued.

Most of the eighteen-gun brigs had been laid up in ordinary, or sold out of the service by 1830, but a few of the later built ones were to be seen on the Coast of Africa through the thirties, such as *Jaseur, Pelorus, Trinculo, Pelican,* and *Childers.*

Distinction Between Brig-Sloop, Gun Brig-and Gun-Boat

With the turn of the century, brig classes were built as fast as they could be laid down.

One must, however, be careful to make a distinction between the brig-sloop, the gun-brig, and the gun-boat which was generally brig-rigged.

The sloop was entitled to a commander, the gun-brig was a senior lieutenant's command, whilst gun-boats were sometimes committed to a master's mate.

These latter were shallow draft, flat bottomed scows, specially designed for work on the coasts of the North Sea.

* Edge says one thousand six hundred and nineteen square feet.

They were knocked together very roughly and as cheaply as possible, and were rather notorious for their slack discipline, nevertheless in the coast blockade, some of them did very gallant work.

Classes of Gun-Boats

The first of these gun-boats, a class of six headed by the *Anniwell* of one hundred and forty six tons, built in 1794, were designed to fight head on, and to take the ground like a barge. Then in 1797 came two classes with drop keels, the *Assault* class of one hundred and fifty eight tons, and the *Eclipse* class of one hundred and sixty seven tons. In 1801 came the *Vixen* class of one hundred and eighty four tons, armed with ten eighteen-pounder and two thirty-two pounder carronades, and the *Aggressor* class of one hundred and seventy seven tons and twenty one sister ships.

These little vessels, which were a speciality of the war, were soon worn out in their rough duties and played no part in the suppression of pirates or the slave trade, but I have mentioned them, as it is very easy to become confused with the different classes of small fry in the Royal Navy, especially as names were continually being duplicated.

Of the genuine brig-rigged cruisers, here is a list of classes for the sake of reference:—

BRIG CLASSES 1795–1812

Date Launched	Name	Rate	Guns	Length gundeck	Beam	Depth of hold	Tons	Number built
1795	*Harpy*	Sloop	16 6prs 12 swivels	95′	27′9″	12′	308	8
1795	*Dispatch*	Sloop	16 32 pr carr	96′	30′6″	12·9	365	8
1797	*Cruiser*	Sloop	16 32pr carr 2 6 pr guns	100′	30·6	12·9	382	81
1804	*Electra*	Gun-brig	16	93′	26·5	12	282	13
1805	*Challenger*	Sloop	16 24pr carr 2 6pr guns	96′	25·10	11·8	282	7
1807	*Apelles*	Gun-brig	12 24pr carr 2 6pr guns	92′	25·6	12·8	251	9
1807	*Rolla*	Gun-brig	8 18pr carr 2 6pr guns	90′	24·6	11	235	107
1812	*Contest*	Gun-brig	10 18pr carr 2 6pr guns	84′	22′	11	179	18

The Tennies or Coffin Brigs

The *Rolla* class of ten-gun brigs, affectionately called *Tennies* by their admirers and *Coffin Brigs* by their detractors, were designed by Sir Henry Peake for channel service only.

It was hoped that they would be a match for the privateersmen infesting the narrow seas, which were often too much for our revenue cutters.

Built as lightly as possible with weather boarding for topsides—that is to say clench built, they were not intended to carry more than six weeks provisions in which trim they carried their ports four feet two inches above the water, were fast, weatherly sailers, easy, good roadsters, (a very important quality), stiff under canvas and very safe. Thus they proved a most attractive lieutenant's command.

Unfortunately the exigencies of the war caused them to be sent all over the world and not to be over worked and over-weighted; they were even loaded down with ten or twelve weeks provisions for seventy five men.

Then indeed these pretty little vessels became both uncomfortable and dangerous.

The lower deck of a ten-gun brig was barely five feet high under the beams: in a stiff breeze the fore and main hatches had to be battened down to keep the lower deck clear of water, and under such conditions the watch below were poisoned by the bilge water effluvia issuing from the pump well and suffocated by the smoke from the galley fire.

All extra provisions and water above six weeks allowance had to be carried above hatches, and it constantly happened that these brigs were hardly in a condition to fight owing to puncheons of water being lashed between each pair of broadside guns. Nor was it long before the new members of this class were being much more heavily built.

The *Cordelia* one of the original weather-board brigs launched at Frinsbury in 1808, on her light draught of water, six feet forward, and nine feet aft, only displaced one hundred and seventeen tons. Fitted for channel service with all her stores, and forty tons of ballast and drawing nine feet ten inches forward and ten feet ten inches aft, she carried her midship port four feet eleven inches from the water. In 1819 the *Beagle* with timbered topsides, and *Sepping's* fitting pieces on a light draught of seven feet nine inches forward, and nine feet six inches aft, displaced one hundred and sixty three tons of water. The *Rinaldo* of the same date sailed on particular service with a draught forward of ten feet eleven inches. and twelve feet two inches aft. Yet after the war several of these litle brigs were fitted as packets, with a third mast, when their crews were reduced from seventy five to twenty seven officers and men and they were still further loaded down with passengers, specie and merchandize.

Though the officers, who handled these little brigs, were superb seamen, it was not to be wondered at if a few of them went missing when employed in packet work backwards and forwards across the Atlantic.

The Pelter Brigs

The still smaller twelve-gun brigs, which were called after one of their number, Pelter brigs, had much less to recommend them than the ten-gun brigs. Several of these were employed against the slave trade, but they were practically useless against the fairy-heeled Baltimore clippers, and the slave-traders laughed at them in derision.

Schooners in the R.N.

The favourite rig of the slaver and the pirate was undoubtedly the long, low rakish, wicked-looking topsail schooner which came from the building yards of Baltimore—But, long before the Royal Navy had any interest in the Slave trade, there were schooners in the service; indeed, the fore and aft rig can be traced back to Stuart times.

It was Lord Colville who first introduced the American schooner into the British Navy.

In 1764 he purchased several schooners from Nova Scotia, of which the draught of the *Chaleur* and others are at the Admiralty, and a model of a similar vessel is to be seen at South Kensington.

(NOTE: Mr. H. I. Chapelle has reproduced the lines of *Chaleur, Halifax* and *Sultana,* and some beautiful drawings of them by Henry Rusk in his *History of American Sailing Ships.*)

These were tubby vessels of conventional design and with the main and fore topsail rig, armed with ten swivels. Schomberg in his 1778 list gives four of them, commanded by lieutenants, the *Placenta, Labradore, Quebec,* and *Egmont.*

By the end of the American War of Independence, a number of very fast schooners had found their way into the service—many of these were prizes; not a few were West Indian built, still more came from the Chesapeake and possibly one or two from the Down East Coast.

Their rigs were as different as their origin. There was the bald-headed Ballahou schooner of the Caribbean; the Nassau privateersman, from which the present day Bahaman sponge schooner can trace her descent: the short gaffed, flat-floored Virginian pilot-boat, the high-sterned pinky from Massachusetts, the fast sailing jib-headed 'Mudian' and fore-topsail and two-topsail schooners of French origin.

American Schooners

In the second American war a fleet of the most beautiful topsail schooners flying the stars and stripes, and heavily armed preyed upon British merchant shipping, and were considered more than a match for our gun-brigs.

Whenever any of these magnificent privateers were captured, their lines were immediately taken off. The lines of half a dozen of these fine schooners are reproduced by Mr. Howard Irving Chapelle in his *Baltimore Clippers,* but those of the *Prince de Neuchatel,* one of the fastest and most renowned of all American privateers, have only recently been unearthed at the Admiralty Curator.

James, the Naval historian, writes as follows concerning these beautiful creations of New York, Boston and Baltimore shipwrights:—

"None can compete with the Americans in the size, beauty, swiftness and seaworthiness of their schooners. They will arm a schooner of two hundred tons with seven guns, including a traversing eighteen or twenty four-pounder, and give her a crew of at least one hundred able- bodied men . . . The American privateer-schooner *Harlequin* of Boston, measured three hundred and twenty three tons and mounted ten long twelve-pounders with a crew of one hundred and fifteen men. Her mainmast (lower mast he means.) was eighty four feet and her foreyard sixty four feet in length. Her bulwark was of solid timber and four inches higher and two inches thicker than that of the British eighteen-gun brig-sloop."

Writing on November fifteenth, 1805 to Lord Barham, the First Lord, Lord Keith C. in C. of the Channel remarked:

"We are now over-run with little privateers: last night (there were) two off the North Foreland and two off Dover: they laugh at the cutters; brig-sloops are the only vessels they stand in awe of. Perhaps some fast American schooners might keep them under . . . "

The dimensions, given on the lines of the captured American schooners, taken off the British dockyards give one an idea of the size and power of these privateers.

Here they are:—

Date Lines taken off	Schooner	Length gun deck	Length keel	Beam	Depth of hold	Tons English	Guns	Remarks
1806	*Flying Fish*	78'8"	60'8"	21'7"	7'10"	150	12	Wrecked off San Domingo, 1808.
1811	*Dominica*	89·6	71·8	23·1	9·3	203	14	
1812	*Sea Lark*	81·3	65·2	22·8	9·10	178	10.12 pr carr	Ex *Fly* sold 1820
1813	*Pike*	93	78·7	24·8	10·6	257	12.12 pr. carr. 2 6 pr guns	Ex *Dart*
1815	*Prince de Neufchatel*	110·8	93·8	25·8		328	17	
1815	*Picton*	101·5	85·6	25·7	10	299	10 12-pr carr 6 6pr guns	Ex *Bonne Foi*
1816	*Musquidobit*	94·7	73·1	24	10·3	220	10	Ex *Lynx* sold 1820
1816	*Grecian*	95·1	74·3	23·10	10·5	224	10 8 18pr carr 2 6pr guns	sold 1822
1817	*Alban*	94·4	78·6	24·7	10·6	252	14	Ex *Wm. Bayard.* broken up 1822.

All these were taken into the Service with the exception of the *Prince de Neufchatel* which broke her back across the dock sill at Deptford.

British Dockyards Spoil Baltimore Clippers

It was contended that the dockyard maties always spoilt these schooners. James wrote bitterly on the subject:—

"If this (i.e. any American schooner) schooner is captured by the British and deemed eligible for the navy, her bulwarks are raised and pierced with ports fore and aft, fourteen carronades, eighteen or twelve pounders, are crowded upon her decks, and she is established (there is no crowding here) with a crew of forty five or fifty men and at least six or seven very young boys. The top-hamper necessarily diminishes the vessel's rate of silling . . . "

And here is what Michael Scott has to say on the subject in *Tom Cringle's Log*.

"All hands were inspecting the *Wave* in her new character of one of his Britannic Majesty's cruisers. When I had last seen her, she was a most beautiful little craft, both in hull and rigging, as ever delighted the eye of a sailor: but the dockyard riggers and carpenters had fairly bedevilled her, at least so far as appearances went. First, they had replaced the light rail on her gunwale by heavy solid bulwarks four feet high, surmounted by hammock nettings at least another foot, so that the symmetrical little vessel, that formerly floated on the foam light as a seagull now looked like a clumsy, dish-shaped Dutch dogger. Her long, slender wands of masts, which used to swing about as if there were neither shrouds nor stays to support them, were now as taut and stiff as church-steeples, with four heavy shrouds of a side and stays and back-stays, and the devil knows what all".

This is how he describes this little vessel when a picaroon "She was a large, shallow vessel, coppered to the bends of great breadth of beam, with bright sides like an American . . . her decks were flush and level . . . she was a very taut rigged hermaphrodite or brig forward and schooner aft. Her foremast and bowsprit were immensely strong and heavy, and her mainmast was so long and tapering that the wonder was how the few shrouds and stays about it should support it: it was the handsomest stick we had ever seen. Her upper spars were on the same scale, tapering away through topmast, topgallant mast, royal and skysail-masts, until they fined away into slender wands".

Besides stiffening up these tall willowy sparred American clippers, the dockyards also cut down the large fine-weather sailplans, for instance *Sea Lark* had her masts reduced nine feet.

***Flying Fish* Class of Bermuda Built Schooners**

Though the lines were taken off, none of them were built on except those of the *Flying Fish*.

This schooner not only had very sharp lines but three masts. A copy of her plans were sent to Bermuda in 1807 and six three-masted twelve-carronade schooners (*Shamrock, Thistle, Mistletoe, Holly, Juniper* and *Bramble*) were built of pencil-cedar after her model.

The English Four-Gun Schooners of 1804-5

Just previous to this, a class of Tom Tit four-gun schooner had been built with the following dimensions:—Length gun deck 46′2″: keel 42′4″: beam 18′5″: depth 8′9″: tonnage 75. There were thirty of them, all built in England except for a dozen in Bermuda, and launched during the years 1804 and 1805.

These were handy little vessels, but with a crew of only twenty, and four miserable twelve-pounder carronades, they certainly did not please British Naval officers. On July 26th 1806 Lord St. Vincent wrote to Rear-Admiral Markham:—

"I have omitted to write you accounts of the schooners, which are no more like

Bermudian vessels than they are like Indian prows: and if any more are built, Surveyor Rule must have nothing to do with them, but the 'Mudian builders left to their own discretions. In fact they are a plague and burthen to all who have them under their orders".

The *Flying Fish* class were a great improvement on these surveyor-designed schooners, which, by the way, were all named after fish such as the *Ballahou, Barracouta, Capelin, Kingfish, Haddock,* etc.

The Classic Class of Bermuda Schooners and Cutters

Finding that these Tom Tit schooners besides being the butt for innumerable service jokes, were too small for the work they had to do, the surveyors designed a new class of one hundred and eleven tons, to carry ten eighteen-pounders carronades, and a crew of fifty men and boys. With their classical names (*Adonis, Alphea, Alban, Bacchus, Barbara, Cassandra, Claudia, Laura, Olympia, Sylvia, Vesta, Zeno bia*) this class were better looking and more useful than the Tom Tits (called the *Whiting* and sometimes the *Haddock* class), but still they were not fast enough for the American and French privateers, even though some of them were rigged as cutters.

Then when the *Flying Fish* class came out in 1808, though very fast, they were looked upon as diving bells. An officer writing in the United Service Journal of 1831 described these three-masted schooners as "perfect flying-fishes, going slap through the seas without rising to surmount them: they were frightful to behold on such occasions, and I have little doubt that the *Shamrock* with poor Abraham Bowen went down like a diver, head foremost: these craft were too ticklish for so stormy a station as Halifax."

But there was the usual reason for thes schooners being sowet; they were too heavily armed with ten, and sometimes when the spare gunports were filled, with fourteen carronades on their decks. They had beautiful sections, and properly ballasted and suitably rigged should have proved easy to handle and sea-kindly, as well as being very fast.

Dominica* Capatured By *Decatur

The *Dominica,* was also rigged as a three masted schooner; When captured by the American privateer *Decatur,* captained by that famous French picaroon, Captain Dominique Diron, this schooner was apparently armed with twelve short twelve-pounders, two long six-pounders, one brass four-pounder and a short thirty two-pounder on a pivot. She carried a crew of eighty eight all told, of whom eighteen were killed and forty two wounded, all her officers except for the surgeon and one midshipman being either killed or wounded.

The Bermuda Corvettes

During the Napoleonic wars, Bermuda builders made a tremendous reputation for themselves: not indeed for their construction of schooners, after the surveyors' plans, but for beautiful flush-decked, fine-lined corvettes on their own plans.

Local tradition credits a man named Shedden or Sedden with being probably the designer, whilst Messrs. Goodriche of St. Georges were the builders.

There were six of these corvettes *Driver* and *Dasher* built in 1797; *Martin* and *Atalante* in 1807 and *Morgiana* and *Sylph* in 1809.

The dimensions given in *Driver's* plan are:—

Length gundeck 107′: keel 83′10″: beam 29′6″: Depth of hold 16′. tons burthen 402.

They were armed with sixteen twenty-four-pounder carronades two long nine-pounders, two twelve-pounders carronades, and manned by one hundred and twenty five men all told.

In the West Indies these corvettes were extremely popular: with their flush decks and unusually good ventilation they had excellent accommodation for both officers and men, and were considered very healthy ships. Being constructed of Bermuda cedar wood, which, besides being very brittle,is exceedingly buoyant, they were said to require as much ballast as a thirty six-gun frigate, and when carrying sail in a stiff breeze, there they were sheets of spray from stem to stern; on the other hand in a gale of wind the lay hove to with dry decks; whilst few vessels could out-point them going to windward.

The *Sylph* was wrecked on Southampton Bar, North America, on January the seventeenth, 1815, with the loss of all hands except her purser and five seamen.

Atalante was unluckily lost on November the tenth, 1813, on the Sister's Rocks whilst making for Halifax in a fog.

And *Martin* came to grief on the coast of Ireland on December the eighth, 1817, and was sold out of the service.

Pickle and Her Sisters

There were three other vessels built in Bermuda which made a great name for themselves and these were the sister-schooners *Pickle, Skipjack,* and *Pincher,* all launched in 1826, and of one hundred and eighteen tons burthen with an armament of four eighteen-pounder carronades, and one eighteen-pounder long gun on a pivot.

Their dimensions were:—

Length Gun Deck	68′ 8″
Length Keel	54′
Beam Extreme	21′ 2″
Depth of Hold	9′ 9″

We shall hear a good deal of these war schooners in a later chapter.

General Bentham's Ugly Ducklings

Perhaps I should also mention General Bentham's schooners, built between 1796 and 1798, the *Redbridge, Milbrook, Netley,* and *Eling* of sixteen guns and one hundred and forty eight tons burthen. They were terribly ugly but fast under certain conditions: their chief interest being that they had sliding keels and were fitted with non-recoiling eighteen-pounder carronades.

CHAPTER III

AGAINST THE WEST INDIAN PICAROON

"No more the geese shall cackle on the poop,
No more the bag-pipe through the orlop sound,
No more the midshipman, a jovial group,
Shall toast the girls and pass the bottle round.
In death's dark road, at anchor fast they stay,
Till Heaven's loud signal shall in thunder roar;
Then starting up, all hands shall quick obey,
Sheet home the topsail, and with speed unmoor".

Elegy composed by Robert Scott, eldest brother of Sir Walter Scott, before the Battle of the Saints, April 12th, 1782.

West Indian Station

WHETHER in time of war or peace the most popular of all stations for the Royal Navy in the days of oak and hemp was always the West Indian Station.

It was also considered the smartest station, where discipline was at its highest pitch and ships were in the best order.

Let me quote from Brenton:—

"There are few sights more gratifying to seamen than a well-regulated ship of war with her people at quarters in the West Indies.

The straw-hats, made by themselves from the beautiful leaf of the palmetto, the white dresses of the seamen and marines, the admirable cleanliness and good order in every department (the bags and bedding being shaken and aired every morning in fine weather) the regularity and order of the store room, the thorough ventilation of the ship from the pump-well upwards, the neatness of the sails and rigging and the perfect readiness, with which every manoeuvre is performed, render her a picture which a British officer will gaze on with delight and a foreigner with awe and admiration".

It was the station where the young officer had the most chance, not only of distinguishing himself, but of enjoying himself.

Yellow Jack and Quick Promotion

Then the scourge of yellow jack gave promotion where the luck of a smart cutting out affair was absent. Yet the chance of prize money was always present right down to the middle of the eighteenth century, for it was a war station above all others. Here the Royal Navy contended in turn with the Dutch, the French, the Spaniards and the Americans; and when we had peace with all these nations, fighting and prize money enough was found in the suppression of the buccaneer, the pirate and the slaver.

Thus from the time of Cromwell—one might even go further back and say Queen Elizabeth—there was glory and honour besides pieces of eight to be found in West Indian waters.

Here many a great name was made—One thinks at once of Barrington and Rodney, and Hood. But we are not dealing in this book with major operations, but with the work of the young lieutenant in command of a tiny tender or of the passed-mate in charge of a pinnace creeping up a Cuban coral-studded channel with muffled oars.

Throughout the West Indies the names of certain naval officers were household words a hundred years ago; but now their deeds of valour, their high spirited escapades, and their romantic histories are, for the most part, forgotten, or else become legendary amongst the descendants of the old Creole stock and the coloured folk.

The Pedigree of a West Indian Gentleman of Fortune

It is curious how the buccaneering type seems to have repeated itself right through into the nineteenth century.

The Buccaneer of the Spanish Main was followed by the Freebooters of Tortuga and Port Royal, the Freebooter by the pirate of Nassau and the Bahama Cays—and then came the Cuban picaroon of the Napoleonic wars, who in his turn eventually gave place to the Columbian and Baratarian Corsair. Lastly, as if the peerless beauty of the Antilles had not been sufficiently smirched by blood stains, came that heartless monster, the Guinea Captain.

Against these gentlemen of fortune, these Hispanola picaroons and dealers in black ivory, the Royal Navy waged a steady war, in which many a famous Admiral of the Red or hard-bitten Commodore laid the foundations of his fortune. Though the flash frigate and the dashing corvette played their part, it was the command of a rakish sloop, an over-worked gun-brig, or of a Bermuda built schooner, which was the surest step to promotion for an officer of spirit.

Specialists in Small Craft

Certain officers, too, became specialists in small craft, the first of a class of seamen who fifty years later were spoken of rather contemptuously in the service as 'brig-officers' or 'briggies'.

Such officers as Jack Perkins, Jeremiah Coglan, Michael Gitton, or Timothy Scriven were content to command a one-gun felucca with a single lateen sail or a deck-over frigate's pinnace, but being without influence, or aristocratic and political connections, they rarely reached further than the first or second rung in their profession. They were the men, however, who were the scourge of the French and Spanish privateersmen, and the conquerors of the pirate and the slaver.

A Post-Captain Who Could Not Read

One of the most remarkable characters that ever held the commission of George III was Captain John Perkins, R.N., whose nick-name in the West Indies was Jack Punch.

His origin is shrouded in mystery, though it was rumoured that he was the offspring of a union between a titled officer and a coloured lady of Port Royal. His appearance, indeed, especially his dark, sallow visage, gave colour to this scandal, and the island of San Domingo seems to have been his domicile in his youth.

On the other hand, many of his friends claimed that he was a pure bred Englishman, born at the village of Kingswood which lies on the right bank of the Avon in the county of Gloucester.

In his prime he was a long, lean, slenderly built man with sharply marked features of mahogany hue. His shrewd, sparkling eyes and firm set jaw gave more than a hint of his active, resolute nature, otherwise there was little indication of that daring, acuteness and unusual enterprise, such as his legendary exploits would lead one to expect.

With all his reputed activity of mind, he had one great deficiency—the most amazing deficiency in a Captain in the King's Navy—he could neither read nor write!

"Old King Cole, though a merry old soul
Nor read nor write could he;
For to read or write was useless quite,
As he kept a secretary.
So his mark for Rex was a single X
And his drink was a ditto double,
For he scorned the fetters of four and twenty letters;
And it saved him a vast deal of trouble".

Jack Perkins, we are told, had a poor memory, for he could never remember the names of his officers, so contented himself with addressing them in old Merchant ship style as simply 'Mister'. It was also rumoured that his memory was equally defective regarding his own children. He was a true sailor of his time, in that there was hardly a port throughout the Caribbees, in which he did not have a wife installed: in this he resembled the famous French picaroon, Captain Love, his one time prisoner and one of the very few who got the better of this illiterate naval officer.

As a sailor, and especially as a schooner commander, he appears to have been beyond compare, though none of his famed exploits are to be found in the gazette—possibly because he never took the trouble to report them. I first find his name as a commissioned officer, in command of the ten-gun schooner, *Endeavour* in 1782. How long he had he already served in the Royal Navy cannot be ascertained at this distance of time, but one extraordinary fact is certain and that is that he passed the whole of his service upon the Jamaica Station, without ever once coming home.

A Prisoner in San Domingo

During the short peace, which followed the American War of Independence, Jack Perkins was the central figure in a most umpleasant adventure. He was caught in the terrible maelstrom of horrors, which took place in San Domingo during the struggle between black and white, complicated as it was by that of Royalist and Republican.

He was accused of gun running, providing the blacks with arms, and without proper trial thrown into Jeremie gaol and condemned to be first tortured and then hanged.

The truth seems to have been that the San Domingo whites owed him a grudge for his activity against the trade of the island during the war.

That Perkins was even then an officer of some importance and notoriety is proved by the fact that Lord Effingham and Admiral Affleck sent the sloop *Ferret*, (Captain Nowell) with a request to the Jeremie authorities that Perkins should be delivered up to the commander of His Majesty's sloop.

The Council of Commons at Jeremie instructed their president to send the following reply:—

> Sir,
>
> However agreeable it has been for us to have you amongst us, our desire would have been not to retard your voyage to the Cayes; our occupations alone have been the cause of your staying here twenty-four hours longer than you intended.
>
> The law imperiously commands us to retain Mr. Perkins and send him to the Colonial Assembly.
>
> We are
> Your obedient and most humble servant
> Plique, *President du conseil.*
> Jeremie. 16th February, 1792.

Luckily for our hero Captain Russell in His Majesty's frigate *Diana* appeared off Aux Cayes on February the seventeenth with a cargo of provisions, sent as an act of charity from the Government, Admiral Affleck and the principal inhabitants of Jamaica. At a public dinner given by the assembly to Captain Russell, the latter spoke up boldly on behalf of

Perkins. He declared that he had satisfied himself of the absolute innocence of that officer, that he had not been legally tried owing to the distracted state of the Colony and yet lay under the sentence of death. "Grant me his life" said Russell firmly, "Do not suffer these people to be guilty of the murder of an innocent man, by which they will drag down British vengeance upon the whole island".

The Assembly, by this time well primed with good wine promised that the notorious officer should be released from the dungeon, in which he lay awaiting death.

The following morning Captain Russell sent an officer for the order of release. Back came this reply.

> 'As it was a promise made after dinner they did not think it binding and the imperial voice of the law called for his execution'.

On reading this impertinent letter Captain Russell declared solemnly before his officers on his own quarterdeck that 'he would sacrifice as many Frenchmen as there were hairs on Perkin's head if they murdered him'.

It was at this psychological moment that the *Ferret* came sailing in from Jeremie and hove to.

There was no time to lose for the execution had been ordered to take place on February the nineteenth.

"Hands up anchor!" roared the enraged Russell. Then away went both ships under a cloud of canvas. Though Jeremie was on the other side of the island the distance was covered in record time. The *Diana* hove to outside the port, with her decks cleared for action, guns run out, tompions out and her crew thirsting for vengeance should Jack Perkins have been murdered.

Meanwhile the gun-brig ran in, and as a backed topsail stopped his way, Nowell's gig was dropped into the water and he pulled ashore with bending oars, clutching in his fist the following peremptory note, having also received verbal instructions as how he should act should there be any hesitation.

> His Majesty's ship *Diana* off Jeremie
> February 24th, 1792.
>
> Sir,
>
> I applied to the provincial assembly at Aux Cayes for the liberation of Lieutenant John Perkins of His Britannic Majesty's Royal Navy and my application was immediately and of course complied with.
>
> Monsieur Billard, the president, promised me an order to your assembly to deliver him up to me.
>
> That order had not arrived at L'Isle de Vache, where I lay, before I sailed, which must be no impediment to your sending him off to me in safety immediately. If, however, it should unfortunately be otherwise, let it be remembered that I do here by, in the most formal and solemn manner demand him. Captain Nowell knows my resolution in case of the least hesitation.
>
> I have the honour to be, sir,
> Your obedient humble servant,
> T. M. Russell, Captain of the *Diana*.
>
> To M. Plique, President of the Council at Jeremie.

As Captain Nowell stepped ashore with Lieutenant Godby, he was surrounded by an excited mob of three-hundred men armed with sabres, amongst whom stood the president, who, after slowly reading the letter, said with some haughtiness:—

"And suppose I do not?"

"In that case", replied Captain Nowell icily in his best French, "You draw down a destruction you are little aware of. Captain Russell has allowed sixty minutes for you to decide—you see, sir, thirty of them are elapsed!".

Then an angry voice called out:

"You shall have him, but it shall be in quarters". At this Captain Nowell deliberately drew his sword from its scabbard and said with deadly emphasis:—

"Sir, order that fellow out of my sight or he dies!".

The president with a bitter grimace was forced to comply, and after a few more attempts to combat the resolute captain, gave orders for the release of Lieutenant Perkins.

One account declares that Perkins was actually standing under the gallows with the rope around his neck, when the messenger arrived with the order for his release.

Another describes the horrid dungeon in which he lay, with the rack, in which he was about to be stretched, standing ready without the prison. A third statement places the prisoner, reduced to a skeleton from starvation and in rags, lying in bilboes aboard a brig of war, at anchor off the town.

It was lucky for Perkins that his case was in the hands of two such resolute officers, both of whom had distinguished careers and ended high up the Admiral's list.

Marshall's account ends thus:— "Captain Russell saw him led into the *Ferret*'s boat, then wore with the ship's head off the land and carried a *most adventurous and enterprising officer and good man* in triumph to the Commander-in-Chief at Jamaica, to whose prayers the sanguinary democrats of the new French regime had refused him".

I have given this story in such detail in order to show the determined way in which naval officers of that date fulfilled their orders and stood by their comrades.

We next hear of Lieutenant Perkins soon after the outbreak of war in 1793, commanding the schooner *Spitfire*, a French prize, brough into service by Commodore John Ford, commanding the small Jamaica squadron of nine ships. In her, Perkins played his part at the taking over of the ports of San Domingo in answer to the cry for help from the Royalists.

In October 1793, the little *Spitfire* had disappeared and Perkins had command of another schooner, the *Marie Antoinette*.

> *Note:* (Extract of despatch from Commodore John Ford, dated *Europa* Mole of Cape St. Nicholas, October 21st, 1793).
>
> "... You will also acquaint their lordships that I seized upon my arrival here, a large schooner in the service of the republic, commanded by Monsieur Auquetin, formerly a lieutenant of the *Jupiter*; and as she is a very fine vessel, mounting ten six and four-pounders, I have taken her into His Majesty's service. The schooner was at that time called the *National Convention*, but formerly the *Marie Antoinette*, which last name I have thought proper to continue and have given the command of her to Lieutenant Perkins, an officer of zeal, vigilance and activity".
>
> *(Naval Chronicle 1817. p 342)*

An Officer of Great Merit

Rear-Admiral Hyde Parker, who succeeded Ford in the command of the Jamaican Station, seems to have been as favourably impressed by the illiterate lieutenant as the Commodore had been; and on July the fourteeenth, 1799 he wrote to Lord Spencer, the First Lord, in this strain:—

> "The want of small vessels and the desire of providing for Captain Perkins, who certainly is an officer of great merit in this country from his perfect knowledge of almost all the ports and harbours, were the inducements which led to my venturing in giving orders for the purchase of a very fine brig, almost new, and in every respect fit for the King's service ... ".

This want of small vessels hardly seems borne out by the Navy List, which gives no less than seven sixteen-gun sloops, six brigs (including the *Drake* of sixteen guns, into which he had promoted Perkins in 1797), four fourteen-gun schooners and three cutters, whilst

Vice-Admiral H. Harvey, in command of the Leeward Islands Station had over a dozen sloops and twelve schooners.

The vessel brought by the Admiral was the *Arab* of twenty-two guns, a privateer brig. But Jack Punch was not the first officer appointed to command her, for a very distinguished sailor, the Hounourable T. B. Capel preceded him.

In April 1801 Perkins, with a detachment of the Buffs under Colonel Blunt, took possesion of the island of Eustatia, for which successful operation he was posted into the thirty two-gun frigate, *Tartar*. In July 1803 he distinguished himself by playing a prominent part in the chase and capture of the *Duquesne*, 74 guns. It was the *Tartar*, which, outsailing the other British ships, hung onto her like a bull-terrier baiting a bull.

Right at the end of his service, Jack Perkins, after being a favourite up at the Penn for over twenty years, somewhat smirched his reputation for astuteness by allowing the famous French privateersman, Captain Love, to slip through his fingers, after having caught him by chance. And it was soon after this event that Captain Perkins either retired or was superseded.

Famous West Indian Privateersmen

Between 1803 and the peace of Paris the war in the West Indies seems to have been mostly waged by French and Spanish privateersmen, who found quite a profitable living in cutting out rich West Indiamen and other merchantmen from the large British convoys.

Of these French and Spanish Corsairs, Captain Love, Jacque Mathieu and Dominique Diron were the best known. Captain Love was called the 'King of the Picaroons' by the officers and men of the Jamaica Station, but for sheer daring he could not surpass Jacca Mattu, as his own men called him. Dominique Diron was a very stubborn fighter, renowned in the American Naval history for his capture of the British naval schooner, *Dominica*, when commanding the American privateer *Decatur*.

Going back to the seventeen nineties, the greatest name amongst West Indian privateersmen was that of Pierre Olanger, but he was considered little better than a pirate by the British Cruisers; indeed, most of these West Indian picaroons became pirates or else slavers when the peace came; and even during the war generally considered that all was fish that fell into their net.

Their boldness, too, in their fishing is scarcely believable. They actually swarmed round the British Islands of the West Indies, and even ventured close into the Naval Stations.

Both Captain Love and Jacque Mathieu were accustomed to personally visit Port Royal and Kingston, where they had agents and accomplices.

Droghers and even fishing canoes were constantly intercepted off South Negril and in Bluefields Bay, and Jacque Mathieu made a practise of heading his little ballahou schooner *Maringouin* (Anglice Mosquito) into the Pallisadoes after dark; then he would launch a light canoe, drag it over the narrow spit of sand, and calmly paddle across the harbour to Kingston. Here he would spend the day learning all about the merchantmen in port, their sailing dates and destinations; then after loading up with as much fresh meat, vegetables and fruit as his canoe would carry, he returned after night fall by the same way, and paddled off to his schooner, which was waiting for him in the offing.

Love was also in the habit of visiting Kingston incognito; he generally took passage in a 'force trader' or 'contrabandista' from St. Jago de Cuba to Port Antonio, and then crossed the Island. His enquiries were even more businesslike and particular, for he always learnt all he could about every man of war on the Station, her best points of sailing, her captain's character, and even such confidential orders as 'secret instructions'. For this purpose he frequented the coffee houses and billiard rooms where British Naval officers collected and listened to all the latest station gossip whilst passing himself off as an Englishman.

At Dignity Balls and in Mary Bottom he was persona grata, and even sang that celebrated ballad:—

"If you want a bit of fun,
You'll find it down in Mary Bottom".

in the midst of a roystering crowd of middies.

The Spaniards were far less daring and enterprising than the French privateersmen. Captain Love contended that they were never bold enough in their undertakings and that their timidity often got them into scrapes, and led to their capture and destruction. Our merchantmen, too, constantly drove them off without much difficulty.

They were, however, rather fond of raiding,—landing and attacking lonely houses and stealing negroes, even upon the coast of Jamaica. They were run more or less on the co-operative plan, the captain of a Spanish privateer being chosen chiefly for his skill in navigation, the men themselves generally deciding their course of action in the face of an enemy.

Captain Love, Prince of Picaroons

Owing to his indomitable bearing and consummate boldness, many officers on the Jamaica Station, were convinced that Love was a Britisher. There was indeed good reason for this belief; to begin with, the French privateersman spoke English without any sort of accent, but then his French was as pure as his English. Many contended that he was an Irishman, but this he always strenuously denied.

That he had been at school in Scotland he could not deny, for, by a strange coincidence, when he was captured by the *Desiree*, her Scottish master recognised him—they had been at school together!

The following description of Love was written by one of the officers of the *Desiree*.

"This singular man was about five feet, ten inches in height, admirably proportioned and extremely active, with a shrewd, penetrating eye and a pleasing, intelligent countenance... He was a perfect linguist, well-read, of polished manners and very pleasing address, and a most entertaining companion".

Three Times Captured and Three Times Escapes

During the War of the French Revolution, Love was captured by the *Thetis*, and sent home as a prisoner aboard the frigate *Proselyte*.

Love, and a French naval officer were given the run of the captain's quarters, and during the night of the *Proselyte*'s arrival in Plymouth Sound, whilst there was the usual bustle and confusion, Love and his fellow prisoner were left to themselves in the after-cabin, with just the usual sentry on the door. Hanging level with the stern windows was the jolly-boat. Somehow or other they contrived to lower the boat into the water without being noticed, then dropping quietly into her, unhooked the falls, and let her drift away on the tide until it was safe to pull ashore at a lonely spot. With money and Love's good English the rest was easy.

His next escape was still more daring. He was caught aboard an American prize, he had just captured, by the frigate *Tartar*.

The unkind hinted that Jack Punch and Captain Love were old cronies, who had had many a game of bowls together in the past, and that the Captain of the *Tartar* actually connived at his prisoner's escape.

The story goes that Love passed himself off as the American owner of the prize—Before her capture by the *Tartar* he asserted that the French picaroons had headed up all the specie aboard in a salt beef cask and had buried it on the sandy shore opposite which the *Tartar* and her prize had come to an anchor. Perkins allowed Love the jolly-boat with two seamen to row him ashore and dig up the treasure. After pointing out to the dull witted seamen where they were to dig, Love unconcernedly wandered off into the woods and was never seen again, either by the chagrined captain of the *Tartar* or his crew. They soon heard of him, however, at his usual game of masquerading in Kingston as an Englishman.

He was not long at liberty before he was again captured under much the same conditions by the frigate *Desiree*.

That gallant lieutenant, the honourable W. Pakenham, of the *Desiree*, on boarding a schooner was met by a polite gentleman, who, volunteered the information that he was her master and that he had been captured two days previously by a French picaroon.

This tobacco-chewing, drawling, inperturbable sailor was, of course, Captain Love, who was on his way to St. Jago to superintend the sale of this, his latest prize. He spun the same yarn for Pakenham's edification, that he had tried so successfully aboard the *Tartar*.

Again on seeing the approaching man of war his captors had taken his box of specie ashore and hurriedly buried it in the strand of the cove, which was within an hour's pull of the captured schooner. He begged Pakenham's permission to go ashore with four of the schooner's crew (his own men, of course) in order to dig up the box. It could not take more than an hour. But Pakenham was not so easily bamboozled by the plausible imitation Yank.

"I should not be at all surprised if you were not Captain Love himself", said the lieutenant, half in earnest, half in doubt. At this, one of Pakenham's boats' crew spoke up:— "Please, sir, he is the man, I recognise him. I was serving aboard the *Thetis* when we captured him".

British Boats Repulsed in the Puerto Escondido

At this the privateersman broke into a careless laugh, and admitted that he was that celebrated picaroon.

Whilst the *Desiree* anchored in Cumberland harbour, young Pakenham was sent off in the prize to search for Captain Love's schooner, which, it was reported, lay moored in the narrow entrance of Escondido (the hidden port) eight miles east of Cumberland Harbour. Love himself actually warned Pakenham to be careful as his schooner mounted fourteen guns and was manned by one hundred men.

Of all the snug retreats frequented by the picaroons on the South side of Cuba, such as Rio Cre, Yatina, Trinidad, the Isle of Pines, Bayamo, Batabano, the Colorado, Barraco, and the numerous small cays of the Archipelago de los Canarreas and the Jardines de la Reina, Puerto Escondido was considered one of the safest from attack.

Having discovered the privateer, and even exchanged a few shots, Pakenham ran back to the frigate and informed his captain that the schooner could only be taken by the frigate's boats.

At this Captain Ross got under way and anchored off the entrance of Escondido soon after night fall.

The passage into this pirate's lair was very narrow, with an ambush generally prepared on the starboard hand where a beach of white sand was backed by high rocks and bush, in the midst of which several deep caves could conceal any number of men.

On the other shore, thick mangrove bushes made such a thicket, as to discourage riflemen.

The *Desiree*'s boats, however, as they pulled in were fired on from both banks, and as they gave way in haste to get through the bottleneck, where they were not only galled by the 'Bush Rangers' or 'Rock Doves', as they were called, but plastered with showers of grape from the schooner, (moored broadside on across the narrowest part) they ran hard and fast ashore on a shoal, which ran out in a long spit from the shore.

The cutting out party were properly trapped. When at length they succeeded in getting one of the cutters over the reef, after tremendous efforts, she was almost at once brought up again by a hawser stretched across the entrance.

For about three hours the boat's crews stood it out. The night was dark with no moon, and only the flashes from the schooner's guns and the red of the rifle fire, indicated the positions of the enemy. Whilst the marines returned the fire, the seaman struggled to haul their boats clear, but it was soon found that the further they hauled, the further they got on to the reef, and the shallower the water.

At last with the serjeant of marines and a seaman killed, a number of men wounded including Pakenham, with a rifle ball through each arm, the boats were compelled to retreat.

When they arrived onboard the *Desiree*, Captain Love, who had warned them against making the attempt, declared that nobody but himself could have cut the schooner out from such a position.

As soon as it was daylight, the frigate was worked close up to the weather point of Escondido, from whence she opened fire on the schooner from her quarter-deck guns, until the latter had warped further in. At any rate the frigate's fire could not have done much harm, as only the schooner's masts could be seen when she opened fire.

Spanish Conspirators Overheard and Love in Disgrace

Owing to Love's well known reputation for the good treatment of his prisoners, he was allowed great lenity by Captain Ross, and very soon became a bright and valued ornament of the midshipman's mess.

In this way, much of his extraordinary history became known to the *Desiree*'s officers. That he often drew the long bow in describing his adventures was probable, nevertheless he seems to have been the beau ideal of the romantic corsair.

On the Spanish Main, the Bahama Sea and throughout the Antilles 'to be as generous as Captain Love' was a common saying; he was as prodigal in helping the needy as he was humane in the treatment of his captives. He was reputed to possess fabulous riches and like the true sailor of his day possessed a wife in every port—and not only a wife but in the towns of Spanish America and on the French islands he owned houses and slaves, and he was wont to entertain in the most lavish manner. With such a slippery customer, who had two most daring escapes to his credit, it was necessary to take every precaution; yet, in spite of this, Love might have worked his will had he not been over-heard conspiring with the Spanish prisoners by a black carpenter's mate, who happened to understand Spanish.

Every evening after his work this man was in the habit of setting his tools upon a grind stone, which was kept within the manger-board (*Note:* a strong bulkhead, on the fore part of the lower deck, to stop the rush of water through the hawse-pipes from poring aft; the manger being the space between stem and the manger board).

Here, one night, he found several of the Spanish prisoners sharpening their knives. A second time this happened. A fresh lot of prisoners (there were fifty to sixty on board) were sharpening their knives, which, on his appearance, they hastily concealed from his view. But the black carpenter's mate was as sharp as one of their Spanish knives and the next evening he hid himself within earshot of the manger. The knife sharpeners were planning to seize the ship as she lay at anchor.

The quarter-watch on deck were to be knocked on the head, those who resisted were to be knifed, and the whole plot to be carried through under the leadership of the notorious picaroon, Captain Love.

The latter was evidently bent on carrying out the good precepts which he had impressed upon the mids of the *Desiree*.

"Take immediate advantage of every circumstance. The man of action must never for an instant let his head go 'wool-gathering'", were his words. It was remembered also that one day he had remarked casually that during the last war, when his health was beginning to suffer from the climate, the English had kindly sent him a trip home, which had set him up again: and he supposed that they would again perform a like friendly act, nevertheless he was willing to bet that before he had been a month aboard the prison hulks in Port Royal harbour, he would take French leave.

No one had offered to take his bet, though he had assured his listeners that it would be punctually met, should he remain in durance vile beyond the stipulated month.

Such talk only served to make the suspicion that Love was concerned in the Spaniards' plot all the stronger. Captain Ross at once had the dangerous privateersman ironed and put in charge of the sentinel at his own cabin door. The Spaniards, also, were deprived of their long murderous knives.

The following morning the conspirators were brought before the Captain, and interrogated. Love defended himself with the utmost eloquence in vehemently indignant and even sarcastic tones:—

"Permit me to assure you, sir, that though in my life I have performed some rash actions I am not yet mad enough to undertake so desperate, ridiculous and barbarous an enterprise. You have caused me to suffer an indignity never before put upon me.

Be pleased to treat me, sir, with that lenity with which I have always treated your countrymen when my prisoners—that is all I ask.

I solemnly disclaim having had any intention of participating in the murderous plan just described".

But the Captain of the *Desiree* was not to be persuaded by all Love's eloquence, and the Corsair remained shackled at the cabin door, where his sprightly, jovial spirit entirely left him, and he sat in a state of utter dejection like a moulting eagle in captivity.

However, he had barely got used to his leg-irons before he was transferred to the *Bellerophon*, seventy-four guns, which was encountered off San Domingo on her way to Jamaica.

Old Tommy, as Admiral Sir James Duckworth was called, paid Love the compliment of placing him in irons with two sentries over him aboard one of the prison-hulks, which in 1803, lay moored in a row across the harbour.

However, sure enough, before the month of his wager was up, both Kingston and Port Royal were raised to a high pitch of excitement by the news that the Prince of Picaroons had escaped—vamoosed into the air as it were, leg-irons, sentries, and all.

Nothing more than vague rumour came out of the Admiral's enquiry into Love's escape.

The sentries appear to have been disaffected Germans, who had evidently been heavily bribed. A canoe must have taken off the prisoner and his guards for at this date one of Port Royal's famous sharks, going by the name of Port Royal Lion, used to swim round the prison ships in order to gobble up the remains of the prisoner's dinners. This shark was such a check on escaping prisoners and deserters that strict orders were given against his being shot at or molested in any way.

Love's Schooner Sunk By H.M.S. *Elk*

No more was heard of the famous French privateersman until 1806. On the first of October of that year, the brig-sloop *Elk*, Captain Morris, sighted a large schooner off Navassa. In a nine hour run, during which the chase had led the *Elk* all round the compass in her endeavour to find out the brig's worst point of sailing; the two ships were hidden from each other by a furious storm of wind and rain.

The *Elk* bore away before the wind to save her spars, having already, by hard sail carrying, sprung her main-topmast. The chase, which was Captain Love's schooner, the

Alliance, of five guns and seventy-five men, rounded into the wind and dropped her sails, a common picaroon's trick, by which he hoped that his pusuer would run by him, and so find himself away to leeward of his quarry when the sky cleared.

In this instance the result was not so happy for the Frenchman, for the *Elk*, blinded by the sheets of driving rain, ran straight into the *Alliance*, cutting her almost in two—then, riding clean over the sinking schooner, passed on into the gloom. But just at the psychological moment, the well-known figure of Captain Love was recognised at the falls of the privateer's stern-boat, and before the sinking vessel was lost in the murk, the jolly-boat with the captain aboard was seen to pull clear. As soon as the wind took off and Captain Morris dared to haul his brig up, she was headed back, and she was just in time to save the men from the wreck, though nothing could be seen of the boat with her lone occupant. Whether he had swamped or made his escape, no more was ever heard on the Jamaica station of the great French privateersman.

Jacca Mathieu, and His Ballahou Schooner *Maringouin*

Rivalling Love in boldness, to which he added a spice of pure mischief, Jacque Mathieu made his reputation first in a long-winged felucca, then in a typical 'balahou' schooner of the Caribbean Sea.

His escapes from under the guns of British cruisers even more remarkable than Captain Love's escapes from British limboes.

In his little felucca Jacca was one day overhauled in a hard wind by a British sloop of war. He at once lowered his sails without resistance and the sloop hove to along side him.

The captain of the sloop, who had been on deck watching the chase since sunrise, retired to his cabin for some welcome refreshment, but he had scarcely sat down before his stern windows were broken and his decanters swept off the table by a discharge of shrapnel. Swearing mightily he reached the deck in time to see the felucca luffing round to windward under his quarter.

It was just on nightfall, and before the sloop could be rounded onto the right tack and sail set, the felucca was hardly to be distinguished, stretching away into the wind's eye, laying up two points closer than was possible for the square-rigged sloop.

A few hundred rounds were sent after him, but Jacque Mathieu got clean away.

In his incredibly swift *Maringouin*, the before mentioned ballahou schooner, Jacca became so bold that he would heave to until his pursuer was within range; then when the first round from the man of war's bow-chaser went skipping by, he would let draw his sheets and in a few tacks work out of shot.

His chief head-quarters was a small port lying under a conspicuous rock on the North side of San Domingo, east of Cape Haytian or Cape Francois, as it was generally called by the French.

There was a fort on the rock, called Monte Christo by the Spaniards, and La Grange by the French, and under its guns French and Spanish privateers considered themselves safe from British cruisers.

Nevertheless men of war boats occasionally were successful in cutting out privateers from under the Monte Christo fort.

One one occasion these doughty picaroons caught a tartar. What appeared to be a large West Indiaman lay becalmed off the great Lion Rock of Cape Francois. At sun up, a flock of Monte Christo privateers headed by Jacca Mathieu, came swooping down upon her under their sweeps and did not discover that their quarry was a well-known British frigate until they were almost under her guns.

As soon as the sea breeze made, the well camouflaged man of war made sail and opened fire upon those of the picaroons that were within range. Through the bad sailing of the frigate, which was worn out, the enemy had a good chance of escape; but she had the advantage of the wind, and by means of slinging shot and sea chests and turning half her crew into their hammocks, she was made to go to windward much better than was her wont. By noon she had one of the privateers, heading on the same tack, on her lee bow. This craft suddenly flung round in a bold attempt to cross her hawse and gain the weather guage. As the two vessels converged, it seemed from the deck of the frigate that the little schooner could not possibly cross her bows. But when it was recognised that this craft was the *Maringouin* and that Jacca Mathieu himself was at her helm, the excitement aboard the cruiser became intense.

The brave privateersman sent everyone of his crew below, and stood alone in a shower of lead, which poured from the bow guns, marines and small arms of the frigate. He seemed to bear a charmed life. The schooner's decks were ripped up, her sails torn, her spars wounded and still he came on, steering his little ballahou as close as she would lie without shivering her headsails. It was touch and go—Would he scrape clear? The moment came when he was almost under the frigate's forefoot. Indeed so near a shave was it that his lee runner actually hooked over the cruiser's jibboom end. The jibboom bent like a trout rod.

"Hooked, by God!" yelled a voice on the frigate's forecastle.

"We have him under the forefoot!" roared the first lieutenant, hailing aft.

"Bonjour, Messieurs!" called Jacca, lifting his hat with an impish grin.

Then the runner leaped clear and the ballahou was free, and went leaping away into the wind's eye, followed by a few wildly aimed shots from the muskets of the marines.

The frigate had better luck with the second of these Monte Christo picaroons.

Her commander did not possess Jacca's nerve and, instead of trying for the weather berth, bore away before the wind with every flying kite in his locker set. It was not until sundown, however, that the frigate got up to her and made the capture.

Shortly after this, Jacca had still a narrower escape. This time he was chased into the Bight of Leogane, where he ran his shallow-draught ballahou into the shoal water along the shore, where the man of war could not follow. Night drew on, and it seemed that Jacca Mathieu must escape—then at half past eight the wind petered out. The *Maringouin* lowered her sails. The frigate kedged and sent away her boats in chase of the elusive privateersman.

It soon grew too dark to distinguish the chase, but the noise of her sweeps gave her away. The boats pulled into the darkness whence came the rasping creak of the sweeping. But when this stopped, they were at a loss for the sky was overcast and there was no moon. However, with muffled oars they pulled on in the direction from which the sweeping had last been heard.

Then there came a strong whiff of garlic and tobacco smoke. A second later two masts could be faintly distinguished within point-blank range. The boats let fly a volley of small arms. And splashes in the phosphorescent water all round them told of a somewhat ragged reply.

As the boats gave way in the confident expectation of grinding alongside the ballahou in a moment or two, the black outlines of the schooner's main and fore sails were seen to be rising, and hauling cried mingled with the sharp clop of musketoons and the spit of bullets. On came the boats, heading for each quarter of the privateer—their bowmen sprang up, ready to hook on.

"Vast pulling!" came the order. Then, at the very moment when a leap would have taken the lieutenant in command over the low bulwarks of the *Maringouin*, there came a chattering noise under the schooner's knife-like stem, her sails filled with a clap, the land-breeze had reached her and she was off. Pulling their best the boats could not hold her and soon dropped astern.

Then a burst of red flame and a reverberating roar came from her bow chaser, but, once again, Jacca got clean away.

A few days later the British cruiser spoke an American merchantman, who reported that Jacque Mathieu had limped into Monte Christo with his pumps going hard, his deck torn up by a thirty-two-pound shot and many of his crew lying wounded under a gaily coloured awning.

Mathieu Captured

It was not until Jacque Mathieu deserted his little *Maringouin* for a fine brig that he was captured, and that took some doing as the following report testifies:—

Princess Charlotte
December, 13, 1804

Sir,

I have the honour to inform you that at ten a.m., Cape Antonie East four leagues, made all sail in chase of a brig: and after a hard chase of seven hours with a fresh breeze, came up with her in latitude 20° 50′ longitude 85° 32′, having steered South the whole of the chase.

After firing four or five shot at her, she struck and proves to be the French privateer brig, *Regulus*, from Guadeloupe, commanded by Citizen Jacque Mathieu, pierced for fourteen guns, but only eleven mounted (having thrown two overboard with her boats and spars in the chase) and eighty four men. She is a very fine vessel, sails remarkably well, is coppered, and is in my opinion perfectly adapted for His Majesty's Service.

I have the honour to be, etc.,
F.F. Gardner.
(The Hon. F.F. Gardner)

To Sir J. T. Duckworth, K.B. etc.

The *Princess Charlotte* was a forty-gun frigate, late the French *Junou*.

The Guadeloupe Privateer *Buonaparte*

Guadeloupe on the leeward island station was even more of a centre for French privateers than the ports of San Domingo. From this base they fairly battened upon the rich West Indiamen and sugar droghers of Barbadoes.

The most famous of all these Guadeloupe letters of Marque and privateersmen was the brig *Buonaparte*, mounting eighteen nine-pounders and manned by close on one hundred and fifty men.

Here is one of her exploits taken from the Barbadoes paper of August the ninth, 1804.

"His Majesty's schooner, *St. Lucia*, Captain Bettesworth, arrived last night from Antiqua also the Mail-boat. By these arrivals we learn the following particulars of a very gallant action between his Majesty's ship *Hippomenes* and the *Buonaparte*, French brig of eighteen nine-pounders and one hundred and forty-six men, in which the enemy owe their escape only to the misfortune of our ship having too many foreigners on board, whose dastard spirit made them shrink from the action.

His Majesty's ship *Hippomenes*, Captain M'Kenzie, cruizing to windward of this island, fell in, in longitude 58° latitude 18°, with the *Buonaparte*, brig, which, mistakening the *Hippomenes* for an African ship, (i.e. a slaver) being disguised purposely to decoy the enemy's cruizers, bore down on her; when a smart action ensued, which lasted for some time: and the enemy, being to windward, at length fell on board the *Hippomenes*.

Captain McKenzie, with the greatest promptitude, seizing the occasion to prevent the enemy's escape, had her bowsprit lashed to the mainmast, calling upon his crew to follow him in boarding, and secure the victory.

He instantly rushed upon the enemy's deck, followed by his officers and about eight men only, when a smart contest ensued, and the Frenchmen were driven from their quarters, and beat abaft the mainmast. Seeing, however, that they had to cope with so few, they soon rallied, and the whole crew being now engaged with this small band of heroes, they were almost all cut to pieces. Captain McKenzie received fourteen severe wounds, his first lieutenant, Mr. Pierce, and Purser, Mr. Colman, were killed, and the master wounded. Thus overcome, they were obliged to retreat and had but just time to regain the ship (Captain McKenzie falling senseless into her main chains) when the lashing gave way, and the enemy fell off, and without wishing to renew the contest, crowded all sail and escaped.

The *Hippomenes* has gone to Antiqua to refit and we are happy to understand that Captain McKenzie, although his wounds in general are severe, and three of them in the head, is likely to recover".

This vivid account gives one a very good idea of the old cut-and-thrust warfare when boarding was the favourite and most successful of British naval tactics—so different from the 'long bowls' of modern action.

***Buonaparte* Beaten Off By West Indiamen**

The same newspaper, the *Barbadoes Mercury*, a little over a year later, came out with the following headlines in large type.

DEFEAT OF BUONAPARTE NOT THE GREAT!!!

BUT

THE CELEBRATED PRIVATEER OF GUADELOUPE

Then came an account of a most gallant action.

On the eighth of November three West Indiamen, the *Thetis, Ceres* and *Penelope*, thirty-one days out from the Channel on their passage to Bridgetown, were attacked in 13° 26′ N., 57° 30′ W. by the *Buonaparte*, which came up under English colours at seven in the morning.

As she ranged up, the picaroon fired two broadsides into the leading Britisher, which was the *Thetis*. Captain Charnley of the latter, seeing that the Frenchman intended to lay his ship alongside to leeward, wore round on the other tack. The *Buonaparte* was thus obliged to take his weather quarter, her crew lashing her to the mizzen chains of the *Thetis*.

Then came an hour's desperate fighting "twice they set us on fire on the quarter deck with stink pots and other combustibles, and made four very daring attempts to board with at least eighty men out of their rigging, foretop and bowsprit, but were most boldly repulsed by every man and boy in the ship. At the conclusion a double-headed shot from our aftermost gun carried away his foremast by the board and that took away his bowsprit and main topgallant mast. He then thought it was time to cast us off", ran the report of Captain Charnley.

The other two Indiamen did their best to second the *Thetis*.

"We began firing at nine and did not leave off till after twelve". Wrote the Captain of the *Ceres*.

He does not seem to have a very experienced crew, for he goes on:—

My ship was on fire three times by neglect of the people with their cartridges, but by the exertion of the crew it was soon extinguished.

They behave with the greatest spirit and I believe would have fought to the last, though one half of them were foreigners. I had several shot in the hull and my rigging and sails were very much cut. The small shot and grape came aboard us like hail, though they did not hit one man. I had two men blown up by the cartridges taking fire, who are very much burned.

The *Penelope* could not have been of much help to the other two, as she had ten of her guns dismounted, one of the troubles of carronades.

The *Buonaparte*, having dropped clear of the *Thetis*; the latter hauled her wind and set about knotting and splicing her cut rigging, whilst her consorts pounded the dismasted privateer but without much effect. The *Thetis* stood into action again as soon as she had repaired her rigging and engaged for another hour.

"But", says her skipper, "finding it impossible to take him owing to his number of men and having no surgeon to dress our wounded, I thought it best to steer our course for this island".

He had two men killed, and his second mate and eight men wounded.

In a letter home, he wrote:—

> "The *Buonaparte* privateer is the completest ship in these seas. She made too certain of us. Freers, my first mate, behaved most gallantly and fought like a lion: so did Lambert, my second mate. Indeed I cannot say enough for every man and boy in the ship: the greatest part of them stripped and fought naked and I am sure would have died sooner than have been carried. There was one hour's hard work, I assure you. I was near going frequently, as they fired several musket balls through my clothes"

The Captain of the *Buonaparte* only a week or two before had sent a challenge by an American to any of the British sloops on the station.

He was very proud of being called:—

"The Terror of the West Indies".

The three West Indiamen, however, had pretty effectively cut his gallic comb; and when the sloop *Cyane* fell in with the *Buonaparte*, making the best of her way to Guadeloupe, she made a prize of the well trimmed Frenchman without any difficulty and brought her into Antiqua on November the eleventh.

The captain of this notorious picaroon after being a prisoner for a short while, was exchanged and returned to the French naval service, after his experience as a privateersman.

When third lieutenant of the war-brig *Lynx* he was killed on January the twenty-first 1807, during her action with the thirty-two-gun frigate, *Galatea*.

Dominique Diron of the Privateer *Superbe*

One of the most successful of the semi-piratical privateersmen, who operated from the maze of coral reefs and cays on the South coast of Cuba, was Monsieur Dominique Diron, Captain and owner of the notorious picaroon *Superbe*, carrying twelve long six-pounders, two long eight-pounders, and close on a hundred men of all nationalities.

Neither Dominique or his crew were particular as to whom they captured, and neutrals seldom escaped him without having to pay for their freedom with canvas, rope, arms and provisions.

The *Superbe*, after a chase of sixty-seven hours with intervals of close action, during which she suffered severely, was at length driven ashore near Cape Maysi, on the East end of Cuba by His Majesty's twelve-gun schooner, *Pitt*, Lieutenant Michael Fitton, on October the twenty-sixth, 1806. Dominique and his crew hastily bundled ashore, leaving four dead and three mortally wounded aboard the *Superbe*.

When Lieutenant Fitton came to overhaul the picaroon's papers in the cabin of the wrecked *Superbe*, he found an account book with a list of prizes, English, Spanish and American, in Dominique's hand-writing, with the value of each, amounting in all to £147,000, sterling.

Dominique at once fitted out the well-known two-topsail schooner *Juliana*, changing her name to the *Vengeance*, or, more grandiloquently, the *Revanche de la Superbe*.

He then sent by a Jamaican free-trader an invitation to Lieutenant Fitton for a contest to the death. But poor Fitton, the most successful schooner captain in the West Indies since Jack Perkins, had by this time been obliged to make way for a protege of the Admiral's, and was languishing on half pay.

Lieutenant Michael Fitton

No British officer had a higher reputation for gallantry in the West Indies than Michael Fitton.

Of good family, his ancestor being Sir Edward Fitton, Chancellor of Ireland in the time of James II. He was born about 1766 at Gawsworth in Cheshire, afterwards the seat of the Earl of Harrington, and entered the Navy in January 1780 under the auspices of Lord Keppel, as captain's servant aboard the *Vestal*, twenty-eight guns, Captain George Keppel.

Whilst serving aboard the *Vestal*, young Fitton was the hero of a very curious episode in International affairs.

The frigate was in chase of an American packet, and the boy joined the furlers on the fore-topgallant yard when the order went to shorten sail on overhauling the American. As the chase's ensign fluttered down, Fitton noticed what he took to be a man falling overboard from her stern.

He immediately reported what he had seen, and, as a consequence, a bag was seen floating on the water, which was duly picked up. This bag proved to contain the actual manuscript of a secret treaty between the American Congress and the Dutch, the ex-president of the rebel colony, Laurnas, being aboard the packet.

As a result of this capture England declared war upon Holland.

After serving as midshipman and master's mate in several ships, Fitton somehow or other found himself in a position which he was far from appreciating—that of purser of the sloop *Stork*.

The *Stork* happened to be at the Nore during the great mutiny, and that her men remained true and did not join the mutineers was generally credited to Fitton's good influence.

Afterwards the *Stork* was ordered to the West Indies, where at the beginning of 1799 Fitton managed to get an acting lieutenant's place aboard the Port Royal Guardship, the *Abergavenny*. During practically the whole of his time in the *Abergavenny*, he was employed in command of her tenders.

In Command of Tenders

One invariably finds that the most dashing and enterprising officers were in command of tenders in the West Indies in war time—Nelson being a typical example.

To show Michael Fitton's keenness it is only necessary to state that he contributed most of the money towards the purchase of each of his commands, putting up as much as £400 for the last, the schooner *Pitt*.

The commander of a tender had also to find the money to keep her in the smartness of paint, varnish and gold leaf, such as befitted a ship of His Majesty's Service. It may be argued that Fitton's prize money easily paid all such expenses, seeing that between 1799 and 1807 he captured over forty sail including many fine privateers.

But it has to be remembered that the Admiral and the officers and men of the flagship all shared the prize money obtained through his instrumentality, and O'Bryne declares that Fitton himself made very little out of his share in spite of his great success.

His first command was merely a launch armed with a bow-gun. Let me quote from the eloquent William James:—

> "Among the many weary hours to which a naval life is subject, none can surely equal those passed on board a stationary flagship: especially in a port where there is a constant egress and regress of cruisers, some sailing forth to seek prizes, others returning with prizes already in their possession.
>
> During the whole of the year 1797 and the greater part of 1798 the fifty-four gun ship *Abergavenny*, as she lay moored in the Port Royal harbour, Jamaica, daily exposed her officers and men to these tantalizing torments.
>
> At length it was suggested that a small tender, sent off the east end of the island or even into Cow Bay, scarcely out of sight of the harbour, might acquire for the parent-ship some share of the honours that were reaped by the cruisers around her.
>
> A thirty-eight gun frigate's launch having been obtained, and armed with a swivel in the bow, the next difficulty was to find an officer who, to a willingness, could add the other requisites, for so perilous and uncomfortable a service.
>
> It was not every man who would like to be cramped up night and day in an open boat, exposed to all kinds of weather, as well as to the risk of being captured by some of the many picaroons that infested the coast.

An acting-lieutenant of the *Abergavenny*, one on whom nature had conferred an ardent mind, habit, an indifference about personal comfort and in eighteen or twenty years of active service, an experience in all the duties of his profession, cheerfully consented to take charge of the cruiser-boat.

Mr. Michael Fitton soon gave proofs of his fitness for the task he had undertaken: and the crew of the *Abergavenny* could now and then greet a prize of their own, among the many that dropped anchor near them.

With a part of the funds that a succession of prizes had brought to the ship, a decked vessel was at length purchased: with the fruits of her gains, another: and so on until the schooner, whose little exploit we are now about to record, came in her turn to be the *Abergavenny*'s tender".

The *Ferret* and a Big Spaniard

This schooner was the *Ferret*, mounting six three-pounders with a crew of forty-five men and boys.

On October the fifth, 1799, a large schooner, with eight ports aside was sighted off the north east end of Jamaica flying an English pendant and ensign.

As the ensign was large enough for a battle ship, and the pendant longer far than the regulation length, Fitton's suspicions were at once aroused and he tacked to close the stranger, which presently substituted Spanish for English colours.

Though the odds against his little tender were heavy, Fitton never hesitated. His first manoeuvre was to gain the weather-guage. Although he close hauled his sheets, he sailed a little off the wind so as to tempt the Spaniard into his wake. Then, as soon as she fell into the trap, he hauled up on her weather and began a sharp action.

After half an hour's battering the Spanish privateer had had enough of it, and made sail for San Jago de Cuba. The fight had been watched by the inhabitants off the East end of Jamaica, and when they saw the *Ferret* following her large antagonist towards the coast of Cuba, they made sure she was captured, and sent information to this effect to Port Royal. However, Fitton stuck on the skirts of the privateer, and when the breeze fell at sunset, put out his sweeps and slowly overhauled her, getting up to her at eleven p.m. when the action was renewed. The Spaniard's fire was high, cutting the *Ferret*'s sails and rigging to pieces, but as usual, the English gunners aimed at their enemy's hull with good effect and it was afterwards learnt that out of a crew of one hundred, the privateer lost ten killed and eleven wounded, Fitton continued the action until the Spaniard reached Santiago or San Jago, as it was then named, when he had to break off the action against a vessel which was twice his size and mounted fourteen six-pounders.

This gallant affair, like many of Michael Fitton's actions, failed to find its way into the Gazette, but his name and that of the little tender speedily became household words throughout the West Indies.

Fitton's Shark and the *Nancy*'s Papers

It is now time to tell Michael Fitton's shark story, and it is so well told in his own words in the *United Service Journal*, that I will quote them verbatim.

His account was addressed to Ilted Nicholl Esq., His Majesty's Proctor.

"I comply with your request and send the narrative of the shark to accompany the official documents and the shark's jaws in your possession.

The Commander-in-Chief on the Jamaica Station, in the year 1799, ordered Lieutenant Whylie, in the *Sparrow* cutter, to cruize in the Mona Passage in company with the tender of H.M.S. *Abergavenny*, under my command. We beat up hank for hank, and on weathering the East end dined together.

On comparing notes, he had ten six-pounders in the *Sparrow* and I had six three-pounders in the tender, with which we concluded (*after dinner*) that we could capture any sloop-of-war of the enemy and even (*before we parted*) beat off and damnably hamper a frigate.

We parted company the next night in chase, but joined again some days after, off Jacmel, the South side of St. Domingo. At dawn, the *Sparrow* was about six miles in-shore: by signal I asked him on board to breakfast.

Whilst his boat was pulling on board, I seated myself on the taffrail, and observing a dead bullock floating at some distance, which the sharks were tearing and lashing to pieces, I had it towed alongside (we were then in the track of cattle-loaded vessels from Puerto Cavallo, Laquira, etc.) the sharks followed; one of them, much larger than the rest I resolved to catch, and make a walking-stick of his back-bone.

I baited a hook with a four-pound piece of beef; he rubbed himself against it, but seemed shy of taking it: when the lesser ones approached I drew away the bait. I changed it for a piece of pork, which at length he bolted. I played with him with about sixty fathoms of line: when exhausted, I had him hoisted in, and directed some of the men to open the stomach, and take out the piece of pork, which could not be worse—in doing which there was found a bundle of papers tied round with a string!

I have to observe that the nature of the service I was then employed in did not require a mute and reverential deference from the seamen (I was never much deposed to exact it). When the sailor handed me the papers, with a queer look he said, "A packet by G — , sir! I hope it's from England: please your honour (touching his hat) will you look if there's a letter for me—I should like to hear from my old sweetheart".

The papers were in a perfect state, except the envelope: they appeared to relate to a vessel's cargo, and a letter, dated at the island of Curacoa, addressed to an enemy's port, had this commencement:—

"The bearer hereof, my good friend Mr. Christopher Schultz, supercargo of the American brig, *Nancy*, will hand you this". It then entered into a statement of mercantile concerns.

My first idea was that the shark had come from Curacoa: the next that the papers had been thrown overboard by some honest neutral chased by one of His Majesty's cruisers. I therefore hailed the man at the masthead and directed him to keep a bright look out: to which he replied:— "There is nothing in sight, sir, but the *Sparrow* cutter in shore, and her boat pulling on board".

When Lieutenant Whylie arrived on board, he said—but I will first describe him.

Lieutenant Hugh Whylie was of the old school—a perfect seaman, brave of course—yard-arm was his maxim—who had, like myself, waddled to the water as soon as out of the shell: he had finished his education from books scattered on the rudder-head, to him equally authentic and erudite, such as Homer's Iliad, and Hudibras, Jack the Giant Killer, Pilgrim's Progress, etc. In religion, he thought a short prayer, well said, better than a life monastic; and, like most good Christians of that day, abhorred popery and the Pope, who, he believed, had dealings with the devil, yet would he, on the impulse, have jumped overboard to save that 'man of sin'?

He was withal a great admirer of the fair sex, whether black or white; and furthermore the West Indies suited him exactly, it being a 'bra country where you are aye drinking and aye dry'.

Alas! Poor Whylie. He was a good hearted fellow; many a cruise we have had together—'I shall not look upon his like again'.

When he arrived on board he said—but I had better give you the dialogue.

Lieutenant Whylie—"What a devil of a long pull you have given me this morning, and not a breath of air out of the heavens. Come, is breakfast ready—no Banyan day, I hope?".

Fitton—"Well, Whylie, my boy, what luck have you had since we parted company?".

Whylie—"Why, I have taken a French schooner, a Dutch schooner and I have detained on suspicion an American brig".

On his looking round and seeing the shark, he said:—

"Why do you dirty your decks with those cursed animals, you'll be a boy all your life time".

Fitton—"Tell me, Whylie, was the American brig you detained named *Nancy*?".

Whylie—"Yes, her name was *Nancy*: you have not met her, I suppose?".

Fitton—"No, I have not".

Whylie—"Then why did you ask me if the brig's name was *Nancy*?".

Fitton—"Was there not a supercargo on board called Christopher Schultz of Baltimore?".

Whylie—"Yes, his name was Skoolts or Schultz, or some damned Dutch name or other: why, you must have spoke her?".

Fitton—"No, I have not, I never saw her".

Whylie—"Then how the devil came you to know I had detained the brig *Nancy*, Christopher Schultz supercargo?".

Fitton—"The shark you see lying there has brought me full information of your brig, and those papers you see spread out to dry are the papers of your brig *Nancy*".

Whylie—"There's a lie somewhere, Fitton, not far off, for I sealed all her papers up, and gave them in charge of the prize-master, when I sent the brig away".

Fitton—"The papers delivered to you by the master when you overhauled her you have, of course, sent with the vessel, but her *true* papers that prove the owners to be enemies and not Americans, are those you see drying on deck, brought to me by that shark you abuse me for catching".

Lieutenant Whylie stared at me, at the shark, at the papers; then quickly descended the cabin-ladder, calling out "Breakfast ho!—none of your tricks upon travellers; none of your gumption, Fitton!".

By the time we had breakfasted, the sea-breeze came down, two strange sail hove in sight, and away we both started in chase and parted company.

On my return into Port Royal, I deposited the papers in the Admiralty Court and sent the shark's jaws with this inscription:—'Lieutenant Fitton recommends these jaws for a collar for neutrals to swear through'.

On Lieutenant Whylie's return, he found the *Nancy* condemned to him as a prize, by the recovery of the true papers, leaving to Johnathan no resource in future but to swallow the papers himself.

signed Micheal Fitton
Lieutenant, R.N.

In reference to Fitton's last paragraph but one, Captain Frederick Hoffman, R.N., in his journal, *A Sailor of King George*, also describes the incident. He happened to be a lieutenant aboard the *Volage*, twenty-two guns, also cruising in the Mona Passage at that date.

He wrote of the shark's jaws, which are now to be seen in the Whitehall Museum of the Royal United Service Institution;—"I well recollect its being suspended over where the American masters' detained vessels stood when they desired to make oath".

The papers are also to be seen in the Museum.

The *Nancy* was a Baltimore brig of one hundred and twenty-five tons, which left that port on July the third, 1799, under Captain Thomas Briggs, bound to Curacoa; she was captured in the Mona Passage by the *Sparrow* on August the twenty-eighth.

Success of the *Active*

In his next command, the *Active*, a schooner mounting eight twelve-pounder carronades with a crew of forty five men, Michael Fitton took part in operations against Curacoa under the thirty-six-gun frigate *Nereide*, Captain F. Watkins.

Here he chiefly distinguished himself by attacking half a dozen French privateers, which for protection, had taken refuge under the walls of Fort Piscadero, at Port Amsterdam.

In December 1800 on the *Active*'s return to Port Royal after a year's hard service, during which she had captured and destroyed more of the enemy's mosquito gun-boats and picaroons than any cruiser on the station, it was found that she was in need of a thorough repair.

A Cruise in a Felucca

Whilst the *Active* was in the hands of the dockyard mates, Michael Fitton transferred his crew to one of her prizes, the *Nostra Signora de los Dolores*, a Spanish felucca of about fifty tons, carrying one twelve-pounder Long Tom on a pivot.

He sailed out of Port Royal at the beginning of January 1801 for a cruise on the Spanish Main.

Though the little felucca was far from seaworthy with rotten ropes, worn-out sails, a leaky deck, and the weight of her Long Tom carried by a badly sprung main-beam, she proved an excellent decoy, by which means the enterprising Fitton was able to surprise and destroy several of Spain's small fry in the coasting and free-booting lines of business. But under such rough conditions as having to sleep on the ballast in the hold, and brave the exhalations from the bilges, (for the felucca had not 'tween decks) or else on deck to be tormented and infected by mosquitoes, his men soon began to go sick.

For this reason, and because his vessel was almost falling to pieces, Fitton who knew every inch of the coast like Jack Perkins, selected a small cay on the Spanish Main near Point Canoe (Point Canoas). Here he recruited the health of his men, careened his felucca, and did his best to make her more seaworthy. Without even twine to repair his sails, he was forced to cut down his big lateen and converted his ship into a lugger. He then bore up for Carthagena, intending to coast along the Main as far as Porto Bello.

At day break on January the twenty-third, whilst rounding Cape Rosario, the little felucca fell in with the Spanish Guarda-costa, *Santa Maria*, a schooner of six long six-pounders, ten swivels and sixty men.

The *Nosta Signora de los Delores* had no bulwark beyond a low rail, and, like Jacca Mathieu, Michael Fitton took the helm and kept his men hidden under hatches, even his only gun being slung below out of sight.

The guarda-costa to any prudent officer would have seemed far too formidable an antagonist, but Fitton combined dash and daring, and having allowed the *Santa Maria* to run close aboard, quickly hoisted up his Long Tom and got it into action.

For a strenuous half hour, the felucca, with her single gun firing twice as often as the whole broadside of the guarda-costa, more than held her own. Then the Spaniard, who was to windward and in-shore, broke off the action by hauling up for the beach of Virus Isle. But Fitton, in dire need, not only of bosun's stores, but of provisions, was not willing to let his prey escape him in this fashion, so he promptly followed his big antagonist into the surf, and when she grounded, the felucca took the shore within fifty feet of her.

As both vessels fell over, the deck of the tiny cruiser became exposed to the fire of the guarda-costa, whose crew, safe behind their high side were able to make good practise with their muskets. Seeing that his crew were in danger of being picked off one by one, Fitton, crying out for boarders to follow him, leaped into the breakers with a cutlass between his teeth, and his devoted crew, even including those who were on the sick list, jumped into the sea after him.

Those weak with fever nearly drowned, but the rest, headed by their commander, and each man with a weapon between his teeth, swam to the schooner, clambered aboard, and after a sharp struggle carried her.

The casualties in this most gallant affair were:— *Nostra Signora de los Dolores* two killed, five wounded; *Santa Maria als Forans* (to give her her full name) five killed, and nine wounded, including her captain, Don Josef Corei, who lost both his hands by a grape shot.

The next thing was to refloat both vessels. As regards the schooner, this was found beyond the power of the felucca's small crew and after taking out the much-wanted stores, Fitton set her on fire. Having no place to keep his prisoners aboard the little *Nostra Signora de los Dolores*, he was obliged to put them ashore, and they promptly joined the local inhabitants in maintaining a steady fire upon the men of war's men from the shelter of the bush. Fitton, however, was not to be defeated.

The felucca had lost her own anchors and cables in a gale of wind four days before, but with those of the prize he managed to edge his vessel off, though not before he had had to heave his Long Tom overboard.

Four days later, this make-shift tender reached the Black River, Jamaica, where she was forced to put in on her way to Port Royal, having only a gallon of muddy water left aboard.

After this rough experience Fitton and his crew returned to the *Active*.

Having expended eighty pounds in procuring intelligence, this enterprising officer next captured four vessels in the Gulf of Maracaibo, but owing to a swindling agent such disbursement from his private purse did not pay him, and at the Peace of Amiens, he returned home without either promotion or reward.

The *Gipsy* at Curacoa

On the outbreak of the hostilities in May 1803, he returned to Jamaica and was given command of the schooner *Gipsy*, of ten guns and forty-five men, the tender of the *Hercule*, the flagship.

In James' account of the operations against Curacoa in December 1803, Acting-Lieutenant Michael Fitton is the only officer, who shows up with any credit, and it was owing to his invaluable work at Curacoa that he owed his long delayed promotion to lieutenant, dated the ninth March 1804. The captains of the squadron all joined in praising his zeal and judgment in the despatches which he had the honour of himself carrying to the Commander-in-Chief.

He seems to have been the only officer who could act as pilot to the squadron, whilst ashore he dragged the *Gipsy*'s guns to the top of a hill which commanded Amsterdam, and thus proved of great annoyance to the port.

Perhaps Fitton's smartest exploit against the Cuban picaroon's, whilst he was in command of the *Gipsy*, was on January the twenty-first, 1805.

Whilst hove to off Cape Antonio, where he was ordered to meet the frigate *Princess Charlotte*, and deliver her despatches from the Commander-in-Chief, he tempted two schooners and three feluccas of the Spanish privateering fraternity to attempt his capture.

Lieutenant Fitton at once saw his opportunity. Standing off the land, his pursuers in a short while were well strung out, with the largest of them, a fine schooner, well in the lead, and every minute becoming more separated from the rest.

The *Gipsy* had the heels of them all, but as soon as Fitton had decoyed his pursuers well off shore, he payed a hawser out of his stern port to check his way. By this strategy the leader was enabled to get up to him. Then round came the *Gipsy*, up went her ensign and it was the Spaniard's turn to run.

She was forced upon the Colorados reef and totally wrecked; her companions crowded sail to get away; and for the next two or three days, until the arrival of the *Princess Charlotte*, the *Gipsy* was left severely alone.

In 1806 the *Gipsy* was replaced by the twelve-gun schooner *Pitt*, Fitton as already stated contributing four hundred pounds towards the latter's purchase.

On October the twenty-third, 1806 towards evening whilst the *Pitt* lay at anchor within the Mole at Cape St. Nicolas, the lookout reported two sail almost becalmed in the offing. Fitton with the aid of his sweeps was soon in chase. All through the night the crew of the *Pitt* tugged manfully at the heavy sweeps, the schooner hardly ever being able to fill her sails with the fitfull land breeze, however, daylight found her creeping along in the wake of three schooners, the nearest of which proved to be the celebrated French privateer *Superbe*, commanded by Dominique Diron. She was conducting two prizes to the port of Baracoa.

The picaroon hove to whilst her prizes pulled steadily on: she was by no means afraid of the little war schooner. As soon as he was within range, Fitton opened fire with his long sixes, and was replied to by the *Superbe*'s long rights, but before the war schooner could get within effective range, Dominique Diron, having given his prizes a little start, slowly filled away and followed them to the westward.

All that day and all the next night the tired men of war's men tugged grimly at the sweeps in the wake of the picaroon. With the harbour of Baracoa under his lee, Diron did not fear the little *Pitt*, but Michael Fitton was a match for the privateersman and by a supreme effort managed to cut off the *Superbe*, though her prizes got safely into port. With the knowledge that there was no less than five privateers lying in Baracoa, Diron again hove to, to await the onslaught of the *Pitt*.

The action began at four in the afternoon. After thirty-five minutes of rapid fire, the picaroon again made sail, and with a light air headed away for Cape Maysi, with the intention of reaching Ochoa Bay, where there was a force of Spanish troops Fitton did his best to keep between the Frenchmen and the shore, and as the two vessels slowly weathered the point, broadsides were exchanged. With his usual daring, Diron cut across the bows of the *Pitt*, which was as close inshore as she dared go, but he ran it too fine, and the *Superbe* touched the reef and remained hard and fast. The privateersmen at once bundled into their boats and pulled for the shore in a panic, leaving Fitton to take possession of the *Superbe* at his leisure.

The Lieutenant and his crew were worn out by over fifty hours at the sweeps, besides the strenuous effort of working the long guns and carronades in action. Fitton himself had never left the deck for sixty-seven hours, and when the sloop, *Drake*, Commander Robert Nicolas, arrived on the scene, Fitton begged that officer to write a report of the action whilst he turned in.

Rear-Admiral Dacres, commanding the Jamaican station, in his report to the Admiralty wrote:—

"The zeal and perseverance manifested on this occasion, during so long a chase (being upwards of fifty hours at their sweeps, with only two-thirds the number of men the privateer had) the very gallant conduct of, and superior, professional abilities displayed by Mr. Fitton will, I trust, recommend him to the protection of their lordships".

It is hardly believable that after making two more captures, the picaroon *Kou-Fou* and the armed Spanish schooner, *Abja*, Fitton on returning to Jamaica was relieved of his command in order to make way for the son of the new occupant of the Penn, young Thomas John Cochrane, a boy of only seventeen years of age.

Such proceedings were recognised in those days as absolutely fair and legitimate.

Nepotism was considered mere loyalty to one's relations and friends and every commanding officer whether he was the Admiral of a fleet, a post captain, or a young commander, had to try and satisfy the demands of a host of relatives, friends and old shipmates, through whose interest he very probably owed his own advancement.

Michael Fitton was sent home on half pay; he received the thanks of the Admiralty and a fifty pounds sword from the patriotic society. He remained an unemployed lieutenant until April 1811, when he was given command of the gun-brig *Archer* on the channel Station.

In the folowing year he was removed into the gun-brig *Cracker* and distinguished himself doing convoy duty up the Baltic, until the peace, when try as he might he could obtain no further sea employment.

At last in January 1831, he was given the appointment of Lieutenant in ordinary at Plymouth, when he was sixty-five years of age. His duty consisted in looking after the laid-up ships in the Hamoaze, which were slowly rotting at their moorings, their cruising days, like his, long since over.

> "Here, a sheer hulk, lies poor Tom Bowling
> The darling of our crew".

could well have been writen for poor Michael Fitton by Dibdin, for truly this was little more for such an old fire-eater than a living death.

Four years later he was admitted into Greenwich Hospital.

The tough old sailor lingered on until the end of 1852, when he died at Peckham at the age of eighty-seven years.

The Picaroon and the Packet

With Michael Fitton out of the way, Dominique Diron sent out the *Vengeance* to cruise round Jamaica, whilst he himself went in search of further fortune—his movements cannot be traced at this time of day, but it seems probable that he went to Charleston, from which port he later brought out the American privateer, *Decatur*, which, in the summer of 1813 captured the British war schooner *Dominica* after a most desperate and sanguinary contest.

To return to the *Vengeance*, off Pedro point, Jamaica, she fell in with the yacht-like Colonial packet-brig *Charles*.

This little vessel mounted six nine-pounder carronades on carriages. Her crew consisted of a 'gallant old seaman' in command named Cromarty, an old follower of Nelson named Sutherland as mate, and eleven coloured men, and she had two passengers, the master of a West Indiaman and a midshipman, making a total of thirteen souls in all.

Unfortunately her arms chest was so empty that her carronnades had to be discharged by a firestick, there being no match; and her small arms comprised four muskets and the midshipman's dirk.

Against this pigmy force the *Vengeance*, besides broadside guns, musquetoons and swivels, mounted a long brass eighteen-pounder amidships, whilst included in her crew of ninety-five men were thirty well-trained French men-of-war's men, who had lately belonged to the huge first-rate of one hundred and thirty guns, the *Imperial*, which had been destroyed by Admiral Duckworth's squadron off St. Domingo in February 1806.

There was a stark calm raging when the *Vengeance*, a great tri-colour at her peak and the *bloody* flag (indicating that she would give no quarter) drooping from her fore-rigging, came up under her sweeps on the larboard beam of the packet, and poured in a broadside.

The *Charles* soon fired away all her ammunition, and she was then boarded and captured without any difficulty.

The blood-thirsty piratical Spaniards, who formed the greater part of the picaroon's complement, would undoubtedly have put every soul aboard the *Charles* to the sword, had it not been for the gigantic boatswain of the *Vengeance*, a Maltese, who had served many years in the Royal Navy.

A Midshipman's Description of a Picaroon

The captured mid has left an extremely vivid account of this typical West Indian picaroon of the war years.

Her captain was a lean, white-haired, mild little man of some age, who evidently had gained the command through shrewdness and cunning, rather than for any gift of commanding men.

He was an Italian; a good seaman and experienced pilot for those seas, but seemed to the British mid to be entirely worn out and lacking in virility.

The second captain was a Frenchman of a much superior class named Jean Marie, who declared that pure misfortune had driven him to the uncongenial trade of a privateersman.

The crew were mostly brown-jacketted, garlic-eating, cheroot-smoking Spanish desperadoes, whose fiercely-scowling black eyes, and ferocious moustachios were rather a test for the little mid's courage, especially when they fell to quarrelling and fierce Cuban oaths were seconded by the long dagger-like knives of Andalusia.

The deck of the *Vengeance* had scarce space enough for these lounging Ladrones, who lay about on the reed-mats of the Cuban 'hombre de mar', there being no room anywhere to sling a hammock.

At meal times, boiled rice, garnished with rancid oil and garlic, and served up in one huge mess-kid, seemed to be the only fare; and the mixture of smells—the 'hogo' of garlic, the stench of 'ghee' and the fumes of the strong Cuban tobacco were almost nauseating to the nostrils of the gently-nurtured English boy, used as he was to the sorry food and foul atmosphere of a midshipman's berth.

All along the South coast of Cuba extended reef-protected havens, and snug anchorages, hidden in amongst sandy cays, which were only approachable by narrow-twisting channels through a perfect maze of coral heads.

Cumberland Harbour

Skirting the coast to the Westward from the Windward Passage between Cuba and St. Domingo, and first of these piratical lairs was the Puerto Escondido, where Love's schooner defeated the *Desiree*'s boats. Then eight miles on, came the large inlet of Guantanimo, known to the Jamaican cruisers as Cumberland Harbour, being so named by Admiral Vernon in honour of the Butcher Duke.

This extensive harbour was much frequented by British men of war, and was an excellent refuge to which to flee when a hurricane was breeding. Here, clumps of mangrove alternated with morasses and salinas or salt ponds, where, and along the edge of brilliant green Savanas, regiments of flamingoes might be seen searching for molluscs.

High timber hid the turns and twists of the Rio Agua Anima, at the back of which low hills faded into the blue of the Cuban hinterland.

Dashing Youngsters

It was off the rocks by the windward entrance of Cumberland Harbour that Dennis Murray, a wild sprig of an Irish midshipman, in the *Desiree*'s jolly-boat with four ship's boys, caught a small felucca. The surprised Spaniards ran their vessel on the rocks then splashed ashore in a panic, persued by the five boys, whose only arms were the midshipmen's dirk, and boat stretchers.

A still more extraordinary cutting out affair was the capture of the twelve-gun privateer, *Coridad Perfecta* by a boat from the schooner-tender *Mary Ann*, Lieutenant-Commander Smith, off Truxillo.

The boat, commanded by another wild Irish mid named Bowley, and also with a crew of four lads, all of whom were under eighteen years of age, was sent in after nightfall to see if a privateer, which had recently captured the Colonial schooner, *Admiral Duckworth*, was in the harbour.

In the darkness Bowley ran up against the *Coridad Perfecta*, which happened to have all her hands ashore except fifteen men.

The startled picaroons promptly discharged a broadside gun which sank the boat without harming its occupants, who at once scrambled aboard the schooner and joined battle with four times their number of Spanish marineros. But the boys had been so well drilled with the cutlass, that they actually succeeded in driving the Spaniards below and carrying the vessel. For this gallant exploit, Bowley was promoted on completing his six years.

Perhaps the best remembered of these cutting out exploits by midshipmen was that of Edward Henry A'Court.

When the thirty-six-gun frigate *Blanche*, Captain Zachary Mudge, was cruising off the coast of San Domingo, young A'Court with a marine and seven seamen was sent away in the red cutter to bring off a load of beach-sand. Though there was an order against boats on such duty being armed, so as to prevent rash and unauthorised raids whilst ashore, half a dozen muskets had been smuggled aboard the red cutter.

Darkness fell before the boat was loaded, and, as she shoved off, a schooner was spotted lying becalmed under the shore.

A'Court at once pulled for her, carefully keeping in line with her stern so as to avoid the fire of her broadside guns. A volley of musketry knocked out two of his small party with bad wounds. Nevertheless, he held on with the most determined spirit, boarded and carried the schooner, which turned out to be bound to Cape Francois, with forty soldiers on board, commanded by a Colonel, whose excuse for his poor resistance was 'le mal de mer'.

The South Coast of Cuba

To return to the Cuban South coast between Cumberland Harbour and the Cabo de la Cruz, lay the port of San Jago de Cuba, its entrance defended by a large fort on its Eastern side.

Between the Cabo de la Cruz and the port of Trinidad lay the Jardin de la Reyna, an inland sea studded with small cays, sand banks and coral reefs—into which the only channel for craft of any size was the Boca Grande.

There were other shallow passages into this pirates' archipelago, but these were only known to the Caymanian and Montego Bay turtlers, the local Cuban wreckers, picaroons, pirates and freetraders (more commonly called force traders during the war).

From the mouth of the Boca Grande to the inshore Channel, which ran for a matter of one hundred and seventy miles, forty miles of sand bores, of staghorn patches, coral niggerheads, and rock-strewn cul de sacs made the navigation even for shoal draught sloops and feluccas, not to speak of larger schooners and brigs, extremely dangerous and difficult.

Anchorages in water, which was seldom disturbed by more than a passing riple, were numerous off cays, covered with low thickets of brushwood and mangroves, and behind spits of dazzling white coral sand, where the turtles laid their eggs and the pirates in later years buried their treasure.

Very few British officers were capable of piloting anything larger than a frigate's cutter into the Jardin de la Reyna but cruisers constantly sent their boats in on exploring expeditions, as witness this account of the captured mid:—

"When in durance aboard the Spanish schooner, whilst at anchor between the Cayos de Cavillones and Los Hermanos, we suddenly saw . . . an English man-of-war's launch with about sixteen lusty rowers, and an officer. She popped from among the mangroves of one of the cays, in an instant, not far from the schooner, the whole nearly of whose crew were fast asleep; I sprang upon the taffrail and waved my 'deputy straw' (my beaver having been purloined by the Ladrones) and involuntarily called out 'What cheer O' to my brother officer. He shook his head and pointed to the offing; I understood at once the motion meant "not strong enough, ship in the offing . . ." (*Note:* See *Nautical Magazine* 1844, "The Leeward Station").

Under the cautious Italian, Dominique Diron's picaroon was very carefull to avoid capture.

This is well described by the midshipmen:—

"Their first consideration being to keep clear of the men-of-war, the moment the sea breeze set in, they bore round off to the Southward, until out of sight of land, when they gradually hauled upon the starboard tack, midway between the West end of Jamaica, and the Caymans. The moment a sail was seen, they altered the course to avoid her, being quite satisfied with the capture they had made. We sighted three square-rigged vessels to windward, and upon each occasion the bustle and buzz of voices of the unruly crew, were such as to show plainly that anxiety for their own safety was uppermost in their minds, and alertness to obey the orders of their officers was displayed only at such times".

Vengeance* captured by *Gracieuse* and *Gipsy

Very soon after the old Italian had relinquished the command to the more dashing Frenchman, Jean Marie, the *Vengeance* fell a victim to the two Jamaican tenders *Gracieuse*, Lieutenant David Boyd, and *Gipsy*, Mr. Watt, which happened to be cruising in company.

The two man-of-war schooners came up with her off Cape Antonio, Cuba, and captured her after a short resistance.

In his official report to Vice-Admiral Dacres, Lieutenant David Boyd described her as mounting four twelve-pounder carronades and one long brass eighteen-pounder amidships with a complement of eighty-three men. When captured on December the twenty-seventh, 1807, she had been out three months from the port of Trinidad, Cuba, without making a capture, and in the fight she lost eight killed and six wounded.

***Superieure, Flying Fish* and *Pike* at Batabano**

By this date, the British cruisers had begun to play havoc with the West Indian picaroons, which at the renewal of hostilities in 1803 were spread over the whole Caribbean sea like a swarm of wasps.

And not only were the swift schooners and feluccas of the privateersmen being overtaken and captured, but the most snug of their retreat were being subjected to raiding attacks.

One of the most daring of these raids was made against Batabano in September 1806.

The expedition was planned by Vice-Admiral Dacres and the following extracts from official reports of the officers concerned show how well it was carried out.

His Majesty's sloop *Stork*
off the Isle of Pines,
September 9th, 1806.

Sir,

Agreeable to your directions I put to sea from Port Royal on the 25th ultimo with the *Superieure*, and *Flying Fish* and *Pike* schooners.

On our arrival off the Isle of Pines I had the mortification to learn from the pilot (that) the *Stork* could not be carried within thirty leagues of the harbour of Batabano.

I thereby directed Captain Rushworth (to whose activity and exertions I feel highly indebted) to proceed with the *Superieure* and two schooners, after having reduced their draught of water as much as possible, and reinforced them with the boats and a party of seamen and marines from the *Stork*: and I have the pleasure to acquaint you, the object of your orders was affected in a very handsome style: for the particulars of which and his subsequent capture of a Spanish letter of marque I have the honour to refer you to the enclosed letter from Captain Rushworth.

I have also to inform you of the capture of a Spanish schooner of ten guns on the 30th ultimo by the *Pike* after a slight resistance.

I have the honour to be, etc.,
George Le Geyt

To James Richard Dacres Esq.,
Vice Admiral of the White,
Commander-in-Chief, etc.

His Majesty's sloop *Superieure*
Off the Isle of Pines, Sept. 9th, 1806

Sir,

I have the honour to acquaint you, after leaving His Majesty's sloop *Stork* on the 25th of August, off the Isle of Pines, it took as to the 2nd of this month to get off Point Gondas distance NW twenty-two miles from Batabano, where I anchored with the *Flying Fish* and *Pike* schooners at midnight weighed and stood for Batabano, to be off that place before break of day, but owing to baffling winds it took us until daylight. I thought it expedient to land, which I accordingly did, with eighteen men from the *Stork*, thirty-five from the *Superieure* and ten from the *Flying Fish* to guard the boats: but after landing two miles to windward of the battery, the marshy irregular ground so impeded our march, and the enemy perceiving it, sent a party of soldiers to way-lay us in the thick bushes: but the most forward of my party charged and completely put them to the route, after leaving two killed and one badly wounded.

At that period a general alarm had spread, the militia had joined the stationary regulars at the front, aided by the men from the shipping in the bay. Our retreat behind then cut off, we were obliged to rush forward to gain the fort, which I am happy to say was completely carried in three minutes: the enemy retreated in all directions, after firing two guns and a volley of small arms, towards the path we were obliged to pass. The battery consisted of six long eighteen-pounders mounted on travelling carriages, which we spiked; and then proceeded to take possession of the vessels, which consisted of one felucca, pierced for fourteen guns, having one eighten-pounder and twelve blunderbusses aboard; a schooner, pierced for twelve, a French privateer of four and three other Spanish vessels with nine gun each, six other smaller with cargoes, which were saved, and the vesels burnt, not having sufficient men to carry them out.

The next morning came off a flag of truce; from them I learn their loss was considerable. I am happy to add we had only one man badly wounded on the occasion. I also feel it my duty to state the great assistance I received from Lieutenants Russell and Murray and Sub-Lieutenants Blake and Brown. The seamen and marines under my command acted in the most gallant manner.

Two days after I captured a Spanish armed schooner, *St. John*, of three guns and thirty-two men after a slight resistance.

I am, etc.,
Edward Rushworth

George Le Geyt, Esq.,
Commander of H.M. sloop *Stork*.

The *Gracieuse* and *Superieure* were war schooners of French build, as was the three-masted *Flying Fish*.

Gracieuse, mounting twelve guns, was captured off Curacoa on October the twenty-first, 1804, by the thirty-six-gun frigate *Blanche*, Captain Z. Mudge.

Superieure, a large two-topsail schooner of fourteen guns which was taken into the service as a sloop, was caught becalmed along with the *Flying Fish* off Cape Nicholas Mole on June the thirtieth, 1803, by the squadron under Captain Baynton of the *Cumberland*, seventy-four guns.

Both *Gracieuse* and *Superieure* made great names in the West Indies; John B, Smith, and David Boyd were the best known commanders of the former, whilst the latter made the reputations of W. C. Fromow, Edward Rushworth and W. Ferrier.

Unfortunately the lines of these two beautiful schooners were never taken off, as they never left the West Indies, unlike the *Flying Fish*, whose appearance so pleased the Admiralty, that they had her lines taken off and sent out to Bermuda for half a dozen ceder-built schooners on the same plan.

The Corvette *Bacchante*

An other famous vessel of French origin which became the scourge of privateers in the West Indies was the corvette, *Bacchante*, twenty-two guns, six hundred and forty two tons, two hundred men.

She was captured on June the twenty-fifth, 1803, by the forty-gun frigate *Endymion*, Captain Honourable Charles Paget in 47° 10′ N., 20° W., when on her way from St. Domingo to Brest with despatches. A corvette of the largest size, she had the scantlings of a seventy-four and the masts, yards and sails of a sixty-four gun ship. With great beam and length of gun-deck, she had a flat floor, and carried her heavy sail plan with ease—let me quote one of her lieutenants:—

"With a strong wind her inclination was trifling or, according to the seaman's phrase, she was as 'stiff as a rock', an excellent sea-boat, sailed fast and worked well, but required good space for tacking or wearing. In fact she was altogether a very superior vessel of her class, a post ship, yet bore but two lieutenants".

Her sail plan is specially deserving of mention. She was very lofty, being a three skysail-yarder; and in the West Indies young Dacras, who commanded her in 1806, hoisted up a lateen moon raker fourteen feet above the truck of the main skysail mast, which she even carried with a fresh trade abeam.

When she was captured she mounted eighteen long twelve-pounders; as usual the Admiralty crammed more guns into her and besides two long nine-pounders, gave her twenty thirty-two-pounder carronades, which were after a while reduced to eighteen.

Her first commander was Captain Charles Dashwood.

He it was who sent his boats in and gutted the privateering lair of Mariel, a little to the westward of Havana. Under young Dacres—he was only a little over twenty—the *Bacchante* took part in the attack on another notorious picaroon's nest—Samana near Cape Raphael, San Domingo.

In both these affairs it was a case of storming stone forts and then capturing the vessels in the harbour. The success of these dashing boat attacks made the names of Lieutenants James Oliver, Henry Loraine Baker, (afterwards Sir Henry Baker, Bart, C.B.) John Norton, and John Campbell. John Norton, when first of the corvette, was considered one of the smartest first lieutenants in the Service. Though a strict disciplinarian, both mids and ratings were devoted to him.

Owing to the activity of such frigates as the *Desiree, Franchise, Pique, Tartar, Blanch* and *Princess Charlotte* or corvettes like the *Bacchante*, brig-sloops such as the *Racoon, Elk, Scorpion* etc., and innumerable war schooners from the brig *Superieure* down to the little *Haddock* class, there were not many pickings left for private men-of-war on the Jamaican Station.

Shipping on the Coast of Cuba in Wartime

Beyond the specie schooners and feluccas running between Vera Cruz and Havana, which owing to their speed were very hard to catch. The only vessels seen on the coast of Cuba were English cruisers, Spanish and French picaroons, an occasional convoy of homeward bound West Indiamen and sugar ships, and the Jamaican free-traders (or force-traders) as they were more commonly called) their enemies, the guarda-costas and a few local fishermen, who divided their time between turtling and wrecking.

Then when war started with America, numbers of their Baltimore schooners, which had previously carried on a sort of smuggling trade in the West Indies, turned privateersmen; and in a short while a regular swarm of these long-legged, wide-winged, heavily manned American letter of marque schooners came buzzing round Jamaica with such daring that they were often seen within range of Port Royal in broad daylight.

The Force Traders

The force-traders were of very great use to our cruisers for they were of the same kidney as the wreckers, fishermen and turtlers, and thus invaluable pilots for the Cuban coral reefs.

They ran their cargoes in tiny schooners of the Ballahou type, or swift Jamaican sloops, and considering that capture by a guarda-costa gunboat meant either death or a life sentence in the mines, they showed incredible courage.

The West Indian Spaniard was always very half-hearted for the war against England, nor had he any enthusiasm for his Gallic ally, thus everywhere along the Cuban coast the local population were hand-in-glove with the Jamaican 'Traficantes'.

A very notable character at Port Royal during the war was Mother Mann, otherwise known as 'Old Jack', who was generally credited with being one of the richest and most active supporter of the force trade.

English Privateersmen

The only English privateersman hailing from Jamaica was curiously enough a soldier, one Watt, an ex-captain of Marines, who, when serving aboard the *Arethusa* was so smitten with the roving life of a picaroon, that threw up his commission, invested in a lovely little schooner, and made the Bight of Batano his main sphere of operations with the Golfo de los Damas as a secondary paradise for this fascinating game of fox and geese.

English privateersmen mostly operated from Nassau and found a profitable cruising ground in the old Bahama Channel and around the Florida cays. The Nassau picaroon, descendant, no doubt, of the old Buccaneer, used to lurk off the Hole in the Wall on the South end of Great Abaco. His snaky schooner, the spit of which can still be seen fishing for sponges on the Great Bahama bank or in the Abaco Bight, preyed chiefly upon the brigs and schooners running cargoes into Havana fron Vera Cruz, New Orleans and Charleston.

The illustration, taken from the *Naval Chronicle* shows a Bahama picaroon and his capture, an American brig. The Admiraly Court at Nassau, a day's sail away made short work of condemning American smugglers.

The best known of the New Providence privateersmen was old Johnson, whose pretty daughters proved a great attraction not only to the British Naval officers, but to adventurers of every description, who were all nobly entertained at his hospitable board.

Kingston and Port Royal at the Beginning of the Nineteenth Century

Before leaving the Jamaica Station, I will try and give some slight picture of Kingston and Port Royal as they were at the beginning of the nineteenth century.

In the old war days many of the houses in the lower part of Kingston had small belfry-like lookout-places fitted with green blinds and furnished with a telescope. From these spyholes the inhabitants kept a close watch on the shipping, and a strange sail in the offing or a movement amongst the raft could not pass unnoticed, whilst the man of war anchorage, six miles away, at Port Royal, was kept under close supervision.

There was little chance of being able to pay your washer-woman or canoe-man or buggy-driver with the fore-topsail. Indeed, every water front loafer, whether black sambo or copper coloured mulatto, knew when this smart corvett, or that rakish gun-brig, or even that Will 'o the Wisp, the Admiral's tender, was due to sail, and whither her destination or her cruising ground.

The sight of a stranger to the station or a cruiser with a prize in the Western channel, or off Black Rock Point was the signal for a sort of water Derby, in which all the dinahs and dignity ball belles vied with each other in their competition for the trade of the stranger or the doubloons of the prizemasters.

Captain Marryat in *Peter Simple* quoted the old West Indian doggerel:—

'Negro on de shore
  See de ship come in,
De buccra come on shore
  Wid de hand up to the chin;
  Man-of-war buccra
  Man-of-war buccra
  He de boy for me
  Man-of-war buccra
  Man-of-war buccra
Gib pictareen to me'.

Dignity Balls

The dignity balls of Jamaica were even more full of decorum and etiquette and those of Barbadoes, so amusingly described by Marryat. They seem to have been divided into grades—of rank as regards British officers, and of colour as regards the ladies.

Creole, by the way, is not a designation of colour, but of berth. In a description of

Jamaica, written by the purser of the H.M.S. *Weymouth* in 1722, the coloured people were thus divided:—

'The first change, by a Black and White, they call a Mulatto; the second a Mustee; and the third a Castee,—the faces like a coat of arms, discovering their distinction'.

As time went on it became necessary to make further distinctions, as the colour mixture became further removed from the pure nigger or 'black Sambo', as he was called.

Thus, 'quadroons' (quarter-blacks) and even 'octaroons', natives growing ever more proud of their white blood, began to be recognised as the top rank of the coloured population—and the first class Dignity Ball consisted, of no one under the quadroon level of Jamaican society.

No gate crashing was allowed, entry by ticket was strictly enforced, and invitations were regarded as an honour even by staid post-captains, whilst middies could rarely get into a quadroon ball.

One of the amusing sides of these affairs was the delight of the coloured people in representing great personages in contemporary history. For instance a sprightly young lieutenant in begging a pretty quadroon to dance a measure, would find to his astonishment that she would not respond unless addressed as 'Your Majesty', being for the time not a 'fleet washerwoman' but the Empress Josephine!

The favourite role for the Master of Ceremonies—a most important figure in all Dignity Balls—was that of the Duke of Wellington, and a belle, who was known at one time to almost every officer in the Royal Navy, even in her old age was still only spoken of and addresed as Lady Rodney.

There was a vast deal of dignity about a Dignity Ball. The square dances were most punctilious affairs, but young officers, never very well posted in all the intracacies of the curious semi-African, semi-Spanish gandangos, sarabands, and quadrilles, preferred the gavotte and the languishing valse (always spelt in those early days with a V) whilst the middies got action in that other new Bohemian dance the polka, and the typically English galop.

Perhaps the most attractive part of the Dignity Ball was its music which was either Spanish or African in origin, when it closely resembled the 'negro sprituals'.

Unlike modern music it was always extremely melodious, and mere noise, whether cacophonous, screech-like, explosive or saxaphonic, was not even tolerated by the lowest of Black Sambo hops.

Old Port Royal

No history of the Royal Navy can be in any way complete without mention of Port Royal, which even in the days of the roystering buccaneers, of Henry Morgan, and the early sugar trade always had its guard ship.

The old dives and taverns of the Jamaican filibusters were mostly washed bodily away by hurricanes or sunk beneath the wave by earthquake; and practically the only remnant of the buccaneering days is Fort Charles, where a marble tablet records:—

IN THIS PLACE
DWELT
HORATIO NELSON
You who tread his footsteps
remember his Glory.

In 1722 an order in Council decreed:— "That all masters of sloops or vessels employed as sugar drogers in and about this island shall, before they are permitted to pass His Majesty's fort at Port Royal be obliged to bring one load of stones each, in order to repair the damages done to the fortifications by the late violent hurricane".

In this way the little dockyard town with its neat rows of houses, running parallel to the sea, its garrison church, its paved courts and curved wooden verandahs, its green jalousies, and narrow roadways, was built and rebuilt as hurricane, earthquake and fire in recurring succession strove to demolish it.

The Port Royal Anchorage

In the days before the steam engine, the man-of-war anchorage off Port Royal was one of the sights of the West Indies.

In the centre of the fleet was always to be seen the high-sided guard ship, or 'guardo' as she was called.

About the longest lived of these old 'guardos' was the *Shark*, which the unkind used to say 'always crammed with as much miscellaneous rubbish as Old Tom (*Note:* Old Tom of Port Royal was one of that harbour's famous shark's) of Port Royal himself!

The guardship was the unhappy home of a host of bored lieutenants and wild mids, prizemasters and reinforcements awaiting the arrival of the ships to which they belonged, or were joining for the first time.

These restless spirits were the instigators of most of those practical jokes, which at times frightened the dusky beauties of Port Royal into fits, and at others scandalized the staider members of Jamaican society.

Young Tandy's Escapades

One of the most alarming of these middies' jokes, was due to the signal mid of the 'Guardo', who as a flag officer (it was before 1815, when flag-lieutenants were appointed) was responsible for the firing of the morning and evening guns.

A frigate, in firing a salute had, inadvertantly, we will suppose, fired a shotted round over the town to the terror of the inhabitants.

Young Tandy, the signal-mid's reputation as a super-joker was so well known in Port Royal, that he was at once accused of this leaden messenger. To falsely accuse such a noted tormentor was asking for trouble, Tandy at once determined to give the timid Port Royalers real cause for complaint.

He had some imitation wooden cannon balls turned secretly in Kingston. These, unknown even to the captain of the gun, he managed to introduce into the bore of the time gun and for several mornings and evenings sent them skimming over the roof tops of Port Royal.

Scared indignation was at once raised to fever heat, but nothing could be brought home to him in spite of the blackness of his character for such jokes, and the Admiral, with whom he was a great favourite refused to believe any of the insinuations against this 'nonpareil' of a signal officer, whose popularity with the ladies of all colours alone saved him from assault with violence in the streets of Port Royal.

If the guardo remained a fixture on her moorings, this was far from being the case with other ships at the man-of-war anchorage; frigates, corvettes, sloops, gun-brigs, schooners and cutters, they were ever coming or going; and the sight, which always brought the Port Royal critics to the water-front or their look-outs, was that of a British man-of-war coming to an anchor. A smart frigate such as the beautiful *Pique*, or a corvette like the *Bacchante*, would come round Port Royal Point with every sail to royals gleaming in the sun, than as the first gun of her salute went off, away aloft dashed her top-men, and when the smoke of the last gun had cleared away, there she would be lying calmly at anchor, sails harbour-stowed, ropes flemish coiled, yards squared, and boat booms out. Such an example of the old-time seamanship was one of those beautiful sights which machinery has robbed us of.

A smart ship was at once recognised by her method of getting under way or coming to an anchor. When a fleet came in and anchored, the nicest judgment was of course necessary. Each ship was previously alloted her position, and to drop your anchor so as to satisfy the sextant of the staff-captain demanded seamanship of the highest order.

The prison hulks lay moored on the main shore off the Augusta Fort, whilst West Indiamen and other merchantmen anchored over at Kingston. But it was seldom that the unfortunate trader could reach her anchorage without being boarded not only by the Guard-boat on duty, which often went out as far as Cow Bay, but in war time by cutters from the men-of-war, who were always in want of men.

The regular West Indiamen not only had 'stow holes' under the cargo, where they hid all men who were unprotected; but often landed most of their best men in Morant Bay, whence they made their way over land to Kingston.

Rowing Guard

Rowing guard was a duty in all naval ports in sailing ship days, and it was one which was never much beloved by either middies or men. Their night guard at Port Royal was considered a prime cause of sickness, owing to the heavy dews, which often wet the men to the skin, and the land breeze, which in those days, was always reckoned to carry the seeds of fever and ague.

The chief duties of the night guard were the prevention of the often desperate efforts of bluejackets to desert from their ships—at the same time the guard-boat had to row round the prison hulks, which lay at quite a distance from the anchorage; thus deserters could chose a time when the boat was off at the hulks and vice versa; however, the Port Royal sharks were more effective against swimmers than any guard-boat, and a canoe was always suspect in the anchorage after nightfall.

To anyone who loved the beauties of a West Indian night and especially the glories of a tropical dawn, rowing guard must have had its compensations.

Dawn in Port Royal Harbour

The break of day in Port Royal harbour had a peculiar charm of its own. The first glimmer of the false dawn showed the hills which lay in a semi-circle round Kingston, rearing their dark shoulders out of a sea of fleecy white mist, which veiled the coast and the anchorage. Then, as the sun rose in all its glory, and the Eastern sky became suffused with gorgeous colour, this mist took on a golden hue and gradually lifted until it hid itself in the folds and azure hollows of the Blue mountains.

As the watery vapour slowly dispersed, it disclosed a purple sea all aglint with golden spangles, and dotted all over with the tiny spritsails of the canoes, and the wing-like Bermuda mainsails of the Kingston wherries.

Off Port Royal and off Kingston rose rival forests of masts and as the deep boom of the morning gun sounded, up went the red, blue and white ensigns to the spanker gaffs.

But long before this, the beef boats of the fleet had collected at the market wharf, where the middies passed their time of waiting in drinking spruce beer, and the men criticized the skill of the fat Jewish butchers. By the time that the Reveille came ringing across the water, the crowded wharf had begun to empty itself, and the cutters, loaded with fresh beef and vegetables were on their way back to the man-of-war anchorage six miles away.

The waterway across the harbour was always a busy thoroughfare in the old war days. The crews of the beef boats pulling wearily back to their ships often had to cease rowing and stand up with oars raised in salute as that man-of-war magnate, a post captain, swept by his brass-bound gig with her eight proud oarmen in their white duck trousers, blue jackets and low-crowned tarpaulin hats, or beautifully made straws*.

Saucy wherries with merry parties of some leave goers took a delight in scudding past the more humble canoe with its black Sambo at the tiller. Reclining in the stern sheets of such craft might be seen pretty Dignity ladies dressed in lustrous white taffetas, who languidly flirted with gay lieutenants, or red-coated subalterns of the Royal Marines, the affectations of these dusky damsels being an everlasting source of amusement to those officers who had a sense of the ludicrous.

Deadman's Cay and Gallows Point

Ships running in by the Eastern Channel passed Deadman's Cay to port, where in the early days malefactors were hanged in leather jackets and sundried, until wind and weather disintegrated them.

In later years a slight rise a short distance from Port Royal along the Palisadoes, which jutted out into the emerald green shallows became known as Gallow's Point.

Here, during the eighteenth and nineteenth centuries, gallows were erected for the execution of pirates and other miscreants.

Old Port Royal Under The Waves

The course into the harbour from the East led directly over the sunken Buccaneer's city, which, on June the seventh, 1692, disappeared beneath the wave amidst the furies of earthquake and hurricane in the short space of two minutes.

Since that date, the sea floor and the spit of rocks and sand upon which Port Royal is built, has been raised and sunk several times.

Back in 1780, Admiral Sir Charles Hamilton has recorded how the submerged houses were then plainly visible beneath the water.

Between 1824 and 1835 the channel was carefully surveyed and the surveying officers found it quite easy to trace the lay out of the submerged town.

Then as late as 1859 a diver reported that the roofs of the houses were still raised above the white coral sand of the sea floor.

Who knows but that some day this buried port of the old buccaneering times may not be raised above the water once more.

---

* Some captains were fond of dressing their gig's crews in special rig. For instance, as late as 1854, Commander Wilmot, when commanding the *Harlequin*, one of the famous Pantomime brigs, dressed his gig's crew in the spangled tights of Harlequin.

Captain Wallace Houston of the *Tricomalee*, also in the early fifties, went one better than Wilmot, for he figged out his whole crew in red shirts and fancy caps.

Oiled canvas petticoats were still seen at sea as late as 1820, and queues and pigtails did not go out of fashion until some years after the peace.

CHAPTER IV

THE CARIBBEAN PIRATES

"There walks no wind 'neath Heaven
Nor wave that shall restore
The old careening riot
And the clamorous crowded shore,
The fountain in the desert,
The cistern in the waste,
The bread we ate in secret,
The cups we spilled in haste."

The Era of the Adventurer

WITH the termination of the Napoleonic and American wars, fighting men all over the world were either compelled to sheathe the sword or else take up with adventurers, insurgents and outlaws. Indeed the first half of the nineteenth century might well be called the era of the adventurer, for men lived lives of incredible romance, whether at sea, in the wake of a liberator or on the frontiers, beyond which lay the savage and the unknown.

Numbers of British soldiers followed Simon Bolivar, just as whole ships' crews of officers and men went south with Cochrane; but everywhere it was becoming difficult to distinguish the liberator from the pirate, and few of these adventurers escaped a violent end.

Insurgents and Outlaws

With peace in the Caribbean, the Guadeloupe, San Domingo and Cuban privateersmen, whose very nature had been swaddled in blood, could not be expected to exchange the sword for the plough-share; and there were only two courses open to them—either they could join up with the Columbian and Buenos Ayrian insurgents, in which case they took out letters of marque against their own countrymen, or else they went all out for the rover's life and hoisted the skull and cross bones. As a matter of fact there was very little to choose between the two, for it was notorious that South American privateers were too colourblind to distinguish between the red and gold bars of Spain, the tricolour of France, the stars and stripes of the United States, or even the superimposed crosses of the Union Jack. Whether they flew the yellow, blue and red bars of Bolivar, the Texas lone star, or the green wreath of Mexico it made little difference—a prize was a prize and the gold of every country was still yellow.

Jean Lafitte

Of all these adventurers, these picaroons and piratical gentry, the greatest was Jean Lafitte, known throughout the West Indies as the Pirate of the Gulf, and the original of Byron's Corsair. Of whom the following was certainly no caricature:—

"He was the mildest-mannered man
That ever scuttled ship, or cut a throat;
With such true breeding of a gentleman,
You never could discern his real thought.
Pity he loved adventurous life's variety
He was so great a loss to good society."

In the numerous accounts of Lafitte's early life it is quite impossible to separate truth from fiction. Of those few of his followers who lived to old age, each had a different story to tell of his early life, and each was wont to declare that he had it from Lafitte's own lips.

Old Jim Crow, who joined the filibuster in 1817 always declared that Lafitte was the son of a Bordeaux merchant, that he ran away to sea and became loplolly boy aboard a British man-of-war at the age of nine; that he served several years in the thirty-two-gun frigate, *Fox* and finally, having got into some scrape, deserted at Deptford, where he was hidden by a French family until he could be smuggled aboard a vessel in the Downs.

Against this we have Byron's quotation from an American newspaper in his notes to the Corsair, which declared that Lafitte 'was well known to the inhabitants of the city of New Orleans from his immediate connection and his once having been a fencing master in that city, of great reputation, which art he learnt in Buonaparte's army, where he was a captain'.

Mr. Bradlee in his book *Piracy in the West Indies* asserts that Lafitte was born in 1780 either at St. Malo or Bordeaux, that when mate of a French East Indiaman he quarrelled with his captain, left the ship at Mauritius, where he fitted out a privateer and preyed on the English in the Indian Ocean before turning his attention to West Indian waters. He also puts foreward the story that Lafitte was captured by the British and spent some years in the barbarous prison hulks, which accounted for his fierce bias against the English flag.

There seem to have been three, if not four, brothers, of whom Jean was the eldest and leader—the others were Pierre, Henri and Antoine or Mark.

The fencing-master was more likely one of these brothers, who acted as Jean's agent in New Orleans for the disposal of his plunder. Pierre Lafitte was a sailor and a more Stevenson like pirate than Jean.

He had but one eye and an ugly disposition. He was none too friendly with his brother and usually cruised the Gulf on his own.

An Irish captain of Jean's fleet, named Morrissey, was approached by Pierre with the suggestion that he should desert Jean at Barataria, and help Pierre to set up a new pirate's rookery on the Isle de Mugeres off Cape Caoche (Yucatan). But Morrissey feared that the treacherous Pierre, having gained the Irishman's polacca and a reasonable recruiter of men, would then 'slip Morrissey's wind'*

One of the last survivors of Lafitte's company was an American sailor, who ended his days as a butcher, to which profession he had no doubt served a long apprenticeship amongst the Brethren of the Gulf.

He accounted for Lafitte's animosity against the Spaniards by the story that the Corsair had once spent a weary time in a Havana dungeon, forgotten by the casual authorities of that city, and as a proof of this yarn he declared that on Lafitte's wrists and ankles were to be seen great white scars, the marks of the irons.

In appearance Jean Lafitte was the typical corsair of romance—a strongly built, handsome man, about six feet two inches in height, with large hazel eyes, long black hair and a drooping black moustache. His manners were refined, his habits sober and self controlled, and his mien uncommonly thoughtful and serious. He seldom smiled, and was only known to laugh when the tiger in him was aroused.

* The polite seafaring expression for cutting a man's throat.

He was no licentious, rioting buccaneer, but a quiet, retiring family man whose privacy was well-guarded by his devoted body-slaves. Nor did he resemble Byron's Conrad, being no libertine or love-sick swain, but both true and devoted to his Creole wife, who was a native of New Orleans, and by whom he had one child—a son.

In dress as in his generous nature, he seems to have been a kind of Robin Hood.

He was generally clad either in buckskins or a sort of green uniform with an otterskin cap. He was never armed, except when on duty, then he wore a brace of pistols in a sash, pirate fashion, and carried a common navy cutlass.

Grand Terre or Barataria

The island of Grand Terre, which Lafitte renamed Barataria and made his head-quarters about the year 1807, guarded a large lagoon, from which a labyrinth of bayous, swamps, and meres, surrounded by rich savannahs, and studded with islets of tall timber, led inland to the Mississippi and so to New Orleans. This island with its five or six miles of sand dunes, scrub and mangroves had long been known to the turtlers and fishermen of the Gulf. Not far away amongst the muddy bayous was a mosquito-ridden, thickly timbered isle, which was reputed to be the last retreat of Blackbeard the pirate, where he left his treasure buried under a wood shanty, which he had built for the last of his fourteen wives, before going to Charleston to consult with his friend, the Governor of South Carolina.

It seems likely that Jean Lafitte arrived at Grand Terre with a number of adventurers of all nationalities, who were attracted to the spot by its convenience not only as a hiding place, but for smuggling contraband goods into New Orleans, the United States having instituted a strict embargo of foreign goods in the year 1807. Possibly Lafitte might claim to be called the first rum runner and bootlegger.

During the war most of these outlaws and contrabandistas were Frenchmen, and their leaders came to be known as 'boss' or master pirates—the word being evidently introduced by some Dutch picaroon.

In a very short while Lafitte, with his gift for commanding men, obtained a strong hold over the whole nest of ruffians, and began to be spoken of as 'the boss'. He may possibly have been elected by vote to the post of Admiral of this piratical and smuggling community, at any rate he was soon in supreme command, made strict laws, fortified the island and built himself a residence. Whether in naming this wild settlement Barataria, he took inspiration from Don Quixote, or merely made play on his profession of barratry, the word stuck and soon began to be mentioned not only in the Government-Houses of the West Indies but in the chancelleries of Europe.

In the Naval Chronicle of 1814, will be found the following notice of Lafitte's activities:—

> "From America we learn that on a rocky island called Barataria, adjacent to the mouth of the Mississippi, a number of French pirates have formed a regular establishment. From thence they send out numerouse armed vessels, and most grievously infest the coast of Louisiana, plundering and destroying the Spanish vessels, and those of every other nation, the French excepted. The property they thus pillage they deposit within the ramparts of a fort, which for this purpose they have constructed and provided with fourteen pieces of artillery. To give a sort of character to these proceedings, they have formed a tribunal, which they denominate a court of vice-admiralty, and where they condemn without ceremony the property they have thus acquired. After judgment is passed, the merchandise is sold at low prices, but for ready money, and in open market. This market is kept two days a week; and if no buyer be found, the goods are introduced into New Orleans as articles of contraband trade. Information of these proceedings has been given to the Governors-General of the Havannas and of the Floridas."

Though he did little cruising himself, having enough to do to organize the shore end of the business, and run his booty into New Orleans, where one of his brothers acted as agent,

Lafitte kept a sharp eye on his captains, and saw that they kept within the limit of his rules and regulations and carried out his instructions.

He was always contended that his operations were strictly legal that he had a Columbian commission and only preyed upon the Spaniards, but once out of his sight the Baratarian cruisers did not hesitate to swoop upon American timber and sugar ships and even English West Indiamen.

Lafitte was careful to insist on his cruisers flying the flag of the Confederation of South American States, first named New Granada and afterwards the Republica of Granada.

Business with a Spanish Governor

I only know of one record of Lafitte going on a cruise himself, and this cruise had a special purpose. He contrived to capture a Spanish Governor, along with his Confessor and secretary; and accused him of being in league with the American pirate Gibbs. Lafitte rove nooses from his yardarms, and stood the wretched Governor and his priest beneath them, whilst the secretary rushed ashore in search of the fifty thousand dollars ransom money. And when the secretary came off with the doubloons, Lafitte politely bowed his prisoners over the side.

Lafitte Frustrates both Land and Sea Attacks

By 1813 the activity of the pirates of the gulf had become so great that the Governor of Louisiana determined to make a serious effort to stamp out Lafitte and his Baratarian rookery.

He began his campaign by offering five hundred dollars for the corsair's head. Jean Lafitte, with ths spice of sardonic humour to which he occasionally gave way, immediately posted placards in New Orleans offering fifteen dollars for the head of the Governor. The latter, not to be beaten, contrived to find a traitor in the freebooter's camp, who knew the way overland from New Orleans to Barataria.

This man acted as guide to about one hundred soldiers, whose commander had orders from the Governor to burn and destroy the pirate's stronghold and bring all prisoners to New Orleans.

The trail through the bush was just a narrow overgrown track, so narrow and tortuous that single file was a necessity. As the guide crept forward through the tall thickets followed by the line of excited soldiers, sudenly like the long-drawn cry of a bird came the piercing call of a boatswain's whistle, a score of armed men leaped upon the traitor, and before a gun could be fired, had disappeared with him into what seemed impenetrable bush. Thus this small punitive expedition found itself alone and lost in the midst of alligator-haunted swamps and was only too glad to retrace its steps as best it could.

But the Governor was not to be daunted; gathering together all the gun boats and small cruisers of the United States Navy, that were to be found in the neighbourhood, he sent them to make an attack by sea, but again Lafitte proved too wide awake, and this sea expedition was repulsed with ease.

By this date Lafitte's force, which styled itself the Brethren of the Gulf, was reckoned to number over a thousand men, whilst his fleet consisted of over a dozen brigs, brigantines, schooners, feluccas and sloops, headed by his flagship, a beautiful schooner, named *The Lady of the Gulf.*

The British General's Letter

Whilst Governor Claiborne of New Orleans was preparing his third expedition against Lafitte, which was also a naval one, but with troops added to the ship's companies, the pirate of the Gulf was approached by the British, both military and naval commanders making the most crude, bare-faced attempts to bribe the powerful freebooter to come over to their side.

The letter sent to Lafitte by the British General was published in the newspaper *Courier* of

November the twenty second 1814, along with the General's proclamation to the people of Louisiana.

These historical documents are sufficiently curious, and shed such a light upon the methods employed in the Louisiana campaign, that I quote them without any expurgation.

Headquarters, Pensacola
August 31, 1814

Sir,

I have only arrived in the Floridas for the purpose of annoying the only enemy Great Britain has in the world, as France and England are now friends.

I call on you with your brave followers to enter the service of Great Britain, in which you shall have the rank of Captain: lands will be given to you in proportion to your respective ranks on a peace taking place; and I invite you on the following terms—your property shall be guaranteed to you, and your person protected.

In return for which I ask you to cease all hostilities against Spain, or the allies of Great Britain. Your ships and vessels to be placed under the orders of the commanding officer of this station, until the commander-in-chief's pleasure is known: but I guarantee their value to you at all events.

I herewith enclose you a copy of my proclamation to the inhabitants of Louisiana, which will, I trust, point out to you the honourable intentions of my government. You will be a useful assistant to me in forwarding them; therefore, if you determine, lose no time. The bearer of this, Captain Williams, will satisfy you on any other points you may be anxious to learn, as well as Captain Lockyer of the *Sophie,* who carries him to you.

We have a powerful reinforcement on its way here, and I hope to cut out some other work for the Americans than oppressing the inhabitants of Louisiana.

Be expeditious in your resolves, and rely upon the veracity of your humble servant.

Edward Nicholls, Lieutenant-General commanding His Britannic Majesty's forces in the Floridas

To M. La Fete or the commandant at Barataria.

The enclosed proclamation ran as follows:—

Natives of Louisiana! On you the first call is made to assist in liberating from a faithless and imbecil government your paternal soil. Spaniards, Frenchmen, Italians and British, whether settled or residing for a time in Louisiana, on you I also call to aid me in this just cause. The American usurpation of this country must be abolished, and the lawful owners of this soil put in possession.

I am at the head of a large army of Indians, well armed, disciplined and commanded by British officers, a train of artillery with every requisite, seconded by a powerful aid of numerous British and Spanish squadrons of ships and vessels of war.

Be not alarmed, inhabitants of the country, at our approach: the same good faith and disinteredness which has distinguished the conduct of Britons in Europe accompanies them here: and you will have no fear of litigious taxes imposed on you for the purpose of carrying on unnatural and unjust war. Your property, your laws, the peace and tranquillity of your country will be guaranteed to you by men, who will suffer no infringementof theirs. Rest assured that these brave men only burn with an ardent desire of staisfaction for the wrongs they have suffered from the Americans, to join you in liberating these Southern frontiers from their yoke, and drive them into those limites formerly prescribed by our sovereign.

The Indians have pledged themselves, in the most solemn manner, not to injure in the slightest degree, persons of properties of any but enemies to their Spanish or English fathers.

A flag over any door, whether Spanish, French or British will be a certain protection.

Not even an enemy will an Indian put to death, except resisting his arms; and as for injuring helpless women and children, and old men, by their good conduct and treatment to them, they will, if it be possible, make the Americans blush for their more than inhuman conduct, lately on the Escambia and within a neutral territory.

Inhabitants of Kentucky, you have too long borne with grievous impositions: the whole brunt of the war has fallen on your brave sons. Be imposed on no more, but either range yourselves under the standard of your forefathers or observe a strict neutrality. If you comply with either of these offers, whatever provisions you send down shall be paid for in dollars and the safety of the persons, bringing it, as well as the free navigation of the Mississippi, guaranteed to you.

Men of Kentucky, let me call to your view and I trust to your abhorrence, the conduct of those factions which hurried you into this cruel, unjust and unnatural war, at a time when Great Britain was straining every nerve in defence of her own and the liberties of the world; when the bravest of her sons were fighting and bleeding in so sacred a cause; when she was spending millions of her treasure in endeavouring to pull down one of the most formidable and dangerous tyrants that ever disgraced the form of man; when groaning Europe was almost at her last gasp—when she alone shewed an undaunted front, basely did those assassins endeavour to stab her from (sic) her race. She has turned on them, renovated from the bloody but successful struggle. Europe is happy and free, and she now hastens justly to avenge these unprovoked insults.

Shew them that you are not collectively unjust: leave that contemptible few to shift for themselves: let these slaves of the tyrant send an embassy to Elba and implore his aid: but let every honest, upright American spurn them with merited contempt. After the experience of twenty one years, can you any longer support these brawlers for licentiousness, who call it freedom? Be no longer their dupes: accept of my offer. Everything I have promised in this paper I guarantee to you in the sacred honour of a British officer.

Given under my hand, at my headquarters,
Pensacola, this 29th day of August, 1814
Edward Nicholls.

Captain Lockyer. R.N. Visits Lafitte

The naval side of the English bribe to Lafitte must have been even more attractive to the arch-robber.

In a letter intrusted to Captain Nicholas Lockyer, the Honourable W.H. Percy, Captain of the *Hermes,* offered Lafitte the command of a frigate, and if he would only enter his force under the British flag, a sum of thirty thousand dollars, payable at Pensacola.

On the second of September, 1814, the eighteen-gun brig-sloop, *Sophie,* quietly sailed in through the pass and dropped her anchor right in amongst the piratical fleet.

This was a case of putting your head in the lion's mouth with a vengeance.

The sight of every gun being run out and trained upon the daring brig, must have been a test to even the strong nerves of British seamen, but Lockyer never hesitated, and with a flag of truce flying from the ensign-staff of his gig, calmly landed in the face of a hundred armed men who lined the shore.

A low growl of anger rose from the pirates. Scowls of hate were levelled at the two British officers, Lockyer and Williams, as they stepped ashore.

"Spies! Spies! To the death with these spies!" rose the cry. Things were looking ugly for the two lone men, and the boat's crew, who were unarmed, stooped furtively to grasp their stretchers. But at the psychological moment the tall form of Jean Lafitte appeared. At once there fell an uneasy silence amongst the unruly ruffians as they made way for the Boss-pirate. Lafitte advanced to meet his visitors with his usual dignified stateliness.

A Pirate's Diplomacy

It was not likely that bribes by his arch enemies, the English and Spanish, were going to have any influence upon his decision; on the other hand he knew that Governor Claiborne was plotting his destruction and the wiping out of his gang.

Before giving an answer of any sort to the British proposals, Lafitte dispatched the following letter by a trusty runner to the Governor at New Orleans.

Barataria,
September 4th, 1814.

Sir:

In the firm persuasion that the choice made of you to fill the office of first magistrate of this state was dictated by the esteem of your fellow citizens, and was conferred on merit, I confidently address you on an affair on which may depend the safety of this country. This point of Louisiana which I occupy is of great importance in the present crisis. I tender my services to defend it; and the only reward I ask is that a stop be put to the proscription against me and my adherents, by an act of oblivion, for all that has been done hitherto.

I am a stray sheep wishing to return to the fold. If you are thoroughly acquainted with the nature of my offences, I shall appear to you much less guilty and still worthy to discharge the duties of a good citizen. I have never sailed under any flag but that of the Republic of Carthagena, and my vessels are perfectly regular in that respect.

If I could have brought my lawful prizes into the ports of this state, I should not have employed the illicit means that have caused me to be proscribed. I decline saying more on the subject until I have the honour of your Excellency's answer, which I am persuaded can be dictated only by wisdom.

Should your answer not be favourable to my desires, I declare to you that I will instantly leave the country, to avoid the imputation of having cooperated towards an invasion of this point, which cannot fail to take place, and to rest secure in the acquittal of my conscience.

I have the honour to be
Your Excellency's most
Humble servant

J. Lafitte.

From day to day Lafitte put off giving Captain Lockyer an answer, whilst he waited for a reply from Governor Claiborne, but the Governor found that the American Generals were unwilling to trust such an uncertain ally as the master-pirate might well prove to be, and so no answer was sent.

Commodore Patterson U.S.N. Attacks the Brethern of the Gulf

In this dilemma Lafitte took the bold course of going himself in disguise to New Orleans in order to find out how the land lay. And he made the unpalatable discovery that an American expedition consisting of three barges, six gun boats and the schooner, *Caroline,* flying the flag of Commodore Patterson was just about to sail from New Orleans with orders to capture and destroy Barataria.

Even this news did not cause the Frenchman to throw himself on the side of his old enemies.

He at once hurried back to Barataria where he found that in his absence his lieutenants had put the British officers in limbo. Lafitte at once had them released, and with all the politeness of a Frenchman gave them a negative answer and sent them back to the brig-of-war, which all this time had lain under the guns of the pirate fleet.

It had been put forward that the large number of Americans under Lafitte made his cooperation with the British an impossibility.

No sooner had the *Sophie* run through the pass, than Lafitte dashed back to New Orleans to see if he could now persuade the Governor with the news that he had sent the British to the rightabout. But he was too late. Hardly had he left the island before Commodore Patterson with his punitive expedition appeared on the scene, and it was all up with the pirate kingdom of Barataria.

Here is the American Commanders report to the Secretary of the United States Navy:—

"On the sixteenth of September, I made Barataria: some of the vessels showed Carthaginian colours: the pirates formed their vessels for battle near the entrance of the harbour: At half past ten a.m. I perceived several smokes along the shore as signals and at the same time a white flag hoisted at the fore on board the schooner *The Lady of the Gulf,* an American flag at the main and a Carthaginian flag (under which the pirates cruise) at her topping lift . . . The pirates had fired two of their schooners, I hauled down my white flag and made signal for battle, hoisting with it a large white flag, bearing the words:—'Pardon to Deserters', having heard that there were a number of such from the United States Army and Navy there, who wished to return, if assured of pardon, and which the President's pardon offered until the seventh of September . . . I perceived that the pirates were abandoning their vessels and flying in all directions. I went in pursuit of them.

At Meridian I took possession of all their vessels in the harbour, consisting of six schooners and one felucca, cruisers and prizes of the pirates, one brig, a prize, and two armed schooners under Carthaginian flag, both in the line of battle with the armed vessels of the pirates and apparently with the intention to aid them—their crews were at quarters, tompions out of their guns and their matches lighted .... Colonel Ross landed and took possession of their establishments, which consisted of forty houses of different sizes, baldy constructed thatched with palmetto leaves.

I have captured all their vessels in port, dispersed their band, without one of my brave fellows being hurt".

In a later despatch the Commodore continued:—

"The force of the pirates was twenty pieces of cannon and from eight hundred to one thousand men of all nations and colour.

I have brought with me six fine schooners, one felucca, cruisers and prizes of the pirates and one armed schooner under Carthaginian colours, found in company and ready to oppose the force under my command".

He is silent about taking prisoners. As a matter of fact a great many got away into the bush, but he succeeded in capturing Dominique, whom Lafitte had left in charge in his absence.

Meanwhile Lafitte had most daringly gone straight to Governor Claiborne.

In the *Pirates Own Book* there is a crude wood cut of Governor Claiborne introducing Lafitte to General Andrew Jackson.

Lafitte Defends New Orleans

The result of this interview was the participation of Lafitte, Dominque, and some seventy to eighty if his gang, released from prison for the purpose, in the defence of New Orleans on January the eighth, 1815.

A breast-work of cotton bales had been raised along the Levee, and at one end Lafitte and his followers were posted in charge of two batteries of cannon.

These guns were served with such precision, and altogether Lafitte and his men behaved so well that President Madison signed a pardon for the whole lot on February the sixth, 1815.

Many of the old pirates wandered back to Barataria and started their old games, but they were routed out and broken up again the following May.

The Snake Island Community

Meanwhile Lafitte himself actually paid a visit to Washington. He then went on to Baltimore where he ordered a clipper to be built, ostensibly for the purpose of privateering against his old enemies the Spaniards, and he soon provided himself with a fresh set of South American republican commissions. His next destination was Snake Island, which until the spring of 1817 was the headquarters of D'Aure, the self-elected Governor of Texas, and also that romantic Spanish exile, General Mina, who, with money mostly provided by English capitalists, was busy making plans to free Mexico from the Spanish yoke.

On March the twenty seventh, 1817, Mina accompanied by D'Aure's flotilla sailed from Snake Island (or Galveston as it was sometimes called by the Spaniards after Bernardo de Galvez, Governor of Louisiana in 1782).

There is no space for an account of the gallant Mina's campaign, it was short and sweet, for he was defeated and shot on November the eleventh following, whilst D'Aure retired to Matagoda Bay.

Meanwhile the raffle of adventurers left behind on Snake Island had elected a government of their own consisting of a governor, Military Commandant, Judge of

Admiralty, Secretary of State, Mayor de Place, Administrator of Revenue and Marine Commandant.

This Comic cabinet used the schooner *Carmelite* as their House of Commons, but their chief business seems to have been smuggling slaves into Louisiana by the various inlets and creeks between the Gulf and the mouth of the Mississippi.

Lafitte Becomes Lord of the Isle

It was not long after this government had been set up on Snake Island, that Lafitte with about fifty followers arrived in his new Baltimore clipper, a brig which he named the *Pride*. He was received with acclamation, and straightway elected to the absent D'Aure's post of Governor.

Lafitte was thorough in all he did. His first act was to draw up a set of Rules and a form of oath, to which everyone wishing to join the 'Brethern of the Gulf' had to conform.

Lafitte, on landing, pitched his camp amongst D'Aure's tumble down huts facing the beach, which he called Campeachy, but it was better knows as Sacarap. Here the American timber ships used to land their cargoes (sacarap was the local name for a timber ship).

He at once started to build a fort with a fosse round it: and this fort in a short while became the centre of a pirate town housing quite as many men as Barataria.

Once again Lafitte became the most powerful pirate chief the world has ever known, his dominance over his wild followers being as strong as ever.

He now styled himself 'The Lord of the Isle'. His cruisers still made great use of Columbian and Mexican colours, but to these they added a special flag of Lafitte's own devising, known as 'The Red Flag of the River'. His flagship was the fourteen-gun brig *Pride;* whilst for use in visiting ships in the bay he had a beautiful eighteen-oar pulling boat built—a sort of state barge, luxuriously fitted, painted a pale blue with much gilt ornamentation, which he named *Culebra* (the rattlesnake).

In all he had about a dozen cruisers including two rakish swift sailing feluccas and a fine topsail schooner, which had been captured full of slaves.

Slaves were easily disposed of, but there was little sale for prizes, and for many years after Lafitte's demise, the wrecks of his prizes were to be seen rotting on the shores of Texas, mostly around Bolivar Point, Pelican Island and Eagle Grove.

Lafitte's Lieutenants

In his short reign at Glaveston (1817 to 1821) Jean Lafitte did little cruising himself, relegating this duty to his lieutenants. The best known of these were:—

Latham,	an Englishman.
Jean Batiste Marotte,	a Frenchman.
Rigmarten or Belluche Pluche,	a Frenchman.
Girol,	a Frenchman.
Felix,	a Frenchman.
Jim Campbell,	an American.
Churchill,	an American.
Franks,	an American.
Roach,	an American.
Lambert,	an American.
Brown,	an American.
Francis,	an American.

These men got short shift if they disobeyed orders or failed to satisfy Lafitte, as will be seen by the fate of Marotte, Brown and Francis.

Visit of General Long

In 1819 General Long of Texas and his officers visited Galveston with a view of enlisting Lafitte's aid in their campaign against the Spaniards. The pirate's rookery then consisted of the fort and Lafitte's own residence, a Yankee boarding-house, several pretty good log cabins belonging to married followers, the usual taverns and grog shanties and a number of huts and tents.

During the six weeks that the Texans remained on the island as the guests of Lafitte, three rich Spanish prizes were brought in, which had been captured without resistance. The crews and passengers were well treated and sent to New Orleans. When resistance was made the treatment became very different, and no mercy was shown—it being a case of 'walk the plank' for all and sundry aboard the victim.

The Fight at Three Trees

In between cruises, the pirates used to have a little relaxation—fishing, shooting, hunting, and collecting turtle and oysters.

Eagle grove, six miles from Glaveston, was a favourite place for sport as were the Deer Islands and Virginia Point on the mainland, also Red Fish Bar near the Trinity river, famed for its red fish and wild fowl. These sporting expeditions however, often led to trouble with the Caranchahua Indians. A pitched battle was even fought in the middle of Galveston Island near a clump of timber, called the 'Three Trees'. Here three hundred Indians were opposed by Lafitte with two field guns and two hundred men. After three days of true Indian fighting. the Caranchahuas retreated to their canoes and retired to the mainland after having lost thirty killed and a great number wounded.

The Indians landed a second time, but were once more driven off by Lafitte, who was accompanied this time by one of the Texan Colonels. After the Indians had fled, the Brethren of the Gulf camped for the night on the beach, and had a merry sing-song round their bivouac fires, in which we are told the stern Lafitte actually joined.

I can find no instance of a Galveston cruiser attacking an English ship and Lafitte received no visits from the vessels of his Britannic Majesty. But slavers running for Cuba wre constantly snapped up and their cargoes of negroes sold in Louisiana.

The Down-Fall of Marotte

It was the capture of a slaver which led to the downfall of Jean Batiste Marotte.

Marotte and another of Lafitte's lieutenants, named Crow, went in chase of a slaver, which by superior seamanship was captured in the end by Crow. As the prize was a valuable one containing a full cargo of prime black ivory, Marotte, the senior captain of the two became jealous of Crow's prowess. It was unusual for both captains to assemble aboard the prize for the share out of plunder, but Crow, suspecting foul play, sent a message asking Marotte to hand his share to his supercargo. the freebooters then set sail for Galveston. Crow again outsailed the Frenchman, and when Marotte arrived, the former went off in the *Culebra* with Lafitte to settle up the accounts.

Lafitte's account book must have been something on a par with that of Stevenson's pirate, Flint, though probably more neatly kept. We now see an instance of Lafitte's dominance over his men.

A box of watches, about which Crow had informed Lafitte, was not put down on Marotte's inventory. Lafitte at once taxed his lieutenant with trying to conceal it. Marotte promptly lost his temper and spat in his commander's face. The latter, with an icy calmness, at once challenged Marotte to a duel. Pelican Island was chosen as being suitable ground, so away went Lafitte with Crow and Marotte. But at the last moment, the latter lost his nerve, fell on his knees, confessed the theft and implored mercy. Laffitte in his stately manner stalked up to his guilty lieutenant, pulled his nose, gave him a back-handed slap on the face and a good booting; then he ordered him to leave Galveston at once and never dare to show his face again. And that was the end of Jean Batiste Marotte.

Brown Hanged and Sundried

The end of Brown was much more unpleasant. This man was a ferocious giant with a very bad reputation. When he applied to join the Brethren of the Gulf, Lafitte hesitated for six weeks before he would admit him, and then he warned him in the strongest language that if he touched any but Spaniards he should hang.

Off went Brown about October 1819, in command of two gun boats and straightway robbed an American on the Mermantace river.

This at once sent the U.S. Revenue schooner *Lynx* on his trail, On the twenty fourth of October, Brown was run to ground in the Sabine river, but excaped ashore with all his men. The pirates then made their way along the coast, and arrived at Bolivar Point in a starving condition—They made a signal fire and Lafitte sent a boat for them.

On the fifth of November one of the *Lynx's* boats captured a pirate boat in Galveston Bay. Aboard the boat was a man who confessed to being one of Brown's crew and stated that four others were at Glaveston.

We now have the official report of Commander Madison of the *Lynx*:—

"On the sixth of November I sounded the bar preparatory to crossing to apprehend the remainder, but was compelled, by the wind blowing fresh on shore, to go off in the night; and on my again making the land on the eighth, I observed a gibbet erected on the point of Glaveston with a man hanging".

Lafitte had kept his promise with Brown, who had been tried by court martial, condemned there and then, and straightway was hanged.

A contemporary rumour credited the body of the hanging Brown with the most sinister behaviour. Every evening the body turned round and faced the settlement, but during the night it revolved again, and in the morning was seen to be facing out to sea as usual. The superstitious pirates considered this a very bad omen.

The other three members of Brown's crew were handed over by Lafitte who wrote Captain Madison a very polite and conciliatory letter, in which he called himself "Governor of Galveston in the Republic of Texas".

Francis, who was an American crony of Brown, was also tried by drum head court martial for the robbery and ill-usage of some American women on the Sabine river.

Within an hour of his trial he was hanged in Galveston on the frame-work of an old house.

The man who can run a piratical federation with success must possess an unusual gift for commanding men, besides an entirely ruthless nature and fearless disposition. He had to take instant decision and act without hesitation. He had to be able to suppress a drunken riot, or even a serious mutiny by the sheer nervous force of his own personality.

Mutiny Aboard the *Pride*

On one occasion after a successful cruise under Lafitte himself, the men of his own flag ship, the *Pride,* became mutinous after the usual carouse on arrival, and planned to run off with the brig. Lafitte and his officers by putting two and two together gained an inkling of the plot, and without saying a word quietly prepared the cabin against attack.

It came in the middle of the night, but the boss pirate was ready. A terrible fusilade was opened upon the mutineers, who fled forward leaving six of their ringleaders dead in the companionway and a like number wounded.

In the morning Lafitte sternly purged the brig of her mutineers, and some days later their bodies floated ashore at Bolivar Point.

Lafitte's difficulty was that he had no control over his lieutenants when they were away cruising, and their many outrageous piracies at length compelled the United States Government to act.

Lafitte Driven from Galveston

Early in the year 1821, the U.S. fourteen-gun brig *Enterprise,* commanded by Lieutenant Kearny, ancored off the bar of Galveston.

Lafitte in his splendid barge at once rowed off, and carried the embarrassed officer ashore, where the latter remained for several days as the pirate's guest, being entertained and feasted in the most sumptuous fashion. But all Lafitte's diplomacy was useless. Kearny had orders to see that Lafitte evacuated Galveston with all possible dispatch.

It took two months for the French corsair to wind up the many ramifications of his extensive pirate business. Many of his followers including Jim Crow and his wife Sally refused to leave the neighbourhood and settled down to the usual Gulf pursuits of hunting, fishing and smuggling.

Last Years of Lafitte

Lafitte sailed away in the *Pride* with his wife, son and treasure, and for the next five years seems to have been ever on the move—at one time he would be heard of at the Island of Margarita near the Orinoco, next he was at Charleston, South Carolina, ever a popular spot with pirates.

The *Pride* was apparently trying to accommodate herself and her crew to the prosaic life of a trader. Black was the name of her first officer and Jim Cochrane was second. From Charleston Lafitte sailed for the Island of Las Mugeres on the coast of Yucatan. Here he landed, and whilst the brig loaded with salt and dyewoods, set sail for Charleston, the old corsair himself along with one of his old Baratarian comrades, a Portuguese named Manuel Lopez, crossed over in a fishing boat to the Indian village of Silan where he 'took sick and died'. This was in 1826. He was buried in the Campo Santo at Silan, and a tombstone, placed over his grave, gave his name, age and date of death.

Between the years 1821 and 1826 we hear of no captures made by Lafitte or his lieutenants, and it is evident that the pirate of the Gulf had retired from business. Whether he left any treasure, and what became of his wife and son it is impossible to say. It is just possible that some prosperous Charleston family guards the secrets of its descent from one of the greatest and most successful of all rovers.

Though Jean Lafitte played no hand, between the years 1821 and 1826, there seems to have been more real old fashioned 'walk the plank' piracy going on in the West Indies than at any period since the days of Blackbeard.

There was little to choose between the Cuban pirate, the Carthaginian privateer and the Havana slavers, for during this period it was quite common for slavers to turn to piracy, and for pirates to run a cargo of slaves.

The Spanish Free-Booter *Gasparilla*

If Jean Lafitte, the pirate of the Gulf, was a romantic figure, what are we to say of the mythical, Spanish, free-booter, Gasparilla, who, if we are to believe the ravings of the dying one hundred and twenty year old pirate, Panther Cay John, was perhaps the most theatrical figure in the whole rogue's gallery of West Indian piracy.

There is no doubt that such a man as Jose Gaspar or Gasparilla existed between 1819 and 1822, and that he was the head of a lawless band of sea robbers, who preyed upon the shipping of all nationalities from Charlotte Harbour, Florida.

But he is never mentioned by either the United States or British Naval Authorities, who at that time both had numbers of ships specially commissioned to cruise against the pirates.

The story of Gasparilla seems to depend entirely on the testimony of John Gomez, known as

Panther Cay John, who died on Panther Cay in 1900, declaring he was the brother-in-law of Gasparilla, and upon that of John Gaspar junior, Gasparilla's cabin boy, who died at Palmetto, Florida in 1875, when seventy years of age.

Though their relations seem utterly fantastic and unbelievable, there remains one gruesome witness to support them, Gasparilla's graveyard in Turtle Bay, Charlotte harbour, where his victims were buried. This was discovered lying about one hundred yards inland from the beach, on the spot where Panther Cay John declared it to be.

Here amongst the bones of both men and women lay the headless skeleton of the Spanish princess, the heroine of the Gomez story.

According to Panther Cay John, this little Spanish princess was captured, along with eleven ladies-in-waiting and attendants, on her way home from Mexico; and on her refusing to enter the pirates's harem, Gasparilla had her beheaded.

On the islet of Cayopelean there used to be a prehistoric burial mound, fifty feet high, which on being opened disclosed a great number of skeletons, together with gold and silver ornaments. These were, of course, of unknown age, probably thousands of years; but, on top of this mound of bones, an observation tower had been built, which was said to be that of Gasparilla, upon which he kept a man on the lookout, watching the waters of the Gulf.

And the island of Gasparilla was stated to have been reserved by the Spainard for his own private quarters, consisting mostly of a large harem.

Gasparilla's Letter

There is one other item in the Gasparilla history, which may have some authenticity, and that it is his letter, addressed to a passenger aboard the Philadelphia ship, *Orleans,* captured off Cape Antonio, Cuba, in September 1821, by Gasparilla's fourteen-gun corvette. Here it is:—

At sea and in Good Luck.

Sir,
Between buccaneers, no ceremony; I take your dry goods, and, in return, I send you pimento: therefore we are now even. I entertain no resentment.

Bid good day to the officer of the United States, and tell him that I appreciate the energy with which he has spoken of me and my companions-in-arms. Nothing can intimidate us: we run the same fortune, and our maxim is that the goods of this world belong to the strong and valiant.

The occupation of the Floridas is a pledge that the course I follow is conformable to the policy pursued by the United States.

Richard Coeur de Lion.

This letter was written in French, and the last paragraph alluded to the activity of the United States in clearing Florida of all who opposed her occupation of that territory in 1819.

At that date the coast of Florida seems to have been the headquarters not only of Gasparilla, but of other long-forgotten pirates, such as Baker, Caesar, old King John, and that one-eyed Frenchman, Pierre Lafitte, the brother of the great Jean.

The End of Gasparilla

Gasparilla's end, according to Panther Cay John came in the spring of 1822 at a time when he was considering the abandonment of his old haunts in Charlotte Harbour, owing to the annoying activities of the American authorities in Florida.

A large ship had been sighted from the Cayopelean lookout tower, almost becalmed off the Boca Grande Pass. She was pronounced to be an English West Indiamen.

Out went Gasparilla in a small sloop, with thirty five men followed by Pierre Lafitte with a like number. Panther Cay John was left ashore with ten men in charge of the pirate settlement in Turtle Bay.

In the fight that ensued, Gasparilla was beaten off, whilst Pierre Lafitte turned tail and fled without taking any part in the action.

Seeing that he had caught a tartar, Gasparilla took a couple of turns of the sloop's anchor chain round his waist and then with the anchor in his arms leaped overboard.

His crew were captured and hanged at the yardarm with the exception of the cabin boy John Gomez junior, who spent ten years in New Orleans gaol.

Lafitte got away and so did the elder Gomez with his ten men.

U.S.N. Captures of Pirates 1821–1822

Young Gomez declared that the English West Indiaman turned out to be an American cruiser, in which the case the official report should be found amongst the U.S. Naval records.

But on November the thirtieth, 1822, the Secretary of the Navy sent the President of the U.S.A. the following list of piratical vessels captured during the previous twelve months, and it will be seen that none of these can be connected with the end of Gasparilla:—

October the sixteenth, 1821. Four schooners of about forty tons each and one sloop of twenty five tons, about one hundred men in all captured by Lieutenant Lawrence Kearny, commanding the U.S. brig *Enterprise* off Cape Antonio, Cuba. Two schooners burnt, the rest sent to Charleston, South Carolina.

October the twenty nineth, 1821, schooner *Moscow* captured by Captain Robert Henley, commanding the U.S. sloop *Hornet*—sent into Norfolk.

November the eighth, 1821, A boat laden with goods captured by Lieutenant Ramage—commanding the U.S. schooner *Porpoise* off Cape Antonio—The crew escaped, the boat destroyed.

December the twenty first, 1821, A schooner of about thirty five tons captured by Lieutenant Kearny—the crew of about twenty five escaped.

January, 1822. A Dutch sloop recaptured from pirates by Captain Elton, commanding U.S. brig *Spark.* The prize crew of seven men sent into Charleston, South Carolina.

January the seventh, 1822. Six vessels captured by Lieutenant Ramage, and the pirate's depot, etc., on the coast of Cuba destroyed. Three prisoners taken. Five vessels burnt and one manned.

March the eighth, 1822, Three launches and four barges captured by Lieutenant Kearny at Cape Antonio and destroyed

June the seventh, 1822. Two schooners captured by Lieutenants Perry and Gregory, three prisoners taken.

Panther Cay John's Account

In the account of Gasparilla which Panther Cay John gave to the United States Census officials in 1900, shortly before his death, he made the following statements:—

In 1782 Gasparilla was a high officer at the Spanish Court; he stole the crown jewels and, deserting his wife and children, set sail for the Gulf of Mexico in a ship stolen out of the Spanish fleet. A price being placed on his head by the Spanish authorities, he waged war specially upon that nation.

His buried treasure, lying somewhere in Charlotte Harbour has never been discovered; but the wreck of his sloop lay visible for thirty years in the sand of the Boca Grande Pass.

It is very difficult to separate fact from fiction in the case of Gasparilla, but for the other pirates of his date we have plenty of evidence in the English and American official reports.

CHAPTER V

HUNTING THE CUBAN CORSAIR

"Clap on more sail, pursue,
Up with your fights
Give fire—she is my prize,
Or Ocean whelm them all!"

Ever since peace had come to the world, piracy had been growing in the West Indies, in spite of the presence of large squadrons of national ships.

Raphaelina, The Colorados Pirate

IT will be noticed that most of the U.S. captures reported to the president refer to Cuban pirates.

The Cape Antonio pirates under Raphaelina, lurking behind the Colorados, pounced out on all shipping passing that headland, and were very successful, in fact, by July 1822 this Spanish pirate chief was said to have amassed 180,000 dollars in gold and silver coin, not to mention vast stores of merchandize.

Cuban Piratical Lairs

Another piratical rendezvous lay behind the reefs to windward of Matanzas.

In behind the isle of Pines was another sure retreat for Cuban pirates, and at the bottom of the Bay of Cortez was situated the Pirates Lagoon. Then the harbour of Escondido, and also Cumberland Harbour, were very popular with the local pirates.

Notorious Cuban Pirates and Their Ships

Amongst the more notorious of the Cuban pirate captains were Domingo, who captured the schooner *Pilot*. He must not be confused with Lafitte's Lieutenant, Dominique, nor with Dominico, a merchant, who acted as receiver for the Cuban pirates and disposed of their loot.

Then there was Josef Sabina of the pirate schooner, *La Gata*: Diabolito, whose schooner, the *Catalina*, was captured by the American gun boats, *Gallinupper* and *Mosquito*, in July, 1823; Cayatano Aroganez of the *Zaragozana*: Antonio el Majorcam, who was one of the scourges on the old Bahama Channel. This man was reputed to have been a Spanish Naval officer, who, when the Caribbean sea became too hot for gentlemen of fortune, took to the road and became a highwayman.

Another noted pirate chief was Cofrecina, who was garrotted at Porto Rico in 1825; Manuel Nieves, though he masqueraded as a Carthaginian privateer, was hanged at Puerto Cabello.

Of the more notorious of the pirate ships, mention should be made of *Cienega, Bandera de Sangre* (Anglice Band of Blood) *Moscow, Palmyro, Albert, Tropic, La Gata, Zaragozana, El Diableto, Aristidies* and *Emmanuel.*

British Victims

There is no doubt that at first the English Commander-in-Chief in the West Indies was slow to believe the various reports of piracies. It seemed to him to be chiefly Carthaginian privateers making legitimate warfare on the Spaniards and no records of British ships being attacked came to hand until December the thirteenth, 1821, when a large Liverpool ship fell a victim to the *Jolly Roger*, her captain being tortured and killed, and also her steward.

Then came news that the ships *Martha, Harborough*, and *Alexander* had been taken, the latter having their whole crew murdered.

In 1822 the list of British ships known to have been captured and pillaged contained the names of the *Alpha, Hebe, Zephyr, Vittoria, Industry* and *Protheroe*. This wholesale capture and murder produced a great outcry in our seaports and commercial circles, and questions began to be asked in Parliament.

Though there were nineteen ships on the British West India station in 1819, most of these were too large to follow the pirates into the shallow, coral-strewn waters of their retreats, and even the few, who were suitable, were mostly kept busy running the mails and doing the work of an Admiral's tender.

"The Gulf of Mexico", wrote Harry Keppel in 1826, "is for dollars what the Bank of Newfoundland is for fish: owing to the number of slavers, who, when their trade is slack, are not above doing a bit of piracy, the merchants care not to trust their money to traders, while captains of the Royal Navy were keen freight collectors". There was a regular rate allowed to Captains of men-of-war for conveying treasures.

In the West Indies from Vera Cruz and the Gulf ports it was two per cent—On the other side of the Horn and Cape a half per cent more.

Of this freight only a half went to the Captain, a quarter going to the Admiral of the station, and the remaining quarter to the Greenwich Hospital.

Not only the ships on the West Indian station, but the packet brigs made quite a nice thing out of this.

The pier of Vera Cruz was almost built of British man-of-war ballast—pigs of iron landed to make place for Mexican dollars.

Success of H.M. Schooner *Speedwell.*

The eighteen-gun brig-sloops and ten-gun brigs on the station could not catch the slippery long legged schooners of the pirates—indeed in 1819 there was only one man-of-war, who would overhaul the average fine-lined rover, and this was the man-of-war schooner *Speedwell*, which cruising in company with the U.S. sloop *Peacock*, and schooner-rigged revenue-cutter *Louisiana*, had been instrumental in catching five slavers.

On the sixth of November 1822 the *Speedwell* further distinguished herself by capturing the pirates, *Union* and *Constanzia.*

An Act of Parliament granting head money for all pirates captured after January the first, 1820, together with very forcible instructions from home speedily put the British squadron upon its metal, and so infected Rear-Admiral Sir C. Rowley, the Commander-in-Chief, that he began to dream of pirates and could talk of little else.

Ontario* Takes the Pirate *Veloz

The first case of a pirate being captured by a British warship occurred on December the nineteenth, 1819, when the eighteen-gun sloop *Ontario*, after a long and anxious chase amongst the Colorados, drove ashore and captured the pirate schooner, *Veloz;* and retook a French merchant brig loaded with cargo from two other prizes, a Bremen brig and a Spanish trading schooner. The latter capsized rounding the reef, but the pirates in the French brig opened fire on the *Ontario*'s boats, Lieutenant Whitworth Lloyd and two of his men being wounded.

Eighteen pirates were taken prisoner, and one of them, the boatswain, who had fired the gun at Lieutenant Lloyd was hanged at Jamaica.

It was indeed the hangman of Jamaica who did more to end piracy than any other means.

The U.S. "Mosquito Squadron"

The commanders of the small but efficient U.S. squadron, consisting of the eighteen-gun sloop, *Hornet*, the twelve-gun brigs, *Enterprize* and *Spark* and the twelve-gun schooners, *Porpoise, Grampus, Shark,* and *Alligator*, complained that they could not get their captures condemned at Charleston and looked with admiration upon the quick hangings at Jamaica. However the United States Naval Department acted with much greater liberality than the British Admiralty.

In 1823 Commodore Porter was put in command of what was called the "Mosquito squadron".

Besides the *Hornet, Spark, Grampus* and *Shark* already mentioned, Commodore Porter had under him the corvette *John Adams*, twenty four guns, *Peacock*, eighteen guns, seven three-gun fifty-ton schooners, five shallow-draft barges, and an amazing-looking paddle steamer, the *Seagull* of three guns, built at Hartford, Conn, in 1818 and the second steamer in the U.S. Navy.

The fifty-gun schooners were smart, little shoal-draft schooners on the lines of the *Chesapeake* pilot-boats. One of them, the *Greyhound* was the first command of David Glasgow Farragut.

Mr. Bradlee credits this U.S. squadron with capturing seventy-nine pirate vessels mounting sixty-four guns and carrying one thousand three hundred men. This is a huge figure for a few years work, but it probably includes pulling boats and such small fry, which were little more than the sneak thieves of the profession. It must also be remembered that the "Mosquito fleet" had only one object, the extermination of piracy whereas the Jamaica squadron had many other duties, including the capture of slavers.

By the year 1821, the pirates had become so bold that the English packets were not safe from attack. In that year the schooner *Speedy*, the packet between Jamaica and Bermuda, was attacked off the east end of Cuba by four large piratical craft and only escaped with difficulty from under their broadsides.

Eliza* Attacked by *El Diableto

On September the thirtieth, 1822, the hired sloop, *Eliza,* acting as tender to the frigate *Tyne*, was actually set upon whilst lying at anchor in La Guajaba, just west of Cayo Romana in the Old Bahama Passage.

The *Eliza* was manned by twenty six men headed by a masters mate, name Hugh Nurse and a mid named White; her only gun was a twelve-pounder carronade.

She was attacked by the pirate schooner, *El Diableto*, mounting six broadside guns and with a complement of forty men, and the felucca *Firme Union*, of five guns and thirty five men.

Here is a first-hand report of the fight:—

"At eight thirty p.m. the schooner brought up at a short distance, and without hailing, fired two shots at the *Eliza*. Mr. Nurse immediately opened a fire from his only gun, loaded with round and grape, supported by musketry; and after six rounds, the slaughter on the pirate's deck must have been great, as the cries of the wounded were hideous. The felucca now bore down between the schooner and the *Eliza*, with the evident intention of running alongside the latter, but which she frustrated by getting under her bow and instantly boarding.

The defence of the freebooters was desperate: the captain and nine men were killed and the remaining part of the crew, with the exception of four men, two of whom were severely wounded, jumped overboard—She appeared to have been fully prepared for action. Shot were heating, and the men were armed with cutlasses, each having a long knife in his left hand. On our side two seamen were killed, and Mr. Nurse and six men severly wounded. Perhaps in few actions of the kind has a greater degree of cool and determined gallantry been displayed".

The *Diableto* managed to escape, whilst the *Eliza* was desperately engaged in capturing the felucca.

British Boarders Use the Bayonet

It was probably due to this habit of Spanish Pirates of fighting with a knife in the left hand that the bayonet was introduced into the Service for the same purpose.

In that rare little book *Personal Recollections on Seamanship, Discipline, etc.,* Captain Francis Liardet tells us:— "The crews of the vessels employed in the West Indies for the suppression of piracy, from 1822 to 1825, had a bayonet and scabbard always attached to the cutlass belt. The bayonet had a becket worked to it, like the cutlass, sufficiently large to go firmly on the wrist. The men were taught to use the bayonet in the left hand, while attacking or repelling the enemy with the cutlass: and in this way the bayonet was always in its proper place, if required to be used with the musket".

Grecian* and *La Gata

The next stiff fight was between H.M. cuttter, *Grecian,* commanded by Lieutenant John Cawley, an (officer of long and meritorious service but with no high connections or pull in the Navy) and the pirate schooner, *La Gata* of ninety tons, commanded by the notorious Josef Sabina with a crew of ninety men.

On the twentieth of March, 1823, whilst cruising within the reefs to the eastward of the Isle of Pines, the *Grecian* observed a schooner lying in what was known as the Pirates' Lagoon, at the mouth of Filipina River. This schooner with her raking spars and low freeboard had all the hallmarks of a rover; but it was not easy to reach her as the cutter had to be worked through gaps in the reef, and round coral heads with very little water under her.

However by clever pilotage she came through in safety, and as she sailed up the Bay of Cortez, the schooner hoisted a blood red flag, signifying no quarter, at the fore mast head and a monstrous black banner, decorated with death's head and crossbones, on her peak halliards.

As the *Grecian*, forging ahead very slowly in the light wind, came within range, the pirate opened on her with round, grape and small shot from an eighteen-pounder pivot gun amidships, a twelve pounder pivot gun on her forecastle and her six broadside nine-pounders, all of which were brought across to bear on the cutter.

Anchored close inside the schooner lay a four-gun felucca and two of the usual piratical pulling boats, each armed with a swivel; these also joined in the action.

It was not until one p.m. that the *Grecian* had sailed near enough to commence close action with her popguns, which were only six-pounder carronades.

For an hour there was a violent cannonade at rapid fire, the aim of the pirates as usual being very wild, whilst that of the men-of-war's men did tremendous execution on the schooner's crowded decks.

After an hour of this bombardment the freebooters had had quite enough of it and could be seen taking to their boats.

The *Grecian* at once headed in to board, but luckily for the little cutter, when arrived within pistol shot she grounded in two fathoms water, and the very next moment the schooner blew up. The shore was only half a cable's length away.

"Man and arm boats" came the order from Lieutenant Cawley.

A desperate hand to hand encounter next took place on the beach, and when the pirates were finally put to rout, they left five prisoners in the hands of the *Grecian*'s men, and over thirty dead stretched out on the ground, out of a total estimated at one hundred and twenty, counting the crews of the felucca and gunboats, which took an active part in the struggle on the beach.

The pirate schooner *La Gata*, it seems, was not entirely destroyed, as a quantity of prize goods were found in her hold.

The prisoners were taken back to Jamaica and hanged at Gallow's Point.

This gallant action should have brought his long overdue promotion to old Cawley, but this was not gazetted till he paid off the *Grecian* on May the eleventh, 1825. Before this occurred he found two further opportunities of distinguishing himself. The first was the salving of the eighteen-gun sloop *Scout*, which had stranded on a reef. The second was the rescue from a bare rock in the Gulf of Mexico of twenty one ship-wrecked British subjects on November the fifth, 1822.

This was a fine piece of work for which he received the Royal Humane Society's Medal, it had required cool courage and clever seamanship, a tremendous surf running at the time.

Walcott and Roberts Capture the *Zaragozana*

Of all the many actions with pirates in the West Indies, that of the boats of the *Tyne* and *Thracian* against the dreaded pirate schooner, *Zaragozana* obtained most notoriety.

At the beginning of the year 1823, Admiral Sir C. Rowley detailed the *Tyne*, twenty six guns, Captain John Edward Walcott, with the eighteen-gun brig-sloop, *Thracian,* Captain John Walter Roberts under his command, to cruise along the North coast of Cuba and sweep the Old Bahama Channel clear of pirates, with special instructions reference the notorious *Zaragozana*, which had slipped out of Havana in January, having cleared as an armed merchantman, through the number of her men and guns should have made the Spanish authorities suspect her honesty.

This duty of pirate hunting was an arduous one for both officers and men, necessitating a great deal of boat service in the hot sun.

Four hundred miles of Cuban coast line, consisting of a maze of coral reefs and cays, had to be carefully searched.

With little protection from the malaria and yellow fever mosquitoes and sandflies, even at the best season of the year, it was not a healthy service, and Captain Walcott, himself, had to invalid as soon as it was over.

Lieutenant Hobson Captured by the Pirate Arogonez

The first move in the hunt was in favour of the pirates, for Lieutenant Willian Hobson with twenty men in a small tender was captured by the chief of the rovers, Captain Cayatano Arogonez, of the *Zaragozana*, a swarthy, black-whiskered Spaniard with a very uncertain temper, who was possessed with an arrogant contempt for his hunters, and was acknowledged to be the master pirate of the Old Bahama Channel.

So little did the West Indian pirate—or any pirate for that matter—consider the lives of his victims, that their life or death often depended on the ruffian's temper at the moment.

Cruelty was a speciality of the Spanish rover. Mutilation of their victims gave these human monsters pleasure. Authentic accounts of the torturing of prisoners are innumerable and too horrible to repeat; but the point must be stressed that it went far beyond mere callous indifference to human suffering for the hideous cries and groans of the victim and his wriggling twists and turns in his agony were witnessed by the pirates with a gloating pleasure. They were even known to accompany the groans of their miserable prisoners with the tinkling and strumming of guitars and zithers, and they sang ribald buccaneering staves as their dying victims pass away.

It will thus be seen that the situation of Lieutenant Hobson and his men in the hands of such a man as Arogonez was a very critical one. Whips were rigged at the foreyard arms of the pirate schooner, and the rope had actually been placed round Hobson's neck, when a sudden wave of caution—one cannot call it mercy—overtook the pirate captain, and he ordered his prisoners to be unbound and the yardarm whips to be unrove. After two or three days, during which they suffered no ill treatment, Hobson and his men were allowed to return in their own boats to the cruisers in the offing.

The next trick in the game fell to Walcott. On a small cay in the port of Maranjo, a large dump of eleven hundred casks of wine and spirits, part of the pirate's plunder, were discovered.

This was subsequently sold at Jamaica for six thousand pounds. After paying Colonial duty and Government claims, two thousand pounds were left to be shared amongst the captors.

Pirates Hanged at Port Royal

Soon after this, the pirate was further roused from his complacency by news of an execution at Port Royal.

Ten pirates were hanged on February the seventh, 1823. Before daylight they were taken under escort of the fiftieth regiment and the town Guard down to the water front at Kingston.

They were then put aboard two wherries along with the Town Guard and the sheriff and taken across the Gallows Point out on the Palisadoes.

Here a huge gibbet had been erected by order of Admiral Rowley, and the execution took place inside a hollow square formed by a guard of fifty soldiers.

The execution was reported in almost modern style in the West Indian newspapers, with the dying speeches and scaffold behaviour of each pirate. One of the pirates, one Pedro Nonde, a huge and immensely powerful man, who was covered with the scars of half-healed cutlass wounds, had to be hoisted up to the gibbet a second time, the first drop having quite failed to break his neck.

Arogonez Murders his Nigger Cook.

This summary execution of the first prisoners taken by the *Tyne*, coming on top of his release of Lieutenant Hobson seemed to the warped mind of the *Zaragozana*'s captain to be the height of ingratitude and treachery.

His paroxysms of rage soon affected his crew until the schooner resounded with oaths and execrations. Apparently a sort of ritual was gone through in the form of oath taking, whereby each man swore never to grant quarter to an Englishman; and to blow his vessel up rather than surrender.

But this was quite insufficient to appease the rage of Arogonez. An immediate victim was a necessity so the black cook, who being a native of Jamaica was thus a British subject, was hauled forth howling for mercy.

Rough treatment soon reduced his howls to whimpers. He was quickly spreadeagled in the rigging. For twenty minutes he was made a target for knives and pistol bullets, care being taken to avoid mortal wounds.

At last, tiring of their sport, the pirates poured round after round into the body till it hung dead in its lashings.

The witness of these terrible proceedings was an American, an old Bahama Channel pilot, whose profession apparently gave him freedom from molestation.

Shortly afterwards the two British cruisers encountered this same American pilot in the harbour of Neranjos, and he informed them that the vessel they were in search of was cruising off Baracoa.

Captain Walcott offered the pilot one thousand dollars to accompany him; but the latter declared that his life would not be worth a moment's purchase should such an action on his part come to the ears of the Cuban pirates, as it could not help but do, for very fisherman, farmer and petty tradesman ashore seemed to be league with the freebooters: he therefore begged to decline the handsome offer.

The *Tyne* and *Thracian* were now carefully disguised as the most slovenly and shorthanded of merchantmen.

Capture of the *Zaragozana*

On the thirty first of March, 1823, the long low hull of a black schooner was seen under easy sail, standing in towards the open roadstead of Playa de miel. The men-of-war headed in as if intending to make the anchorage likewise. But the pirate for it was the *Zaragozana*, was not to be deceived, and, after three hours slow sailing in a light wind, he was seen to loose his flying kites and with every rag set steer a course for the Puerta de Mata, a veritable North coast Escondido.

The swift *Zaragozana* soon ran away from the English cruisers, and when at one thirty p.m. they arrived outside the entrance, which was no more than a cable's length in width, the schooner was discovered, already securely moored across the mouth of the port.

In the light dropping wind it meant hours of the most tricky pilotage before the ships could work within range; so the pipe of 'Man and arm boats' was sounded.

Whilst Captain Roberts was left in charge of the ships with orders to work in shore as quickly as possible, Captain Walcott himself and the First Lieutenant (Amos Plymsell) of the *Thracian* led the way in their pinnaces, which each carried boat carronades in their bows.

It was not until three p.m. that after a hard pull the boats arrived within range of the schooner, then with a crash the whole pirate's side burst into flame, whilst from the concealment of the bush on either side came volleys of small arms. At the same moment the red and yellow bars of Spain, which had been hanging at the pirate's peak, were replaced by a black flag, of such a size that its drooping fly almost touched the water.

As they advanced, the boats opened a steady fire both from their carronades, and from their marines and small arms' men.

As long as they had water between them the pirates plied their guns well, but as the boats dashed up alongside the schooner with the usual stentorian British cheer, the Spanish valour melted away. With the exception of the Captain and a few of the stoutest hearted, not one of the polyglot crowd of ruffians stayed to face the cold steel of the British bluejacket, but leapt wildly overboard and swam for the shore.

Somehow or other, in spite of the almost impenetrable mangrove forest and bush, the boats' crews managed to round up twenty eight prisoners including Cayatano Arogonez, who never left his schooner.

Meanwhile Captain Roberts and Mr. Bull, acting master of the *Tyne* had succeeded in working their ships through the most intricate channel to within gun-shot of the captured *Zaragozana*. This was considered one of the most brilliant pieces of boat service since the war, the pirates lost ten killed and fifteen wounded whereas the attack only suffered one killed and five wounded.

The *Zaragozana* prisoners were all hanged on a gigantic gallows on the Palisadoes at Port Royal to the great satisfaction of Sir Charles Rowley, who sailed for home very soon after, being succeeded by Vice-Admiral Sir Lawrence Halsted.

Pirate Schooners Become H.M. Cruisers

Before he went, however, he increased the effectiveness of the Jamaica squadron by adding three celebrated pirate schooners to the British Navy—these were the *Union, La Gata,* and *Zaragozana*. The first was allowed to keep her name, but the La Gata was renamed *Lion* and the *Zaragozana — Renegade.*

The *Union*, before turning pirate had been well known on the Jamaica station as the *City of Kingston*, built at Kingston in 1821. The *La Gata* was a Baltimore schooner built in 1821, whilst the *Zaragozana* was built at Baltimore in 1820.

The dimensions of these schooners, as given in the Admiralty list, were as follows:—

Name	Tons	Length Gundeck	Length Keel	Beam	Depth	Where Built	When
Union ex City of Kingston	84	59′ 9″	44′ 6¼″	18′ 3¾″	6′ 10″	Kingston	1821
Lion ex La Gata	88	61·8	43·0¾″	19′ 4″	5′ 9″	Baltimore	1821
Renegade ex Zaragozana	115	76·3	59·10¾″	19′ 2″	7′ 4″	Baltimore	1820

As regards armaments, the Admiral wisely refused to allow the dockyards to raise bulwarks on these beautiful little schooners, or to stuff them full of guns.

The *Union* and *Lion* besides a long Tom amidships on the usual pivoting carrriage had a twelve-pounder carronade per broadside: *Renegade* being larger was rated as a four gun schooner. She was also given a complement of thirty five men as against thirty one for the other two.

As soon as they were re-fitted, the three ex-pirates were sent out to cruise against their own kidney; and very successful they were, though it was hard, trying work for the men.

Cruising in Company

At first *Union* and *Lion* worked in company under Lieutenant-Commander W. Hobson.

Hobson took the *Lion* with master's mate J.B.B. McHardy as his second in command. Lieutenant-Commander James Marriot had the *Union* with senior mate Francis Liardet as his First Lieutenant.

Here is what Liardet wrote regarding this service:

"When it is considered requisite for vessels to cruise in narrow, shoal and dangerous waters, it would be disirable that they should cruise in pairs. I speak from experience. I was sometime employed against the pirates in the West Indies, most of which time, the *Lion* and *Union* schooners cruised together, under the late much lamented Captain Hobson. We were continually and successfully employed in the most dangerous and out of the way places on the Coast of Cuba, and I believe I may assert, that when on our cruising ground (from the nature of the service and the want of good charts) that we were seldom above a week without one or other of the schooners being on shore, and frequently in situations in which one must have been lost without the help of the other.

In many cases the *Lion,* or the *Union*, was so hard and fast on shore, that the one afloat was obliged to take up a position right astern, with all her anchors down, and all cable out, and heave her off by main strength, and frequently obliged to remove everything out of her, even to the crew, and in some situations in danger of losing both vessels.

You may therefore suppose what either of these vessels would have done singly, when we found so much difficulty with the greatest assistance from each other: and on several occasions this service had to be performed under the fire of the pirates from the shore".

Commanders Against Pirates Picked Men

It was a job, of course, for picked men and men who were acclimatized.

Hobson was afterwards Governor of New Zealand: Lieutenant Commander Charles Elliot, who commanded *Union* and *Renegade* in turn, went out to China as a member of Lord Napier's mission and succeeded Sir G. B. Robinson as Chief Superintendent of British Trade in China. Lieutenant-Commander Henry Love, who commanded the *Union*, in 1824, had a very high reputation in the Service. He claimed to have suggested the use of paddles for steam-vessels. After commanding the famous *Columbine* on the West India station, he became a sub-commissioner of pilotage for the port of Southampton, and superintendent of Lights, buoys and beacons between Beachy Head and Portland for the Trinity House.

Francis Liardet, who was descended from an old Swiss family, ended his days as Captain of Greenwich Hospital. No officer had a greater reputation in the Service, both for seamanship and gallantry. Six different times did he leap into the sea to save a man overboard.

The first time was from the brigantine *Forester* in Portsmouth Harbour: he was carried away by the stong ebb, and picked up with the man he went after when they were at their last gasp.

The second time was from the *Jaseur*, eighteen guns, when off the Cape of Good Hope: he jumped into a heavy sea to save a man who had fallen from the main topsail yard.

The third time was again from the *Jaseur* when she was off the East coast of Africa, going seven knots under stunsails. This time he dashed into a sea full of sharks to rescue a mid-shipman.

In all the glorious annals of the Royal Humane Society he was probably the recipient of the greatest number of medals.

Whilst serving in the *Union*, Liardet was severely wounded in action on July the twenty fifth, 1823 and upon his recovery he was promoted to the command of the *Lion*.

War Schooners *Assiduous, Magpie* and *Monkey*

Besides the three famous ex-pirate schooners *Lion, Union* and *Renegade*, there was a very smart little schooner tender, named *Assiduous*, which unfortunately has not found a place in the Navy List; and all we know about her is that Admiral Halstead had two war schooners built from her lines, the *Magpie*, at Jamaica in 1826, and the *Monkey*, at Bermuda in 1827.

Their measurements therefore, should give a guide to the size of the *Assiduous*, and were as follows:—

Name	Tons	Length Gundeck	Length Keel	Breadth	Depth
Magpie	70	53′ 3″	42′	18′	7′ 3″
Monkey	68	56′	48′ 8½″	17′ 10″	7′ 4″

Magpie was armed with two nine-pounder long guns, and two eighteen pounder carronades. These were evidently considered to have over-weighted her, for *Monkey* was only given two Twelve-pounder carronades and a five-and-a-half pounder howitzer. Their complement was thirty five all told.

It seems very probable that the *Assiduous* was another captured pirate schooner, but this is impossible to prove. Her life in the Royal Navy seems to have been a short one.

Between November 1824 and May 1825, she was employed under Lieutenant Richard Dowse in hunting Cuban pirates.

In the twenties the fear of pirates was so great that merchantmen were convoyed between West Indian ports, and the war schooners were constantly interrupted in their pirate hunting in order to convoy some merchantman to Belize, Tampico, Vera Cruz, or the ports of the new Columbian republic.

Of course these were short trips, but sometimes they were very unpleasant especially during the hurricane season.

These West Indian schooners had to be carefully sailed, and in a blow their logs record topmasts and yards being sent down and jibboom rigged in—The schooners all carried yards on the foremast, even to royals, and also had a full suit of stunsails.

Log of the *Renegade*

The *Renegade* was specially lofty and heavily rigged, and on one of her cruises she carried away her trestle-trees on the foremast, which only the previous cruise had been badly sprung.

This was in 1825, and a few extracts from the Captain's log book may give a better idea of the strenuous life aboard one of these schooners in bad weather.

Renegade Port Royal to Savanilla (Columbia) and back

July 2. Weighted and made sail by South Channel. Heavy sea. Close reefed fore and mainsails and stay foresail. Struck main-topmast and foreyard.

July 4. Set balance-reefed mainsail and close-reefed fore-topmast staysail. Strong gales.

July 5. Heavy sea. Close reefed. Pumped ship every hour.

July 8. Anchored Savanilla—Put Consul and Mrs Fouché ashore.

July 11. Made sail out of harbour.
4.30 Sprung foremast—Shortened sail. Sent foreyard, topsail yard and topmast on deck. Close-reefed foresail and staysail. Anchored St. Martha.

July 12-18. Employed fishing foremast, painting outside of schooner and mastheads and spars, also wooding and watering.

July 21. Anchored Port Royal.

Renegade Port Royal to Casilda (Cuba) and back

Nov. 2. Left Port Royal.
Set flying jib and royal; up fore sail, down gaff topsail and mainsail. Struck main-topmast, sent topgallant yard on deck.

Nov. 30. Arrived Casilda Harbour.

Dec. 3. Sailed from Casilda.
Cape Cruz N. W. Out first reef of topsail. Set topgallantsail. Found starboard trestle-tree carried away. Sent topsailyard, topgallantyard and mast on deck.

Dec. 10. Saw schooner to windward. Out boats and cleared for action.
11. a.m. Spoke *Zelme*, Columbian privateer, hove to and she sent a boat.
Secured guns and made sail for the Morro, Havana.

Dec. 12. Anchored in St. Iago de Cuba.
Making new trestle trees.
Noon got cross trees over.

Dec. 14. Fidded topmast and topgallant mast. got lower and topsail yards up, bent topsail. P.M. Made sail. 4.15 came to in lower anchorage. Wm. Power, boy deserted from boat.

Dec. 19. Arrived Port Royal—Sent Mr. Pentham to hospital. 2.15 arrived H.M.S. *Isis*. In port H.M.S. *Serapis, Valorous*, and *Britomart.*

This was the last cruise of the Renegade.

On December the twenty seventh a survey was held upon her, and on December the thirty first she was taken into the dockyard and dismantled. On January the third, 1826, her crew were discharged into the different ships in the harbour, and at sunset Lieutenant Bolton hauled down his pendant and the schooner was handed over to the charge of Captain Charles Elliot of the *Serapis*.

British and American Cruisers Work in Company.

During the years 1824 and 1825, I find the English cruisers *Speedwell, Lion, Union, Renegade* and *Assiduous*, schooners, *Grecian* cutter, together with the boats of the frigates *Diamond,* forty six, *Dartmouth,* forty two, and *Hussar,* forty six guns, working in company with the vessels of the United States Mosquito Squadron.

Here are a few scattered extracts from the logbooks of the *Lion* (Lieutenant Liardet), and the *Union* (Lieutenant Love).

Log of the *Lion*

Lion cruising

Oct 19, 1824.	Sandy Cay WSW 3 miles. Sent boats manned and armed to schooner at anchor in shore. 1.30 p.m. boat returned. Schooner laden with salt. 8.30 p.m. weighed and made sail along shore to Westward. 9 p.m. grounded in five and half feet, furled sail laid out anchor astern to haul off, but tide falling.
Oct. 20.	5 A.M. Hauled off into nine feet of water. 7 p.m. grounded in eight feet of water, laid anchor out. 8 p.m. hove her off and made sail to Westward.
Oct. 22.	Boarded coasting schooner from Havana.
Oct. 28.	Point Francesca S.E. by S. half a mile. Made sail in company with United States schooner, *Terrier.* (61 ton shallow-draught Chesapeake-type, bought specially for pirate hunting, commanded by Lieutenant Paine).
Oct. 30.	*Terrier* in company. Cape Antonio West seven miles.
Oct. 31.	9 p.m. Despatched boats manned and armed in company with *Terrier*'s boats in search of pirates.
Nov. 1.	A.M. boat arrived with news of having captured a piratical felucca, with two Americans that had been taken out of schooner *Rainbow* of Elizabeth City, North Carolina. P.M. Weighed and made sail. Five boats joined with crew of French ship lately captured by piratical schooner. Depatched boats in shore and made sail in chase of a ship supposed to be the captured French ship. 8 p.m. Squally. *Terrier* in company. 11 p.m. Fired five shot under stranger's forefoot. Hove to and boarded her, proved to be ship from Bordeaux bound to Havana.
Nov. 3.	Examined Corrientes Bay in search of pirate's prize. 7.30 p.m. Anchored in five fathoms, *Terrier* in company.
Nov. 4.	Discharged four Frenchmen into *Terrrier*. Made sail, *Terrier* and boats in company.
Nov. 5.	Rocky Point N½E fourteen miles. 3 p.m. observed a ship at anchor under land. Made all possible sail in chase. 5 p.m. Closed the *Union.* 7 p.m. Tacked and made all possible sail, ship bearing N½E. Light airs and variable. 8 p.m. Employed getting boats and prize ready for going away to ship at anchor.
Nov. 6.	Anchored in 1½ fathoms. Strange ship about one cable distant—found her to be French ship *Calypso*, taken by the pirate, crew of which we had on board; and that the boats had taken a small boat with bags of coffee and one man and two boys in a lagoon about a mile off. Boats returned having captured a felucca.
Nov. 7.	St. Phillips Bay. Sent boats to bring off coffee.
Sunday.	Found in the woods. P.M. Hauled schooner alongside *Calypso* and got two hundred and fifty bags of coffee on board. 2.30 p.m. Hauled off to anchorage. Getting anchor laid out and hove up.
Nov. 9.	Employed warping ship *Calypso* out.
Nov. 11.	Pocky Point S. by W. ten miles. 5.30 weighed and made sail. *Terrier* and prizes in company. Punished J. Kelly with forty two lashes for getting drunk on shore whilst getting off the coffee.
Nov. 13.	Rounded Cape Antonio.
Nov. 14.	Bonavista E. 3 miles. 4 p.m. observed schooner and sloop at anchor under the land. Found them to be droghuers.
Nov. 16.	Grounded and hove off. Sent boats in shore (*Lion* was making her way round to Havana searching for pirates as she went, having left *Terrier* and the prizes behind).

Nov. 18. Grounded and hove off.

Nov. 19. Anchored Havana; found H.M. schooner *Speedwell* lying here. (Four men, including J. Kelly deserted here).
As soon as she had reprovisioned the *Lion* sailed again in company with the U.S. Barge *Gallinipper*.

Dec. 1. Parted company with *Gallinipper*. Found lying at Sandy Cay U.S. schooner *Terrier* and prizeship *Calypso*.
Commander of *Terrier* informed us of felucca swamping astern of her during strong gale of November the eighteenth.

Dec. 2. Discharged American seaman, G.W. Baily, captured in pirate felucca into *Terrier*. Made sail, set square sail and reefed topsail.

Dec. 4. 8.10 Anchored, Fort of Matanzas S. by W.
Lying here H.M. schooner *Speedwell* and U.S. ship *Hornet* and schooners *Grampus* and *Porpoise*.
(Here the *Lion* stayed some days refitting).

Dec. 8. Scrubbed hammocks, white washing lower deck, scraping hold, washing ballast. Carpenter repairing boat, sail-maker repairing mainsail.
(December the fourteenth found the *Lion* cruising on the North coast of Cuba).

Dec. 14 Light breezes. Observed a sail standing to Westward.
6.30 a.m. Stranger tacked and made all sail. Showed our colours to a schooner under Spanish government flag. Got the studding-sail booms on the yard and made all possible sail in chase of her.
5. p.m. Light airs—schooner S.E. by E. one and a half miles sweeping away.
5.20 p.m. ranged up under her starboard quarter and sent boat away to board her under cover of the gun. She proved to be the schooner *Relampayo*, thirty nine days from Mennasseh bound to Havana with one hundred and fifty slaves on board. Sent mate Crispin and ten men on board to take charge of her. Took twenty men out of her, leaving the captain and two there. Supplied her with six bags of bread for the slaves.

Dec. 16. Matanzas S. ½ W. twenty miles.
Spoke the Columbian privateer brigantine *Joseph*. Burnt blue light for convoy to distinguish us from privateer.

Dec. 17. Arrived at Havana with prize.
At this date Columbian privateers (which it was often difficult to distinguish from pirates) swarmed round the coast of Cuba.

On December the thirtieth, Lieutenant Liardet writes:—
"Observed four strange sail—Made sail in chase of two schooners. Showed our colours to two Columbian cruisers in chase of a brigantine. Tacked—Working to windward to close cruisers".

11.50 "Cruisers firing at brigantine to make her heave to". January 12, 1825. Found the *Lion* at anchor in five fathoms, Point Yeacos, Mona Cay N.N.W. fourteen miles.

"8 p.m. Arrived H.M. schooner *Assiduous* with a sloop, her prize; weighed and dropped down abreast of prize sloop".

Log of the Union

The best log for the first six months of 1825 is that of Lieutenant Love, commanding the *Union*.

Jan. 18, 1825. Sent *Union*'s cutter and gig with cutters of *Dartmouth* and *Assiduous*, manned and armed, under Lieutenant Love to examine creeks in neighbourhood of Cayo Blanco and off Cayo Alacian.

Jan 19. Made sail, *Assiduous* in company. 9. a.m., grounded in seven feet, forced her off with sails.

There were no captures this cruise and on January the twenty eighth, *Assiduous* and *Union* worked into Havana Harbour under their sweeps. Here they found H.M.S. *Dartmouth*, *Pyramus, Diamond,* and *Lion*.

Here also on February the eighth Love turned his hands up and punished Absolam Davy with forty eight lashes and Isaac Taylor with twenty one for theft.

There could not have been much chance for either pirate or slaver during Feburary 1825, for besides the American Mosquito fleet and a number of Columbian privateers, there were the following English men-of-war ranging the coast of Cuba:—

Diamond, forty six, Captain the Lord Napier, *Dartmouth,* forty two, Captain J. A. Maude, *Grecian*, cutter, Lieutenant John Cawley, *Speedwell* schooner, Lieutenant W. H. Castle, *Renegade*, schooner, Lieutenant James O'Brien, *Lion*, schooner, Lieutenant Francis Lardet, *Union,* schooner, Lieutenant H.O. Love, *Assiduous,* schooner, Lieutenant Richard Dowse.

Captures in the Nicholas Channel

On March the fourteenth, *Lion, Union* and *Dartmouth* left Havana and on the afternoon of the seventeenth brought up with Rocky Cay, S.W. by W. and Mono Cay N. by E.

At sunset the frigate sent her barge and two cutters under Lieutenant Ward with three midshipmen and thirty nine men to join forces with the schooners, who with the boats in tow headed into shoal water until the schooners themselves could go no further.

They were anchored somewhere in the neighbourhood of the Cayo Cadiz in the middle of the Nicholas Channel. Nothing happened until March the twenty eighth, when the waiting schooners at one thirty saw flashes in the offing. By this date the boats of that extraordinary little war steamer, the U.S. galliot, *Seagull* had joined in the hunt. At two twenty the boats returned to the anchorage with the news that they had captured a pirate schooner armed with a twelve-pounder on a pivoting carriage, of whose crew they estimated ten or twelve had been killed.

As usual the pirates had fired wildly, and done little damage only two Englishmen being wounded out of a large force of boats headed by the U.S. barge, *Gallinipper*, under Lieutenant W. W. McKean.

The pirates had hidden their schooner up a creek behind trees, nevertheless out of thirty five men, eight were killed and nineteen captured.

The pirate captain produced Spanish papers, but these proved to be forged, and as cases of American goods were discovered aboard her there was no doubt of her guilt.

On March the twenty ninth, the victors started to work through the reefs; at eleven they passed the Columbian privateer *Penesola* lying at the anchor, and by noon had rejoined the frigate *Dartmouth.* The American account says that a small topsail schooner was also catured though her crew escaped ashore, and Captain Maude confirms this.

On the following day one of the prizes went hard and fast ashore in a heavy squall. The boats of the *Lion* and *Union* were able to save her cargo but the schooner herself had to be set fire to. The pirates were taken to Key West by the American war ships; The *Union* and *Lion* followed them and anchored there on April the first, 1825.

Boats of *Icarus* Capture Pirate Diableto

The most notable capture in the years 1824-1825 was that of the notorious pirate schooner, *Diableto*, by Lieutenant Charles Croker, First Lieutenant of the little *Icarus*, and master's mate (acting lieutenant). J. B. B. McHardy in the boats of the gun-brig and a hired Spanish launch.

The pirate schooner was discovered in a creek behind the Cayo Blanco near Trinidad, Cuba, on August the twentieth, 1824.

Her crew did not put up much of a resistance. Many of them jumped overboard, swam ashore and hid among the mangroves. But the greater number took to flight in four large pulling boats, after five pirates had been killed and a number wounded by the fire of the boats.

Aboard the *Diableto* were found the master and eight hands of the American brig *Henry*, who had been treated with great brutality and were to have been put to death the following day.

The *Henry* was found hard and fast in a creek, a mile above the schooner along with a deserted sloop with part of the *Henry*'s cargo on board.

As the *Henry* could not be floated, she had to be burnt, but the *Diableto* was brought off and it is quite possible that she became the *Assiduous*, which was commissioned by Lieutenant Commander Richard Dowse in November.

Pirates in the Gulf of Batabano

Within the isle of Pines in 1824 most of the small cruisers collected in an effort to extirpate this nest of pirates.

Lieutenant William Holt, first of the frigate *Hussar*, who when first of the *Ferret* had distinguished himself in the action with *Dolores*, was sixty seven days in charge of the *Hussar*'s boats working in the Gulf of Batabano.

Here on the previous June the *Lion* and *Union* had captured the pirate *Flor de la Mar* and a number of piratical gun boats. In the spring of 1824 the *Speedwell* caught a pirate felucca off the Isle of Pines. The island itself was searched for freebooters by George Snell, mate of the *Icarus*, a very active boat officer, who for a while had command of a captured schooner.

With the Jamaica Squadron on one side of Cuba and the American Mosquito squadron on the other, piracy from the old Cuban hiding places had become a difficult business by 1826, and most of the freebooters were turning to the slave trade as being much more profitable game.

The Danish Schooner *Vigilant*

But the pirate still lurked in the West Indies.

At the present day, running as a packet between St. Thomas and St. Croix, is a little fore and aft schooner, named the *Vigilant*. In 1825, this historic vessel captured a pirate that had been making the Puerto Rico passage very unpleasant.

The *Vigilant* must be one of the most interesting relics of the old Napoleonic war years.

She was built at Baltimore as long ago as 1800, and started life as the slaver, *Nonsuch* of Wilmington, S.C. About forty years ago a print showing her hold full of slaves use to hang in the Moravian Mission at St. Thomas in the Virgins.

It was in 1825 that she came into the possession of the Danish Government, who fitted her out as a cruiser.

Under the Danish Captain Irwinger, and with thirty Danish soldiers on board in addition to her crew, she sailed in search of a pirate, found her and followed her in amongst the reefs and cays.

As the soldiers were hidden below, the pirate thought she had an easy prey, and after a few rounds had been fired, ran alongside with the intention of boarding. Then up sprang the soldiers, and the corsair found he had caught a tartar.

The *Vigilant*, as the Danes had renamed her, brought back four prisoners, who, according to rumour, were hanged at St.Thomas.

After this, having done her job, she was sold into private ownership, and under one of her owners, is said to have been suspected of piracy in her turn. As far back as 1860, she began carrying the mails through the Danish islands under charter to the Government. She lost her square yards in about 1850, but this does not seem to have affected her speed, for she has no difficulty in making the forty eight mile run between St. Thomas and St. Croix in four hours, being punctual to a minute in the strength of the Trade.

In the hurricane of 1876, she sank in eleven fathoms off St. Croix, but was raised and refitted; then in 1916, she again fell a victim to a hurricane, but was once more refloated; this time a good deal of her timbering was replaced, and she is considered to be as fit for her work as ever she was.

English Harbour Antigua after the War

The economy forced upon the Admiralty by the British Government at the end of the long years of war had reduced the ships on most stations, but nowhere perhaps to such an extent as upon the Leeward Island station as it used to be called.

The once busy dockyard at English harbour, Antigua, was almost deserted: the Commissioner had gone, the Master-attendant had gone. The storekeeper passed an idle time watching over empty storehouses. The boatswain of the yard had still a couple of negro shipwrights under him; but no caulkers, smiths, or joiners remained; and the man-of-war that put in for repairs had to hire labour and make with its own staff or import from elsewhere what it required in the way of fittings.

From Trinidad to Porto Rico and from Curacoa to the Grenadines, the pendant of a British man-of-war, with the exception of tenders and packets, had become almost as scarce as it is at present day; yet the lofty sails and raking spars of the South American picaroon and of her sisters, the slaver and the pirate, were to be met with everywhere.

Red Eyes, The Pirate

If the wreckers of the Bahama Bank had begun to complain that their peculiar business was not as brisk as it had once been, the ballahou schooners of St. Vincents and St. Kitts and the sugar droghuers of Barbados had a very different story to tell.

It was whispered that receivers of stolen goods were making fortunes in St. Eustatius and St. Thomas. Extraordinary reports of pirates were carried from island to island by the inter-island traders.

Negroes who had been been fishing off the land spoke with goggle-eyed awe of being held up and their fish stolen by a heavily armed schooner, which was painted green on one side and white on the other, and which somtimes flew a Dutch and sometimes an English ensign. This sinister craft, it was whispered, belonged to none other than the terror of the seas, Red Eyes the pirate.

The Pirates' Dumping Ground at Saba

But the most mysterious affair in the whole West Indies was the piled up wreckage on the east side of Saba, which had come to be called the Pirates' Dumping Ground.

It was significant that only eighteen miles to windward lay Oranjestad, the port of St. Eustatius, where it was confidently rumoured that a large piratical agency existed, run by two Americans named Stiles and Martin.

In the roadstead under the lee of the island, barques, brigs, schooners, sloops and feluccas would be seen standing off and on, waiting until one or other of these men went off to them. After which they would either be unloaded by lighters, or sail for an unknown destination. But this seldom took place in daylight. They invariably sailed after dark, especially after being unloaded—and there seemed to be some connection between the number of wrecks on Saba, and the number of vessels in the roads of Oranjestad.

At last news of these suspicious happenings reached the Pen at Jamaica, and Admiral Halsted sent the eighteen-gun ship-sloop *Grasshopper* down to investigate.

Commander A. Crawford had been down to Dutch Guiana in order to procure Dutch slave papers, without which no cruiser had any authority to detain vessels of that nation.

On his way back the *Grasshopper* was overtaken by a hurricane, in which she sprung her main-mast below the partners; and on the twentieth of September 1827, put into English Harbour, Antigua, for a refit. This, it is not surprising to find, was a slow job. However at the end of October she ran down to her cruising ground in the Virgins.

At St. Kitts Captain Crawford learnt that suspicious vessels often passed Basseterre heading for St. Eustatius and Saba.

He then sailed into the Oranjestad Roadstead, where he anchored at sunset. During the night the boats of the sloop searched every ship in the Roads, but failed to find one that answered to the descripiton of any pirates on the Admiral's list, nor did they succeed in identifying any vessel as a rover's prize.

So at dawn, Crawford weighed again and steered from Saba, intent on examining the Pirate's Dumping Ground.

The Dutch Island of Saba is one of the most extraordinary in the whole West Indies. it consists of the cone of an extinct volcano, whose sides rise sheer from the sea. Its inhabitants live in the crater, their town being called Bottom. They are an honest, hardworking lot, and speak English. They have not intermarried with the blacks, and still boast fair complexions and red cheeks, which is not really very surprising for they are descended from pure Scottish and Devonshire stock for the most part, refugees originally from the Civil war, with a sprinkling of Morgan's buccaneers, whom he marooned there in 1665 for being troublesome.

In spite of the taint in their blood, these simple folk were honest boat builders, who had nought to do with pirates of any sort. Their boats were actually built at Bottom, and had to be lowered down the steep path, called significantly the Ladder, before they could be launched.

Now let me quote from Captain Crawford's journal for his description of the Pirate's Dumping Ground.

"Arrived abreast of its (Saba's) eastern extremity, we discovered and opening or Channel between the island and a low, rocky cay that lies to the westward at the distance of about half a mile.

Into this channel we cautiously ran, having the yards braced by, and keeping the lead going as we advanced. The soundings were found to be most irregular. At one cast the man in the chains had twenty fathoms, and at the next perhaps not more than five. So that the navigation over this bed of coral-formed spicula was anything but comfortable, particularly as our Admiralty charts threw no light whenever upon the darkness, in which we groped our way.

Having run about a mile into this passage, we came abreast of a cliff, smooth and sheer as a wall, and which rose without a break to the height of seven or eight hundred feet. A smooth sandy beach, white and glistening, about fifty yards wide, separated this cliff from the water.

Along the whole of this beach, which no surf seemed ever to have disturbed, so calm and unruffled did it appear, were scattered numerous fragments of wreck, amongst which the hull of one vessel seemed entire.

On examination, however, she was found to be so much injured, that, could she have been floated (a difficult process where the ground outside was a bed of coral), she would have been found almost worthless.

Her name still plainly legible on her stern was *La Felicité de Marseilles* and she appeared to have been the last plundered and then left to rot.

We counted the fragments of ten or eleven different vessels, the names of which were all undecipherable except *La Felicité* and another called the *Orinooko*. This latter was evidently an English ship, but we were unable to make out to what port she belonged.

Few places could have been selected more convenient for the purpose of freebooters.

The situation, until you are actually abreast of the beach, is perfectly concealed and as little likely to be visited as the most unfrequented spot in the West Indies.

Being near both to St. Eustatius and to St. Thomas, where a secure and ready market was always found for plunder and where it was pretty well known the pirates had agents and friends, no position could have been better fixed upon.

Before I had been long on the station, two Americans, who under pretence of carrying on mercantile business at St. Eustatius, were deeply implicated in those piratical transactions, had to fly that island: and I have no doubt that others equally notorious, though not publicly denounced, were at the time resident in St. Thomas. In fact, without co-partners on land, who first contributed to the outfit and afterwards disposed of the plunder, those gentry could not have existed at all".

Though the *Grasshopper* cruised for more than a fortnight in the Virgins, and as far as the east end of Porto Rico, she had no sight of Red Eyes or any other local rover—no doubt they had all been warned to keep clear.

In fact' I can only find record of two of these windward Island pirates being captured—The first was the *Vigilant*'s prize, and the second was the pirate schooner, *Las Damas Argentinas*, taken by the eighteen-gun sloop *Victor*, shortly before the *Grasshopper*'s arrival on the station.

The story of the latter capture can be told in considerable detail.

The Pirate *Las Damas Argentinas*

Towards sunset on an October day in 1827, the typical rakish American schooner of Baltimore lines and low freeboard hove to under the lee of Saba. Her black sides, which were unrelieved by the bright band of the honest Yankee trader, and the carefully tarpaulined Long Tom amidships damned her in the eyes of the Saba natives, though she was loaded with a cargo of coffee and sugar and bore the name *Boliver—Baltimore*, on her stern. Aboard her, too, was one of the Martin family of St. Eustatius—In a short while the Dutch Governor of the Island came hurrying down the Ladder, and was soon closeted in the schooner's cabin. Presently he emerged, carrying a leather bag, which his boatman reckoned held five hundred dollars in silver coin.

Then throughout the night the Saba shore-boats were busy transferring the *Boliver*'s cargo to the land. When day broke to the astonishment of the simple islanders, the schooner's stern had been newly painted, and instead of *Boliver—Baltimore*, the name now read *Elizabeth of Saba*. The explanation was clear—The five hundred dollars was the cost of Dutch registry, and when the schooner sailed, she hoisted the Dutch ensign, politely dipping it in farewell to the Governor.

The previous history of this Baltimore schooner came out later on at the trial of the pirates.

It appeared that she was a very fast Baltimore clipper, of the true Maryland breed; she had arrived at St. Thomas, flying the stars and stripes and commanded by a man named Quincy, who evidently handed her over to owners in St. Thomas, who were none other than piratical agent of receivers.

She was provided with a crew of from forty to fifty men, and that most convenient piece of paper for a corsair, a Buenos Aires letter of marque. Apparently she was only one of a dozen pirate vessels using this device—and preying upon the world's shipping, though by their commissions confined to cruising against Spanish and Portuguese vessels only.

The *Bolivar*, since leaving Saba under her new name, had been in to St. Thomas twice to refit, and had again changed her name to *Las Damas Argentinas* as befitted her commission, and her latest captain was a young Majorcan.

A Flourishing Business

Her prizes along with those of the other pirates were sent into the Islands of Saba, St. Thomas and St. Eustatius, where the Dutch Governors were undoubtedly in league with the local agents of the rovers. The prizes were condemned under the flimsy pretext that they had been picked up as derelicts, and their cargoes were distributed through the islands of St. Thomas, St. Eustatius, St Martins and St. Bartholomews, and sold for the benefit of the captors and their agents.

Such a flourishing business could hardly be kept quiet, for in those days the hall marks of the ships of different nationalities were easy to see. For instance the merchant brigs—then the most common rig in the seven seas—of England, America, France and the Northern countries could not be mistaken for those of Portugal and Spain.

Thus when the English Governor of St. Kitts, the Honourable Stedman Rawlins, heard that a British-built brig with a crew of half a dozen dagoes Spaniards and other Mediterranean nationalities), had backed her topsail off Saba and sent to St. Eustatius by the packet for a crew of runners to take her across, his suspicions were aroused. He at once sent one of his staff off to St. Eustatius to make careful enquiries. The A.D.C. nosed about Orange town, and what he learnt caused him to take a boatman and row off to the anchorage.

His first visit was to a newly-painted black brig, the vessel which had recently been brought across from Saba. He found the name *Aurora* freshly painted upon her stern, but it had been so roughly done in such thin paint that he was able to decipher *Carriboo* of Liverpool beneath the new surface.

Here was the name of a vessel which was long overdue, and which had been last reported as far away as Gibraltar.

He found that she had anchored off Orange town "in distress", whereupon the Governor, acting as a prize court of vice-admiralty, had ordered one third of her cargo to be landed as payment for the work of salving her—in other words for payment of the crew of negroes, who had helped to sail her across from Saba.

Of course Martin, the pirate's agent, was put in as valuer. The brig's cargo consisted of crockery, dry goods, iron ware, etc., valued at one hundred and forty thousand dollars.

The A.D.C. before returning post haste to Basseterre, also learnt from his black boatman of the curious sinking of a French brig which had arrived in the roadstead two days previous to the English brig. This vessel, according to common report ashore, had sunk in deep water, her cargo being pigs of lead.

But the aide's boatman assured him that all her cargo, consisting of French manufactured goods, had been landed in the night, after which she had been ballasted with St. Eustatian beach rock, and with a number of auger holes bored through her bottom, allowed to sink well clear of the shipping in the deepwater outside the anchorage.

As a result of the A.D.C.'s enquires, the gun-brig *Emulous* was sent to St. Eustatius. She arrived there before the somewhat slack agent of the freebooters had begun to unload the brig; and without any 'by your leave' carried off the spurious *Aurora* to Basseterre.

Meawhile H.M. ship-sloop, *Victor*, Commander George Lloyd, arrived off Saba; and very quickly learnt all about the mysterious English Brig and much else of a suspicious nature from the very flustered and thoroughly frightened Dutch Governor. Whether Captain Lloyd had previous information about the pirate is not certain, but he evidently wormed all he needed to know from the Governor, for no sooner had he got aboard than the *Victor* was squared away to the Southward with stunsails and every flying kite set.

H.M.S.*Victor* Captures *Las Damas Argentinas*

After a run of forty miles, the *Victor* sighted a rakish, black schooner lying becalmed off the North end of St. Kitts. Here was her quarry, the notorious *Las Damas Argentinas*. As the *Victor* lost the dying Trade wind, she let fly her bow chaser at the pirate; once, twice, three times was an iron ball sent skipping across the sea in its vain effort to reach the schooner. This caused the latter to hoist Dutch colours. For a while the two vessels lay becalmed, just out of range of each other, then with a clap, the schooner's sails filled, and away she bowled for her only refuge, the roadstead of St. Eustatius and, she hoped, the protection of the Dutch Governor.

When she brought up under the Orange town fort, she lowered her Dutch colours as the anchor went down, running up in their stead the flag of the new Buenos Airian Republic.

Evidently the priate captain considered that his best chance lay in trusting to his Buenos Airian commission, dated February 1826, rather than the protection of the slippery Governor, who, he realised, would not hesitate to sacrifice *Las Damas Argentinas* in order to save his own skin.

At this date, September the sixth, 1828, the *Golden Rock* of Admiral Rodney's day had fallen from its high estate. No longer was it the chief mart in the West Indies; many of the large warehouses along the shore were in ruins; seven instead of seven hundred vessels lay in the roadstead—The Governor of Statia was now very small beer, and sure enough, when the *Victor* sailed into the anchorage and proceeded to fire the customary salute, the Governor grew pale and lost his nerve, just as his compatriot at Saba had done.

An armed boats crew pulled from the man-of-war aboard the pirate schooner.

The lieutenant was met by a suave young man, who produced his authority to sink, burn and destroy the enemies of the new South American republic, in explanation of the brass thirty-two pounder Long Tom amidships, and his two score of swarthy, bewiskered gallow's birds.

The rest of *Las Damas Argentinas* prizes were Spanish, and therefore came within the terms of the Buenos Airian commission.

It appeared that the two brigs had been taken off Gibraltar. The pretence of proceeding within the law was kept up by the pirate captain, whose name was Joseph Lazaro Buysan; he informed the captains and some passengers, who were aboard the two brigs, that their cargoes were contraband.

The pirate and her prizes were steered for the Canaries, where the crews and passengers of the brigs were landed. Capain Cook of the *Carraboo* represented that they would be in hard straits on the island of Lanzarote, where they were to be landed without money to pay their way, whereupon the young Minorcan gave him twenty dollars and French Captain ten dollars, truly a deed of marvellous magnanimity on the part of a pirate captain.

However this merciful treatment had no effect upon the St. Kitts jury, and the whole crew of the *Bolivar* ex *Elizabeth*, ex *Las Damas Argentinas*, was condemned to be hanged with the exception of two cabin boys and five men who had been recruited at the Canaries, and a blackshmith, who when the schooner had refitted at Charlotte Amalie, St. Thomas, had been shipped aboard by his boarding house keeper, to whom he owed thirty dollars. The cook of the pirate, who had been pressed out of a Portuguese prize was also reprieved. But when the prize crew proceeded to shackle this Mediterranean Corsair and his crew to a length of chain-cable, and herd them into the gloom of their own steerage, the Minorcan showed that he could curse fluently in a number of languages, and not least in the language of seamen, the well adjectived tongue of Great Britain.

The *Victor*, without awaiting any diplomatic negotiation, calmly sailed away for Basseterre with *Las Damas Argentinas*, taking her from under the guns of the Dutch fort without a murmur from the Governor, who sighed a great breath of relief as soon as the two vessels were over the horizon.

The trial of the pirates took place at St. Kitt.

Two of the rovers, whose English was the most fluent, turned King's Evidence.

The piracy was proved by the capture of the French brig, the *Carraboo* and an American ship named the *Peru* of Nantucket.

The Pond Pasture at Basseterre with its grove of silent palm-trees, beneath which the gallows were erected is still a place to be avoided after dark, where "Jumbies" frighten 'poor black nigur'.

Here, facing the upper end of Basseterre Roads, twenty-eight of the pirates were hanged—the pirate captain, his two Spanish mates and eight of his crew two days after the trial, then two days later ten more of his crew and a day later the remaining seven. Once again the Commanders of the American Mosquito fleet were loud in their praise of British methods of justice.

Whether the *Las Damas Argentinas* affair had anything to do with it or not, certain it is that towards the end of the twenties, the West Indian pirate, who flew the flag of the Carthaginian or Buenos Airian picaroon, and was not averse to running a cargo of slaves, seems to have made the Cape Verds his headquarters.

Probably it was mainly because the Cape Verds were rejoicing in a business-like Governor, who played the Dutch game with even greater skill. In reading Captain Marryat's 'Pirate and Three Cutters' many must have wondered if his pirates were not over-coloured. Yet there is only too much evidence to show that he was by no means drawing the long bow, and that his beautiful schooner, the *Avenger*, with her ruffiany crew were drawn from life.

Let me quote a short paragraph written by the editor of the United Service Journal in June 1829:—

The Practice of Piracy

"The practice of Piracy, accompanied by every barbarous and wanton aggravation, has become so alarmingly prevalent, as to call for some prompt and decisive measures for its suppression. Unarmed ships are scarcely safe in our own waters; but the Gulf of Florida, Caribbean Sea, and whole sea-board of South America on one side, and the Levant and Greek Archipelago on the other, swarm with lawless Buccaneers. It appears a consequence of national regeneration in the case of the Greeks and South Americans that other ties, as well as that of allegiance, should be shaken off.

A recent letter from the Agent of Lloyds at St. Michael's Azores, states that His Majesty's ship *Undaunted* had been there, and is now about these islands cruising for the protection of British interests. It is hoped this act of Government will lead to the interception of the notorious pirate, who lately attacked the *Admiral Benbow*".

The Sinking of the Packet *Redpole*

A more serious affair than the attack on the *Admiral Benbow* was the sinking of the ten-gun packet brig, *Redpole*, which left Rio on August the tenth, 1828, and was attacked by the Buenos Airian pirate, *Congress* of eighteen guns off Frio.

The little *Redpole* after a close action of an hour and a quarter went down with her colours flying, every man aboard being either killed or drowned.

Cape Verd Port of Entry for Pirates

Porto Praya, the port of entry of San Jago, Cape Verd Islands, was the port used by no less than five pirates in 1830. It no doubt paid the Governor and inhabitants to allow them to enter and clear without molestation.

The pirate brig *Estrella*, two hundred and ninety tons, eight guns, fifty-three men, commanded by Don Franisca, otherwise J. Comas, was the most notorious. For she had disposed of booty several times at Porto Praya.

When H.M.S. *Talbot* called there in the autumn of 1830, the *Estrella* was reported to be hanging about the island waiting for the *Louisa, Mackay*, from London. The man-of-war made a short hunt without success, but as she was bound for the Cape, she could not make an exhaustive search.

Other well-known pirates making Porto Praya their rendezvous were the schooners, *Primeira. Galega*, ninety tons, three guns, forty men; *Restauradora*, one hundred and sixty tons, 3 guns, thirty men, *La Primeira* ninety seven tons, one twenty-four-pounder, twenty-seven men and *Urania* one hundred and eighty two tons, five guns, seventy-one men. All these pirates belonged to Havana, and had cleared from St. Jago, Cuba between May the twelfth and September the sixth, 1830, under Spanish colours and the pretence that they were slavers.

In those days the seas were crowded with untold numbers of two masted, smart, tall rakish craft; and men-of-war had to be very wide-awake—even the most innocent to all appearances often turning out to be the worst offenders.

Last Cruises Against West Indian Rovers

Here is an extract from the logbook of the Captor of *Las Damas Argentinas*:—

June 25, 1828. Fresh breeze and clear. Running out of Basseterre Roads. One p.m. fired a gun to bring a stranger to. Two p.m. came up with the chase, the Danish schooner, *La Laure*, eight guns, thirteen men, St. Thomas to Guadeloupe, laden with indigo, ten passengers. Sent two officers and seven marines to take her into St. Kitts.

Two-thirty p.m. made sail to overhaul a schooner to the Northward. Three p.m. hove to and boarded the schooner *Carolina* from St. Thomas to Martinique. Three-fifty p.m. anchored. Schooner a cable's length astern.

La Laure was given up by the civil authorities. We hear no more of this suspicious schooner, which was to all appearances going about her lawful occasions; but evidently she was a law-breaker of some sort or other, or the stubborn Danish Governor would never have given her up.

In the spring of 1831 pirates were again reported on the coast of Porto Rico, and in the Virgins. The Columbine, Commander Gabriel, sailed from Antigua on April 23rd on search for these rovers, but failed to find any traces of them.

It was however, such fast sailing cruisers as the first of the Symondites that so frightened the black flag fraternity that they gave up business in the Caribbees, and took up new cruising grounds on the trade routes of the South Atlantic and Indian Ocean.

CHAPTER VI

COAST OF AFRICA 1807-1818

"T'is liberty alone that gives the flow'r
of fleeting life it's lustre and perfume,
And we are weeds without it."

Last Convoy of British Guinea Men

ON Ocotber 22nd, 1807, the last convoy of British Guinea-men, consisting of five ships protected by the brig-sloop, *Favourite,* sixteen guns, Commander Frederick Hoffman, sailed from Sierra Leone and after seven weeks arrived at Barbadoes.

During the passage Captain Hoffman and his officers frequently visited the Guineamen; and he declared that he found them orderly and clean, and the slaves healthy.

These slaves had been obtained at the great slave mart at Bence Island—The principal slave dealer, a mulatto, had bought them from the neighbouring tribes in exchange for that staple food, rice; a few, too, were prisoners caught trespassing on the rice grounds. That want of food was a great recruiting agent was only too evident. Indeed Hoffman described how a black woman offered him her eleven year old son for a cob—about four and sixpence.

British Slave Trade Stamped Out

On January 1st, 1808, the British and American trade in slaves was forbidden by law.

Yet gamblers in human lives persisted for a while even under the red ensign, though detection meant confiscation of the ship and a fine of one hundred pounds for every slave. However through the efforts of the African Institution, the great British anti-slavery society, the punishment of transportation was added, and this finally stamped out all British slave trading by 1811.

American Slavers Captured by British Cruisers

It was not so easy to combat the American Guineamen, as there was no war ships of that nationality stationed on the coast with instructions to enforce the law, however in 1808 two Yankee slavers, the *Amedie* and *Africa* were captured by British cruisers in the West Indies and condemned at Tortuga.

This only caused the American captains to obtain Spanish papers and fly Spanish colours.

Great Britain's Futile Negotiations

The British Government offered Spain a gift of eight hundred and fifty thousand pounds, and a loan of ten million dollars to abolish the slave trade, but she refused—very probably because her hold over Cuba was so slight at that time that she knew she could not carry out her bargain.

French slavers were, of course, as liable to capture as any other French merchantmen during the war years, and in 1808 some half dozen of them were captured and condemned at the Cape and in the West Indies.

Great Britain concluded a treaty with Portugal in 1810, by which the latter agreed to confine her slaving to her own African dominions. This meant in practice that any Portuguese ships, which shipped their slaves North of the Equator, were liable to capture.

Commodore Irby

The first commodore on the African Coast was Captain the Honourable Fred Paul Irby of the thirty-eight-gun frigate, *Amelia.*

Irby, besides being a most gallant and extremely efficient sailor, was one of those modest, kind-hearted, humane commanders whose officers became his devoted friends, and whose ship's company were a happy family.

The second son of Lord Boston, he went to sea in December 1790, after being educated at Eton College; but he was only fifteen years of age when he played his part in the glorious action of the first of June, 1794, aboard the seventy-four gunship *Montagu.*

The following extract from his letter to his father gives more than a hint of the writer's modest personality:—

> ". . . . On the morning of the first of June we set at it about twenty-five minutes after nine o'clock.
>
> There were three ships upon us till the *Royal George* came to our assistance. There was a three-decker and an eighty gunship upon us for an hour and twenty-five minutes—we physicked them!
>
> Poor Bennett! The first shot that they fired at us took off one of his legs: he had it cut off, and I can venture to say there never was a man in the world who behaved with greater bravery and patience than he did. The same shot killed a seaman, and the third broadside killed Captain Montagu: he stretched out his hand and said, 'Oh, Mr. Donelly! Mr. Donelly!' (that is our First Lieutenant) and instantly expired. The ball entered his neck, and went out at his shoulder. We broke the French line, and Lord Howe gave us the credit to say that this ship behaved as well as any in the Fleet.
>
> Our present Commander, Mr. Thomas Larcom, is a very good man, but cannot make up for the loss of our poor dear Captain. Bennett is in a fair way, thank God."

In the Battle of Camperdown

In the battle of Camperdown we find Irby serving as Second Lieutenant aboard the twenty-eight-gun frigate, *Circe,* Captain Peter Halkett.

Hamilton's Letter

Besides being Admiral Duncan's repeating-frigate, the following extracts from letters to the editor of the United Service Journals shows the important part played by the *Circe* and her officers.

> ". . . . I beg leave to offer a few remarks on the . . . Dutch fleet coming out of the Texel on the 7th of October, 1797, as I consider the credit of that part of the Service is due to the memory of the late Admiral Sir Peter Halkett who commanded the *Circe* frigate at that time.
>
> On the first of October 1797, Admiral Duncan proceeded with the fleet to Yarmouth Roads, leaving the *Circe* frigate, Captain Halkett, *Active* cutter, J. Hamilton Commander, and *Speculator* lugger, H. Hall Commander, to watch the Dutch fleet.
>
> On the sixth of October, I sent a boat to board a galliot, and the officer returned and reported to me that the master had told him the Dutch fleet was coming out in the morning. I immediately went on board to try and get some further intelligence, when the Master again informed me that 'he had brought a pilot from Amsterdam, who showed him a note from one of the Dutch captains of a Dutch man-of-war stating that he, the pilot, must be on board at six o'clock the following morning, as the fleet was going to sea.'
>
> I then stood off to the *Circe,* which lay about seven miles distant and related to Captain Halkett the information I had just received who answered:—
>
> 'We have been off here too many years to believe in any such stories', but ordered me to keep close in and watch their movements: which I did, and fired several shot through the red buoy at the mouth of the Texel and sunk it, with a view to annoy the enemy in coming out.

On the 7th of October, at about six a.m. saw all the Dutch fleet get under way and come out of the Texel, when I made sail and joined the *Circe* and Captain Halkett ordered me to keep to windward and reconnoitre so as not to be taken.

After this I sailed along the whole of the enemy's line and counted the number of line-of-battle ships, frigates, etc., which I communicated to Captain Halkett, who was then hard-pressed, being chased by three Dutch men-of-war: and when I ran up alongside of him and shortened sail, he observed he 'never saw a vessel sail so fast as the *Active'.*

The enemy chased us about thirteen leagues from the Texel, when Captain Halkett hailed me and said they could see a squadron to the W.N.W. which he supposed (and which afterward turned out) to be Captain Trollope coming from Yarmouth, and that I was to go and join him: and as it was by this time nearly calm, I put off in my boat and rowed about ten miles. I went on board the *Russell* and related to Captain Trollope the intelligence of the Dutch fleet being out, and he ordered me to let my boat go astern and for me to stay on board the *Russell:* and in about two hours after, the *Beaulieu* frigate hailed us and said the body of the enemy's fleet was right ahead.

On the morning of the 8th, as soon as Captain Trollope had made out the force of the enemy, he gave me a dispatch for the First Lord of the Admiralty (Lord Spencer) with orders to land at the first place in England and to proceed without a moments delay to the Admiralty and at the same time despatched the *Vestal* frigate to call Admiral Duncan's fleet out of Yarmouth Roads.

The First land I made was Cromer, it blowing a fresh gale from W.S.W. Having beaten the frigate completely out of sight and being at this time doubtful if she could possibly get up that day in time to call out the fleet, I hesitated about disobeying my orders, which I at last fortunately resolved to do—tacked and worked the cutter up at the back of Yarmouth sands firing guns, with the signal flying for an enemy's fleet being at sea.

I immediately went on board the *Venerable* and gave Admiral Duncan the information of the Dutch fleet being at sea, when he desired me to lead the fleet where I considered it most likely for him to fall in with them . . . . "

(signed) J. Hamilton
Commander of H.M. Packet *Widgeon*
Dover

Richardson's Letter

Here is the second letter, which was written by Rear-Admiral Sir Charles Richardson K.C.B., who was First Lieutenant of the *Circe* at Camperdown.

"When the *Vryheid's* masts went by the board, her position was, perhaps, two cable's lengths on the weather quarter of Admiral Duncan's flag ship, the *Venerable.* Both ships ceased firing; but the action continued both ahead and astern of them

(The *Circe* being the Admiral's repeating frigate was close to the *Venerable).*

I said to Captain Halket:—'If you have ever read the history of the Dutch wars, you will be aware, that De Winter will run all risks to get on board some other Dutch ship, as De Ruyter and other Dutch Admirals did formerly.

It is evident that the *Venerable* cannot have a boat that will swim. I therefore volunteer my services to take him out of his ship, before he can effect his escape, if you will give me the jolly-boat only'. He replied, 'If you can find volunteers you have my permission.'

In a minute the boat was lowered, and manned with four seamen and myself. There was too much sea to approach the *Vryheid* on the weather side and a whole raft of masts and yards was under her lee.

Leaving a boat-keeper in the boat and accompanied by the other three men, I scrambled over the wreck, and on reaching the quarter deck found De Winter on his knees holding a square of sheet lead while a carpenter was nailing it over a shot hole in the bottom of a small punt about twelve feet in length, which was to have been launched for the Admiral's use and escape.

Putting my hand upon his shoulders and telling him he was my prisoner, I demanded his sword, and promised to conduct him to Admiral Duncan in a safer boat than that on which he was engaged.

He said:—'This, my destiny, was not foreseen', and walking; aft with me, he directed my attention to a small bureau which contained his public and private papers, and begged me to save it from being plundered. I promised him it should not be opened and gave him to understand that Admiral Duncan would ratify that promise. De Winter than took leave of a

2. The Capture of the Spanish Slave Vessel *Delores* by H.M. Brig *Ferret*, 4th April 1816.

From an coloured lithograph by G. F. Lambart, after the painting by W. J. Huggins.

[*Facing page 96.*

3. The boats of H.M.S. *Morgiana* capturing the Slaver *Esperanca*, December 11th, 1819.

From a water colour in the National Maritime Museum.

[*Facing page 97.*

young officer (I believe his nephew) who was desperately wounded, and accompanied me to the gangway, the officers and crew making way for him, and many kneeling took their leave of him.

To get into the boat we had to recross the raft of masts and spars alongside: and two of my boats crew, one on each side, supported the Admiral.

Notwithstanding the carefulness observed, however, De Winter stepped on a portion of the main topmast about the centre of the spar: but from its having no rigging attached to it, it turned round and the Admiral disappeared. Whilst expecting his rising, I observed the crown of his head lifting some canvas, which was lying over the craft, and a sailor in a moment slit the sail with his knife, and we had the happiness to save our gallant prisoner's life.

In rowing towards the *Venerable,* De Winter expressed a wish that I should restore him his sword, in order that he might personally deliver it to Admiral Duncan, saying at the same time, 'I hope to have the honour of presenting you with one more valuable'. I complied and he had his desire gratified".

This involuntary bath of the Dutch Commander-in-Chief was not mentioned aboard the *Venerable,* and neither Admiral Duncan and his officers or the Dutch Admiral's fellow prisoners had any inkling of it, until a ship-broker coming aboard the flag-ship at Yarmouth related that it was all in the London papers.

Irby, after Camperdown, followed his captain into the *Apollo* frigate, in which he was wrecked on the 7th January 1799, on the coast of Holland.

From April 1800, when he was promoted, he was commander of the *Volcano,* bomb, in the Baltic till January the 14th, 1801, from which date he commanded the eighteen-gun brig-sloop *Jalous* in the North Sea until he was posted in April 1802.

After a short period in command of the Harwich Sea Fencibles, Captain Irby commissioned the *Amelia* in October 1807.

Having distinguished himself off L'Orient and in Basque Roads, etc., in May 1810 Captain Irby was ordered to proceed to Teneriffe and look out for some English slavers, who were reputed to be under Spanish colours.

In this he was successful, capturing the *Gallicia* and *Palafox,* which were both condemned on his return to England.

It was his cleverness in carrying out this duty that caused the African Institution to beg the Admiralty to appoint him senior officer on the Coast of Africa.

During his service as the first Commodore especially appointed to combat the slave trade, Irby was lucky if he could count on the help of the gun brig. On November the 25th, 1812, the gun brig *Daring* was run on shore and burnt by her commander, Lieutenant W.R. Pascoe, to prevent her being captured by the French frigates *Arethuse* and *Rabis.*

In 1811 an Act had been passed empowering Governors of Colonies to sieze and prosecute all slave ships, and this act induced the Governor of Sierra Leone, to fit out at the expense of the Colony, the Colonial schooner, *Princess Charlotte.*

With such means the Commodore could not hope to put much of a check upon such a profitable trade; but, that his efforts were not entirely futile may be judged by the following Government returns.

Slaves Released, Prize Money Paid 1810-1812

Year	Slaves Released	Prize Money Paid
1810	594	£17090
1811	1362	£35556
1812	1185	£36620

The following slavers were brought into Sierra Leone for adjudication during the three years of Captain Irby's command.

Slavers Captured 1810-1812

Date of Adjudication	Name of Slaver	Master of Slaver	Number of Slaves
	1810		
April 9	*Lucia* (brig)	Wing	Not specified
April 21	*Doris* (schooner)	Mestre	" "
May 2	*Marianna* (schooner)	De Souza	" "
May 10	*Esperanza* (schooner)	Vincente	" "
July 3	*Zaragozano* (brig)	Dolz	" "
August 2	*Merced*	Viamonte	" "
August 2	*Floridana* (schooner)	Jearrean	" "
August 2	*Vincidor* (brig)	Mariamio	" "
August 14	*Sant Jago* (schooner)	Serano	" "
September 17	*Pez Voilador (schooner)*	Guadabens	" "
September 17	*Cirilla*	De Los Reys	" "
September 17	*Hermosa Ritu*	Montani	" "
October 13	*Diana* (schooner)*	Berthe	" "
November 21	*Marquis de la Romana*	Vilalta	" "
November 21	*Maria* (brig)	Madsen	" "
December 15.	*Pearla* (brig)	Milbury	" "
December 15	*Maria Dolores*	Backhouse	" "
	1811		
January 11	*Vivillia*	Rodriguez	" "
January 11	*Anna* (brig)	Rees	" "
January 11	*Lucy* (brig)	Wolver	" "
March 9	*Marianna*	Sanna	" "
March 20	*Saint Antonio Almos*	Comacho	" "
June 26	*Nostra Signora de Dolores*	De Landa	" "
June 26	*Amelia*	Campbell	" "
July 16	*Hawke*	Taylor	" "
July 22	*Capac*	Sylvester	" "
July 23	*Paloma*	Yellechi	" "
August 26	*Havanna* (brig)	Agicola	98
September 16	*Confianza Veloz* (brig)	Mendoza	No return
October 15	*Paquette Volante* (schooner)	Lopez	38
October 15	*Urbano*	Salazar	59
October 29	*Calypso* (brig)	Ferreira	13
December 16	*Venus* (brig)	De Malta	21
	1812		
January 19	*Prazeres*	Braga	Not Specified
February 11	*Princeza da Beira* (schooner)	Wallis	56
February 24	*Pepe* (schooner)	Castilia	75
March 7	*Dezanganas* (brig)	Musgrato	23
March 10	*Flor de Porto* (schooner)	Abrien	112
March 17	*Destino* (brig)	San Peyo	23
March 25	*Saint John* (brig)	Pinto	10
March 31	*Lindeza* (brig)	De Silva (mate)	143
April 2	*Maria Primero*	Periero	403
April 4	*Felis Americano* (brig)	Cardogo	35
April 5	*Urania*	Izabel	Not Specified
April 5	*St. Miguel Triumphante*	Boos	133
June 12	*Centinella*		No Return
October 17	Orizonte (schooner)	Viera	11
October 17	*Flor d'America* (brig)	Pientzneau	363
November 14	*Andorinha*	Mazza	270
November 20	*Neuva Constitucion* (sloop)	Mestre	81
November 20	*Vigilant* (sloop)		53

* American under Portuguese colours—Condemnation reversed on appeal.

Dual Between *Amelia* and *Arethuse*

The *Amelia's* service on the coast was brought to an end on February the 2nd, 1813, by a terrific dual with the French frigate *Arethuse.*

This famous sea fight, which ended in the antagonists dropping apart exhausted, is very full described in *James' Naval History.* With half his ship's company incapacitated by wounds, and most of the remainder by sickness; and with his frigate hardly seaworthy, her sides being pitted with plugged shot holes, her masts and spars scarfed and frapped and her rigging a mass of knots and splices, the Commodore was forced to make the best of his way home.

Commodore Browne Destroys Slave Factories

Captain Thomas Browne of the *Ulysses,* forty-four guns, was appointed to succeed Captain Irby as commodore on the West coast of Africa.

He found the slave trade generally on the increase both in the Bights and along the windward coast. One of his first actions was to destroy the remainder of the English factories.

The first to go was Captain Fraley's Bangara factory on the Congo; then a Mexican betrayed two slave merchants, father and son, who posed as Spaniards under the names of Don Ricardo and Don Felipe Drax, but were in reality Englishmen of the name of Drake.

Lieutenant Robert Hagan Captures Forty Slavers

The Colonial schooner, *Princess Charlotte,* commanded by Lieutenant Robert Hagan, descended upon their barracoons on the Rio Pongo and Rio Basco, and destroyed three hundred houses and a great quantity of stores, but the chief culprits escaped.

Hagan, one of those ubiquitous Irishmen who trace their descent back to the O'Neill princes, was a very great thorn in the side of the slavers.

Between November 1815 and May 1823, whilst in command in turn of the Colonial cruisers, *Princess Charlotte,* and *Prince Regent,* and the gun-brig *Thistle,* he captured forty slavers and freed four thousand Africans.

Perhaps his most noteworthy success was his capture of the pirate *Paz,* when in command of the brig *Prince Regent.* The *Paz* was greatly superior to his little brig, both in guns and men and put up a strong resistance.

When the *Thistle* left Sierra Leone for home in the year 1823, he received a piece of plate from the judges and members of Council and a hundred-guinea sword from the merchants with addresses of thanks.

Though he was knighted and posted, this was his last sea service.

The destruction of the barracoons of English slave-traders left large districts at the mercy of the far more cruel Spanish, Portuguese and half-caste merchants.

Browne's Captures, 1813-1815

In two years Commodore Browne's squadron captured thirty slavers, the official returns showing:—

1813	634	slaves	released	£17,280	prize	money.
1814	560	"	"	£27,995	"	"
1815	626	"	"	£17,940	"	"

(A new regulation cut down the bounty for slavers captured and slaves released).

Brisk* Captures Piratical Slaver *Union

The *Brisk,* eighteen-gun sloop, Captain Henry Higman, paid off on August the 31st, 1815, after twelve months on the coast, during which time, she captured five slavers—the most gallant of these captures was that of the piratical slaver *Union,* a schooner pierced for fourteen guns but mounting only six.

This vessel, after a chase, was becalmed fifteen miles from the war-sloop, Captain Higman at once despatched his boats under his first lieutenant, John Dewar. After a long hot row, the *Union* was boarded at midday and carried in the face of a desperate resistance, most of her piratical crew being driven over-board into the sea.

The *Favourite,* twenty-gun corvette, Captain John Maxwell, paid off at Portsmouth in 1814, after nine months on the coast during which time she captured four Portuguese slavers and took part in the destruction of the slave barracoons on the Rio Pongas.

Comus up the New Balator

The *Comus,* twenty-two-gun corvette, Captain John Tailour, was the first man-of-war to ascend the New Calabar river as high as Duke's Town where she captured seven Spanish and Portuguese slavers after a most determined resistance and much bloodshed in 1815.

Commodore Browne Leaves his Station to Convoy Indian Trade Home

Commodore Browne happened to be at St. Helena when the news of Napoleon's escape from Elba reached that island. The homeward bound fleet of East Indiamen, who were also making a stop at St. Helena, as was their custom, at once begged the Commodore to convoy them home.

As their cargoes were reckoned to be worth ten million sterling the Commodore decided to leave his station and see these valuable ships safe home.

Though he received no further employment from the Admiralty the Honourable East India Company rated him a large sum for the usual reward of a service of plate.

Commodore Sir James Yeo

Sir James Yeo was appointed Commodore in the autumn of 1815 and he sailed for the coast in the forty-two-gun frigate *Semiramis.*

The Admiralty had promised him a squadron of small cruisers which could hunt the slavers out of their lairs in the steamy African rivers, but when the time came for him to sail he found that all these vessels were required to guard Napoleon at St. Helena. He thus had chiefly to rely upon the little Colonial schooners, *Queen Charlotte, Princess Charlotte,* and the brig *Prince Regent,* whilst in place of the *Comus,* he was given the *Baun,* twenty guns, Captain William Fisher.

The *Baun* was one of the Levant class of ship-sloops, built in 1812 and measuring four hundred and sixty six tons.

She distinguished herself on the 5th of March, 1816 by laying alongside and boarding the slaver *El Temerario,* of sixteen guns and eighty men, after a long running fight, and ten days later she made another good capture, the *San Antonio* with five hundred and five slaves.

The _Queen Charlotte_ and French Slaver _Louis_

On the 11th March 1816 off Cape Masurada, the *Queen Charlotte,* Colonial schooner, overhauled the French slaver, *Louis,* which had just arrived on the coast from the West Indies.

With the war hardly yet over, the Commander of the *Queen Charlotte* immediately opened fire on the Frenchman refusing to be searched, and a desperate engagement took place in which the French slaver did not haul down her colours until she had accounted for double the number of British to her own men killed. One return gives twenty-four British to eleven French killed, but another gives the numbers as twelve to three French.

The *Louis* was duly condemned, but on appeal the judgment was reversed, the arguments being that the slave trade was legal in France, that British cruisers no longer had the right since the peace to search French ships, and finally that the British Government must not 'force the way to the liberation of Africa by trampling on the independence of other states in Europe'.

Weakness of British Government

It was evident that our politicians had blundered. Indeed as the conquerors at the end of a world war, and the masters of the Five Oceans, our rulers could have made what terms they chose, not only with France, but with Spain, Portugal and any other European power regarding the outlawing of the slave trade

At the same time the Admiralty, by their niggardly treatment in alloting vessels to the coast of Africa blockade showed that they were far from realising the difficulties before our cruisers.

Influence of the African Institution

Had it not been for the power and influence of the African Institution, it is probable that neither the Government nor the Admiralty would have awakened to their duties.

Whilst Sir James Yeo was struggling to patrol the African coast from Cape Verd to the equator with less than half a dozen cruisers, a seventy-four, two frigates, three sloops and one or two ten-gun brigs were kept dodging to and fro off St. Helena as a guard for Napoleon.

Ferret and *Dolores*

One of these guardships, the little *Ferret,* Commander J. Stirling, was lucky enough to capture a slaver on her way home.

The *Ferret,* which had formed one of Sir George Cockburn's squadron escorting Napoleon to St. Helena, sailed for England with dispatches on March the 27th, 1816.

On the 4th of April, when nearing the equator in 305 15° 40'W, the gun-brig sighted a polacca-rigged brigantine, which had all the hallmarks of the new type of rakish Baltimore-built slaver, and wail was immediately crowded in chase.

The *Ferret* was a clipper-built American privateer schooner which, after being captured by the British, had been re-rigged as a brig, and quite spoilt by the heavy-handed dockyard maties. From being a low-sided, whippy masted, slackly-rigged schooner, she was converted to a taut, over-sparred brig. And as if her new outfit aloft had not been enough to make her crank, the dockyard had replaced her light rail by solid bulwarks, through the ports of which the red tompions of no less than fourteen eighteen-pounder carronades were poked, which greatly added to her chances of turning turtle in the first squall.

Thus she had to be handled with the greatest care and skill however, both Commander J. Stirling and his First Lieutenant, William Holt, were equal to the occasion.

Like the coffin brigs, in order to carry the water required for her passage home, the little *Ferret* had to strike ten of her carronades down into the hold in order to make room on deck for water-butts. This necessity no doubt improved both her stability and her sailing powers, for it was found that she was slowly overhauling the chase.

This vessel was the Spanish slaver, *Dolores,* which was also an ex-American privateer of the war which was just over.

She had, however, a much superior armament to that of the gun-brig. This consisted of a thirty-two pounder Long Tom amidships, four long nine-pounders and two long twelve-pounders carronades.

The *Ferret* had been chasing for some hours before she arrived within range of the slaver's long gun, which at once opened upon her. The Guineaman's aim was to bring down a spar and lame the little gun-brig, and in an hour's practice whilst the *Ferret* was closing on him, he did succeed in cutting up her rigging a good deal and also caused a number of casualties amongst her crew.

The four little pop-guns, which the gun-brig had mounted, did very little harm, when the two vessels were near enough for them to be brought into play; and it was the accurate fire from the muskets of the marines which in the end drove the Spaniards from their guns and caused the Captain of the *Dolores* to haul down his flag.

The *Dolores* was found to have two hundred and seventy five slaves on board, all in very good condition.

Giuseppe Fornaro Ex Bluejacket

This was due to her Supercargo, Guiseppe Fornaro, a man, who besides being one of the most humane, afterwards became one of the most successful of Cuban slavers.

This man was a Venetian; the son of a small farmer and market gardener. As soon as he could escape from school, he went to sea in a Levantine corn mistico. After various youthful adventures of the Don Juan type, in which both the stiletto and bullet played their part, he volunteerd aboard the English Line-of-battle ship, *Culloden,* Captain Sir Thomas Troubridge, in preference to a life amongst Greek pirates and Turkish gaolers.

Whilst serving in the *Culloden,* he had the mortification of watching the battle of the Nile, whilst the *Culloden* lay stranded on the point of Aboukir. On the *Culloden* paying off, her crew were transferred to the *Barfleur,* in which Collingwood had his flag.

Fornaro lived in this man-of-war world for two years without putting a foot ashore, it is therefore not surprising if he ran at the first opportunity. This occurred at Plymouth, where he managed to get aboard a Guineaman, which had put into port in order to replace a sprung foremast.

Guiseppe Fornaro found the British seamen aboard that London Guineaman a wilder and even more depraved lot than the Levantine cut-throats with whom he had often been thrown during his Mediterranean coasting days. But their captain was a sober, capable man who maintained discipline by liberal use of a belaying pin. The Guineaman was slow, roomy and well found. She loaded five hundred men, women and children in the Bight of Benin, and after a ten weeks' passage landed all her slaves except three in a healthy condition.

At Jamaica the unlucky Fornaro was pressed into the frigate, *Tamar,* which, after cruising with some success in the West Indies, was sent at the commencement of the short peace, to Havana with a load of Spanish prisoners.

Here Fornaro once more contrived to escape from the British Service, by swimming ashore during the night in defiance of the sharks.

He next signed on board a Spanish slaver of the old precontraband days, a roomy, full-built vessel of three hundred tons, in which he worked his way up to mate and finally to supercargo.

In the fight with the *Ferret* he very nearly lost the number of his mess, being shot through the neck. When he recovered from his wound Fornaro had no difficulty in obtaining command of a slaver; and owing to his cleverness in avoiding the English cruisers, his humanity and care of his slaves; and the good condition in which he invariably landed them, he soon became the favourite commander in the Havana trade, the shares in his command always bearing the highest price in the market. He speedily amassed a large fortune, married, bought an estate, and settled down in Cuba; but again fell a victim to a British cruiser when persuaded to go as a sort of Commodore over three slavers on one last trip to the coast.

The *Dolores* was taken to Sierra Leone where she was condemned.

Whilst Sir James Lucas Yeo was commodore on the coast of Africa, the full tide of postwar economy at the Admiralty set in, and for the latter part of his period of command he only had the *Cherub* corvette, Captain George W. Willes, a very distinguished officer who we shall hear of again commanding the *Brazen* with great success.

Sickness Aboard the *Semiramis* and Death of the Commodore

In 1818 the *Semiramis* became very sickly, and she was ordered home by way of Jamaica. Here she buried her purser on the 17th July, then in 40° 40′ N 50° 45′ W on the 31st of August, the body of the Commodore himself was launched into the deep.

He was only thirty-six years old, so that general debility could hardly be the correct diagnosis for his disease, which we are told he bore with the utmost fortitude.

He was just one more fine British seaman sacrificed in the cause of freedom, for there is no doubt he fell a victim to the West Indian mosquito like many others in his ship's company.

During his period on the coast, I find the following returns:—

Captures 1816-1818

1816	2711 slaves	released	£12,269	prize	money.
1817	1028 "	"	£26,325	"	"
1818	1643 "	"	£25,705	"	"

In 1817, after long negotiations Spain agreed to abolish her slave trade North of the Equator for the sum of £400,000, which was paid by the British exchequer.

CHAPTER VII

COAST OF AFRICA 1818-1821

"My father was a Cormantine, my mother was a Ningo
For two old knives, one piece cloth.
They sell-ee-me-by jingo".

(West Indian negro ditty).

Commodore Sir George Ralph Collier

TO succeed Sir James Lucas Yeo in the arduous and unhealthy duties of Commodore on the West coast of Africa, the Admiralty picked Sir George Ralph Collier, Bart., K.C.B., out of the Captain's list, in which practically every name was known for distinguished war service of one sort or another—and it would have been difficult to have made a better choice.

In May, 1818, Sir George was forty-four years of age, an officer of immense experience, tremendous keenness and unrivalled industry.

He was prepared for his profession at the Maritime Academy, Chelsea, which must have provided a most efficient schooling, for when he was a midshipman in the *Carysfort* a mess-mate declared young Collier to be a good astronomer, marine surveyor and draughtsmen and an excellent linguist, possessed of a good knowledge of French, Spanish and Italian.

In 1799, Collier was First Lieutenant of the *Isis* at the capture of the Dutch squadron in the Texel.

Vice-Admiral Mitchell sent him home with his dispatches, which, of course, meant promotion.

He was at once made Commander of the eighteen-gun ship sloop, *Victor,* and in September, 1801, distinguished himself by his most determined chase, and sinking of the French corvette, *La Fleche,* in the Indian Ocean. This action gained him his post rank (April 22, 1802). He was then appointed to the *Leopard,* fifty guns, which he brought home and paid off on February the 24th, 1803.

A Successful Frigate Commander

His next ship was the *Champion,* twenty-four guns; and out of her he went to the *Minerve,* thirty-two guns, in February 1806.

After capturing a great number of prizes on the coast of Spain in this frigate, he removed in 1807 into the *Surveillante* thirty-eight, and accompanied the Copenhagen expedition, being again chosen for the honour of bearing home the dispatches announcing the capture of the capital and fleet of the Danes.

From this date until Wellington's entry into France across the Bidassoa, Collier in the *Surveillante* did yeoman work on the coast of Spain, being most of the time in charge of a small squadron of sloops and frigates.

In the American war he was specially selected to command the heavy fifty-six-gun, fir frigates, *Newcastle* and *Leander,* built for the purpose of combating the heavy metalled frigates of the Americans.

Whilst Captain John Hayes in the *Majestic* with *Endymion* and *Pomone* under him watched New York. Sir George Collier in *Leander* with *Newcastle* and *Acasta* watched Boston. His chief quarry was the *Constitution,* remarked at the end of this tour of inspection:—

"You are a larger ship, but I do not think your men are as stout as ours in the *Constitution"*. Whereupon Sir George sent his challenge to the American frigate in these words:—

"They may be very little, but their hearts are in the right place and I will thank you to inform the American captain that if he will come out and meet the *Leander,* I will pledge my word and honour that no British ship shall be within twenty leagues—and further, if my ship mounts more guns than the *Constitution,* I will throw the additional guns overboard".

However, the *Constitution* waited until Collier was refitting at Halifax before slipping out to sea.

Captures *Prince de Neufchatel*

As showing the Commodore's eye for a ship, when in chase of the elusive *Constitution,* he captured the famous American privateer, *Prince de Neufchatel,* which not long before had played such havoc with the attacking boats of the *Endymion.*

Instead of sending her to Bermuda or Halifax, where she would have sold for a good sum, Collier sent her to England with dispatches regarding the American Squadron and in his letter suggested that the Admiralty should buy her, or at any rate, take note of her lines. Her lines were actually taken off at Deptford, but the dockyard officials allowed the beautiful little vessel to break her back across the dock sill*.

A Yankee Non-Plussed

Following on the capture of the *Prince de Neufchatel* came an amusing encounter with an American brig, whose master boarded the *Leander* to complain of his mutinous crew.

To their amazement, after saluting Captain Collier and the group of officers standing round him on the *Leander's* quarterdeck he burst out with:—

"I callate and opine that yew'll do a tarnation share of mischief to the durned English sarpints and play the devil's game with their rag of a flag". He went on to remark that he recognised the *President* at once by her black painted masts and sides and the cut of her sails. Then, addressing himself directly to the astonished Commodore, he reminded Commodore Decatur of their having met recently in New York.

Sir George fell in with this mistake, took the man below, and even went so far in a spirit of fun to leave a track chart open on the table with "*President* from New York on a cruise" scribbled across it—this made the Yankee shipmaster all the more convinced of the ship's identity, and he collapsed with amazement when told, who was really entertaining him.

Following upon this incident came the chase of the *Levant,* so criticized by James, but the account of McDougall, First Lieutenant of the *Leander,* clears Collier of all the blame; the *Leander* returned to England from Canada in July 1815 with fifty-two transports containing twelve thousand troops under her convoy.

Captain Henry John Leake of the *Myrmidon*

When the Commodore hoisted his broad pendant aboard the *Tartar,* forty-two, the Admiralty were still starving the coast of Africa squadron and Collier had to combat the fast growing slave trade with a couple of corvettes, and an odd sloop, and a couple of gun-brigs. However, if he was short of ships, he managed to collect a fine lot of officers under him. His most able second-in-command was Captain Henry John Leake, who on his return from Africa was made a K H for his services on the coast.

* Her plans can be seen at the Admiralty Curators. Her lines and sail plan are also beautifully reproduced by my friend, Mr. Howard Irving Chapelle, in his *History of American Sailing Ships.* I give her history in my *Opium Clippers,* for her model was used in the design of *Red Rover,* the first opium clipper.

Leake's last service in the war had been as lieutenant of the brig-sloop, *Persian.*

As showing this officer's presence of mind and promptitude of action, one day found the *Persian* off Cape Trafalgar, her decks crowded with French prisoners, and only Leake, a quartermaster and two seamen on watch. All of a sudden the prisoners made a rush aft. Leake seized a cutlass from the arm's box, threw another to the quartermaster and the pair held the French at bay till the men below came up to their assistance.

Captain Leake sailed for the coast of Africa in May 1819, in command of the twenty-gun corvette, *Myrmidon.* This vessel, along with the *Hermes, Valorous, Hind,* and *Larne,* was built on the lines of the famous French, *Bonne Citoyenne,* of five hundred and eleven tons. These *Bonne Citoyenne* models never came up to expectation, which is not surprising for that ship's design was much overrated by her contemporaries, and the copies were further spoilt by being fifty tons smaller and ten feet shorter.

The *Morgiana,* Captain Strong

A much more useful vessel than the *Myrmidon* for catching slavers was the eighteen-gun ship-sloop, *Morgiana,* which was commissioned December 1818 by Captain Charles Burrough Strong, a man who had fought under Nelson, had seen a great deal of hard service, was enthusiastically reported upon by his captains, and was one of the most highly respected and thought of officers in the service.

His command; the *Morgiana,* was a very intersting craft, one of the famous flush-decked Bermuda-built sloops.

Flush-decked craft were always much healthier than frigate-built, especially in the tropics, and these sloops, with their excellent accommodation, were undoubtedly the most suitable vessels of their date for slave catching on the African coast.

Unfortunately only one other of the Bermuda sloops was still in the Service at this date and this was the old *Driver,* built in 1797. She followed the *Morgiana* out to the coast.

The *Morgiana* mounted a two nine-pounder guns, and sixteen twenty-four-pounder carronades, and carried a complement of one hundred and twenty five men. Her tonnage was three hundred and ninety tons burthen, and her dimensions were:—

Length of gundeck 107 feet: length of keel 83′10″: breadth 29′11″: depth 14′8″.

The *Pheasant,* Captain Kelly

Another of Sir Ralph Collier's squadron was the *Pheasant,* corvette, an old design of Sir William Rule's built at Southampton as far back as 1798, on the plans of the old *Merlin.*

Though only three hundred and sixty five tons burthen, the *Pheasant* was more heavily armed than the *Morgiana,* mounting eighteen thirty-two pounders carronades and two six-pounder guns. Her dimensions were:—

Length of gun-deck 106′1″: length of keel 87′9$^{7}/_{8}$″: breadth 28′3½″: depth 13′9″.

She was commanded by Benedictus Marwood Kelly, another officer who had seen a great deal of service, especially in the West Indies. He was also an old hand on the Guinea coast, having served there in the *Adamant* as far back as 1807.

Another very experienced officer under Collier was Lieutenant Robert Hagan, who was promoted from the Colonial brig, *Prince Regent,* into the gun-brig, *Thistle,* in May 1819.

The Pelter Brigs

The only vessels in the squadron, which were able to hunt out the slavers in their lairs up the rivers, were the twelve-gun brigs, called "Pelter brigs", after one of their number.

There were eighteen of these tiny one hundred and eighty one ton brigs built in private yards in the years 1812 and 1813, from a design by the surveyors, Rule and Peake.

As compared with the despised coffin-brigs, it will be seen that they were even less attractive for general cruising:—

Pelter-brig *Thistle:* 181 tons:
Coffin-brig *Rolla:* 235 tons: 8 18-pr carr., and 2 6-pr guns.

Name	Length gundeck	Keel	Breadth	Depth
Thistle	84′:	70′:	22′ 2″:	11′
Rolla	90′:	73′7″:	24′ 6″:	11′

In design, like the coffin-brigs, the Pelter Brigs were good enough: but they were invariably overloaded with provisions etc., and this spoilt their sailing, which in proper trim, was not bad off the wind, though not equal to that of the slavers they had to catch, which even at this early date were being mostly supplied by Baltimore builders.

These Pelter brigs must have been most uncomfortable to live aboard on the sweltering coast of Africa. The lower deck barely five feet under the beams, was crowded to suffocation, often thick with the smoke of the galley fire (there was no room for the galley above) and generally horribly tainted with the smell of bilge water issuing from the pump-well.

Tenders on the Coast

It was owing to the difficulty of navigating deep corvettes up the unsurveyed rivers that started the fashion for tenders on the coast.

This was a fashion which had been started in the West Indies as far back as the 1770's.

Nelson's first command was a tender of the Lowestoffe's the schooner *Gayton,* in which vessel, he says; "I made myself a complete pilot for all passages through the islands situated on the North side of Hispaniola".

This was in 1777 when Admiral Gayton was Commander-in-Chief at Jamaica. In the following year we find him in another tender, called the *Little Lucy,* after Captain Locker's daughter.

The officers mostly to be found commanding tenders were young men of the Nelson type, burning for action, and more intent on glory than prize money.

The tenders on the coast of Africa were either the property of the Commodore or of one or other of his captains. They were ex-slavers, purchased at Sierra Leone after being condemned.

The constant heavy boat work of an African cruiser with its long, hard pulls in the steamy heat up miasmic rivers in boiling sun, or tropical rain was considered, and rightly, to be the chief cause of fever; and tenders were found to be much more healthy for both officers and men.

There were never very many tenders: Here is a complete list of the privately owned tenders:—

1822	*Augusta*	tender to	*Myrmidon*
1826	*Hope*	" "	*Maidstone*
1828	*Cornelia*	" "	*Eden*
1828	*Little Bear*	" "	*North Star*
1829	Paul Fry	" "	*Sybille*
1829	*Dallas*	" "	*Sybille*

Following these tenders, two very famous ex-slavers were bought into the Service, whose careers were extraordinarily successful under the white ensign.

These were the *Black Joke* and *Fair Rosamond.*

French Slavers

When Commodore Collier arrived upon the coast, he found the slave trade booming.

His position indeed was sufficient to take the heart out of any keen commander, for the Bights simply swarmed with French slavers, none of whom was he allowed to touch.

In October 1821 the following slavers with French flags and papers were boarded in the river Bonny by the *Myrmidon.*

Brig	*L'Isis*	of	Nantes	with		slaves.
"	*Leger*	"	"	"		"
"	*Prince*	"	"	"		"
"	*L'Active*	"	"	"		"
"	*L'Eugene*	"	Havre	fitted	for	"
"	*L'Alcide*	"	Nantes	"	"	"
Schooner	*Fox*	"	Martinique	"	"	"

In the same month the *Snapper,* Pelter brig, boarded on the coast:—

Schooner	*Y*	of	Guadeloupe	fitted
"	*Leverette*	"	Nantes	"
"	*Matilde*	"	Guadeloupe	"
"	*Caroline*	"	Martinique	full cargo
Brig	*Neptune*	"	Cayenne	fitted
"	*Pilote*	"	Nantes	full cargo
"	*Clarisse*	"	Nantes	fitted

In 1824 our ambassador in Paris bitterly declared to the French minister that the French flag was shielding villains of every nationality. (Note. See Buxton).

In his very last report Commodore Collier supplied evidence of one hundred sail of slavers clearing from the Bonny and New Calabar rivers in 1821, the greater number of whom flew the white flag of France.

The Story of the *Rodeur.*

One of the most tragic of all the horrors in which the slave traffic abounded was the experience of a French slaver.

On January the 24th, 1819, the French slaver *Rodeur* of two hundred tons sailed from Havre for the Bonny river, where she anchored on the 14th of March.

Aboard the *Rodeur,* under the care of her captain was a boy of twelve years of age, named Romaigne, the son of a rich Guadeloupe planter.

This boy kept a diary, which for a vivid account of a terrible 'middle passage' cannot be surpassed in its simple recording of what took place. It is reproduced in full in the introduction to *Slave Ships and Slaving* published by Marine Research Society of Salem.

The first entry in this human document entended for the eyes of his mother, was written on the outward passage:—

> "It is now just a week since we sailed; but indeed, it is not my fault that I have not sooner sat down to write. The first two days I was sick, and the other five were so stormy that I could not sit at the table without holding. Even now we are rolling like a great porpoise, yet I can sit very well and keep the pen steady. Since I am to send you what I do without copying it over again at the end of the voyage, I shall take what pains I can; but I hope, my dear mother, you will consider that my fingers are grown hard and tarty with the hauling all day on the ropes, the captain being determined, as he says, to make me a sailor.
>
> The captain is very fond of me and is very good tempered: he drinks a great deal of brandy, he is a fine handsome man and I am sure I shall like him very much."

The *Rodeur,* which had a crew of twenty-two men, took on board one hundred and sixty negroes. This was accomplished in the usual brutal style, and here are a few extracts from the boy's diary.

"Since we have been at this place, Bonny Town in the Bonny river on the coast of Africa, I have been more accustomed to the howling of these negroes—At first it alarmed me, and I could not sleep . . . Today one of the blacks whom they were forcing into the hold, suddenly knocked down a sailor and attempted to leap overboard. He was caught, however, by the leg by another of the crew, and the sailor, rising up in a passion, hamstrung him with a cutlass. The Captain, seeing this, knocked the butcher flat upon the deck with a handspike.

I will teach you to keep your temper,' said he with an oath, 'He was the best slave of the lot'.

I ran to the main-chains and looked over; for they had dropped the black into the sea when they saw that he was useless".

The *Rodèur* sailed on the 6th of April, and whilst the Captain walked the deck 'rubbing his hands and humming a tune' in great good humour at having six dozen prime marketable slaves. But the boy wrote in his diary;—

"Their cries are so terrible that I do not like to go and look down into the hold. At first I could not close my eyes: the sound froze my very blood; and, one night, jumping up in horror, I ran to the Captain's stateroom. The lamp shone upon his face; it was a calm as marble, he slept profoundly and I did not like to disturb him."

His next entry told of the first tragedy of the passage:—

"Today word was brought to the Captain, while we were at breakfast, that two of the slaves were dead, suffocated as was supposed, by the closeness of the hold: and he immediately ordered the rest should be brought up, gang by gang, to the forecastle, to give them air . . . They had no sooner reached the ship's side, than first one, then another, than a third sprang up on the gunwhale, and darted into the sea, before the astonished sailors could tell what they were about. Many more made the attempt, but without success; they were all knocked flat to the deck, and the crew kept watch over them with handspikes and cutlasses till the Captain's pleasure should be known with regard to the revolt.

The negroes, in the meantime, who had got off, continued dancing about among the waves, yelling with all their might, what seemed to me a song of triumph, in the burden of which they were joined by some of their companions on deck. Our ship speedily left the ignorant creatures behind; their voices came fainter and fainter upon the wind; the black head, first of one, then of another, disappeared; and then the sea was without a spot: and the air without a sound.

When the Captain came up on deck, having finished his breakfast, and was told of the revolt, his face grew pale and he gnashed his teeth, 'We must make an example', said he, 'or our labour will be lost'. He then ordered the whole of the slaves in the ship to be tied together in gangs and placed upon the forecastle, and having selected six, who were known to have joined in the chorus of the revolters and might thus be considered as the ringleaders, he caused three of them to be shot, and the other three hanged, before the eyes of their comrades".

After this dreadful scene it is not surprising to hear that the boy could not sleep, that "Cold sweats broke over my body", and that at last he began to pray to loudly that he actually awoke the Captain.

Not satisfied with shooting and hanging, the Captain next had the slaves confined in the lower hold; when fifteen days out the sailors who slung down the provisions from the upper hold reported that the negroes were suffering from red eyes, a deadly form of ophthalmia.

Young Romaigne probably did not know that since leaving the coast the allowance of water for each slave had been cut down to no more than half a glass a day.

All the ship's doctor could do was to shrug his shoulders and remark:—

"C'est embetant, ma foi! Mais c'est la nostalgie!"

The Captain, however, declared that every slave cured was so many dollars in their pockets, and insisted that the infected negroes should be transferred to the upper hold and treated.

Apparently the disease was not uncommon, and patients were known to recover, sometimes with the loss of an eye but generally with just a dimness of vision.

As the *Rodeur* neared the Equator, the usual calms and squalls were experienced, but, though heavy downfalls of rain solved the thirst problem, opthalmia and dysentry raged amongst the negroes.

The first member of the crew to find his sight affected, caught the complaint from sleeping on the grating, covering the slave-hold.

The French boy's next entry in his diary was written as his sight was leaving him:—

> "All the slaves and some of the crew are blind. The Captain the surgeon and the mate are blind. There are hardly enough men left, out of our twenty-two, to work the ship. The Captain preserves what order he can, and the surgeon still attempts to do his duty, but our situation is frightful . . . All the crew are now blind but one man. The rest work under his orders like unconscious machines; the Captain standing by with a thick rope, which he sometimes applies, when led to any recreant by the man who can see. My own eyes begin to be affected; in a little while, I shall see nothing but death . . . .
>
> Mother, your son was blind for ten days, although now so well as to be able to write, I can tell you hardly anything of our history during that period. Each of us lived in a little dark world of his own, peopled by shadows and phantasms. We did not see the ship, nor the heavens, nor the sea, nor the faces of our comrades.
>
> We rolled along in our dreadful pain, with no other steersman than fate: for the single individual of the crew who was our last hope and stay, had added a thousand fold to the calamity of his fellows by sharing in it himself . . . . We were blind, stoneblind—drifting like a wreck upon the ocean or rolling like a cloud before the wind.
>
> The Captain was stone blind, yet had hopes of recovering his sight, while most of the others were in despair. A guard was continually placed, with drawn swords, at the store room, to prevent the men getting at the spirit-casks and dying in the frenzy of intoxication. Some were cursing and swearing from morning till night, some singing abominable songs: some kissing the cruicifix and making vows to the blessed saints. A few lay all day long in their hammocks, apparently content to starve rather than come abroad for food. For my part, I snatched at anything I could get to eat: cookery was unthought of. I thought myself fortunate when I was able to procure a cupful of water to soften a biscuit as dry and hard as a stone.
>
> Then there came a storm. No hand was upon the helm, not a reef upon the sails. On we flew like a phantom ship of old, that cared not for wind or weather, our masts straining and cracking; our sails bursting from their bonds, with a report like musketry; the furious sea one moment devouring us up, stem and stern, and the next casting us forth again, as if with loathing and disgust. The wind, at last, died moaningly away, and we found ourselves rocking, without progressive motion, on the sullen deep. We at length heard a sound upon the waters, in like of the smooth swill which remained after the storm, and our hearts beat with a hope which was painful from its suddenness and intensity: it was like the splashing of a heavy body in smooth water: and a simultaneous cry arose from every lip on deck and was echoed by the men in their hammocks below and by the slaves in the hold. Our cry was answered! And for some minutes, nothing was heard but an interchange of eager cries.
>
> The Captain was the first to recover his self-possession and voices sank into silence when we heard him speaking the approaching vessel with the usual challenge.
>
> 'Ship ahoy! Ahoy! What ship?'
>
> 'The *Saint Leon* of Spain. Help us for God's sake!'
>
> 'We want help ourselves' replied our Captain.
>
> 'We are dying of hunger and thirst. Send us some provisions and a few hands to work the ship—and name your own terms'.
>
> 'We can give you food, but we are in want of hands. Come on board of us and we will exchange provisions with you for men'. answered our Captain.
>
> 'Dollars! dollars! We will pay you in money a thousand fold, but we cannot send. We have negroes on board; they have infected us with opthalmia, and we are all *stone-blind*!'
>
> At the announcement of this horrible coincidence, there was silence among us, for some moments, like that of death. It was broken by a fit of laughter, in which I joined myself; and before our awful merriement was over, we could hear, by the sound of the curses which the Spaniards shouted against us that the *St. Leon* had drifted away.
>
> This vessel, in all probability foundered at sea, as she never reached any port".

The first of the *Rodgeur's* crew to regain his sight was the man who had preserved it longest, and it was due to him that the tragic slave ship ever reached her port.

The boy scribe also regained his sight. The Captain and four others only regained the sight of one eye, whilst five other men of the crew began to see dimly, but the surgeon and the remaining eleven hands had lost their sight entirely. Of the slaves thirty-nine never recovered their sight, whilst an eye was lost or the sight injured of all the rest.

On the 21st June, 1819, Guadeloupe was sighted. That morning the Captain called all hands and had every negro brought up on deck. Young Romaigne though he was about to return thanks to God for their miraculous escape, but this devil in human shape had no such intentions.

The cargo of slaves was insured and the underwriters had to make good every lost negro, so the Captain ordered the mate to pick out the blind negroes, tie pieces of ballast to their legs and throw them overboard.

This monstrous command was carried out by the crew without a single murmur of remonstrance; thus the thirty-nine blind slaves gained a merciful release from the cruelties of this world, whilst the slaver saved his pocket, and, as he callously remarked; avoided turning his ship into a hospital for blind negroes'.

Morgiana* and *Esperanca

The most gallant cutting out exploit in 1819 seems to have been the capture of the Spanish schooner, *Esperanca,* by the *Morgiana.*

After a long chase the *Morgiana* had almost arrived within range of the schooner when the wind petered out in the heat of the day.

The boats were at once lowered away for a long, hard pull in the scorching sun.

I may be here of interest to describe the usual routine before boats were sent away from a ship on a cutting out job.

First of all that the men should not be sent away fasting, when as in this case it was nearing the hour of noon, they were piped to dinner without waiting for the master to make his report of:—"Twelve o'clock, sir, by the sun". with that magniloquent response:—"Make it so".

As soon as the people had swallowed an unusually hasty meal, bluejackets were mustered round the capstan and marines in the waist that the boarding party might be selected.

Though in the old days a cutting out expedition was usually a volunteer affair, as every single member of the crew was always eager to go, the first lieutenant or the officer commanding the boats had to pick and choose, their chief difficulty being to make excuses why those not chosen had been excluded.

"The best hands must remain in charge of the ship", was the usual pronouncement of the first lieutenant in answer to the universal cry of:—"May I go, sir".

With the composition of the cutting out party settled, the lucky ones who had been chosen, were mustered with their arms for inspection. Each seamen stood in line with his polished and sharpened cutlass at the slope over his right shoulder, and his muffled oar held upright with the loom in his left hand and the blade aloft.

The jollies in their redcoats made a splash of colour against the whites, in which the bluejackets of all smart ships on the coast were clothed.

They too were inspected by the marine officer, an inspection of muskets and accoutrements being much what it is at the present day.

Whilst this was going on, the bosun and gunner saw to it that the boat coxswains had certain extras in their boats, such as grapnel-hooks, to each of which about five fathoms of inch and a half line were spliced; blue lights; match tubs; and even lighted match, as well as ammunition for the boat carronades, when these were carried.

The next job was hoisting out the boats. This was a mad scramble in a badly run ship, but a smart, orderly evolution in such a crack vessel as the corvette *Morgiana,* which could hoist out her six boats and have them manned and armed and alongside, all ready for service, in the short space of ten minutes.

As it was likely that the boats would not be back before dark, it was the custom for the ship to signal from the peak with one or more battle-lanterns, whilst the boats showed their position by blue lights, when necessary.

There was one more preparation which was never overlooked by an experienced first lieutenant, and that was some identification mark such as a piece of white or coloured calico, stitched round the left sleeve of each border, so as to avoid confusion in the dark.

Before the cutting out expedition had gone far on their way, it was by no means unusual to find that an extra mid or two and perhaps an extra bluejacket had somehow smuggled himself aboard one or other of the boats.

The wise officer in command, having make half the distance between the corvette and the chase, would then give his men an easy with a bite of biscuit and a sip of six-water-swizzle.

Though this was not done by the *Esperanca,* slavers very often triced up boarding nettings; then it was that the tomahawkmen or "slashers" were warned to be ready; and 'mince his meshes' was the well-known cry.

Gallantry of Midshipman William Mansell and Marine Lord

As the boats arrived within range of the slaver, a final easy was given for the men to get their wind before the last dash alongside.

"Trust to your cold steel rather than *flash of fire*", was the final admonition of William Mansell, a mid of ten years service, who was commanding in the *Morgiana's* gig.

As the boats pulled in, cold shot were dropped into them from the slaver and the first of these knocked down and badly bruised young Mansell, as he sprang up in the stern sheets of the gig. He was up again in a second, and was the first to gain the schooner's deck, supported by a marine named Lord. For two minutes or so these two had to withstand the cut and slash of the Spanish crew whilst the rest of the boarding party were trying to gain a footing on the deck.

Whilst Mansell kept the slaver's Captain and another man in play, the marine cut down the helmsman. The midshipman succeeded in disabling and badly wounding the *Esperanca's* Captain; and he was then almost swept off his feet by the impetuous rush of his own bluejackets to his succour. The slaver was speedily carried after two of her men had been killed and six wounded; the *Morgiana's* casualties being three wounded including the gallant midshipman, who received his promotion for this action, his claim being warmly pressed by Wilberforce himself. Until February, 1822, he acted as *Morgiana's* first lieutenant, but he was one of those officers without influence, and after being in the Coastguard, he retired from the Service in 1838 when still a lieutenant, having been appointed secretary of the Metropolitan Public Carriage Office.

A Slaver of Eleven Tons

By the year 1819, the inhuman custom of packing slaves into the hold of small vessels, overlapping each other like sardines, had become rife. On July the 30th, 1819, the *Pheasant* captured a tiny schooner of only eleven tons, named the *Nora Felicidade.* Aboard this pigmy craft besides a captain and ten seamen were no less than seventy-one slaves. In the main hold, measuring eighteen feet by seven feet eight inches at its main breadth, and with only a height of one foot eight inches under the beams, were seventeen men shackled in pairs by the legs, and twenty boys, lying one on top of the other. These were stored on top of their provinder, consisting solely of yams.

4. The Prize Vessel *Neptuno*, commanded by Mr. R. B. Crawford (Midshipman of H.M.S. *Esk*) with one gun and five men beating off the Spanish Pirate *Carolina* carrying ten guns and ninety men, commanded by Captain Antonio Soumath, in the Bight of Benin, March 20th 1826.

From a coloured Aquatint by Edward Duncan after the painting by W. Joy.

[*Facing page 112.*

5. H.M. Brig *Black Joke*, Lieutenant Henry Downs (Tender to H.M.S. *Sybille*) engaging the Spanish Slave Brig *El Almirante* in the Bight of Benin.

From an Aquatint in colour by Edward Duncan after a painting by W. J. Huggins.

[Facing page 113.

The women were even more crowded: in a hold nine feet four inches by four feet eight inches with a head room of one foot eight inches, lay thirty-four emaciated negresses.

When released scarcely a single negro could stand on his feet—being weak from starvation as well as crippled by cramp.

It is to be feared that this was by no means the worst case of over-crowding at this date as well as later.

Punitive Expedition up the Pongas

In the early days as well as later, the cruisers had a good deal of service ashore against chiefs, who needed to be taught a lesson.

During the spring of 1820, a punitive expedition was undertaken by Captain Leake against King Mungo-Brama, the chief of the Ponga river, who had murdered an officer and several men belonging to the gun-brig *Thistle* and he kept three alive as prisoners.

With one hundred and fifty bluejackets and marines from the *Myrmidon, Morgiana, Thistle,* and *Snapper,* and one hundred and eighty black soldiers of the second West India Regiment, he first of all destroyed a strongly stockaded battery, mounting four guns; he next defeated Mungo-Brama, with a force of five thousand warriors in a pitched battle, released the prisoners, and afterwards burnt no less than eight kraals or, as they then called them, 'mud towns'.

It is to be feared that this most successful little affair led to Brigadier-General Sir Charles McCarthy underestimating the fighting powers of West Africans, which was the prime cause of his death at the hands of the Ashantis.

Catching slavers and making punitive expeditions were by no means the only duties of commanders on the Guinea Coast. Often great powers of diplomacy in negotiation and treaty making were required in an R.N. captain or commodore, and in such work few naval officers were found wanting.

In January 1820, Commander Strong of the *Morgiana* was promoted and succeeded by Commander Alex Sandilands, who, in his turn, gave place in May 1820 to Commander William Finlaison, who was promoted from the *Tartar.*

Finlaison found his first duty on assuming the command of the corvette was a diplomatic one, and he was successful in composing the differences between the British merchants and the native chiefs in the river Gambia.

Success of the Tender *Augusta*

During this year of 1820, we find the first tender operating upon the coast of Africa. This was the schooner *Augusta,* belonging to the *Myrmidon* and commanded by a very gallant officer, Lieutenant F.A. Smith, who had been for the previous eighteen months a master's mate of the *Tartar,* and who, in the attack on the slave trade towns of the Pongas had lost an eye. Smith in his little *Augusta* made several captures, and it is probable that his success led to the purchase of other condemned slavers by commanding officers of his squadron.

The Case of *La Jeune Estelle*

The worst example of cold-blooded cruelty on the part of a slave captain in 1820 was the case of the *Jeune Estelle.*

On the fourth of March, after a long chase the boats of the *Tartar* boarded *La Jeune Estelle* of Martinique. Her master, Olympe Sanguines, declared that he had been plundered of his slaves by a pirate—it was quite common for one slaver to steal from another in this piratical way, so that his statement seemed quite probable if it had not been for the uneasiness and alarm, exhibited by the crew of the Frenchman.

This caused the Boarding officer to order a search of her hold. Whilst the bluejackets were below, faint groans were heard coming from a headed up cask—The cask was quickly opened, and two little negro girls of about twelve years of age were found within, in the last stage of suffocation. These girls were revived and taken aboard the *Tartar,* where they were immediately recognised by a man who had some little while back been taken prisoner by the schooner, *Swift* of New York, Captain Richards. In making further enquiries, the Commodore discovered that this same Captain Richards had died at a place on the coast called Trade Town, leaving behind him fourteen slaves including these two girls.

Shortly after his death Sanguines (a suitable name for such a ruffian) had landed at the head of an armed boat's crew, and carried off the fourteen slaves aboard his ship.

During the chase, the *Tartar* had passed several casks floating on the water, evidently thrown overboard by the slaver, and there was a horrible fear that the rest of the slaves had gone to their death in these casks. However the commodore, in order to make certain, had a further search of the slaver made.

On top of the water casks in the hold was a rough platform giving a space of only twenty-three inches between it and the tops of the casks. Within this space and jammed between two casks, a wretched negro, more dead than alive, was discovered.

With this discovery the French Captain turned abusive and threatened to prosecute Sir George Collier for daring to search a ship under the French flag. At this, the Commodore considered the advisability of sending the ship to Senegal for adjudication by the French commissioner, M. Schmoly.

The difficulty was that the slaver was in no condition to make the long beat to windward.

As the Captain was able to prove that the half dead negro had been purchased by him for eight dollars worth of brandy and iron, the angry Commodore was obliged to let this slave remain aboard the slaver, but he took the two girls.

It is interesting to know that they were brought up by the Sierra Leone missionaries; and, in 1824, one was happily married whilst the other was chief monitor of the Church missionary school at Leopold. When upbraided for breaking the laws of his country by Sir George Collier, the slave captain retorted that he knew upwards of forty captains slaving under the French flag. Against these French slavers the British squadron were powerless; as an instance there is the case of the *Marie.*

The *Marie* Case

On January the 21st, 1820, the *Morgiana,* Captain Sandiland, took possession of the Martinique schooner, *Marie,* which was lying in the roads of Gallinas with one hundred and six slaves on board.

The *Marie* was taken to Sierra Leone, where the slaves were landed. The Captain of the slaver, one Guyot, fell ill and died at Freetown, but the mate, Auguste Lepelletier, who succeeded him, proceeded to law, protesting against the detention of the ship and the forcible landing of the slaves; the right of search by the English having been refused at the aix la Chapelle congress in November, 1818. The British Government was forced to make reparation for this violation of the law of nations, and the *Marie* was sent to Senegal.

In this trouble with the French, the English only scored once. The *Myrmidon* caught a Frenchman, named *La Catherine* which Captain Leake succeeded in getting condemned, as having committed an act of piracy.

***Carlotta* Capsized**

The sorely tried British Commodore and his captains were much tempted to go outside the law, or at any rate, interpret it in their own favour.

Early in 1821 the *Myrmidon* boarded the Spanish schooner, *Carlotta,* off the Gallinas settlement: this vessel had the reputation of making an occasional piractical cruise between slaving voyages. She had no papers of any sort, and no slaves on board, in addition her officers contended that she was going to load south of the line. Unable to discover sufficient reason for detaining her, and doubtful if she would be condemned at Sierra Leone, the Commodore had her towed to leeward, and, after receiving a deposition from her crew, released her off Cape Coast Castle.

She immediately beat back round Cape Palmas to the Gallinas, where, in confirmation of the Commodore's suspicions, she took on board two hundred and sixty slaves.

The day after sailing from the Gallinas, this schooner was capsized in a tornado off St. Ann's, and sank. The whole of her slaves being leg-ironed below went to the bottom with her.

Her master, who, all the time that she had been detained by the *Myrmidon,* had been on board, though his crew swore that he was ashore, with two of the crew, were the sole survivors and after many hardships managed to make the shore in the *Carlotta*'s stern-boat.

When next the old Commodore paid a visit to Sierra Leone, he found this rascal confortably lodged in the British hospital enjoying the luxury of British charity.

Subterfuges and False Logbooks

Besides the French slavers, another trial for the British squadron in those early days was the Portuguese slavers, who appeared on the coast, and when overhauled, contended that they were going to, or had taken their slaves aboard, to the southward of the Equator.

For instance, in February 1821, the *Morgiana* captured the *Emilia* with three hundred and sixty nine slaves from Onim in Bight of Biafra. Her master, when interviewed by the Commodore, declared that he had come from Malembo, which is south of the line. Nevertheless, there was proof that he had only left Onim three days previously, and, if there had been any doubt on this point, the fresh, unhealed wounds of the hot irons on the raw flesh of the wretched slaves, who were branded like cattle, gave the lie to the slaver.

Most of the Portuguese and Spanish slave masters kept two log-books—one for inspection by a British cruiser, the other for navigation purposes.

At Whydah in March, 1821, the boats of the *Tartar* boarded the brig *Victoria,* which was busy landing her slave goods, whilst six or seven hundred slaves were waiting to be shipped at the barracoons ashore. Yet this vessel could only show a licence from the Government of Brazil, authorising her to take slaves south of the line.

The Slave-Traders—Da Souza

Whydah was the headquarters of the great slave merchant Da Souza, known throughout West Africa as Cha-cha. He was the slavebroker of the King of Dahomey. His origin was shrouded in mystery, many fantastic tales being told, but it seems pretty certain that he was a mulatto from Rio de Janeiro—an escaped criminal, according to some authorities.

When he first appeared in slaving circles at Havana, he was a very young man, and claimed to have been an officer of Dom Pedro's Imperial Guard.

In his report to the Admiralty of December 1821, Commodore Collier remarked:—

"The slave trade at Whydah is conducted to a very great extent by a Portuguese renegado, named Da Souza, who, banished from the Brazils, has fixed himself at Whydah, where he is agent or slave factor to the Brazilian nation and lives in prodigious splendour, assumes the rights and privileges of a person in authority, granting papers and licences to the slavetraders in all the form and confidence of one empowered to do so by the Portuguese Government."

The extent of the slave trade at Whydah may be judged by the number of Portuguese vessels anchoring off this port and Lagos annually, being generally calculated at one hundred.

Theodore Canot in his memoirs wrote:—
"I consigned the *Estrella* to one of the most remarkable traders that ever expanded the African traffic by his genius.

Senor Da Souza—better known on the coast and interior as Cha-cha—was said to be a native mulatto from Rio Janeiro. I do not know how he reached Africa, but it is probable the fugitive made part of some slaver's crew, and fled from his vessel, as he had previously abandoned the military service of Brazil. For a while his days are said to have been full of misery and trouble, but the Brazilian slave trade happened to receive an extraordinary impetus about that period; and gradually the adventurous refugee managed to profit by his skill in dealing with the natives and by acting as broker among his countrymen.

He loved the customs of the people. He spoke their language with fluency of a native. He won the favour of chief after chief. He strove to be considered a perfect African among Africans; though, among whites, he still affected the graceful address and manners of his country. In this way, little by little, Cha-cha advanced in the regard of all he dealt with, and secured the commissions of Brazil and Cuba, whilst he was regarded and protected as a prime favourite by the warlike-king of Dahomey".

Da Souza's palace-like mansion was built near an abandoned Portuguese fort on a situation picked for its beauty. This he filled with every luxury that money could buy.

Wines, food, delicacies and raiment were brought from Paris, London and Havana. The finest women along the coast were lured to his settlement. Billiard tables and gambling-halls spread their wiles or afforded destruction for detained navigators... Sometimes commanders from Cuba or Brazil would be kept months in this perilous nest, while their craft cruised along the coast in expectation of human cargoes.

In a book published in New York, in 1860, called *The Revelations of a Slave Smuggler,* a story of passion and jealousy is told in which Da Souza and an ex-nun are the central figures.

This refers to his early days in Cuba, when he is described as a youth named Da Souza, who claimed to be a Brazilian officer of the Imperial Guard of Dom Pedro, but I believed him to be a mulatto'.

In the autumn of 1839, the narrator again encountered Da Souza at Whydah, and was invited to dine in his palace, and in accordance with the custom of the coast offered a temporary wife.

"You shall have French, Spanish, Greek, Caucasian, Dutch, English, Italian, African or American". Said Da Souza laughing, "or, if you prefer an old flame, there is Donna Emillia". This was the ex-nun, who had been abducted from the gloomy iron-barred convent of Oritava.

One more extract from Canot's description of this remarkable slave-dealer:—

"When he saillied forth, his walk was always accompanied by considerable ceremony. An officer precede him to clear the path, a fool or buffoon hopped beside him, a band of twelve musicians sounded their discordant instruments, and a couple of singers screamed, at the top of their voices, the most fulsome adulation of the mulatto".

Don Pedro Blanco

The only slaver who does not seem to have had his moral vitality sapped by the insidious traffic and vitiating climate was a Malaga master-mariner, named Pedro Blanco, who in 1813 had the courage to build his barracoons amids the desolate mud spits and reedy marshes of the sluggish river Gallinas.

In such a wild pestilential spot it required a man of unusual character, not only to survive in his soul-deadening surroundings, but to succeed in his abominable trade.

Yet, this slender, haughty, swarthy-faced Spanish Don never sank into the usual worn-out drug-taking voluptuary, though for fifteen years he never left his fever stricken station or even crossed the bar of the Gallinas river.

Like all the high caste slave traders, he kept Oriental state and surrounded himself with every luxury, including a seraglio, in which each favourte had her own separate establishment in African style, whilst Don Pedro himself lived on a small island, with his sister as his only white companion.

At one time his power and influence along the coast exceeded even that of the great Cha-cha of Whydah; and innumerable tales were told of his arrogance and cruelty.

He is said to have shot a sailor dead for refusing him a light to his cigar—a deadly insult to a Spaniard.

His house servants for the least offence were chastised with rods. He put no value beyond the African market value upon life. Yet he was magnificently generous both to natives and to whites. Canot tells the following characteristic story of this generosity:—

"His memory was remarkable. I remember one night, while several of his employees were striving unsuccessfully to repeat the Lord's prayer in Latin, upon which they had made a bet, that Don Pedro, taking up the wager, went through the petition without faltering. The slaver insisted on receiving the slave which was the stake and immediately bestowed him in charity on a captain who had fallen into the clutches of a British cruiser".

This story of topsy-turvy morality is certainly hard to beat.

Mongo John

Up the rivers Nunez and Pongas, at this early date, the traders were mostly semi-European or American—The chief of the Rio Ponga slave-dealers was the man named Ormond, known on the coast as Mongo John. His father was reputed to have been a Liverpool Irishman and his mother a chief's daughter. Whilst he was being educated in England, his father's death in Africa left him stranded high and dry whilst yet a boy. He shipped to sea, was pressed into a British man-of-war, and for five years played the part of Gun-room steward. As soon as he was paid off he returned to Africa where he found his mother and a host of coloured relatives in possession of his father's property.

Jack Ormond, with his dash of white blood, was equal to the situation, and soon was in his father's shoes, the owner of lands, houses, barracoons and slaves, and before the year was out he had declared himself 'Mongo'—an African term, meaning the 'Chief of the River'.

He lived even more like an African chief than either Da Souza or Pedro Blanco, with the neighbouring Foulahs and Mandingoes fawning upon him. His seraglio was mostly filled with native girls, presents from chiefs, who wished to curry favour with him.

Mongo John in his prime was a stout, burly, black-eyed broad-shouldered, short-necked man; but the enervating climate, adided by drink and drugs soon drained his vitality and wore him out until he became no more than a cipher in his own headquarters at Barralong.

In the very early days there was a villainous Englishman, known as Don Ricardo, amongst these river slave magnates. He also was an ex-sailor, with a swarthy face and cold, glittering eyes, a pure piratical type. He was head of the house of Villeno and Company, and had his chief barracoons at New Tyre in the Kambia. A ruffiany nephew, named Philip Drake, or, coast fashion, Don Felipe Drax, was his right hand man.

Their trade was put a stop to by the *Princess Caroline,* whose commander accused them of being English renegades. Though the precious pair managed to escape at the point of the pistol, and took refuge in the bush, their slave pens at Rio Basso and New Tyre were set fire to and destroyed.

Duke Ephraim

Up the Old Calabar at Duke Town, which was fifty miles from the entrance, there was no outstanding trader or broker, the whole traffic in slaves being in the hands of the reigning chief, known to the slaver captains, legitimate merchantmen and men-of-war as Duke Ephraim. He was one of those African despots, who delighted in human sacrifices, and beheaded a man if he so much as crossed his shadow.

In August 1821, Captain Christopher Knight took the *Snapper* up the Old Calabar and anchored off Duke Town.

On going ashore the British officer was horrified to see five heads separated from their bodies lying in the market place, having just been decapitated as a funeral offering.

He boldly went and remonstrated with the chief, only to learn that just before his arrival no less than twelve persons, including three English palm oil traders, had been beheaded on the beach in full view of all the shipping.

"Me die, one tousand go with me", declared Duke Ephraim proudly.

In dealing with such a potentate, it behoved the Guinea captain to tread warily, for the least imaginary offence of lack of kou-tou would keep him waiting months for a cargo, or, if serious enough in the eyes of the chief, send him away with an empty hold.

Up the Bonny, New Calabar and Anthony rivers there were also no intermediaries between the natives chiefs and the captains of the slavers.

H.M.S. *Thistle* Disguised as a Palm-Oiler

In these early days few slavers seem to have been captured once they were clear of the coast, and most of the success of the squadron was through boat-work up the African rivers.

It would not be true to say that the cruisers were always outpaced by the slaving brigs and schooners. Few slavers, whether Baltimore-built or otherwise, could get away from the Bermuda-built corvette, *Morgiana.* Here is a typical capture of hers.

On February the 14th, 1821, in 3° 50′ N 3° 30′ E. she overhauled the schooner, *Emilia,* which was two days out from the river Lagos with three hundred and ninety six slaves on board, and though the schooner tried her best, the chase was a very short one.

The *Myrmidon,* also, was equal to the fastest of the slavers in a breeze.

In September 1821, when cruising off Cape Formosa, a sail was sighted from the masthead at day-break, and at 2.30 p.m. the *Myrmidon* came up with the schooner *Adelaide,* from Padagary in the Bight of Benin with two hundred and thirty two slaves.

But the gun-brigs found that only strategy or luck could bring them alongside a slaver in the open.

On her spring cruise of 1821, the *Tartar,* with the Gun-brig *Thistle* in company, ran round the coast from Sierra Leone to Fernando Po. On this occasion the *Thistle* was sent ahead, disguised as a slaver. Their success was not great, few captures from open roadsteads being made.

At Quitta they learnt that a Frenchman had just left with three hundred and eighty slaves and at Whydah a Brazilian brig, which pretended to be a palm oiler, was examined by the *Thistle.*

At this date, the demand for slaves south of the line was so great that the supply ran out, thus many of the Brazilian traders were tempted to run the gauntlet of the British cruisers and try for slaves in the forbidden Bights to the north of the line.

This brig was found to be all ready for slaves with water casks full, farina laid in and shackles piled ready. She was consigned to Da Souza, and the Commodore sent orders to the *Pheasant* to watch her.

Captures in the Bonny River

Continuing his cruise the Commodore took the opportunity of surveying the coast between Cape Formosa and Fourchee Point. This valuable work was never neglected and

Captain Leake of the *Myrmidion* was credited during his Commission with surveying six hundred miles of coast.

Arrived off the eastern entrance of the Bonny, Commodore Collier was preparing to send the *Thistle* and the *Tartar's* boats up the river, when a schooner was noticed anchored in the channel. As the *Tartar* could not weather the West Sandhead, she anchored, whilst Lieutenant Hagan in the *Thistle*, went ahead with Spanish colours flying.

He had barely made the entrance before a native canoe left the side of the anchored schooner and came off to the gun-brig.

This canoe contained the native pilot who had brought the schooner down, and he hoped to get his trip back by piloting the supposed newly arrived slaver. He was, however, no sooner alongside than he realised his mistake and was about to paddle away when Lieutenant Hagan 'with that presence of mind and activity I have so long known him to possess' (Commodore's report) jumped into the canoe, followed by a bluejacket and his head krooman, and thus prevented the pilot from getting away.

With the frigate in the offing and her boats not yet lowered, Hagan determined to capture the schooner by means of the pilot's canoe and a little stratagem.

Charles Lyons, an admiralty mid, then acting as master of the *Thistle* and 'an officer of great merit', (Commodore's report) and thirty men secreted themselves in the bottom of the canoe and ordered the natives to paddle it back to the anchored slaver.

At the schooner's hail, Lyons replied in Spanish that the brig was a Spaniard bound in for slaves, and that the frigate just visible in the offing, was an English palm-oiler. At this, the suspicious officers of the schooner, who were standing by their stern chasers all ready to fire into the canoe, were sufficiently satisfied to return to their supper in the cabin. The canoe then came on and was run alongside with a cheer, all further deception being abandoned.

A volley through the stern windows proved a slight check to the boarders, Lyons, a seaman and a marine being wounded. This volley was described by Commodore Collier as 'the drunken obstinacy of the supercargo, who as well as the master is American, English and Spanish by turns'. The volley was promptly returned. Unfortunately a number of female slaves were on deck at the time, and many of these in their terror leaped overboard, to be at once seized by sharks.

In the confusion of the moment whilst Lyons and his bluejackets were clambering aboard the slaver, the canoe slipped away and gave the alarm up the river.

The prize proved to be the *Anna Marie* of Cuba, Juan de la Roche, master, with upwards of four hundred and fifty slaves. Though she had only cleared from Duke Town the day before, already the slaves were in a sad plight—over thirty in the last stage of dysentry and many down with fever. The males were leg-ironed below in pairs and many were bound so tightly with rope lashings that the manila, in some cases, had eaten through to the bone.

Lieutenant Knight from the *Tartar* was sent on board to take charge, and he was greeted with screams and shouts for air and water, and a wild attempt of the slaves to break out over the quarterdeck barricade.

A number of blunderbusses pointing below were evidence of how the Spainards maintained order, but Lieutenant Knight succeeded in quieting the negroes without recourse to firearms.

Whilst he was engaged with the slaves the Spanish crew had been mutilating the schooner's rigging, cutting away every rope within reach.

This vicious behaviour caused them to be ironed in the hold directly the slaves had been released. As soon as possible over two hundred of the slaves were removed to the *Tartar*, where it was thought advisable to place the crew, especially the supercargo, who, in his rage at being captured, had been behaving like a maniac. He was undoubtedly of British or American birth, though he swore he was a naturalized subject of Spain.

The *Anna Maria* turned out to be the same vessel that had been brought into Sierra Leone the previous year by the *Myrmidon,* and liberated again because the prize courts were considered unable to deal with her case.

The Commodore, a most humane man, was the first British officer to take the slaves out of slavers into his own ship for attention and medicine. He also refused to send away his prizes to Sierra Leone for adjudication until he had succeeded in restocking them with pure water and yams.

Whilst the *Thistle* was dealing with the *Anna Maria,* the *Tartar's* boats under Lieutenants Marsh and Graham pushed on up the river and after a tedious row, boarded a Portuguese slaver in the face of a fire of grape and musketry.

This capture proved to be the *Donna Eugenia* from Pernambuco with a royal licence to slave at Cabenda or Malemba, south of the line, but, with eighty five slaves already on board from *Duke Ephraim's* barracoons.

After their adventure in the Bonny, the two lieutenants reconnoitred Duke's Town and the Old Calabar anchorages, making prizes of the *Constantia,* a small schooner of seventy-three tons, and the *Gaviao,* another Brazilian, who found slaves unprocurable south of the line.

Commodore Collier's Report

During 1821, the slaving in the Bonny and Old Calabar rivers was booming, and the efforts of the cruisers were of very little account. Between July 1820 and October 1821, one hundred and ninety slave cargoes were taken from the Bonny, and one hundred and sixty two from the Old Calabar.

Indeed Commodore Collier, in his last report before sailing for home, dated twenty-seventh of December, 1821, wrote very gloomily of the position.

Here are a few extracts:—

"It is true that certain powers have abandoned the trade entirely; but, not withstanding this, my full persuasion is that this infamous traffic in amount is no less than it was; and numberless opportunities of personal observation justify may saying that in the manner of conducting it, its cruelty and brutality, it cannot be surpassed".

He then proceeded to report on the slavers of different nationalities, after giving American cruisers the following pat on the back.

"American officers had on all occasions acted with the greatest zeal . . . the most perfectly unanimity prevailed between the officers of H.M. Squadron and those of the American vessels of war". (Note:—The following U.S.N. ships visited the African coast, 1820-1823. Frigate, *Constellation;* ship-sloops, *Peacock, Hornet, Erie,* and *Ontario;* brig, *Spark;* and schooners, *Grampus, Shark, Alligator* and *Porpoise.*

Spark and *Grampus* spent more time on the coast than any of the others. Both caught slavers at sea, but the bulk of the work fell to little revenue cutters, working in the West Indies, such as the *Alabama* and *Louisiana.* These were small schooners of only about fifty tons burthen. It should be stated that American so called revenue cutters were all schooner-rigged).

"French slavers", reported the Commodore, "are occasionally to be found on all parts of the coast: her colours being protection everywhere, but the principal resort of the French slavers is the river Bonny".

Regarding the Spanish slavers he wrote:—

"Although by her treaty Spain has relinquished the trade, her subjects infects the coast of Africa still: in the period of the rains they become most active . . . and I am quite satisfied that, as suits the views of the masters of the Spanish slaving schooners, they at one time act as pirates against all vessels, then under the flag of Atigas act as South American cruisers, and then, when it shall better serve them, return to the practice of slaving".

Of the Portuguese, he reported:—

"The Portuguese will cling to the slave trade as long as it shall be possible: the profits are so large as to induce all risks, the vessels of this nation range every part of the coast, whether north or south; enter every port and creek where a slave is to be purchased; and many small vessels under this flag are still employed in supplying the slave factories of Princes Island and St. Thomas."

The Commodore next described the condition of the slaves in captured slavers and his efforts to save their lives.

The slaves were found fettered in pairs, jammed one within the feet of the other, lying in filth, racked with fever, dysentry and other horrible African diseases, and often the dead still shackled to the living. Helped in his remedies by the untiring surgeon of the frigate, Mr. Patten, and the assistant surgeon of the *Thistle,* Mr. Bennett, the Commodore removed every sick slave from the captured slavers to the booms of the *Tartar,* where they had every attention: at the same time such precautions were taken aboard the frigate against infection that only one member of her company was attacked by fever and he soon recovered. This was the ship's assistant surgeon.

Besides the reports of the Commodore, we have the reports of General Sir Charles McCarthy to Earl Bathurst.

In the months of July and August 1821, whilst cruising in the Bight of Biafra, the *Myrmidon* boarded and examined sixteen slave vessels, only one of which, the Portuguese schooner, *Adelaide* could be sent for adjudication in accordance with the provisions of the public conventions. During the same period the *Pheasant* on the leeward station found six slavers at Whydah and Badagry, equipped with boilers, irons and water-casks, but with no slaves on board and therefore untouchable.

Snapper visited the Old Calabar and Lagos during these months and found one Spaniard, six Portuguese, and three French slavers, only one of which could be sent for adjudication.

On her next cruise the *Myrmidon* again found the Bonny river swarming with slavers.

Owing to the fact that the chiefs of the Bonny and Calabar districts levy a tax on each slave-ship, a register had been kept. Lists from this registry were sent to Sierra Leone, but at first they were considered exaggerated and incredible, though afterwards they were found to be only too correct.

The Story of Bishop Crowther

A very notable man in the history of West Africa was rescued as a boy from the clutches of the slave traders in the year 1821.

The town of Oshogun in Yoruba land was raided by the Fulahs, and amongst those carried off were a mother and her three children two girls and a boy of eleven years. The boy, named Adjai, was eventually sold in the slave market at Ijaye and marched in a slave gang to Lagos, where he was put aboard a Portuguese slaver.

The ship was captured by the *Myrmidon,* and her negroes taken to Sierra Leone, where Adjai was educated.

In 1864 this liberated slave was consecrated as the first bishop of the Niger Territories. He was the famous Samuel Crowther, to whom the spread of Christianity in West Africa was mainly due.

Myrmidon's Boats up the Bonny

The gallant old Commodore, Sir George R. Collier, sailed for home in the summer of 1821, leaving Captain Kelly of the *Pheasant,* senior officer on the coast until the arrival of his successor. Collier did not long survive his trying three years of duty on the pestilential coast, dying on March the 24th, 1824.

The following reports written by Captain Leake of the *Myrmidon* will give a good idea of the hard service performed by her during the summer and autumn of 1821.

The first is dated off the River Bonny on the 12th of September, and runs as follows:—

"After completing my water in the Bay of Fernando Bo, I put to sea to search the Bonny, if weather would permit. I anchored off Anthony Point on the evening of the 9th of August, and at daylight next morning dispatched the boats under Lieutenant Bingham to intercept any slaves he might find there. In going up the Anthony river instead of the Bonny was ascertained that it was a much shorter cut to the anchorage of the slave vessels in the latter river, and that it enabled the boats to surprise them by day break.

They found no less than six French vessels all trafficking for slaves: the first they boarded was a brig with one hundred and fifty men on board. The captain informed Lieutenant Bingham that there was a Spanish brig and a schooner in the creek full of slaves and their crews on shore in a state of mutiny. He immediately pulled in the gig (with pinnace in company) to search them.

Upon approaching, he fired a musket or two to make them hoist their colours and to prevent their slaves from jumping overboard, which numbers were in the act of doing: they took no notice of this, but upon coming within pistol shot, they hauled up their ports and commenced a heavy fire of grape. The contents of the first gun, I am sorry to say, took the stern sheet of the gig, and severely wounded Lieutenant Bingham, Mr. Deschamps midshipman, John Morgan, sergeant of marines and one seaman. This resistance being so unexpected, the commanding officer apparantly dying from a wound in the breast and the vessels keeping up a warm fire, he judged it expedient to withdraw the boats.

Immediately on receiving this intelligence, I dispatched Mr. Edwin with a reinforcement of twenty-nine men to attack them: but he, having assertained that the vessels had made every preparation to defend themselves by lashing several hundreds of iron bars round them and laying a platform of the same athwart from the upper part of the bulwark, and their awnings so taut nailed down that no entrance could be effected but by one man at a time; under these circumstances I judged it unpracticable for our boats to board, and the weather being extremely bad I was unwilling further to expose my men. I therefore conceived it my duty to take the ship up the river in order to punish the renegades for their insolent conduct.

I was further induced to the attempt through a representation made to me that the King of Bonny had ill-treated our merchants trading with him for palm oil, detaining them unnecessarily six or seven months, while the slave ships received their cargoes in the short space of one, and they (our merchants) felt satisfied the appearance of a man-of-war would be of the greatest importance to their trade.

Taking every possible precaution of sounding repeatedly upon the two bars, laying buoys down, and waiting for clear weather, the proper time of tide and a fair wind, which necessarily in the rainy season on this coast caused much delay, I am happy to say I crossed the bar in safety, carrying 3½ fathoms and anchored in the Road of Bonny a little after sunset on the 31st of August.

The Spaniards, on seeing the ship, immediately escaped ashore and sent me a joint letter acknowledging they had done wrong in firing into the boats, and entreated I would take their vessels and spare their lives. To this, of course, I made no reply; but, finding that all the slaves had been sent on shore, and that the natives had taken away all their cargo and provisions much time was lost previous to our taking possession in making the King deliver them up again, which, however, I at length effected by threats and intimidation. On board of them we found one hundred and fifty four slaves in the brig, and one hundred and thirty in the schooner: the former is a remarkably fine vessel of two hundred and fifty four tons, mounting twelve carriage guns, and at the time she fired upon our boats had a complement of seventy-five men, thirty of whom had been taken from the schooner".

The names of the slavers were *Caridad* and *Nueva Virgen* and both had been fitted out at St. Jago de Cuba. The *Myrmidon* conducted them to Sierra Leone, where they arrived on November the 4th, having lost fifty-one of the slaves on the passage up. Both vessels were condemned.

On his arrival at Sierra Leone, Captain Leake wrote the following despatch, dated November the 7th.

"I have visited the Old Calabar, Rio del Rey, Bimbia river and the Cameroons, I am sorry to say without success. Information travels so quickly from river to river by the creeks of this country that the news of my having taken the vessels from the Bonny had reached a week before I could appear off them: the slavers became alarmed, shipped what slaves they could, put to sea, and thus escaped me. A Spanish felucca bound to the Havanna sailed with two hundred a few days prior to my boats searching the Old Calabar, and a Portuguese brig with the same number for Bahia sailed three days previous to my anchoring in the Cameroons. From the former river there had sailed within the last eighteen months, one hundred and seventy seven vessels with full cargoes, more than half of them were under the French flag, the others Spaniards and Portuguese.

These accounts have given me, not only from the Kings and chiefs of the rivers, but from those who were eye witnesses of the shipments and sailings.

The vessels reported in my last to have left the Bonny between July and November 1820, with eighty-six that have already sailed this year, added, with thirty-five from the Bimbia and Cameroons will make the number four hundred and twenty four, many of them carrying from five hundred to one thousand slaves; and allowing the very moderate average of two hundred and fifty, each vessel will make one hundred and six thousand slaves from the four Northernmost rivers in the Bight of Biafra in eighteen months—and by far the largest half under French flag.

I had purposed next to visit the rivers Danger and Gaboon, but my ship, having been exposed to the incessant rains of a very long and severe season, and my officers and men suffering much from the same with a good deal of actual sickness and fever; and finding, on making these rivers, I had not sufficient men left to man the boats, I was compelled to quit the coast for this place to procure refreshments.

Nothing, by way of stores had arrived; my ship being in a bad state from want of sails, rope, etc., and many seamen short of her complement, I do not feel authorised to leave till I get a supply".

Activity of French Slavers

These reports were, to say the least of it, discouraging, the hard work of the cruisers being of so little avail. Nor could the *Snapper,* now under Lieutenant Christopher Knight, report any better success.

Whilst running down the coast from Sierra Leone to Cape Mount during October 1821, she fell in with nine slavers—eight of these were French and could not be touched, and the other was a Dutchman which escaped.

French slavers were also seen at the Gallinas and at Sherbar. On the windward coast from the island of Goree to the mouth of the Gambia, and on again to Cacheo and Bissao, the Portuguese were most active, and besides sending slavers to Brazil and Cuba, had a number of small craft running slaves to the Cape De Verd Islands.

The slave traders of Cacheo actually went up the Rio Grande in armed sloops and boats, rushed the native kraals during the night and carried off as many negroes as they could capture. This method of stealing slaves was called *Panyarring.*

The rivers Nunez and Pongas were visited by the gun-brig, *Thistle*—but she was only able to bring out the *Rosalia* with sixty slaves, bound to the Havana. This vessel was Spanish though with no regular papers, and during the unhealthy season had lost eight of her crew in the Pongas.

There was a very unpleasant incident in 1821. The *Pheasant* put a prize crew aboard a Brazilian slaver, called the *Volcano*. The slaver's crew managed to overpower and kill all the prize crew with the exception of two kroomen, one of whom they carried off to the Brazils, but the other, Quashie Sam, a native from Cape Coast, managed to escape and brought the news to the British Authorities.

CHAPTER VIII

COAST OF AFRICA 1822-1827

"Oh, the old Commodore, the rum old Commodore,
A queer old Commodore is he;
For the bullets and the gout
Have so knocked his hull about,
He will never be more fit for sea".

Commodore Sir Robert Mends

SIR George Collier was succeeded on the coast of Africa by Commodore Sir Robert Mends in the *Iphigenia*, forty-two guns, who arrived out in February 1822. The new Commodore was another distinguished war veteran and a much shot up one.

As far back as the American War of Independence he lost his right arm, shattered by a cannon ball, and at the same time received some lead in his left knee. This was at the siege if York Town. He was removed to a ship, which caught fire and burnt, Mends being saved by his hammock-man, who took him up in his arms and was only just in time to get into the last boat with him.

In 1782, he served in the *Conqueror*, when Rodney defeated Comte de Grasse. This time he had a splinter wound in the head and his jaw was fractured.

In 1793, he was lieutenant of the *Colossus* in Lord Bridport's action off L'Orient, and this time he was severely wounded, burnt and bruised and blinded for some days through the bursting of a lower deck gun.

In 1796, when commanding the eighteen-gun sloop, *Diligence*, he captured the Spanish twenty-two-gun brig, *La Natividad*, after an action of three quarters of an hour off Porto Rico. This time he got off with a musket ball in the remaining arm.

In 1809, he commanded the *Arethusa* when she captured the forty-six-gun frigate, *Niemen*. He was the only person wounded aboard the English frigate, receiving a splinter in the forehead, which affected his eyesight, and gave him trouble for the remainder of his life. Such a gallant veteran, besides Knighthood and a wound's pension, had many a foreign order, such as the Grand Cross of Charles III and the Cross of the Victory of Asturias.

The Mends were a distinguished naval family, and there are still many officers alive, who served with Sir Robert's nephew, Admiral Sir William Mends of toggle and becket fame.

Under Mends, the African squadron was reinforced by the Levant class ship-sloops, *Cyrene*, twenty guns, four hundred and fifty one tons, and *Bann*, twenty guns, four hundred and sixty six tons, both built in 1812; and the *Driver*, eighteen-gun, Bermuda-built, flush-decked ship-sloop, sister ship of the *Morgiani*, arrived on the coast in 1821.

The *Bann* which was no stranger to the Bights was commanded by Captain Phillips, who at the end of a succesful four months cruise was obliged to invalid, after four bouts of fever.

Indeed the *Bann* suffered severely from the climate, and in the spring of 1823 was hurried off to Ascension, having lost her purser, gunner, captain's clerk, two midshipmen, twenty bluejackets, five marines and four boys. Phillips was succeeded by Lieutenant G. W. C. Courteney from the *Cyrene*.

Lieutenant Mildway Up The Bonny

On his arrival at Sierra Leone, the new Commodore found the *Myrmidon* refitting. On the 11th of March, 1822, the two men-of-war proceeded down the coast in company, the *Iphigenia* having on board the new Governor, General Sir Charles McCarthy, who had been appointed to take over the forts from the African company. Both the Commodore and the General were new to the coast. After visiting Dix Cove, Cape Coast Castle, Annamaboe and Accra, where he dropped the Governor, the Commodore proceeded with the *Myrmidon*.

At Appam a Portuguese brig was caught loading, with twelve slaves already on board. At Whydah a Portuguese schooner with three out of her cargo of two hundred and fifty slaves was captured.

The Commodore put Lieutenant G. W. St. John and a prize crew aboard the schooner, and sent her ahead. At Lagos she found five slavers, one of which had one hundred and eighty seven slaves on board and so was liable to capture.

Arrived of the Bonny, the ships were anchored in the offing, whilst their boats were sent up the river under the command of Lieutenant George William St. John Mildmay of the *Iphigenia*. Crossing the bar soon after daylight on the 5th of April, the boats came in sight of the shipping, lying off the town, at about seven o'clock. Of the anchored vessels, two schooners, four brigs and a brigantine were undoubtedly slavers.

As soon as Mildmay was near enough for the colours to be distinguished he hoisted ensigns on the boat flagstaffs. The slavers, which were about four miles away at once put springs on their cables and began to heave round so that they could bring their broadside guns top bear.

Directly the boats were within range, the two schooners opened fire, and after a short while two of the brigs, and the brigantine, hoisted French colours and joined in. The boats advanced steadily under a heavy fire for twenty minutes, and lost two men killed and five wounded before they were able to get alongside.

The slavers did not mind the fire from the boat carronades and musketry, but they were not willing to face cold steel, and, as the bluejackets boarded, they retreated below.

Whilst they kept clear themselves, they put muskets in the hands of the slaves and ordered them to fire up the hatchways. This, of course, brought retaliation, in the course of which many unfortunate negroes were killed.

The captures proved to be:—

The Spanish schooner, *Yeanam*, 306 tons, eight long eighteen-pounders, two long nine pounders, fifty-five men, three hundred and eighty slaves.

Spanish schooner, *Becua*, 180 tons, eight long eighteen-pounders, one long nine-pounder, forty-five men, three hundred slaves.

French brig, *Vigilant*, 240 tons, four twelve-pounder-carronades, thirty men, three hundred and forty-three slaves.

French brig, *Petite Betzey*, 184 tons, four nine-pounder-carronades, twenty-five men, two hundred and eighteen slaves.

French brigantine, *L'Ursule*, 100 tons, four nine-pounder-carronades, twenty-seven men, two hundred and forty-seven slaves.

There was also a French brig, named *Le Theodore*, which took no part in the action though her crew were believed to be aboard one of the other Frenchmen aiding in her defence.

Close at hand was a housed-over brig, which turned out to be the palm oiler, *William Rathbone*, from Liverpool.

As usual many of the terrified slaves leaped overboard and were taken by the sharks.

Aboard the *Yeanam*, four slaves were killed and ten wounded. A poor little girl, ten years old, lost both her legs, and another girl lost her right arm. Another little girl of but twelve years of age was found fastened to a heavy chain, ten feet in length.

In the *Becua*, whose crew had hurriedly deserted her, a lighted match was found hanging over the open hatch of the magazine. This villainous attempt to blow up the schooner with her slaves and captors was only just frustrated in time.

Enquiry revealed the fact that the five slavers fully expected to capture the boats, in which case every man about them was to have been put to death. The prizes were sent as usual to Sierra Leone for adjudication.

On the passage the *Yeanam* became separated from the others and sank in a tornado with three hundred and eighty slaves on board.

Morgiana's Captures

Captain Christopher Knight of the *Morgiana*, during his last cruise to leeward before sailing for home, made the following captures:—

7th March 1822. Spanish schooner, *Duchosa Estrella*, 100 tons, one gun, thirty-four slaves, from trade Town for Porto Rico.
23 March. Brazilian schooner, *L'Adolphe*, 169 tons, eight guns, from Picanning for Bahia.
13 April. Brazilian schooner, *Taminha*, 137 tons, six guns, from Porto Novo for Bahia.
13 April. Brazilian schooner, *Zefiro*, 190 tons, two guns, from Whydah for Bahia.
13 April. Brazilian schooner, *Amelia*, 120 tons, four guns, from Whydah for Bahia.
13 April. Brazilian polacre, *Desengano*, 60 tons, two guns, from Whydah for Bahia.
15 April. Portuguese brig, *Esperanca*, 189 tons, two guns, one hundred and forty-nine slaves from Lagos for Para.

Midget Slaver of Dona Marie de Cruz

In the autumn of 1822, the *Bann* under Captain Phillips, was the most successful of the British cruisers, capturing no less than six slavers in the Bight of Biafra between August the 27th and December the 3rd.

The *Thistle*, Lieutenant Robert Hagan, was also cruising in the Bight of Biafra, and on the 3rd August 1822 boarded the midget slaver, *San Jose Hallaxa*, a seven ton schooner, which had put back to the Old Calabar after a vain attempt to reach Prince's Island.

This vessel was owned by the callous Dona Maria de Cruz, daughter of the notorious ex-governor of Prince's Island, Don Gomez. On leaving Duke's Town the schooner contained thirty slaves—ten of these had died of starvation. One woman had gone crazy from drinking sea water, and in order to stop her fearful shrieking, she had been flogged to death. This was not the first nor the last speculation in slaves made by this inhumnan Governor's daughter.

This was one of the *Thistle*'s last captures before Hagan was promoted and sailed for home in the spring of 1823.

This distinguished officer entered the service in December 1807, aboard the *Surveillante*, when Commodore Sir George Collier was her captain.

From November 1815, Hagan had been on the coast of Africa commanding in turn the *Princess Charlotte*, *Prince Regent* and *Thistle*. During this long term of service he had captured forty slavers and liberated four thousand slaves, a record which few officers have equalled.

Before he sailed for England, the members of the Council and Judges of Sierra Leone presented him with a piece of plate and a letter of thanks, whilst the merchants, on their part, gave him a sword valued at one hundred guineas with a similar address.

He was knighted in 1835 and posted in 1843. His last service before retiring was as Inspecting Commander in the Irish Coast Guard.

1823. A Sickly Season

The gun-brig, *Snapper*, also went home in 1823. These cruisers were replaced by the twenty-six-gun corvette *Brazen*, Captain George Wickens Willes, and the eighteen-gun sloop, *Victor*, Commander Thomas Prickett.

Commodore Sir Robert Mends having sailed round the West African station, went onto the West Indies, but here the *Iphigenia* was attacked by yellow fever, both officers and crew suffering severely. Sir Robert, thereupon, sailed for home and paid her off.

It seems that the Admiralty had made a rule that the Commodore should not remain on the station during the rainy season, which was considered then to be the most unhealthy time of the year.

In 1823, the Commodore commissioned the forty-two-gun frigate *Owen Glendower* at Chatham, having prevailed on the Lords of the Admiralty to allow him to stay on the coast through the rainy season. This was a fatal decision, for it so happened that 1823 was a very sickly season.

Though the West coast of Africa and especially the Bights had such a bad name for fever and disease, in some years the squadron was often quite free of illness; than a year came round that more than decimated it.

On September the 1st, 1823, the Commodore went down with cholera, and he died on the 4th, a sacrifice in the cause of humanity, after forty-four years of arduous and brilliant service.

His eldest son, a midshipman of the *Owen Glendower*, followed him on December the 5th, dying from fever caught up the slave rivers of the Bights in the previous June.

The Ashanti Campaign

The suppression of the slave trade was considerably over-shadowed in 1823 by the Ashanti war.

In 1821, on the Royal African Company ceasing to exist, the Governor-in-Chief of the West Coast of Africa, General Sir Charles McCarthy, as we have already seen, took over the Gold Coast forts. He repudiated the treaty, made by Mr. Dupuis, the British Consul, at Kumassi, and decided to defend the Fantees against their oppressors. For this purpose he collected all his available force at Cape Coast Castle. This consisted of the Royal African Corps, the Cape Coast Militia, a detachment of the West India Regiment and a very mixed lot of native levies.

Without the aid of the Royal Navy, the clash between this motley crowd and the war-like Ashanti would have been even more disastrous than it was. The Royal African Corps, for instance, was just a scalliwag corps, as we used to call such levies in the Boer War, consisting of all the tough characters obtainable from the British Army as officers and non-commissioned officers, and undisciplined natives in the ranks.

The campaign may be said to have started in July 1823, when ten thousand Ashanti went on the warpath and advanced towards Cape Coast Castle. Major Chisholm, commandant of Cape Coast Castle, managed to collect a force of about three thousand men, consisting of militia, native levies and volunteers.

Under the command of Captain Laing of the militia and Lieutenant John King, 1st Lieutenant of the *Driver*, who had volunteered his services, this force managed to hold up the Ashanti advance for four months by skilful bush fighting, and then by cutting off their supplies, at last forced the Ashanti warriors to retire.

Lieutenant King returned to his ship with a wounded leg and fever: the *Driver* then departed for the South American station.

Another naval officer, who distinguished himself in the Ashanti war was John Jeayes, master's mate and acting first lieutenant of the *Snapper*. When the gun-brig sailed for home,

Jeayes volunteered into the Colonial brig, *Prince Regent*, which was to co-operate with the troops.

Gallant Death of Sir Charles McCarthy

In January 1824, the Ashanti again advanced in their thousands. By this time General Sir Charles McCarthy had arrived on the spot.

With the heart of a lion, but no idea of bush fighting, Sir Charles boldly led out his troops against the savage enemy. Of three columns of levies, he took command of the post of danger, facing the main Ashanti force. This column only numbered five hundred natives under a dozen white officers with a much diminished company of white troops, in front of whom stood Sir Charles, conspicuous in his red tunic and white cock's plume.

The clash came at Assamacow on January the 21st. The thin line of the advancing troops suddenly came out into a clearing, and the next moment a murderous fire from their hidden enemy mowed them down. Nothing but their belief in the invincibility of the white man held the coast levies to their ground, and as their white officers were shot down, they began to waver, and at last to slink away into the bush. But the whites, both officers and men, hung on grimly and it has even been asserted that McCarthy would have succeeded in keeping the hordes of howling Ashanti at bay, if some fool at the base had not supplied him with kegs of vermicelli under the impression that it was gunpowder.

With the failure of his ammunition, the general and his small band of white men, who had by this time been reduced to less than a dozen, most of them wounded, could only sell their lives as desperately as possible on the ground on which they stood. When the Ashanti warriors dashed in upon them with spear and assegai, their chief in hopes of large ransoms, vainly attempted to save the lives of the General and the eight officers who still stood upon their feet; but, with no thought of surrender, these few invincibles fought on until each was ringed with foes. Then came the end, a glorious end, such as has never been forgotton amongst the Ashanti, the story being handed down from father to son.

Amazed at such a resistance, the king of the great Ashanti nation had the head of the general cut off from the spear-pierced body and carefully embalmed. It henceforth became a fetish, which, on festival days, was paraded with great pomp through the streets of Kumassi.

Years after, when the embalming had lost its effect, the skull was mounted in gold and used as the King's drinking cup. When Prempeh's palace was captured in the last Ashanti war, a skull covered with Arabic writings was discovered, and this was supposed to be the famous skull of the great white chief.

The heart, too, of the general was preserved and sent back to the King. In accordance with the common African superstition, this was then eaten by the chief and his warriors in order that they might acquire the white man's courage.

Amongst the Fantees, Sir Charles McCarthy's name is still preserved in many of their songs, and their most sacred oath is 'By Wednesday and McCarthy'.

The retreat of the only survivors of this battle, one-hundred and forty-nine men under Lieutenant Erskine, was covered by the gallant little brig, *Prince Regent*.

It was now touch and go whether Cape Coast Castle itself would be able to hold off the advancing Ashanti. Luckily for the defence of the fort it had been re-equipped with modern guns by Captain Charles Bowen of the *Driver* in July 1823, before the last threat of the fierce tribesmen, but it would have been speedily starved out had not the *Prince Regent* managed to procure a fresh supply of provisions.

Even so the situation of the defenders was looking desperate when the forty-six-gun frigate, *Thetis*, Captain Sir John Philliamore, C.B. and the twelve-gun pelter brig, *Swinger*, arrived on the scene with a further supply and a detachment of the Royal African Corps.

On the 21st May, 1824, another fierce battle took place in which the British lost eighty-eight killed, six hundred and seventy-eight wounded and eighty-eight missing. Amongst the wounded was the fire-eating Lieutenant John King, who, on the *Driver*'s arrival from Brazil, had leaped ashore in eagerness to play the soldier again. This time he received his well-earned promotion.

Between July the 4th, and July the 11th, there was again severe fighting in which bluejackets and marines from the ships, under Andrew Drew, the first lieutenant of the *Thetis*, played a gallant part.

The war dragged on until on August the 7th, 1826, the Ashanti suffered their worst defeat at Dodowah. Finally in 1831 the proud warrior King was at last compelled to sue for peace from Governor George Maclean, Administrator of the Gold Coast.

Commodore Charles Bullen

The death of the old Commodore left Captain Grace of the *Cyrene* senior officer of the coast. But when John Filmore arrived out in October to take over the *Bann*, he assumed the chief command as being senior on the list to Grace, who, rather than dispute the command on a technicality, sailed for home in the *Cyrene*. Filmore appointed himself to the *Owen Glendower* and sent Lieutenant G. W. C. Courtenay to the *Bann* from the *Cyrene*. This double shuffling did not last for long however, for Filmore returned to England in January 1824 and the *Owen Glendower*'s first lieutenant, George Woollcombe became acting captain for a short while before being appointed acting captain of the *Bann*, and finally, on promotion, to the command of the *Victor*, eighteen guns, in February, 1824. For over six months the station suffered badly for want of a Commodore, and the cruising against the slave traffic was very spasmodic.

The new commodore commissioned the *Maidstone*, forty-six guns, on December the 12th, 1823. The choice of the Admiralty fell upon Captain Charles Bullen, and no better man for that arduous post could have been selected.

Bullen was an old friend and mess-mate of the dead commodore, and one of the most popular officers in the service, which he had entered as far back as 1779. Like Collier and Mends he had seen a great deal of service, being a veteran of both Camperdown and Trafalgar, where he had acted as flag captain to Northesk. Nor was he a stranger to the coast, having been mainly instrumental in 1801 when commanding the *Wasp*, eighteen guns, in saving the colony of Sierra Leone from a powerful combination of native chiefs.

On arriving out on his station he found the Ashanti war raging and the slave trade booming: yet the Admiralty were still blind to the needs of the African squadron, which could well have done with some of the West Indian schooners.

West African Squadron 1825

At the beginning of 1825, the squadron consisted of:—

Maidstone	46 guns	Commodore's broad pendant
Atholl	28 guns	Captain James A. Murray
Brazen	26 guns	Captain G. W. Willes
Bann	20 guns	Commander G. W. C. Courtenay
Esk	20 guns	Commander W. J. Purchas
Victor	18 guns	Commander George Woolcombe
Redwing	18 guns	Commander D. C. Clavering
Conflict	12 guns	Lieutenant John Chrystie
Swinger	12 guns	Lieutenant John Scott

The *Atholl* was an experimental ship, built of larch from the Duke of Atholl's estate in 1820. That she was well built is proved by the fact that she was still going strong as a troop-ship in 1858.

The *Brazen* was built at Portsmouth in 1808 from a design by Sir J. Henlowe. She ended her days as a church ship and after twenty years of this duty was broken up in 1848.

Bann and *Esk* were built by Seppings in 1812 on the lines of the *Levant*, with the famous diagonal timbering of that surveyor, so that they were solid masses of hardwood, coated with cement and coal-tar and caulked within and without.

None of Seppings' corvettes were fast, there being no give about them and they also at a disadvantage on the coast owing to their tall spars which poking up above the horizon, were a bad give-away to any approaching slaver. *Victor* was perhaps the most useful ship in the squadron, being one of the brig-sloops of three hundred and eighty tons, built after *Cruiser*. The Pelter brigs, *Swinger* and *Conflict* were too slow to catch a slaver except by strategy.

False Tonnage in Brazilian Licence Papers

Commodore Bullen found the callous cruelty and depravity of the slave trade worse than ever.

In 1824, two Brazilian vessels were captured by the *Victor*, whose tonnage was doubled in their licence papers—These were the *Diana* and *Dos Amigos Brazilieros*. Portuguese law allowed five slaves to every three British tons. The *Diana* was registered as a vessel of one hundred and twenty tons, though her true measurement was only sixty-six tons. She was caught with one hundred and fifty-six slaves loaded at Badagry.

The *Dos Amigos Brazilieros* only measured ninety-five tons, though she was registered as being one hundred and forty-six tons. She had a crew of eighteen, and two hundred and sixty slaves on board.

Another Brazilian, the *Aviso* with a crew of thirty-three and four hundred and sixty-five slaves loaded at Bagadry, was caught by the *Maidstone*—her licence made her two hundred and thirty-one tons, whereas she only measured one hundred and sixty-five.

The slave decks of these three ships were in a truely terrible state, even for slavers. *Diana* had small-pox raging aboard. The *Dos Amigos Brazilieros* had a number of infants and negresses about to become mothers, whilst the *Aviso*, for the run across, had barely twenty days' provisions and less than than twenty days water.

The report of February, 1825, stating that three thousand men, women and children, more than half of them still alive, were thrown overboard by the slavers during the passage, is scarcely to be wondered at when this terrible over-crowding is realized.

Bloodhounds in Slavers

One of the latest devices of the slave-captains was the employment of fierce dogs, half bloodhound, half mastiff. A resident of Freetown wrote in the Sierra Leone *Gazette* of December the 11th, 1823:—

"Having gone off to the slave-vessels lately sent into this harbour, I was struck by the appearance of some very fierce dogs, of the bloodhound species, natives of Brazil: and, on inquiry, found that they had been taken on board for the purpose of assisting their inhuman masters in coercing the unfortunate victims of the lawless cupidity.

They had been trained, it appears, to sit watch over the hatches during the night, or whenever the wretched beings were confined below, and thus effectually precluded them from coming up. This abominable system is, I understand pretty generally practised on board the slavers from Bahia and Cuba".

The notorious Theodore Canot never dared to go to sleep without a bloodhound guarding his bed.

Another Midget Slaver

There is no doubt that men who embarked in the slave traffic became absolutely callous to human suffering, and looked upon slaves like so many head of cattle or sheep. But no Guinea captain seems to have been more indifferent to suffering than the lady Donna Marie de Cruz of Prince's Island.

Another of her tiny cockboats was captured by the *Victor*. Lieutenant Scott reported that in a space with only eighteen inches under the beams twenty-three slaves were stowed, six of whom had already died, and all of whom were in a state of actual starvation. The burthen of this schooner, the *Maria Paguena*, which had sailed from the Gaboon river, was only five tons.

One more example from the *Victor*'s log, to show the callousness of slave traders. In June 1824 she overhauled a lugger off the Kittan coast. Before she could get alongside, the slaver's longboat was launched and pulled away for the shore, leaving the lugger (*L'Henriette Aimée*) with all her slaves still chained below, to wreck herself in the heavy surf.

The crew of the slavers in cases of wreck or foundering never showed the least thought for the slaves.

It was about this date that the English palm-oil brig *Accession* came upon a water-logged wreck lying on her side with thirty-one blacks clinging to the mast. The crew of the *Accession* hacked a hole in the side of the slaver, and took out ten slaves, who were still alive. It appeared that one hundred and thirty-eight of the slaves had been previously taken off by the slaver, *Viajante*, but as she already had six hundred and twenty-two negroes on board, no more could be taken so they were left to perish.

Redwing's Bad Luck With Her Prizes

In 1825, the eighteen-gun sloop, *Redwing*, Commander Clavering, arrived on the coast. This vessel was peculiarly unlucky with her prizes.

In November 1819, she was on the St. Helena station under commander Fred Hunn, on the dull job of watching over Napoleon.

Bored with this monotonous life and urging as an excuse the many piratical acts of slavers, Commander Hunn, who was a half-brother of Canning and somewhat of a privileged officer, proceeded to capture the French slaver, *Sylphe*, with four hundred slaves from the Bonny. This excess of zeal led to a great deal of diplomatic correspondence, at the end of which the slaver was returned to the French.

In October 1825, the boats of the *Redwing* were dispatched up the Old Calabar under her first lieutenant, Card.

Two Spanish slavers were found up the river, and after a sharp exchange of volleys, the Spanish schooner, *Teresa*, with one hundred and ninety-nine slaves was captured. The crew of her consort, a brigantine named *Isabella* fled to the shore, leaving two hundred and seventy-three slaves on board and papers dating back to 1816.

Both vessels were sent to Sierra Leone for adjudication and neither arrived.

The *Teresa* capsized in a tornado and only six of her slaves were saved. The *Isabella* was recaptured by one of the many piratical slavers, which hung about the coast, and was taken to Cuba.

Young Crawford in *Neptuno* Fights off a Pirate

The pirate, which recaptured the *Isabella*, may possibly have been the same vessel that attacked the *Neptuno*.

On March the 6th, 1826, the *Esk* captured the Brazilian brigantine, *Neptuno*, and the sloop, *Esperanza* from the River Benin or Formosa.

On the wearisome passage to Sierra Leone the *Esperanza* soon outdistanced the *Neptuno*. The latter besides ninety-two slaves and four of her slave crew including the Brazilian master, had a prize crew consisting of Richard Borough Crawford, a midshipman of twelve years standing, in command, a master's assistant named Finch, (a lad of only sixteen years) five bluejackets, and a ships boy of seventeen years, named Olivine.

After a fortnight of calm weather, a nice steady breeze sprang up on the morning of March the 20th.

Wearied out by his long spell of watchfulness, young Crawford was asleep in the usual officer's quarters aboard a slaver, which was a sort of box on deck, much like a kennel, and indeed called by the Spaniards and Portuguese a 'dog-house'. Officers of slavers generally were obliged to sleep in these dog-houses on deck, for both forecastle and cabin were given up to the living freight.

Presently Crawford was awakened by the slaver's captain, who pointed with great uneasiness to a large brig, which was coming up astern, and seemed to be in chase of the *Neptuno*.

At first Crawford thought the brig might be the *Redwing*, but the Brazilian captain kept warning him with the word 'Ladrone! Ladrone!' (Pirate! Pirate!).

The little *Neptuno* was armed with two six-pounders, and Crawford ordered these guns to be loaded, and spare powder and shot to be brought on deck. He also hoisted the red ensign at the peak and put the brigantine under all sail. When, however,it became evident that the brig astern had the legs of the *Neptuno*, Crawford shortened sail and hove to.

As the stranger, a large brig mounting ten broadside guns and two swivels, ranged up within hail, her dirty appearance, crowded decks and noisy ruffiany crew proclaimed her to be anything but a man-of-war. Crawford, convinced by her appearance that the slave captain was right, let draw his foresheet and fitted away again, but this action speedily brought a shot from the pirate, which passed between the *Neptuno*'s masts. At this the intrepid Crawford exclaimed:—

"I will have a shot at her if I die for it". And he immediately fired one of his popguns. The gun missed fire; and his badly scared crew now flung themselves upon his, begging him not to irritate the corsair, which had run up French colours.

By this time there was only fifty yards between the two ships, and a hail came from the pirate, ordering Crawford to come aboard with his papers. The wide-awake midshipman begged to be excused as he had no boat.

Whereupon a boat put off from the side of the brig containing five swarthy, bare-breasted oarsmen and a man at the tiller, wearing no waistcoat, but with his villainous face shaded by a wide Havana sombrero. This man was just about to spring aboard over the low bulwark of the brigantine, when Crawford, no wit impressed by his truculent bearing, warned him at his peril to stay in his boat.

This drew forth an angry exclamation in Spanish. "Damned rum French", remarked Crawford in a low tone to the slave captain, who was at his side, "They are nothing but a set of piratical Spaniards". With a fierce oath the man in the Panama hat then ordered Crawford to get into the boat.

The latter pretended to agree and asked him to wait whilst he fetched his papers. He then cautioned his men to keep on the alert, and on no account to allow any of the Spaniards to gain a footing on the deck.

Down in the cabin and out of sight, Crawford carefully primed his pistols.

Returning to the gangway with his pistols held behind his back, in the hope that they would not be noticed, he next ordered the pirate to pull back to the brig without him.

The latter, however, catching sight of one of the pistol butts, sprang to his feet and caught at the rigging in order to swing himself aboard.

Crawford without a moment's hesitation thrust his pistol against the man's breast bone and fired. The corsair's officer fell back dead across the gunwale of his boat.

A second pirate now jumped up, but the undefeatable Crawford, holding his other pistol in both hands, took deliberate aim and shot him through the heart, so that he too dropped dead. A third member of the boat's crew, an Irishman, who had been translating Crawford's words to his commander, now begged for mercy.

The latter calmly ordered this Irish renegade and the three men remaining of the boat's crew to jump into the water and hang on by the gunwale.

By this time the brig was in a furious hubbub, and presently opened a heavy fire upon the *Neptuno* in spite of the fact that her boat was still alongside.

At the first crash of splintered wood, the prize crew, with the exception of a man named Frost and the boy Olivine, all ran below. As they deserted the deck, Crawford damned them all for a set of cowards.

"Don't say all, sir", cried Frost, "for I will stand by you as long as there is a button on your jacket".

The boy also cried out:—

"Well done sir, kill them all".

The Brazilian captain also offered his assistance against the pirate. And so this strange one-sided fight began. Frost took the helm, the slave-captain brought ammunition, whilst Crawford and the boy loaded and fired the puny six-pounder.

The pirate luckily made no attempt to run alongside and board, contenting herself with firing her broadside guns and swivels at point-blank range; but whereas her aim was high and mostly through the rigging, Crawford's popguns went through the sides and every round did execution on her crowded decks.

After two hours' firing, a shot from the pirate at a lower elevation passed through the *Neptuno*'s hold, killing a negress and taking off a girl's arm, whilst a splinter flew from the brigantine's side and sculped Crawford's forehead to the bone. Still undaunted, he was taking aim at a crowd of men upon the pirates forecastle, when Frost called out:— "Your head's wounded, sir, let me have a crack at them!".

Crawford with one hand severely hurt, the bone of his forehead broken, and by this time utterly exhausted from the violent work of loading and firing the gun, stood back.

Frost took careful aim and fired.

Screams from the brig proclaimed his success. It was the last shot fired in the action.

"They've had enough! They don't like your papers!" sung out the Brazilian captain.

He was right, furious quarrelling could be seen and heard going on aboard the brig, in the midst of which she filled her sails and bore away before the wind.

All the honours of this extraordinary action belonged to the indomitable midshipmen. With the excitement and tension over he collapsed upon the deck. All hands rushed to tend him. The Brazilian captain, who well knew what would have been the fate of every white man aboard but for young Crawford's valour, fetched wine.

As for two kroomen who were members of the *Neptuno*'s crew—they exhibited their admiration by squatting down in front of the hero, and, after staring him intently in the face, burst into loud peals of laughter.

When the little brigantine arrived at Sierra Leone, everyone, both afloat and ashore, vied in showing the brave midshipmen honour; and presently from England came the welcome news that the Admiralty had promoted him.

The Brazilian captains evidence before the Court of the Mixed Commission is worth quoting:—

Question: 'Who shot the Spanish officer?'.
Answer: 'It was Senor Crawford'.
Question: 'Who shot the other man in the pirate's boat?'.
Answer: 'It was Senor Crawford'.
Question: 'Who fired the gun?'.
Answer: 'It was Senor Crawford. Me see no one fight much but Senor Crawford. I tell you me fear too much: me poor man: have wife and family at Bahia: but

> English mariner's fear more bad than me: before this me hear English mariners brave past all men: this time me no see it: one or two men not fear very much, but fear a little bit'.

That this action of Crawford's was no mere haphazard piece of sheer recklessness is shown by that officer's subsequent history, of which I shall have something to say later.

The Tender *Hope*. Lieutenant William Tucker

In the history of the Royal Navy's suppression of the slave trade, gallant action, which have never found their way into history books, are without number. There were even ships flying the pendant, which won renown on the coast but were never shown on the Navy List. Of such was the tender *Hope*.

On the 29th September, 1825, the *Maidstone* captured a beautiful Spanish schooner, named *Legunda Gallega*, just out of Lagos with two hundred and ninety-two slaves. As soon as she was condemned by the Mixed Court at Sierra Leone, the Admiral bought her and renamed her the *Hope*.

His reason for buying her is set forth in the following letter written to the Admiralty in 1826.

"She was purchased on my own account at Sierra Leone in January last for the shelter and comfort of the officers and crews of my boats when detached on distant service in this unhealthy climate, to prevent, as much as possible, their contracting fever from being exposed to the tremendous heat by day and the heavy dews by night".

The *Hope*'s burden was one hundred and forty tons. She was armed with long traversing twelve-pounder, and four of Govers eighteen-pounders. Lieutenant William Tucker, second officer of the *Maidstone*, was placed in command of her, supported by R. Lamport Pengelly, Admiralty midshipman, George Williams, assistant surgeon, eighteen seamen, five marines, and eight kroomen.

Tucker was a very experienced officer in dealing with slavers, besides being a very smart one in all other respects.

In his early days when serving in the East Indies he attracted the attention of the Commander-in-Chief, East Indies, the famous Admiral, Sir Henry Blackwood, through his close attention to navigation. But on Blackwood offering him a master's warrant—he was then rating as mate—he declined with these words:—

"I hope one day, Sir Henry, to see my flag flying, as yours is now".

At this time he was serving in the *Liverpool*, commanded by Captain (afterwards Commodore Sir F. A.) Collier. The *Liverpool* was employed on the Mauritius station and took part in the attack upon Ras-col-Khym in the Persian Gulf, when he was nearly creased in a night attack on the camp, two midshipmen close by him losing their lives in this way.

During the five months that the *Liverpool* cruised in the Mozambique channel and off Madagascar, her boats captured five slavers; and the most conspicuous officer on this boat-service was Tucker, who was often away from his ship six weeks at a time.

Tucker ended this commission in the Bombay-built teak ship, *Ganges*, and when she paid off in 1822, he was reported upon as 'a credit to the Service and an honour to the ship he belonged to'.

Previous to serving in the *Maidstone*, he had been in the *Pyladese* and *Atholl*, and had become as experienced on the West Coast as he had been on the East.

The first success of the little *Hope* was the capture off Whydah of the Spanish schooner, *Nicanor*, on May the 20th, 1826, with one hundred and seventy-six slaves on board. Lieutenant Tucker's orders were to scour the Bight of Benin and keep a special watch on Lagos, Whydah and Badgry.

The *Hope* and *Prince of Guinea*

The beginning of September, 1826, found the tender inspecting the Whydah roadstead for the hundredth time. There were no less than twelve vessels lying there awaiting the convenience of Da Souza.

One of these was a specially fine specimen of an American-built clipper-brig, brand new, measuring two hundred and eighty tons (American) armed with a twenty-four-pounder traversing Long Tom amidships, four long nine-pounders, two long six-pounders and two swivels with a crew of seventy-two all told.

This vessel had just come across from Rio de Janeiro with a licence to load seven hundred and one slaves.

Her water-casks were filled, her slave-deck laid and her farina and yams all on board.

Convinced that she would be off in a very few days, Tucker sailed out of the roadstead and, after putting the horizon between the *Hope* and the Whydah shipping, lay in wait for the *Prince of Guinea*, as she was called.

Our experienced slave-catchers were no wit less wide-awake than the wily Guinea captains themselves, and every kind of ruse was brought into play in order to get within range of a suspected slaver.

On this occasion Lieutenant Tucker lowered all sail and lay drifting on the calculated course of the slaver with only the thin wand-like masts of the *Hope* showing against the sky and no patch of canvas, glaring white in the sun, to warn the approaching slave-brig.

Everything worked out as he had expected. No sooner had the *Hope* disappeared from sight than the *Prince of Guinea* began to take her cargo of black ivory aboard. In three hours, six hundred and eight men, women and children had been crowded onto her slave deck, and, as the last canoe left her side, her anchor was broken out, her topsails, already hoisted and held in the spilling lines, were let fall and sheeted home, and without any fuss or cheering, she slipped away from the anchorage in true slaver fashion.

At daybreak the following morning, there she was, almost within range of the *Hope*'s guns—but not quite. A long, weary chase now began, and the schooner took twenty-eight hours to overhaul her sufficiently to be able to open fire.

The action began on August the 6th, 1826, in Latitude 3° 22′ N., Longitude 4° 11′ E. The heavily armed *Prince of Guinea* put up such a desperate fight that, after two and a half hours' of close action, she was no nearer being captured than after the first broadside. Three of the *Hope*'s guns had been dismounted and her commander, who was serving the Long gun himself, had been wounded.

He now determined to run alongside the brig and board in spite of the great disparity in numbers, but he was too faint from loss of blood to head the boarders himself; young Pengelly, however, was only too delighted to take his place.

As the two vessels ground together, the British Bluejackets, with a thunderous cheer, swept over the low rail of the *Prince of Guinea*.

Pengelly at their head was shot in the side as he leaped over onto the brig's deck, but he never faltered for an instant. He was ably backed up by the assistant surgeon, who seems to have been as proficient with a cutlass as he was with a surgeon's knife. For a few minutes the clash of steel was sharp, but the motley crew of a Brazilian slaver, even though more than three to one, could not stand for long against the cut, slash and thrust of the trained fighting man, and presently they laid down their arms and begged for quarter.

They had suffered severely, thirteen being killed and eleven wounded, whilst down on the slave-deck three of the unhappy negroes lay dead and eleven were wounded.

Aboard the *Hope* the casualties were negligible, being put at three wounded, including the commander and second-in-command.

According to the Commodore's second report of the action, sixteen slaves were drowned in an attempt to swim to the boats of the *Hope*, and twelve more died on the passage to Sierra Leone—the report does not say if any of the wounded were amongst these.

Both Tucker and Pengelly were immediately promoted for this gallant action.

The *Hope*'s next capture was the Spanish schooner *Paulita*, four days out from Benin with a cargo of two hundred and twenty-one slaves. She was captured on the 6th of December in 5° 4′ N., 4° 42′ E., after a chase of several hours.

This time Tucker had to contend with disease, for smallpox and dysentry were found to be raging on the slave-deck, causing twenty-eight deaths before the schooner reached Sierra Leone.

On receiving the news of his promotion to commander, Tucker sailed for home, but before he left the coast, Commodore Bullen presented him with a watch with the inscription "liberated 1003 fellow creatures from the bonds of slavery".

As usual on promotion Tucker found himself out of employment for a time and then had to be content with a coastguard appointment. However, the year 1839 found him back on the coast in command of the sixteen-gun brig-sloop, *Wolverine*, with which vessel he captured no less than fourteen slavers.

Commodore Bullen's Report

I will bring this chapter to a close with a copy of Commodore Bullen's Report to the Admiralty of May the 22nd, 1827, dated from the *Maidstone* at the entrance of the Sierra Leone River:—

"I have the honour to acquaint you for information of my Lords Commissioners with particulars of my late cruise in the Bights of Benin and Biafra for the suppression of the slave trade.

On the 11th of March, I weighed from Accra Roads, intending to run down the different anchorages in the Bight of Benin in order to detect and detain vessels carrying on the trade under the Brazilian flag in direct opposition to the true intent and meaning of the treaty entered into with Portugal, and furnished with irregular licenses to touch at the Islands of St. Thomas and Prince's as designated in their Lordships' letter dated the 14th of January 1826[1].

On the evening of the 13th (March 1872) I came off to Whydah and commenced by detaining the *Trajano*; on the following day off Bagagny the *Venturoso* and *Carlotta* and off Ajuda the *Fontadoro*; on the 16th off Lagos the *Provindencia* and on the 22nd off the Benin River the *Conceicao Packet de Rio*, making a total of six vessels seized for carrying on the illegal traffic in non-conformity with the existing treaty in so short a distance.

The whole of these vessels, having valuable trade cargoes I instantly manned, armed annd despatched to Sierra Leone for adjudication in the Mixed Commissioned Court.

Standing in need of water, I made the best of my way to Prince's Island, where I arrived on April the 3rd. On the following day I was joined by the *North Star*[2].

From Captain Arabin I received the returns of his having captured the Spanish schooners, *Fama da Cuba* in the river Old Calabar with one hundred slaves on February the 7th, and the *Emilia* with two hundred and eighty two slaves in the river Bonny on January the 31st; also the Brazilian brigs, *Conceicao de Maria* with two hundred and thirty-two slaves off Lagos, four hours after she took them on board on the 4th March, and the *Silvenhina* at the entrance of the Old Calabar on the 12th March, making a total of eight hundred and eighty slaves in four vessels.

---

[1] This refers to the treaty with Portugal, concluded in 1826, which though recognising Brazil's independence, made her a party to Portugal's agreements with Great Britain with reference to the abolition of the slave trade.

[2] The *North Star* was one of the twenty-eight Donkey frigates, mounting twenty-eight guns and measuring five hundred tons. Sir William Symonds criticised these vessels very severely. He wrote that they could neither fight nor run away: that it was dangerous to be on board them and that their bad sailing was the chief cause of our ill success in the American War.

In addition also to the captures made by Captain Purchas of H.M. sloop, *Esk*, of the *Lynx* and *Invincible*, the former with two hundred and sixty-four and the latter with four hundred and forty slaves, fully detailed in my letter No. 15 dated the 20th of February, I this day received letters from him announcing his being necessitated to deviate from my orders and proceed to Sierra Leone before the appointed time for his officers and prize crews, in consequence of having fortunately detained the Brazilian vessels, *Venus*, with one hundred and nine slaves on the 6th of February, and *Dons Amigos*, with three hundred and seventeen on the 8th of February while cruising in the Bight of Benin.

Having dispatched the *North Star* to Sierra Leone for her officers and men detached in prizes, I left Prince's on the 8th of April with intention of examining the rivers in the Bight of Biafra before the expiration of my command: and on the 10th sent the pinnace and cutter, manned and armed, under command of Lieutenant Lyall, to search the Old Calabar.

The afternoon of the same day a suspicious vessel was seen from the masthead between me and the Island of Fernando Po. In consequence of light winds at dark I lost sight of her, but about 10 p.m. by aid of the moon she was again seen about seven or eight miles distant. At this instant, the wind being light, Lieutenant Morton, first of this ship and who has served with me ever since I commissioned the *Maidstone*, volunteered his services to take charge of the cutter and gig and endeavour to intercept her: and it is with feelings of great pleasure I acquaint their lordships that, after a hard and fatiguing pull, at midnight he succeeded in bringing to the Brazilian brig, *Creola*, with a cargo of three hundred and nine slaves, out two days from the Old Calabar river, and making a total of 2,494 liberated by the *Maidstone* alone since my command on this station.

During my stay I found that since my leaving here on the 11th of March no less than six Brazilians had passed for slave cargoes in the Bight of Benin, several making it a constant practice of now anchoring and getting their cargoes from Dutch Accra.

Being short of provisions and weak-handed from so many vessels away, as well as unable to spare the time, I dispatched the two gun-brigs, on their joining, to cruize for the interception of these vessels during my absence to windward.

The *Conflict*, Lieutenant Wakefield, had already detained two fine class vessels under the same circumstances of being furnished with irregular passports.

Having concluded my arrangements to leeward I weighed on the 6th instant from Port Antonio, Prince's Island, with my prize in tow for Sierra Leone, which river, after a very short passage of fifteen days and with loss of only twenty slaves since capture, I am just entering".

The *Maidstones* Commission

The *Maidstone* paid off on September the 15th, 1827. Her first lieutenant, Charles Morton whose service afloat from first joining in October 1807, had been under the command of the Commodore with the sole exception of the years 1812-1814, when Bullen was on half pay, was promoted.

Between May 1824 and June 1827 the *Maidstone* had captured nineteen vessels and liberated 2,595 slaves. 5 others had been condemned without slaves.

The squadron during Commodore Bullen's command had disposed of fifty-nine slavers and 1,081 slaves. This fine work was not accomplished without payment in British lives. The *Maidstone* lost seventy-two of her ship's company from fever during her commission and had twenty-nine lieutenants, four pursers and two surgeons appointed to her at different times.

Her last service was in co-operation with Lieutenant Colonel Sutherland in bringing the Ashanti war to a successful conclusion.

The Commodore, after being Superintendent of Pembroke Dockyard, where, as usual, he was exceedingly beloved, was appointed captain of the *Royal Sovereign* yacht.

In 1815 he had received the C.B.: in 1835 he was knighted and awarded the K.C.H.; and on April the 18th, 1839, he was advanced to the rank of Rear-Admiral, November the 9th, 1846, to Vice-Admiral and July the 30th, 1852 to Admiral.

CHAPTER IX

THE COAST OF AFRICA 1827-1830

"Come, messmate, and tip us your flipper,
Whilst I knot all my yarns up together
Here's yarns for the flag-ship and skipper,
And yarns of fresh gales and foul weather.
Here's yarns of the barge and each boat,
Here's yarns when the foe cried 'peccavi';
Here's yarns for the jollies afloat,
And a gallow's tough yarn for Old Davy".

Commodore Francis Augustus Collier

CAPTAIN Francis Augustus Collier, C.B., one of Nelson's happy band of heroes, was appointed commodore on the coast of Africa in place of Commodore Charles Bullen, with his broad pendant in the *Sybille,* forty-eight guns.

Collier, who was serving in Nelson's flagship at the Battle of the Nile, and afterwards in the *Fondroyant* under Sir Edward Berry, was considered one of the keenest and tautest officers in the Service.

His last piece of work had been the crushing of the pirates in the Persian Gulf, when commanding the *Liverpool,* fifty guns. In the official report he is spoken of as 'rendering the most ardent and efficient aid' to Major-General Sir William Grant Keir, who with three thousand troops was in charge of the shore end of the expedition in which Ras-ool-Kyma, the pirate town, was taken, its fortifications destroyed, and all its vessels burnt or sunk.

Lieutenant William Turner

Collier's first lieutenant in the *Sybille,* William Turner, was one of the most popular officers in the Service, albeit he was without any aristocratic label, being the son of the well-known Portsmouth wine merchant. He had already served a commission in the *Sybille,* when she bore the flag of Sir Charles Rowley in the West Indies; but he was not destined to remain long in her on the coast for the frigate's very first prize after her arrival out was to prove Turner's first step to fame.

The Famous *Black Joke*

This was a brig owned in Bahia, called the *Henriquetta,* which was the fastest and most successful slaver on the coast.

Between 1825 and 1827 she made six voyages, landed 3,040 negroes in Brazil and cleared £80,000 for her lucky owner. She was making her third voyage of the year.

It was a little after eight bells, midnight, on September the 6th, 1827, when the *Henriquetta* was first discovered, reaching off the land on the frigate's lee bow. There was a fine fresh breeze and the *Sybille* at once crowded sail in chase. The brig had only taken her cargo of five hundred and sixty nine slaves aboard a few hours previously; but, confident in the unrivalled speed of his vessel, her captain made the fatal mistake of trying to cross the frigate's bow in order to get to windward, and this daring move brought her within gun shot.

Though she was heeled under a heavy press of canvas with the spray flying over her weather cathead, the *Henriquetta* for all her speed could not out-distance the skipping balls from the *Sybille's* bow-chasers, and after several rounds had screamed through her rigging, she hove to in token of surrender.

Three weeks later, on September the 26th, a metamorphosised brig, with a slender pendant flying at her main-royal-masthead, could be seen lying at the Sierra Leone anchorage.

This was the *Sybille's* new tender, *Black Joke,* commanded by Lieutenant William Turner, with a complement of fifty-five men, and armed with a long eighteen-pounder on a pivot amidships.

Of all the slavers converted into slave catchers, the famous *Black Joke,* ex *Henriquetta,* was without a doubt by far the most successful.

She was not the first vessel to be given this curious name in the Royal Navy.

Origin of her Name

In 1793 there was a ten-gun lugger of that name attached to the fleet under Lord Howe. Two years later we find the same lugger under Admiral Duncan in the North Sea. In 1811 the French captured a hired cutter of four guns in the Channel, which had the name of *Black Joke,* and it is very likely that there were earlier vessels than these with this name on their trail boards.

It seems to have been quite a well-known term in the eighteenth century for a dance of the nature of an Irish jig. This jig went to an air which was sung in Chetwood's *The Lottery* (1732) in Guy's *Achilles* (1733) and in *Don Quixote of England* (1734).

In the same year the tune was used for the first song in the anonymous opera, *The Whim,* translated from the French and performed at Goodman's Fields. Again Henry Brereton Code used it for his widely known song *The Sprig of Shillelagh.*

That it was the name given to a dance tune does not explain the meaning of the two words, but I am told that 'joke' or 'jook' is an old north country word for duck, thus the *Black Joke* was probably the *Black Duck.*

So much for the name of the new brig tender, which was so soon to be dreaded by every slaver between the Gambia and the equator.

Unfortunately the *Black Joke* never left the coast of Africa, and her lines were never taken off, as would undoubtedly have been the case, had she ever been in a naval dockyard.

We can only conclude that she owed her existence to the brains of a Baltimore shipwright, for nowhere else at this date could vessels of her speed be turned out.

As regards her lines, we only have one thing to go on besides her extraordinary sailing powers. This is a statement made by one of her commanders, Lieutenant Ramsay. He declared that she would *forge astern in a calm.*

The usual effect upon the later clipper-ships of motion caused by a swell and of the flapping of sails was headway and not stern way.

Such vessels as the tea clippers, *Ariel, Titania, Spindrift,* and their like used to make three to four knots by the flap of their sails.

That *Black Joke* made stern way seems to prove that she was more akin to the modern racing yacht in her bow and stern lines, for many well-known prize winners have been found to tow lighter stern first than bow first.

According to contemporary reports her burthen was about two hundred and sixty tons. I have been lucky enough to find a note of her length and beam at the Admiralty library under the heading of 'tenders'. Here, her gundeck is given as 90 feet 10 inches, her beam extreme as 26 feet 7 inches, and beam for tonnage as 26 feet 3 inches.

That she was an extremely handsome little vessel to look at is proved by the well-known print of Huggin's picture.

Like all Baltimore vessels her scantlings were probably on the light side. Whilst she flew the pendant she was worked to the bone.

That she was not considered worth a refit was possibly due to the Admiralty's efforts at economy, but that her model was not preserved reflects upon both the Admiral commanding the station and the Lords of the Admiralty themselves, when it is remembered that her success as a slave catcher was not only the talk of the Service itself, but of shipping people generally.

The Ship-Sloop *Primrose*

Second only to the *Black Joke* in her success during Commodore Collier's period of command was the little ship-sloop *Primrose,* which was commissioned for the coast by Commander T. S. Griffinhoofe on August the 4th, 1827.

This vessel had already had an adventurous career. She was a member of that large family of eighteen-gun brigs, which owned the *Cruiser* of 1797 as their name ship, and did the work of the present day destroyer in the time of Howe, Jarvis, Hood and Nelson.

The *Primrose* was actually an improved *Cruiser,* of better model and sweeter lines.

The draught of her lines is signed by both Rule and Peake, and gives the following dimensions:—

Length between perpendiculars	108 feet
Length of keel for tonnage	87 feet
Breadth extreme	28 feet 7 inches
Depth in hold	13 feet 6 inches
Burthen in tons	$382^{47}/_{94}$
She was built at Portsmouth in 1809	

During her first commission she was commanded by C.G.R. Phillott, who after accompanying Sir Joseph Yorke to Lisbon, spent two hard years in the North Sea. Then she had some unpleasant convoy work escorting the Quebec trade.

It was on the 12th March, 1814, that the *Primrose* fought her extraordinary night action with the Falmouth packet, *Duke of Marlborough,* Captain John Bull, under the impression that she was an enemy ship.

Though the little packet brig only carried a broadside of popguns and a crew of thirty-two men, she held her own most valiantly until the mistake was discovered. Convinced that he had to do with an enemy, Captain Bull made every preparation for resistance. Boarding nettings were slung up and stuffed with spare sails, mattresses and hammocks. A spare topsail yard was lashed across the stern as a boarding boom, and her topsail sheets were stoppered.

It was a case of flags being indistinguishable and night signals in the shape of blue lights unseen. Captain Phillott had, of course, to stand his courtmartial and receive a censure, whilst the gallant Captain Bull was presented with a sword of honour. Captain Phillott continued to command the *Primrose* until 1818, when he was posted after a West Indian commission.

In 1824 the beautiful little brig was converted to ship-rig along with many others of her class. This, it was contended, turned a smart-sailing efficient brig into a slow inefficient ship, and there was much searching of hearts amongst the peppery old hands.

It is impossible to say how much the sailing of the *Primrose* suffered—it would appear to be very little, if her success in catching slavers is taken into account. But it was soon proved that these conversions spoilt the little eighteen-gun sloops. For instance, the *Pandora* after conversion to ship-rig took part in the cruise of the Experimental Squadron of 1825, and her crew contended that she had completely lost her sailing power; besides being deeper in the water owing to the additional weight aloft, she actually spread less canvas when on a wind by one hundred and fifty feet.

There was a brig, too, which gaver her name to *Fly Martin,* that Admiral who, when commanding the Mediterranean fleet was renamed Pincher Martin.

The *Fly* as a brig was a flyer; but as a ship young Billy Martin, the son of Admiral Sir T. Byam Martin, found her a precious dull sailer, and concentrated all his efforts into making her a smart ship at drill.

From 1824 to July 1827 the *Primrose* was on the West Indian station under commanders John Stoddart, George Vernon Jackson and Octavius Vernon Harcourt. On paying off, she was at once refitted for the coast of Africa.

Successful Commission of the *Esk*

With the arrival of the *Primrose* on the coast, the *Esk* went home. Captain Purchas had had a most successful commission, in fact Commodore Collier wrote in his report that she had captured more slavers and lost fewer men than any other ship in the Squadron. Between July 1825 and February 1827 the *Esk* had captured nine Brazilian, Dutch and Spanish slavers and liberated 2,249 slaves.

Commander Purchas finished up his commission by helping to settle the new naval stations at Fernando Po. He arrived at Spithead on May the 1st, 1828 with a good freight of ivory and gold dust, and was at once posted for his good work.

Black Joke* and Spanish Privateer *Providencia

It was not until January 1828 that the *Black Joke* began her spectacular career as a British cruiser.

She sailed from Sierra Leone on the 5th in company with the *Sybille* and *Esk.* A week later a schooner was sighted working off the land. All three ships immediately made sail in chase. The slaver was a smart sailer, and she played every possible trick that seamanship could devise even to throwing her guns overboard. The frigate and the sloop were soon run out of sight, but to her astonishment the slaver found that she could not shake off the new addition to the West African squadron, and on January the 12th, Lieutenant Turner had the satisfaction of capturing his first prize, the Spanish schooner, *Gertrudes,* with one hundred and fifty five slaves on board.

The next adventure of the *Black Joke* was by no means so satisfactory.

Early on the morning of April the 2nd, 1828, a little before daylight a large brig was sighted not far from the island of St. Thomas. Directly she was chased, the brig stood away from the *Black Joke,* whose enthusiastic crew had already begun to reckon up their prize money when, to their astonishment, as the sun came blazing up over the horizon, the stranger tacked and stood down towards the *Sybille's* tender.

As soon as the two vessels had closed, both hove to within hail of each other. The stranger then sung out to say that he would send a boat aboard the *Black Joke.* Preparations to launch a boat could be seen going on board her, and then the same voice had to admit that he had not a boat that would swim, the sun had evidently played havoc with their planking. Whereupon Lieutenant Turner, who evidently took greater care of his boats, sent his master's mate, E. L. Harvey, and two seamen across to the stranger.

As soon as the mate had disappeared over the brig's rail, one of her officers and five men jumped into the *Black Joke's* boat and rowed off to her.

Lieutenant Turner received the officer politely at the gangway. The latter with very little ceremony at once demanded to see the tender's papers.

By this time Turner had become anxious about his men, being far from reassured by the appearance of this officer and his wild-looking seamen, but he produced his commission and Commodore Collier's order to cruise. It then appeared that two days before the Spanish brig, which was named the *Providencia,* had been boarded by the *Sybille,* and that her Captain had shown the Commodore his commission from the King of Spain to cruise as a privateer against the vessels of the South American states.

The domineering officer of the *Providencia* next demanded that Commodore Collier's order to cruise should be sent aboard the Spaniard so that the signature could be compared with that which the Commodore had signed on the back of the *Providencia's* commission.

This was too much for Turner's patience, and he not only refused point blank, but detained the astonished officer and two of his dusky seamen as hostages for Harvey and his two bluejackets.

The next move came from the captain of the privateer, who calmly suggested that fifteen bluejackets should be exchanged for the fifteen of his crowd of dagoes, and the two ships should then sail in company to Prince's Island.

To this extraordinary proposal Turner's refusal was even more stiff and curt.

Then the privateer, without any warning, let fly her whole broadside of seven guns into the *Black Joke.* Turner at once filled his topsails and, taking up a raking position on the Spaniard's bow, pumped grape from his Long Tom into him for two whole hours.

At the end of this time the *Providencia,* which was almost unrigged, with spars wounded, sails torn and running rigging hanging in bights, hoisted a flag of truce and returned the *Black Joke's* master's mate and two bluejackets.

These three had had a most unpleasant time during the action, and would undoubtedly have been killed by the cut-throat crew of the brig had not her captain intervened in their favour.

The *Providencai* refused to disclose her casualties, which were heavy. The crew of the *Black Joke* escaped scot-free owing to the usual dago practice of aiming high.

It then appeared that the *Providencia* had mistaken the *Black Joke* for a Columbian privateer, for which she was searching.

It was a costly mistake, for, whilst the tender sent her hands aloft to mend her damaged rigging, the Spaniard lowered her flag to half-mast and set about burying her dead.

This two hours' action at close range between the *Black Joke* with one long gun and fifty-five seamen and the *Providencia* with fourteen guns and eighty men was the first of a number of duels in which the tender invariably came out on top.

That no official notice was taken of this incident was a proof of the condition of the high seas as this date, when all kinds of letters of marque, sporting strange unknown flags, swarmed from Florida to the River Plate and from the Rock of Lisbon to the Cape.

Black Joke Captures *Vengador* (Ex *Prince of Guinea*)

The cruising of the *Black Joke* yielded no further excitement until the 16th of May, 1828, when she captured the Brazilian brig *Vengador,* mounting eight guns with a crew of forty-five men and no less than six hundred and forty five slaves on board.

The *Vengador,* which offered no resistance, turned out to be the *Prince of Guinea,* which had been captured two years before by the *Hope.*

At this date it was the custom to sell condemned slavers at Sierra Leone. As a rule their agents at once bought them back and in a very short while they were at their old games under new names.

Sometimes slavers were even sold at Lloyds. This stupid proceeding, which was popular because it was profitable from a prize money point of view, was put an end to in 1836, when an Act of Parliament was passed, which forbade the selling of captured slavers.

Black Joke Captures the Pirate *Presidente* and her Prize

On the 27th of August, Lieutenant Turner paid a visit to the Whydah anchorage. As the *Black Joke,* which by this time was well-known all along the slave coast, headed in, three vessels, two schooners and a brig, hurriedly weighed their anchors and boldly sailed out to meet the man-of-war. The largest of these was a heavily armed schooner, which was seen to be directing the other two by signals.

The *Black Joke* was soon within hailing distance of her, but her reply to Turner's hail was a broadside, which was instantly returned by the brig. The other two vessels at once altered course to assist their consort, but Turner handled his swift clipper with such skill that he was able to extricate himself from a very unequal conflict. He then stood off under easy sail, the large schooner following cautiously in his wake without attempting to renew the fight. That night, when the moon rose at half past eleven, the schooner was sighted on *Black Joke's* weather quarter, but her consorts were out of sight.

The drum was immediately beat to action and the watch below came tumbling up on deck. Turner at once tacked the tender, and placing her cleverly athwart the hawse of the oncoming schooner, brought her to close action. The latter, however, was ably handled and again and again avoided the man-of-war's efforts to run alongside and board.

The action had continued for more than an hour with great spirit on both sides, when the schooner suddenly bore up under every sail he could set in an endeavour to escape.

This gave the *Black Joke* a stern chase, but by 4 a.m. after a heavy fire of both round, grape and musketry, Turner at length succeeded in running aboard his opponent, though the two vessels were going over seven knots through the water. With a deafening cheer and flashing cutlasses the active bluejackets hurled themselves over the low rail of the schooner.

The enemy stood to it with hanger, pike and battle-axe, and for some minutes a desperate hand-to-hand struggle took place, the men-of-war's men being greatly outnumbered.

However as soon as their Captain fell to the deck mortally wounded, the schooner's crew laid down their arms and cried for quarter.

There were no slaves on board and the schooner turned out to be the well known pirate *Presidente,* mounting one long pivot and six broadside guns, with a crew of ninety-five men, thirty of whom, including their captain, were killed or wounded.

Against this heavy casualty list, the *Black Joke* had only one man killed, which speaks well for the cutlass drill aboard the tender.

In the cabin of the *Presidente,* Lieutenant Turner found a pirate signal book; and, when at daylight a brig was sighted upon his weather quarter, he hoisted the private signal 'to close'. This was obeyed without hesitation by the other vessel, which was quickly captured. She turned out to be the Portuguese brig, *Hosse,* which had been taken and plundered a few days before by the pirate schooner. The *Presidente* was sent to Sierra Leone in charge of a prize crew, but was wrecked on the passage up. Her crew were tried as pirates, but were acquitted for want of sufficient evidence; the *Presidente* also had a privateer's commission which, however, had long since expired, and in any case this did not entitle her to capture a Portuguese vessel.

The *Black Joke* was awarded salvage for the recapture of the *Hosse.*

The tender's last piece of service was under the command of Lieutenant Turner took place on September the 14th, 1828, when she assisted the *Primrose* in capturing the *Zephorina* with two hundred and eighteen slaves on board.

On November the 14th, 1828, Lieutenant Turner handed over the *Black Joke* on promotion to another officer of the *Sybille,* Lieutenant Henry Downes.

During his command of the *Black Joke,* Turner had liberated nine hundred and nine negroes and earned a nice sum in prize money for his shipmates aboard the *Sybille,* who presented him with a sword, valued at two hundred guineas, and bearing the following inscription:—

"A token of respect and regard from Commodore Collier, the Captain, officers and ships company of H.M.S. *Sybille* to Captain Wm. Turner for his zeal and gallantry while Lieutenant commanding the *Black Joke* tender".

Black Joke Captures *Almirante*

In August 1828, a very superior slaver had dropped her anchor in Lagos Roads. This was the clipper brig, *Almirante,* flying Spanish colours, pierced for twenty guns, but only mounting fourteen, four of which were long nines and the rest eighteen-pounder Govers.

Of 360 tons burthen, she had formerly been ship-rigged under the name of *Oroonoko,* but had been altered to a brig at a cost of 35,000 dollars.

Being very notorious on the coast, Commodore Collier was very anxious for her capture, and gave orders for the *Black Joke* to keep a close watch upon her. Though the latter was one hundred tons smaller, manned by fifty seven seamen, marines and kroomen as against the slaver's eighty ruffians of all nationalities and armed with her long pivoting eighteen and little twelve-pounder carronade against the slaver's Govers and long nines, no one in the coast of Africa squadron had the least doubt of her being able to take on the big Spaniard—yet the captain of the *Almirante* laughed at the idea of the *Black Joke* capturing his splendid vessel, and even boasted, amongst the slaving fraternity of what he would do to the little man-of-war tender; and whilst he was ashore buying slaves, he gave his mate orders to weigh and stand out to sea, ready for battle, should a cruiser be sighted.

The *Almirante* began to embark her slaves in January 1829. On the 19th of that month the *Black Joke,* which had been hovering about in the offing, ran into the Roads of Lagos and took note of the fact the slaver was about half loaded.

Lieutenant Downes then stood off until he was once more out of sight of the anchorage.

On the 28th of January the *Almirante* sailed for Havana with four hundred and sixty-six slaves on board.

Lieutenant Downes had carefully calculated her most likely course, which was not, of course, the direct course for the Antilles: and his calculations proved to be correct, for at daybreak on the 31st the slaver was sighted from the *Black Joke's* masthead, standing to the southward under a press of sail. One may imagine the keenness and excitement aboard the little man-of-war, as she gave chase to the vessel, which she had been patiently watching for since the previous August.

The wind was very light, and by half past nine had died away altogether. "Out Sweeps" was, at once, the order aboard the *Black Joke,* then for nine hours until six p.m. the crew of the tender strained at their long ash oars and actually rowed the little brig thirty miles.

"About 5 p.m.", wrote the commander of the *Black Joke,* "we had neared the chase sufficiently to smack a shot at her, and at 5.45 she shortened sail, fired a gun to windward and hoisted Spanish colours: afterwards she wore twice; giving us her broadside each time; but, though from having no bulwarks our men were all exposed, without effect".

As the sun set and darkness closed in, Lieutenant Downes cleverly manoeuvred under his sweeps so as to baffle every attempt of the *Almirante* to rake him, for he did not consider it prudent to take his vessel into close range of the slaver's powerful broadside.

So the night passed and dawn on February the 1st found the two brigs still becalmed and within a mile and a half of each other.

No doubt by this time after their long hours at the sweeps the *Black Joke's* crew were badly in need of rest, and Lieutenant Downes wisely gave them time to recruit their strength.

All through that long hot morning the two antagonists lay idle, all possible preparations for action having long ago been made by both crews.

Then at 12.30 p.m. a breeze sprang up from the Westward and the *Almirante* headed as if she meant to close with the *Black Joke* and wipe out her puny opponent. Outnumbered in both men and guns, Downes determined at all costs to outmanoeuvre his big enemy. First of all, he tacked to get upon her weather quarter, then after a short stretch, he tacked again and edged down to close. By 2.30, he had gained the position he wanted, within grape range under her stern.

The Captain of the *Almirante* immediately wore round and let fly with his larboard broadside. Three tremendous cheers came from the *Black Joke,* and off went her Long Tom and carronade, double shotted and carefully aimed for the slaver's crowded deck.

At 3.15 finding that he was so heavily out-gunned Lieutenant Downes determined to put the struggle to the test by the time-honoured British method of boarding. The helm of the *Black Joke* was put up and her sails trimmed. The quartermaster was ordered to lay the tender alongside the enemy, but before this manoeuvre could be carried out, the wind fell away to a flat calm.

However the *Almirante* was able to get her starboard broadside to bear and let fly again with round and grape. This broadside might have been disastrous to the *Black Joke,* but it was badly directed and passed overhead.

At 3.30 a light air put the flogging sails to sleep, the slaver at once made another attempt to wear round. The vessels closed, but the *Black Joke* was much the handier craft at manoeuvring in a light air, and Downes was able to get into a commanding position upon the *Almirante's* larboard quarter, from which he raked the slaver for twenty minutes, making such good practice that when the commodore inspected the quarter and stern of the Spaniard afterwards, he vowed he had 'never in his life witnessed a more beautiful specimen of good gunnery'. Indeed, at the end of this deadly twenty minutes, the *Almirante's* stern frame and taffrail had been turned into a sieve, her fire was silenced, and a hail came across the water announcing that she had struck her flag.

On going aboard to take possession, the prize crew found the deck of the Spaniard abandoned to the dead and dying, the men having been mown down beside their guns at half-pistol shot. Of her officers only the third mate remained alive, the Captain, first and second mates and boatswain being all killed, whilst the total casualties of the slaver were fifteen killed and thirteen wounded as against six men wounded aboard the *Black Joke.* During the last few minutes the tender's fire had been so hot that the survivor's had deserted their guns and taken refuge amongst the slaves below.

This was one of the most determined actions ever fought by a slaver. On drawing the charges from the guns afterwards, a round shot and two of grape were found in each. The Spanish captain, however, made the usual mistake of all Latin nations of aiming high in order to dismast his opponent, with the hope that, then he could sink her at his leisure; but the showers of musket balls from the despised carronade of the *Black Joke* made a clean sweep of the *Almirante's* decks.

The latter had several men in her tops, who had been promised special rewards for every officer they could pick off. She was found to be in excellent fighting order, all the running gear had been unrove, from the fairleads on the lower rigging and frapped snugly round the masts. The topsail sheets were stoppered, the peak halliards were stoppered in two places, the lifts replaced by chain slings, and every bit of lumber on deck thrown overboard. The damage to the hulls, masts, sails and rigging was severe in both ships.

The starboard main shrouds of the slaver were cut off at the same level as if by the single blow of an axe. This turned out to be the work of the black cook of the man-of-war, who had vowed to do his bit as a free African. He had somehow managed to insert two fathoms of chain into the muzzle of the long guns as it was being loaded, and this chain shot had taken disastrous effect upon the *Almirante's* main shrouds.

Whilst the dead were being hove overboard and the decks cleaned up, a shrewd bluejacket suddenly sung out to his mate, who was about to slide a body through the open port:—

"Avast there! That fellow's an officer. Let's overhaul him a bit before he goes overboard".

They did so and found a belt, heavy with doubloons round the dead man's waist.

The *Almirante* proved a valuable prize. After being condemned, she was repurchased by the slaver's agents at Sierra Leone and was soon back in her old trade.

Like Turner, Downes was generously rewarded by his grateful commodore. This time it was an object d'art in the shape of a vase of polished 'Heart of oak' with a silver-gilt ornamentation and the inscription:—

"A tribute of admiration and respect to Lieutenant Henry Downes for his gallant conduct, when in command of the tender *Black Joke*".

The famous little brig's next capture was the Brazilian brigantine *Carolina* with four hundred and twenty slaves on board. This took place on the 6th of March, 1829, and shortly afterwards her commander, having suffered severely from the climate, was invalided home.

He had released eight hundred and seventy five negroes from bondage and, on his arrival home was at once promoted to commander.

He was succeeded by Lieutenant Edward Iggulden Parrey, an officer of the *Primrose* who, a short while before, had distinguished himself, in command of the sloops boats.

Saucy Jack Captured by *Primrose's* Boats

Parrey's first capture with the *Primrose's* boats was a very notorious Portuguese slaver of four guns, forty men and two hundred and five slaves. This vessel turned out to be the famous American privateer, *Saucy Jack,* which during the war had captured no less than six ships, six brigs, nine schooners and two sloops. This was surely an ignominious end for the most successful privateer out of Charleston. Shortly after the capture of the schooner *Saucy Jack,* Lieutenant Parrey took the boats of the *Primrose* up the Nunez on an exploring expedition.

Up the Nunez

At this date the Nunez was a favourite slave river. Once inside the shoals and sandbanks at the river's mouth, it was fairly easy navigation up to Rappace. Low mud-banks, covered with the repulsive forms of alligators soon gave way to the overhanging boughs of the virgin forest, full of chattering monkeys and screaming parrots.

On the north side of the sluggish stream the natives were warlike and uncertain, and Parrey kept away from this bank. At the Sand Island anchorage he found two slavers, one Spanish and the other French—these with no slaves on board could not be touched. Opposite the native town of bamboo huts a Liverpool brig, named the *Locheil,* swung to her anchor. Nobody could be seen aboard her and she had the most dishevelled appearance with blistered sides, rigging anyhow, and the paintwork peeling off her deckhouses. On boarding her Lieutenant Parrey found her captain, mate and her whole crew lying dead in their berths below.

After the unpleasant task of burying the dead, Parrey weighed her anchor, took the brig out of the river and handed her over to the *Primrose* which convoyed her to Sierra Leone, where her agent paid over one hundred and ninety pounds in salvage.

Dutch Galliot Slaver ex English Yacht

Parrey's next adventure was up the Cachao river in charge of the pinnace. After a hard pull against the strong ebb a Dutch galliot was surprised taking her slaves aboard and quickly made a prize on January the 15th, 1829.

This vessel turned out to be an ex-English yacht, which had once belonged to Alderman Sir William Curtis, a keen member of the Royal Yacht Club, when she was called *Die Yonge*

Vrou. In her prime this galliot not only cruised with the Royal Yacht Squadron but often accompanied George IV when he went afloat in the yacht *Royal George.*

Her come-down in the world was as great as that of the *Saucy Jack.* She was disguised under the name of *Aurelia* and had thirty eight slaves on board.

Soon after her capture Parrey was picked upon by the Commodore for the coveted command of the *Black Joke.*

Cornelia Captures *Venus*

It must not be supposed that the *Black Joke* was the only tender to distinguish herself at this date. The *Eden,* twenty-six guns, Captain William Fitzwilliam Owen, had a brig tender named *Cornelia,* armed with one long seven-pounder pivot gun and two six pounders. She gave Samuel Mercer his first push up the ladder, for it was whilst under his command that she captured the notorious piratical slaver *Venus* of three hundred tons, eleven guns and eighty-eight officers and men off the old Calabar.

Mercer was only an acting lieutenant at the time and this capture procured him his promotion.

There is an interesting model of the *Venus* to be seen in the musuem of the Royal United Sevice Institution at Whitehall, which was presented by the son of Samuel Mercer. The *Venus* was captured by surprise on November the 16th, 1828.

Mercer's successor in the command of the *Cornelia* was Henry Kellett, then first lieutenant of the *Eden.*

This officer afterwards became very distinguished, first of all as a surveyor, then for his gallantry in the first Chinese war, and finally as an Arctic explorer.

In February 1829 Kellett captured the slaver *Mensagera,* on the bar of the Bonny river. This was a dangerous place, where the assistant surgeon and ten men of the *Victor* were drowned in 1825.

The bay between Fouche Point and Rough Corner Point is encumbered with sandbanks, through which run the shifting channels forming the mouths of the New Calabar and Bonny rivers.

In those early days there were no helps to navigation, and a lookout on the foreyard and a leadsman in the chains were always a necessity long before reaching the first bar.

The Tenders *Little Bear, Paul Pry* and *Dull Ass*

Another tender which did good work in 1828, was one belonging to the *North Star,* which was aptly named the *Little Bear.* On October the 30th she captured the slavers *Arcenia* and *Estrella do mar* in 3.50 N 9.30 E.

The successes of the *Black Joke, Cornelia* and *Little Bear* induced Commodore Collier to buy two more slavers after they had been condemned at Sierra Leone.

The first of these was a schooner, which he renamed the *Paul Pry,* the second was the *Black Nymph,* a fine brig of between three and four hundred tons, which he renamed the *Dallas,* as a compliment to a service friend of long standing—unfortunately this name became transformed in the Service into the *Dull Ass,* in spite of the fact that the brig had been considered one of the fastest slavers on the coast. The fun-loving bluejackets soon had other variations of *Paul Pry* in use, such as the *Peeping Tom* and the *Little Inquisitive.*

A Case of Prize Money Law

One of the captures of the *Paul Pry* caused an important case in the Admiralty Court. This was the *Donna Barbara,* taken in St. George's Bay on March the 15th, 1829 with three hundred and fifty slaves bound to the Brazils. Acting-Lieutenant Brown, the commander of the *Paul Fry,* handed the slaver over to Lieutenant E. Harvey, who had been sent up the coast with orders for the tender in one of the *Sybille's* boats. Harvey took the *Donna Barbara* to Sierra Leone, she was condemned by the Mixed British and Brazilian Commission, and the slaves emancipated.

Then Sir Charles Robinson, the Admiralty judge, decreed that the commander, officers and crew of the *Sybille* were not entitled to a moiety of the proceeds of the slave ship nor to the bounties on the slaves.

The Commodore at once appealed against this decision, which was against all rule and custom in the Royal Navy regarding private tenders ever since the days when Nelson commanded the tenders, *Gayton* and *Little Lucy*.

The King's Advocate in his defence stated that the *Paul Pry* was fifteen hundred miles from the *Sybille* when she made the capture, and contended that she was not a member of the squadron which the Commodore commanded.

The Counsel for the *Sybille,* in his advocacy of the frigate's rights, declared:—

"The practice of allowing boats belonging to ships of war to go in quest of slave vessels had been productive of the best results. During the seven years prior to the adoption of this plan the whole squadron only captured 9,679 slaves, while in the three years since the adoption of the plan 12,470 slaves had been seized and emancipated".

As was only to be expected the Court reversed Robinson's decision and gave the prize money to the *Sybille.*

Paul Pry in a Tornado

The last piece of service on the part of the *Paul Pry* ended most unfortunately.

After a chase since daylight, the little tender by four p.m. was almost within a range of a large armed slaver. The brass six-pounder, mounted amidships, which was the tender's only weapon, was being got ready for the usual warning shot whilst aft on the quarter-deck the small arms, in the shape of dozen muskets, lay ready loaded with their muzzles pointing forward. The breeze was freshening, and the commander of the *Paul Pry* kept taking his eyes off the chase to look to leeward, where an ominous black arch of cloud was rapidly rising above the horizon.

This arch was the sure sign of an approaching tornado.

"See all clear for shortening sail" sung out Browne. Then in the same breath, as he turned his eyes to the chase. "But give her a shot first".

Bang went the six-pounder, with the peculiar report of a brass gun, and, as the muzzle had been well greased, a ring of smoke followed the ball in the direction of the slaver.

The crew of the *Paul Pry* had just time to note the splash, as the shot plunged into the sea in the wake of the slaver, when again came the urgent command of Lieutenant Browne:—

"In fore-royal! Stand by everything! Shorten sail!"

As he spoke, the spars of the schooner came upright, the canvas flogged the masts and then hung listless, a sudden chilly damp made itself felt—this was the usual moment of calm before the tornado. Then came a resounding crash and a steely-blue zigzaging streak of lightning from out of the blackness overhead; with it came the wind, hissing, roaring, screaming. It took the *Paul Pry* aback, and over she went to port until the water, rushing through the bulwark ports, was up to the hatch coamings.

"Drop the peak! Trice up the tack! Hard up the helm!" Came the orders. Then as the schooner began to pay off, she slowly righted. And now the floodgates of heaven were opened and down came the rain.

The noise of it made the last order of the Lieutenant almost inaudible—"Square the yards!" He yelled at the top of his voice, and even as the men ran to the braces, they were stricken.

The pile of small arms aft, which had been protected from the rain by a tarpaulin, suddenly began going off. The mate, who was second in command, was the first to fall with both legs shattered below the knees by musket balls. And he was followed by several of the crew. It is difficult to picture the scene of horror and confusion. The black, gloomy heavens, spouting their tropical rain, were split every few seconds by shafts of lightning. The ship shuddered under the shock of the terrific clap and clatter and reverberating rumble of the thunder; her decks resounded with the patter of rain, each drop of which made the noise of a shrapnel ball falling on a tin pan; the wind screamed, and howled through the rigging, whilst loose ropes' ends flogged against spar and sail, yet distinguishable in the midst of all this hurly-burly came the deep groaning of the wounded men.

The chase, which had disappeared into the murk, was forgotten—Sails and wounded men had to be attended to. Apparently there was no assistant surgeon on board. The mate was in the worst case, for his mangled legs were spouting blood. Tourniquets of spunyarn were hurriedly applied, and he was carried below. Then a council of Lieutenant, gunner, bosun and steward decided that amputation was immediately necessary. The French cook undertook the terrible job: with his carving knife he cut the shattered parts away; and with clever seamen's hands his assistants took up the arteries and strapped and padded the stumps, then he turned his attention to the other wounded men.

As the various wounds were being dressed, night came down; the tornado had passed on, leaving a light wind and confused rolling sea, in which the *Paul Pry* tumbled and tossed to the agony of the sufferers. When daybreak came, the horizon was bare, there was no sign of the slaver. Browne at once altered course for Fernando Po. Luckily one of the corvettes of the squadron was found there and the wounded men were at once removed to her.

A few day later the Commodore arrived, and, on learning of the sad happening aboard the unlucky *Little Inquisitive,* sold her out of the Service.

Dallas Captures *Madre De Dios*

Unlike the *Black Joke,* neither the *Paul Pry* nor the *Dallas* made much prize money for the *Sybille.* Possibly the fact that they were commanded by oldsters—master's mates, who had lost much of their fire, and all hope of promotion, instead of smart young lieutenants like the *Black Joke's* commanders, had something to do with it. But certainly both the schooner and the brig had the name of being unlucky.

The *Dallas,* however, ended up her service with a really good prize after a long spell of chasing slavers that were either empty or protected by the French flag.

It was the rule aboard all cruisers on the African coast for the signalman on duty to proceed to the masthead at break of day.

One clear morning, when the *Dallas* was barely moving in the lightest of air, down from aloft came the welcome cry of "Sail Ho!"

The eagle-eyed singleman announced that the vessel in sight was a schooner: presently he sang out that he could detect the white splash of sweeps at work. But for three hours the *Dallas* crept along as fast as the chase without having recourse to sweeping. Then the breeze failed altogether and the order went forth:—"Haul up the courses; out sweeps".

The bluejacket of the present day has no conception of this hard duty of rowing a three hundred ton vessel in the tropics for hours on end.

The method usually adopted was this. After the sweeps had been passed out of the ports, the looms were swiftered together, so that the blades should cut the water at equal intervals, and the time was kept by beat of drum.

It is not to be wondered at that the sailor of the sail was as thin as a lath, yet from head to foot one mesh of beautifully firm whip-cord muscles.

Hours of pulling at long sweeps in the broiling sun needed such stamina as cannot be produced by modern artificial means.

Aboard the *Dallas* the second-in-command was an Irish mid, and he did his best to stimulate the rowers by calling out in his rich brogue:—

"Now for it, bhoys! Now for it! A gold chain or a wooden leg!"

In the short-handed tender it was a case of all hands at the sweeps: and all day the sweeping continued without an easy, except for an occasional dash to the scuttle butt for a mouthful of tepid water.

As the sun went under, the welcome breeze came ruffling along on the water, the idle sails were once more filled, the sweeps were laid in, and the men threw themselves down on the deck for a well-earned rest.

When last seen at dusk, the slaver's hull could just be distinguished from the deck of the *Dallas*. The question was, what course would the slaver take throught the night? She might bear up and when well to leeward, haul off the land again, or she might stand on for a few hours and then tack, keeping her wind, or she might down all sail and trust to the tender running past her without seeing her.

The Commander of the *Dallas* decided to bear up and run before the wind until midnight and then make sail and work off shore till daylight.

This course of action worked successfully. At daylight the chase was visible about seven miles in shore. The wind was light, the water smooth, and the brig slipped along so cleanly that only the passing bubbles told of her speed.

All day the chase continued with the *Dallas* slowly gaining until by sunset the two vessels were only two miles apart. The night fell down black and moonless, and again the chase was lost to sight. But this time the slaver, being well in the Bight, could no longer bear up, but either had to hold her wind or lay to.

At 8 p.m. the *Dallas* tacked and stood close-hauled off shore, and at daybreak the schooner again showed in shore of the brig. There was a moderate breeze all day and once again the *Dallas* slowly gained. Towards sunset the low land to leeward of Lagos became visible. Still the slaver continued to stand in until it looked as if she was bent on running ashore.

She evidently drew less water than the *Dallas,* which hung on with the lead going until after dark. Then at last came the order:—

"See all clear for going about".

The words were scarcely out of the Lieutenant's mouth before the mid on lookout with a nightglass glued to his eye sung out:—

"She's standing across our bows."

The breeze was freshening. The slaver had gone about in hopes of being able to cross the man-of-war unobserved.

The next order was:—

"Get the gun ready and give her a shot as she comes upon the bow".

The Long Tom was almost loaded to the muzzle. The order to fire was given—The ball sped on its journey, but no effect could be seen.

Directly the *Dallas* was in the schooner's wake, she was put round on to the same tack. The breeze by this time had so increased that both vessels were dangerously heeled. However the brig continued to gain though she could not hold quite so good a wind.

The gun was fired, when it could be brought to bear without the helm having to be eased. Slowly the brig crept nearer until suddenly the well-known smell of the black man assailed the nostrels of her crew, and brought the welcome intelligence that the chase had slaves on board.

Soon the slaver was within musket range, and the marines received orders to try and pick off the man at the helm. This caused the schooner's helmsman to yaw about in his attempt to avoid the bullets, and as soon as the tender obtained an overlap on the slaver's lee quarter, there came the welcome hail of:—

"We strike! we surrender!"

"Let go everything then". Ordered the *Dallas*'s Commander.

"We can't unless you cease fire".

The marines grounded their muskets. Then, as each vessel rounded into the wind with thundering canvas, each commander began to roar out rapid orders for taking in sail.

In these modern days it is not necessary for a sailor to have, what used to be known as 'a reeftopsail voice', but in the last days of sail this was considered a very necessary attribute in a watch officer.

The bellowing of the after guard, the hauling cries of the Spaniards and the clatter of shaking canvas, were soon almost drowned by the shrieks and yells which came from the frightened blacks in the hold of the slaver.

Ten minutes later and the jolly boat of the *Dallas* was alongside the slaver, which turned out to be the *Madre de Dios*. There were three hundred and sixty slaves aboard her. The Long Tom and musketry of the brig had done some damage aboard her, besides shattering the wrist of a poor negress with a babe at her breast. The helmsman, who had stuck to his post since sundown, had been killed and some of the crew had been wounded.

Such was the end of a chase which had lasted for over sixty hours.

Loss of the *Redwing* in a Tornado

Considering the large sail-plans of our brigs of war, it speaks well for the seamanship of their officers that so few were overwhelmed by the fierce breath of the West African tornado. But in 1828 the eighteen-gun brig-sloop, *Redwing,* disappeared and her fate was not cleared up for over a dozen years.

At last in the year of 1841 the captain of the Spanish slave schooner, *Flor de Porto Rico* informed Don Leon John Banes, Governor of the Island of St. Vincent, Cape Verds, that he had seen the *Redwing* in chase of two slavers.

At the approach of a tornado this slave captain wisely lowered every sail, but the *Redwing* and two other slavers carried on: and when the storm struck them, they all three capsized in full view of the *Flor de Porto Rico,* not a soul being saved.

Don Leon passed on this information to Commander Denman of the brig-of-war, *Wanderer,* being one of thoses Spanish grandees, who were very well disposed towards British Naval officers.

A Pelter Brig and an Old Sea Dog

A vessel which did a great deal of hard work upon the coast in the eighteen twenties with rather disappointing results was the little one hundred and eighty one ton, twelve-gun, brig, known in the Service as the "Pelter" brig.

Of such were the *Thistle* commanded by Robert Hagan, the *Snapper,* commanded by Christopher Knight, which in 1821 sailed sixty miles up the Old Calabar River, the *Swinger* and *Clinker* commanded in turn by George William Matson from November 1825 to Ocotober 1830, the *Conflict,* commanded by George Smithers, and the *Plumper* commanded by John Adams.

These little vessels were the laughing-stock of the swift slave brigs and schooners, which, whilst waiting for their caroes, often came out from such anchorages as Whydah and Lagos and amused themselves by trying their 'rate of sailing' against the 'Pelters', thus finding out the exact qualities of these tiny men-of-war and their cruising station.

As one Naval officer put it:— "A pug-dog after a hare would be a no more ridiculous sight than a fourteen-gun pelter in smooth water after a slaver".

These old brigs of the Napoleonic era, war-worn from much hard work, as most of them were, were generally commanded by lieutenants, who had been knocking about as long as their ships, and were well-known characters in the Service.

Typical of his type was George Matson, previously first lieutenant of the *Esk,* who was known as old 'Rough and Ready'. He was one of those old sea dogs who from long service afloat was never at his ease ashore.

As he put it in his quaint way:—"There's no spring or elasticity about dry land. Give me something for the sole of my foot on blue water and you may keep the land and welcome. Born at sea, bred at sea, I desire to die and to be buried at sea. I've made many a meal of fish, it is but fair that fish should make a meal of me".

Matson was the kind of officer that in now quite extinct. He was wont to wonder how people could be content to remain on one spot of land, a most unnatural mode of existence in his opinion.

Like his old brig, Matson was a bit behind the times. His times were those of the press gang and the cat o' nine tails, of the blockade and the fleet action. But though he had seen hard times, he was not a hard officer and when he paid off the *Swinger* in July 1826, he was presented by his crew with a dress sword, belt and epaulette in token of their very great esteem.

Though the command of a 'pelter' brig was considered a heart-breaking job by most smart young lieutenants, it suited such an officer as Matson, whose promotion was long overdue and to whom prize money was always a welcome addition to his pay.

And when on his run down the coast from Sierra Leone, the Guinea captains came out to show him up, he delighted by guile or superior seamanship to defeat the swaggering Dons and Dagoes, even though he knew he could not touch them, being empty.

Matson Entertained by a Pirate

Off Cape Coast Matson was once entertained by a pirate unawares. He had boarded a felucca at anchor, but which proved to be untainted by any whiff of the negro. he was received with great politeness by the Spanish captain and regaled with champagne, claret and cigars. This in no way surprised Matson, for he knew that many of the Spanish captains in the slave trade were high-born hidalgos, who took to the life more for the sake of excitement than for any desire for a fortune cemented by the blood of many negroes. Nor was he averse to champagne, though he did not consider it compared with a strong norwester of good Jamaica rum.

Not very long after Matson had been entertained in this way, that same long-limbed felucca captured the *St. Helena,* schooner, and murdered her crew. She was nothing but a pirate!

In the passage down the coast old hands like Matson usually put in at Accra for a stock of poultry and eggs, which could be bought fairly reasonably with Spanish dollars or the usual cut-money of the coast. The eggs were, of course, more the size of pigeons' eggs, and the hens of the long-legged scraggy jungle-fowl variety.

The Great Slave Mart of Whydah

Whydah in the eighteen twenties was undoubtedly the biggest slave port and mart on the coast.

The actual town of Whydah was one and a half miles in-land situated on the shore of a shallow lagoon which was barred from the sea by a quarter-mile ridge of beach.

The beach station of Whydah, where traders landed, consisted of no more than half a dozen store houses and huts on the edge of a high patch of jungle trees. To gain this miserable assemblage of shacks a bad surf had to be braved, and it was safer to employ natives to bring off anything in the way of provisions and water-casks.

The anchorage itself was about a mile out in seven fathoms. Here the empty slavers tossed for months at a time. West Africa was never the land of hurry and hustle, and the lordly Cha-cha always kept the Guinea captains in suspense till a few hours before their cargoes were to be received on board.

On one occasion Matson sailed into the Roads of Whydah and found thirty slavers waiting to load. The old brig tacked about the anchorage whilst George Matson inspected each slaver in turn. Their crews amused themselves by making ribald jests about the lumbering old Pelter brig, which formed a great contrast to their slim, rakish clippers.

By the end of the twenties the boom in the slave trade was so great, and negroes in sufficient quantity so hard to come by, that many slavers took to piracy pure and simple, whilst others preyed upon each other.

The Piratical Slaver *L'Antonio*

I have already quoted a note from the United Service Journal of 1829, to show the prevalence of piracy and I have told the story of Benito de Soto and the piracy of the *Morning Star* in *The Blackwall Frigates*.

The *Defensor De Pedro* was far from being the only slaver, which turned pirate: though she put such a scare amongst the homeward-bound East Indiamen that they asked for convoys from St. Helena, also preyed upon the slavers, masquerading as the famous tender *Black Joke*.

Another piratical slaver was the *Antonio*, she was condemned at Sierra Leone in 1831, was bought and turned into a yacht by the Earl of Harborough, from whom she was bought by Captain Thomas Horsburgh, and became the famous opium clipper, *Nymph;* sailing in her old age under Dents House flag.

Canot Captures a Stolen Slaver

The notorious slave trader, Theodore Canot, who at this stage of his career was as much afloat as ashore in Africa, actually bought a condemned slaver in Sierra Leone and fitted her there with a nine-pounder Long Tom amidships for the express purpose of capturing a full slaver.

He had heard of a vessel almost loaded in the Rio Nunez, whose mate had taken possession of her through the simple method of poisoning her captain. This vessel Canot considered fair game. Having employed a spy to tell him when her cargo was complete, he boldly sailed up to Furcaria with the intention of capturing her before she left the anchorage.

However the slaver had got wind of his pretty scheme, and being of light draft, retreated up the river to Kakundy.

Canot was not the man to be baulked in this manner. As soon as night fell, and guided by the best native pilot on the river, 'whose skill' as Canot expressed it, 'was kept constantly under the lee of my pistol', the slave trader took two boatloads of ruffians with muffled oars and shaded lanterns up the narrow reaches of the river.

Let me quote the entertaining Frenchman.

"We fell like vampires on our prey in the darkness. With a wild hurrah and a blaze of our pistols in the air, we leaped on board, driving every soul under hatches without striking a blow! Sentries were placed at the cabin-door, forecastle and hatchway.

The cable was slipped, my launch took her in tow, the pilot and myself took charge of the helm, and, before daylight, the prize was alongside my schooner, transhipping one hundred and ninety seven of her slaves with their necessary supplies".

The poisoner mate was ashore carousing with the chief of Kakundy, and on discovering the rape of his craft, mustered three canoe loads of warriors under the lead of his black Majesty himself, and came paddling downstream in a great hurry to regain his vessel. However a few rounds of grape from the nine-pounder soon took the fight out of the negroes.

Escape From a Cruiser

This happened in the midst of the rainy season, and when Canot reached the sea he found the calms of a sweltering July delayed his passage up the coast.

It was ten days before the favourable current and an occasional draught from the Sou-west took him to the longitude of the Cape Verds. But here he had a narrow escape from capture; and, after describing the slave chase from the cruiser's side of the deck, it may be perhaps of interest, to hear the slaver's. Canot's descriptions are so very vivid that they are always worth quoting in full:—

" . . . . the tenth day found us rolling from side to side in the longitude of the Cape de Verds. Day broke with one of its customary squalls and showers. As the cloud lifted, my look-out from the crosstrees announced a sail under our lee. It was invisible from the deck, in the folds of the retreating rain, but in the dead calm that followed, the distant whistle of a boatswain was distinctly audible. Before I could deliberate, all my doubts were solved by a shot in our mainsail and the crack of a cannon. There could be no question that the unwelcome visitor was a man-of-war.

It was fortunate that the breeze sprang up after the lull and enabled us to carry everything that could be crowded on our spars.

The slaves were shifted from side to side—forward or aft—to aid our sailing. Headstays were slackened, wedges knocked off the masts, and every incumbrance cast from the decks into the sea. Now and then a fruitless shot from his bow-chasers reminded the fugitive that the foe was still on his scent.

At last the cruiser got the range of his guns so perfectly, that a well-aimed ball ripped away our rail and tore a dangerous splinter from the foremast, three feet from the deck. It was perilous to carry a press of sail on the same tack with the weakened spar, whereupon I put the schooner about, and, to my delight, found we ranged ahead a knot faster on this course than the former.

The enemy went about as quickly as we did, but her balls soon fell short of us, and, before noon, we had crawled so nimbly to windward that her topgallants alone were visible above the horizon".

Canot Suppresses a Mutiny

Canot having escaped the cruiser was not to land his stolen cargo without further trouble.

One dark night, when the schooner was approaching the West Indies, the mate disappeared overboard, the suspicion being that he had been put over the rail by some of the crew.

The second mate's demeanour was also far from pleasing Canot. This man along with five seamen had been shipped in the Nunez from the despoiled slaver.

Canot at last broke him, sent him forward and threw his 'dog-house' over board. This treatment only accelerated the brewing mutiny. This again is most vividly described by this entertaining slave trader.

"It was a sweet afternoon when we were floating along the shores of Porto Rico, tracking our course upon the chart. Suddenly, one of my new assistants approached with a sociability common among Spaniards and, in a quiet tone, asked whether I would take a cigarillo.

As I never smoked, I rejected the offer with thanks, when the youth immediately dropped the twisted paper on my lap. In an instant I perceived that the cigarillo was, in fact, a billet rolled to resemble one. I put it in my mouth, and walked aft until I could throw myself on the deck, with my head over the stern, so as to open the paper unseen. It disclosed the organization of a mutiny under the lead of the broken mate.

Our arrival in sight of San Domingo was to be the signal of its rupture, and for my immediate landing on the island. Six of the crew were implicated with the villain, and the boatswain, who was ill in the slave hospital, was to share my fate".

Landing Slaves in Cuba

"My resolution was promptly made. In a few minutes I had cast a hasty glance into the arm-chest, and seen that our weapons were in order. Then, mustering ten of the stoutest and cleverest of my negroes on the quarterdeck, I took the liberty to invent a little strategic fib, and told them, in the Soo-soo dialect, that there were bad men on board who wanted to run the schooner ashore among rocks and drown the slaves while below. At the same time I gave each a cutlass from the arm-chest, and supplying my trusty whites with a couple of pistols and a knife a piece, without saying a word I seized the ringleader and his 'colleagues'.

Irons and double-irons secured the party to the mainmast or deck, while a drum-head court martial, composed of the officers and presided over by myself, arraigned and tried the scoundrels in much less time than regular boards ordinarily spent in such investigations. During the inquiry we ascertained beyond doubt that the death of the mate was due to false play. He had been wilfully murdered as a preliminary to the assault on me, for his colossal stature and powerful muscles would have made him a dangerous adversary in the seizure of the craft.

There was, perhaps, a touch of the old-fashioned Inquisition in the mode of our judicial researches concerning this projected mutiny. Whenever the culprit manifested reluctance or hesitation, his memory was stimulated by the cat".

To cut this courtmartial short, I may add that the six men were flogged and then put in irons. It was thought necessary to treat the mate with more severity. Some proposed making him walk the plank: others that he should be sent adrift on a raft, well ballasted with chains. But Canot ended by marooning him in shackles on Turtle island with a beaker of water and three days' food.

Hardly had the schooner filled away from the cay than a bank of white cloud, followed by an impenetrable fog, warned Canot of the approach of a white squall, but before he could shorten sail, the blast arrived and over went the schooner on her beam ends, luckily the mainsail burst from its boltropes or the slaver would have turned turtle, the rudder being out of water.

Canot blamed himself for not keeping a sharper lookout, but he was soon his impurtable self again, "happy to find that our entire loss did not exceed two slave children, who had been carelessly suffered to sit on the rail".

Being "without papers, manifest, register, consignees or destination", it was necessary for Canot to exercise unusual circumspection in landing his cargo.

About nine miles East of Sant Jago was a secluded cove, at the head of which was a spacious barn belonging to a Catalonian 'ranchero'. Canot being 'partial' as he expressed it, to Catalans, confided in this rancher.

Through him the Governor-General was informed of the slaver's arrival and received his percentage.

In the same way the mouth of the Captain of the port was kept shut. Canot himself mysteriously disappeard for a time, the local pilot, for the usual price, taking over the commander's responsibilities. This was chiefly for the object of avoiding minor officials, whose 'consciences had not been lulled by the golden anodyne'.

The slaves were landed, and, after forty-eight hours rest, marched to Santiago—Head money was paid and the whole cargo speedily sold through brokers.

Whilst Canot was enjoying the proceeds, his crew were also lounging about Havana. One of them, on losing his money in a gambling hell, went to the French Consul for relief.

Then, indeed, the whole story came out and the order was signed for Canot's arrest. Warned in time he made himself scarce, until all possible witnesses against him had been taken off by a 'convenient press-gang'. After which he was left in peace with his ill-gotten gains. As the wily slave-dealer remarked:—"Things are managed very cleverly in Havana—when you know how!"

Lieutenant Adams Captures the *Maria*

To return to Lieutenant George Matson, inspite of her poor sailing capabilities, when he paid off the *Clinker* in October, 1830, he had emancipated 1,400 slaves, and this good work gained him his promotion.

Another officer, who made a great reputation as a slave catcher, was John Adams, first lieutenant of the *Atholl,* who, on January the 6th, 1830, took command of the *Plumper.* This Pelter brig, when commanded by Lieutenant E. Medley arrived home 'defective' in December 1828, she was also dreadfully crowded, having forty prisoners on board, charged with piracy.

Adams was no stranger to a 'Pelter' brig, for instance in 1824 he had commanded the name ship, 'Pelter', herself on the Newfoundland Station.

Adams distinguished himself whilst commanding the *Plumper* by boarding and taking a slaver in his gig with a crew of only five men. This vessel was the *Maria* of six guns and forty-four men, but only one hundred and thirty-three Spanish tons.

She had been out eleven days; she had five hundred and twelve slaves on board and was so crowded that already smallpox, dysentery and other dreadful African diseased had broken out aboard.

The Squadron Attacked by Putrid Fever

The prize crews of captured slavers were always considered the most fruitful source of contagion when there was much sickness in the African Squadron.

The constant and fatiguing boat-work up the slave rivers was also held responsible for much fever. The work of the mosquito was not even dreamt of at this date, and fever was always put down to the miasmic mists rising off mudbanks and to the effluvia of rotting tropical vegetation.

During the last year of Commodore Collier's command a putrid fever, as it was termed, attacked the Squadron, and the flagship *Sybille* seems to have suffered worse than any other ship. Yet the Commodore had taken every precaution he could think of to ward off the effects of the deadly mists, which at times enveloped the coast.

At sunset every single man aboard the *Sybille,* whether he was the officer of the watch or the mate of the hold, the Commodore's cook or the loplolly boy, had to don a specially issued blanket, suit, consisting of 'frock and trousers', so that to quote one of the *Sybille's* mids—"all hands looked like so many polar bears".

The first ship to catch the contagion was the *Eden.* During a passage of a month between Sierra Leone and Fernando Po, she buried forty-seven of her company, including the acting commander Badgley, two midshipmen, two assistant surgeons and her carpenter.

Some of these including her commander had been taken ill before leaving Sierra Leone and Lieutenant Tambs from the *Hecla* had been put aboard to carry on his duty.

When the *Eden* arrived at Fernando Po, Lieutenant Tambs, Lieutenant Kellet and her master were the only officers on their feet.

Her Captain, W.F.W. Owen, was in charge of the new colony at Fernando Po, and he must have been horrified when he discovered the sad condition of his ship, which he had been eagerly expecting. Shortly after the arrival of the *Eden* at Fernando Po, Captain Owne's relief, Colonel Nickolls, arrived with his staff aboard the sloop, *Champion.* The new surgeon for the colony and his two assistants were landed sick in their cots on the Monday morning—One of the assistants died on the Tuesday and the surgeon on the Wednesday.

The Settlement of Clarence Cove

This was an unfortunate start for the new English settlement at Fernando Po, and gave it a very bad reputation for health from the very start.

The use of Fernando Po as a base for the West Coast Squadron had been first suggested by the Grenada sugar planter McQueen, who in 1816 had explored the mouths of the Niger.

His suggestion was supported by Sir Thomas Fowell Buxton, and, in 1830, the English Government obtained the session of the island—the Clarence town settlement in Clarence Cove being started by Captain Owen. But the members of the Mixed Commission could never be induced to exchange Sierra Leone for Fernando Po, owing to its sinister reputation.

Freed slaves were employed to clear the ground and drain it; two Colonial schooners ran regularly between Clarence Cove and the Bonny and Calabar rivers ostensibly to fetch back yams and live stock, and in this way the squadron were kept informed of all slavers in those rivers.

A superintendent from England, an old soldier was responsible for the work of the settlement: when asked how he was carrying on, he was wont to reply that "He had one gang digging graves, as usual, and the other making coffins until further orders".

Yet Fernando Po owed her fever entirely to the windward coast. Both the *Eden* and the *Champion* had picked up the fever at Sierra Leone. When the *Sybille* arrived there just before the rainy season was due, she found the whole Colony in a panic.

It was a certain 'due up', as the sailors expressed it, if you caught the contagion, which was diagnosed as 'putrid yellow fever'—an extremely virulent kind, accompanied by the usual 'black vomit'. Instances of anyone surviving an attack were so rare as to be almost unknown—usually it was ill, dead and buried within forty-eight hours.

Lying in the stream close to the *Sybille* was a lately arrived prize, which had lost every soul aboard excepting a boy.

The surgeon of the *Sybille* already had a number of cases when she arrived at Freetown and he considered that the ship had received the infection from a party of marine artillery-men, who had been taken on board at Fernando Po, and that the severity of the attack was due to foul air generated in the ship's hold.

Her maindeck, fore and aft, was soon lined on both sides by the sick in their hammocks.

As man after man succumbed, after a terrible parozysm during which the fatal black vomit was a sure precursor of the end, there was as great a feeling of panic aboard the frigate as there was at Freetown, Sierra Leone.

Throughout her commission the *Sybille* had been a happy ship with a grand lot of officers.

A Softened Martinet

Up to the date of this visitation she had been usually healthy, owing as all hands acknowledged, to the care and watchfulness of Commodore Collier and her surgeon, Dr. R. M'Kinnall. The old Commodore was a taut hand and considered something of a tartar in the Service, but this terrible visitation of yellow jack softened him to an incredible degree and almost broke down his stern self-control.

Day and night he was on his feet. He had by an unflinching severity brought the *Sybille's* company to the highest pitch of discipline. But as officer after officer, man after man died, the old Nelsonian relaxed his iron rule and won the devotion of all hands by his unfailing sympathy, kindness and attention.

Occasionally the devil in him awoke and he started to raise Cain, but it quickly subsided again and, worn out by his unceasing patrolling amongst the sick and a touch of fever, the old lion nearly succumbed himself, though his tough frame and unconquerable resolution pulled him through.

In his devotion to the sick he was ably backed up by three very exceptional officers, his surgeon, Doctor M'Kinnall, his master, old Tom Collins, and his purser, George Moxon.

It is hard to say which was the most popular with the ship's company, the refined, literary, science-loving doctor, the weather-beaten, bluff old master, a sailor of the old school and old shipmate of the Commodore, or the talented purser, who was the life and soul of the Dog Watches.

Old Tom Collins

Old Tom Collins, who had out-lived all his own kith and kin, and thus stood alone in the world, was the friend of every man aboard; whenever he was off duty, he was to be found by the side of a sick man, trying his best to hearten the *Sybille's* dispirited crew.

For weeks he never flagged. The frigate left Sierra Leone and sailed for the Bights. Still man after man was stricken, man after man died.

Old Tom Collins, like the Commodore was pronounced too tough to be touched. But one day his servant sickened and the next morning was dead. This boy had been more like a son than a servant to the old man, who had taught him to read and write and even the rudiments of arithmetic. From that moment all hands noted a change—in a few days the master sickened, twelve hours later he was dead.

The news of old Tom's death struck the last spark of life out of all hands, consternation seized upon the bravest. The day of old Tom's death the *Sybille* anchored in West Bay, Prince's Island. The old man wished to be buried at sea, so the boats of the *Sybille* with muffled oars pulled slowly out of the harbour, carrying the coffin well weighted with thirty-two pound shot.

It would be hard to imagine a more impressive scene—The very heavens reflected the gloom that was in every heart, for a vast bank of cloud denoted the rapid approach of a tornado: it was soon so dark that the officer officiating as chaplain could hardly read his prayer book, and as he pronounced the words:—'We therefore commit his body to the deep', the storm burst with peal upon peal of thunder, and flash on flash of lightning, and rain like a waterspout.

As the whole scene was lit up, the well-weighted coffin was seen to leap more than half out of the water. For a moment it hovered upon its end and then amidst the terrific clatter of thunder sank from sight.

Again amidst the torn-up water it reappeared to the accompaniment of a salvo of heaven's artillery; and a horrible noise like the death-rattle in unnumbered throats seemed to proceed from it. One after the other the boats pulled madly for the *Sybille,* until only the senior officer's boats remained. The superstitious seamen were convinced that spirits were contending with devils for the soul of Old Tom. Three times the coffin showed itself, before it sank for ever. The explanation was of course simple. Until the water could get into the coffin and the air out, it would not sink, and it was held on end by the shot at the dead master's feet. But when the boats arrived alongside, and spread their story through the ship, the panic, induced by the fever, was increased by a crop of the most grisly yarns of a supernatural character.

Doctor M'Kinnall's Heroism

Then it was that Doctor M'Kinnall came to the rescue and gave an exhibition of unselfish courage, such as deserves to be ever remembered in the Service. Finding that his cheery demeanour, had no power to allay the terror of the fever that was now gripping all hands, he determined upon a demonstration of his own fearlessness of the contagion.

Amongst the sick, whose hammocks crowded the main-deck, lay a sailor who was at his

6. Action with the Spanish Slave Frigate *Veloz Passagera* captured by boarding by H.M. Ship *Primrose*, Commander William Broughton, off Whydah, Bight of Benin the 6th September 1830.

From an Aquatint in colour by Edward Duncan after a painting by W. J. Huggins.

[*Facing page 160.*

7. H.M. Brig *Pantaloon*.

From a lithograph by H. John Vernon in the National Maritime Museum.

[*Facing page 161.*

last gasp. Doctor M'Kinnall, in such loud tones that every head was turned to listen, told his sick-bay attendant to fetch him a wine-glass. Then, as the black vomit burst from the sufferer's lips, he filled the glass with it and, holding it on high, called the attention of everyone to what he held in his hand. Then he laid back his head and tossed off the horrid mess, draining the wineglass to the last drop. And not content with this amazing exhibition of fortitude, he went straight on deck and remained there for two hours in the sight of all the watch, so as to prove to everyone that he had taken no precaution, such as an emetic, to nullify the effects of the terrible draught.

This supremely gallant, if horrible action, went far to allay the panic aboard.

On her arrival at West Bay, the *Sybille* was so short-handed that it was not easy to carry on duty. Her old master was dead, her young purser was dead, indeed, no less than one hundred and five officers and men had lost the number of their mess.

In desperation the Commodore determined to sail for that pleasant recruiting place for sick ship's companies, St. Helena.

Just as the *Sybille* was about to sail, her tender, the *Dallas* arrived and was ordered to attend her.

The Commodore and the Captain of the *Orwell*

On their arrival at St. Helena, the *Dallas* was given practique, being quite healthy, but to the Commodore's rage the frigate was placed in quarantine.

Lying at anchor at St. Helena was the Indiaman, *Orwell,* which was on her passage home from China. Several of her men offered to volunteer aboard the short handed frigate, but the indignant captain of the Indiaman refused to allow them to leave his ship and swore he would 'repel force by force'.

This was too much for the already sorely tried temper of the Commodore, who was smarting at the indignity of the quarantine. Leaning out of the frigate's quarter-gallery window, he roared out the following answer to this provocative message:—

"Go back and tell him to remember the *Leander* in Madras Roads". This referred to a like trouble between the Royal Navy and the Honourable East India Company. And as he drew his head in, he could still be heard growling:—

"I'll sink him, by God! I'll sink him at his anchors!"

It was just at this critical moment that the crack forty-two-gun frigate, *Pallas,* Captain Lord Adolphus Fitzclarence, homewardbound from India, came sailing into the Roads. Up went a string of flags aboard the *Sybille,* and the signal officer of the approaching ship was surprised to read the signal:—'Man and arm boats!'

In a very few moments the frigate's boats with their men, resplendent in clean white frocks, white trousers and white hats, were pulling into the anchorage at a racing stroke in hopes of some kind of a spree.

But it all fizzled out. The *Orwell's* captain gave up his men, the Commodore recovered his temper, and with theatricals and a ball the fair sirens of Jamestown soon dulled the memory of the recent horrors suffered by the flagship's company.

High Jinks at St. Helena

Commodore Collier, released from quarantine, landed and took up his quarters with the Governor, an old shipmate of his. The officers, in turn, were allowed to accept the hospitality of the chief merchant and ship-chandler of St. Helena, who was known throughout the Service at Thol-thol. This man, who had once been a private in the St. Helena regiment under the Hon. East India Company, kept open house for officers of the Navy and never thought of presenting a bill, his stock phrase being:—

"The Honourable John Company pays for all". whilst the frigate was being 'stripped to a gantline', as it was called, for a thorough overhaul aloft and alow, the Commodore sold his tender, the *Dallas,* to a merchant of St. Helena. This man cut down her lower masts to give her more stability, gave the command to a strange shipmaster, who was 'on the beach' at Jamestown, and sent him off to Cape Town for a cargo.

In this way the unfortunate *Dull Ass* fell into bad hands, for her new master loaded a cargo at the Cape on the credit of his owner, then ran across to a South American port, where he sold his cargo, brig and all, and disappeared with the proceeds.

Before the frigate sailed for home, there were gay doings afloat and ashore.

At the ball the Yamstock young ladies and the Governor's daughters were fairly danced off their feet. The fun was kept up till daylight. Then came a late supper of deviled drumsticks and bones, ham, etc., and on top of this the untirable Naval officers called for horses and went for a gallop. The next night saw a dinner at the Governor's where soldier and sailor fraternised under the influence of many parting cups.

Nor must some description of the theatricals be forgotten in this picture of St. Helena in the days of the old Wooden Walls and the East Indiamen.

The first piece was "She stoops to conquer", followed by "Raising the wind". The actors and actresses were all provided by the frigate, though the female costumes of Miss Neville and Miss Hardcastle, played by two of the *Sybille's* midshipmen, were superintended and fitted with much fun and laughter by the fair Yamstocks. Tony Lumpkin's mother was played by the acting master of the frigate with the aid of an enormous fan and such voluminous skirts that he found it harder to keep his feet on the stage than upon the rolling deck of the frigate when running before a gale.

These amusements were followed by picnics, and before the ships sailed amidst vows of eternal devotion, there was even a naval wedding at the little church on top of Ladder Hill.

There was many a sad heart in St. Helena when the old *Sybille* weighed her anchor one morning in May and sailed majestically out past the Mundens, the Sugar-loaf and the Deadwood, with the homeward-bound or paying-off pendant streaming away behind her, its fish-bladder bobbing in her wake, her extemporary band playing "The Roast Beef of Old England" at the top of its pipes, and a mast-head man standing on each truck waving a boat flag.

Primrose and *Veloz Passagera*

As usual there was a short interregnum whilst the old Commodore was going home and the new was on his way out—they seldom waited to be relieved directly their time had expired, but placed the station in the hands of the senior captain.

It was during this interregnum that one of the smartest slaver actions ever fought took place. This was that of the *Primrose* and *Veloz Passagera.*

The *Primrose,* in her cruise during the summer of 1830, discovered that in one district at any rate slavers seemed to have given up business.

On the southern shores of the Bay of Lovengo, the Spanish and Brazilian barracoons were found to be all destroyed. This did not help the unfortunate captives of the slave-trading chiefs. On the side of a hill close to the town the bones of close on one hundred negroes were found. The King of Loango told the officers of the *Primrose* that he had been obliged to butcher these slaves as there were no slave ships to hand and he could not afford to feed them.

These captives had formed part of a large caravan bringing ivory to the coast, and there being no slaver or even dealer to rid him of them, he had been forced to knock them on the head. In lamenting the unavoidable waste of black ivory, the King boasted that he could easily provide for eight slave ships a week, allowing four to five hundred blacks for each ship.

During the years 1829 and 1830 every cruiser had orders to keep a close watch upon a large frigate-built, full-rigged slaver, named *Veloz Passagera,* which was hovering about the coast in her endeavour to fill up with from 1,400 to 1,500 slaves.

Many of the squadron had boarded her in Whydah Roads, including the *Primrose.*

Edward Harris Butterfield, who had been long on the coast in the *Atholl, Sybille* and *Black Joke,* had been promoted from the last named having been one of her mates in the *Almirante* action. He was now First Lieutenant of the *Primrose;* and happened to be the officer of that ship, who boarded the *Veloz Passagera* in Whydah Roads. He recognised one of the slaver's officers, Alexander Nocetta, and a seaman, as having been aboard the *Almirante,* when she fought the *Black Joke.*

Such vessels as the *Veloz Passagera* were something of a rarity amongst the slave ships, which were mostly brigs, brigantines and schooners, though I can give other instances of three-masters.

As far back as July 1826 Captain Willes of the *Brazen* reported:—

"The rivers are full of all description of vessels slaving, the French in great numbers and the Dutch under the French flag. There is a Spanish corvette, the *Sultan,* of fourteen guns, fifty-six men, lately arrived on the coast from Bordeaux, she will take seven or eight hundred slaves when ready. There is also a large Spanish frigate-built ship at Gaboon, which will take as many if not more. She came last from Martinique. I have sent to Sierra Leone since I parted from the Commodore (on 8th May last) a Dutch schooner with two sets of papers and a Brazilian ship with twenty-five slaves on board, six hundred being ready for her at Lagos, making in the whole nine hundred and sixty since I have been on the coast".

The *Veloz Passagera* was an old Spanish war corvette, a vessel with five feet more beam than *Atholl,* which was the largest cruiser on the coast since the departure of the *Sybille.*

But even she was not the largest vessel trafficking for slaves, for in February, 1829 the British consul at Bahia wrote to warn the Commodore about a four-masted Portuguese ship, the *Sophia,* which sailed for the coast on the 5th of that month. This giant slaver was owned by Don Jose de Santiago of Libson. She had a Portuguese master, a Dutch supercargo, a French mate, a Brazilian second mate, and a large crew of every nationality except British.

On September the 3rd, 1830, Commander William Broughton took over the command of *Primrose,* Commander Griffinhoofe having died at Ascension in February. Commander Broughton who was the son of a distinguished circum-navigator, Captain W.R. Broughton, and grandson of Sir Thomas Broughton bart., was new to the coast, but he had seen a lot of service, especially in the East under Sir James Brisbane, and had also served in the West Indies.

With such an experienced first lieutenant as Butterfield he was not likely to miss any opportunities, and it so happened that he had not been four days aboard when the notorious *Veloz Passagera* was fallen in with.

The *Primrose* had picked up her new commander at Princes Island, and being ordered to cruise in the Bight of Benin, she was heading for Badagry in about 4° 30′ N 4° E when at about 5.30 p.m., a sail was reported.

All possible canvas was at once crowded in chase, but the weather was hazy, and for some hours the sail was lost sight of—then, all of a sudden, at 11.30 p.m. she was discovered, close to and standing towards the *Primrose* with her yards hard on the back stays. The two vessels passed within hail on opposite tacks. Captain Broughton, hailed the stranger but obtained no answer. He therefore fired a warning gun to leeward, but again the big stranger made no sign. The *Primrose* was then tacked in her wake and ranging up on the weather quarter of the *Veloz Passagera,* fired two shotted muskets over her and ordered her to heave to.

At this she rounded into the wind with her topsails shaking and Lieutenant Butterfield was sent aboard to examine her. The quick eyes of the old *Black Joke* mate took in the situation at a glance. The large crew of the slaving corvette were all at quarters, armed and in readiness for a fight.

As the *Primrose* changed her bearing, so did the gun crews of the *Veloz Passagera* traverse their guns, keeping them carefully trained on the little sloop. The officer, Alexander Nocetta, conducted Butterfield onto the quarterdeck where another, who spoke English informed him politely that the Captain was ill and unable to come on deck.

However, the Captain himself, one Jose Antonio de la Vega, stood at the foot of the companionway. Keppel who met this man eight years later described his as a handsome, intellingent-looking Biscayan.

Butterfield asked to be allowed to go round the vessel's decks. This the Captain refused to allow, but he volunteered the information that he was going to Princes Island for wood and water, and also produced his papers. Three times Butterfield asked to be allowed to see round the ship and three times Captain de la Vega gave a firm refusal. However the experienced eyes, ears and nose of the *Primrose's* first lieutenant had seen, heard and smelt enough. He returned to the sloop and made his report.

Thereupon Captain Broughton hailed again, ordering the slaver's captain to come aboard the *Primrose,* but no notice was taken. An unshotted gun was then fired, whereupon someone aboard the *Veloz Passagera* sung out in English that they would neither send nor receive a boat during the night, as they could not see whether the *Primrose* was a British cruiser or a Columbian pirate.

At this, Broughton called across that he would stay by the *Veloz Passagera* during the night and board her at sun-up.

In his official report, he says:—

"Finding I had much the advantage of her in sailing and wishing to avoid the effusion of blood by a night action with a vessel crowded with slaves, I remained by her till morning".

At daylight on the 7th of September, the *Primrose,* which was the windward of the two vessels bore down upon the *Veloz Passagera* with a union jack at the fore, pendant at the main and ensign at the peak, thus showing plainly enough that she was no Columbian picaroon.

Arrived within half pistol shot, Broughton hailed to ask if the slaver was ready to receive the sloop's boat. Once more the Spanish captain sent back a refusal. At this the commander of the *Primrose* called out that if she did not heave to in order to allow his boat alongside, at the expiration of five minutes, he would let her have a shotted broadside.

The imperturbable Don Jose shrugged his shoulders and replied that the man-of-war could do as she like, and the impetuous Alexander Nocetta added in Spanish "that they would all go to hell together".

At the end of five minutes, bang went the *Primrose's* broadside and immediately the whole side of the *Velox Passagera* burst into flame with the return broadside. Again the *Primrose* fired, and then Broughton, placing himself at the head of the boarders, ordered his quartermaster to lay the *Primrose* alongside her antagonist.

The high side of the slaver was well above the rail of the little sloop and for a full quarter of an hour the boarding party struggled to obtain a footing against pikes, cutlasses, bayonets and cold shot. a pike hurtled past Broughton and struck quivering in the fore-deck on the man-of-war. Then a second severely wounded him in the abdomen and he fell from the rail of the *Veloz Passagera* into his own ship's fore-chains. But the stalwart Butterfield was in close support, and when his captain cried out that he was done for, proceeded to cheer on the boarders, sweeping his way onto the slaver's forecastle with a death-dealing cutlass.

The motion of the two vessels as they ground together and then fell apart in the long, heaving swell, made the task of the boarders both difficult as well as hazardous.

Nevertheless once Butterfield seconded most stoutly by acting* lieutenant Foley, acting master Fraser and a midshipman named Bentham, had got a footing on her deck. He carried her in ten minutes—But it was a very sharp and bloody ten minutes.

The forecastle head of the *Veloz Passagera,* where a last desperate resistance was made by some twenty men, who imagined that no quarter would be given, was a perfect shambles.

Yet, as usual in such actions, the crew of the man-of-war escaped in a wonderful manner. Besides the Captain, wounded severely, his intestine being partly cut through, one seaman and two marines were killed, Watts the boatswain and one marine were dangerously wounded, Fraser, the master, and two men were severely wounded and Bentham, the midshipman and five bluejackets were slightly wounded out of a complement of one hundred and thirty five men including twenty five kroomen.

The doctor, Lanes, who was suffering from fever, crawled out of his berth to attend to the wounded. Two of these were riddled with grape, others had to be probed for musket balls, and most of them were suffering from pike and bayonet wounds.

Of the slavers crew, no less than forty-six were killed and twenty wounded, including the Captain, who had to have his arm amputated; these casualties were out of one hundred and fifty five men of all nations, who formed her crew. Six of the wounded died in spite of the efforts of the *Primrose's* surgeon. In the hold of the *Veloz Passagera* five hundred and fifty five slaves were stowed, five of whom had been killed by the broadsides of the *Primrose.*

Commander Broughton was so incensed by this fierce resistance, that he brought home twenty-eight of the slaver's crew including her mate, Alexander Nocetta, in order to have them tried for piracy under a special commission (issued in the tenth George IV). At the trial Nocetta said he was an Italian of Spanish descent, who had shipped in Havana at ninety dollars a month.

An American seaman, named Curtis Gulpin, said he had shipped at Havana at forty dollars a month. Amongst the prisoners were also another American, a Swede and a Frenchman; the rest being Spanish.

Lieutenant Butterfield, mishipman A. J. Bellingham and other members of the *Primrose's* crew gave evidence of the engagement, but the court pronounced the prisoners not guilty of piracy and they were sent back to Havana.

This capture was one of the finest pieces of work in the whole history of the Royal Navy's efforts to suppress the slave trade, and it was celebrated by the following typical 'Come all ye' which gives a very accurate account of the engagement. This used to be sung in many a forecastle sing-song by old *Primrose* hands, and was published in the *United Service Journal* under

Galley Yarns

Come all you gallant sailors bold, that to the seas belong,
Oh, Listen unto me, my boys, while I recount my song;
'Tis concerning of an action that was fought the other day,
By the saucy little *Primrose,* on the coast of Africa.

One evening, while we the deep with gentle breezes plough,
A sail is seen from our mast-head, hard on the weather bow;
The gloom of night now coming on, of her we soon lose sight,
But down she bears, about five bells, as if prepared for fight.

Yet here she overreach'd herself, and prov'd she was mistaken,
Thinking by passing in the dark, that she could save her bacon,
For British tars don't lose a prize, by fault in looking out,
So we brought her to, with much ado, at eleven o'clock about.

* Owing to her time on the coast through a very sickly season, most of the *Primrose's* executive were acting, as were her purser and doctor.

All hands were called to quarters, our guns were clear'd away,
And every man within the ship, was anxious for the fray;
Our first lieutenant went on board, her hold to overhaul,
And found them training of their guns, to the boatswain's pipe and call.

To get near the main hatchway, our officer contrives,
But some ruffian-looking rascals surrounded him with knives;
For well they knew we peace must keep, unless that we could tell,
That slaves were actually on board, detecting them by smell.

Striving this object to attain, he firm resistance met,
So then return'd on board in haste, fresh orders for to get;
Says he:—"It is a spanking ship, I'm sure that she has slaves,
And bears from sacred house and home the wretches o'er the waves".

"Oh! Very well!" our Captain cries, "for her we will be by,
And on the morrow's coming dawn, a palaver we will try;
For should we now attempt to make a pell-mell night attack,
I fear our fight would heavy fall upon the harmless black".

So early the next morning, we gently edged away,
Our Captain hail'd the stranger ship, and unto her did say—
"If you don't send your boat on board, and act as I desire,
Although you bear the flag of Spain, into your hull I'll fire".

The Slaver swore that all our threats should not his courage scare,
And that th'assault of such a sloop was quite beneath his care:
Our Captain calls, "Stand by, my lads' and when I give the word,
We slap off two smart broadsides, and run her right on board".

The signal then was given, a rattler we let fly,
And many a gloomy Spaniard upon her decks did die:
"Now fire again! my British boys, repeat the precious dose,
For round and grape, when plied so well, they cannot long oppose".

Now peals the roar of battle strife, now British hearts expand,
And now the anxious sailor pants to combat hand to hand:
With grapnels and with hawsers we lash'd her to our beam,
Although the muzzles of her gun did o'er our bulwarks gleam.

"Away, my men!" the Captain cries, "'tis just the time to board",
Upon her decks we jump'd amain, with tomahawk and sword;
The conflict now was sharp and fierce, for clemency had fled,
And streams of gore mark'd every blow—the dying and the dead.

Our Captain heads the daring band, to make the *Veloz* strike,
But soon received a dangerous thrust, from a well-hove boarding pike.
We thought 'twas all "clue up" with him, although he cheered us on
And we determined every man, the slaver should be won.

We beat them on the main-deck till they could no longer stand,
When our leader sings out "Quarter" some mercy to command;
But now the sherry which we made, with panic fill'd the horde,
For some dived down the hatchways and some leap'd overboard.

Close to their scudding heels our lads did their attentions pay,
Cutlass in hand, to hold their own—to capture more than slay;
Through slippery gore we fought our way, the quarterdeck to gain,
And in loud cheers her mizen peak soon lost the flag of Spain.

Our prize we found was frigate-built, from Whydah she sail'd out,
With near six hundred slaves on board, and eight score seamen stout;
Equipp'd with stores of every sort, the missile war to wage,
And twenty long guns through her ports seem'd frowning to engage.

Of those that were made prisoners, they all were put abaft,
And we with well-arm'd sentinels paraded fore and aft;
We pick'd up all the slaughter'd men, and hove them in the deep,
Where, full in number fifty, they take their final sleep.

And twenty more disabled Dons, with eyelet holes and scars,
Were treated by our surgeon, the same as our own tars,
For when they struck no time was lost, to the *Primrose* they were sent,
And arms, and legs, and broken heads, strict ordeal underwent.

Our chief was badly wounded, likewise the master too,
One midshipman, the boatswain, and nine of the our ship's crew;
Besides three seamen killed outright, who thus resigned their breath,
And in the hour of vict'ry gain'd a patriotic death.

So now my story to conclude, although beyond my might—
I write these lines to let you now, how loyal tars can fight;
So toast the health of those brave lads that bore the palm away,
And beat the Spanish ship *Veloz* on the coast of Africa.

Conflict's boats and *Nympha*

The *Primrose* had been over three years on the Coast, and the capture of the *Veloz Passagera* was the signal for hoisting her homeward bound pendant. She accompanied her magnificent prize to Sierra Leone, and then sailed for home.

On her way north, the sloop overhauled the gunbrig, *Conflict,* on the first of December off the Gambia. Lieutenant Smithers was in chase of a slaver, but hardly had the *Primrose* made out the two vessels, before it fell down a flat calm.

The *Conflict* was not to be balked of her prey, and she at once sent away her cutter in charge of her master, Rose, with orders to board and search the chase.

As soon, however, as the boat came within range, the slaver, a large schooner, opened fire upon her with great guns and small arms, and the first broadside wounded several of the cutter's crew. At this show of her teeth on the part of the slaver, Rose wisely drew off and made a signal for reinforcements.

The *Primrose* was too far away to be of use, but the little pelter brig quickly sent away for her other boat. As soon as she arrived on the scene Rose pulled into the attack, each boat taking a side. As in the case of the larger *Veloz Passsagera,* a most desperate resistance was put up by the slaver's crew, who actually went on fighting till they were forced over the side and drowned.

The casualties on both sides were heavy indeed considering the small number engaged. Eleven of the boarders were wounded more or less severely, whilst the slaver lost seventeen men either killed or drowned. She turned out to be the *Nympha* bound to Boa Vista, Cape Verd Island, and owned by Colonel Martinez, the Portuguese government agent there. There were one hundred and sixty seven slaves on board, in a miserable condition, the survivors of a much larger cargo.

In accordance with the tenth George IV, the Captain and crew of the slaver were tried as pirates, but as usual nothing came of it.

***Falcon* and Pirate**

The doings of pirates and the work of our men-of-war against pirates are continually to be found reported in the newspapers at this date.

But here is a newspaper report for which I can find no scrap of evidence. It is taken from the Evening Standard (price 7d) of December the 15th, 1830, and runs as follows:—

"A most gallant action had just taken place off the Island of Ascension. His Majesty's ship *Falcon,* thirty guns, fell in with a pirate mounting fifty guns and having a crew of two hundred and fifty men.

After two hours fighting *Falcon* made the pirate a prisoner. On reaching Ascension Island the officers of *Falcon* sent the pirates ashore in companies of twenty in the long boat and hanged them on the island, reserving only the captain and mate, who were taken to Bermuda for trial".

The *Falcon,* as it happened, was one of the ten gun coffin-brigs about which controversy was then raging in the Navy. At the date of this imaginary encounter she was on the West Indian station under the command of Commander H. G. Colpoys.

CHAPTER X

THE ROYAL YACHT CLUB AND THE SYMONDITES

"A Sailor I've been, and have ploughed the salt sea, sir,
And, of all sorts of lives, still a sailor's for me sir".

Yachting Enthusiasts

EVER since the days of the Merry Monarch, the aristrocracy of England following the royal example had always shown great interest in the Royal Navy, and it was the custom of every great family to send one member at least into the Service—the fool of the family, if we are to believe Marryat, though a long list of famous admirals can easily refute this semi-serious contention.

Besides these well-born professional sailors, towards the end of the Napoleonic wars, an ever growing number of amateur sailors were to be found among the ranks of the nobility, the landed gentry and the merchant princes, these latter being mostly West Indian sugar planters and East Indian nabobs.

The Cork Water Club

The first club of yachtsmen was, of course, the Cork Water Club, of which Lord Inchiquin was a lively member.

This club, founded in 1720, flew an Union flag with a Royal Irish harp and crown on a green field in the centre. It seems to have combined dining with yacht racing, for by its rules, 'Admirals' were forbidden to bring more than two dishes of meat and two dozen of wine for the entertainment of the club, nor were long tail wigs, large sleeves or ruffles allowed to be worn by any member.

The Irish yachts, which were started from the Castle of Haulbowline were bluff, round-bowed cutters with highly ornamented sterns, They were pole-masted with short-gaffed and loose-footed mainsails, and two headsails.

Fouls whilst racing sometimes led to cutlass-work amongst these exciteable Irishmen.

The Cumberland Society

In England ever since about the middle of the eighteenth century there had been racing upon the Thames, and under the patronage of H.R.H. Prince Henry Frederick, Duke of Cumberland, these shallow-draught, clinker-built, Thames racing cutters in 1775 became known as the Cumberland Sailing Society, generally called the Cumberland fleet.

As befitted a membership, which had a close connection with the City of London, we are told that on non-cup racing days, a match was often made for a turtle, which was served up at the dinner after the day's sport.

Neither the Irish or the Thames yachts ran to any size, nor were these yachtsmen concerned with anything beyond boat-racing, eating and drinking.

The Royal Yacht Club

But on June the first 1815, forty-two gentlemen met at the Thatched House Tavern in St. James's Street and founded the Yacht Club, a condition of membership being the owning of a yacht of not less than ten tons burthen.

In September 1820, George IV honoured the Yacht Club by allowing it to use the prefix royal, then in 1833 William IV directed that "as a mark of His Majesty's gracious approval of an institution of such national utility, it is his gracious will and pleasure that it shall henceforth be known and styled the Royal Yacht Squadron, of which His Majesty is graciously pleased to consider himself the head".

Lord Yarborough, First Commodore of the R.Y.S.

The words 'an institution of such national utility', were a reference to the great part played by the Royal Yacht Club in the improvement of ship design in the Royal Navy. Ever since its foundation, and still more since the Earl of Yarborough had been elected Commodore in July 1827, the club had shown as much interest in naval architecture and naval tactics as the Admiralty itself. In its early days, Lord Yarborough was continually taking the Royal Yacht Squadron for a cruise in formation; and a special signal book was issued, of which I have a copy dated 1830, in which is set out an order of sailing in two divisions, starboard and larboard, with coloured diagrams for such evolutions as tacking in succession, wearing in succession, forming line abreast, sailing by the wind in a line to bear up and form two columns, etc.

The Commodore was a matter of fact far keener on ship design and smartly executed tactical exercises than on racing, and his heart was undoubtedly with the Royal Navy. His first yacht was the *Falcon*, a brig of one hundred and fifty-five tons, which became one of the first of the opium clippers when he built his second *Falcon*, a full-rigged ship of three hundred and fifty-one tons in 1824.

This beautiful vessel was built by List of Wootton Bridge, near Cowes, and was intended to represent the very last thing in twenty-gun flush-decked corvettes.

Lord Yarborough not only led and drilled the Royal Yacht Squadron with this splendid flagship, but he went out with the Experimental fleets, and even took part in the Battle of Navarino, flying, it is said, the flag of the Admiral of the Isle of Wight.

Although Lord Yarborough was the most kindly man without a hard word for anybody, he maintained strict naval discipline aboard the *Falcon*, his crew of fifty-four choice hands actually signing a paper setting forth 'the usefulness of a sound flogging in cases of extremity and their perfect willingness to undergo the experiment whenever deemed necessary for the preservation of good order'.

Probably no club ever had such an excellent first commodore as the Royal Yacht Squadron.

On his death some humorous verses on the difficulty of electing his successor were written by Lord Winchelsea, which began as follows:—

> "When time took old Yarborough down by the stern,
> And the *Kestrel** returned with the Commodore's urn,
> There was mourning at Cowes, lamentation at Ryde,
> For the jolly old tar was the whole island's pride.
> He was bluff in his bearing and broad in his beam
> His club was his child and its doings his theme".

The Marquis of Anglesey and His Cutter *Pearl*

Next to Lord Yarborough, perhaps, the most well-known of the early members was that one-legged Waterloo veteran, the first Marquis of Anglesey.

Like his Commodore the great cavalry leader showed the keenest interest in the improvement of warship design. He was the owner of two cutters, both built in the year of Waterloo. These were the famous *Pearl* of 113 tons and the *Liberty* of 42 tons.

* The *Kestrel* was the Earl of Yarborough's last yacht, a brigantine of two hundred and two tons, which at his death was bought by the Admiralty and served a commission on the South east coast of America. The famous *Falcon* had been sold in 1836).

The *Pearl* was one of the most celebrated yachts in the squadron. Throughout her long life, she remained under the Marquis' ownership until his death in 1853; and there were very few vessels that were able to sail past her. She was built at Colchester by the Frenchman Sainty, notorious as the builder of swift smuggling cutters.

The Man-of-War Cutter

In treating of small craft design in the Royal Navy, the cutter deserves more than a passing mention. Tracing her descent from the coasting hoy and the seventeenth century service ketch, the British war cutter has scarcely received justice from historians, for the simple reason that her duties seldom brought her into the limelight and, at the same time, she was generally commanded by an old lieutenant, who, lacking influence and aristocratic connections, and with no hope of further promotion, had, as a rule, degenerated into a grog-drinking sluggard, though still a superb seaman.

Lord St. Vincent used to say that a good officer was thrown away in a cutter whilst a bad one had no business there.

Thus it came about that practical seamen of poor education and little pretensions to good breeding were the usual run of cutter men.

Nevertheless, though not often noticed in the Gazette, the cutters besides carrying out their revenue duties, played a great part in combating the enemy privateersmen in the Channel, the North sea and elsewhere.

These British cutters were built all round the coast—Leslie in his "Old Seawings, Ways and Words" had a drawing of a cutter on the stocks on the grassy verge of a cliff edge—but every port and fishing village contributed its quota. And the men who clenched them together built by eye and seldom put pencil to paper, yet in the main their results turned out superior to those of the Admiralty's scientific designer's, so that it came to be recognised that purchased vessels were superior in speed and seaworthiness, if inferior in strength of build, to those of the surveyors.

The old English cutter was clench-built with plenty of flare forward, a moderately rounded and, later, a straight stem, greatest breadth about one third of the length from the stem head, generally abreast of the mast, steep floors, a deep heel, square transom and raked rudder post. According to Professor Laird Clowes the rig was introduced into the navy about 1763.

Every sail that could be set on a single-masted vessel, found a place in a Naval cutter's inventory. Writing of the revenue cutter *Dwarf*, of the eighteen twenties in his "Sailor's Word Book", Admiral Smyth says, she had royal studding sails, sky-scrapers, moon-rakers, stargazers, water sails and ringtails.

The bowsprit was always a running one, and the forestay set up with lanyards and dead-eyes to the stem head. The mainsail was loose-footed, with a gaff which in early days was quite short but gradualy increased in length till the sail was almost square.

In the eighteenth century, the square yard was carried very low, so that the topsail, was cut with a tremendous arch in the foot in order to clear the forestay.

There were three great periods of cutter-building in the Royal Navy 1778/9, 1806/9 and 1817/20, then, chiefly through the interest of Lord Yarborough, the Marquis of Anglesey and other keen members of the Royal Yacht Squadron, a number of yacht-like revenue cutters were built, following the lines of some of the famous cutter yachts, such as Lord Anglesey's *Pearl*, Joseph Weld's *Arrow*, Lord Belfast's *Louisa*, the Earl of Chesterfield's *Therese*, the Duke of Norfolk's *Swallow* and Captain the Honourable R. Greville's *Scorpion*.

King of Dover, A Master-Builder

The best known builder of cutters for the despatch and revenue service between 1780 and 1800 was undoubtedly King of Dover, the builder of the famous brigs, *Weazle* and *Speedy*.

His vessels seem to have been mostly built on spec and either purchased by the Admiralty whilst in frame or after launching.

He was evidently a favourite of the surveyors and a man of influence; he was a daring designer and his other vessels showed many of the characteristics of his big cutters, such as cut-away ends, rockered keels, raking stem and stern posts and much dead rise.

Sainty Builds The Ship-Sloop *Pearl*

The Frenchman "Sainty" of Colchester owed his chance to the Earl of Anglesey, being represented in the Navy List by the cutter, *Emerald*, and the ship-sloop *Pearl*, of twenty guns and five hundred and fifty-eight tons, built at Colchester in 1828.

In his autobiography Admiral Lord Clarence Paget had this to say about the latter vessel:—

"She was built by Sainty on the enlarged lines of my father's yacht, which was the clipper of these days. It was a graceful compliment to him to give me (the command of) this vessel, as he had proposed her construction. She had all the attributes of the cutter *Pearl*, was marvellously fast but not very weatherly.

The *Paddy* From Cork Beats The *Emerald*

The *Emerald*, which was made tender to the Royal Yacht, was considered the fastest cutter in the navy until a wonderful Irish cutter yacht came to Portsmouth in 1832 and licked the stuffing out of her. This was the *Big Paddy*, otherwise called the *Paddy from Cork*, a cutter of one hundred tons, designed and owned by Mr. Caulfield Beamish and built under his directions at King's Quay, Blackrock, Cork. In 1830 the *Big Paddy* made her name by beating every opponent in the Belfast, Isle of Man and Clyde regattas of that year. She even managed to hold her own in a friendly match with Lord Anglesey's *Pearl* considered 'the fastest cutter in the three Kingdoms'. though there was a light breeze, smooth water and a strong lee-going time, the *Pearl*'s best weather and the *Paddy*'s worst.

The old Marquis, who entered the Yacht Club with the *Pearl* as an original member in 1815, seldom consented to race, but in 1825 he was goaded into matching the *Pearl* against Joseph Weld's *Arrow*. But in accepting the challenge, he remarked "If the *Pearl* is beaten, I'll burn her as soon as we get back". The match was for five hundred pounds, from the yachts moorings in Cowes Roads round a mark boat in Swanage Bay and back. Luckily for the *Pearl* she won by ten and a half minutes, it was her last match.

The *Paddy*, though one hundred tons burthen, was of very light draught and her rise of floor was said to be as much as thirty degrees. In her old age she was converted into a tugboat on the river Lee.

Sainty and Beamish were far from being without rivals. Joseph White of Cowes was another designer and builder, who owed his chance to the interest of R.Y.S. members.

His finest cutter was probably the *Stag*, launched in 1827, which was considered even faster than the famous *Diligence*; both of these flew the Revenue Stripes.

Not all revenue cruisers were cutters.

There was a wonderful little brig, the *Prince of Wales*, of one hundred and sixty tons, built at Cowes in 1822 and stationed at Stranraer. She was so noted for her speed and sea qualities, that she was brought south to take part in the Experimental Squadron of 1832. She was built by Mr. Jelly of Cowes.

As regards the cutters, Captain Symonds R.N. built the *Sylvia* of seventy tons in 1827, whilst Captain Hayes R.N. built the *Arrow* one hundred and fifty seven tons in 1825, and *Seaflower* of one hundred and sixteen tons in 1830.

The surveyor, Seppings, built the *Magpie* class of cutter tenders (*Magpie, Lark, Quail, Raven*and *Starling*) in 1829.

EXAMPLES OF R.N. CUTTERS

Date Built	Name	Tons	Length Gundeck	Length Keel	Beam	Depth of Hold
1778	*Flying Fish*	190	75′	51′ 5″	25′ 8″	10′ 5″
1778	*Expedition*	151	69′	49′ 2″	24′	10′
1790	*Hind*	161	71′·8	52′ 4″	24′ 3″	9′ 7″
1806	*Surly*	137	63′	46′ 9″	23′ 6″	10′ 2″
1809	*Pigmy*	193	82′·6	70′ 6″	22′ 8″	10′ 6″
1809	*Dart*	127	62′·7	47′ 7″	22′ 5″	10′
1810	*Dwarf*	203	74′·6	56′	26′ 1″	11′ 8″
1816	*Linnet*	81	55′·6	44′ 5″	18′ 6″	7′ 6″
1817	*Diligence*	160	70′·8	52′ 3″	24′	11′
1819	*Vigilant*	161	67′·3	51′ 4″	24′ 3″	10′ 7″
1820	*Emerald*	86	57′·3	45′ 9″	18′ 9″	9′ 1″
1825	*Arrow*	157	64′	48′ 8″	24′ 9″	9′ 2″
1827	*Stag*	130	66′·1	52′ 6″	21′ 10″	9′ 10″
1830	*Magpie*	108	68′·9	49′ 6″	20′ 3″	9′
1830	*Seaflower*	116	60′	46′ 11″	21′ 8″	10′ 6″

The Yacht Club Backs Lieutenant William Symonds

It must not be supposed that the members of the Royal Yacht Club were content to show off the speed of their yachts against noted men-of-war without actively interesting themselves in the building programme of the Admiralty.

We have seen how the Marquis of Anglesey was responsible for the building of the *Pearl*, sloop of war: it was chiefly through Lord Vernon that Commander Symonds was commissioned to design the famous *Columbine*, though he also had the backing of many other members notably the Commodore, Lord Anglesey and Vice-Admiral the Honourable Sir Charles Paget.

In 1822, whilst cruising about the Mediterranean in his yacht, the *Transit*, the Honourable George Vernon was astonished by the smart way in which a little yawl yacht worked out of Valetta harbour. On making enquiries he discovered that this yawl was the *Nancy Dawson*, designed and built by the intendant, a Naval officer named Lieutenant William Symonds.

A warm friendship was soon struck up between the two families of Vernon and Symonds; and the two yachts, *Transit* and *Nancy Dawson*, were raced against each other with results all in favour of the latter. At the end of the Malta season Symonds embarked his family in three small yachts of his own build, the *Nancy Dawson*, a three-masted lugger, called the *Fortune's Favourite* and a still smaller boat, the *Sal Shapes*.

Whilst the *Transit* sailed for England direct, the smaller yachts sailed for Leghorn.

Here Symonds found a very famous yachtsman, Lord Byron, aboard his schooner, the *Bolivar*, which romantic vessel had the indignity of being beaten by the little *Nancy Dawson*.

Another anecdote of Byron at this period is mentioned in Symond's autobiography.

An officious brig-sloop, the *Despatch*, objected to Byron flying a pendant and ordered him to haul it down. There would have been a dual to avenge the indignity, had not the commander of the *Despatch* taken himself off.

The year 1824 found Lieutenant Symonds back in England, where he published his pamphlet on Naval Architecture. In the following year through the interest of George Vernon and his other yacht club friends he was appointed First Lieutenant of the Royal Yacht, *Royal George*, with the command of her tender, the ten-gun brig, *Calliope*, which he quickly changed from a slow to a fast sailer, by altering the position and stand of her masts and her ballasting. As Symonds himself explained, though 'great breadth of beam and extraordinary sharpness' were the characteristic features of his system of designing, he paid very careful attention to stowage, the stand of the masts and the cut and set of the sails.

Symonds Designs The *Columbine*

Symond's pamphlet roused a great deal of interest both at the Admiralty and in the public press and gained him the backing of a large number of influential people. Though Lord Melville and Admiral Sir George Cockburn favoured him, that troublesome and ineffective body, the Navy board, being greatly offended by his pamphlet, became his implacable enemy, and when he was commissioned by the First Lord to design the *Columbine*, tried to make his chief supporter, George Vernon, sign a bond for twenty thousand pounds as a guarantee. However Symonds' friends in the Royal Yacht Club, headed by Lord Yarborough, and George Vernon, not to speak of Vice-Admiral the Honourable Sir C. Paget, the commander of the *Royal George* and also a full member of the club, were too strong for the Board's opposition and the bond was never signed whilst the designing of the *Columbine* went ahead.

The Experimental Squadron 1825

In the year 1825 *Calliope* was allowed to join the Experimental Squadron and Symonds declared that his little brig beat the lot of them.

This, the first of the Experimental Squadrons, cannot be better described than by the verses of an able seaman of the *Pandora*, which ran as follows:—

Twas on the 21st of March, from Spithead we made sail,
With the Experimental Squadron, in a sweet and pleasant gale;
The wind from E.S.E., my boys, through the Needles we did go;
With British colours flying, we made a gallant show.

The first was the *Phaeton*, our noble Commodore,
The *Pylades*, and *Champion, Orestes* and *Pandor*,
The *Rose* also in company, to the westward we did steer,
To try our rate of sailing without any doubt or fear.

We sailed with the wind right aft, full forty leagues or more,
Until we spied a signal, made by our noble Commodore,
To haul our ships up to the wind, as close as they could be,
To try which was the best, both Large[1] as well as Bye.[2]

To our Commodore the praise is due, he sails so very fast,
But he carried away his bowsprit[3], and endangered his mainmast;
The *Pylades* sails very well, but sorry am I to say,
She lost three of her bravest tars when her fore-topmast broke away[4].

The *Champion* and *Orestes* too, both carry a press of sail,
But rig the *Pandora* as a brig[5], and she'll show them all her tail;
The wind blows from the Eastward, into Scilly we must go,
To put our ships to rights a bit, and then to Portsmouth ho!

---

1 Sailing with a fair wind.
2 Sailing with a foul wind.
3 The *Phaeton*, forty-six-gun frigate, had an iron bowsprit and mast for trial but they did not answer.
4 The *Pylades*, eighteen-gun sloop, designed by Sir Robert Seppings, the surveyor, lost her fore-topmast over the side, whilst three men were aloft furling her fore-topgallantsail, in a strong blow.
5 The eighteen-gun brig-sloop *Pandora* had been altered to a ship which put her deeper in the water, and cost her her good sailing qualities, spreading less sail on a wind by one hundred and fifty yards than before and failing to hold so good a wind.

The eighteen-gun corvette, *Champion*, had been designed by Captain Hayes R.N., the designer of the *Arrow* cutter, which had proved superior to the revenue cutter, *Basilisk*, designed by Seppings.

The eighteen-gun corvette *Orestes*, from the Board of the School of Naval Architecture, under the direction of Professor Inman, was intended to be an improved *Rose*, which had been built to their designs but to Admiralty dimensions in 1821.

After this first cruise all these experimental ships were altered. *Orestes* had her masts shifted and her sail area increased: *Pylades* had her mast positions changed and her keel deepened by a foot. But the experiments led nowhere, though after three cruises Tinchan, the naval architect, places the *Orestes* first, the *Plyades* second and the *Champion* third, his placing is suspect owing to his being personally interested.

A Letter of the Duke of Portland

In the autumn of 1825 Symonds handed over the *Calliope* on promotion to commander; and by the turn of the year the *Columbine* was in frame at Portsmouth and receiving a great deal of attention and admiration.

Amongst others, the fourth Duke of Portland saw her and fell in love with her, with the result that he laid down the beautiful little *Pantaloon* at his building yard at Troon to Symonds' design.

Before doing so, the Duke wrote the following letter explaining his intentions to Commander Symonds.

19 Cavendish Square,
London,
May 15, 1829.

Dear Sir,

Having occasion to trouble you with a letter on one subject, I will write upon two.

The first subject on which I must write to you is to know where I should pay my subscription to the widow of the late Mr. Frost.

The other subject is one which does not press so much, but which, if you give me credit for being as sincere an admirer of your system of ship-building as I really am, will not surprise you.

I think it will appear to you very plain that between the necessity of economy and the indisposition of the Navy Board, the Admiralty is not likely of itself to sanction at present any further experiments.

In order to force them upon it, it had occurred to me to be possible to build a ship myself: and when built, to offer it to the Admiralty at a moderate price, provided, on trial, it beat a great majority (seven out of ten) of their own vessels of the same class, which might be tried with it.

My first idea was to have given full scope to both your favourite ideas, not only of building, but rigging, and to have built a ten-gun vessel to be rigged as a ketch. But seeing the great prejudice against this mode of rigging, when applied to vessels of the size of a gun-brig, amongst naval men, and considering the impossibility of prevailing against a prejudice (if such it is) I next turned my thoughts to the equipment of a vessel of smaller description, between a cutter and a gun-brig, but as I cannot find out that there is a class of vessels of that description, I have also abandoned that notion.

I, therefore, have been obliged to revert to the idea of building a gun-brig: and from the inquiries I have made of the usual length of the gun-brigs in H.M.'s Service, I have concluded that one built on your plan, would approach very near to the dimensions of the *Harlequin**.

This is the present state of my intentions, and I wish in this stage to submit them to your consideration, whether the attempt would be likely to be conducive to the further introduction of your system or otherwise: and if you should be of that opinion, what would be the precautions necessary to be taken to obviate any objections hereafter to be made by the Admiralty.

* This refers to the yacht *Harlequin*, a ketch of 292 tons, built for Lord Vernon, on Symonds' lines in 1828, and converted to brig-rig the following year. This yacht must not be confused with the Naval brigs of that name: apparently Vernon pulled the *Transit* to pieces and used her timbers.

> I have little doubt that if their consent was previously asked it would be refused. But I do not see how they could refuse a trial of the vessel when actually built, or to take it at a moderate price in cast it should be display the great superiority which, if faithfully built on your principles, I have no doubt it would.
>
> I have not heard yet that my boats are finished†: when they are, I should be very glad if you could be tempted to superintend the trials of their respective merits.
>
> Ever, dear sir,
> Yours very sincerely
> Scott Portland

A word should perhaps be said concerning this fashion of Pantomime names both on the Royal Yacht Club and in the Royal Navy.

This was due probably to the popularity of the Pantomime "Mother Goose", first performed at Covent Garden in 1806 and to the great success of Joseph Grimaldi as the clown.

In 1828 the Duke of Portland named his new ketch of one hundred and fifty-six tons, built on the lines of the *Columbine*, the *Clown*.

Columbine, First of the Symondites

The *Columbine*, which was launched at Portsmouth on the 4th of December, 1826, was a great success from the start.

She was a very pretty ship and many sailors will tell you that good looks are a sign of good qualities all round. Certainly this was the case with the *Columbine*, for she was noted for her sea kindliness as for her speed; and she was one of those rare vessels which had no vices, behaving like a thoroughbred in every situation.

In the *United Service Journal* she was highly praised and proclaimed to be 'one of the prettiest and fastest vessels of her size that ever swam'.

Charlie Napier declared '*Columbine* is indeed a sweet vessel, the regular American clipper, and does infinite credit to her constructor'.

Her crew voiced their opinion of her in the following forecastle song, which will be found in *Slight's Chronicles* of Portsmouth.

Of all the ships that e'er were built
To sail the ocean's brine, sir,
Throughout the fleet not one can beat
Our saucy *Columbine*, sir.
For she's so strong, so tight, so stiff,
And does the rest outshine, sir,
Huzza! for him that laid the plan
Of the saucy *Columbine*, sir.

The *Trinculo* may do her best,
And the *Alert* so fleet, sir,
Alert she is, but then she's not
Alert enough to beat, sir,
Our bonny bark at any time
Shall run her out of sight, sir;
And though we sail just like a witch
We've lots of room to fight, sir.

We do not fear the *Challenger*,
The *Sapphire* or the *Tyne*, sir.
The *Wolf* may growl, but, fair or foul,
No beating *Columbine*, sir.
The *Acorn* and the *Satellite*,
Their efforts, too, may try, sir,
But if they beat the *Columbine*,
Why, hang it, they must fly, sir.

† This paragraph refers to five little ten-tonners of various designs, named *Punchinello, Grimaldi*, etc., which were built entirely for experimental purposes.

8. Captain Sir William Symonds, K.C.B. Surveyor of the Navy.

From a lithograph after the painting by Phillips. In the National Maritime Museum.

[*Facing page 176.*

9. J. B. B. McHardy as a Lieutenant and as a Rear-Admiral.

From a pencil drawing and a litho vignette in the National Maritime Museum.

[*Facing page 177.*

As an epoch-making vessel in the progress of Naval ship design, the *Columbine* must be considered one of the most important warships of the last days of wood, hemp and canvas in the Royal Navy. To her success Sir William Symonds owed his appointment to the post of surveyor; though it must be confessed that she would never have been built but for the keenness and influence of his friends in the Royal Yacht Club, who not only had to overcome professional jealousy and prejudice, but practically agree to imdemnify the Admiralty should she turn out to be a failure.

Her sucess led to the building of a whole fleet of sailing men-of-war of all rates, from the majestic one hundred and sixteen gun, first rate, *Queen*, down to the little schooner, *Bermuda*; and these vessels were known throughout the world as 'the Symondites'.

Characteristics of the Symondites

That the innovation in design was a radical one may be realised by a glance at the midship section of a pre-Symondite and that of a Symondite.

Symonds, himself, gave a very simple demonstration of the difference by joining his thumbs together and making a midship section with his hands open, then turning his joined thumbs uppermost and bringing his fingers together.

His vessels were, in fact, wedge-shaped under water instead of being rounded like a barrel.

The Barque-Rig

The *Columbine* was a flush-decked, eighteen-gun sloop, and was barqued-rigged. And here again was a radical innovation, showing great enterprise on the part of her designer. Just at this time there was a prejudice against the brig-rig, and many of the famous eighteen-gun sloops were beng changed from brig to ship-rig, to their great detriment as was seen in the case of the *Pandora* and others. The *Columbine*'s barque-rig may have been a surrender to the Admiralty, yet there is a curious parallel in the French Navy.

In 1801 a corvette a batterie barbette, named *La Diligente* was launched, but her constructor resigned in a pique and seemed to have died of chagrin because she was not rigged in accordance with his opinion.

But directly she was rigged and fitted in every way upon his plan she proved a great success, and for many years was considered the fastest vessel in the French Service: and here is the significant point—she, also, was barque-rigged. Though the French tried in vain to build after her model, they never succeeded in producing a vessel which could rival her sailing qualities.

The fashion of three masts for such small vessels soon passed and in 1834 *Columbine* was re-rigged as a brig, and this was found to be a great improvement all round.

The plan shows her as refitted with two masts instead of three.

Here are the measurements given on the plan.

		feet	inches
Length between perpendiculars		105	0½
Length of keel for tonnage		84	0⅛
Breadth of extreme		33	6¼
Breadth moulded		32	8
Depth in hold		7	11
Draught (light line) Forward		8	3
	Aft	12	10½
Draught (fitted for sea) Forward		13	10
	Aft	15	0
Displacement (light line)		257 tons	
Displacement (fitted for sea)		502 tons	
Burthen in Tons		492	

Symonds, himself, was given command of his vessel and was allowed to chose his officers, Lieutenants J. Welch and E. Wilson. His son Tom Symonds (afterwards a very noted Admiral) and his nephew Louis Tindal joined the *Columbine* as midshipmen.

The Experimental Squadron of 1827

During the summer of 1827 a second Experimental Squadron was sent to sea under Sir Thomas Hardy with his flag in the *Pyramus* (a forty-two-gun frigate modelled on the *Belle Poule* and built in 1810).

Besides the *Columbine*, the experimental ships consisted of the following:—

Challenger,	28,	Captain J. Harrison, designed by Captain Hays.
Tyne,	28,	Captain J. K. White, designed by Sir R. Seppings.
Sapphire,	28,	Captain Henry Dundas, designed by Superior class of shipwrights apprentices.
Wolf,	18,	Commander Geo. Hayes, designed by Captain Hays.
Acorn,	18,	Commander Edward Gordon, designed by Sir R. Seppings.
Satellite,	18,	Commander J. M. Laws, designed by Sir R. Seppings.
Alert,	18,	Commander Sam Burgess, designed by Sir Wm. Rule.

All these ships were untried and just off the stocks with the exception of the old *Alert*, which was launched as a brig-sloop in 1813.

Though the first cruise, which lasted to the end of May, proved *Columbine* to be superior to the rest of the Experimental ships on all points, Symonds was far from satisfied with her trim, and was allowed to shift his masts further aft and give her more after canvas.

There was, of course, the keenest rivalry between the different ships and their supporters urged their claims by running down their opponents in every possible way.

During the first two cruises the ships were told to stow four month's provisions and as much water as possible.

When Doctor Inman, of the Naval College who was mainly responsible for *Sapphire*'s lines was told by the Victuallers chief clerk that *Columbine* had handed in receipts for four month's provisions and fifty tons of water, he remarked:—

"If Captain Symonds had taken the provisions in at one side, he has thrown them overboard on the other, and Lord Vernon has indemnified the purser".

Another enemy of the *Columbine*, Mr. Secretary Croker of the Admiralty, when he sent out the order for the squadron to complete to six months' victualling office allowance for the third cruise, said:— "The *Columbine*'s death warrant is signed!". And he was considerably astonished when told that she had stowed the six months' provisions in addition to forty-five and a half tons of water, "all below, except two lime-juice cases".

This was confirmed by Sir Thomas Hardy's report on *Columbine*'s stowage, which ran as follows:—

"The bread in the bread room, and a bin in the centre of the 'tween-decks, the provisions under hatches (except two lime-juice cases on the lower deck) the whole of the stores in the store-rooms, the sails in bins round the 'tween-decks—ship in good order and ready for sea".

Thus was a great triumph for Symonds as when unable to deny the superior speed of *Columbine*, inability to stow her full allowance for foreign service was put forward.

As soon as the trials were over Symonds was posted and the *Columbine* under Commander C. Crole was sent to the Halifax station.

The Duke of Portland's *Pantaloon*

We now come to Symond's second great success, the ten-gun brig *Pantaloon*, built through the enterprise of the Duke of Portland at his own yard at Troon.

Symonds himself went North to superintend her fitting out, and the making of her sails. Let me now quote from his own diary:—

"At length in the early part of the summer (1831) the *Pantaloon* was launched and tried against the *Clown.* After this we sailed in company to Plymouth, to join the Channel Squadron under Sir Edward Codrington.

We tried immediately, though only three weeks off the stocks: and made a spectacle of the squadron, composed of the *Caledonia*, flag-ship, the *Prince Regent, Asia, Revenge, Donegal, Talavera, Barham, Curacoa, Stag, Pearl* and *Charybdis*. Our victory was reported to the Admiralty, after many trials and in all weathers".

Sir Edward Codrington's report was decisive enough, for its first paragraph ran as follows:—

"Caledonia" at sea,
28th July, 1831.

Sir,

The several trials which we have had of the sailing of His Grace the Duke of Portland's brig "Pantaloon" have all tended to satisfy me of her being able to outsail every ship and vessel under my command under any circumstances of wind and weather in which sail can be carried, and the proof which she gave yesterday was so decisive that I consider any further trial with this squadron as useless . . .

To Captain the honourable George Elliot
Admiralty

The dimensions of *Pantaloon* are of interest when set alongside those of the *Rolla*, the pioneeer ship of the ten-gun brig class, which the Duke of Portland hoped the *Pantaloon* would make obsolete.

Date Built	Name	Tons	Guns	Length Gundeck	Length Keel	Beam	Depth of Hold
1807	*Rolla*	235	8 18-pr carr 2 6-pr guns	90	73·7	24	11
1831	*Pantaloon*	323	2 6-pr guns	90	71·4	29·4	12·8

Fincham gives *Pantaloon*'s top speed as nine knots four fathoms close-hauled in smooth water, and with all sail set before the wind in moderate weather twelve knots.

She was immediately bought into the navy and made tender to the Royal Yacht.

Captain Symonds was now on the full flood of success. The Lord High Admiral (the Duke of Clarence), after inspecting the *Columbine*, had suggested his designing a large frigate, but the Navy Board had succeeded in squashing this project; and it was not until Sir James Graham became first Lord of the Admiralty in November, 1830, that anything further came of it.

Symonds Appointed Surveyor

In the spring of 1832 'those Spiders of the Navy Board', as old Lord St. Vincent called them, were abolished. Then in June Sir Robert Seppings was retired upon superannuation. (Joseph Tucker, the joint-surveyor, having retired in 1831). This left the way clear for the supporters of Captain Symonds to urge his appointment, and on June the 9th, 1832 he became Surveyor of the Navy.

The appointment of a naval officer to this technical post, which had always been held by a civilian aroused a great deal of criticism and dissatisfaction, and Symonds speedily found the whole strength of the dockyards from the master shipwrights down to the apprentices in the School of Naval Architecture pitted against his rule.

If it had not been for the strong support of his noble friends in the Royal Yacht Club and the backing of many senior officers in the navy, he would have found it hard to make any headway. He was lucky, or possibly clever, in getting two very capable men appointed to his staff. John Edye, late chief foreman of Chatham dockyard, was made his chief clerk and his professional advisor, and Oliver Lang was made his chief draughtsman.

On May day 1832, the fifty-gun frigate, *Vernon*, was launched at Woolwich, having been built to his design, in five months by the father of Oliver Lang, and soon afterwards the first pair of Symonds' sixteen-gun, four hundred and thirty ton, brig-sloops, the *Snake* and *Serpent*, were launched, the first from Fletcher's Thames yard and the second from Woolwich dockyard.

The *Snake* was just in time to take her place in the Experimental Squadron of 1832.

Lord Belfast's Yacht *Waterwitch*

Hardly had the new surveyor taken office before he found that he had a new competitor against him—namely Joseph White, the famous Cowes yacht-builder.

White received his order to design and build a gun-brig from the Vice-Commodore of the Royal Yacht Club, the Earl of Belfast, a man of great energies and enthusiasms, who had suddenly tired of the long dual betweeen his cutter, *Louisa* and Joseph Weld's *Alarm* and was seeking new worlds to conquer.

White's task was not an easy one, taking the measurements and the tonnage of the successful *Pantaloon* he was to build a brig that should not only be her superior in speed, but in all the qualities considered necessary in a man-of-war.

In his effort to please Lord Belfast, White surpassed himself—the little *Water Witch* was his chef d'oeuvre; he never produced a sweeter vessel though he was responsible for many beautiful yachts, being considered the chief builder to the Royal Yacht Club; had constructed some of the fastest of the revenue cutters, notably *Vigilant* and *Stag*; was renowned in the China Seas for his superb opium clippers, such as *Audax* and *Astarte, Denia* and *Wild Dayrell*; and finally, had a whole fleet of racing fruit schooners to his credit.

Lord Belfast was one of those 'fighting macs', who was never happy unless he was in the thick of a contest or dispute of some sort, and he was far from being afraid of the publicity of the press, thus the early history of his gun-brig yacht may be followed step by step in such journals as the *Sporting Magazine*, the *United Service Journal*, the *Nautical Magazine, Bells's Life* and the *Advertiser*.

In the *United Service Journal* of 1835, the naval Architect, William Henwood, gave a table of calculations for twenty British men-of-war of each rate, from which I have taken those for *Waterwitch* and *Columbine*:—

	Waterwitch	*Columbine*
Length at Load water-line	88′ 11″	102′ 7″
Breadth extreme at water-line	28′ 9½″	33′ 2¼″
Depth from water-line to lower edge of keel rabbet	11·142′	13·4′
Draught of water forward	10′ 2″	14′ 4¼″
Draught of water aft	14′ 6″	14′ 10¾″
Displacement in tons	330·8	524·8
Centre of gravity of ditto before middle of load-water-line	1·67 ft.	4·25 ft.
Displacement before centre of gravity	5804 cu. ft.	9435 cu. ft.
Displacement abaft cèntre of gravity	5774 cu. ft.	8933 cu. ft.
Difference of fore and after bodies in tons	86/100	14 3/10
Distance of centre of gravity of fore-body from centre of gravity of the Displacement	16·44 ft.	18·79 ft.
Distance of centre of gravity of after-body from centre of gravity of the Displacement	16·52 ft.	19·84 ft.

These calculations are also given by A.F.B. Creuze in his Treatise on Navai Architecture.

Here is what Henwood says of the *Waterwitch*:—

"It remains merely at present too take a passing notice of the *Waterwitch*, lately purchased into the Navy and which appears to possess very superior sailing qualities. The points in this vessel, which distinguish her from others, and perhaps especially from those with which she has been placed in competition, are the proximity of her centre of gravity to the middle of her length and the very near equality of her tendencies to pitch and scend".

As regards her scantling, Lord Belfast gave the newspapers the following account:—

"The *Waterwitch* has very high bulwarks, scantling far exceeding that of ordinary vessels and moreover, a solid bottom. She is, in fact, a mass of timber. He (Lord Belfast) profited by the experience of what was urged against the *Pantaloon* yacht, which vessel outsailed all the old-fashioned ships in Sir Edward Codrington's squadron, but was found not to have a solid bottom nor the proper quantity of timber for a man-of-war, and the latter was put in before she was taken into the King's service . . . *Neptune* is quite right as regards her stern being upright and consequently not so handsome as if it had been more overhung. But being built for a man-of-war, the intention, which had completely succeeded, was to enable her to run two guns out astern without a platform, which most vessels are obliged tc have, and which is exceedingly inconvenient in as much as it takes up a considerable portion of the quarterdeck".

In the well-known print of the *Waterwitch*, beating Sir Pulteney Malcolm's Experimental Squadron this ugly stern is plainly in evidence, but the first alteration made by the Admiralty on purchasing her, was to give her a very handsome counter—apparently they thought the advantage of being able to fire her stern-chasers was negligible.

The Experimental Squadron of 1832

Lord Belfast persuaded Captain George Pechell R.N. to take command of the *Waterwitch* for her trials with the Experimental Squadron, which consisted of:—

Donegal,	78, flagship, taken from the French 1798.
Vernon,	50, new frigate by Wm. Symonds.
Dryad,	42, designed by Henslow 1795.
Stag,	46, similar to American *President*.
Castor,	36, new frigate by Sir R. Seppings.
Tyne,	28, built by Sir R. Seppings 1826.
Nimrod,	20, built by Sir R. Seppings 1828.
Orestes,	18, designed by School of Naval Architects 1824.
Trinculo,	16, old Rule 18-gun-brig built Bursedon 1809.
Snake,	16, new-gun brig 430 tons by Wm. Symonds.
Prince of Wales,	Revenue Brig of 200 tons, built at Cowes April 1806, had a thorough repair at Plymouth in 1823. Lieutenant Oliver, her commander had commanded her for twenty-one years on the coast of Scotland.

When the *Waterwitch* joined the Squadron during the first week of August, there had been several trials, in which the ships had had a chance to 'tune up', and these had shown that the remarkable old revenue brig had the heels of the squadron.

The new surveyor's ships, *Vernon* and *Snake* were absent on the new brig-yachts first trial.

Waterwitch's weight of provisions and water was given as one hundred and sixty tons; in a test which lasted from noon till seven on August the twelfth the four leading ships bore from the flag at the finish.

Waterwitch	W¼S	6½ miles and 48 yards.
Prince of Wales	W by S	4 miles and 327 yards.
Castor	SW by W¾W	3 miles and 220 yards.
Nimrod	NW by W	2¼ miles and 307 yards.

Admiral Malcolm's report ran as follows:—

"In our trial today on a wind with a moderate royal breeze and smooth water, going from two and a half to four knots, the *Waterwitch* had a very considerable advantage of all the squadron, particularly in weathering. The *Castor* and *Prince of Wales* were nearly equal and both these vessels gained on the *Orestes* and gained and weathered a good deal on the *Donegal* and *Nimrod*".

On the following day, the Admiral reported:—

"We had a fine royal breeze from the West today and were going from four to five knots, and in a trial of four hours and a half, the *Waterwitch* weathered on the

Castor	1½ miles.
Prince of Wales	2¼ miles.
Trinculo	3½ miles.
Donegal	5¼ miles.
Nimrod	5¼ miles.

On August 27th the *Clown*, with the Duke of Portland on board, and a schooner yacht, the *Campodoro*, of one hundred and six tons joined in the trials and, said the Admiral, "went to windward quite as well as any of the squadron". *Waterwitch*, however, was not present.

On September the 2nd *Waterwitch* left Plymouth with the squadron and in light westerly breezes and smooth water had her first opportunity of showing her stern to *Snake* and *Vernon*, which vessels in the order named led the rest of the experimental ships.

The Lords of the Admiralty in the Admiralty steam-yacht *Lightning* now arrived to watch the trials and on September the 4th an eight hour trial to windward in a fine easterly breeze took place. During the whole day *Waterwitch* led with *Snake* and *Vernon* in second and third places, then just before the end, the wind fell and in the swell the brigs could not keep the wind in their sails and this allowed the *Vernon* to creep up and head *Snake* by half a mile and *Waterwitch* by a quarter of a mile.

On the next day the squadron was tried before the wind in fine weather, thirty miles being covered in six hours by the *Donegal*.

In this time the *Waterwitch* gained

1½ miles on the *Snake*
3¼ miles on the *Vernon*
4½ miles on the *Castor*
6¼ miles on the *Stag*
7 miles on the *Nimrod*
11½ miles on the *Donegal*

On September the 6th the wind was Easterly, a fine breeze with a little swell.

"At noon", reported the Admiral, "the *Waterwitch* parted company, having carried away her bobstay and Captain Pechell being desirous to return in her to London immediately. The *Waterwitch* beat the *Snake* a little today and in her various trials with the Squadron, she has certainly shown herself to be a fine vessel and a fast sailer".

His report on the *Prince of Wales* and the *Snake*, which two brigs ranked next to the *Waterwitch*, are worth quoting:—

"The *Prince of Wales* is a remarkably fine little brig; a fast vessel on a wind; and a lively sea-boat. She held way with the *Vernon* on a wind, when blowing strong".

"The *Snake* is a very fine brig. When it blows strong and there is a head sea she weathers on the *Vernon* in a surprising manner, but in smooth water she has no advantage over her. She goes well 'large', but not quite so fast as the *Vernon* and *Castor*".

The result of these trials was a hot paper warfare between the supporters of the *Waterwitch* and the *Snake*. But Lord Belfast and Captain Pechell had the last word in the following letter to the *Nautical Magazine*, dated October the 4th, 1832.

Sir,

The proceedings of the Experimental Squadron, as reported in your last magazine for this month, are pretty nearly correct; except that a brig, named *Waterwitch*, gave another brig, called *Snake*, as decided and complete a dressing, both by the wind, before the wind, and off the wind as any vessel ever yet gave another.

Secondly, I agree with your informant that *Waterwitch* did display some superiority in light winds: superiority enough to beat the whole squadron: but she displayed a much greater superiority in strong breezes and a head sea, which does not appear to be at all in accordance with the feelings of your informant, whose whole, sole and only consolation seems to be that *Waterwitch* 'could not stand the head sea that was running': if she could not, why did not *Snake* (after a trial of four hours and a half, with leave to put her guns, etc., below) come up with her?

As for stability, the report of the inclination or heel was a conclusive proof as to the superior stability of *Waterwitch*.

The telegraphic communication alluded to 'that the *Waterwitch* was satisfied with her superiority' was inconsequence of a previous signal made to the Admiral before starting that morning—'that *Waterwitch* intended leaving the Squadron that afternoon for England'.

Your informant labours under a dreadful mistake when he states *Snake* always started to leeward, he intended to say *Waterwitch*, not *Snake*, as in every trial, *Snake* was invariably on the weather quarter of *Waterwitch*; and if he will take trouble to recollect, he will remember that in every trial by the wind, *Waterwitch* spared *Snake* a reef in his topsails or royals or flying jib.

The correctness of these statements are well-known on board the flagship.

On September the 4th the following trial was made (in the presence of the Board of Admiralty) by the wind under all sail for eight hours on the larboard tack, with a fine breeze from the Eastward, which continued steady for seven hours and during which time *Waterwitch* had considerable advantage over the whole squadron.

It afterwards fell nearly calm: the *Waterwitch* being ordered to tack by signal, nearly becalmed and bowing a short head swell, stood nearly still, while the *Vernon* coming up two points, with the sea on her quarter, was enabled to weather the *Waterwitch* by a short distance.

It must be recollected, however, that the *Waterwitch* at starting was upwards of a cable's length to leeward of the *Vernon*. The *Snake* at the end of the trial was about two miles to leeward.

September the 5th Wind E by S, Course W by N, rate of sailing from six to seven knots; length of trial, six hours; under all sail: studding sails on both sides below and aloft.

Ships of the Squadron	Distance from *Waterwitch* at starting	Bearing from *Waterwitch* at starting	At conclusion of trial	Distance gained by *Waterwitch*
Vernon	½ mile	N by E	E by N	2 miles
Castor	½ mile	North	E ½ S	3½ miles
Stag	½ mile	E by S	E by S ½ S	5 miles
Donegal	5 miles	W by N	E by S	12 miles
Snake	500 yards	N by W	NE ½ E	2 miles

September the 6th. Wind E by S. Course SSE; Scilly bearing ENE fifty miles: length of trial four hours: the Squadron carrying double-reefed topsails and topgallantsails.

Ships of the Squadron	Distance from *Waterwitch* at starting	Bearing from *Waterwitch* at starting	At conclusion of trial	Distance gained by *Waterwitch*
Vernon	300 yards	NNW	N by W½W	3 miles
Snake	300 yards	NNE	North	1 mile
Castor	400 yards	N by W	NW by N	4½ miles

> The ships generally in this trial had their hammocks down, some of them their guns run in the *Snake* ordered by the Admiral to put guns, anchors, cables and whatever might be deemed an impediment to her sailing below: but their stability was not equal to the *Waterwitch*.
>
> *Signed* Belfast
> George Pechell, Capt. R.N.

Waterwitch and _Pantaloon_

Previous to joining the Experimental Squadron Lord Belfast had gone in search of the *Pantaloon*, which as tender to the Royal Yacht, had constantly shown off her beauty and her speed before the crack yachts of the Royal Yacht Club.

But *Pantaloon* was not to be found, and the supporters of *Waterwitch* insinuated that she had been sent out of the way on purpose, but as a matter of fact *Pantaloon* was carrying the mails out to the fleet off Lisbon.

According to the late Charles Ratsey, who was aboard the *Waterwitch*, Belfast chased the *Pantaloon* right away to the coast of Portugal where he succeeded in having a successful trial of sailing with her, but I can find no record of this trial and fear he is confusing it with a later occasion.

There were two points upon which everyone agreed that *Waterwitch* had the advantage.

The first was in her beautiful bow with its long, gradual curves, which made the sharpest of Symondites look bluff, and the Seppings models veritable colliers.

When Joseph Weld inspected the brig on the stocks it was her long bow which he pronounced would beat the *Pantaloon*.

As proof of this, on suggestion apparently of Lieutenant S. C. Dacres, her commander, the *Pantaloon*'s bow was altered in the spring of 1833, to the very great improvement of her sea worthiness in a head sea, as well as of her speed in rough weather.

Ratsey's Sails

The second great advantage possessed by the *Waterwitch* were her beautifully cut Ratsey sails. G. R. Ratsey, the sailmaker, was aboard the *Waterwitch* during the trials and one day the Admiral sent for him.

When he arrived aboard the *Donegal*, Sir Pulteney Malcom asked him:— "I want you to tell me what there is about your sails that makes them so superior to those of all the fleet".

Hardly were the trials over before the following paragraph appeared in the October the 1st issue of the *Times*.

"The Board of the Admiralty, having expressed its very great admiration for the beautiful; symmetry and standing of the sails of the *Waterwitch* yacht, made by Mr. Ratsey of Cowes, have ordered that the sails of the men-of-war shall in future be cut in a similar manner".

It was not until November that Lord Belfast was able to satisfy his ambition in trying the *Waterwitch* against the *Pantaloon*.

He caught her in Falmouth on her way out to the Tagus and arranged with her commander, Lieutenant Dacres, to have a contest the following day. At 8 a.m., therefore on November the 23rd, the *Waterwitch* weighed her anchor and beat out of Falmouth harbour with two post captains and the master of a Falmouth packet on board.

The wind was strong at SSW and the brig was under double-reefed topsails, foresail, jib and fore and aft mainsail.

Pantaloon came out at 10 a.m. and *Waterwitch* at once bore down and rounded to close on her weather quarter.

Then at 11.15 a.m. both brigs filled away on the starboardtack in a heavy sea and strong SSW wind under courses and topgallant sails over reefed topsails, *Pantaloon* being about a couple of cables to the ENE of the *Waterwitch* at the start.

After four and three-quarter hours' sailing, the *Waterwitch* was five miles dead to the windward to weather of the Lizard, whilst *Pantaloon* had only just fetched to windward of the Black Head.

At 4 p.m. the *Waterwitch* hove round and ran back, and at 4.30 hauled her wind on the weather beam of the *Pantaloon*. Both vessels then tacked to the Southward, *Waterwitch* maintaining her position with her square mainsail in the buntlines.

At 6 p.m. the two brigs tacked to the Westward together, the wind still strong from the SSW. At midnight they lost sight of each other in the darkness, and after burning blue lights, which were not answered, *Waterwitch* returned to Falmouth, whilst *Pantaloon* continued on her course for Lisbon.

When the summer of 1833 came round, the Admiralty still showed no sign of wishing to buy *Waterwitch*, whereupon Lord Belfast amused himself by showing off his brig's paces against every man-of-war that came out of Portsmouth.

His favourite manoeuvre was to sail round them, often sparing canvas; he had a smart crew on board and sometimes he would make tack for tack and each time the *Waterwitch* came round she would have her ropes coiled down first, very often by as much as a minute and a half. He could generally spare a sloop or gun-brig his topgallant sails, and he would run ahead of a line of battleship or heavy frigate with his mainsail hauled up.

His chief victims were the new Symondites, the clippers of the Service, and his ostentatious attentions must have been exceedingly galling, especially as each time the *Waterwitch* showed up a Government vessel, a full and most damning report would appear in *Bell's Life* and other journals and papers which supported Lord Belfast.

Before joining the Experimental Squadron in 1832 Lord Belfast gave the following information to the press:—

"Her sails are the same size as those of a ten-gun brig, nor has she any advantage in being without fittings below, having all the bulkheads up with the exception of the one, which ought to divide the captain's cabin from the gun room, which was omitted to make a larger and more airy cabin for my friends. She has her full weight of stores, etc., on board, as if provisioned for five months, with eighteen-pounder carronades and two long six-pounders, three boats, all spars etc., on deck . . .

I should not have the least objection to change her eighteen-pounders to twenty-four-pounders, and sail any square rigged vessel now in England for whatever sum they please".

With regard to the *Waterwitch*'s sail area, the following comparison with that of her life-long rival, the *Pantaloon* is of interest, when taken in conjunction with their sail plans.

Sails	*Waterwitch*	*Pantaloon*
Fore and main royals	255 feet	260 feet
Fore and main topgallantsails	535 feet	610 feet
Fore and main topsails	1210 feet	1160 feet
Fore course	1250 feet	1196 feet
Main course	1620 feet	1580 feet
Jib	620 feet	530 feet
Flying jib	325 feet	295 feet
Fore and aft mainsail	1830 feet	1650 feet

The Race Round the Eddystone

Before the yachting season of 1834 opened, Lord Belfast dismantled the *Waterwitch* as a man-of-war and refitted her as a yacht; he also improved her appearance by fitting a false counter to her chopped off stern.

At first it was rumoured that he proposed racing her against Weld's invincible *Alarm*, but in the end the brig's only race proved to be the one thousand pounds' match against C. R. M. Talbot's schooner, *Galatea* of one hundred and seventy tons.

Lord Belfast in his enthusiastic fashion had challenged any square-rigger afloat to a race from the Nab round the Eddystone and back, and the *Galatea* with her square foretopsail was allowed to consider herself a square-rigged vessel. The match aroused a tremendous amount of interest, not only amongst yachtsmen, but with the betting fraternity.

As regards the former, Captain Davis, representing the Southampton yacht skippers, went over to Cowes with a commission to back the *Galatea*, and all the money he could put up was promptly covered by Charles Ratsey (the father, by the way, of the late Tom Ratsey, one of the finest men that ever cut a sail or handled a tiller) and a few of *Waterwitch*'s supporters, who afterwards invested their winnings in a piece of plate commemorative of the race. But such betting was modest compared to that which took place at the London sporting clubs, where, it was stated, fifty thousand pounds changed hands.

The *Waterwitch*, besides her regular crew, had Admiral Ratsey, Charles Ratsey and many other experts aboard. The Admiral was in charge, whilst Ned Corke, considered the finest helmsman in the Solent, who had been at the helm of the *Louisa* in all her races with the *Alarm*, took the brig's tiller.

The start from the Nab was arranged for 10 a.m. on Monday, September the 1st, 1834, but when the day arrived, it was blowing so hard from the westward that the Commissioners of Portsmouth Dockyard, who were to start the yachts, would not venture outside the harbour. Meanwhile the two antagonists lay hove to off the Nab, the *Waterwitch* with topgallantsails ready to set over single reefed topsails and the *Galatea* with a double reefed foretopsail and single reefed mainsail.

At last, after waiting sometime, those in charge of the racers agreed to start themselves and away they went with the schooner nicely placed on the brig's weather bow.

The ebb was running and they headed off into the Channel on the starboard tack; the *Waterwitch*, going to windward in marvellous fashion with the weather leaches of her topsails just on the quiver, when about a third of the way across the Channel, was able to tack upon *Galatea*'s weather. During the afternoon the wind, which had been at gale force in the early morning, petered right out and at 7 p.m. the racers were off Dunnose, with *Galatea* about two miles to windward. The calm was little more than a lull, for it breezed up and blew very hard during the night. Against the wind and flood tide it was a case of short tacks along the shore, which was of great advantage to *Galatea*.

When off Old Harry *Waterwitch* reefed both topsails whilst in stays and we are told that it was considered a very smart piece of work for a yacht's crew: it left insufficient men, however, on deck to board the main tack, and at one moment it was feared that the mainsail would blow to pieces before the tack could be hauled down.

In the reach across West Bay, the *Waterwitch* once more got the schooner under her lee, and in the hard wind the smaller vessel was forced to clew up her fore topsail and content herself with her fore and aft canvas.

At 7 p.m. on Tuesday the *Galatea* had a slight lead off Berry Head, but once more the wind freshened at sundown, and off the Start she carried away her jibboom and whilst clearing the wreck, got too close in under the Bolt head and lost the tide.

But now came the most thrilling part of a very thrilling race. No arrangement had been made about rounding the Eddystone, and the racers were free to leave it either to starboard or port. As it happened they actually met, with one intending to round it to port and the other to starboard.

The illustration is a careful copy of a sketch, which was given to me by the late Mr. Thomas Ratsey. This was taken from a painting of the scene by the marine artist Schetky and shows the two vessels converging.

As a matter of fact the incident was a good deal closer than it is shown in the painting.

It was two o'clock in the morning, a very dark wild night, and both brig and schooner were very hard-pressed. Ned Corke, like every racing helmsman of any worth, was not wasting any room at the mark, and he rounded so close to the rocks that the breaking seas actually burst over the brig's rail. As the *Waterwitch* fell off before the wind with her mainboom to starboard and the lighthouse on her starboard beam, the *Galatea* was suddenly observed looming through the murk to port and evidently heading to cross her bows. But there was no room for such a manoeuvre. With this Ned Corke roared out in a stentorian hail, which reached the schooner through all the noise of wind and surf, of shaking sails and the hauling cries of the men sheeting home the brig's royals:—"Ease your helm, or we must either sink you or go ashore on the rocks".

The *Galatea*, heavily pressed with her flying square sail already set and her stunsails half set, had just room to luff under the stern of the *Waterwitch*; but, in doing so, she shipped a sea which broke in her fore staysail and split it from clew to head.

The ebb had been running about two hours, and the *Galatea*, on rounding, at once hauled in for the land to get out of the tide.

The question was, should *Waterwitch* follow her? In match-sailing it is a golden rule to stay with your opponent if you are leading and never let him run away on his own.

However, on this occasion Corke would not follow the schooner inshore.

"Let them go where they like", he said, "we'll steer ships course up Channel".

Daybreak found the *Waterwitch* under every sail she could set running before a fine fresh breeze in mid Channel, whilst *Galatea*, in under the land, showed up quite five miles astern. The flood carried the brig to Portland Bill; but with the ebb setting down channel, the schooner, in out of the strength of the tide began to pull up.

However *Waterwitch* managed to maintain her lead and without further incident finished by rounding the Nab at 2 p.m. on the 3rd, just twenty-five minutes ahead of the *Galatea*.

The last three survivors of this race were Talbot, who when he died was senior member both of the Royal Yacht Squadron and of the House of Commons, young Ratsey and a boatman named Barwick, who were the two youngest men aboard the *Waterwitch*, being both twenty years of age. The brig, by the way, carried a crew of eighty, none too many as it happened in such a hard wind.

This race brought the unusual qualities of *Waterwitch* once more before the Admiralty and in October, she was purchased into the Service.

Attempt by Seppings to Improve Ten-Gun Brigs

In spite of the very considerable prejudice against them in the Royal Navy and many complaining letters in the Service journals, Seppings continued throughout the twenties to build the notorious ten-gun coffin-brigs.

Taking the average, four to five were built every year, and in 1829 no less than nine were sent afloat. However in the following year, so great was the outcry about the slow-sailing of our small cruisers on the coast of Africa, that Seppings determined to try and produce a satisfactory slave catcher.

For the ten-gun brig he was quite satisfied with the under water lines of Peake's design. Nor was he wrong in this for the design itself was a very clever one, and it was entirely over-loading, over-gunning and perhaps over-sparring which had brought such opprobrium upon it.

Seppings was not the man to give way to clamour of any sort, and his idea for a good slave-catcher was a cut-down ten-gunbrig. So in July 1830 the *Nautilus*, which had been built in 1823, was launched with the following structural alterations—the forecastle head was done away with altogether, the high bulwarks were considerably lowered, and ports constructed so as to allow water on deck to clear away quickly.

The lower rigging was set up to the bulwark stanchions so that there were no projecting channels or chain plates to drag in the water when the brig was healed.

The carronades, which so blocked up the decks, were stowed fore and aft when not in use, the carriages being bolted to the ship's side.

Below decks side binns were done away with and the warrant officers were berthed in one large cabin instead of several small ones.

The *Curlew* was built on these plans. Then in March, 1831, the *Brisk*, built at Chatham in 1819, and the *Charybdis*, built at Portsmouth in 1823, were cut down and launched at Portsmouth. In May 1832 the *Griffon* and *Forester* were built on the same plans, as was the *Lynx* built at Portsmouth in 1833.

In 1834, the *Buzzard* was built at Portsmouth. She differed, however, from the others as she was given a little more free-board.

The Cut-Down Brigantines

Nautilus and *Curlew* retained their ten guns and brigrig exactly as the rest of the ten-gun brigs—but the other six were specially armed for chasing slavers with a pivoting long gun amidships and two carronades. They were also rigged as hermaphrodites or brigatines.

In 1837 the last of these cut-down Peake designs was launched—this was the *Termagant*, built at Portsmouth.

Though her plain-sail consisted, like that of the others, of square sails at the fore and fore and aft on the main, she was also provided with some additional light sails to be set flying on the main. These were square main-topgallantsail, topsail and main course. At the same time these sails were supplied to *Brisk, Charybdis, Griffon, Forester, Lynx* and *Buzzard.*

For about ten years these brigantines worked hard to capture slavers; they were, of course, too slow for the Baltimore-built slavers, but on the whole they did a lot of useful work without receiving any praise.

Dolphin and *Bonetta*

They were soon put in the shade by Symond's two sister brigantines, *Dolphin* and *Bonetta* which were launched in 1836.

The following dimensions show the difference in size and power:—

Name	Guns	Tons	Length deck	Breadth	Depth
Brisk	3	235	90′	24′ 6″	11′
Buzzard	3	231	90′	24′ 8″	11′
Bonetta	3	319	90′ 7″	29′ 3″	14′ 6″

Seppings also built four little vessels of one hundred and eighty two tons and six guns, with the following dimensions: length deck 80′, length keel 64′ 5½″, breadth 23′, depth 9′ 10″.

The first two of these sister ships were the brigantines *Viper* and *Hornet*, launched in 1831; then came the schooner *Cockatrice*. launched in 1832 and finally the schooner *Spider*, launched in 1835.

These were nicely designed vessels, but too full in their lines to be able to compete with the new Symondites, and they were mostly used to run the mails and as despatch boats in the West Indies and down the South American coast.

The Symondite Sixteen-Gun Brigs

Perhaps the most useful all round cruiser ever designed by Symonds was his sixteen-gun brig, which was built to fill the place of the famous eighteen-gun brig-sloop of the *Cruiser* class, which by 1830 was pretty well worn out from long service and hard usage.

The *Snake* Class

There were several classes of these sixteen-gun brig-sloops, the first being the *Snake* class, built between 1832 and 1837, and consisting of *Snake* and *Serpent*, built at Limehouse, *Harlequin* and *Lily*, built at Pembroke. *Ringdove* and *Sappho*, built at Plymouth, *Wanderer* and *Wolverine*, built at Chatham, and *Racer*, built at Portsmouth.

Their dimensions were as follows:—

Tons	Length Gundeck	Length Keel	Breadth	Depth
428 2/94	100′ 6″	78′ 7″	32′ 4″	15′ 2″

The *Grecian* Class

Then during the next ten years, the *Grecian* class of sixteen-gun brig-sloops were built. These consisted of:—

Grecian and *Persian* built at Pembroke.
Pilot and *Acorn* built at Plymouth.
Bittern and *Albatross* built at Portsmouth.
Fantome built at Chatham.
Arab built at Chatham.
Elke built at Chatham.
Heron built at Chatham.

Their dimensions were as follows:—

Tons	Length Gundeck	Length Keel	Breadth	Depth
485	105′	82′ 7″	33′ 6″	14′10″

Both these classes had a complement of 130 men. The 1839 and 1847 changes in armament will be found in the appendices, also their spar dimensions.

The *Cygnet* Class

The next class of Symondite brigs was the *Cygnet* class, built between 1840 and 1847. This consisted of:—

Cygnet and *Heroine* built at Woolwich.
Ferret and *Philomel* built at Plymouth.
Hound built at Deptford.

They were evidently intended specially for hunting slavers, being smaller than the sixteen-gun briggs, with an armament of:—

2 32-pounder 32 cwt. 6 ft. 6 in. guns
and
6 32-pounder 25 cwt. 6 ft. guns

Their dimensions were:—

Tons	Length Gundeck	Length Keel	Breadth	Depth
358 18/94	95′	74′10″	33′ 3″	13′ 0″

Captain F. B. Montresor, who commanded the *Cygnet* between 1845 and 1847 bears the following testimony to the little brig and her crew.

"... I could not have joined any ship in the squadron with a better set of officers and a better ship's company .... She was a dear, sweet, little craft, fast sailing and with a splendid lower deck. To me the *Cygnet* seemed as nearly to represent a floating Utopia as any ship could. Fancy a ship in such moral discipline that I could give the petty officers leave to go on shore for two hours and find every man on board at the end of that time, and that in a place abounding in grog".

The Packet Brigs

This *Cygnet* class must not be confused with the *Crane* class of Symondite packet brigs, which with the advent of the steam packet were taken off the Mail service and sent out to foreign stations—mostly to the coast of Africa.

The measurements of these little packets agreed exactly with those of the *Cygnet* class except in the matter of depth, which in the packets was 14′ 8″, the former also only mounted six guns. They consisted of the *Crane*, launched at Woolwich on the 28th May, 1839; *Express* and *Swift*, built at Deptford; *Ranger* and *Alert*, built at Rotherhithe; *Penguin* and *Peterel* built at Pembroke, and the *Linnet* built at Cowes.

The *Siren* Class

The finest class of brig-sloops ever built by Symonds as well as the largest was the *Siren* class, built between 1841 and 1853.

The six brigs of this class were:—

Siren, built at Woolwich, and *Helena, Camilla, Atlanta, Mosquito* and *Rover*, all built at Pembroke with the following dimensions:—

Tons	Length Gundeck	Length Keel	Breadth	Depth
549	110′	86′ 9″	34′10″	14′10″

During the *Siren*'s first commission, Lieutenant G. B. Nott wrote to his brother, Captain G. N. Nott, from Calcutta on April the 13th, 1843 in the following enthusiastic terms:—

"The *Siren* is, without exception the finest brig I ever beheld. She carried ten week's water, and four months' provisions for one hundred and twenty five men, under hatches; works beautifully, always within ten points: and her common rate of sailing is eight and a half knots on a bowline. She has never strained a rope-yarn; and the running gear we now use is the same we rove in England, eighteen months ago. The accommodations are splendid for a brig, the quarters most roomy: and she carries her twenty-five hundredweight guns without complaining in the least.

As yet we have not seen a man-of-war to try with, except the *Lily* at the Cape of Good Hope, and the difference of sailing between us was too ridiculous for comparison".

Lieutenant Nott fails to mention an encounter which took place shortly after the *Siren*'s sail against the *Lily*—and considerably humbled the pride of the occupants of the brig's ward room and gun room.

The *Siren*, whilst working through the Mozambique Channel, with the land on either side out of sight, fell in with a slaver to which she immediately gave chase.

Presently it fell a flat calm and the *Siren* was left motionless, but to the astonishment and chagrin of Commander Smith and his crew, the slaver, with her sails flapping against the masts, gradually lengthened the distance separating the two vessels until she disappeared over the horizon.

The explanation of this marvellous performance on the part of the slaver is very simple. Directly the breeze failed, the experienced captain of the Brazilian vessel at once dropped his anchor, which the commander of the sloop never thought of doing, with the result that he was rapidly carried away by the strong Mozambique current, no one aboard apparently being sufficiently observant to note the *Siren*'s drift.

The Experimental Brigs

In the year 1844 five experimental twelve-gun brigs were built from the designs of five different naval architects. Sir William Symonds designed the *Flying Fish*; White of Cowes, the designer of the peerless *Waterwitch*, was responsible for the *Daring*: Messrs. Read, Chatfield and Creuze of the late school of Naval Architecture produced the *Espiegle*, John Fincham, the master ship-wright, made the plans of the *Mutine* and Blake, master ship-wright at Portsmouth, those of *Osprey*.

The following were the principal dimensions of these brigs:—

Name	Tons	Length Gundeck	Length Keel	Beam Ex.	Depth	Draught F'ward	Aft
Daring	425	104′ 0″	83′ 0½″	31′ 0½″	15′ 2″	12′ 5″	16′ 9½″
Flying Fish	445	103′ 1″	81′ 7″	32′ 0½″	14′ 8″	13′ 6″	14′ 7″
Espiegle	439	104′ 8″	83′ 7¾″	31′ 6½″	13′ 1¼″	12′ 9″	14′ 9″
Mutine	428	102′ 0″	81′ 2″	31′ 6″	13′ 7″	12′ 8″	14′ 2½″
Osprey	424	101′ 3″	80′ 4″	31′ 6½″	13′ 6″	12′ 2″	15′ 1″

Another important measurement to be taken into consideration in a man-of-war was the height of the lower port sills above the water. These were as follows:—
Daring 4′ 5″; *Flying Fish* 3′ 10″; *Espiegle* 5′; *Mutine* 4′ 9″; *Osprey* 4′ 6″.

When it became known that these brigs were to be tested in the most exhaustive sailing trials possible against the two crack ten-gun brigs, *Pantaloon* and *Waterwitch*, and the sixteen-gun brig, *Cruizer*, which had been built on Rules lines in 1828, the keenest interest was aroused not only in the Royal Navy but amongst yachtsmen and shipping people throughout the Kingdom.

Ackerman published five lithographic prints, drawn by H. J. Vernon, showing the brigs under sail with one of the new cracks in the centre of each picture.

Captain A. L. Corry was made commodore in charge of the brigs, with his broad pendant in the steam-frigate *Firebrand*.

This officer had greatly distinguished himself in the Mediterranean fleet between 1835 and 1839, when commanding the *Barham*, fifty guns; known as a crack yachtsman, he was considered the smartest jockey in the Service, being one of those sailors who seemed to have been born with that instinct for getting the best out of a ship under sail whatever the conditions.

After beating Symonds' *Vernon* hands down with the *Barham*, he offered to change ships and backed himself to bring the *Vernon* in ahead of his own ship.

Under such a man a very high standard of seamanship and sailing tactics was needed and the command of an experimental brig was by no means a position to be envied by slackers or indifferent seamen.

During the trials the officers of the brigs had to be ever lastingly taking angles and jotting down observations, for the Commodore required a full hour to hour return of the following points from each ship whilst the sailing trials were in progress:—

Quantity of set sail changes in sail set—rate of sailing—points off the wind—angle of mainyard with the keel—angle of lee-way—common inclination—angle of pitching—angle of scending by the stern—time of pitching from and to a horizontal line—position of helm state of sea—greatest roll to windward (when close-hauled) angle of greatest lurch to leeward and the same to windward with the time taken in rolling through the greatest inclination when before the wind.

It is not surprising, therefore, that the commanders of the brigs were very carefully chosen.

Commander H. J. Matson, having paid off the *Waterwitch*, was appointed to White's new crack, the *Daring*. He was considered one of the smartest brig officers in the Service.

Commander Robert Harris, chosen for the command of the Symondite, *Flying Fish*, though he had had much experience in brigs, having served in *Algerine, Ferret, Onyx* and *Pantaloon*, was chiefly known for his gunnery and seamanship, he held the highest certificate from the *Excellent* and displayed the supreme form of seamanship in heaving down the *Melville*, seventy-two guns, at Chusan, China.

Mutine was in charge of R. B. Crawford, and was his first appointment since his unfortunate court-martial.

Commander T. B. Thompson of the *Espiegle* had served in the *Columbine* under Tom Henderson, in the *Pique* under Rous and Boxer, and in the *Magicienne* under Burnett Mitchell and Warren on the coast of Syria.

Commander Frederick Patten of the *Osprey* had recently commanded the *Rapid*, ten-gun brig, on the South American coast. He was one of those life-saving officers, having jumped overboard on three different occasions to save men in the water.

The *Waterwitch* was given to Commander T. F. Birch, a nephew of the famous Admiral, Sir James A. Gordon, K.C.B. After serving in the *Pique* under Rous he had been first of the *Scout*, 18 on the West coast of Africa, and afterwards commanded the *Lynx* and *Wizard*.

Edmund Wilson, who took over the *Pantaloon*, had been in the *Columbine* during her first commission, his last service being the command of the *Cygnet*.

The last of the Experimental brig commanders was Edward Gennys Fanshawe of the *Cruizer*. He seems to have been the only one who had not had previous service in a brig and unfortunately for him, he found himself appointed to the slowest vessel of the whole squadron.

There were fourteen trials between the eight brigs, beginning on October the 29th, 1844, and ending on December the 2nd. In these trials *Daring* magnificently tuned up and sailed by Matson and in spite of a troublesome leak, was easily first on nine out of thirteen starts.

The record of these trials was afterwards published with Captain Corry's report in great detail; at the same time there was a great deal of correspondence between the supporters of each brig in the Service Journals.

It may be asked why did not *Pantaloon* and *Waterwitch* do better? The reason seems to have been that they were short-handed with only eighty men compared to the one hundred and ten of the new brig's.

The racing was very strenuous and from the constant wetting and fatigue the brigs soon had an average of a dozen men a piece on the sick list. The *Daring* owing to Matson's popularity, had the best crew and was very smartly handled.

To modern eyes her design is not as attractive as that of the little *Waterwitch*.

The following table giving an 'Order of Merit' is not really as informing as it would have been if the brigs had started in the modern way across an imaginary line and given courses which included beating, reaching and running. Vessels, too, were often thrown out or lost their position by carrying away booms, sails and gear, though repairs were very smartly executed and mishaps which would have made a modern yacht give up the race were either made good or put up with.

It was difficult with new rope rigging to keep it properly set up.

As an example of smart repairs, I take the following from the report of the first trial.

11.50 a.m. *Osprey* carried away main-royal halliards.
11.56 a.m. *Osprey* set main royal.
11.55 a.m. *Pantaloon* carried away main topgallant halliards.
12 noon *Pantaloon* set main topgallant sail.

The brigs were beating to windward under single reefed topsails in a moderate Westerly breeze with long swell, their mean rate of sailing being five knots two fathoms. *Espiegle* was absent, setting up her rigging, and *Mutine* had parted company.

The mean rate of sailing under different conditions compares well with that of large yachts of a much later date, except, of course, to windward.

In the last trial, for instance, in a strong-beam breeze, the brigs mean rate of sailing was ten knots.

EXPERIMENTAL BRIGS. ORDER OF MERIT.

Ship	1st	2nd	3rd	4th	5th	6th	7th	8th	Start
Daring	9	1	1	—	—	2	—	—	13
Flying Fish	2	5	5	2	—	—	—	—	14
Espiegle	1	3	3	1	1	—	2	1	12
Waterwitch	—	2	—	3	3	1	2	1	12
Pantaloon	1	1	1	1	1	2	1	1	9
Mutine	1	—	3	3	4	—	—	—	11
Osprey	—	2	—	3	1	4	1	1	12
Cruizer	—	—	1	—	2	3	3	3	12

At the end of the trials Commander Matson wrote the following letter to Mr. Joseph White, the designer of *Daring*:—

My Dear Sir,

We have had only one trial since I closed my last letter: with respect to the *Daring*, it was the same story over again: but I am able to give you a much better account of the *Waterwitch*, who showed her strength, and hung pretty close to our lee quarter.

On the 28th of November tried sailing by the wind in fresh breezes, most of the brigs being under single-reefed main and double-reefed fore topsails, and occasionally topgallantsails! *Daring* had single-reefed fore and main topsails and for a short time main topgallantsail: but as I had it all my own way, I took in and kept under easy sail, winning the race in a canter.

Waterwitch carried a press of sail all day, had topgallantsails set almost all the time, and appeared to stand up admirably.

Osprey carried away her jibboom and *Cruizer* her main topgallant yard soon after starting: and *Mutine* missed stays in the first tack and afterwards carried away her jibboom, the third since leaving port. *Pantaloon* did nothing.

We were sailing for the most part against a head sea, and she therefore went bodily to leewards, although they have filled all her tanks with salt water. At the end of six hours and a quarter's trial we had gained as follows:— On *Waterwitch* 1,500 yards: *Espiegle* 4,800 yards: *Flying Fish* 7,500 yards: *Pantaloon* about five miles, but her distance could not be measured as she was barely in sight: *Osprey, Mutine* and *Cruizer* were out of sight, dead to leeward, about eight miles distant. Had I carried topgallantsails I might have been another mile to windward: but as the weather was thick, I did not think that any angles could have been taken, moreover I wished to show that we could beat them all under less sail. The *Waterwitch* lost a great deal every time in tacking, she had not men enough to work her properly, having twenty-two men on her sick list, out of her small crew. All the brigs have very large sick lists, averaging from fifteen to twenty owing to their being so very wet. *Daring*'s sick list had always been the smallest.

I have now only eight, and we have very seldom exceeded ten, mostly boys and marines who suffer from seasickness.

One of my officers yesterday received a note from a friend on board the *Firebrand*, who says there is but one opinion on board the *Firebrand* respecting *Daring*. I have written several letters respecting her capabilities, copies of which I will send you with this letter.

I think the *Espiegle* is decidedly rising in the scale and I think that the *Mutine* would have beaten the *Flying Fish* yesterday, had she not carried away her jibboom. I never saw her make so good a start, she is generally the very worst. The Commodore gave me an order to supply my spare-jibboom to *Mutine*, thinking, I suppose, that *Daring* is the least likely to carry one away. I am glad of it, for I hope to get another in its place a couple of inches stouter.

December the 3rd off the Lizard. We made a glorious finale yesterday, running into the channel, we tried with the wind a beam going ten and a half knots, under all plain sail except royals. At starting *Daring* was number six in the line, but she soon passed them all, and led the field in fine style, gradually increasing her distance every half hour. At the end of a four hours' trial we had gained as follows:—

On *Espiegle* 2,400 yards: *Mutine* 2,540 yards: *Flying Fish* 3,080 yards: *Osprey* 3,200 yards: *Waterwitch* 4,800 yards: *Cruizer* 5,605 yards: *Pantaloon* 10,000 yards. You will see that although the *Daring* beat them all so much, the other four large brigs were very near together, only eight hundred yards difference between them.

The little *Waterwitch* did very well, she cannot be expected to run with the large brigs, but she showed herself off in comparison to the *Pantaloon*. The *Waterwitch* tried to carry a fore-topmast stud sail, but it did her more harm than good and she took it in.

Pantaloon was sailing on her beam ends all the afternoon. I certainly never saw a man-of-war heel over so much before, she must have sailed with an inclination of thirty degrees. She does not appear to be any stiffer than before she filled her water-casks.

At the end of the trial yesterday we were close inshore, about three miles from the Wolf Rock, the Commodore then made the signal to part company and make the best of our way back to the rendezvous, off the Lizard.

I put the canvas on the *Daring* and we were at our post by daylight, where we met the Commodore, the only vessel in sight. The *Osprey* made her appearance this afternoon, but at sunset neither of the others had arrived.

December the 4th. Our trials are now over, and we are making the best of our way to Plymouth, with orders to chase the *Firebrand* to the Eddystone; the wind is light and baffling and it depends more on chance than on good sailing who gets there first. However I mean to see what I can do by daylight. Perhaps I may not have time to add anything more than to offer my sincere congratulations on your success in giving to the Service so matchless a brig as the *Daring*.

I am, etc.,
H. J. Matson.

To Mr. Joseph White,
Ship-builder. East Cowes.

As regards the reference to *Pantaloon* filling her water-tanks, Captain Corry had issued orders that no vessel was to fill her tanks with water for ballast: but on the Lieutenant commanding *Pantaloon* reporting her 'unsafe without ballast', he was allowed to fill his tanks.

The better health of the *Daring*'s crew is accounted for by the correspondent of the *Morning Herald*, who wrote:—

"The sailings have proved a service of the most trying description for the officers and men.

The former have been unceasingly employed after breakfast (which took place before daylight) till the close of the day ended the trials, and it need scarcely be dwelt upon that the accounts come to hand, speak of cold and wet jackets and broken spars and that many of the vessels were perfect shower-baths compared to the others. In these respects the *Daring* is said to be infinitely more comfortable and accommodating to her crew, from her elevated bows and large forecastles giving nearly the accommodation of a half deck in bad weather, whilst her stability far exceeds the surveyor's vessels; with a capacity for stowing two months provisions more than any vessel of the squadron, at the same time twenty-three tons less by measurement than the surveyor's *Flying Fish*, which is unable to take three month's provisions".

As soon as the brigs reached Plymouth, the expert correspondent of the *Naval and Military Gazette* published an order of merit, which he contended was agreed upon by the officers and crews of the brigs. This order was as follows:—

Daring, Espiegle, Flying Fish, Waterwitch, Osprey, Mutine, Pantaloon and *Cruizer*.

Daring was immediately taken into dock for her leak to be stopped and a defected plank on each side was replaced.

Other ships had alterations made which it was hoped would improve their sailing.

Mutine for instance, had her false keel increased so as to give her more depth of water.

Whilst *Mutine, Osprey, Waterwitch* and *Pantaloon* sailed from Plymouth on January the 15th, 1845, for the west coast of Africa and Indian Ocean, *Espiegle* and *Flying Fish* were ordered to cruise together between the Eddystone and Lands End, and during a month's trials *Flying Fish* was considered the best sailer to windward and *Espiegle* going free.

On March the 4th, the two brigs sailed for further trials with the *Daring*—Again the *Daring* had the best of it, in eight trials to windward and three off the wind, beating the *Espiegle* five times out of eight, whilst the latter beat the *Flying Fish* five times out of eight, and *Flying Fish* managed to beat *Espiegle* three times.

These brig trials had very little effect upon the future designs of gun-brigs, whose day, except as training ships, was very nearly over, their place in the Service being taken in the fifties by snaky-looking, barque-rigged, screw gun boats of *Pioneer, Mohawk* and *Arrow* classes, which were laid down respectively in 1854/5 and 6. These were handsome little ships and their commanders were very proud of them.

Note: (*Arrow Class*. $476^{68}/_{94}$ tons, 160 H.P. armed with two sixty-eight-pounders and two twelve-pounder Howitzers. Dimensions, Length gun-deck 160′: length keel 143′ $4^{3}/_{4}$: breadth 25′ 4″: depth 13′ 3″.

Arrow, Beagle, Lynx and *Snake* were built at Blackwall by Mare, and *Viper* and *Wrangler* by Green.

Mohawk Class. $669^{79}/_{94}$ tons, 200 H.P. armed with two sixty-eight-pounders and two thirty-two-pounders. Dimensions, Length gun-deck 180′: length keel 163′ 7½″: breadth 28′ 4″: depth 14′.

Mohawk and *Sparrowhawk* were built by Young at Limehouse: *Osprey* by Fletcher at Limehouse, *Lapwing* and *Ringdove* by White at Cowes; *Coquette, Wanderer, Assurance* and *Surprise* by Green at Blackwall: *Alacrity, Vigilant, Renard* and *Foxhound* by Mare at the Orchard Yard, Blackwall.

Pioneer Class. $868^{49}/_{94}$ tons, 350 H.P. armed with two sixty-eight-pounders and four thirty-two-pounders. Dimensions, Length gun-deck 200′: length keel 179′ 5″: breadth 30′ 4″: depth 14′ 6″.

Pioneer and *Flying Fish* were built at Pembroke; *Intrepid* and *Victor* by Wigram at Blackwall, and *Roebuck* and *Nimrod* by Russell at Millwall. This class had two funnels instead of one, between the fore and main masts.

It would not be fair to finish this sketch of the Symondites without mentioning the surveyors eighteen-gun corvettes and twenty-six gun and 36-gun frigates and their rivals.

As we are mostly concerned with the smaller ships, I will take the eighteen-gun corvettes first. The first of these little full-rigged ships to be built by Sir William Symonmds was the *Rover* of six hundred tons built at Chatham in 1832.

There is a very interesting letter by her commander, Charles Eden, of her doubling of Cape Horn, which is worth quoting as showing how a corvette behaved in the worst weather this world can provide.

"... I sailed from Rio on the 14th of October last, perfectly crammed with stores and provisions for the squadron. The store keeper at Rio informed me that I had got more in than any ship had ever taken before. Besides my own four months' provisions, I had fifty-five casks of rum, besides oatmeal, chocolate and several small things stowed in the after hold. The fore and main holds full to the hatches: on the lower deck oak plank etc.: on deck spars, etc. In fact she was so deep that, looking at her in Rio harbour I fancied it would be impossible to keep a dry jacket in her: she was drawing 14′ 6″ forward and 15′ 7½″ abaft.

We went to sea and within one week of our leaving Rio to within one week of our arriving at this place (Valparaiso) we had a succession of very heavy gales of wind and at times a most tremendous sea (unfortunately for me, always foul). For eighteen days (at different periods) we were under close-reefed maintopsail and trysails, and for some days under trysails alone: and I can safely say I never was in any ship so dry or so easy. This is the opinion of everyone on board. I have often seen the watch walking the weather gangway, when the ship has been under this sail, as unconcerned (as far as the fear of getting a wet jacket from her shipping water) as if they were on board a three-decker.

She did not ship *one sea* the whole of her passage: one small one struck her and stove in a port; and that is the extent of the damage done to her. We carried our quarter-boats (one a six-oared gig) and a canoe hoisted up astern; neither of them were touched.

But what surprised us, and myself more particularly, was her weatherly qualities under that sail. On no one occasion did she make a point and a half leeway. This was proved for several successive days by reckoning.

I had a long passage (I only arrived here yesterday, December the 12th) five days of which I was at the Falkland Islands. A French corvette sailed fourteen days before me and only arrived here six days ago. Most of the merchant ships have been seventy or eighty days, in fact, they have had hardly any arrivals lately: but those that have come in say they have experienced worse weather this summer off Cape Horn than ever before".

A year later the *Rover* again doubled the Horn from the Eastward, but this time in the depths of winter, and here are a few extracts from the letter of her new commander, A. S. Hammond.

Valparaiso, July 23rd, 1836.

"... We have just arrived here from Rio de Janeiro after an exceedingly boisterous passage round Cape Horn in the depth of winter and never was I more delighted (and the whole of my officers likewise) with a vessel. We have tried her in all sorts of weather from a calm with a heavy, rolling sea to as hard a gale as I ever witnessed and worse seas, and she has behaved nobly.

We ran thirteen and a half knots off Cape Horn with a jury topmast, having previously, in a very hard gale off the Falklands, found our main mast very badly sprung, which I attribute to the badness of the spar ... Coming up this coast off Cape Pillar, under closereefed topsails and reefed courses, with a high sea on, we were going seven and eight knots: I am sure one of the old twenty-eight-gun ships (to one of which I belonged three years) would not have been going five, and making with that perhaps three points leeway: whereas we were scarcely making half a point ...".

These letters will make astonishing reading for anyone who has rounded the Horn in a steel barque of the latter end of the nineteenth century.

They were sailors and they had ships in those days!!

Rover's dimensions were:— Length gun-deck 113′: length keel 109′ 9″: breadth 35′ 5″: depth 16′ 9″.

In 1836 Symonds launched the *Dido*, which celebrated little ship gave the expression 'cut a Dido' to the Service, owing to her smart reputation during her first commission in the Mediterranean, but her name is chiefly remembered with that of her second captain, Harry Keppel, on the Eastern station, where he helped Rajah Brooke to join Borneo to the British Empire.

Dido was larger than the *Rover* with a tonnage of 731 tons; length gundeck 120′: breadth 37′ 6″ and depth 18′.

Symonds built two sister ships of the *Rover*, namely *Arachne* and *Terpsichore*, both launched in 1847, and two sister ships of the *Dido*, namely *Daphne*, launched in 1838 and *Calypso* in 1845.

The Symondite class of six rate frigates consisted of the twenty-six gun *Vestal* (1833), *Cleopatra* (1835), *Carrysfort* (1836), *Iris* (1840), *Spartan* (1841), *Juno* (1844), *Amethyst* (1844), *Creole* (1845), and *Alarm* (1845).

Vestal registered nine hundred and thirteen tons and her dimensions were:— length gundeck 132′ 6″, Keel 101′ 6″: breadth 40′ 7½″: depth 10′ 6″, and the rest of the class only differed slightly from these measurements.

Of the fifth rates, Sir William Symonds launched the thirty-six gun frigate, *Pique*, at Devonport in 1834, and followed her with the *Cambrian, Flora, Active* and *Sybille*.

Throughout the thirties and forties there were very few rivals to these Symondites.

Admiral the Honourable George Elliot designed the eighteen-gun *Modeste*, 562 tons, and the ill-fated, but exceedingly beautiful, twenty-six-gun, *Eurydice*, of 908 tons.

Modeste was tried against *Rover* and *Eurydice* against *Spartan*; and the very detailed reports of these trials go to show that there was very little in it, the Symondites winning in their particular weather and the Elliot ships in theirs, due allowance being made for the blindness of keen partisanship on the part of the naval officers concerned in the trials.

With regard to the *Pique*, she also was most exhaustively tried against the *Castor*, built in 1832 by Sir Robert Seppings and the *Inconstant*, built in 1836 and designed by Captain Hayes.

These three ships were considered the last word in frigate designs, during the thirties. Under the most highly thought of captains in the Service, these three large frigates were continually being tried against each other with varying results, and the excuses put forward by the captain who found himself astern during a trial, show the great keenness and high seamanship shown.

Their most exhaustive trial was under the direction of Sir J. J. Gordon Bremer in the *Hercules* seventy-four: this had been immortalised by the Artist O. W. Brierly, of whose paintings there is a fine lithograph.

The three ships were very closely matched, and their captains tried various experiments in order to improve the sailing of their ships, guns, provisions and water were the chief playthings in the trimming of the frigates, for instance, when after a beat in a strong breeze and heavy head sea, *Castor* signalled:—

"*Castor* too deep: six month's provisions: not fair trial!".

Rouse of the *Pique* replied:—

"*Pique* flying light: three week's provisions: can you send me sand and salt water?".

The point of this was that Rous knew that Lord John Hay, commanding the *Castor*, had thirty tons of extra ballast on board.

The dimensions of these frigates were as follows:—

Frigate	Tons	Length Gundeck	Length Keel	Breadth	Depth	Draught of water F'ward	Draught of water Aft
Castor	1283	159′ .8″	133′ 7″	42′ 8″	13′ 6″	12′ 8″	15′ 2″
Pique‡	1623	160′	131′	48′10″	14′ 7″	13′ 2″	16′10″
Inconstant	1422	160′ 1″	132′	45′ 5″	13′ 7″	12′ 9½″	15′ 5″

Armament Upper Deck 22 32-pounders
† Quarter Deck 10 18-pounders
‡ Forecastle 4 18-pounders

† Afterwards replaced by 32-pounders.
‡ When they were first commissioned these 36-gunships were rated as 3rd class frigates: *Pique* was later given 4 more guns and made a 2nd class frigate with sail area of that class.

DIMENSIONS OF MASTS AND YARDS

	Pique Masts		*Pique* Yards		*Castor* and *Inconstant* Masts		*Castor* and *Inconstant* Yards	
	length ft. ins.	Diam. ins.	length ft. ins.	Diam. ins.	length ft. ins.	Diam. ins.	length ft. ins.	Diam. ins.
Main Mast from deck								
lower side of trussel trees	57 6	34			57 6	32		
Head	17 0				17 0			
Total length	100 0		91 0	22	100 0		86 6	21
Main topmast	62 6	20½			59 6	19½	62 0	13½
Main Head	8 4		65 0	14½	8 0			
Main Topgallant	28 0	11½	41 6	10	27 0	11	40 0	9½
Main Pole	19 0		29 6	6	18 0		28 6	6
Fore Mast from deck to								
lower side of trussel trees	52 8	32			52 8	30		
Head	16 0				16 0			
Total length	93 1		78 6	19	93 1		74 6	18
Fore topmast	55 0	20½	55 6	12½	52 6	19½	54 0	12
Fore Head	7 6				7 1			
Fore Topgallant	25 0	10	36 6	8½	24 0	9½	35 0	8½
Fore Pole	17 0							
Mizen-mast from deck to								
lower side of trussel trees	48 4	24			48 4	22½		
Head	12 0				12 0			
Total length	73 8		61 9	14½	73 8		58 0	13½
Mizen topmast	44 6	14	45 0	10	42 6	13½	43 0	9½
Mizen Head	6 0				5 9			
Mizen Topgallant	21 0	8	29 6	7½	20 0	8	28 6	7
Mizen Pole	14 0		22 0	4½	13 6		21 0	4½
Gaff			41 0	9			41 0	9
Spanker booms			58 0	13½			58 0	13½
Bowsprit ex housing			43 6	34			41 6	30
Housing			18 0				17 3	
Jib-boom including housing			45 6	14½			43 6	14

AREAS OF SAILS OF 2nd and 3rd CLASS FRIGATES

	2nd Class feet	3rd Class feet
Main Course	4018	3571
Main Topsail	3518	3208
Main Topgallant sail	1318	1213
Main Royal	609	553
Fore Course	3092	2578
Fore Topsail	2661	2432
Fore Topgallant sail	1026	944
Fore Royal	485	450
Driver	2452	2236
Mizen Topsail	1678	1533
Mizen Topgallant sail	679	625
Mizen Royal	332	307
Mizen Jib	1626	1481
Fore Topmast staysail	725	665
Total area	24219	21976

This sketchy account of the small Symondite classes and their rivals would not be complete without my giving the cost of the various ships, when completed and ready for sea.

A comparison with modern costs will show how science has increased our liabilities.

Here are the figures:—

Ship	Guns	Tons	Cost £
Castor	36	$1283^{68}/_{94}$	29,578
Pique	36	1633	33,001
Inconstant	36	1421	30,922
Vestal	26	913	21,383
Dido	18	731	14,969
Grecian	16	484	10,356
Siren	16	549	10,889
Childers	16	385	9,757
Daring	12	426	9,231
Flying Fish	12	445	9,723
Mutine	12	428	9,501
Espiegle	12	443	9,723
Saracen	19	228	8,106
Bonetta	3	319	6,510

The largest ship built by Sir William Symonds was the three-decker *Queen* of one hundred and ten guns and 3083 tons. She cost eighty-three thousand pounds. This was lower than Sir William Rule's three-deckers, the *Royal William, Sir George* and *Trafalgar* of one hundred and twenty guns and 2694 tons, which cost respectively £89,640, £90,817 and £99,227.

Eighty-gun ships such as the *Vanguard* and *Superbe* cost £62,115 and £65,535, whilst Symonds' famous fifty-gun frigate, the *Vernon* of 2082 tons cost £48,487.

The times were shortly coming when building expenses were to be doubled and even trebled; but this did not occur till the days of oak and hemp were over, and the Admiralty, which ever since the peace had strained every nerve in promoting all possible economy, were obliged to ask the Exchequer for millions, where before they were hesitating about thousands, in order to provide the nation with strange turreted armour-clad and wire-rigged monsters of destruction.

CHAPTER XI

COAST OF AFRICA 1831-1832

Praise de Lamb,
Hallelujah!
Fight for de brederen
in de Congregation,
Hallelujah!
Praise de Lamb,
Hallelujah!
Fight for de sisters
in de Congregation,
Hallelujah!
(African Rowing Song)

Magnificent Hayes

COMMISSIONED at Plymouth on the 24th May, 1830, the *Dryad,* forty-two-gun frigate, sailed on the 29th, of September for the West Coast of Africa, flying the broad pendant of the new Commodore, John Hayes, C.B. known throughout the Service as 'Magnificent' Hayes.

The nickname commemorates his consummate seamanship in saving the line of battle ship *Magnificent* in Basque Roads on the wild night of December the 16th, 1812.

A Piece of Old Time Seamanship

This was always considered in the days of the Wooden Walls as a supreme example of seamanship, demanding every attribute of the real sailor—courage, coolness, judgment, fore-sight, and a knowledge of a ship's particular capabilities and the strains and stresses that her hull and rigging could bear. One tiny miscalculation, one moment's loss of nerve, one second's hesitation, and the ship and every life aboard would have gone to Davy Jones' Locker.

On the evening of the day in question, the *Magnificent*, a seventy-four-gun ship, brought up about midway between the Chasseron Reef and that of Isle de Ré in sixteen fathoms. She was all ready for bad weather with her courses reefed and top-gallant yards on deck. At eight o'clock with the wind increasing in squalls the topgallant masts were struck, half an hour later the ship was veered to a cable and a half.

It was not a dark night, but there was no moon. The greyish white line of surf could be distinguished from the ship as it broke on the reef which lay a bare quarter mile astern and on the starboard quarter. At nine p.m., the ship having dragged into ten fathoms, the small bower was let go and the topmasts and topsail yards struck. The next order was to heave in on the best bower, but when three quarters of the cable was in, the anchor caught fast on a rock. The *Magnificent* was, in fact, in amongst a network of rocks, one of which was right under her keel. The wind, by this time, was blowing a full gale from WSW with a heavy sea and driving rain. The inboard part of the cable fast to the hooked up anchor was cut and bent to the spare anchor. A leadsman was ordered into the chains and a quartermaster attended the deepsea lead at the gangway. Men were also stationed with axes by the sheet and spare anchors ready to cut them adrift directly they were wanted.

At daylight, on the quartermaster reporting that the ship was driving according to the drift of the the lead line, the spare anchor was cut away. This stopped the vessel's dragging for the moment. The ebb tide now began to come away in its strength. The gale was still increasing, and a high sea, breaking ahead of and outside the ship, showed that she was absolutely surrounded by rocks. With the wind slowly veering to the Westward, the reef about a cable's length away, lying SSE and NNW, was white with a furious surf, set up by the lee-going tide. The seamanship required to save the *Magnificent* was how to cast her clear of the reef and make sail with yards and topmasts down. All hands stood by with their lives depending on their captain's judgment and seamanship and their own smartness in carrying out his orders. The first order from Captan Hayes was to hoist the fore-yard two-thirds up. Whilst this was being done, a spring was passed from the starboard quarter to the spare cable, but even as the hawser was being got along, the spare cable parted! as the ship still held, on, the sheet anchor was kept at the bow. Captain Hayes' next order was to hoist the main yard two thirds up, and make the quarter spring fast to the cable of the small bower. Whilst this was being done the topmen aloft were stopping up the topsails and courses with spunyarn stops and casting off and making up the gaskets.

When this was done one man was left aloft to attend to each stop with particular orders not to let go and loose the sail until that sail was named. The yards were next braced sharp up on the port backstays for making sail on the starboard tack. Tacks and sheets and the halliards of the main and mizen staysails were now manned and the spring taken to the capstan.

Captain Hayes took advantage at this psychological moment to make a short speech through his speaking trumpet. His words came clear and stern:—

"This is a case of life and death! If my orders are executed properly the ship will be saved! If not every soul aboard will be drowned within five minutes!"

It must be realised that the ship lay head to wind: as the spring was hove in, her quarter would be hove to windward, then directly her sails could fill on the starboard tack, they were to be sheeted home and the staysails set, and it was hoped that the ship with reefed courses, (the yards only two thirds up to allow of close-reefed topails being set) the topsails close-reefed and lower staysails would have no difficulty in clawing off.

Unfortunately as they hove in on the spring after the cables had been cut, the sea would not let her cast to port and round went her head towards the reef.

The oldest seaman in the ship thought that all was lost; but clear and calm came the order through the trumpet:—

"Sheet home foretopsail! Board the foretack! Haul aft the foresheet!"

With her foreyards flat aback, away went her head and she began to gather stern way.

"Helm hard a starboard!" Was the next order, followed by:—"Square main and mizen topsail yards! Keep the mainyard braced up!"

As the wind came aft of the beam the squared mizen topsail was set. Directly the wind was right aft, the after yards were braced up, the helm ported, and the *Magnificent*, having pivotted on her helm, came to on the starboard tack and headed away South with the wind on the beam.

"Keep her South!" was Hayes' last order to the quartermaster, then in a voice that all could hear:—"The ship is safe!"

This manoeuvre of Captain Hayes is a classic example of the old-time seamanship. The following points specially should be noted:—

1. The thoughtout preparation such as stopping up the topsails so that they could be set quickly.
2. The setting of reefed topsails over reefed courses when the topmasts were housed—the parels of the yards came only just above the caps, and the sails could not have been set if the courses had been in their normal position instead of two thirds of the way up.
3. When the spring was unable to pull the ship's s stern over against wind, tide and sea,

Captain Hayes without a moment's hesitation took the only possible action that gave his ship a chance in forcing her onto the starboard tack by wearing short round. But he had no room to come ahead so he gave her stern way by keeping both mainsail and foresail aback.
4. Finally he helped her with the mizen topsail and the helm, the latter hard astarboard to help the head off whilst she had stern way.

Designs of Captain Hayes

Captain Hayes, besides being a great seaman was a skilled designer with a complete knowledge of the shipwright's craft. His uncle was the master shipwright at Deptford Dockyard and was anxious that his nephew should succeed him and perhaps end up as surveyor of the navy. For five years Hayes was taught theoretical designing and practical ship-building by his uncle, but on that old gentleman succumbing to an attack of gout, he threw his compasses and drawing-board away and entered as a midshipman aboard the *Orion*, seventy-four-guns, commanded by Sir Hyde Parker. Through much service afloat and much hard fighting, Hayes always maintained his interest in ship designing, and, as soon as the peace brought leisure, he turned to his old love with much zest and published a pamphlet on ship design, which attracted a great deal of attention in the Service.

His first piece of work for the Admiralty, was the *Arrow*, a cutter of one hundred and fifty seven tons and ten guns, which was employed in protecting the oyster fisheries and the suppression of smuggling, commanded (at the request of Captain Hayes) by Lieutenant John Powney, K.H.

On the *Arrow* proving a success—according to James she possessed 'stability under canvas with little ballast, great buoyancy, better stowage and swifter sailing qualities than any model yet designed by known schools of naval architecture—Hayes was commissioned to design the eighteen-gun ship-sloop *Champion*, which took part in the experimental trials of 1825.

And shortly before sailing to take up his command on the coast of Africa Commodore Hayes had completed an R.N. cutter, called the *Seaflower*.

After several trials on the Solent in which, it was stated, the *Seaflower* showed a great superiority over the cutters on the station, the Commodore was allowed to take his latest design out to the coast as a tender.

That Commodore Hayes was a popular as well as a capable commander we have ample testimony. Here are the words of one of his lieutenants in the *Dryad*.

"The presence of the Commodore was always a source of pleasure to those who served under him: he combined, with a high reputation as an officer, a scientific mind and the kindest of tempers, a perfect knowledge of seamanship in its superior as well as subordinate branches. He could fit the rigging, rig the ship, govern and work her afterwards in so masterly a manner, that, from the officer to the merest boy on board, he was sure of confidence and support in any enterprise in which he might engage: in short, he could build, rig, govern and sail the ship with equal ease and credit".

As his commander in the *Dryad*, the Commodore had William Turner, only lately promoted for his gallant work when in command of the *Black Joke*.

A fellow officer of Turner described him at this time as 'a man of whom every one spoke well, and of bitter material in truth must have been that being who could bear other testimony of him'.

Of the other officers of the *Dryad*, both the senior lieutenant, Henry Huntley and the surgeon, Peter Leonard, published their private logs of the commission, so that we have a very clear view of the conditions prevailing on the coast during the years of the *Dryad*'s commission, namely 1830-1832.

***Dryad*'s Passage Out**

After sailing from St. Helen's on the 29th September, 1830, the *Dryad* put into St. Mary's, Isles of Scilly, for a supply of fresh stock.

In those days St. Mary's was a busy port with a flourishing trade and the anchorage was generally crowded with shipping from large barques and brigs down to small coasting schooners and ketches, whilst the anchorage of New Grimsby across the flats was often packed from end to end with Cornish fishing luggers.

On the 6th of November, the *Dryad* anchored at Porto Praya, St. Iago where the Commodore received information of two pirates which were preying upon the Cape Verd shipping. He at once interrupted his passage to Sierra Leone, and sailed on the 8th of November in search of the pirates.

On the following day a Brazilian brig was boarded. She proved to be one of the Portuguese 'trade ships', sixty-nine days out from Angola in ballast and bound to the Cape Verds to load salt for Brazil.

These 'trade ships', as they were called sailed to the West coast with cargoes of spirits, tobacco, gunpowder and cloth, with which the negro cargoes of the slavers were purchased. And it was usual to take a return cargo of salt from the Cape Verds.

On November the 11th, 1830, the *Dryad*, anchored at Porto Grande, St. Vincent, and it was learnt that four schooners had only lately left that port—two of these were Spanish slavers but the other two, which flew French colours, were said to answer to the description of the pirates. Thereupon the Commodore continued his tour of the islands, anchoring at St. Lucia on the 13th, at Port St. George, Island of St. Nicholas on the 15th and in English Road, Boa Vista on the 17th. Here the *Dryad* took on board the guns and an anchor of H.M.S. *Erne*, which had been wrecked on the Island of Sal in 1819. The Portuguese Government Agent, Colonel Martinez, had been responsible for the salvage and the grateful Lords of the Admiralty had presented him with a handsome silver salver with a suitable inscription. They may or may not have known that he was one of their most formidable enemies, considered the largest slave trader on the African coast and the owner of more slavers in Havana than any other dealer in black ivory. His relations with the British were evidently friendly enough and the surgeon of the *Dryad* treated his wife for ophthalmia during the frigate's stay at Boa Vista.

Here further news was received of the pirates. A French vessel had been attacked in the Bay by one of them quite recently, but had succeeded in beating her off.

As the Commodore could obtain no further information about either rover, he sailed on November the 19th for Sierra Leone.

On November the 29th, the numbers of bats and shore birds circling round the ship, gave those new to the coast their first hint that the land was close under the horizon.

The next excitement was the sight of two vessels to windward. These proved to be *Plumper* and a rakish looking slaver which she was examining.

Though the slaver had three hundred negroes on board and was bound from the Sherboro to Guadeloupe, she had to go free as her papers and colours were French.

The *Plumper*, however, was able to give the Commodore all the latest news about the station, including the successful actions between *Primrose* and *Veloz Passagera* and *Conflict* and *Nympha*.

The following day the *Dryad* sighted the Mountains of the Lion showing like a line of azure clouds above the thick brick-dust coloured haze, which lay along the horizon. With only a very light breeze coming off the land, it was well into the afternoon before the frigate picked up the Sierra Leone pilot.

He came aboard in a boat pulled by four negroes and proved to be a sturdy six foot black, who answered to the name of Prince Stober.

He was a character, typical of Freetown—a freed slave, who during the week piloted vessels in and out of the river and on Sundays played the sky pilot as pastor of the methodist conventicle.

The picturesque anchorage in the Sierra Leone river with the low wooded Bullim shore on one side, and Freetown with its scattered houses backed by an amphi-theatre of hills on the other, was not reached until daylight on December the first, 1830.

Freetown, Sierra Leone, in 1830

From the anchorage, Freetown, with its gaily-painted bungalows, and plank huts, its wide grassy streets, its luxuriant foliage of fruit trees such as banana, orange and pawpaw with its background of high timber, tall cotton woods, African oaks, etc., looked most attractive, but ashore it was more true to its reputation of being a whited sepulchre.

Built on a hillside of brittle sand and iron stone, its shingle roofs, jaluseed window-frames and unevenly boarded walls were the prey of the bug-a-bug or white ant. Red oxide dust and iron mould cloaked it.

High up at the back stood the Citadel, Fort Thornton, the Hospital and at the very top the new barracks.

Freetown at this date was a rambling, polyglot town surrounded by native kraals of the typical African mud-hut type, each of which was dignified by the name of the town.

Two of these towns reserved for liberated slaves were given the names of Wilberforce and Murray. Settler Town was occupied by Nova Scotian settlers. Maroon Town housed maroons from Jamaica. Soldier and Gibraltar Towns contained discharged soldiers from the West India Regiment and the Royal African Corps.

A significant appurtenance to every European's dwelling was what Indians would call a chokidar's hut. This was a low, wooden box which was used to house the Krooman, whose duty it was to guard the dwelling through the night. These were mostly the well-known, so-called dog-kennels, which were such a conspicuous sight on the decks of most slavers, being used as deck cabins by the officers of these over-crowded vessels; they were no larger or more savoury than the ordinary English pig-sty.

At this date there was only one inn in Freetown, only two billiard-tables, but any number of shops and stores, well stocked with British goods. A church that was so large, that at one time some scandal was caused by it being used as a market place, stood in the centre of the town. It was said to have cost near eighty thousand pounds.

In the broad streets practically every race in Africa could be seen from tall, slender Foulahs and Serawoolahs with their roughly-fashioned golden rings to intelligent, athletic-looking Mandingoes, driving their bullocks. Freed slaves, semi-educated and intent on fooling new comers—they had been known to sell their less sophisticated brethren back into slavery again—were everywhere, though the latest arrivals were safely lodged in what was known as the Liberated African Yard.

The English villas and their grounds were generally surrounded by hedges of wildpine-apple or of a typical flowering creeper, the cultivated ground being mostly cassada, cocoa and fruit.

There was a racecourse, even at this early date, where little tats from the Gambia competed, and all the tricks of horse racing were practised. The track lay between the road and the river about two miles from Freetown and being open to the sea breeze was a favourite place for riding and driving before the dinner hour, when the sinking of the sun and the breath of the salty breeeze combined to revive the exhausted European.

The anchorage off Freetown was not usually as empty as it is shown in Huggins' pictures. Usually it was well stocked with masts and yards, amongst which might be seen the tall masts of such a frigate as the *Dryad*, towering above the trucks of general merchantmen, timber droghers, and the rakish looking prizes, sent in by the preventive squadron.

Cotton wood canoes plied everywhere about the harbour, or crowded round a new arrival amongst the shipping, from which noisy black washerwomen sought for custom or sturdy kroomen with filed front teeth and tattooed arrows on each temple asked to be engaged.

The Timber Trade

The chief trade of Sierra Leone at this date was in African timber a business which had been started by a merchant named MacCormac, in 1816. The wood, the African oak and teak, was cut by native Bulloms and Timmannees and floated down the river on rafts to storehouses on different islands, where from fifteen to twenty small merchantmen were always to be seen loading the logs. As the ships were up the rivers for sometime, it was a very unhealthy trade for their crews, and in December, 1830, when the *Dryad* was at Sierra Leone, an English barque lay in the Mellacoree, which from captain to cabin boy had not a single member of its crew left alive. Yet in spite of its unhealthiness the trade was very profitable at this time. The ships came out in ballast, which they discharged on the ballast ground, a little above Freetown over on the Bullom shore.

The Dreaded Miasma

Though Sierra Leone was by no means as bad for mosquitoes as many places on the coast, it was very far from being the health resort many of its old hands declared it to be.

Miasma—the dreaded mist which rose from rotting vegetation—was the cause of all fever in the medical opinion of that day.

Let me illustrate this fear of miasma by an anecdote of Commodore Bullen.

One day during the rainy season when sun and rain succeeded each other at short intervals, Sir Neil Campbell, then Governor of Sierra Leone, sent off to the flagship to invite the Commodore to breakfast at eight o'clock.

Commodore Bullen excused himself with the message that he made it a rule on the coast of Africa not to land before ten o'clock in the morning.

Thereupon the Governor sent back his A.D.C. with the polite reply that he would put off breakfast till ten o'clock and that he would take a ride in the meantime

"Which way was he riding?", asked the Commodore of the A.D.C.

"To the westward, along the beach road by King Tom's point". Thereupon the Commodore led the young soldier to the ship's side and pointing to the land, said:—

"There goes the Governor, now do you wonder why I won't land before ten".

A sheet of low lying mist covered the shore, in which the Governor and his horse were completely hidden with the exception of his cocked hat and feather, which were plainly visible bobbing up and down to the horse's trot, just clear of the top of the mist. It was not very long after this that Sir Neil Campbell succumbed to the climate.

When the *Dryad* was on her passage out the conversation in wardroom and gunroom constantly turned upon the unhealthiness of the climate of West Africa. Old hands told hair-raising yarns for the edificaton of those who were making their first visit to the station.

The new chums warded off the dread fear of fever by making a joke of it, as has ever been the habit of the British, and the stock sally aboard the frigate was:—

"Oh poor so-and-so, yes, I remember him well. He went out in the *Dryad* and died three days after her arrival at Sierra Leone".

But the doctor's first visit to the hospital showed him not only the dread diseases of fever and ague amd dysentery, but all the plagues of Africa such as boils and blains, dropsy, and that trying eruptive complaint known on the coast as craw-craw.

Of the ravages of fever he had an object lesson before his eyes in the few emaciated wrecks, eleven in number, who were the survivors of thirty-eight fever victims, lately landed by the *Plumper*.

This brig had lately been up in the Rio Pongas and had anchored so close to the shore that her yards, like those of the frigate *Firebrand* in the St. Iago de Cuba, brushed the overhanging branches of the noble forest trees. And night and morning the Pelter brig was enveloped in a thick impenetrable mist, which rose from the shiny ooze, which fringed the river banks.

It was therefore not surprising that on her return to Sierra Leone, she landed thirty-eight fever victims.

The Kidnapping of Freed Slaves

Whilst the *Plumper* was up the Pongas, a female slave escaped from one of the slave barracoons and rushed down to the brig's boat, which had just landed. She had been kidnapped from Sierra Leone, and Adams received evidence of more than one hundred other negroes in Joseph's barracoons, who had been kidnapped from the colony.

In the same month, December, 1830, the *Favourite* boarded a slaver under French colours, on board of which several of the slaves spoke a little English and had undoubtedly been kidnapped from the kraals of the liberated slaves. This kidnapping was further confirmed by the gun-brig *Conflict* which arrived in Sierra Leone on December the 17th with a French schooner containing fifty-one slaves, two of whom declared that they had been taken from Regent's Town. These two were landed by orders of the Mixed Commission and the slaver taken to Goree for French jurisdiction.

The usual method of kidnappers was to entice the negroes, especially the children, out of the kraals and take them down to Cockle Bay, where they were hustled into waiting canoes, paddled across to the Bullom shore and from there quickly transported to one or other of the slave rivers.

To such a height had this kidnapping grown, that the Bay had been rechristened Pirate's Bay.

The Case of the *Virginie*

Kidnapping freed negroes from Sierra Leone was not always a very safe game to play.

On March the 20th, 1831, a French sloop of fifty tons named the *Virginie* arrived at Sierra Leone. She had sailed from the Plantain Islands for Guadeloupe with a cargo of ninety-two negroes, supplied by a black slave trader named Corker. A number of these slaves had been kidnapped from the Colony. Her crew only consisted of eight men, but she had on board as passengers to Guadeloupe, the master and ten men of another French vessel, which had stranded on the coast.

In such a small vessel every inch of space was taken up below and the women had to be stowed in the arms Magazine.

The captain of the *Virginie* by his monstrous cruelty and daily flogging of the slaves soon roused them to a state of suppressed fury.

The Sierra Leone slaves took the lead and the women managed to pass them arms through the partition; then, watching their opportunity, on March the 12th they rose upon the crew, and after a sharp fight in which the brutal captain and every Frenchman except the badly wounded cabin-boy were killed, they gained possession of the sloop.

The eleven passengers took no part in the fray, preferring to seek a refuge up the rigging, where they remained for some hours in a state of terror.

At last the leader of the slaves persuaded them to descend, having promised them their lives if they would take the *Virginie* back to Sierra Leone. When they reached the deck, they were severely manhandled and, after being stripped to their blood-stained shirts, were clapped into irons below; and they were made to understand with many ferocious gesticulations that they would be killed if the land was not sighted by a certain day.

However with these sore and weary passengers taking turns at the helm, the land was made successfully. When the boarding officer went out to the *Virginie*, he was greeted by a freed slave from Sierra Leone, who in his broken English was able to relate what had happened.

In explaining his own presence he told how he had been captured by the slaver trader whilst carrying rice in his canoe to the Sherboro.

The *Virginie*'s decks presented a strange sight as she slowly ran into the anchorage.

A black sentinel, naked except for a straw hat, which he had placed rim uppermost on his head with the crown stove in to fit his woolly pate, stood over the Frenchman at the helm with a drawn sword.

Another negro strutted about the deck clad only in an embroidered waistcoat with three heavy silver watches dangling by their chains from his neck. Others wore striped shirts with cutlasses buckled round their middles, whilst one or two proud blacks sported no other covering but a dress coat.

The decks and sails of the sloop still bore evidence of the fight in the many blood-stains everywhere; whilst below the French prisoners in leg irons and only their shirts were pitiful objects, filthy, bruised, bleeding and starved.

The boarding officer was received with wild cries of joy by the slaves, but the Frenchman did not feel safe until an English officer and party of bluejackets took charge.

Slave stealing in the Colony had been a scandal of some years; indeed the commander of the *Dryad* had once captured a slaver aboard of which was a negro who had been three times kidnapped from Sierra Leone and three times recaptured, by H.M. ships *Brazen, Maidstone* and *Esk*.

The Mandingoes were proved to have been guilty constantly of buying liberated slave children for about five pounds a piece and then selling them to the traders up the slave rivers.

Black Joke's Commanders

Since Turner had left the *Black Joke*, the little brig had been looked upon as a certain step to promotion. Downes, who followed Turner, had been in the Service twenty-four years when the *Almirante* action brought him his long awaited step. He was succeeded by Lieutenant E. J. Parrey from the *Primrose*, who after capturing the schooner *Christina* with three hundred and forty eight slaves on the 11th of October, 1829, was promoted to the rank of commander on the 10th February following.

When Parrey left on promotion, the tender's senior mate, William Coyde, became acting commander for a time. Coyde captured the brigantine *Manzanares* with three hundred and fifty four slaves on the 1st April, 1830 and then gave place to Lieutenant William Ramsay, the first of the *Atholl*.

That Scotsman's first success was the capture of the brigantine *Dos Amigos* on November the 9th, 1830, in 3° N 9° E.

But previous to this capture Ramsay had, had a most disappointing and fruitless month overhauling French slavers, whom he was not allowed to touch. He was even stretching the international law in boarding them.

During October 1830 he overtook and examined no less than five Frenchmen, having on board one thousand six hundred and twenty two slaves, all loaded in the Bonny.

Then in the following month, he found as many as ten large Frenchmen lying in the Old Calabar, waiting to load their cargoes of black ivory. Thus the Spanish brigantine was like manna from Heaven.

Capture of the *Dos Amigos*

The *Dos Amigos* ran out of the river Cameroons about 9.30 a.m. of the 9th, but at the mouth of the river met the gig of the *Black Joke*, under her mate R.K. Jenkins and flying a large white ensign.

The cunning little slave-catcher herself was also waiting outside, but sufficiently below the horizon as to be unobserved from the river entrance.

The slaver, on seeing the white ensign, at once wore round on her heel, and ran up the river again with the intention of landing her slaves before the boat could reach her.

The Bay of the Cameroons is a mass of reefs and shoals through which and round Cape Suellaba, the southern point, the ebb runs with such velocity that the best of oarsmen in the sharpest of gigs cannot stem it. The gig with her sail set to the sea breeze, which was just making, and her crew rowing their hardest, was only just able to round the Dog's head shoal and follow the brigantine up the sixth fathom channel.

The *Black Joke*, in the offing, also hauled up her kedge, and with all her flying kites set began to thread her way through the many shoals and sand spits with the intention of going to the aid of her boats. Just inside the entrance the gig was joined by the cutter, which had been up the river during the night spying out the land, and was on her way back to the brig when she met the gig.

It was about ten miles up the river to King Bells Town—Peter's Town as some called it. Yet so strong was the stream that the swift brigantine did not reach the anchorage till sunset, with the gig, followed by the heavier cutter, a good two miles astern.

As the boats came in sight of King Bell's Town, thirty canoes could be counted alongside the slaver, all busy landing her slaves in a fury of excitement. When, half an hour later, Jenkins pulled alongside, the sun had set, the anchorage was in darkness and the wretched slaves had been driven away into the bush by the King Bell's people.

At daybreak the following morning the tall spars of the *Black Joke* were sighted from the town, as the brig wended her way up the river.

As soon as the man-of-war had brought up opposite the town King Bell sent his son off to ask what she wanted:—

"I am going to fire your town about your black wooly heads if you don't hand over the slaves of the *Dos Amigos*" was Ramsay's reply.

The flustered son of the King leaped into his canoe and paddled off in a hurry. Presently he returned wih an offer of twenty five negroes provided the *Black Joke* held her fire.

Don Juan Ramon de Muxica, the captain of the *Dos Amigos*, admitted that he had embarked five hundred and sixty three slaves and that these had been landed again and the coppers for cooking their own food thrown overboard. Commander Ramsay, without the coppers, was naturally unable to reship the slaves, having no means of feeding them, and thus he was checkmated by the cunning slaver.

However he had the vessel, which turned out to be an unusually fine specimen of a Baltimore model. Ramsay had a careful survey made of the *Dos Amigos* by his two mates, Coyde and Jenkins; and as the *Black Joke* was badly in need of rope and her decks in need of caulking, he relieved the *Dos Amigos* of sixty fathoms of two inch rope, one hundred fathoms of one and a half inch, several balls of spun yarn and ten pounds of pitch. He also took over a few yarns for his ship's company, who had had no fresh provisions for a couple of months.

With a crew of fifty-three kroomen and three Spanish prisoners, Jenkins took the *Dos Amigos* up to Sierra Leone in twenty-seven days.

Here the brigantine was again surveyed by the representatives of the Mixed Commission, who were horrified to find the *Dos Amigos* was short of twelve casks of provisions and seventeen bags of rice. Upon which Jenkins explained that each krooman received half a pound of rice a day as well as salt junk, whilst three bags of rice were thrown overboard being infested with vermin.

The *Dos Amigos* was condemned in February 1831 and at public sale purchased on account of his Majesty's Government by order of the Commodore, who converted her into a tender and renamed her the *Fair Rosamond.*

Lieutenant Castle Takes Over the *Black Joke*

In February 1831, Ramsay, being badly in need of a change from the stuffy cabin of the little tender, was appointed first lieutenant of the *Dryad*, and a very experienced slave catcher in the shape of William Langford Castle, was appointed to the command of the *Black Joke*.

Castle, it will be remembered, had commanded the five-gun schooner, *Speedwell*, in 1822-1823 against the Cuban pirates. Then he went as first lieutenant to the ten-gun brig *Helicon*, and in 1824 to the ten-gun brig, *Beaver*. Besides being first lieutenant of the *Isis*, fifty guns, flag of Admiral Sir L.W. Halstead in the West Indies, he had served in that capacity aboard both the *Sybille* and the *Dryad*, and he persuaded the Commodore to give him an opportunity to get his promotion through a cruise in the lucky *Black Joke*.

He had barely changed places with Ramsay when his opportunity came.

On the 14th of February, 1831, the Spanish schooner *Primeira* loaded three hundred and ten slaves at the Gallinas.

On February the 22nd in 6° 20′ N 11° 32′ W, she was overhauled by the *Black Joke*, which fired several blank rounds to bring her to with no effect.

As a tornado was coming on and Castle was afraid that the chase might slip him in the thickness of the driving rain, he at length fired a shotted gun, which brought the *Primeira* up with sails shaking and booms cracking.

Two of the unfortunate negroes in the hold of the slaver were killed by this one shot, as well as the cook, whilst two slaves, the mate and four of the crew were wounded.

The *Primeira* was only one hundred and thirty tons burthen and her slave deck a bare two feet two inches under the beams; the slaves were very nearly stifled and consisted of one hundred and eleven men, forty-five women, ninety-eight boys, fifty-three girls and four babies, and as if this was not sufficient, the schooner was still further crowded by a number of abominably filthy monkeys.

A merchant of Sierra Leone was implicted in this vessel, as it was proved that she had gained her bread supply from him.

This was Castle's only capture whilst commanding the tender, for he was almost immediately transferred to the acting command of the *Medina*, twenty guns, where he remained until promoted on October the 29th, 1831, whilst Ramsay went back to the *Black Joke*.

Medina* Captures *El Juan

Whilst in command of the *Medina*, Castle captured the Spanish brig *El Juan*, with four hundred and seven slaves on board. During the chase, the *El Juan* being heavily pressed, heeled over so much that the frigthened negroes made a rush for the grating over the main hatchway.

Fearing that they were attempting to rise, the crew fired through the grating until all was quiet in the hold. After the brig was captured Castle went aboard the slaver and afterward declared that he had never seen such a carnage in his life, as had taken place in the hold of *El Juan*. As the negroes were brought on deck frequently the living and the dead were found shackled together.

Huntley's Cruise in the *Seaflower*

When the *Dryad* and the Seaflower cutter arrived out at Sierra Leone, the senior lieutenant of the *Dryad*, Lieutenant Henry Vere Huntley, took command of the cutter for her maiden cruise on the slave coast. Her complement consisted of three midshipmen, an assistant surgeon, a carpenter's mate and a boatswain's mate, five marines, twenty-three bluejackets and ten kroomen. She was armed with an eigtheen-pounder carronade, mounted on an elevated slide, one of those contraptions, from which the carronade generally upset each time it was fired. Her only other artillery was a light brass six-pounder field-gun, mounted on the ordinary wooden ship's carriage.

Of small arms there were five stands for the marines and six for the bluejackets.

On her way to the Bights the *Seaflower* had no sight of a ship, slaver or otherwise, for several weary weeks. The monotony of a slow run down the Gold Coast was relieved by a day or two spent visiting each of the forts, whose commandants were only too pleased to entertain the officers of passing men-of-war.

It is, perhaps, hardly realised that slave catching was a terrible monotonous job, in which prizes were as scarce as currents in a sailor's duff. Long spells of idleness upon a heaving swell under a windless sky were the ordinary everyday experience of a cruiser on the coast of Africa. Except in the rains, the brazen sun glared down day after day upon a glittering sea.

As the vessel swung her mastheads backwards and forwards across the sky, every timber groaned, every block cheeped, every rope flogged against shroud or spar, whilst on deck the pitch bubbled in the seams, and below the scuttling cockroaches left their loathsome trail over everything.

Under such conditions the wise commander did everything possible to keep his people interested and amused, as well as fit.

Sing-songs, single stick and boxing matches, dancing and every kind of old ship-board game, such as slinging the monkey, were encouraged in the dog watches: but directly eight bells was struck, strict silence and no light were rigidly enforced.

At this date, when a slaver could not be condemned unless she had slaves aboard, it was the practice of the Guinea captains to load their black cargoes at sunset, leave their anchorage soon after dark and hope to be to seaward of the waiting cruiser by daylight.

To counter this proceeding it was the custom for cruisers to stand out thirty or forty miles from the coast during the night, and as soon as daylight approached, to run in-shore until the tops of the trees fringing the beach could be seen from the masthead.

The *Seaflower*, after her arrival in the Bight, carried out this practice for some weeks before a sail was sighted—a schooner, out of Whydah, failed to run out of sight of the waiting tender when dawn spread its rose flush over the heavens.

Lieutenant Huntley with his assistant surgeon and senior midshipman were at breakfast.

The mid had just been voicing his dream of the night before, in which a slaver had been chased with success, when 'Sail Ho!' came down through the skylight.

The tender was standing in close-hauled against the fresh land breeze. The booming of the surf could be plainly heard, though only the tops of the highest trees in the bush fringing the beach were visible.

The slaver, with studding sails boomed out, could be seen down to her tops. As the order to set the gaff topsail was called out aboard the cutter, the slaver's square-sail suddenly vanished.

"She's round" cried half a dozen voices. And so it was, the slaver had luffed up and began to beat back to Whydah Roads in the hopes that she would be able to discharge her slaves unseen by the cutter.

All was disciplined excitement aboard the *Seaflower*. Whilst her popguns and small arms were loaded, a mid with a telescope at the masthead reported every movement of the chase.

"She has thrown a boat overboard", came down from aloft. "They are cutting away her anchors" "The stern boat had been cut away". And so on.

Slowly but surely the sturdy cutter gained, it being her best point of sailing and the schooner's worst. As they drew in shore, the wind came still more ahead and both vessels lay down to the stiff breeze with sheets hard in and the sprays flying over the bows.

"They are throwing bags and casks overboard". Screamed the mid at the masthead of the *Seaflower*.

Then the chase began firing guns and jigging a square flag up and down on her fore signal halliards. Would she get her slaves ashore in time? Up to the masthead went Huntley—unless he could swear to having seen slaves leaving her side she could not be adjudicated upon.

In amóngst the crowd of shipping ran the schooner. On the beach, men could be seen hurriedly launching canoes, then dashing through the surf and paddling furiously towards the anchored shipping, behind which with her topsail aback the schooner proceeded to hide herself.

Presently the canoes, now crowded with negroes could be seen returning to the beach. For a moment or two their black hulls were almost hidden in the spray of the heavy surf, then a rush of blacks dashed up the white sand into the green bush.

This was all that could be seen from the masthead of the cutter. Huntley was unable to swear that the canoes had gone alongside the chase, hidden, as she was, behind the anchored craft.

Confident that she had nothing to fear, the schooner then stood out of the Roads.

The disappointed commander of the *Seaflower* at once had a musket fired as a hint that the schooner was to heave to for examination.

No notice was taken, for the report had not been heard aboard the slaver, being drowned in the booming of the surf. This gave the tender an excuse for firing a shotted gun. The six-pounder was trained upon the slaver and fired. A white splinter tore away from her weather rail between the two masts, and a white fountain of spray showed where the ball had plunged into the sea beyond.

Up into the wind went the slaver and lay plunging in the head sea with hers sails shaking.

Lieutenant Huntley himself went on board her, and found every evidence of slaves having been very lately aboard, but the law required that not even one, but two slaves, had to be found aboard in order to qualify the vessel for adjudication at Sierra Leone.

Having warned the slave captain to pay more attention in future to the signals of a British crusier, the disgruntled lieutenant returned to his own vessel. Both ships now headed back for the Whydah anchorage, where seventeen slaves were awaiting De Souza's convenience.

After sending her boats aboard every slaver in the roads, the cutter, having now cruised her prescribed time and being nearly out of wood and water, headed away for West Bay, Prince's Island, where the Commodore was expected.

The *Seaflower* had not been many days in West Bay before the *Dryad* arrived with her two tenders, the *Black Joke* and *Fair Rosamond.*

As Lieutenant Castle had been transferred to the *Medina*, the *Black Joke*, as well as the *Fair Rosamond*, was in need of a commander.

Lieutenant Huntley as senior lieutenant was given his choice. He was naturally, more eager to command the famous slave catcher, *Black Joke*, than take over an untried vessel. But the Commodore pointed out that the *Black Joke*, was nearly worn out, wanted recoppering, and without a thorough structural repair, which was out of the question on the coast, could hardly hope to last another six months, where as the *Fair Rosamond*, was nearly new and in excellent condition. Huntley thereupon took the Commodore's advice and selected the *Fair Rosamond*, whilst Ramsay went back to the *Black Joke*.

H.M. Schooner *Fair Rosamond* (ex *Dos Amigos*)

The *Fair Rosamond* had been carefully measured at Sierra Leone and her lines taken off by the Commodore.

As she became one of the most successful of cruisers in the slave trade, besides being a remarkably interesting model from the designer's point of view, her measurements are worthy of being put on record: viz:

Length of gundeck	74′ 11¼″
Length of keel	61′ 1½″
Breadth Extreme	23′ 2¼″
Breadth for tonnage	23′ 0¼″
Breadth Moulded	22′ 8¼″
Depth of hold	10′ 4½″

Draught in her best trim with three months provisions.

Forward	7′ 6″
Aft	11′ 10″
Ballast	35 tons
Number of Men	44

Armament a long nine-pounder on a pivot amidship and a small shifting carronade.

Burthen in tons	172 27/94

The *Fair Rosamond* was even more of a wicked-looking craft than the *Black Joke* with her raking masts and low freeboard.

In model she resembled closely the typical American pilot boat of the deep Baltimore type, with unusually short overhangs, especially aft, and a fiddle-head gracing a handsomely curved cut-water and knife-like bow lines.

Altogether she was a very smart and pretty little vessel, and a command not to be sniffed at by the most fastidious of flagship lieutenants.

It was found that though the *Black Joke* had the legs of the *Fair Rosamond* when on the wind, the latter had the best of it as soon as sheets were eased. In the Navy List the *Fair Rosamond* was always described as a schooner, but it should be realised that she was very much of a two-topsail schooner, with topsail and topgallant sail on the main, and a large square mainsail, which was set flying like the square foresail.

When she was sent home at the beginning of 1837, the Portsmouth naval architects and shipwrights looked with horror at her tall sail plan and they were not content until they had cut down her sail plan by over two thousand feet, thus very materially affecting her sailing powers in light winds. But directly the ex-slaver reached her cruising station, you may be sure that the longer spars and bigger sails were sent aloft.

The comparison of the two-sail plans is of interest as showing the pig-headedness of the dockyard trained naval shipwright.

	Original plan feet	Cut-down plan feet
Boom mainsail	1840	1700
Square mainsail	1750	1534
main topsail	910	—
Main topgallant sail	240	—
fore course	1782	1440
fore topsail	935	860
Fore topgallant sail	412	325
Fore Royal	224	—
Jib	450	435
Fore staysail	530	530
	9083	6824

It will be noticed that the fore royal and main topsail and topgallant sail were done away with.

There is no note about flying kites, but stunsails and a ringtail were, of course, provided; and in the sail plan a gaff topsail and a flying jib are shown. In her rigging plan there is one very interesting fitting. In order to give spread to her shrouds, the lower deadeyes were shackled to iron plates, which were bolted to the sides, but held by struts quite a foot outside the bulwarks; this was owing to the roundness of her sections, and the very considerable tumble-home of her bulwarks.

The plan of *Fair Rosamond*'s upper deck is of interest not only as showing how the deck of an American built slaver was arranged, but also for is pivoting guns and their positions.

Black Joke* Captures *Marinerito

The Commodore ordered *Black Joke* to cruise in the Bight of Biafra and the *Fair Rosamond* in the Bight of Benin. With half her officers and men away in the three tenders it was not possible for the *Dryad* to do more than made a leisurely cruise up and down the coast. Her tall spars gave her away to the slaving fraternity long before she could gain a sight of her prey and thus the Commodore depended upon his tenders and gunbrigs for prizes. The West coast squadron was, as a matter of fact, worse starved than ever in 1831, and even Rear-Admiral Warren at the Cape was kept extremely short of ships.

Besides the *Atholl* and the eighteen-gun ship-sloop *Favourite*, the Commodore only had the Pelter brigs, *Conflict* and *Plumper*, besides the tenders.

In January 1831, the *Plumper*, Lieutenant S. Sullivan commanding arrived at Sierra Leone with a prize, a Spanish schooner of one hundred and eighty tons, which had a crew of forty besides five hundred and four negroes loaded in the river Gallinas.

At the time of capture of this slaver, the *Plumper* had only six white men aboard and was depending almost entirely upon her Kroomen.

On resuming command of the *Black Joke*, Ramsay sailed at once for Fernando Po in order to take on board a set of sweeps which had been sent out from England for the tender's use.

At Clarence Cove Ramsay found a Colonial vessel at anchor, whose master, Mr. Mather, informed him of a heavily-armed Spanish brig which was on the eve of sailing from Duke's Town.

This vessel, he described as being the finest slaver that had been on the coast for some time, with a crew of picked men and armed with one pivot and four broadside guns. She was evidently in very great order and discipline and no one was permitted to go on board.

Captain Mather had even dined ashore with her officers, who made no secret of their intention of fighting. They laughed at the idea of being taken by the *Black Joke*, and, as for the gun-brigs, they did not sail fast enouth to get near her.

Ramsay at once up-anchored and sailed to intercept this arrogant slaver. The *Black Joke* dropped her anchor off the bar of the Old Calabar on the evening of April 23rd, but stood out to sea during the day, so as to be out of sight of any vessel coming out of the river.

As usual this little brig, the scourge of all slavers, was in luck. At 11 a.m. on April the 25th, a large brig was sighted in the Nor-West, coming out of the river. *Black Joke*'s topsails were immediately lowered, with the result that the stranger was within sight from the deck before she recognised the tender.

There was a fresh Sou-Westerly breeze blowing, and the chase, instead of standing down, bore away to the SE under all sail with the intention of crossing the *Black Joke*'s hawse and sailing between the Main and Fernando Po.

All day long the *Black Joke* steadily gained upon the fast-sailing slaver, until at about 9 p.m. the latter was just within range of her Long Tom. As the two vessels got under the lee of Fernando Po, they ran into a flat calm.

The chase swung idly round the compass until the *Black Joke*'s head was pointing straight at her starboard beam. A shot was fired ahead of the slaver, as a hint to surrender, but the confident Spaniard immediately replied with three guns from her starboard broadside.

It was now bright moonlight and dead calm, without the least motion on the water, the two brigs being right in the middle of the passage between the Cameroon mountains and Fernando Po.

Ramsay ordered his new sweeps to be manned; and as the *Black Joke* slowly drew up on the slaver, she opened upon the tender with a steady fire of grape. One of her first rounds struck down a bluejacket on the forecasle head, named Isaac Fail, who was at once carried below to the assistant surgeon, Mr. Douglas.

Only an occasional round was fired from the *Black Joke* as she approached, and this was aimed high, just to distract the aim of the Spanish gunners and to avoid injuring the black ivory below. For a whole hour, from 1 to 2 a.m. the tender was under a heavy fire of round, grape and musketry. Ramsay had his two guns loaded to their muzzles with grape and musket balls, but the captains of the guns were given strict orders not to fire until the *Black Joke* ground alongside the slaver and the order to board was given.

Ramsay ordered the sweeps to be laid in at the last, for a light air sprang up, just sufficient to give the brig steerage way and she glided forward as if she was slipping over ice.

Two steady men were then told off to lash the vessels together at the psychological moment and the rest of the crew were ordered to lie down, with cutlass, pike and boarding-axe in hand, ready at the word to spring up and follow their commander over the slaver's rail.

The *Black Joke* carried her way in a marvellous fashion, and for two or three tense moments nothing was heard but the hiss of water under her cutwater.

Then, of a sudden, an Irish voice broke the silence aboard the slaver.

"Come aboard, ye English blackguards, and fight us fairly".

At this Ramsay, who was sitting on the port gunwhale, watching every move of the enemy, his sword point resting on the deck, spoke up in his broad Scottish accent:—

"I'm coming, mon, I'm coming as fast as I can".

As the *Black Joke* came up, Ramsay gave the signal to his old one-eyed boatswain's mate, Peter Kenney, who, after a piercing whistle on his pipe, cried out in a stentorian voice "All hands to board!" And as he sprang across the deck, in readiness to jump as the two ships touched, he yelled for a rope 'to lash the devil with;' but there was no time owing to the amazing fashion in which the *Black Joke* carried her way.

Even in that light air so great was her speed that she cannoned off the slaver and only Ramsay, Bosanquet, his mate, Peter Kenney and nine men were quick enough to gain the slaver's deck.

Then pandemonium broke loose. Every gun on both vessels was fired off. Every Britisher was cheering, even to the wounded man below, who waving his hat over his head, cried in a strong but slowly dragging voice:—

"Hurrah! boys, hurrah! God bless King William!" As the last word came out, his hand dropped, his head fell back, and he died in the arms of the surgeon.

On the slaver's deck the clash of steel, punctured by pistol shots, told of a desperate fight waging between Ramsay, Bosanquet, Peter Kenney and the nine bluejackets against seventy-seven ruffians of every nationality. Below on her slave deck shrieks and guttural shouts came from her terrified cargo.

With some yards of water separating the two vessels, things began to look pretty serious for Ramsay; but, aboard the tender, a tiny mid, Hinde by name, not fifteen years of age, at once took charge, ordered all hands to the starboard sweeps, and got the *Black Joke* back alongside the slaver and lashed. He then boarded the latter at the head of the remainder of

Black Joke's crew, only leaving behind one or two wounded men. Another of the tender's middies, young Pearce, after receiving a pistol-ball through his hat, found himself out-fenced by a gigantic Spaniard, who, with a blow of his cutlass knocked him overboard, but the boy, though he could not swim, managed to catch a hold and with his sword in his teeth promptly climbed back again by way of the fore sheet.

As usual mere numbers could not withstand the impetuosity of the bluejackets, and, after a sharp clash of steel for a few hectic minutes, the Spaniards gave way, and ran below, crying for quarter.

The slaver turned out to be the very vessel the *Black Joke* had been told to watch for.

She was a brand-new clipper of three hundred and three tons, named the *Marinerito*, and flew Spanish colours. She was fifteen feet longer and had greater beam than the *Black Joke*, and was armed with one long pivoting Spanish eighteen-pounder and four, what were called, short-long broadside eighteen-pounders against the tender's two eighteen-pounders. Her crew consisted of twelve officers and sixty-five men, of whom thirteen were killed, or drowned overboard and fifteen wounded, four dangerously.

Against this the *Black Joke* out of her complement of six officers and thirty-eight seamen and marines had one seaman killed, Lieutenant Ramsay severely wounded, Mr. Bosanquet, the mate, wounded by a sword cut across the neck whilst in the act of boarding, and five men wounded.

Nor did the famous little *Black Joke* herself escape scot-free: besides having much of her standing and running rigging cut through and many of her spars wounded, her larboard bow and quarter were both stove in by the heavier side of the *Marinerito*.

The hatches of the slaver were found battened down over the negroes, and the very first duty of the victors, after the Spanish crew had been overcome, was to open the hatches, when a terrible state of affairs was revealed.

The living were crouching in agony upon the bodies of the dead.

Those who were capable of crying out, gasped plaintively for water, others pointed to their throats.

Ramsay immediately had a large tub filled and placed in the middle of the slave deck. Instantly there was a rush of the released negroes, and many, who had seemed to be dying, sprang to life from under the feet of the more robust.

Then, in the midst of the tragedy, there came a ludicrous incident. The woolly bullet-heads of the negroes became wedged in the tub, as they fought to get their lips to the water, and until they could be prized adrift, many of the eager drinkers were in real danger of either suffocation or drowning.

Others, like thirsty dogs, lapped up the drops that fell to the deck, as the water in the barrel was splashed over. The scrimmage was soon relieved by jugs of water being passed round—Here again they gave evidence of their terrible thirst, by draining the jugs at a draft and then madly biting the china with their teeth until every jug was in atoms.

Even so their thirst was not relieved and, when later, they were landed, they tried to lap up the salt water by bending over the side of the boat.

Out of four hundred and ninety six slaves, twenty-six were found dead—suffocated—whilst one hundred and seven were at their last gasp.

Ramsay at once ran into Clarence Cove with his prize and hurriedly landed the slaves as the only chance of saving their lives—yet, even so, only forty-seven out of one hundred and seven could be kept alive.

Spanish slave crews always went in terror of a slave rising, and generally warned the British rescuers against allowing the negroes to go free and unironed. Yet in the report of this action we read:—"All slaves appeared to be fully sensible of their deliverance and upon being released from their irons expressed their gratitude in the most forcible and pleasing manner . . . The poor creatures took every opportunity of singing a song, testifying their thankfulness to the English, and by their willingness to obey and assist, rendered the passage to Sierra Leone easy and pleasant to the officers and men, who had them in charge".

Bosanquet, took charge of the prize, and with two or three of her crew, to serve as witnesses before the Mixed Commission, and those of the slaves who were considered by the doctor to be in fit condition.

Though he made the passage in twenty-five days, in that time twenty-five more negroes had died.

Those who survived the dreaded hospital at Clarence Cove were afterwards shipped aboard the *Plumber*, which took a month on the passage up to Sierra Leone and in that time lost twenty of the negroes.

Nor did the tragedy of the *Marinerito* end here. The remainder of her crew were conveyed in the *Atholl* to the Island of Annobon, where they were turned adrift.

Nine of these men shortly afterward set out in three canoes for the Island of St. Thomas. The remainder preferred to build a boat for that purpose, and apparently paid for their food and lodging by selling their clothes.

After refitting at Clarence Cove, where the *Dryad* found her on May the 2nd, the *Black Joke* returned to her station in the Bight of Biafra.

About the middle of June when cruising off the Bonny she actually picked up one of these Annabon canoes with three starving, half-dead members of the *Marinerito*'s Spanish crew. They told a tragic tale—they had seen no land since leaving Annobon, the canoe containing their provisions and water had been swamped and lost, and for the past ten days they had had nothing but occasional rain-water they were able to catch in their mouths.

When the Commodore fell in with the *Black Joke* on June the 23rd, two of these men were still aboard her, the other having been landed on Prince's Island. They believed that their companions in the other two canoes had all perished in a heavy tornado, which they encountered.

Acting upon the strong recommendations of Commodore Hayes, the Admiralty at once promoted Ramsay, Bosanquet and Douglas, the assistant surgeon.

Fair Rosamond Captures *Potosi*

The *Fair Rosamond* was not long in proving her value as a cruiser, her first chase showing that it would take a very fast slaver to escape her.

On July the 20th, 1831, a slave-laden schooner, coming out of Lagos in the evening, saw what appeared to be a slave-ship heading in for the anchorage.

However when the two vessels were within four miles of each other, some suspicion that the approaching vessel was not what she appeared to be invaded the wary Guinea captain's mind; and he took in his kites, ready for an instant change of course.

It was then about five o'clock, within an hour of darkness, and there was no moon. On came the stranger, laying a course close-hauled on a wind for Lagos, whilst the loaded slaver stood on before the wind. As the two vessels passed each other at the limit of signalling distance up went the Spanish ensign to the peak of each ship.

The night was very dark and the wind fresh and squally. Hardly had the loaded slaver been lost to sight before the stranger, which was, of course, the *Fair Rosamond*, had hauled round in her wake with every sail set.

All night long, the little schooner kept her course to the Southward, laying down to a spanking breeze on the beam. It was an anxious night for Huntley and his eager crew, for it was so dark that not even the sharpest eyes aboard could detect the loom of the Spanish schooner ahead. Before daylight every man was at his station, the Long Tom amidships was cast loose and made ready, and every preparation made either for a hard chase or a sharp action.

As dawn approached every eye was glued to the horizon. To sharpen the eyes of the lookouts aboard his cruisers Commodore Hayes offered a dollar per hundred of slaves captured to the lookout, who sighted the slaver captured. To this reward the commander of the *Fair Rosamond* added another eight dollars; but these incentives were quite unnecessary for every man aboard was keenness itself, and hardly had the false dawn proclaimed itself, before half a dozen voices roared out the welcome words of 'Sail Ho!'

There was the slaver in plain view, about seven miles on the lee beam. The first manoeuvre tried by the Spaniard was an attempt to cross the hawse of the *Fair Rosamond* and thus get up to windward of her; but she soon found that the latter was too fast for any game of that sort. She then bore away before the wind, setting her squaresail, studding sails and flying kites. The Spanish schooner proved to be a very fast vessel, and was able to hold her own in the lulls, but the *Fair Rosamond* came up on her very quickly in the puffs; and as the wind freshened so the cruiser gained, until, at the end of a six hour's chase, the slaver was within range of the *Fair Rosamond's* long gun and matters were looking pretty desperate for her.

Overboard went her spare spars, her boats, and even casks of provisions, but still the *Fair Rosamond* closed on her. A warning shot was sent whistling over the Spaniard's mastheads, and was seen to plump into the sea ahead, sending a fountain of white water up out of the deep Atlantic blue. This evidence that the cruiser had her range, urged her to fresh efforts. She now cut her anchors away and set her men to wetting the sails so that interstices between web and woof might be close up and the canvas hold the wind better.

These efforts of the Spanish captain—and no one could sail these clipper-lined Baltimore-built brigs and schooners better than the Spanish and Portuguese—produced a definite increase of speed, and with the wind lulling away again, the *Fair Rosamond* dropped back a bit.

Nor were Huntley and his officers backward in trying to improve their schooner's speed: whilst experiments in trim were made, the sextant and azimuth compass were used to show the smallest alteration in distance or bearing. Weights, and even the hands themselves were moved from one part of the deck to another and the result carefully noted in the Vernier.

Again the breeze freshened and *Fair Rosamond* lessened the range. The nine-pounder was trained upon the slaver's spars in the hopes of crippling her. The result of this second shot was distastrous to the slavers topmast and lower stunsails on one side, the boom and lower stunsail yard being knocked away. The Spanish captain at once altered his helm until the wind was on the other quarter and cut away the damaged gear.

After firing several more rounds at her sails without doing more than make neat round holes, Huntley at last ordered the gun to be depressed. At the very next shot the white splinters were seen to fly from the taffrail and the helmsman fell forward over the wheel—dead.

This was enough. The slaver hauled down her flag and hove to with everything still set except her stunsails. But Huntley was up to this old trick. Directly the boarding boat was lowered the slave captain meant to fill away, leaving the *Fair Rosamond* to pick up her boat before taking up the chase again. It was now late in the afternoon and the Spaniard hoped with luck to give the man-of-war the slip in the approaching darkness. But Huntley did not heave to until he was abreast of the slaver and within fifty yards of her. Then he hailed her:—

"Lower your sails down instantly and come aboard".

"No intende Inglese".

There were no linguists aboard the *Fair Rosamond*. No one could speak Spanish, so Huntley tried the slaver in his best French.

"No intende Francese". Whined the Spanish captain with a miserable shrug of his shoulders and holding out his hands in supplication.

Lieutenant Huntley was a determined man with very little patience and a good deal of easily aroused irritation in his composition.

He well knew that the Spaniard was lying. Turning to his six marines, who stood in a line like so many ramrods, with their muskets ready primed, he gave the order:—

"Marines fire at his jib halliard block and do so until the halliards are cut away".

The delighted marines soon proved their markmanship by downing the sail.

"Well done, marines! Now the peak halliard block on his fore gaff".

One round was sufficient, the Spanish captain gave in and hailed in very good English to say that he would come aboard.

"Very good—cease firing, marines", said Huntley, his temper restored by the success of his manoeuvre.

The slaver turned out to be the Spanish schooner, *Potosi*, with over three hundred slaves on board, a beautiful model like all slavers at this date and probably straight from the stocks of some Baltimore shipwright. As usual after a long chase the slaves were found half dead from want of air, water and food—three in fact did die.

Sending her prize away to Sierra Leone for adjudication, the *Fair Rosamond* ran into Lagos Roads and deposited the Spanish captain and his crew aboard one of the empty slave ships lying there.

A Decoy Paid out by Huntley

The *Fair Rosamond*'s next adventure off Lagos was not so satisfactory.

She was running along the land towards sunset within sight of the anchorage when a large brigantine was noticed getting under way. The slaver made sail and stood off to sea in the gathering darkness. The tender was round after her at once, and fearing to lose her in the night Huntley cocked up his long gun at its greatest elevation and fired, but the round fell short.

Until 2 a.m. Huntley and his senior mid were able to keep sight of the chase through their night glasses, then heavy rain fell and blotted her out. However at daybreak there was the chase only four miles away. Unfortunately the wind dropped down as the sun rose and recourse had to be had to the sweeps. These were worked with a will, though sweeping in the heat of the tropics was the most killing job, a and the most hated of all work aboard a small cruiser. By 8 o'clock the chase was within range and lowered down her sails in token of surrender. As was his usual practice, instead of sending a prize crew aboard the slaver right away, Huntley ordered the captain to come aboard the *Fair Rosamond* with his papers. To the amazement of all hands, the slave captain calmly announced that he had no slaves aboard, his cargo was in the barracoons awaiting him.

"Then why this chase and all this trouble?" burst out the commander of the *Fair Rosamond.*

"Oh! I just wanted to compare the speed of my brigantine with that of your little man-of-war". Returned the captain in a very off-hand way.

"Well, now that you have gained the knowledge, you shall pay for it". Declared the short-tempered Huntley through his teeth. He was the kind of officer on whom it was very unwise to play such tricks.

Calling to his senior mid, he said:—

"Take ten good hands: unbend his sails: unreave his running rigging; throw overboard his guns, his gunpowder and every weapon of any sort that you can find. Make his crew range his cables on deck with the inner ends secured, then let go both bowers and run the cables out to the clinch".

The midshipman carried out his orders to the letter. The brigantine's yards were soon swinging about without their braces; then as their lifts were unrove they became cock-billed in every direction like a vessel in mourning. Next her head dipped and her stern came out of water as the cables ran out. Then a big splash told of her fine long pivot gun going overboard.

Morillé, muttered the Spanish captain as he watched it go.

"Now your craft is ready for you", said Huntley. "You see the price of learning that your vessel sails slower than the cruiser. You can now get your anchors and make sail—remember the cost before you think of playing any more tricks with a British man-of-war".

The Spaniard was careful to keep silent for fear of further reprisals, but there was murder in his scowl as he went over the side.

The sea breeze had arrived by this time, and the *Fair Rosamond* filled away on her weary task of standing off and on.

The slaver went back to Lagos and eventually got away with some four hundred slaves on board. She managed to elude the tender in spite of a special watch being kept for her.

Drunken Palm Oilers

Cruising on the African coast is not all chasing and prize making: and the *Fair Rosamond* had little success during the rest of the summer, her only capture being a small prize of little value.

Her crew did, however, have an hour or so of excitement when two brigs with their yards boxed all ways were sighted on the horizon.

It was at first concluded that here was a pirate busy at his trade. But the brigs turned out to be British palm-oilers, who had lost their officers from fever, and whose crews, having got at the rum casks, were drunk to a man.

The British palm-oil trade at this date took almost as great a toll of human life as the slave trade. Most palm-oilers came limping into London, Liverpool or Bristol with less than half their hands alive. Where ague and fever had failed to kill, it was a case of

"Drink and the Devil had done for the rest
Yo! ho! ho! for a bottle of rum"

Fair Rosamond* and *Black Joke* Capture *Regulo* and *Rapido

The Palm-oilers were, however, very useful to the cruisers in giving information about slavers.

It was whilst the *Fair Rosamond* was refitting at Clarence Cove at the beginning of September, 1831, that she learnt of the Spanish Slavers, *Regulo* and *Rapido* from a British palm-oiler just out of the River Bonny. As these were large brigs they could not cross the bar of the Bonny except at spring tides, and as the moon was not full for another week the tender had plenty of time to finish her refit and then run the one hundred and thirty miles from Clarence Cove to the mouth of the Bonny.

The captain of the palm-oiler declared that the two slavers had decided to sail in company for mutual protection and were determined to fight their way to sea should the *Fair Rosamond* or *Black Joke* put in an appearance.

The *Regulo* mounted fourteen long twelve-pounders and the *Rapido* four broadside eighteen-pounder carronades and a Long Tom eighteen-pounder on a pivot amidships.

As against this armament the *Fair Rosamond* had but her Long nine and small carronade. Also she was very short-handed, for out of her complement of forty-five men, ten were away in the prize and there were a number of fever patients unable to do duty.

The palm-oil skipper showed great amazement at the temerity of the tender in proposing to attack two such heavily armed and strongly manned slavers as he assured Huntley the *Regulo* and *Rapido* were.

"The *Black Joke* will be somewhere handy, as it is her station", was Huntley's reply to the merchantman's doubts. "With her long eighteen-pounder we shall be more than a match for

"You may think so—two guns and a half against nineteen". Replied the palm-oiler. "If you trouble them, they'll sink you for your pains or my name's not Hemingway".

If we succeed in falling in with them, they will soon be in Sierra Leone". Declared Huntley confidently.

When the *Fair Rosamond*'s commander returned on board, he gave orders to his first lieutenant, the senior mid, John James Robinson, that the schooner was to be refitted and ready for sea in three days, which would allow three days to reach the Bonny.

Young Robinson was a most reliable officer, his keenness being only equalled by his resourcefulness, whatever the situation, and at the end of three days, on the evening of the 7th September to be exact, the little schooner weighed from Clarence Cove with every sail spread to a light land breeze.

"She glided out of the Cove in so silent, stealthy and motionless a manner that she almost seemed sensible of her errand". Wrote her Captain.

The following evening found her riding to a small kedge beyond the outermost shoals of the Bonny in such a position that her masthead lookout could command both channels leading out of the river.

The slavers might be expected at the top of the tide, which was at six o'clock in the morning. Daybreak broke on the 9th without any signs of them.

Aboard the tender, MacIlroy, her assistant surgeon, had to report ten men unfit for duty from fever, including the gunner, who had charge of the powder magazine.

Awnings were spread and the fever patients slung in hammocks on deck so as to get the benefit of the fresh sea breeze, for it was evident that the slavers could not appear before the next high water.

Early in the afternoon the ship was thrown into excitement by the lookout crying "Sail Ho!" However this soon proved to be the *Black Joke*, arriving as usual in the nick of time.

She dropped her kedge close to the *Fair Rosamond* and Lieutenant Ramsay at once lowered his boat and came aboard the schooner.

It was the first time the two tenders had met since parting for their respective stations in the previous March. Ramsay and Huntley, besides being lieutenants of the same standing were old friends. Huntley, at the moment, was the senior, for the news of Ramsay's promotion for the *Marinerito* action had not yet reached the coast. Huntley, whose station was the Bight of Benin, and not Biafra, first of all apologised for poaching on the *Black Joke*'s preserves, urging as some extenuation that he considered circumstances demanded it.

Ramsay, happy in the thought that the *Marinerito* business would give him his promotion, laughingly replied that he was quite ready to let the *Fair Rosamond* have whatever fighting there was going.

Huntley then asked the Scotsman what information he had received about the two slavers. Ramsay told him that only the previous day he had boarded a French slaver, whose captain had declared that there were two slavers up the Bonny, one of them an old sixteen-gun man-of- war brig (the *Regulo*), who intended to sail together, when they considered they would be more than a match for the dreaded *Black Joke*. This bore out the statement of the palm-oil captain, Hemingway.

On the following morning, September the 10th, at high water, the words "Sail Ho!" were roared from the masthead of the *Fair Rosamond*. The lookout was Tom Peter, the head krooman, who had the smartest eyes in the ship.

Up the rigging went Robinson with his glass, taking the ratlins two at a time.

"Two ship come". Asserted the krooman, pointing towards the river mouth.

"Two brigs under a cloud of sail". Sung out Robinson.

This was the signal to get the schooner ready for eventualities. There was no violent hurry. The approaching slavers were still below the horizon from the deck and it would not do to show a sail until the two tenders were discovered. Also there was a clock calm where the man-of-war lay, the sea breeze not having made yet.

The sick were carried below, the awnings taken in, the guns made ready, and the headsails hoisted in stops. For nearly an hour after they had been sighted the slavers ran on under the land breeze before they noticed the upper spars of the cruisers showing above the horizon.

At half past nine, evidently somewhat nonplussed to see that there were two ships on the horizon instead of the little *Black Joke* on her lonesome, as they expected, the two slave brigs anchored just inside the outer bar.

It was at this moment that a light sea breeze reached the tenders, who weighted their anchors and made all sail, the *Fair Rosamond* getting away first, as the *Black Joke* had a heavy bower down in twenty fathoms, and this gave the schooner a lead of half a mile or more.

Fair Rosamond, slipping along in her usual silent fashion led the way along the edge of the Baleur Bank in from two and a half to three fathoms of water. Though the sea was scarcely ruffled by the light breeze, a long heavy swell was rolling in without a break like so much oil, and the men-of-war had to avoid being bumped on the hard sand of the bank, which would have been fatal to themselves as well as to their enterprise. The *Black Joke*, owing to the worn and rough state of her copper and an injured false keel could not hold the speedy *Fair Rosamond* and in spite of every effort, slowly fell astern.

At 1 a.m. the sea breeze reached the slavers, which had been lying becalmed ever since they had anchored. After some signalling with their bunting, both weighed and stood out to sea, as if determined to fight it out with the cruisers.

Under topsails, topgallantsails, jib and boom mainsail, and with the Spanish colours at the peak, the two brigs came steadily on with the *Regulo* leading.

For perhaps twenty minutes they came on and then, all of a sudden, the *Rapido* lost her courage, bore away and setting all her stunsails and flying kites made a run for the river, with the evident intention of landing her slaves before the cruisers could get up. Deserted by her partner, *Regulo* was forced to follow suit or risk certain capture.

Both vessels manoeuvred very smartly, their kites being set in almost man-of-war time. When they put their helms up *Fair Rosamond* was still on the far side of the Baleur Bank, between three and four miles from them with *Black Joke* perhaps three quarters of a mile astern of her.

Between the Baleur Bank and the outer bar lay a number of sand spits through which the channel threaded itself in many twists and turns.

The slavers had pilots aboard but Huntley as he bore away round the end of the bank and set his stunsails and squaresail had only his judgement to trust to, besides a new chart of Commodore Owen's surveys. On every side of the *Fair Rosamond* the sea broke heavily upon the numerous shoals. It was certainly ticklish navigation, and there was no stopping to sound the way, in fact both slavers and cruisers were wetting their sails and making every effort to increase their speed.

As the channel narrowed the wind freshened and the water grew rougher until nothing but a turmoil of broken water showed ahead of the schooner.

Owen's bearings were, however, faultless and the anxious Huntley picked his way without touching. As the *Fair Rosamond* approached the bar, no break could be seen in the line of breakers, into which the schooner flung herself with the sprays flying over her yardarms and her low bulwarks hidden in the froth and fury of her passage.

For a few tense moments she was more under than above water, then she ran hissing into the deep smooth river. She crossed the second bar about a mile and a half astern of the *Regulo*, which in her turn was the same distance behind the *Rapido*. *Black Joke*, having picked up in the rough water, came into the river about four hundred yards astern of the *Fair Rosamond.*

Above the second bar there was a depth of ten fathoms for some seven miles. Five miles up lay the anchorage of the palm oilers, who were all Britishers. Their crews lined their rails as chase and chaser threaded their way through them.

As the *Fair Rosamond* passed each ship, a roar of cheers burst from it until the whole fleet of barques, brigs and brigantines resounded with deep British cheers.

One gallant palm-oil skipper pulled alongside the man-of-war schooner with eight of his crew armed with muskets, and, as he leaped aboard, called out heartily:—

"Brought some volunteers, sir, you look so weakly manned".

"Thank you", returned Huntley, "We do want men, but it will be a case of cold steel: your men should have cutlasses, not muskets".

At this the brave old captain dashed back aboard his for cutlasses, but the *Fair Rosamond* was moving so fast that he was unable to catch up with her until all the excitement was over.

Huntley certainly was short of hands for the approaching fray, for besides himself, Robinson and the assistant surgeon, he could only muster ten bluejackets, four marines and six kroomen.

About two miles above the anchorage of the palm-oilers, a large tributary ran into the Bonny from the Eastward. Into this the slavers turned and were soon hidden from the *Fair Rosamond* by a mile of low land covered in high grass and low jungle. As the slavers ran down inside, the *Fair Rosamond* ran up outside, but young Robinson, up on the schooner's topgallant yard could see over the jungle and note every action of the slavers.

"The leading brig is throwing her slaves overboard". Called down the midshipman.

"Canoes are going alongside both brigs". Was his next announcement. "They are trying to land the slaves."

As the *Fair Rosamond* swept round the bend into the side stream, there was the *Regulo* within point blank range, evidently hard and fast in the mud. Around her were a crowd of canoes, into which a black mass of Africans were crowding in a wild state of panic.

Screams, shouts, angry orders and even pistol shots denoted the desperate efforts of the slaver's crew to get rid of their terrified cargo.

Fair Rosamond at once dropped a shot over her. This was the signal for a stampede to the shore on the part of the canoes; then down fluttered the red and gold bars of Spain from her peak.

Running close under her stern, Huntley warned her captain that if a canoe came off to her or a single man was landed, he would open fire again; then the *Fair Rosamond* passed on, leaving the brig to be taken possession of by the *Black Joke.*

Mean while the callous crew of the *Rapido* could be seen throwing her slaves overboard still shackled together, and by the confused noise of splashing and shrieking it was evident that either crocodiles or sharks were busy upon the victims.

By the aid of his glass, Huntley could see that her guns were trained upon his schooner, whilst the sun flashed on the points of the bayonets and pikes in the hands of her crew.

The *Fair Rosamond* had downed her stunsails as she slid round the sand spit marking the turn into the side steam, for she then had the light breeze abeam. The water was like glass through which the schooner cut without any sound louder than the hiss of a snake.

As she drew near to the *Rapido*, a commotion in the water ahead told of a pair of drowning slaves. The dinghy was dropped over, a boathook was thrust down through the bubbling water and most luckily hooked up the chain, then two half-drowned young Africans were pulled into the boat, shackled together, the right leg of one to the left leg of the other. They were taken aboard and put below.

As the *Fair Rosamond* arrived within point-blank range of the *Rapido*, her pivot gun was brought to bear upon the deck of the brig, which by this time had either landed or drowned the whole of her cargo of four hundred and fifty slaves.

The shot just missed her fore rigging and, passing over the deck, plunged into the mud of the river bank. At this the slaver's crew showed signs of wavering.

"Let them have it, marines, keep the panic up". Roared the schooner's Commander.

The four marines of the *Fair Rosamond* just had time to get off two rounds apiece before the tender was alongside. As she poked her jibboom through the brig's fore rigging, Huntley with a yell of "out cutlasses and board", leaped across her rail, followed by young Robinson, the four faithful marines and two bluejackets, Morris and Oliver. But before they could get to grips the Spanish crew hurled themselves below out of range of the British steel, leaving their captain alone on deck. This man, Don Felippe, as he named himself, was a fine upstanding specimen of a Spaniard, and like most of the Guinea captains, no coward.

With a flourish of his sword he advanced to receive the boarders, then realising that he could do nothing single-handed, he calmly sat down to await his fate.

The cowardly crew of the *Rapido*, were found crowding in her cabin and after slave hold, to the number of sixty-one men, three of whom had been wounded. Two of their number had also been killed by the fire of the marines.

The shorthanded Huntley was somewhat perplexed as to how to deal with so many prisoners,

The short twilight of the tropics was almost over and night was upon them. With any resolution the slaver's crew could have overpowered his few men by mere weight of numbers.

In such a case he wisely ordered that they should come up the companion ladder one at a time and he cautioned them to leave all arms behind on pain of being shot without ceremony.

They were a miserable, disconsolate lot of men as they came slowly out onto the deck. One by one they were carefully searched and then shoved below on the main-slave-deck, captain and all. As the last one disappeared into the dark, pestiferous hold, the hatches were put on and a heavy chain cable coiled on top.

Meanwhile the *Black Joke* had laid the other slaver, the *Regulo*, aboard and captured her without resistance. Most of her crew of fifty-six men had jumped overboard in a mad attempt to swim ashore. Of her four hundred and sixty slaves two hundred and twenty were found to be still aboard, the rest having either been landed or thrown to the sharks.

A palm-oil trader, who arrived in the river a month later counted no less than one hundred bodies, some of them terribly mangled, lying on the shore, shackled together two and two.

The *Regulo* was found to have only eight of her long twelves mounted, but even so she should have been a match with her large crew for both tenders combined.

By the time that both slavers were in order with their crews confined below, it was low water and all four vessels were aground in thick, black, slimy, evil-smelling mud.

It was found impossible to move them except at the top of the tide, and even so, the *Regulo* had first to be lightened. Thus it was nearly a week before the two tenders and their prizes were out of the Bonny. In that time many difficulties had to be overcome. Deluges of tropical rain alternated with stifling heat, which hid the four ships in wreaths of steamy mist, and made the hard work of kedging and warping through the mud a matter of superhuman endurance. The pestilential climate, of course made the daring seamen pay a heavy toll. Two of the *Fair Rosamond*'s crew died on the night of the capture and the fever victims increased daily.

Then the *Black Joke*'s surgeon discovered three cases of small-pox aboard the *Regulo*. Ramsay at once ordered the negroes to be landed.

The shores of this tributary of the Bonny consisted of swamps backed by jungle with here and there a small native village, a mere cluster of huts. It was evident that the slaves had been brought from afar for none of the local blacks could understand their language and the villages refused to receive them.

At midnight they arrived back on the shore, and their moaning and wailing, as they cried to be taken aboard again, could be heard for the remaining hours of darkness, but at daybreak they had all disappeared—into the river, said one, taken by wild beasts, said another, at any rate the crew of the*Black Joke* never saw the two hundred and twenty slaves of the *Regulo* again.

Before leaving the river, Huntley and Ramsay paid a visit to the King of Bonny a palm-wine-drinking decadent chief, who was spoken of in words of contempt by his disgusted subjects.

"He no proper king like him fadder—he nebber hab cut off man's head", was their main criticism.

The British officers could get no promise out of him that he would make a stand against the slavers. He admitted.—

"Spaniard man do very wrong to drown poor black man". Then he ended the conference by saying:—

'Gib my compliment to my brudder, King Wil'em. Tell him send me 'dash' ".

With neap tides coming on it was no easy pilotage getting the ships out of the muddy tributary and down to the palm-oil anchorage, but in this work two British palm-oil captains lent invaluable aid.

The two half-drowned lads, who had been picked up by the *Fair Rosamond*'s dinghy, turned out to be the means of condemning the *Rapido*, for all her other slaves having been thrown overboard or landed, it was upon their evidence alone that she was condemned. The difficulty was to find an interpreter who understood their language, for they proved to be a very different race to the usual coast negro and had probably been brought from Central Africa in a caravan.

In every possible way they tried to show their gratitude to their rescuers. They were never idle always joining in the ship's work from the first moment when of their own accord they took brooms and helped the deck sweepers.

Then, whenever the commander of the *Fair Rosamond* came on deck, they always fell on their knees before him and kissed his hand.

A word remains to be written about the two slave captains. Don Felippe was bitterly accused of cowardice by Don Raymond of the *Regulo*. As the latter explained to his captors:—

"When we first weighed and you saw us sailing in line, we had agreed to engage you among the shoals, trusting that with our local knowledge and good pilots we could give you the slip and possibly enveigle you into the shallows and wreck you. When that coward turned and ran, I had to run also but I knew all was lost.

At Havana they maintained I was a match for any of your small cruisers and here I am captured by a one-gun schooner and twenty men".

At this he covered his face to hide his tears. He was apparently just married and both his own and his wife's fortunes were embarked in the *Regulo*, so that he looked upon himself as completely ruined. Indeed such was his dejection of spirit that he died at Sierra Leone, whilst the adjudication of the two slavers was proceeding.

One more note before we leave the Bonny. It should be noticed that French slavers no longer infested that river. This was owing to the revolution of July 1830, which brought in Louis Philippe, who was in favour of abolition and granted the right of search during the ten years, 1831 to 1841. This caused the few French captains who remained in the trade to sail under Spanish or Portuguese colours.

Black Joke Repaired at Clarence Cove

After the capture of the two slavers in the Bonny, the *Black Joke* sailed for Clarence Cove, and she had not been long at the anchorage before the Commodore arrived.

Hayes determined that the beautiful little brig should be thoroughly repaired. She was hauled up on a rough kind of slip and the *Dryad*'s carpenters and their mates, helped by some of the island carpenters, set to work upon her twisted keel, ragged copper and torn planking.

With the Commodore superintending, the work started at the beginning of October, but it did not get along very fast owing to all the carpenters going down with fever.

The settlement, ever since it had been started, had been suffering severely from fever and cholera. On the 7th November one of the island carpenters died, and the ship's company of the *Dryad* were so affected by the prevailing diseases, as well as ulcers which were most difficult to heal, that on the 9th, Commodore Hayes decided to take his ship away for a week, leaving the work on the *Black Joke* in the hands of the captain of the *Atholl*, which had arrived at Clarence Cove on the previous day.

Hardly was the *Black Joke* afloat once more before news arrived from England of Lieutenant Ramsay's promotion. This caused a shift round in the commands of the tenders. Lieutenant Huntley, not satisfied with his luck in the *Fair Rosamond*, evidently persuaded the Commodore to let him have the *Black Joke* for a spell.

And Commodore Hayes was so pleased with young Robinson's part in the recent capture that he made him an acting lieutenant and gave him command of the*Fair Rosamond.*

This change took place in December 1831.

Fair Rosamond Coppered at Ascension

In the spring of 1832, *Fair Rosamond* was sent to Ascension for a respite from the unhealthy Bight of Benin.

Unfortunately two of her men had been down with small-pox caught from the slaves of the *Regulo* and Captain Bate, Royal Marines, the popular commander of the garrison, thought it wise to order her into quarantine.

The little war schooner was sent round to a small bay, called Comfort Cove. Robinson was not the man to waste time, and having managed to obtain a sufficient number of copper plates, he hove the schooner down and coppered her. The crew slept ashore in tents and landed for their meals after working aboard the ship during the day. The *Fair Rosamond* lay out in the full strenghth of the S.E. Trade, but ashore it was hot and stuffy. To the astonishment of Robinson, his men began to go down one after another with dysentery until twenty-five out of forty-five of the crew were laid up.

This was not really surprising, as after a scanty fare of ship's beef and bread, the men began to 'live high', as they expressed it, on an abundance of fish, turtle, fruit and vegetables.

However, MacIlroy, her assistant surgeon, took such care of his charges that after a spell that was severe while it lasted they all recovered; and the schooner with a new copper bottom and her men once more fit for sevice returned to her station.

Black Joke Makes Her Last Capture

On February the 15th, 1832, the *Black Joke* made her last capture: this was the Spanish schooner, *Frasquita*, with two hundred and ninety negroes, caught as she came out of the Bonny.

Black Joke Sails Round *Brisk* and *Charybdis*

A few weeks later the *Black Joke* was waiting outside the Bonny for her old antagonist, the *Almirante*, which under the name of *Cherouka*, was known to be loading negoes up the river. Whilst he lay in the offing on the tiptoe of expectation, the *Isis*, with Admiral Warren appeared over the horizon, with two new slave catchers, the brigantines *Brisk* and *Charybdis*.

Great things were expected of these cut down ten-gun brigs: two of the smartest lieutenants in the service, each with a distinguished record on the West African coast, were appointed to command them—these were Lieutenant E. H. Butterfield, who took over the *Brisk*, and Lieutenant R. B. Crawford, who was given the *Charybdis*.

There was a new broom at the Admiralty in the shape of Sir James Graham, and though he made many improvements in the service, one of his less successful changes was to do away with the West African Commodore and put the station under the Admiral at the Cape.

Warren was a distinguished officer with a splendid fighting record, but he had no experience of the coast.

His first order to Huntley of the *Black Joke* was to try rate of sailing with the two brigantines. The result was not long in doubt, the famous ex-slaver, according to those who witnessed the trial, walked round and round them in a cable's length.

Black Joke's End

The Admiral, not too pleased at the exhibition made of his pet brigantines, then went on board the *Black Joke* and inspected her. The inspection ended in a rough survey, at the end of which the Admiral ordered the greatest of all slave catchers to make the best of her way to Sierra Leone, where she was to be burnt as no longer considered fit for service.

The stern Admiral little realised the consternation, not to say despondency, on the station, which was caused by his peremptory order.

Leonard of the *Dryad* voiced the general feeling amongst the slave catchers when he wrote:—

"... this favourite vessel—the terror of slave dealers and scourge of the oppressors of Africa, has done more towards putting an end to the vile traffic in slaves than all the ships on the station put together ... many a slave dealer would give a greater price for her than she originally cost, were it only for the purpose of destroying almost the only object of dread in his illicit traffic.

Her demolition will, therefore, be hailed as the happiest piece of intelligence that has been received at the Havannah, and wherever else the slave trade is carried on, for many years".

The *Dryad*, after a welcome holiday at Ascension had arrived at Sierra Leone on January the 28th, 1832, the day after the new commander-in-chief of the African station had arrived there in the *Isis*, fifty-two guns, with the new slave catchers, *Brisk* and *Charybdeis*. The *Dryad* left Sierra Leone in the wake of the *Isis*—the Commodore being anxious to communicate with his three tenders, *Black Joke, Fair Rosamond* and *Seaflower* before sailing for England.

Owing to the hospitality of the well known British merchants, Bannerman and Hanson, at Accra, the Commodore was induced to spend a week there, and was thus too late to put in his word on behalf of the *Black Joke*.

He found Huntley waiting for him at Fernando Po, with an order from the Commander-in-chief that the Commodore was personally to see to the destruction of the poor little tender.

Though extremely mortifified Commodore Hayes had no alternative but to obey orders, though this went sorely gainst the grain.

When this was learnt in Fernando Po, he received a petition from the freed slaves there begging that he would not destroy the famous brig. And when he was taking final leave of Clarence Cove and about to step into his gig, he was surrounded by a crowd of Africans, men and women, who knelt before him and even embraced his legs, their voices all raised in one last appeal not to injure "poor *Black Joke*".

With his three tenders in company, the Commodore returned to Seirra Leone at the beginning of May. He was determined that the other two tenders should not have the *Black Joke*'s fate, so he took them home with him.

It is a great pity that he did not think of taking off the lines of the brig before she was burnt, but probably he was in too great a hurry to hoist the homeward bound pendant and grudged every day that kept him in Sierra Leone.

Huntley had the sad job of dismantling the *Black Joke* and selling her masts, sails and stores by auction: then on the 3rd May, 1832, she was set on fire.

Many a liberated black, watching the flames and smoke rising from the anchorage must have wondered at the sight, little recking that the greatest friend of the African native and the greatest enemy of the cruel dealers in human lives was slowly going to her end, lamented by every officer and man on the station.

A few days later the Commodore sailed for England.

Brisk Captures *Prueba*

On the very day that the *Black Joke* was destroyed, one of Warren's two pets, the *Brisk* made her first capture.

Her log entries show a very typical chase and capture in the Bights. 2nd May, 1832. Position at noon, Lat. 2° 19′ N. Long. 50° 5′ E (Dead Reckoning) West Bay, Princes Island S73 E 142 miles.

2.40 p.m. Calm and Cloudy—light rain. Chase E.S.E. 10 miles.
9.40 a.m. Calm. Lowered quarter boats and sent them in chase—Employed Sweeping, trimming and making sail to all catspaws. Broke three sweeps.
Noon Light airs and variable. Chase E.S.E. 7 miles. Noon position 3° 19′ N. 3° 36′ E. (observed). Prince's Island S. 48 E. 140′.
P.M. Light airs and hazy—employed as in forenoon.
2 p.m. Observed the boats make a signal 'a prize'. Having boarded and captured the Spanish schooner *Preura* (sic. the name of the slaver was *Prueba*) with 312 slaves on board from Bonny to Havannah. In sweeps.
4.30 p.m. A breeze from the Westward.
5.30 p.m. Shortened sail. Hove to on the starboard tack in company with the slaver. Employed making the necessary arrangements.
7.50 p.m. Filled on the starboard tack.
8 p.m. Light breezes and cloudy. Prize in company.
4th May, 8 a.m. Sent provisions on board schooner for the prize crew and preparing for departure in charge of Mr. Fox, midshipman, Mr. Oades, master's assistant, seven seamen and one marine.

On August the 27th, 1832, Lieutenant Butterfield, on promotion to commander, gave up the command of the *Brisk* to Lieutenant Josiah Thompson and went home in H.M.S. *Southampton*.

Crawford Captures a Fort Single-Handed

Lieutenant Crawford was not so fortunate. In a small cruiser such as the little *Charybdis*, one unsympathetic or disagreeable officer was quite sufficient to turn a happy ship into an unhappy one, and just about this time there was a crop of courtmartials, almost wholly due to bad tempers and incompatable natures.

Lieutenant Crawford had the misfortune to fall foul of his master, who took the first opportunity of running him in for the breaking of regulations such as altering the *Charybdis* and using up stores in his efforts to improve her, both in her internal arrangements and rig. One of these disagreeable courtmartials was the result.

Technically Crawford was proved to have been in the wrong and to the general indignation of the navy was dismissed the Service though recommended to mercy. The Admiralty revoked the sentence but left him on half pay.

Thus, instead of slaver-hunting in the Bights, we find him serving as a volunteer aboard the steamer, *Phlegethon*, in the first China war.

It was not long before young Crawford distinguished himself in a second extraordinary victory against odds. It was during the attack on Amoy. A certain fort with a battery of eleven guns was annoying the shipping very much from a commanding position on a hill.

Crawford, after taking stock of the fort, suggested to Captain McCleverty of the *Phlegethon* the possibilty of taking the fort by surprise.

They were standing on the steamers bridge, which extended between her two paddle boxes, and some of the officers of the 49th regiment, which was on board, were also watching the fort from this position.

Captain McCleverty, in answering Crawford, said he thought it a bit too risky. But, on one of the soldiers sneering contemptuously that it was all very well to talk about such an exploit but another matter to carry it out, McCleverty was nettled.

Turning to the officers of the 49th and out of hearing of Crawford, he said sharply:— "You are mistaken, gentlemen, Crawford means what he says".

The old skipper considered they were reflecting upon the honour of his cloth, and a further sneer so irritated him that he sent away his first lieutenant in the gig with six picked hands and allowed Crawford, himself to take four volunteers in the jolly boat.

It sounded a hair-brained scheme but a golden maxim in war is "L'audace! toujours de l'audace!" and away dashed Crawford, urging on his four gallant volunteers with such a will that they soon left the gig astern.

The eager young lieutenant leaped ashore, and without waiting to see if he was followed, scrambled like a goat up the steep one hundred and fifty yards slope and, doubling round to the back of the fort, entered by a small postern gate.

Right opposite him, within a few yards, were some forty or fifty Chinese soldiers, lying about and smoking, whilst others were working the guns, which were being fired upon the passing ships.

The power to act instantly without a moment's hesitation was only equalled in Crawford's nature by his utterly fearless gallantry.

He was armed with a slug-loaded double-barrelled fowling-piece, and a brace of pistols. Bang! Bang! Bang! Bang! went his four rounds into the lolling Chinamen, who, with screams of fear, were so panic-stricken that they actually jammed themselves in the main door of the fort as they rushed headlong, without even looking round at their single attacker.

In the meanwhile, Ryves, the *Phlegethon*'s first lieutenant, with the gig and jolly boat crews were toiling up the steep escrapment, intent on making a frontal attack, when the sudden rush of Celestials, with trailing pikes and matchlocks and terrified mien, brought them to a sudden halt.

Then, whilst they were settling the hash of the fugitives on the hillside, Crawford, alone within the battlements of the fort, proceeded to hoist the Union Jack in place of the Imperial dragon. It so happened that the steamer *Nemesis* was passing at the moment with the General Commanding-in-Chief, Sir Hugh Gough, and his staff on board, who, watching the whole gallant episode, cheered Crawford's action to the echo. Twenty minutes later Crawford and Ryves were fighting their hardest to retain the fort against a Chinese counter attack.

Ryves was wounded, but, aided by a party of the 49th, which were quickly landed from the watching *Phlegethon*, Crawford succeeded in holding the fort against ten times his number of Celestials.

This gallant affair was proudly told throughout the China Expeditionary Force, and, when it reached the ears of the Admiralty, Crawford was given the command of the new experimental brig-sloop *Mutine*.

Courtmartialled For Flogging a Mutinous Seaman

Crawford's was not the only Courtmarital that aroused a great deal of criticism and dissatisfaction in the R.N. at this time.

On the 22nd March, 1832, the old eighteen-gun brig, *Pelorus*, captured the *Secunda Theresa*, a beautiful Spanish slaver on her first trip.

During this passage up the coast to Sierra Leone, Lieutenant de Sausmarez, the prize master, had a great deal of trouble with a refractory seaman.

On his arrival off Freetown, he found the *Black Joke*, lying at the anchorage awaiting her end. She had, of course, outstripped the Commodore and the other tenders on the passage up the coast.

After consultation with Huntley, young de Sausmarez had his mutinous seaman flogged. The commander of the *Pelorus*, R. Meredith, was a great opponent of flogging and had issued the strictest orders against it being resorted to aboard his ship. He was horrified on learning of his prizemaster's action and directly the latter rejoined the *Pelorus*, put him under arrest. For eighteen months that unfortunate officer remained under arrest, being eventually sent home in the *Curlew* to stand his Courtmartial, when the Court at once acquitted him and fully justified his action.

Slaver Becomes Squadron Yacht

The end of the slaver *Secunda Theresa* is interesting. She was bought and turned into a yacht by captain (afterwards Lieutenant-Colonel the honourable R. F. Greville, a keen member of the Royal Yacht Squadron, (for so the Royal Yacht Club was designated after July 1933 in accordance with the wishes of the King as a "mark of His Majesty's gracious approval of an institution of such national utility").

The *Secunda Theresa* after being sold at Sierra Leone, was sent home under the name of *Dispatch*. When Greville bought her, he called her the *Xarifa*, after the heroine of Lockhart's Ballad.

I find the following glowing account of her in the United Service Journal 1833:—

"The *Xarifa*, brig yacht, belonging to the Honourable Captain Greville, arrived at Milford on the 14th instant (March 1833), from Portsmouth on her way to Madeira and the Caribee Islands.

This beautiful vessel forms the perfect beau ideal of naval architectural symmetry. The long low rakish look and airy tracery of Cooper's fanciful "Water Witch, appear realized in the *Xarifa*; whilst, within, all her equipments evince the simplicity and elegance of the proprietor's taste.

It has never fallen to our lot to inspect a more beautiful vessel: and we are persuaded, notwithstanding Captain Chamier's hit at the Yacht Club, that had he seen the *Xarifa* he would have suppressed his sarcasm. She was built at Philadelphia expressly for the slave trade . . . During the late tremendous hurricane she was upon a lee shore off Brighton, but carried sail admirably, and worked herself out of the scrape without difficulty".

CHAPTER XII

AGAINST THE CUBAN SLAVER

"I remember the black wharves and the ships,
And the sea-tides tossing free
And Spanish sailors with bearded lips
And the beauty and mystery of the ships
And the magic of the sea".

Early Captures of Slavers in the West Indies

IT was not until the pirate menace had been conquered that the slaver became the main quarry of the Royal Navy in the West Indies.

Previous to the year 1826 captures of slavers were few and far between.

The *Union* captured the *Eugenia* on November the 1st, 1823, and the *Lion* captured the *Relampayo* on December the 14th, 1824, but these were gifts of fortune, in the midst of their pirate hunting.

In August, 1826, there is the following characteristic entry in Harry Keppel's breezy log:—

"Left (Port-au-Prince on August 6) in the early morning just in time to share prize-money with the *Aurora* and *Harlequin.*

Observed the frigate *(Aurora)* fire a shot across the bows of a schooner under Dutch colours; between us she had no chance of escape. She proved to be Spanish from Africa with two hundred and sixty seven slaves on board, which, as their heads were shaved and greased, the looked, before we got close, like so many thirty-two pound round shot".

Keppel was serving in the *Tweed,* twenty-eight guns, Captain Frederick Hunn.

H.M. Squadron of Ex-Pirate Schooners Broken up

In the year 1826 the ex-pirate squadron of schooners was broken up. Both *Lion* and *Renegade* required so much repair after their constant encounter with the coral fangs surrounding the coast of Cuba that the Admiral reluctantly sold them.

What happened to the *Assiduous* is not on record, but after 1826 there is no further mention of her.

It also seems likely that the *Union* gave place to another vessel of the same name, whose plans may be seen at the Admiralty Curator's. This *Union II,* in design, was an exceedingly interesting schooner being one of the earliest examples of a vessel with pivoted centreboard. She had two of these, one on each side of the mainmast, with chain lifting tackles at their after ends. With great flare forward, almost flat bottomed with great beam, and a wide transom, her measurements were as follows:—

Length between perpendiculars	80′ 2″
" of keel	71′ 4″
Breadth extreme	24′ 0″
Depth	10′ 9″
Draft forward	6′
Aft	6′ 6″

The lines, which were taken off in 1823, are very roughly draughted, but beautiful drawings of the plans are to be seen in Mr. Howard Irving Chapelle's book, *The History of American Sailing Ships.*

The origin of this schooner is not known.

A Lieutenant of the U.S. schooner, *Grampus,* named Finch, was reported to have declared she was an American-built slaver.

On the other hand the schooner *Minx,* built at Bermuda, 1831, which is noted in the Admiralty list as 'similar to Union', was of the same tonnage and dimensions of the ex-*City of Kingston,* and the *Firefly,* built at Bermuda in 1830, which had a centre-board like the *Union* II, is described in the Admiralty records as 'similar to an American schooner'.

Bermuda War Schooners

Not content with the two little schooners, *Monkey* and *Magpie,* built on the lines of the *Assiduous,* Admiral Halstead had the three schooners, *Pickle, Pincher,* and *Skipjack* built at Bermuda in 1827.

These were perhaps the most successful of all the West Indian war schooners. The Admiral was very proud of them. A record at the Admiralty says that they were built from a draught prepared at Jamaica, and there is no doubt that their chief architect was the Admiral himself.

They were exact sister ships of one hundred and eighteen tons burthen, rigged as topsail schooners and armed with an eighteen-pounder Long Tom on a revolving carriage amidships and two eighteen-pounder carronades-two other carronades being added later when it was seen that they were stable enough to carry the additional weight.

Their dimensions were:—

Length gundeck	68′ 8″
Breadth extreme	21′ 2″
Depth	9′ 9″
Keel	54′

The plan shows a fine able schooner with a good turn of speed. Their usual complement was from thirty-six to thirty-nine men.

They proved very popular in the Service and there was always much competition amongst ambitious young officers to get appointed to one of these three Halstead schooners.

Yet life aboard a little war schooner was something like that in the early torpedo boats, plenty of knocking about and hard lying. Like the torpedo boats they were an excellent training for a young officer, especially in navigation, pilotage and seamanship. They also taught those great qualities in commanding men, self-reliance, self-control and quick initiative, the importance of which can never be overestimated.

The snare in commanding a small vessel was, of course, the danger of a too easy relaxation of discipline, which in the end brought the 'briggy', or 'brig-officer' into disrepute.

Such officers as Hobson, Love, Liardet, and Bolton must have been stirct disciplinarians.

In their logbooks one often finds as many as twenty-four lashes of the cat awarded for such a misdemeanour as insolence.

Life on the schooners in peace time was far more full of exciting incident than aboard larger ships, and some officers loved their freedom and adventurous cruises so much that they hated to leave them.

Such a one was Lieutenant Edward Holland, who between July 1826 and December 1830, when he was obliged to invalid, commanded *Monkey, Nimble, Union, Minx* and *Firefly* in turn.

Commander A. Crawford of the *Grasshopper* accused Admiral Halstead of having the 'cacoethes construendi' so strong upon him that he preferred to build cedar wood schooners at Nassau and Bermuda to buying captured slavers of the superior Baltimore model for the Service.

But in the above list of Holland's commands will be noted the name *Nimble*. This schooner was bought by the Admiral and was just such a Baltimore model as Commander Crawford suggests.

H.M.S *Nimble* Ex *Bolivar*

The *Nimble,* in the Admiralty records is described as 'ex *Bolivar*', built Jamaica 1822, purchased 1826.

She was a large topsail schooner of one hundred and sixty eight tons, with the following dimensions:

Length of gundeck	83′ 7″
Length of Keel	64′ 7⅝″
Breadth extreme	22′ 2″
Breadth for tonnage	22′
Depth	9′ 5″

She was commissioned on August the 1st, 1826, by acting-lieutenant Holland who was given three mates (Dartnell, Fletcher and Lewis) and a complement of forty-one men.

Her armament consisted of an eighteen-pounder Long Tom on a pivot amidships and four broadside eighteen-pounder carronades.

Holland was quick to rectify the usual faults of the dockyard in converting a vessel into a man-of-war.

His two foremost carronades, were sent to Kingston for alteration, the two inner fore topmast shrouds were done away with, the topmast stunsails were enlarged, and the ship was trimmed with pigs of iron ballast until she drew six feet nine inches forward and eleven feet five inches aft.

The *Nimble* soon made a name for herself as a successful slave catcher.

It should, perhaps, be noted that a previous *Nimble* in the Service had been a fourteen-gun cutter, purchased in 1781 and commanded in 1796 by that gallant officer, Jeremiah Coglan.

Loss of the *Magpie*

It says much for the way in which British Naval officers handled these schooners, that so few of them came to grief in bad weather. The rig has always been a favourite one with American seamen, but Britishmop officers were considered more at home in square rig. Nevertheless with the exception of the *Magpie,* all the West Indian naval schooners survived many years of tropical squalls and worse.

The *Pincher,* indeed, was caught napping in the comparatively calm waters of the Isle of Wight in 1838 and capsizing, went down with all hands. This was entirely due to open hatches, and officers who were strange to her, and indeed, to war schooners of any description.

The *Magpie's* end was equally tragic. On August the 27th, 1826, she was cruising off the Colorados Roads at the Northwest end of Cuba under Lieutenant Edward Smith.

A pirate had been very active off Cape Antonio and Smith had been sent off in search of the river. Unfortunately the little schooner was without a companion.

After being becalmed during the afternoon, the *Magpie* got the land breeze about 8 p.m., and proceeded under reefed mainsail, whole foresail, square-topsail and jib.

An hour later the wind suddenly shifted from West to South and a black squall cloud was noticed over the land. The mate of the watch at once called Lieutenant Smith, the hands were turned up and the *Magpie* prepared for the approaching squall.

Slowly the lurid cloud swelled and swelled until the whole sky was covered, the light breeze died away: the schooner lost steerage way and began to roll in the smooth water with a chattering of blocks and flogging of canvas, as a long swell lifted her hull.

All hands were on deck at stations, knowing what they had to expect.

Suddenly a white line of foam could be distinguished, rapidly approaching the schooner and a moment later the roar of the wind could be heard. The *Magpie* was without steerage way and what little canvas she had set was caught aback.

Down she lay in the darkness, till the white foam came creaming over her low rail.

"Axes to the masts", roared Lieutenant Smith. "Cutaway the weather lanyards". But there was no time. Over went the schooner, until everyone found himself struggling in the water. A zigazag flash of lightning lit up the gloom, showing two leaning masts against the sky, but no hull, the *Magpie* was sinking.

The boat, which was on the booms between the masts floated clear: in the darkness men in a panic attempted to climb into her; under went her gunwale, she rolled over and floated keel up. Amongst those still above the water were the Commander, the mate, Maclean, and the gunner's mate, named Meldrum.

Though it was pitch dark, the squall had passed and it was calm again.

The more active of the crew clambered up onto the keel of the boat, others hung on as best they could, but their only chance lay in righting the boat. Smith ordered the men off the keel and after several attempts the boat was righted. Whilst two men got in and began to bail with their hats, the remainder of the survivors hung on round the gunwale.

The fear in everyone's mind was, of course, sharks, and scarcely had the bailers got to work before someone cried out:—

"A shark! A shark!"

Instantly there was a wild scramble to get into the water-logged boat, and again it capsized—In their wild panic the men fought for their grip of the boat, and it took sometime before the collected voice of their commander, assuring them that it was a false alarm, could calm them and bring them to their senses.

Once more the boat was righted and the slow business of bailing recommenced. So the night passed—Daybreak found nine souls out of twenty-four still alive, and by 10 o'clock on the 28th the boat was almost clear of water.

Then again came the fearful cry of "Sharks! sharks! sharks!" and over went the boat again in the panic that ensued.

There was no doubt about it this time. For a while the sharks kept off, alarmed by the wild struggle and splashing that was going on. Then they gradually swam closer and closer, until with a rush they actually passed over the boat and between the terrified men who were hanging for dear life to the gunwale. Still no one had been touched, but this could not last long.

Again the sharks, fifteen in number, approached, and this time the men felt the sand-paper-like skin of the monsters rubbing against their legs and bodies. Then came a shriek, followed by another. The water round the water-logged boat became tinged with blood.

A man was caught by the leg: he threw up his arms and disappeared. A second followed him beneath the wave.

But even in the midst of the carnage, Smith kept cool and cheered on the men, urging them to go on clearing the boat of water.

In the midst of it a shark seized him by the leg—though suffering torture he held on to the stern sheets of the boat. The leg had been bitten off above the knee, but he gave no sign for fear of frightening the men, who had again taken up the bailing. Again Smith was attacked, the shark catching hold of the other leg, and he could not avoid a low moan escaping him. His hands loosed their grip and he was just disappearing when the two men who were in the boat bailing, caught him by the arms and succeeded in pulling him into the boat. Here he lay, submerged to his waist in water, throughout that hot, grilling day, with the sun glaring down, but not a drop of water to ease his burning thirst, nor of course, food to maintain his strength.

Seeing that his end must be near, he called the youngest survivor to him—a ship's boy named Wilson, and said:—

"You are young and, I think, most likely to survive. Tell the Admiral that I was bound for Cape San Antonio, in search of the pirate, when the squall capsized us. Tell him that the men have done their duty and no blame is attached to them. I have only one favour to ask him—to promote Meldrum to be a gunner".

With this he shook hands with each survivor and said Goodbye,

The insufferably hot day passed, yet still their commander remained alive, and from time to time he cheered them on in a low, husky voice.

As soon as the sun had set, the sharks appeared again—Sharks are always twice as daring and voracious after dark.

As they nosed up against the gunwale, which only lifted a few inches above the water, the scared men shrank back from the serrated teeth and cruel eyes, the boat gave a lurch and upset; and the dying commander rolled out and was never seen again.

When the terrible melee with the sharks was over, four men only lay shuddering across the keel of the overturned boat, which rolled with a sluggish sickly motion in the midst of a sea of blood.

Maclean, the young master's mate, now rose to the occasion and strove to rally the spirits of his three companions, Meldrum, the boy Wilson and another seaman.

As soon as the fins of the sharks had once more disappeard, he besought his surviving comrades to get down off the keel and right the boat, as being their only chance. But with the exception of Meldrum, the terror of the sharks, the pityless sun, the want of food and drink, and this ghastly prospect of a slow death took the spirit clean out of the boy and the bluejacket.

Though they righted the boat and had almost managed to clear the water out of her, these two about 3 a.m. in the morning both became delirious and before either Maclean or Meldrum could stop them, had sprung overboard and sank from sight.

Dragged down by the sharks was the horrible thought of the two survivors.

However neither Maclean nor Meldrum were of the kind that gave in, and though utterly exhausted, kept at the bailing till the boat was dry. Then they lay down side by side and fell into a sound sleep.

They awoke to find the sun high in the heavens, the sea with hardly a ripple and blank to the horizon. The outlook appeared desperate. Without a mast, sail or oars, without food or water, with the horrible end of their shipmates ever before their eyes, the two men sat silent, one in the bows, the other in the stern.

The terrible torture of thirst swelled the tongues in their mouths and made speech difficult and painful. As the days passed each began to envy the quick fate of their shipmates.

They looked at each other and realised that the same horrible thought was passing through each brain. Just a slash with a sheaf knife, a spurt of blood, the black swollen lips glued to the wound and a sudden relief from the intolerable torture of thirst. It was so easy.

One of them fell forward on his knees and his piteous lips moved in prayer—At once his example was followed. A hoarse mumbling of words with little sense and much repetition gave relief to each. The horror in their eyes was cleared away for a while.

As the glowing red ball of the sun sank beneath the horizon, they lay back listlessly, knowing that through the long hours of the night there would be no hope of rescue. Of the two, Maclean had grown so weak that he could scarcely raise his head.

The second night passed. The boat rocked gently in the slight fitful breeze, and the castaways, relieved of the burning sun-rays, again were refreshed by sleep.

With the first coming of light, they searched the horizon for a sail, one looking to the East and the other to the West. Suddenly a hoarse strangled cry broke from the parched lips of Maclean, and Meldrum following the line of the mate's pointing finger, saw a square shaft of white on the horizon, to leeward.

A ship was beating up towards them. And now came the long-drawn-out agony of suspense. Would she pass close enough for that speck of a boat with its two wildly-waving occupants to be seen?

At first all seemed hopeful, she was heading directly for them—then, the tower of canvas suddenly came upright, the sunlight on the sails faded, she was going about, and heading away at right angles. They could now see what she was, a merchant brig, probably American, with black topsides, and cotton canvas.

The wind was light and inclined to be patchy. As the brig stood away, despair crept into the eyes of the two *Magpie* survivors, yet they watched her every movement, unable to look away, they knew that unless she quickly tacked again, all hope of rescue was gone.

Then, just as the agony of suspense was becoming intolerable, round she came again and once more headed directly for the boat.

This time she came on, slowly and still more slowly as the breeze continued to lighten, until she was within half a mile; by which time both men were waving their jackets and trying their best to shout.

But once more, just at the very moment when they made sure she had seen them, the brig slowly came up into wind and headed away on the other tack.

Maclean flopped down in the stern sheets and covered his face with his hands, then looked up in amazement as the hoarse, cracked voice of Meldrum came to him.

"By God, I'll swim to her!"

For answer Maclean pointed to where a sinister pointed wedge cut the water away to leeward.

"It's our last chance", urged the gunner's mate, He was a strong swimmer, the brig had little more than steerage way. The only risk was a shark.

"Don't tell me if you see a shark after me. I shall splash, but shan't look behind me. I'd rather die without knowing, if I must".

"Don't do it, Meldrum, you're throwing away your life", said the mate, then with a piteous voice gave the other his last messages for his wife.

The gunner's mate with a quick, fervant prayer, jumped overboard with a loud splash and began swimming strongly after the brig, splashing with both legs and arms at each stroke.

Hardly was he fifty yards from the boat than Maclean saw three fins go by—three sharks were following the swimmer. Unable to keep silent, he shouted encouragement with his raucous voice.

Another fin passed. The sharks were only kept off by the splashing. Still Meldrum swam on, his eyes fixed on the brig watching for a face to show above the rail.

When he had gained two thirds of the distance, and Maclean could hardly distinguish him, he felt his strength leaving him. With a last kick he threw himself half out of the water and shouted with all his might. A head poked over the brig's rail, looked with shaded eyes for perhaps half a minute and then waved an arm. The next moment all was bustle aboard the brig. A boat was swung out and lowered; and in a very short while the two survivors of the *Magpie* were saved.

The whole tragic story was told in the subsequent court martial at Port Royal by the young master's mate.

The court was deeply affected by the recital of the tragedy, whilst the two, who alone had survived, were in tears.

However the gallant Smith's dying request was acceeded to—Meldrum was promoted to gunner—Maclean, at the same time, received his lieutenant's commission, afterwards going into the coastguard service.

From the year 1826 the slave trade of Cuba increased by leaps and bounds, for instance in 1827 between January the 3rd and December the 31st, twenty-seven slavers sailed from Havana for the coast of Africa, whilst between January the 3rd and December the 27th, 1828, sixty-three slavers left Havana.

From the beginning of 1826 for about twenty years, the chase of the slaver in the West Indies was the chief business of the Jamaica squadron.

Union Captures *Magico*

On the 21st of January, 1826, the schooner *Union,* commanded by Lieutenant Lowe, was cruising on the North East coast of Cuba under the orders of Captain Hobson of the *Ferret,* ten-gun brig, when the Spanish brigantine, *Magico* was sighted.

After a long chase the slaver at last ran ashore near the Port of Manati on the 22nd, her crew and about two hundred negroes getting safely ashore.

When Lieutenant Lowe went aboard the stranded vessel in order to take possession, he found one hundred and seventy nine slaves still on board the *Magico,* many of whom proved to be severly wounded.

Evidently the Spaniards had used their swords freely in an effort to force the terrified negroes overboard, and there were from twenty to thirty dead bodies floating in the sea round the brigantine.

As the *Magico* was being searched, a burning length of match was discovered leading to a barrel in the powder magazine.

Slavers of this description were as bad as the worst of the pirates.

The *Union* had another exciting chase amongst the reefs and shoals of the Bahama Bank on the 27th of April, 1826, after the Spanish brigantine, *Palowna.* In the strong breeze the slaver had the heels of the little schooner, but as long as she was within range, the *Union* fired steadily at the *Palowna's* masts in the hope of disabling her, and this fire was smartly returned.

After keeping sight of the chase for two whole days, Lieutenant Lowe lost her at dark on the 28th, being then amongst a veritable labyrinth of rocks on the South-West end of the Bank. He, thereupon, wisely anchored.

The Spaniard, carrying on recklessly in the stiff breeze, speedily holed herself on a coral head and being force over it by her canvas sank in deep water.

The pilot of the *Union,* who spoke Spanish, afterwards met one of the *Palowna's* crew at Xebarra, who informed him that only the Captain, himself and one other man had reached the shore in her stern boat out of a crew of twenty-nine men and one hundred and sixty five slaves. Nor had the *Union's* gun-practice with her Long Tom been useless for three Spaniards had been killed and one wounded during the chase.

On the 5th of March, 1826, the *Speedwell,* Lieutenant Bennett, whilst cruising near the Grass Cut Cays in the Gulf of Providence, came across the wreck of the Spanish slave brigantine *Orestes* and was able to rescue two hundred and thirty eight negroes alive.

Nimble And Slaver *Guerrero* Run Aground On The Bahama Bank

Chasing slavers on the Great Bahama Bank was a game which needed clever piloting amongst the coral heads, and the cruisers often had to take great risks, especially on dark nights.

The *Nimble* was very nearly sacrificed to the coral fangs in making her first capture in December 1827.

On the 19th a strange sail was sighted near the Orange Cays, and the little war schooner immediately made sail in chase.

The fugitive soon showed what she was by her fast sailing, and all day long the chase continued with the *Nimble* slowly gaining, but it was not until dark that she overhauled her quarry.

As she ranged up astern, the slaver suddenly bore away across her bows to rake her, and, at once, a brisk action commenced. This was at 6.16 p.m. In half an hour the slaver had had enough of it, for she stopped firing, luffed up into the wind as if she was heaving to, and, after blazing off a blank cartridge, burnt a flare.

Believing that the chase had struck, Lieutenant Holland ceased fire and prepared to send a boat aboard. But he was taken in by a regular slaver's trick. Having induced the *Nimble* to cease fire and back her topsail, the Spaniard filled way and ran for the Florida coast.

The war schooner was quickly after her, but it was dangerous work as the water under their keels grew less and less.

Suddenly it was realised that they were running over a shoal, and at the first agitated cry of the leadsman the *Nimble's* helm was put down; but, as she came round in stays, her keel could be felt dragging over the hard coral with that sinister grating, which was just as if the little vessel knew her danger and was shuddering with fright. For a few moments she carried her way and then stuck fast.

At the very same moment a tremendous crash and horrid yelling told of the Guineaman in trouble. She was also hard and fast on shore, and the crash told her pursuer that her masts had gone by the board.

No more yelling came from the slaver, though lights along her deck showed where she lay, pounding heavily. The *Nimble* was in the same predicament, but nothing could be done until daylight when the war-schooner's boats were sent alongside the slaver.

At sun-up the *Nimble* managed to haul off into deep water, after sacrificing her false keel, rudder, anchors and cables. But there was no floating the slaver, which proved to be the Spanish brig *Guerrero,* better known as the *San José*, of fourteen guns and ninety-five men with over five hundred slaves.

Only one hundred and twenty slaves and twenty of the *Guerrero's* crew could be accommodated aboard the *Nimble;* but luckily for all concerned three American wreckers came off from the coast soon after daylight, and took the remainder of the crew and slaves off the wreck.

The *Guerrero* being abandoned as unsalvable, a course was set for Key West, but on the way the Spaniards either overpowered or bribed two of the wrecking sloops, which managed to give the rudderless *Nimble* the slip.

On arrival at Key West, Lieutenant Holland soon found that he would become involved in international complications, if he handed over his slaves to the American authorities.

After a few days of vain argument, he wisely decided to sail for Havana, where, in spite of the unseaworthiness of the *Nimble* after her night's bumping on the reef, he arrived on December the 29th.

Cruisers and Their Prizes Unpopular at Havana

Havana was no more sympathetically inclined towards the damaged slave-catcher than Key West, but in the Spanish port Lieutenant Holland at any rate had the help and support of the British Consul-General.

The arrival of British men-of-war and captured slavers was a never failing source of irritation to the people of Havana, who one and all, were either financially interested or owed their living to the slave trade.

The merchants of Havana, indeed, did all they could to put the British cruisers off the scent and even bribed foreign merchantmen to report false cases of suspected pirates, so as to get the men-of-war out of the way when slavers were expected on the coast.

Grasshopper* and *Xeres

Thus in June 1827 the *Grasshopper* was misled by the master of a Prussian barque, who told Commander Crawford that he had been chased by a pirate off Matanzas.

The sloop at once put to sea, but Crawford, after cruising for a short while off Matanzas without seeing any sign of a pirate, wisely bore up for Cape San Antonio.

At daylight the following morning, June the 27th, when the *Grasshopper* was off the Western end of the highland of Rosario, a large topsail schooner was sighted hull down on the starboard bow, standing in for the Colorados on the port tack, the wind being moderate from South East.

In order to make the pass through the reef, the stranger had to cross the cruiser's bow; and the *Grasshopper,* running along the coast with her royal and topgallant stunsails and other flying kites set, seemed certain to cut her off from the reef. Perceiving that this would happen, the slaver gradually kept away until she had the wind on her starboard quarter. For a while the war-sloop closed on the chase, but as the wind fell lighter and lighter, it was seen that the chase was no longer getting nearer. Presently the slaver gybed her booms over and brought the wind right aft; then as the last breath of air petered out, she manned her sweeps.

Meanwhile aboard the *Grasshopper* every possible means of improving her speed was taken. Guns were moved here and there to alter her trim, the pumping-engine was set to work wetting the sails, the best helmsman was sent to the wheel, whilst Crawford and his officers with their eyes glued to their sextants, kept measuring the distance between the two vessels. The calm did not last long and as the day advanced, the breeze freshened again and steadied. Once more the sloop was gaining, and soon a boat, spare spars and other fittings from the slaver came floating by, an indication that she was being hard-pressed and was lightening herself of all moveable weight. Towards sunset the wind was fresh enough at times to compel the *Grasshopper* to lower her royals. It was scarcely dark before the moon, which was near the full, rose directly astern and showed the schooner, as if cut out in silver, laying down to it about six miles ahead.

Any keen racing yachtsmen can realize the excitement aboard the sloop.

The *Grasshopper* was one of the *Cruiser* class of eighteen-gun-brig-sloops, which had lately been given three masts and ship-rig. Luckily the new spars and masts, which were fitted at Woolwich, were very light and had not spoilt her sailing powers as much as might have been expected, indeed her commander contended that she never chased anything that she did not overhaul.

In a trial of sailing of four hours with the *Arachne,* considered the fastest sloop of the class in the West Indies, the *Grasshopper* had had a little the best of it, both ships being on a wind under courses, single-reefed topsails, topgallant sails, jib and spanker and going about eight knots.

According to Crawford, Admiral Halstead in his effort to improve the sloop, shortly after the commander had left her, succeeded only in spoiling her by removing her short poop, giving her squarer, heavier yards and bringing her more by the stern.

But at the date of this chase, the little sloop was considered by her officers to be in perfect sailing trim, yet the slaver seemed to be holding her own in an astonishing way.

Towards midnight a haze gradually hid the schooner from every eye except that of White, one of the mates, who had superlative sight. He maintained that he could distinguish her and that she was keeping her course. But at 2 a.m. Captain Crawford, with his eyes glued to his night-glass, suddenly discovered that the chase had hauled up and was crossing the *Grasshopper* on the larboard tack.

He at once set a course that would keep the schooner a point on the starboard bow, the sloop having all her larboard (the term 'port' not then being in common use) stunsails set. The slaver's change of course, which she had evidently hoped would not be noticed, was the cause of her capture.

By seven in the morning she was within range, and a warning shot caused her to round to and give in after a chase of twenty-six hours' duration, covering two hundred and twenty miles.

The slaver proved to be a fine, new, clipper-built schooner of two hundred tons and five guns.

She had only left Havana five months before and had three hundred and ninety two slaves out of a shipment of four hundred, which the Captain declared he had taken aboard in the Bight of Benin, but which it was believed had been taken out of a Brazil slaver by an act of piracy.

The Piratical Slaver *Fama De Cadiz*

This stealing of slaves by one slaver from another was very common at this date. Two years later the *Fama de Cadiz* arrived at Havana after landing three hundred slaves at Santa Cruz.

This notorious piratical slaver had actually robbed other slavers of close on one thousand negroes. She had, however, a terrible middle passage, when small-pox and other diseases reduced her slaves to no more than three hundred, and her large crew, said to number one hundred and fifty seven cut-throats of all nations, down to sixty-six. The survivors of her slave cargoe were landed in such a miserable state that they sold as low as one hundred dollars a piece.

In the *Xeres,* as the *Grasshopper's* capture was called, the slaves, both men, women and children, proved to be unusually healthy and cheerful in spite of having been battened down for twenty-four hours. Another surprise was the presence aboard of a Spanish naval officer, who declared that he had been given leave to make the trip by Admiral Laborde, commanding the Spanish squadron at Havana.

The crew proved to be the usual fierce, black-whiskered lot of dagoes. They and the slaves were set ashore at Havana.

At this date by Spanish law these captured slaves were apprenticed to masters for seven years, their masters being obliged to feed, clothe and look after them. At the end of the seven years they were supposed to be set free, but with Cuba a mass of cupidity and corruption from the Governor downwards, it was extremely rare that these so-called apprentices ever received their freedom, any trumped-up charge of misdemeanour being sufficient to prevent it.

Whilst he was getting the *Xeres* condemned, Captain Crawford counted nearly a dozen brigs and schooners fitting out for the slave trade; and he found that he could buy shares in these vessels on the stockmarket, the value of the shares depending chiefly upon the reputations of the different captains.

Grasshopper* and *Firme

It was well into November, and the *Grasshopper* had covered a great deal of ground before she made her next capture. Whilst cruising under the lee of Martinique the sloop sighted a large brigantine coming down under all sails, having just run out of the passage between Martinique and St. Lucia. With the wind strong at West by South, about two points before the beam, the stranger came steadily on, whilst the *Grasshopper* without alteration of course or canvas made preparation for action.

Carronade slides were brought athwart ships, ports shipped, hammocks piped down, and one by one so as not to attract attention, the men were sent aloft to be all ready to cast off gaskets and stick out stunsails at the order "Make sail".

By 8 a.m. the stranger was abeam.

The sloop then went about, letting out a reef and setting her topgallantsails whilst in stays.

No sooner had the *Grasshopper* sheeted home than the brigantine, satisfied of her identity, hauled her wind and, dowsing her stunsails, trimmed away for Martinique on the starboard tack. As the wind was less in shore, the chase, which was half courses down, was rapidly closed. At 9.30 a.m. she saw that this would not do so she gradually bore away until the wind was upon her starboard quarter.

The *Grasshopper* at once ran up starboard stunsails and kept away a couple of points, so that the courses converged.

But the chase succeeded in crossing, and as soon as she bore well before the beam, Captain Crawford bore away till he had her a point on his starboard bow, both ships being now under all possible sail, steering WNW, with the wind on the starboard quarter.

With the wind slowly easing up as the sun neared the zenith, the slaver began to increase her distance. Aboard the sloop the drooping canvas was wetted and light weather staysails were got up out of the locker and set flying. Then about four bells, 2 p.m. the wind freshened and the *Grasshopper* began to close until two bells in the first dogwatch, when again it began to fail.

William Warren, the sloop's most efficient first lieutenant, was anxious to try a shot, but Captain Crawford would not even allow the log to be hove or a bucket of water to be drawn for fear of checking her way; and he still less would consent to yawning off his course for the time necessary to sight and fire the shot.

He however allowed a shot to be fired wide without yawing just as a warning. This raised a cheer as the chase was seen to let fly her royal halliards.

Men aboard the *Grasshopper* were beginning to shake hands and congratulate each other in momentary expectation of the slaver rounding to. But up went the brigantine's royal again; and with darkness falling and the moon not rising before ten, there seemed every chance of the chase being lost to sight.

Luckily for the sloop, the wind breezed up again until the masts were bending and booms creaking with the strain. For a couple of hours cruiser and slaver splashed along at twelve knots, then down came a heavy squall.

Aboard the *Grasshopper* royal and topgallant stunsails were smartly got in, and, as soon as the bustle of shortening sail and the clatter of the squall was over, the rising moon showed the chase, barely three cables off on the starboard bow, lying broached to with her sheets all gone and her sails flying. The man-of-war ranged up on the slaver's weather quarter; and as the squall showed no signs of lessening, topsails were reefed and all made snug, whilst the boarding party pushed off in the cutter for the chase.

She turned out to be the Spanish brigantine, *Firme,* of two hundred and eighty five tons, two months from the Bight of Biafra with four hundred and ninety five slaves alive out of five hundred. She was armed with a long twenty-four-pounder swivel gun and four short eighteen-pounders, her crew totalling forty-eight including three passengers.

This brigantine was not a new clipper from the Chesapeake like the *Xeres,* but one, which, though she must have been very fast in her day, was almost worn out, and the squall had been too much for her.

Several chain-plate bolts had drawn in her upper works, her running gear had carried

10. The capture of the Two Topsail Slave Schooner *Bolodora* by H.M. Schooner *Pickle*, Lieutenant J. B. B. McHardy on the 6th of June 1829, after a chase of Fourteen Hours and an Action of One Hour and Twenty Minutes within Pistol shot.

From an Aquatint in colour by Edward Duncan after the painting by W. J. Huggins.

[*Facing page 240.*

11. The Capture of the Spanish Slave Brig *Midas* by H.M. schooner, *Monkey* on the Great Bahama Bank June 27th, 1829.

From an Aquatint in colour by Edward Duncan after the painting by W. J. Huggins.

[*Facing page 241.*

away and sails had torn, and being in imminent danger of losing his masts the slave captain had felt compelled to give in.

As the *Firme* had to be taken to Havana, Captain Crawford decided to put into St. Kitts for maize and rice; and by sun-up the next morning both ships lay at anchor in Basse-terre Roads.

A Humane Slave-Captain

And now for once one can bear testimony to a humane slave-captain.

When Crawford and the *Firme's* captain went aboard the brigantine after breakfast, this is what he saw—I quote his exact words:—

"I found all the slaves, men, women and children, a remarkably fine, healthy race—fat, sleek, good humoured—and, to all appearances, happy and contented. It was quite a pleasure to witness their joy when the captain of the *Firme* stood upon the deck. They all crowded round him, and in every way the could testified the pleasure they felt at his presence, showing by their action, that they looked upon him as their friend and father. Not one moody or sullen-looking black did I observe among the whole".

This unusual Guinea captain proved to be none other than Guiseppe Fornaro of the *Dolores,* now know as Don Juan Sandemo.

This was his nineteenth voyage and second capture. He had sailed from Havana in January, 1828, with the *Xeres* and another schooner under his orders. The slaves had been embarked at Popoe on the Gold Coast on the 18th of October and were destined for Guadeloupe. The three vessesl were to have kept company and he had actually issued a code of signals for their use, but in a blow off the Canaries the little squadron of slavers had been dispersed.

Captain Crawford was so pleased at the condition of the slaves that he presented a memorial, couched in very strong terms, in favour of Fornaro, to the Captain-General of the Cuba, when they reached Havana.

When the *Grasshopper* arrived at Havana with her second prize, her unpopularity was so marked as to cause Crawford to take special precautions. Even the pratique officer and head of the Adnano had had an interest in the captured vessels and plainly showed their displeasure on boarding the sloop. And when the Commander landed to pay his respects to the Governor, a jeering, scowling mob, crowded the landing-place and at one moment it looked as if his gig's crew would be forced to use their stretchers.

When he returned aboard, his First Lieutenant announced that there was a strong rumour that an attempt was to be made after dark to capture the *Firme,* and even to set fire to the *Grasshopper.* Crawford at once took precautions, additional marines were sent aboard the slaver, and every night he had boats rowing guards round the two vessels.

The captain himself went about his business in the port in half expectation of a cuchillo neatly placed between his ribs in the true Spanish manner and he took very good care not to be ashore after sunset.

The adjudication of the *Firme* took about a week, and then, as soon as the slaver had been delivered over with complete inventory (a very important item) to the charge of the British Commissioner, the sloop sailed for her station to windward.

Spanish Trickery

As showing the lengths to which the Spaniards would go in combating the endeavours of the Royal Navy to suppress the slave trade, a couple of Spanish war schooners did their best to hide a slaver from the British cruiser by keeping between the former and the latter.

It was about five o'clock in the afternoon when the *Grasshopper,* in beating to the Eastward in order to open the Gulf, came upon the three schooners running in for the land under the same sail. The glass soon revealed that the inside schooner was longer and lower in the water than the other two, also her paint was rusty and weather stained and her sails much bleached from wear. The sloop was at once eased off the wind a couple of points so as to close the suspicious vessel: but it was too late, she slipped in between the heads of a little Puerto Escondido, which lay between Havana and Matanzas and was not even noticed on the Admiralty chart.

As the chase, with topgallant and royal stunsails set as an evidence of her flight, slipped through the narrow entrance, the sloop threw several shot after her; and then, as it was nearly dark and Crawford was unwilling to risk an unpleasant international incident, he backed his topsail to await the Spanish warships, which on his first shot bore up in his direction.

The Commodore's corvette now arrived on the scene, as well as the two schooners.

As the schooners headed for the *Grasshopper's* hawse and the corvette for her wake, Crawford thought it prudent to clear for action and keep good steerage way for manoeuvring on his vessel, in case of a misunderstanding which might lead to a regrettable incident, as diplomacy would describe it.

However as the slaver had evidently escaped the sloop's clutches, the Spaniards did no more than try and fool the British as to the former's business. As the corvette passed under the *Grasshopper's* stern, the Commodore hailed that he had overhauled the stranger and that she was only a small trader with fruit and wine from the mother country.

Crawford replied that it was indeed curious that she should run from him, refuse to heave to on being fired at, and still more put into that tiny hidden port when she had Havana close aboard under her lee. With this the British sloop made sail to the Northward, whilst the Spaniards remained hove to off the entrance, covering their hidden countryman.

Skipjack and *Maria*

Admiral Halsted's new schooners were not long in proving their worth as slave catchers, but he was careful to put old experienced lieutenants in command of them at first.

The *Skipjack's* first commander was Lieutenant J. Pulling, one of those deserving officers who had seen much service but little promotion. He had the ill-luck to be acting master of the *Atalanta* when she was lost on the Sister's Rocks off Halifax Lighthouse in a thick fog in November 1813.

He had subsequently distinguished himself in the coastguard service in Hampshire in many affrays with smugglers.

On being appointed to the *Skipjack* in December 1826, he soon began to be somewhat of a scourge along the North coast of Cuba. He was too experienced to get caught in the many traps laid for him, but in November, 1828, he certainly had a narrow shave.

On the morning of November the 29th a suspicious schooner was discovered heading along the coast a few miles from Havana.

After a short chase and exchange of rounds from their Long Toms, the slaver led the war schooner in towards a village, called Jaymanita, some nine miles west of Havana.

The passage to the port led through unbuoyed reefs and shoals, but the slaver, knowing her ground, was able to run in under full sail and anchor. Immediately shore boats came off and proceeded to remove the slaves in spite of the *Skipjack's* fire.

The latter had to send a boat ahead to sound before she dared sail in, but she succeeded in anchoring in eleven fathoms within half a mile of the slaver at 8 p.m. The boats were at once manned and armed and sent away. Though they pulled their best, they were too late; and before they could get up the last shoreboat full of negroes had paddled off.

A minute later, when the boats were still a cable's length away, the slaver blew up.

The whole of the after part of the schooner was blown to atoms but forward in the forecastle an emaciated, half-dead negro was found. The slaver turned out to be the *Maria,* one hundred and sixty tons, one long twelve-pounder, Captain Don Francisco Romero, with two hundred and thirty three slaves shipped in the Old Calabar on May the 21st.

Slave Ports of Cuba

With the neighbourhood of Havana being so well watched by the British cruisers, slavers soon made a practice of landing their caroges all round the coast of Cuba.

A few years later the British consul reported that out of twenty-five cargoes of negroes landed in six months, nine were landed at Guanima, four near Trinidad, three at Manil, two at Camarisca, one at Puerte de Guano, one at Cabanos, one at Banes, one at Cogimar, one at Santa Cruz, one at Canimar and one near St. Jago di Cuba.

Juragua, a little to windward of St. Jago, was another favourite port of entry for slavers, nine cargoes, making two thousand eight hundred and three slaves, being landed there in the year 1838. (Buxton).

There was also a regulation of the port of Havana in favour of slavers. No vessel was allowed to enter the port between sunset and sunrise with the exception of slavers. They had this privilege granted to them in defiance of the treaties entered into by Spain. This is not to be wondered at when the Governor-General himself reckoned on making a fortune out of his commission.

Losses in 1828

The year 1828 was fatal to two of the schooners on the Jamaica station.

On the 17th of March, *Union,* commanded by Lieutenant C. Madden, was wrecked off the East end of Rose Island, New Providence, without the loss of life. At this distance it is impossible to say whether this was the vessel whose lines were sent to the Admiralty in August 1828, or not. That there was no blame attached to Madden was proved by his being placed in acting command of the *Speedwell* in June 1829.

On December the 18th, 1828, the schooner *Kangaroo,* Lieutenant Anthony de Mayne, was lost on the Hogsties Reef off Cuba, all her crew of forty-five being saved.

The *Kangaroo* had not been mentioned before. She was a six-gun schooner, which seems to have been employed only in surveying.

British Cruiser's Success in 1829

The year 1829 proved to be the most successful year the British war schooners in the West Indies ever had in their efforts to suppress the slave trade. This was, in part, due to the mistake of the slave owners, merchants and brokers of Havana in despising these little vessels.

The British consul, writing to the Earl of Aberdeen on July the 11th, 1829, remarked:—

"The practice of arming large vessels for the slave trade to resist His Majesty's small schooners had been much in vogue amongst the Havana slave traders during the year past; and although the result of all such contests must be evident from the circumstance that no schooner has ever yet been defeated in her attempt on a slave vessel, yet as the disparity of force may excite the Spaniards to fight, there is reason to fear the loss of valuable lives if this system of resistance is longer permitted . . . "

Again he wrote on July the 17th:—

"The activity and gallantry of His Majesty's schooners on this coast seem likely to give a most effectual check to the trade in slaves by running the speculators in this odious traffic and capturing their largest and finest vessels . . . "

Monkey* Captures *Josepha* and *Midas

The little *Monkey,* the smallest of all the war schooners, was the first to distinguish herself by capturing a vessel of more than four times her tonnage.

The commander of the *Monkey* was Lieutenant Joseph Sherer, an officer of eighteen years service, who had been with Parry in the *Hecla* during his two first polar voyages, and he had been a lieutenant of the *Victor* when she captured *Las Damas Argentinas.*

He succeeded the following officers in the command of the *Monkey,* Willoughby Shortland, Duncan F. Campbell, Fred. W. Foote and J. B. L. Hay; and his first success was the capture of the Spanish schooner, *Josepha* (ex *Fortuna*)* near the Berry Islands with two hundred and six slaves on board on April the 7th, 1829.

The *Monkey* was lying ready to pounce in that favourite lurking place of the war schooners, Slaughter Harbour, which was little more than a large pool of water, formed by the Stirrup Cays, with a difficult entrance over a bar of scarcely two fathoms.

Slavers constantly passed within sight of this retreat, and so convenient was it for the smaller English men-of-war that Lieutenant Shortland of the *Skipjack* actually laid down moorings there in 1831, from which the schooners could slip and be at sea and so on to their prey in a few minutes.

When the little *Monkey* came sailing into Havana with the big *Josepha* in her wake, the seamen aboard British traders in the port slapped their thighs and swore that it was a case of the *Speedy* and *Gamo* over again.

The slave trading fraternity of Havana were, however, so incensed that Sherer had to be as careful as Crawford to avoid a stiletto in his back and again there was talk of an attempt at recapture.

As soon as the *Josepha* had been condemned, Sherer was glad to hurry away to his station in the Florida Channel.

As the *Monkey* rounded Bemini from the South about 9 a.m. on June the 27th, 1829, there lay a large brig at anchor on the Bank, some six or seven miles away. Her topsails were lying in the buntlines and mastheaded, and the sight of the war schooner caused her to up anchor and stand away under easy sail.

The wind was very light and when the *Monkey* was within about three miles, the brig again anchored; and this time it was evident that she meant to resist capture for she got a spring on her cable so as to be able to slew her broadside in any required direction.

She also kept her topsails set with the yards slung and the sheets stoppered.

As soon as the *Monkey* had worked within point-blank range, which took some time in the paltry air, the brig fired a wild ill-directed broadside. Lieutenant Sherer held on until he knew that every shot from his popgun would go home: then, ranging up across the stern of the anchored brig, he opened a brisk fire.

After half an hour's bombardment, a hail came from the after end of the brig, saying she had surrendered, but forward on her topgallant forecastle a number of men still kept up a fire of musketry. However a few more rounds of grape and canister from the *Monkey's* Long Tom settled the business. The victory was almost bloodless; the *Monkey* had not a man hurt whilst the brig had only one killed and three wounded, the man-of-war firing high for fear of injuring the slaves.

The prize proved to be the *Midas*, ex *Providencia,* of three hundred and sixty tons, mounting four long eighteen-pounders and four medium twelve-pounders with a crew of fifty-seven men. She was a very well-known slaver on the coast of Africa. As usual in such captures the ownership of the *Midas* was put upon the dead man, one Gabriel Galan, who happened to be the first mate and supercargo. This proceeding was in order to conceal the identity of the real owners in Havana.

---

* When two names are given, it generally signifies that the slaver had already been captured by our cruisers under her original name, but had been bought in by the owners and sent slaving once more under the new name.

This practice was not put an end to until the British Government forbade the sale of captured slavers.

If the arrival of the *Monkey* in the Havana with the *Josepha* as a prize made a stir amongst the seagoing and mercantile population, the arrival of the same mosquito-like schooner with the even larger *Midas* caused even greater gnashing of teeth. To show the discrepancy in size, the boom of the brig's fore and aft mainsail was as long as her captor.

Five of the *Midas* crew turned out to be British subjects and two were American.

As the U.S.N. schooner *Grampus* happened to arrive at Havana the day after the *Monkey* and her prize, the Americans were formally handed over to her Commander.

Of the British, one was a free black of Jamaica. The others had belonged to a Liverpool ship which had been wrecked on the coast of Cuba.

They were sent home, tried for piracy at the Old Bailey and condemned to death, but their sentences were commuted to transportation for life.

The *Midas* had sailed from the river Bonny with five hundred and fifty seven slaves and had lost one hundred and fifty seven on the passage. So terrified were the negroes by the action that as soon as they were released from the hold they started jumping overboard; and in this way thirty were drowned.

It may be imagined that the crew of the *Monkey,* consisting of twenty-six men had their hands full. On the passage to Havana, a matter of thirteen days, nine more negroes leaped overboard, whilst sixty-nine died of small-pox and dysentery.

Ten more died before the anchor had been down in Havana harbour a week; and the rest to the number of two hundred and eighty were in such a state of starvation and illness that the *Monkey's* surgeon reported:—

"It had hitherto been impossible to make out the descriptions of their persons and marks that are inserted in their certificates of emancipation".

The enterprising Admiral Halsted was succeeded in the command of the West India station in 1827 by Vice-Admiral the Honourable C. E. Fleming with his flag in the *Barham,* fifty guns, thus he did not have the satisfaction of witnessing the success of his new schooners in overtaking and capturing the swiftest and most heavily-armed of the Cuban slavers.

One after the other the new schooners arrived in Havana with their prizes. the capture which, with that of the *Midas* by the *Monkey,* caused the greatest sensation in the West Indies was the *Pickle's* conquest of the *Bolodora.*

Lieutenant John Bunche Bonnemaison McHardy

On the first of January, 1828, in reward for his meritorious service against the West Indian pirates, Lieutenant John Bunche Bonnemaison McHardy was given the command of the schooner, *Pickle,* in succession to Lieutenant John Walker.

Few men had had greater experience in the arduous service of the small cruiser against the picaroon, pirate and slaver of the West Indies.

One of those midshipmen who had been laid on the shelf at the end of the war, he proceeded out to the West Indies at his own expense, but his enterprise succeeded and he quickly obtained a vacancy in the sloop, *Bermuda,* Commander John Pakenham. This was in November 1816. The little brig, however, came to grief on the dreaded Tampico bar, shortly after he had joined her. His next ship was the twenty-gun corvette, *Esk,* Captain G. G. Lennox on the Jamaica station, and from her he went to the surveying schooners, *Landrail* and *Kangaroo,* under Master-Commander Anthony De Mayne. In these little vessels he became a master-pilot for the Caribbean. In the spring of 1821 he returned home to pass his examination and this being duly accomplished, he was at once ordered back to the West Indies, where after serving a short while in the *Nantilus,* eighteen guns, and the *Sybille,* Sir Charles Rowley's flagship, he received his appointment as second in command of the *Lion* in February 1823.

After being attached to the *Gloucester,* seventy-four guns, Commodore Sir Edward W.

C. R. Owen, whilst he convalesced from fever in America he was next appointed acting-lieutenant of the gun-brig, *Icarus*.

Besides distinguishing himself in the capture of the pirate schooner *Diableto,* he was in the affair off the Isle of Pines, where Lieutenant Laton and four seamen were captured and murdered by the pirates. He also took part in the capture of two schooners, two feluccas and four piratical row-boats.

Pickle* and *Bolodora

The *Pickle* was always a very popular little ship. She outlived all her sister schooners in the West Indies by some years, and men were content to serve in her year after year. For instance, J. Finlay, who was appointed clerk, when she commissioned, served fourteen years in her.

In the year 1829 the *Pickle's* cruising ground was along the North East coast of Cuba from the windward passage to the Old Bahama Channel.

Her first slaver was sighted off the Bahia Narango on February the 19th, a schooner running to the Westward along the coast. All sail was at once made in chase. At 1.30 p.m. the slaver, seeing that the *Pickle* was fast-overhauling her, put her helm down and ran ashore about a league east of the Puerto Padre.

The *Pickle* had shown her colours, but until she grounded no flag was hoisted aboard the stranger, but it was then noticed that she was flying a large Spanish vane.

The crew of the slaver, assisted as usual by the local fishermen, managed to land all the slaves with one exception, before the *Pickle's* boats were able to get up. McHardy was not the man to give up tamely and he actually landed and made a search, but not a trace could he find of either slaves or crew, who had all been quickly smuggled away. The slave found on board was ill and died forty-eight hours after the capture.

The slaver turned out to be the *Golondenia,* a small schooner, mounting one nine-pounder gun, which had left Havana the previous August.

As a rule slavers that were run ashore were too badly bilged to be salvable, but McHardy managed to heave the *Golondenia* off the ground undamaged.

Cruising after slavers was far from being all chasing and fighting. In examining the logs of the West Indian war schooners, one only finds the excitement of a capture or a chase at long intervals like plums in a sailor's duff.

In between one reads of the every day round in which the most common entry was perhaps:—"exercised great guns and small arms". There was no need of sail drill aboard a war schooner—this the trade wind and the hurricane attended to, so that, reefing, sending up and down topmasts, and yards, rigging in and out jibboom, and sticking out and taking studding sails were almost daily entries. It must be remembered, also, that the West Indian war schooners could not stow more than a small amount of water and provisions, thus 'wooding and watering' upon some uninhabited cay or up a little-known creek were welcome incidents in a cruise, when the men had a chance to haul a seine and the officers a stroll ashore with a shot-gun.

It was not until June, 1829, that the *Pickle* made her next capture. At daybreak on the fifth of June when she was three leagues to the Nor-west of Port Narangos, a suspicious-looking two-topsail schooner was made out to the Eastward, heading along the coast towards the *Pickle.* The science of camouflage was just as well understood in those days as it was in the Great War. Not only had the *Pickle* been disguised to look like the usual West Indian coaster, but her actions were such as would not arouse suspicion; thus, an hour later, when the stranger showed signs of heading in-shore to land her slaves, the war schooner was at once headed out to sea.

The ruse succeeded and once more the other resumed her course. Next the *Pickle* was tacked in-shore in order to get between the stranger and the land, but McHardy was careful to behave as if he had a very different object in view. It was well for the *Pickle* that she was very carefully disguised and behaved in tacking like the usual short-handed merchantman, for the slaver had taken a pilot aboard the day before, who knew the war schooner well.

As soon as McHardy was satisfied that he had cut off his quarry from the land, the wind being North East and the slaver dead in the winds eye from the *Pickle,* he threw of all the camouflage, which had made the slaver mistake him for a droghuer, and made all sail in chase. The main topmast, which up to that moment had been on deck, was smartly mastheaded and the gafftopsail set; and the flying jibboom, which was also in board, was likewise rigged out.

The stranger at once took alarm and headed away, close on a wind on the starboard tack.

This was the *Pickle's* best point of sailing and she was soon weathering and fore-reaching on the chase. As usual every trick known to seamen was played on both sides. Each vessel wet her sails, experimented with her trim, shifted heavy weights up to windward and slung round shot in nettings or even, in the case of the man-of-war, sent a watch to their hammocks.

However by four in the afternoon the *Pickle* was within range and at 4.20 she showed her colours and fired a shotted gun.

The *Bolodora,* for so the stranger was named, carried on without a sign. At 6.30 with darkness coming on. McHardy sent several more round shot skipping after the chase, whose crew approached their captain with the request that he would bear down and snuff out his tiny antagonist.

But the slave captain was wise in his generation... "Not while there is a chance of avoiding it", he replied.

As the night closed in, serene and beautiful, but dark and overcast, the *Pickle* gradually worked up under the lee of the *Bolodora,* but taking great care by altering course to prevent the slaver passing to leeward. It was so dark that the chase would have been lost to sight but for the hawk eyes of James Stewart, the *Pickle's* signalman. At 8.45. and again at 8.58, the *Pickle* tacked, so as to keep between the chase and the land to leeward. At 9.15 the *Bolodora* tacked and started to bear away, but the *Pickle* was too quick for her, quickly setting her big squarer sail the war schooner kept her place to leeward. Towards midnight with the *Pickle's* log showing seven knots through the water, the *Bolodora* was rapidly being overhauled. Then in answer to a warning shot, the latter shortened sail and bore down to engage. The little man-of-war was all ready for action with her big antagonist, her topsail sheets were stoppered, her main gaff and yards chain slung and the big squaresail, which had been lowered at 11.15, all ready to haul up and set at a moment's notice. Every man of her crew except the Commander and helmsman were lying down round the guns.

The *Bolodora* headed to pass under the *Pickle's* stern with the object of raking her, but this was prevented by the man-of-war going about.

Twice Lieutenant McHardy hailed, but not a sound came from the slaver. A third time he hailed and then—crash! Her whole side burst into flame. One British seaman mortally wounded was the result of the broadside.

"Mr. Fowell", called out McHardy calmly to the senior mate, who was in charge of the *Pickle's* Long Tom, "take care to depress your fire and don't throw away a shot".

"Aye, aye, sir, I'll take good care not to spoil his maintopsail, as I know you would like to rig the little *Pickles* as a two-topsail schooner", came the quaint reply out of the darkness forward, where only the merest glimmer of a battle-lantern showed the two wooden quoins tommed under the breach of the gun in order to depress it sufficiently.

Both the long gun and the carronades were loaded with an extra canister of musket balls, but the fire was reserved until the *Pickle* had been manoeuvred into a position on the *Bolodora's* port quarter.

A hot night action then began.

A light breeze was blowing. The moon had set and except when the blaze of her guns lit up her decks, the slaver could only be distinguished from the *Pickle* as slightly darker than her back-ground of sea and sky. When the reddish-yellow light of the gunfire was reflected against the smoke rising from the gun-muzzles and against the white surface of her cotton sails, a certain confusion could at times be noticed along her crowded decks. But the *Pickle* was not having it all her own way, for the *Bolodora's* musketry was very sharp and well-aimed and the war schooner had no solid bulwark, only a low rail. Luckily her crew had been well-trained by the experienced McHardy, and all her guns were served in a crouching position. The old yacht-racing order when on a wind of 'Heads down!' was action discipline aboard the *Pickle.*

McHardy had introduced another innovation, her braces were worked from the lower deck.

For an hour and twenty minutes the action continued within pistol shot distance—then the slaver's mainmast fell, shot away about six feet above the deck. Barely had the crash of its fall ceased before a voice was heard hailing from the slaver, and a long voluable sentence in Spanish and broken English could be distinguished.

From this it was gathered that the *Bolodora* had received several shot in his foremast, had most of his rigging cut away, and not a sail standing: that the Captain was wounded and in bed; that eight of her crew were killed and seven wounded besides the captain; that the speaker himself was wounded and, in fact,—he wished to surrender.

Lieutenant McHardy at once ordered the speaker to send a boat aboard, but he replied that he had none that would float.

He was then told to keep near at hand till daylight, when the *Pickle* would then take possession, and he was warned that if so much as a single musket shot was fired, no quarter would be given. From the fierce way in which she had fought and also because she had shown no colours, McHardy was inclined to believe that the capture was a pirate, so he took every possible precaution.

As it fell calm at the end of the action, the *Pickle's* sweeps were manned to keep her in a commanding position.

The surgeon now set to work upon the wounded. This he had been unable to do during the action, for this reason—no light could be kept going below owing to the concussion of the Long Tom!

The wounded were ten in number including Mr. James Cook, the surgeon himself, and W. N. Fowell, the mate, who both had what were called slight wounds. The worst cases were now removed to the Captain's cabin. Of the killed all were members of the crew of the Captain's gig and Horner, the first to be killed, who had shown great gallantry, was mourned as the best hand in the ship.

Those of the crew who were unhurt were busy until daylight knotting and splicing rigging and doctoring wounded spars. The mainsail was full of shot-holes, and at the first signs of dawn was shifted.

The two carronades were hors de combat as was usually the case with these wretched pop-guns after half a dozen rounds.

The crew of the *Bolodora* were equally busy during the night. With daylight it was seen that she had sheeted home her foretopsail and was showing Spanish colours in her fore-rigging. She also showed an inclination to creep away, whereupon the *Pickle* set her squaresail and ranged down on the slaver's larboard quarter with every sound man of her crew at stations.

Young Fowell was then sent aboard the slaver to take charge, and his first action was to haul down the Spanish flag.

The *Pickle's* boat came back with a scowling, dark-coloured man, one Bonifacio Echelacu, the captain of the *Bolodora,* whom McHardy well knew by reputation. He was, in fact, a certain notorious ex-pirate captain, an outlaw in Spain, who was forbidden to comand a Spanish vessel, yet apparently a fit instrument for the slave traffic.

The *Bolodora* also turned out to be the *Mulata* of evil repute, whose papers bore a warning over the signature of Commodore Collier, commanding on the coast of Africa.

She was a fine two-topsail schooner of two thirty five tons, with a deck ninety-four feet long, and mounting two long twelves and two long eighteens, being pierced for sixteen guns. Of her crew of sixty-two men, ten had been killed and fourteen wounded. The *Pickle's* crew of thirty-nine all told, including six small boys and two sick men, had suffered a loss of four killed and ten wounded.

As the ex-pirate stepped on board the little war schooner and glanced round her decks, he seemd quite overcome with chagrin and amazement.

His first request was for the surgeon to examine his head, which had been badly hurt by the fall of the *Bolodora's* mainmast. He was afterwards sent to the prison hospital at Havana, where he died.

Aboard the slaver, the master's-mate and his small prize crew found their hands full.

On deck the *Bolodora* was a raffle of gear, dismantled guns, broken spars, dead and wounded men, and what were still more difficult to deal with—a number of drunk men, some of them reeling about the decks, others too far gone to stand erect. Fowell, to his disgust, also found that the main topsail was like a sieve, shot full of holes. All the small sails, too, had been wantonly slashed and cut about by the drunken crew, before they had thrown their small arms and cutlasses overboard.

In his report McHardy, who was a judge, declared that the deck of the *Bolodora* was more like that of a pirate than anything else.

The bluejackets, almost dead-beat from the long night of fighting and re-fitting after a day of chasing, nevertheless managed to clear up the mess. The chief difficulty was the lack of leg irons for securing the prisoners.

McHardy decided that he would tow the *Bolodora* into Xibarra before going on to Havana. The two vessels anchored in that port on the 7th of June and the English war schooner soon discovered that she had put her nose into a hornet's nest. So great was the feeling against her, that not only could she get no assistance from the port authorities, but the inhabitants showed that given the smallest opportunity they would attempt to retake the *Bolodora.* But the crew of the *Pickle* were not to be defeated. They rigged and set up jury-masts aboard the *Bolodora*, and they made stocks the better to secure their prisoners. Then they sailed away for Havana where the prize was condemned before the Mixed Court of Commissioners, the crew of the slaver marched off to gaol, and the slaves, to the number of three hundred and thirty five, who had been shipped at Popoe, landed and apprenticed amongst the different sugar estates.

Only two of the West Indian schooners were sent across the Atlantic to pay off. These were the *Pickle* in the autumn of 1830 and her sister ship, the *Pincher* in 1837.

The *Pickle,* still under the command of Lieutenant McHardy arrived at Plymouth on September the 26th, 1830. Before paying off, the little schooner was inspected by the port admiral, Sir Manley Dixon, and found to be in such a high state of efficiency and discipline that McHardy's name was most favourably brought to the notice of the Lords of the Admiralty and he was promoted to the rank of commander 'for his meritorious services'. The *Pickle*, too was much admired before being sent back to the West Indian Station under Lieutenant T. Taplen at the beginning of January, 1831.

The high state of the *Pickle* is mentioned here in order to show that lax discipline was by no means to be expected in these Tom Tit cruisers, as officers in crack frigates and ships of the line were so fond of asserting. In fact whether the schooners were smart or slack, happy or miserable, like every other ship of war, and merchant ship for that matter, depended entirely on their commanders.

The Saucy *Columbine*

In the year 1830 Vice-Admiral Sir E. C. Colpoys succeeded Vice-Admiral the Honourable C. E. Fleming in the command of the West India Station.

The station had lately been joined on to the North American station and the commander-in-chief now spent more than half his time at Halifax and Bermuda, contenting himself with a leisurely winter cruise through the West Indies. In his absence the old Jamaica and Windward stations were left in charge of a senior captain; and it was from this moment that the importance and smartness of the West Indian station began to decline.

Between 1830 and 1832 that beautiful little sloop, the saucy *Columbine,* commanded by those two most gallant and popular officers, James Wallace Gabriel (June 1830—July 1831) and Henry Ommanney Love (July 1831—March 1834) was for sometime S N O Jamaica.

On March the 13th, 1831, the Commander-in-chief wrote from Jamaica to Sir William Symonds:—

"Columbine is the admiration of all who look on her".

Whilst Love was S N O, there occurred a nasty insurrection of the negroes in Jamaica, and bluejackets had to be landed in order to protect Montego Bay and other towns from the insurgents.

Whilst the larger man-of-war, mostly eighteen-gun sloops, such as *Columbine, Champion, Grasshopper, Hyacinth, Racehorse* and *Rose,* wandered rather aimlessly through the islands, having a good time socially, but very little serious work, the little war schooners were kept busy on the Bahama Bank and round Cuba, maintaining a ceaseless watch for slavers.

***Monkey* Wrecked on Tampico Bar**

Very occasionally one or other of them was detached to Vera Cruz, Tampico, Belize or Cartegena, and given the chance to pick up a freight of specie.

It was on one of these occasions that the little *Monkey* came to grief on May the 13th, 1831. She was wrecked on the dreaded bar of Tampica of which Harry Keppel writes:—

"A more uninviting open roadstead could not be: in-shore the mouth of a large river, a bar and heavy surf breaking across and beyond; we lay at single anchor ready to face foul weather".

Crossing the bar was always a risky business and at times quite impracticable. The channel was ever changing and even after a strong Norther there was seldom more than twelve feet of water on the bar in the deepest part. Once over the bar there was from three to five fathoms. On those days the beach and river banks in the rains were encumbered with large mahogany trees, washed down the river by the floods. It was a long row to the watering place, which was above high water mark, and watering parties had many adventures with turtle, alligator and even sharks.

Large boats were sometimes turned end over end on the bar and the loss of life there was heavy, however though the *Monkey* was lost, all her crew were saved.

The Havana and Gulf of Mexico Traffic

Slavers making for Havana and the Gulf of Mexico would not have had much of a chance to escape the little cruisers between the years 1830 and 1832 for the ground was continually being quartered, or rather the sea and cays searched by schooners, *Firefly, Kangaroo* (a three-gun schooner in place of the wrecked surveying craft) *Minx, Nimble, Pickle, Pincher; Skipjack* and *Speedwell.*

It should, however, be recognised that the seas were very much fuller of ships, and the traffic very much greater in those days than it is at present.

It was by no means unusual for as many as twenty sail of American brigs, brigantines, schooners and barques of from one hundred to four hundred tons to pass within musket shot, and even within hail, of the Great Stirrup Cay daily.

The greater number of these were making for the Havannah, their usual route being to make the Hole in the Wall, then the Stirrup and if the weather was threatening to sail through the N.W. channel, but if fair to cross the Great Bahama Bank to South of the Cat Cays.

Most of these vessels came from Baltimore, Charleston and the Chesapeak and were hard to distinguish at any distance from the usual slaver of American build. It was therefore necessary for the R.N. war schooners to overhaul and give each in turn a careful look over.

Bahaman Wreckers

Wrecks, in such a concourse of ships, were, of course, frequent, many of them being slavers. The conch, or native Bahaman, from New Providence, made a good living in his small sloop or schooner, sponging, turtling and wrecking—but in those days wrecking was specially profitable and most of the snug anchorages, such as Slaughter, would be shared between the war schooners, keenly alert for slavers, and the wrecking schooners, as wide-awake for wrecks.

As in the case of the Cornish wreckers the conch fraternity have been accused of decoying vessels on to reefs.

One of the best known of the wreckers was a mulatto named Elis, who had obtained a grant in perpetuity of Great Stirrup Cay, one of the Berry Islands. Here he lived happily with his wife and family, in a comfortable house made of drift lumber.

He had cleared twelve acres of bush, on which he grew Indian corn and vegetables He also possessed cows, pigs, goats and poultry; and had several boats for fishing and a handy sloop for sponging and wrecking. With a bold shore and good anchorage off his cay, he was well-known to the officers of the war-schooners, and was often used as a pilot in the more difficult parts of the Bahama Bank.

CHAPTER XIII

CAPTAIN TROTTER AND THE PIRATE *PANDA*

"A quick run to the South we had, and when
we made the Bight,
We kept the offing all day long and crossed
the bar at night.
Six hundred niggers in the hold and seventy
we did stow.
And when we'd clapped the hatches on
T'was time for us to go!"
(Old Slaver's Chanty).

The Piracy of the Mexican

THE outstanding event on the coast in 1833 was the capture of a pirate by the ten-tun brig, *Curlew*, Commander H. D. Trotter, who, having served half his Commission on the East coast, had only lately arrived on the station and taken over the duties of senior officer in the Bights.

This is a very good example of the thorough way in which the Royal Navy policed the seas and with bull-dog tenacity kept on the trail of the miscreant until he was brought to justice.

On the 2nd May, 1833, Trotter was at Fernando Po and on the 9th captured a slaver with two hundred and ninety slaves off that island. Towards the end of the month, the *Curlew* put into Port Antonio, Prince's Island, where Captain Trotter was shown an old copy of the Salem commercial *Advertiser* by a resident American merchant named Gould. In the *Advertiser* was a long account of the piracy of an American brig, the *Mexican*, by a cuban schooner of the Baltimore clipper type.

The *Mexican*, a brig of two hundred and twenty seven tons, with a crew of thirteen men, commanded by Captain John G. Butman and owned by the famous Salem ship-owner and philanthropist, Joseph Peabody, sailed from Salem for Rio de Janeiro on August the 29th, 1832.

As was very usual with Salem and other merchantmen at that date besides one hundred bags of salt petre and one hundred chests of tea, the *Mexican* carried specie in silver for the purpose of purchasing a return cargo. This silver, packed in ten boxes holding two thousand dollars apiece, was stored in the run under the cabin floor. But every man aboard knew where the specie was stowed.

The story of the piracy was told in after years with much detail by Captain Thomas Fuller, the last survivor of the *Mexican*'s crew, besides being written down by John Battis, at the request of his son.

On sailing day the crew assembled at Peabody's store-house. All appeared on time except the cook, Ridgley, a coloured man. Knowing that he boarded with a Mrs. Ranson on Becket Street, the rest of the crew set out to find him.

He appeared strangely reluctant to go aboard, making all kinds of excuses and when at last they got him out of the gate, he was sent into a wild state of terror by a black hen, which flew up on to the fence and flapping her wings, crowed lustily.

This the darkey declared was a most unlucky omen for the *Mexican* and he could hardly be persuaded to go aboard.

From the first day of the voyage both the Captain and Mr. Reed, the mate, kept a close look-out for pirates, whilst in the foc'sle, many a lurid piratical yarn was spun.

At 4 a.m. on the morning of the 20th of September when the brig was in 33° N. 34½° W. the mate warned the lookout to keep a sharp eye, as there was a vessel about, which had just crossed the brig's stern and gone to leeward.

Before daylight the lookout, standing between the knight-heads, noticed a vessel crossing the bow and heading to windward. He sang out, but even with his night glass the mate could see nothing.

At dawn the *Mexican* was standing South East, the wind being light at Sou-sou-west.

About five miles off on the brig's weather quarter was a topsail schooner, heading on the same course.

Directly the captain came on deck at six bells, seven a.m. he took his glass into the maintop and overhauled the stranger. He noticed that she had a large crew: he counted thirty men on deck besides a hand looking out from the fore-topgallant yard.

This roused his suspicions: and, as the schooner did not appear to be a very fast sailer, he ordered all sail to be piled on the *Mexican* .

Young Battis, who had gone up to loose the main royal, remained on the yard whilst it was mastheaded and, after a good look round from his airy perch, reported a brig right ahead.

From the rapid way in which the schooner ranged up on the beam of the *Mexican*, it was concluded that she must have had a drag out before—one of those devices in common use with ships of the picaroon and piratical fraternity.

However by eight bells, breakfast time, she went ahead as if she was after the other brig. Whereupon Captain Butman altered course to the westward, but this at once brought the schooner down upon him under a press of sail.

The *Mexican* had two short carronades, but these proved useless for the only shot on board proved to be far too big for the bore.

In a very short while the schooner's intention was put beyond doubt by a round as a hint to heave to. Captain Butman at once backed his mainyard, upon which the schooner did the same with her foresail and at the same time hoisted Columbian colours, being then about half a mile to windward.

John Battis's description of the pirate schooner gives an excellent idea of the true corsair of that date.

"She was a long, low, straight topsail schooner of about one hundred and fifty tons burthen, painted black with a horn of plenty painted white; masts raked aft, and a large main-topmast, a regular Baltimore clipper. We could not see her name. She carried thirty or more men with a long thirty-two-pound swivel amidships with four brass guns, two on each side".

The pirate hailed in English from the schooner's forecastle.

"Where are you from and what is your cargo?"

"Salem", returned Captain Butman, "With tea and saltpetre".

"Send your boat aboard and bring your papers". Captain Butman replied that his only boat was leaky.

"Come aboard quickly or you'll be for trouble", roared back the angry voice.

"It's no use", said Butman, turning to his mate, "I must go myself. Give me four men. That man is in earnest".

The following men pulled Captain Butman over to the pirate—Jack Ardissone, Thomas Fuller, Benjamin Larcom and Fred Trask.

The captain, fearing that the worst would happen to him and his boat's crew, shook hands with his mate before shoving off, and told him to do his best for the ship if he never saw him again.

Dead Cats Don't Mew

As Captain Butman was steering for the schooner's gangway, he was roughly ordered to go under her fore chains, upon which five black-whiskered ruffians, with pistols in their belts and long Spanish knives up their sleeves, jumped into the boat.

One of these called out in Spanish for instructions. Back came the sinister command in the same language:—

"Dead cats don't mew! Search her and bring aboard all you can. You know what to do with them!"

At this Ardissone, who understood Spanish, whispered that all was over, then burst into tears.

Someone suggested pulling off for the other brig, which was now in plain sight. But young Fuller said scornfully:—

"I'll stay and take my chance with the boys". They then pulled back to the *Mexican*. On reaching her deck, each pirate drew his knife. Two of them drove the Captain below, with threats of instant death. A moment later the mate came up, ordered the crew to muster aft and get the money on deck. Just as Luscomb and Battis stepped into the companion, the boatswain of the pirates, as it afterwards turned out, came up and ordered the three desperadoes, who were loafing about the deck, to set upon the two men of the *Mexican*. Both were at once struck over the head with the long Spanish knives. Young Battis's head was saved by his Scotch cap and a large cotton handkerchief inside it, both of which were cut right through. At this point, the mate Reed pluckily interfered.

Whilst the boxes of specie were being passed up on deck, the third mate of the schooner, the commander of the five men aboard the *Mexican*, hailed his vessel, which at once sent a boat with sixteen men aboard to take the treasure across to the pirate. Having ferried the specie across, the pirate's boat returned to the *Mexican* with nearly another dozen men.

Then as a search for loot began, the knife-play of the pirates grew rougher and their intentions more murderous.

Nine of them set upon the Captain, Battis and Jack Ardissone in the cabin. Captain Butman had his speaking trumpet broken over his head, whilst knives were flourished in his face.

Chased by other pirates, Battis tried to jump out of the stern window, meaning to catch the davit falls of the stern boat, which was still alongside, and pull himself on deck.

But Ardissone caught him by the ankle. The pair then fell or jumped from the steerage into the hold, Jack Ardissone breaking two ribs in doing so.

As the brig was in ballast and the hold clean swept, the two men by this means reached the forecastle, where most of the *Mexican*'s crew had taken refuge.

I will now quote John Battis verbatim:—

"We hadn't been there long before the mate, Mr. Reed, came rushing down, chased by the boatswain of the pirate, demanding his money.

The mate then told Luscomb to go and get his money, which he had previously given Luscomb to stow away for him in some safe place: there were two hundred dollars in specie, and Luscomb had put it under the wood in the hold.

Luscomb went and got it, brought it up and gave it to the pirate, who untied the bag, took a handful out, retied the bag, and went up on deck and threw the handful of money overboard so that those on the schooner could see that they had found more money.

Then the pirates went to Captain Butman and told him that if they found any more money, which we hadn't surrendered, they would cut all our throats.

I must have followed them into the cabin, for I heard them tell the captain this. Previous to this, we of the crew found that we had about fifty dollars, which we secured by putting into the pickle keg, and this was secretly placed in the breast-hook forward. On hearing this threat made to the captain I ran back and informed the crew what I had heard, and we took the money out of my keg and dropped it down the air-streak, which is the space between the inside and outside planking.

It went way down into the keelson. Our carpenter afterwards located its exact position and recovered every cent of it. Strange to say the first thing they searched on coming below was the pickle keg.

The search of our effects by the pirates was pretty thorough, and they took all new clothes, tobacco etc. In the cabin they searched the captain's chest, but failed to get at seven hundred dollars, which he had concealed in the false bottom: they had previously taken from him several dollars which he had in his pocket, and his gold watch, and had also relieved the mate of his watch.

About noon it appeared to be very quiet on deck, we having been between decks ever since the real searching party came on board.

We all agreed not to go on deck again and to make resistance with sticks of wood if they attempted to come down, determined to sell our lives as dearly as possible.

Being somewhat curious, I thought I'd peep up and see what they were doing; as I did so, a cocked pistol was pressed to my head, and I was ordered to come on deck and went, expecting to be thrown overboard. One took me by the collar and held me out at arm's length to plunge a knife into me. I looked him right in the eye, and he dropped his knife and ordered me to get the doors of the forecastle, which were below. I went down and got them, but they did not seem to understand how they were to be used, and they made me come up and ship them. There were three of them and as I was letting the last one in I caught the gleam of a cutlass being drawn, so taking the top of the door on my stomach, I turned a quick somersault and went down head first into the forecastle.

The cutlass came down, but it did not find me: It went into the companion way quite a depth, then they hauled the slide over and fastened it, and we were all locked below.

They fastened the aft companionway leading down to the cabin, locking our officers below as well. From noises that came from overhead, we were convinced that the pirates had begun a work of destruction. All running rigging, including tiller ropes was cut, sails slashed into ribbons, spars cut loose, ship's instruments and all moveable articles on which they could lay their hands demolished, the yards were tumbled down and we could hear the mainboom swinging from side to side. They then, as appears by later developments, filled the caboose or cook's galley, with combustibles, consisting of tar, tarred ropeyarn, oakum, etc., setting fire to the same, and lowered the dismantled mainsail so that it rested on top of the caboose.

In this horrible suspense we waited for an hour or more when all became quiet save the wash of the sea against the brig.

All this time the crew had been cooped up in the darkness of the forecastle, of course unable to speculate as to what would be the next move of the enemy or how soon death would come to each and all of us.

Finally at about three o'clock in the afternoon Thomas Fuller came running forward and informed us that the pirates were leaving the ship. One after another of the crew made their way to the cabin and on peering out of the two small stern windows saw the pirates pulling for the schooner.

(The crew, of course, reached the cabin via the 'tween decks and lazarette).

Captain Butman was at this time standing on the cabin table, looking out from a small skylight, the one means of egress the pirates had neglected to fasten. We told him that from the odour of smoke, we believed they had fired the brig. He said he knew it and ordered us to remain quiet. He then stepped down from the table and for several moments knelt in prayer, after which he calmly told us to go forward and he would call us when he wanted us.

We had not been in the forecastle long before he called us back, and directed that we get all buckets under deck and fill them with water from casks in the hold. On our return he again opened the skylight and drew himself up on the deck. We then handed him a small bucket of water, and he crept along the rail in order to escape observation from the schooner.

The fire was just breaking throught the top of the caboose when he arrived in time to throw several handfuls of water on top so as to keep it under. This he continued to do for a long time not daring to extinguish it immediately lest the pirates should notice the absence of smoke and know that their plan for our destruction had been frustrated.

When the fire had been reduced to a reasonable degree of safety, he came and opened the aft companionway and let us all up.

The schooner, being a fast sailer, was in the distance about hull down. The fire in the caboose was allowed to burn in a smouldering condition for perhaps half an hour or more, keeping up a dense smoke.

By this time the pirate schooner was well nigh out of sight or nearly topsails under, to the Eastward.

On looking about us we found the *Mexican* in a bad plight, all sails, halliards and running gear were cut, headsails dragging in the water, and on account of the tiller ropes being cut loose, the brig was rolling about in the trough of the sea. We at once set to work repairing damages as speedily as possible and before dark had bent new sails and repaired our running gear to a great extent.

Fortunately through the shrewdness and foresight of Captain Butman, our most valuable ship instruments, compass, quadrant, sextant, etc., had escaped destruction. (The *Mexican* had no chronometer), it seems that immediately on discovering the true character of the stranger, he had placed them in the steerage and covered them with a quantity of oakum. This the pirates somehow overlooked in their search, although they passed and repassed it continually during their visit".

So much for the account of that inquisitive and intelligent seaman, John Battis.

He had little more to add. All that night Captain Butman steered north before a strong squally wind with all the sail he could carry.

The next day after tacking to and fro in a Westerly direction, he finally headed the *Mexican* for Salem, where she arrived on October the 12th, 1832.

Trotter of the *Curlew* Hears of the *Panda*.

To return to Captain Trotter at Prince's Island, the American merchant Gould informed the captain of the *Curlew* that a Spanish schooner, named the *Panda*, which had lately been at Port Antonio for provisions, answered very closely to the description in the newspaper of the pirate schooner. Also her crew had been very free in scattering dollars about; indeed they behaved like pirates on the spree.

Finally he said that he believed that the *Panda* was trying for a cargo of slaves in the river Nazareth.

With the newspaper account in his pocket, Captain Trotter hastened aboard his brig and sailed for the coast. The *Curlew* was anchored about nine miles off-shore in the mouth of the Nazareth on the evening of the third of June, 1833.

"Man and arm boats!" came the order, always an exciting one, as darkness fell.

Captain Trotter in his gig took command of the expedition with Maule, a mate, and G. Quinton, the second master, in charge of the other two boats.

The bar was crossed as soon as there was light enough to see, then came a long, hard pull up the river against a strong stream. They had gone a bare three miles, however, when they

12. Rear-Admiral Henry Dundas Trotter as a Captain.

From a painting by George Richmond, R.A.

[*Facing page 256.*

13. H.M. Schooner *Pickle*.

From a painting by W. J. Huggins.

[*Facing page 257.*

came upon the suspected pirate lying at anchor about a mile away. Before the boats could reach her, her crew were seen to hurriedly pull for the shore in her boats.

A Lighted Match to the Magazine

One man only staying behind in order to set the schooner on fire, and he slipped away in a small canoe. Trotter in his swift gig made a dash to cut the pirates off, but could not catch them. As soon as the boats got alongside the schooner, smoke was noticed rising through the cabin skylight. John Turnbull, a seaman, at once leaped below and finding cotton and a lighted match leading to a magazine containing sixteen casks of gunpowder, he most gallantly seized the burning match and threw it overboard.

Next the galley fire was found alight with a cask of gunpowder with the head out alongside it. But the man-of-war's men were in time and this trick to blow up their enemies, (a common one amongst Spanish picaroons, and pirates, as we have already seen), was frustrated.

Nothing in the way of ship's papers was found, but some letters signed by Pedro Gibert and addressed to the boatswain and carpenter of the *Panda*, as well as an unusual number of foreign ensigns and pendants, afforded sufficient evidence to cause Captain Trotter to seize the schooner. Nor was he the man to leave his task unfinished, and by hook or by crook he was determined to get the pirates into his custody.

Five of the *Panda*'s crew at once surrendered, but these had only signed on at Prince's Island. However they were able to strengthen the evidence against the *Panda*, for they declared they had often heard the other hands describe the piracy.

Trotter's next act was to try and make the native chief of the district give up the pirate captain, whom he knew as Don Gibert, and the remainder of the schooner's crew.

Then *Panda* was taken out of the river and anchored alongside the *Curlew*, whilst Trotter went himself and interviewed the chief.

King Pass-All

This man was known as King Pass-all, as his favourite expression was the grandiose one:—"I pass all kings".

In spite of his lordly mien King Pass-all pretended that he had not the power to seize the pirates, who had fled into the bush.

After days of palaver Trotter saw that only force would persuade the old savage.

There was not water enough to bring the *Curlew* in over the bar, so the captured *Panda* was made use of. The schooner was anchored off the town of King Pass-all and the gunner sent ashore with an ultimatum that unless the pirates were brought off within a certain time, fire would be opened.

The *Panda* Blows Up

And now came his first set-back for the indefatigable commander of the *Curlew*—and that a very tragic one.

On the *Panda*'s long twelve-pounder amidships being fired at the expiration of the time-limit, a spark fell on some loose powder in the cabin and exploded the casks of gunpowder in the magazine below. The whole of the vessel's stern was blown out as well as the planking of the portside aft. The schooner healed over and filled, but being in little more than her own depth of water, her crew were able to get upon her starboard rail, where they hung until two of the boats, which were between two and three miles off on their way back to the *Curlew*, were able to rescue them. But the disaster cost four lives. Johnson the purser was picked up dying. Lewis the gunner, who was found in the water, clinging to the torn planking, was fatally injured. A marine was in the same case, whilst one of the kroomen was never seen again. Another marine had to have his leg amputated. Trotter, himself, was hurt, and being jammed between the torn-up deck planking and the bulwark, it was with difficulty that he was extricated before the vessel filled.

Luckily the surgeon, Mackey, had escaped injury. He had jumped into the fore-rigging to see where the shot fell. His escape was the more lucky in that his assistant was at that moment dying of fever aboard the *Curlew*.

The gun-brig happened to be under way, standing in with a light breeze, but she had been hull down when the accident happened.

The wounded were got aboard her as soon as possible, but the purser, gunner and marine died before the boats could reach her.

Besides the loss of life, the loss of stores and weapons was serious. Directly Trotter left for the *Curlew*, the natives swarmed on board and began looting the half-sunken *Panda*.

Trotter on the Pirate's Trail

Trotter, however, was not to be beaten. But before returning to the attack in the Nazareth, he determined to try and catch some of the pirates who had left the schooner at different parts of the coast according to his five Portuguese prisoners.

On June the 20th the *Curlew* sailed for the Gaboon river in a hunt for the *Panda*'s second mate.

This man had apparently sailed for Havana.

Captain Trotter then went to St. Thomas and interviewed that old rascal of a governor, Senor Don Jose Maria de Ferreira, who professed complete ignorance of the pirates.

He next got onto the trail of two pirates, which led to Port Antonio, only to find that they had just left Prince's Island for Whydah.

As senior officer on the coast under Admiral Warren, who, with both the West and East coasts as well as the Cape in his charge, had little opportunity of cruising in the Bights himself. Trotter had to attend to his station, and duty called him to Cape Coast Castle, where he landed one of his Portuguese prisoners, to be put aboard the first cruiser that called there, for the purpose of identifying any possible pirates.

He then went to Whydah and interviewed the great de Souza. According to the latter, one of the pirates, who had left Port Antonio for Whydah, had already sailed for Bahia; whilst the other, as soon as the *Curlew* had been sighted had fled to the King of Dahomey at Abomey.

De Souza offered to send an officer of the *Curlew* under escort to the King of Dahomey, but Trotter was now too short of officers to risk one on what might be a wild goose chase of some week's duration.

There were thirteen slaves waiting to load in Whydah Roads and Trotter went aboard each one of them himself in his search for lurking pirates.

The *Curlew* next looked into the Bonny, but by this time Trotter was down with a really bad bout of fever.

On August the 17th, 1833, the brig arrived at Clarence Cove with her captain dangerously ill. He was carried ashore in his cot to the house of Colonel Nicolls, the Governor, to whose care and kindness he owed his life.

Colonel Nicolls, Commandant at Fernando Po

Colonel Nicolls, who had been much shot up in the war, was one of the best-known characters on the coast. With an eye gone, the muscles of his cheek and mouth lacerated and even his larynx damaged, his voice was peculiar; and as he was a man whose kindly disposition and good heart were accompanied by the hottest and most hasty of tempers, his hospitality was a great entertainment for a fagged-out fever ridden slave-catcher. He had two fixed beliefs—the first was that the climate of Fernando Po was perfect and the second was that ague was beneficial rather than the reverse.

It was about this date that Huntley, now commanding the *Lynx*, found him lying on his bed in a pair of old flannel trousers and a red night cap; his red shell-jacket, glazed cocked hat with its staff-officer's feather, and his sword in its sheath, sharing the bedside table with business papers, powders, sugar, lemons and barley water.

To the commander's greeting of:—

"I am sorry, sir, to see you so unwell".

A Beautiful Ague!

The commandant, with his broken reef-topsail voice, roared back:—

"Not a bit ill—never felt better—I have a bea - ut - iful f - f - fit - of ague".

Besides nursing Trotter through a beautiful ague and a nasty bout of fever, he had news of the pirates for that undefeated sleuth-hound.

It happened that one of the Colonel's officers, Captain Beecroft, had had occasion to go over to the Island of Bimbia, at the mouth of the Cameroons, river, where he was accosted by five Spanish sailors, begging a passage to the Old Calabar. He replied that he would take them to Fernando Po and from there they could get on to the Old Calabar. These men were still at Fernando Po awaiting the opportunity of a passage.

Meanwhile Beecroft had been informed by his agent at Bimbia that a quantity of Spanish dollars had been found at low water mark, which it was supposed had been lost out of their canoe by these Spaniards, when they were landing on the island. The case seemed suspicious and they were confronted with one of the Portuguese taken from the Nazareth. He at once recognised them as part of the *Panda*'s original crew. At which the youngest, a lad of eighteen years, named José Perez, being admitted as King's Evidence, made the following statement.

Evidence of José Perez

"I entered on board the schooner *Panda*, Pedro Gibert, at Havana: she had two iron-guns, and one long brass one abaft the main-mast.

We sailed about thirteen months ago for the coast of Africa on a slaving voyage. About a month after we had been at sea we boarded a ship at night: I believe she was English. We took two coils of rope, two goats, some syrup and sweetmeats.

About twenty days afterwards we fell in with the American brig: first saw her at 6 a.m. I was at the masthead at daylight, but did not see the brig until she was seen from the deck, and I was kept all day at a the masthead for it.

About 8 a.m. we closed her, hailed her to send her boat on board, which she did, then the second officer, boatswain, carpenter and four men jumped into her and made them row back to the brig; the second officer being armed with a cutlass, and the others, with long knives.

Soon after they were on board, the boatswain came to the after part of the brig and hailed the schooner, showing the captain his handfull of dollars, which he threw into the sea.

On this the captain sent the schooner's boat to the brig with some hands and they set about plundering her. They sent the brig's crew to the forecastle and then secured them in the cabin: but, before this, they made them get up the boxes of dollars from below. Then they put some tarpaulins and something else into the caboose and set fire to them and left the brig. But they brought with them ten boxes of dollars, half a cask of butter, about three hundred dollars in a bag, I was told got from the captain, but I did not see it. Then they scuttled the brig's boat, and made sail away from her for Africa.

When we boarded the American there was another brig in sight and when we left her a ship was seen to leeward. When we made the coast, we went to Grand Bassam for water, and were chased off for about eight hours by a frigate, but we made the river Nazareth, to purchase slaves.

After we had been in the Nazareth about two months they sailed for Prince's Island to refit: but before that they cut off the figure-head of the schooner and made her all flush with the bulwarks.

I was left on shore in charge of the slave-house, while the vessel was gone to Prince's: she came back to Nazareth in about a month.

About five months afterwards I heard that a man-of-war brig was at the mouth of the Nazareth and after anchoring she sent her boats up the river to board the schooner. As soon as the schooner's people saw them, they took to the boats for the shore. I was by the captain on shore, and heard the carpenter tell him that he was the last person out of the vessel, and had got her papers.

The carpenter told him also, he had put a barrel of powder in the caboose with a train from it into the cabin, leading to the magazine and had left a slow match burning. He expected before then, he said, to have seen the English all blown into the air together. The captain asked the carpenter what he had made the match of, and was told 'brimstone and powder'.

I was away in the bush but I heard firing on the town and saw rockets, but I believe nobody was hurt.

When the schooner anchored off the town of Nazareth, a few miles outside of the river, in charge of the man-of-war officers, the Spaniards all took to the bush except the captain, who remained in the town, secreted by the King.

Four days after the man-of-war sailed from Nazareth, the schooner *Esperanza* arrived.

Some of the crew of the *Panda* went on board of her.

About a month ago, five of my shipmates and I got a canoe and our captain gave us leave to go where we liked and he gave us all our share of the plunder we had got: the whole was one thousand and sixty dollars, but my share was two hundred and fifty.

We arrived in the Cameroons river about six days afterwards, and hearing that an English schooner was at Bimbia, we went to her, but agreed to say that we were ship-wrecked seamen.

We wanted to get to Calabar or Bonny, but as we could not get there without going to Fernando Po first, we threw most of our dollars away at Bimbia and kept only a few".

This confession was made before Colonel Nicolls, Captain Beecroft and Doctor Basllard, R.N., justices of the Peace for Fernando Po.

The five Spaniards and a sixth, who was caught on Bimbia, were thereupon sent off in custody aboard the *William Harris*, transport, to the Island of Ascension to await events.

The next information came from the Nazareth, where it was rumoured that the pirate captain was negotiating for the purchase of the schooner, *Esperanza.*

By this time Captain Trotter was on his legs again.

The presence of a small English barque, the *Princess Elizabeth*, just arrived at Fernando Po from Liverpool, gave Trotter an idea. He had already tried force on the rascally King Pass-all with disastrous results and he now determined to employ strategy.

After consulting Colonel Nicolls, Captain Fatio, the master of the *Princess Elizabeth* agreed to lend his vessel for a month and take her into the river Nazareth, with an officer and a dozen men from the *Curlew* concealed on board.

Young Matson's Gallant Role

Henry James Matson, one of the mates of the *Curlew*, volunteered to command this forlorn hope.

First of all the barque had to discharge her cargo of salt in the river Cameroons and she was then to go on to the Nazareth under the pretence of wishing to trade.

On August the 29th both vessels sailed from Fernando Po, whilst Captain Trotter trusted to young Matson and Captain Fatio to carry on in the Nazareth, he himself sailed on his lawful occasions, viz, a cruise in the Bights after slavers.

Yet where ever he sent his boats, the undefeatable Trotter always saw that they had Simon Domingo, one of the Portuguese crew of the *Panda*, with them.

Nothing transpired off the Bonny, but at St. Anna de Chaves, St. Thomas, the schooner *Esperanza* was discovered at anchor—and what was more to the point Simon Domingo caught a glimpse of one of the pirates in the town, who hurriedly made himself scarce.

Trotter rushed to the Governor, who treated this information as being a pure fabrication.

Then Holmes, the American, came forward and told Trotter in the strictest confidence that not one but five pirates had landed from the *Esperanza*.

After begging the unwilling Governor to instititue a search, Trotter could do no more, so he sailed for the Nazareth.

Meanwhile on September the 22nd, the *Princess Elizabeth* arrived off the Nazareth from the Cameroons.

Matson had been absent in a prize when the *Panda* had been captured the previous June, so that there was no chance of his being recognised as an officer of the execrated *Curlew**.

---

*Note:

Officers of the *Curlew* in June 1833

Commander H. D. Trotter
No lieutenants

Acting Master	Daniel Quintom
Surgeon	Samuel Mackey
Assistant Surgeon	G. Laurie (died of fever)
Acting Purser	Thomas Johnson (killed)
	Mates
	H. J. Matson (absent in captured slaver)
	F. Maule
	R. W. C. Wichelo (absent in a prize)
Master's Assistant	G. H. Quintom
Midshipmen	Thomas Belgrave
	S. F. F. V. Strawbenzie
	W. Mottley
Gunner	Robert Lewis (killed)
Carpenter	W. Hammond
Clerk	John Chapman (promoted to acting purser)

Officers recently appointed

Lieutenant Malcolm McNeale
Lieutenant Joseph Pike
Surgeon I. K. Ballard in place of Mackey (invalided)
William Merriman Acting Gunner

Nevertheless the natives seemed suspicious and refused to come aboard the barque, though they showed their curiosity by paddling round her in canoes.

The captain of the *Princess Elizabeth*, being ignorant of the river, had not anchored in the usual place; and it was decided to try and quieten the suspicions of the natives by sending ashore for a pilot to take the barque to the proper merchantman anchorage in the river.

Matson, dressed in a red shirt and a Scotch cap, playing the role of mate of the *Princes Elizabeth*, with his two most trusty bluejackets and two kroomen thereupon pulled away for King Pass-all's town.

That he knew for the risks he was taking is proved by the following letter, addressed to his captain:—

Cape Lopez,
September 24th, 1833.

Sir,

As I am about to proceed on what may possible prove a dangerous expedition, I have left a few lines to explain what our movements have been: we arrived at our rendezvous on the 20th; I left on the 21st; I arrived here on the 22nd: the natives are evidently very suspicious of us: several canoes have reconnoitred us, but none would approach the vessel: therefore I conceive the only way to lull their suspicions is to go on shore and ask if they have any trade to make, and gain what information I can respecting Don Pedro; if I see him I shall offer to exchange cloth, etc., for dollars, to induce him to come on board; I shall, of course be guided by circumstances, and act to the best of my judgement. If I am detained I think it would be better to trust to chance for an escape and not sacrifice any more lives in carrying on what would prove an unequal warfare. I hope you will excuse my attempting to give advice, I only request that no lives be lost on my account: if they think proper to make me suffer the fate of a spy, write to my friends and say I have done my duty. With kind regards to all shipmates, I remain,

Your sincere friend and well-wisher
H. J. Matson

To Captain Trotter,
H.M. sloop *Curlew*.

This letter is interesting, not only for its part in the drama of the *Panda* but as revealing the gallant character of young Matson, one of the best-known of slave catchers in after years.

On arriving in the Nazareth, Matson found that the King had lately removed his headquarters some twenty miles to a position near Cape Lopez.

It was a long weary night of pulling, but in those days hours at the oars were a great part of a naval seaman's work. The anchorage, where several Portuguese slaves were lying, was reached soon after daybreak.

On Matson Landing, he was approached and saluted by a polite genlemanly-looking Spaniard, who, however, carried a sword.

This was none other than Don Pedro Gibert, the pirate captain himself. Young Matson was wide-awake, and caught on to this fact through noting the keen way in which the Spaniard looked him over.

After bowing courteously to the dignified Spaniard, Matson walked straight to the King's kraal, where he found the rascally old Chief surrounded by his wives and headman.

The young officer, behaving with the greatest coolness, declared that his vessel had come to trade for elephants' teeth, and that his captain would be glad to see the King on board the following day for his customary 'dash'*, and that in the meanwhile he begged for a pilot.

Luckily King Pass-all happened to be in good humour and replied that not only should he have a pilot, but that he would send his son, Prince Narshin, aboard for the 'dash'.

* On the arrival of any vessel to open a trade with the natives, it is customary to give the Chief what they call a 'dash', which is a present of part of everything you have on board.

No Chief ever neglects coming on board for his 'dash', and without which little or no trade is carried on.

(Admiral Sir Henry Keppel in *A Sailor's Life*).

At this moment, when all seemed to be proceeding satisfactorily for the masquerading Matson, a man came hurrying in and said something to the King, which had the effect of causing every eye to turn upon the supposed mate.

The fact was that the pirate captain, his wits sharpened by his uneasy conscience, had sent this man with a message that he suspected Matson to be a British Naval officer in disguise.

Matson, though he could not, of course, understand what was said, was at once put on his guard by the evident reference to himself in whatever it was that was told to the King: however, though decidedly uneasy, he kept his head and answered all the King's questions respecting the barque's cargo to the latter's satisfaction.

Matson then returned to the beach to wait for Prince Narshin and the pilot. Here he was again accosted by the pirate captain, who asked him to come with him and meet some of his shipmates.

Matson did not hesitate for a moment, though he knew he might be going to his death.

The Spaniard took him to an open shed where a number of dago* seamen were lolling about.

After a short talk about cargoes and freights these men proceeded to question Matson about British cruisers and particularly regarding the movements of the *Curlew*.

During this interrogation the large, handsome black eyes of the man, whom he suspected of being the pirate captain, never left the mate's face. But Matson, though uncertain of everything—of his own safety; of his interrogators' identity with the pirates; of the intentions of the treacherous King, or even whether the hostages for which he had angled so skilfully, would really turn up; nevertheless replied without hesitating and with absolute truth to each question until, in the midst of this testing of his courage and cuteness, in walked the negro pilot and the King's son.

It is difficult to keep this dramatic story of the *Panda* within limits, for again and again some accidental incident influenced the whole course of justice for good or ill: yet through it all one can see the inexorable hand of fate gradually closing upon the pirate captain.

Plot and Counter-Plot at Cape Lopez

The Cape Lopez natives bore a very bad reputation for treachery and murder, so Capatain Fatio was much relived when he at last saw the boat returning.

The King's son and the pilot were shown the usual Manchester bales; and then were filled up with food and drink until, a pair of happy savages, gorged to repletion, they fell into a deep sleep.

That very night, soon after eight bells midnight had struck, the *Curlew* rounded to under the barque's stern and hailed. Matson at once rowed aboard the sloop and informed Captain Trotter of his progress. Then the brig filled away and stood out to sea again.

Luckily neither the hailing nor the noise of the boat being launched and hauled up again was able to wake the two hostages.

Nor indeed did a cry of 'fire': for on this same night the binnacle lamp somehow set alight to the wooden binnacle stand and threatened to burn up the ship.

On the following day there was much excitement at the Cape Lopez anchorage for the barque, *Princess Elizabeth*, sailed in from the river mouth, and the *Curlew* disguised as a slave brig with the Brazilian flag flying, came in from the opposite direction.

The camouflage of the man-of-war proved to be quite successful, for the King who was carousing aboard a Portuguese ship, at once sent two of his headmen aboard the *Curlew*, whilst he himself hurried ashore to be in readiness to receive the newly arrived slave captain.

* Dago was the term applied by British and American seamen to all members of the Latin race, whether Spanish, Portuguese, Italian, Mexican, or South American.

The next move on the part of the *Curlew*'s commander was, however, a bad blunder.

As the King's canoe was seen to head for the shore, a cutter under Lieutenant McNeale left the side of the *Curlew* in chase.

This was a dead give away, for there was no disguising the stroke of men-of-war's men.

The King's paddlers were, also, quite equal to the task of keeping ahead of the cutter and after a desperate race he landed in safety.

However Trotter now had four hostages, including the King's son and a near relation.

These were treated with the greatest kindness and from young Prince Narshin it was learnt that the mate, carpenter and three other pirates had gone to St. Thomas in the *Esperanza*, but Don Pedro, the captain, and a few others of the *Panda's* crew still remained with King Pass-all.

After much shuffling and temporising, the King at length agreed to give up the pirates to an officer of the *Curlew* the following morning.

Captain Trotter determined to go himself in his four-oared gig. Leaving two men in the boat with Quintom, the master's assistant, he proceeded along the beach followed by the other two.

The Surrender of the Pirate Captain

And now came a most dramatic moment. Every eye, whether aboard the ships in the anchorage or ashore, was glued on the captain of the British man-of-war.

Then out of the bush above the beach came the pirate captain, walking with his usual slow dignity.

This man was evidently a good bit of a mystery. To quote a witness, he was one "whose thoughtful, dignified countenance betokened a man long accustomed to command and who, but for having engaged in the dastardly, degrading slave trade, might have been the last to have been brought into his present humiliating situation". He seems to have been scarcely the true type of a pirate captain. His control over his own ruffiany crew was apparently negligable, yet his influence over the drunken old King Pass-all had certainly been great.

As Captain Trotter advanced towards him, he was seen to halt with with his left hand on his sword and his right hand held behind him.

The British officer thinking he held a pistol, sprang forward to catch his arm, but tripped, and the next moment the pair of them rolled in the sand, grappling wildly together.

An instant later each man sprang to his feet. Don Pedro then bowed to his antagonist, as a dignified hint that he surrendered, and walked quietly down to the boat.

With the lion a captive, the jackals rushed in. Almost before Don Pedro had reached the *Curlew* his store had been broken into and a wild scramble took place for its contents, in which many a woolly pate received a hammering.

Some of the *Panda*'s papers, including the muster-roll, and a few bags of dollars were saved from the rapacious Cape Lopez natives, but it was rumoured that the greater amount of the *Mexican*'s dollars had been buried in the beach between Nazareth and Cape Lopez.

As soon as the remaining pirates, Jose Velasquez, Antonio Ferrer and Nicholas Costa, had been sent off by the King, the four hostages were returned amidst great rejoicing in King Pass-all's bee-hive of an African town.

Matson had treated Prince Narshin, who was little more than a boy, with great kindness and on parting had dressed him in one of his old uniforms to the immense gratification of that youth.

It may now be thought that Captain Trotter's long hunt after the *Panda*'s pirates was over.

But this was far from being the case. He now had to hurry back to St. Thomas to lay the mate and his companions by the heels.

However, before sailing, he went ashore to take a ceremonious farewell of the old chief, little imagining that their antagonism was by no means over. As he stepped out of his gig onto the beach, the excited natives made a rush, and in a moment he found himself being hoisted up onto gleaming black shoulders. And in this way he was carried into the presence of King Pass-all in the centre of the town.

All indeed seemed well. Diplomatic relations were restored; the dignity of the flag maintained; and the negro monarch placated with the usual present of rum and tobacco.

The *Curlew* then up anchored and sailed for St. Thomas along with the *Princess Elizabeth*, which needed to wood and water before resuming her business in the Cameroons.

When the *Curlew* arrived at St. Thomas on the 4th October, 1833, eager eyes looked out for the *Esperanza*, but she was not to be seen in the roadstead of St. Ann de Chaves.

The Governor of St. Thomas Befriends the Pirates

The Governor, however, assured Trotter that the pirates had not escaped aboard the schooner. The latter next had a visit from Holmes. This lynx-eyed American at once informed Trotter of the true facts. The pirates had actually purchased a small vessel, which was then lying in the anchorage, from the Governor himself, and had been busy fitting her out when the *Curlew* hove in sight. At which the Governor at once hurried them into hiding.

The incensed Trotter again tackled the slippery governor and vowed he would take his own steps if the pirates were not handed over.

Hardly had he issued this ultimatum before he was informed by Captain Pollard of the American ship, *Henry Hill*, that the *Esperanza* was lying at the back of the island and that, by order of the Governor, the pirates were being marched down to the beach opposite to be put aboard her.

As soon as it was dark, Matson was dispatched in the boats to take possession of the *Esperanza*. This he succeeded in doing, but once more Trotter was balked of his prey, for neither the captain of the schooner nor the pirates proved to be on board.

However the *Esperanza* was detained to go before an Admiralty Court, Trotter's contention being that by bringing the pirates from Cape Lopez to St. Thomas, knowing well that they were miscreants trying to escape justice, the captain had laid himself open to a prosecution.

Having got the better of King Pass-all, Captain Trotter found himself up against a much more formidable antagonist, in the Portuguese Governor of St. Thomas.

It seems hardly credible that a high Government official should protect pirates from their pursuers. But it should be remembered that at this date both slavers and pirates were accustomed to fit out at Havana right in front of the windows of the Governor-General's palace, having gained their immunity by the usual means of a large bribe.

After much quibbling and prevarication the Portuguese Governor was forced to admit that the five Spanish pirates were lurking on the other side of the island. These were Bernardo de Soto, the mate of the *Panda*, Francisco Ruitz, the carpenter and Manoel Bayga, Domingo de Guzman and Juan Antonio Portana, seamen.

The Governor, at last was forced to promise that he would apprehend these men and deliver them up to the British man-of-war.

But is was a case of mañana. Days passed and nothing happened. In this game of wits the Governor was a passed-master, but that bull-dog Trotter held stubbornly to his point.

When he taxed the Governor with selling his own schooner to the pirates, the latter brazenly denied all knowledge of any such transaction. When Trotter offered to bring proof, the Governor pleaded the want of a good interpreter, though Captain Fatio, who was standing at the captain's side at the time, was an excellent one.

The Governor next feigned ill-health, in order to avoid further interviews with the importunate naval captain. In this way he gained sufficient time to arrange for a man to come forward and confess to having sold the schooner to the pirates.

Strange as it may seem, the Governor was not alone in his fight to save the skins of the pirates; besides him, every official and indeed the whole population of the island were on the side of the freebooters, so great is the power of the dollar.

The feeling was not only strong against the British naval officers but against their American sympathisers. Honest Holmes had his house set on fire and barely escaped with his life. Captain Pollard was set upon, knocked about and robbed.

However, in the end, of course, the stubborn Trotter had his way, the five pirates were sent off and the *Curlew* sailed for Prince's Island, where her commander reported the conduct of the St. Thomas Governor and also demanded the apprehension of Captain Cosmé of the *Esperanza*, for aiding and abetting the pirates.

Here, however, he was forced to put up with promises that the Governor's conduct would be enquired into and the captain sent to Lisbon by the first man-of-war.

Trotter had now secured fifteen of the pirates, including the captain, mate and carpenter. He had retrieved some of the dollars, destroyed the *Panda*, confiscated the *Esperanza*, and still his job was not finished, for now came news that Captain Cosmé's trunk, said to contain papers, and letters, showing the intercourse between the Captain of the *Esperanza* and Don Pedro, the pirate captain, were at Cape Lopez. These were also expected to implicate the rascally governor of St. Thomas and others, so Matson was ordered to proceed with the *Esperanza* in search of this important trunk.

King Pass-all and his unruly subjects were considerably surprised to find that the *Esperanza* had now become a prize of the indefatigable Englishmen. But the news that Cosmé was detained, a prisoner at Prince's Island, was the signal for his store to be looted for slaves. In spite of Matson's remonstrances and King Pass-all's vigourous efforts with a long sword, which were aimed at retaining the loot for himself and his four hundred wives, the store was speedily emptied of its contents. Matson then sailed back to Prince's, where the missing trunk had already been sent. The Portuguese authorities examined the trunk in the presence of Trotter, but, needless to say, no incriminating papers could be found.

However Matson had brought news that there was still a member of the *Panda*'s crew hiding in the bush at the back of Cape Lopez.

King Pass-all Has His Revenge

On the 19th of January, 1834, the *Curlew*, with the *Esperanza*, commanded by Matson, in company, once more anchored at Cape Lopez.

Captain Trotter, himself, being laid low with one of his bouts of fever, entrusted the task of getting the remaining pirate to Matson. The latter had no reason to suspect that the King would give anymore trouble, but it so happend that King Pass-all was in the midst of a drinking bout and in a very pugnacious mood; and he ordered Matson and his boat's crew to be seized without ceremony.

Whilst this was happening in the town Lieutenant Pike was sent in the gig to examine a Portuguese schooner, which lay within twenty yards of the beach, but round the point and out of sight of the man-of-war.

Apparently Lieutenant Pike had a boat's crew of kroomen, armed only with cutlasses. He was busy examining the slaver's papers when fifteen or sixteen canoes, crowded with excited negroes, all armed, pushed off from the beach.

They drove the kroomen into the gig, then set upon Lieutenant Pike. He was belaboured till he was half dead, stripped of his clothes and left lying on the beach, naked and scarcely conscious.

When neither boat came off from the shore, Lieutenant McNeale, little thinking what had really happened, set off in the jolly boat, accompanied by the purser and a boat's crew of six unarmed bluejackets to find out what delayed them. No sooner were these ashore than they found themselves prisoners in the middle of a crowd of war-dancing warriors.

Here was a pretty kettle of fish for Captain Trotter to tackle during the lucid intervals that his fever allowed him.

His three senior executive officers, his purser, six bluejackets and ten kroomen in the hands of a drunken African chief, whose people had the reputation of being the most murderous lot of savages on the coast.

Let me now quote Matson in his account of the incident:—

"Captain Trotter, who always fancied that nothing was done while anything remained to do, determined on getting him (the remaining pirate) also; as soon therefore, as his duties as senior officer would permit, he sailed for Cape Lopez.

On arriving there, Captain Trotter being himself very ill in bed, from an attack of fever, sent me to demand of the King the remaining pirate.

On waiting on his Majesty, between four and five o'clock in the afternoon, I found him half drunk and in a towering passion; and on stating the object of my visit he declared he would not give up anyone who had claimed his protection, and that, as Captain Trotter had made war on him, he would make prisoners of all Englishmen, and would now begin by keeping me a prisoner until five hundred pounds was paid for my ransom.

I saw he was very drunk, and had no idea he would do what he threatened, but on the head krooman coming to report that the natives had hauled up my boat, I saw something serious was intended. I was detained a short time in the King's house, and then told to go where I liked.

On proceeding to the beach I found a great commotion and excitement, and was informed that one of the *Curlew*'s boats manned by white men had been captured and the crew stripped naked.

I was conducted to a small hut, where I found McNeale, first of the *Curlew*, stark naked and with both legs in irons. I then returned to the King to remonstrate against this treatment, but found him more drunk than ever. All that I could get out of him was:—"One time, Captain Trotter—me now—I Captain Trotter", and this he kept repeating in answer to my complaints.

While this was going on a white man was brought to the King a prisoner, quite naked, and his face and person covered with blood and dirt. It was some moments before I recognised Lieutenant Pike, second of the *Curlew*.

My first impulse was to throw off my coat to give him, but the old chief ordered me to desist, and on my refusing, he threatened that I should be stripped like the rest.

I thought it politic to comply, but the old brute allowed me to give Pike my pocket handerchief; he also agreed to let NcNeale out of irons.

It was then getting dark and we were marched off by different parties and not allowed to hold any communication with each other.

Prince Narshin, whom I formerly had prisoner on board the merchant barque, took me under his special protection: I asked him to look after the rest, and to give them something to eat: he did so and was very kind and attentive. This young fellow did much to alleviate our sufferings.

I did not close my eyes during that night, being dreadfully tormented by mosquitoes and other vermin: the noise and excitement, too, on the beach made me believe that an attack on the *Curlew* was meditated.

I felt uneasiness on this account: Captain Trotter was very ill: nearly all the officers and part of the crew prisoners: the remainder sickly, and the few that were well were divided between the *Curlew* and the schooner.

A surprise on a dark night might have proved successful and even had the natives been repulsed with loss, the fate of those on shore would have been sealed. While this move was going on, I heard footsteps stealthily approaching the hut in which I lay a solitary prisoner: whispers were exchanged as some person unfastened the door, and I was sure I was about to be assassinated: but it turned out that the intruders were two blacks who came to enquire of me how many whites remained on board the *Curlew* and the schooner.

I pretended to count up numbers and then replied 'One hundred and twenty, or one hundred and twenty-five on board the *Curlew* and twenty-five on board the schooner'.

I believe this exaggeration of numbers prevented an attack.

The next morning we were all taken before the King who received us in great state, surrounded by about forty of the headmen of the place. All the *Curlew*'s men were quite naked except myself, who had been allowed to keep my clothes as well as to wear my sword, on account, as he said of our former friendship. We remonstrated energetically against our treatment, particularly in having been stripped and beaten: he replied that it had been done and could not now be helped; that we should not be released until Captain Trotter paid him goods amounting to three thousand dollars, with a promise not to molest him again, and that if these terms were not agreed to he would send us into the bush where we should die of fever or be devoured by wild beasts.

All remonstrance appeared to be in vain, and two kroomen were dispatched in a canoe to inform Captain Trotter of our predicament and the terms offered for our ransom. The King also permitted Lieutenant Pike to go off in a canoe, to have his wounds dressed under a promise to return.

Captain Trotter wrote to inform us that he was ready to make any sacrifice rather than to allow us to remain another day in so unhealthy a spot, and desired us to make the best bargain we could, adding that he would send the things on shore directly.

After a long negotiation with the King, it was agreed that we were to give him goods amounting to one hundred pounds and that we should be liberated on the receipt of them".

When the ransom was sent ashore, King Pass-all declared that it was not enough, and for two days almost hourly bargaining went on between the King and Matson: however, on the third day the *Fair Rosamond*, Lieutenant-Commander George Rose, appeared on the scene. This beautiful little ex-slaver had been thoroughly refitted at Portsmouth, and her sail plan altered and cut down; however, I can find no evidence of her sailing powers being spoilt, for her commission under Rose, a very capable officer, was a very successful one.

The arrival of another man-of-war was sufficient to frighten old King Pass-all into returning his captives and on the very next day they were received aboard the *Curlew* with cheers. Trotter, of course, was not the man to let such treatment go unpunished. On his demand for his men's clothes and the repayment of the ransom being refused by the King, he sent Matson off in the *Esperanza* to Prince's Island in search of the *Trinculo*.

The *Trinculo* to the Rescue

The *Trinculo* was one of the old eighteen-gun brig-sloops. She was built at Bursledon in 1809, but since then her armament had been reduced to fourteen thirty-two-pounder carronades and her two long nines. She was commanded by James Booth, a 'taut' hand as a strict disciplinarian was called.

When two men were caught fighting on the lower deck, he had their left wrists tied together, then a reef-point fastened to each right hand. They were then told to thrash each other, the first to give in being promised four dozen with the cat.

He also made his officers take star sights and lunars on every possible occasion

Admiral Sir J. C. Dalrymple Hay tells a good yarn re this sight taking. Of course the results were often fudged, the most usual trick being to give a slight variation from the dead reckoning as the result of the stellar observation. But the Irish second Lieutenant went one better by recording in the log the longitude by lunar. But it so happened that the moon did not happen to be in distance with the star noted in the logs, whereupon Booth sent for the delinquent.

"How dare you make this entry, sir? The moon is not even in distance", said the commander angrily.

"Oh I know that", said the unabashed Paddy, "I took the distance betwixt two stars".

"And you call that a lunar observation".

"No, sur, my mishtake", in his rich brogue, "we call that a starling".

Booth was duly discovered at Prince's and sailed home at once, his whole ship's company fairly thirsting for blood, after a long dull eventless cruise.

Directly Trotter saw the *Esperanza* and *Trinculo* approaching the anchorage he made every preparation for a primitive attack upon the town.

The water was too shoal for the ships to join in, but eleven boats were manned and armed.

These opened fire upon the town with rockets, musketry and round shot from the twelve-pounder carronade mounted in the bows of the *Trinculo*'s pinnace.

This bombardment soon drove the natives back into the bush at the back of the town, whence they had previously removed all the women and children and everything of any value.

Some casualties were inflicted, but the blacks, who had collected in large numbers in answer to the sounding of the King's war drums during the previous three or four days, mostly kept out of range.

It had been intended to fire the town, which consisted of the usual bamboo huts, but owing to the wind shifting, Trotter wisely decided not to land and contented himself with the punishment inflicted by the boats.

By this time the *Curlew* had a great many men on the sick list besides her commander, and Lieutenant Pike after his rough handling and exposure was at death's door.

After his settling up with King Pass-all and the Cape Lopez savages, instead of sailing for Prince's Island, where he expected to be relieved as S N O by Meredith of the *Pelorus*, Captain Trotter headed straight for Ascension, where not only his fever-stricken crew, but many sick piratical prisoners speedily recovered.

After a month at Ascension the *Curlew* and *Esperanza* sailed for England, arriving at Portsmouth in June 1834. It was decided not to try the pirates in England, but to send them to Salem for trial, where the *Mexican*'s crew might be found to witness against them.

They were sent across the Atlantic in the ten-gun brig *Savage*, Commander Loney. G. H. Quintom, the master's assistant of the *Curlew*, being sent to give evidence regarding their capture.

Meanwhile it was decided that the case against the *Esperanza* was insufficient to detain her and she was returned to the Portuguese Government.

A few years later she was again seen in the Bights, but this time she was a war-schooner belonging to the Portuguese Navy.

The arrival of the *Savage* in Salem with the *Panda* pirates caused great excitement, for it was the first time a British man-of-war had entered the port since the independence of the U.S.A., also the handing over of the pirates for trial in the States was considered an international act of courtesy that was very much appreciated.

Loney and his officers were almost overcome by the hospitality showered upon them by the town's people, headed by Mr. Joseph Peabody, who insisted upon Daniel Quintom being his guest throughout his stay in America.

The Trial of the Pirates

The *Savage* arrived at Salem on August the 20th, an indictment was found against the prisoners on October the 23rd and on 11th of November the trial opened under the well-known judge, the Honourable Joseph Story.

The excitement and interest that this trial aroused throughout the civilised world was truly extraordinary.

It will hardly be believed how great was the sympathy with the prisoners. In America pamphlets were published and sent out broadcast, alleging perjury on the part of the witnesses, and attributing Trotter's action to the very lowest motives.

The chief supporter of the pirates was Mrs. Child, the wife of their advocate, who actually interviewed the President on their behalf and subsequently published a most violent and travestied description of the whole affair, in which the pirates were presented as foully wronged innocents, and the Royal Navy as the snake in the bosom of civilization.

Even a leading London journal and a royal duke were, for a while misled by these American pamphlets into taking up the case of the pirates .

The Captain, Pedro Gibert, the mate Bernardo de Soto, the carpenter Ruiz, and four others were pronounced guilty. Three of the prisoners were found not guilty and one committed suicide in gaol.

It is probable that a great deal of the sympathy with the pirates was due to the bearing of the captain and mate. Don Pedro Gibert was something of an enigma. Why such a man should have ever descended to piracy it was impossible to explain.

From the day of his capture to the moment of his execution he never lost his calm dignified bearing; always behaved like a man of good breeding and displayed the utmost fortitude.

That the mate, Bernardo de Soto, had had a hand in the piracy was equally surprising, for he had not long before been the hero in a most gallant piece of life saving.

In 1831 he had been master of the *Leon*, voyaging between Havana and Philadelphia. On his return passage he discovered the American ship, *Minerva*, with seventy-two souls on board, stranded on the Bahama Bank, out of sight of land. She had a cargo of lime and had sprung a leak, thus her passengers and crew were in danger from two opposite elements—fire and water.

Shortly before the American ship *Chariot* had passed by without taking any notice of the signals of distress. De Soto stopped and rescued everybody and conveyed them to Havana.

His eloquent advocate made great play with this rescue, even comparing De Soto to the Good Samaritan.

The father of the *Panda*'s mate proved to be an administrator of ecclesiastical rank at Corunna and his wife also of gentle birth.

He himself had passed all his navigation and seamanship examinations to that of the highest grade in Spain, that of Captain or first pilot for the East Indies.

De Soto owed his life to his wife's efforts on his behalf. Crossing from Corunna to Havana, she there obtained many letters on her husband's behalf and then went to Washington and threw herself at the feet of the President. The result was a pardon.

Pedro Gibert and the other men found guilty were executed on June the 11th, 1835, and their actions on the scaffold were reported in the greatest detail by all the American papers. All of them died like brave men, which was not always the case with pirates.

Pedro Gibert, the pirate captain, never would acknowledge his guilt; he mounted the scaffold which bore the gallows, with his usual calm bearing and stately step.

The Roman Catholic priest, standing by the foot of the ladder urged him on with the curious words "Spaniards ascend to Heaven".

One of the pirates, Boyga, had attempted to commit suicide in his cell and, having nearly bled to death, had to be carried onto the scaffold.

To him and the others, Gibert spoke with utmost fortitude:—

"We are going to die, but let us be firm for we are innocent".

The pirate captain then took off his linen collar and handed it to the hangman with the words:—

"This is all I have to part with; take it as a keepsake: I die innocent, but I die like a Spaniard, goodbye brother, we die in the hope of meeting you in heaven".

Prayers were read by one priest, then a second addressed the assembled crowd on behalf of the prisoners, who, he said, maintained their innocence to the last.

De Soto, Reformed Pirate

This extraordinary pirate story had still further light let in upon it by De Soto in after years, when the captain is shown up under two very different aspects.

First I will quote a letter from Matson to the *Nautical Magazine*.

"About two years after this event I visited Havana, being the second lieutenant of the *Pearl*.

On the English consul hearing that I had a share in the capture of the pirates, who had originally sailed from Havana he strongly advised that I should not make myself known, and on no account go ashore after dark, as those men had many friends in the place, who would gladly take an opportunity to revenge their death.

I did not pay much attention to the latter part of his recommendation, and on that very evening went to the opera in company with the captain of the *Pearl*, Lord Clarence Paget and Mr. Schenlez, the judge of the Mixed Commission Court. We had not long been seated in the front row of one of the boxes, before Lord Clarence drew my attention to a man in the pit, who was looking earnestly at our box. I looked at him, but not recognising his countenance, paid no more attention to him. Sometime afterwards Lord Clarence Paget said:—

"Matson, don't look down, but that man has never taken his eyes off you since we came into the box: I should not wonder if he is one of those pirate fellows". I looked again and then recognised my old friend De Soto. There was evidently no harm in the expression of the man's face, so after looking at him for a minute I gave a nod of recognition. His eyes were immediately filled with tears and he appeared much pleased at my noticing him.

. . . Soon after breakfast on the following morning de Soto made his appearance, much to my surprise, on the quarter deck of the *Pearl*.

I offered him my hand, on taking which he was much affected: I then asked him to walk below, but this he begged to be excused doing, and he firmly presisted in refusing: he said he did not forget the difference in our position: he recollected what he had been and had no wish to bring disgrace on a British officer by introducing himself in his apartment. He stated that he merely came on board to thank me for the kindness he had formerly received at my hands. I was certainly not aware that he owed me any thanks. During the eight or nine months he remained a prisoner on board the *Esperanza* under my command, he was in irons in the hold, except when taking his daily walk under charge of the sentinel.

He told me that Perez, who turned King's, or rather State's evidence, was assassinated on the very day he returned to Havana.

We walked the deck for upwards of an hour, when he gave me the whole history of his connection with the *Panda*; he stated that when he joined that vessel as chief mate, he believed she was going on an ordinary slave trading voyage: he was not aware that piracy was intended until they had actually put to sea, when he found that no cargo was on board and that they were to trust to robbery to obtain goods wherewith to puchase a cargo of slaves. This was the only part of his story that I had reason to disbelieve, because, as chief mate he must have known all along that the vessel was without any cargo.

However he emphatically denied that either he or Don Pedro ever contemplated the commission of murder: that piracy then attracted little notice, unless accompanied by the loss of life.

(Perez declared that when Garcia (the boatswain) was ordered on board the *Mexican* he asked De Soto, if the crew were to be despatched. De Soto replied, 'No do not touch a hair of their heads for human life is sweet'. To this Garcia simply answered:—

'Dead cats don't mew!')

They boarded two vessels before they fell in with the American brig, namely an English and a Dutch vessel, but as they had neither money nor other valuables, nothing was taken excepting some cabin stores and a little rope, and none of the crew were in any way maltreated.

After the money had been taken out of the *Mexican* they hurried away on account of another sail being in sight, which they perceived was a man-of-war. It was then discovered that the brig was on fire, and as no person was to be seen on her decks, Don Pedro taxed the boatswain, who commanded the boarding party, with having killed the crew. This he denied having done, but he had in fact secured them all below and then set the vessel on fire. As he received orders not to ill-treat any person, this proceeding gave rise to much ill-feeling between the captain and the boatswain; the latter, being often put in irons and confined by Don Pedro's orders.

De Soto informed me that the fatigue and excitement undergone by his wife in procuring his pardon, brought on a severe illness, of which she died soon after his release.

I was at Havana again ten years after this, being then in command of the *Daring*.

On my sending a message to De Soto, to say I should be glad to see him he came on board.

He did not appear then to fancy that he was inflicting any disgrace by taking a seat and a glass of wine in my cabin. The world had gone well with him since his trial, and he was now undoubtedly a reformed character.

He never looked like a pirate, he had a benevolent expression of countenance and was particularly mild and gentle in his manners.

During ten years he had commanded a large steamer running between Havana and Matanzas, and latterly had become part owner. He told me he had made a considerable sum of money, but had never engaged in the slave trade since his liberation This was strictly true for I heard it confirmed from other sources. He was then moving in a very respectable sphere at Havana and was known generally as Don Bernardo. I made many enquiries about him and heard that he now bore a very excellent character and was generally respected".

An American shipmaster, Captain Nicholas Snell, also records meeting De Soto in after years and hearing the story of the piracy; but the yarn by this time had become twisted into the following:—

After the capture of the *Mexican* there was a grand carouse in the cabin of the *Panda*, when the chief toast was:—

"Here's to the squirming Yankees". Pedro Gibert is represented as hurling many black oaths at the boatswain on learning that those aboard the *Mexican* had not been put to death, and that he cruised for two days in search of her with that object in view.

It is curious that only a year or two previous to the *Mexican* affair, had occurred the piracy of the *Morning Star*, by the Buenos Airian slave brigantine, *Defensor Pedro*, Captain Benito de Soto—no relation, it is presumed of Bernard de Soto, but a pirate who was much more true to type.

The case I have already fully recorded in my book the *The Blackwall Frigates*.

It, too, showed how little distinction there was between the pirate and the slaver, for not long before his capture of the East Indiaman, De Soto had run a cargo of slaves into Havana.

Here again the pirate captain owed his capture and execution to carelessness in not seeing that the pirate's maxim:— "Dead men tell no tales", was properly carried out.

The following letter to Captain Trotter will show that his efforts were duly appreciated:—

Admiralty
16th September, 1835.

Sir,

My Lords Commissioners of the Admiralty, having had under their consideration your exertions while in command of the *Curlew* in the capture of the piratical schooner *Panda* and her crew, and perseverence displayed by you in circumstances of extreme difficulty, and involving you in great personal responsibility, for which, and the protection thereby afforded to American commerce, you have received through His Majesty's Secretary of State for Foreign Affairs the thanks of the President of the United States, are pleased as a mark of the sense which my Lords entertain of your conduct, to promote you to the rank of Captain in the Royal Navy.

I am, sir, your most obedient servant,

C. Wood.

Commander H. D. Trotter.

CHAPTER XIV

THE WEST INDIAN STATION 1832-1842

Oh, 'tis a fine frigate, *La Pique* was her name,
All in the West Indies she bore a great name;
For cruel hard usage of every degree,
Like slaves in the galley we ploughed the salt sea.

At four in the morning the game is begun
To the cock-pit the waisters for buckets must run
Our fore and main topmen so loudly do bawl,
For sand and for holystones both great and small.

O Master Make-clever, you knows him quite well,
He comes up on deck and he cuts a great swell;
It's 'Damn your eyes' here and 'Damn your eyes' there,
And straight to the gangway he takes a broad sheer.

Half a dozen he starts, and so he goes on;
You're sure of a hiding, boys, every one;
For soldier or sailor he cares not a damn,
But he'll hide you as long as you're able to stand.

Our decks being wash'd and our sheets being home,
It's stand by your hammocks, boys, every one;
Seven turns with your lashings, black clews and black shows,
It's All the world over, and over she goes.

(Note. And so on for an innumerable number of verses. The name of the ship was sometimes given, sometimes concealed, but *La Pique*, a very smart ship, seems to have been the original vessel immortalised by this foc's'le bard.)

Speedwell's Success

IT is curious the way in which each little R.N. schooner distinguished herself in turn. In the task of catching slavers in the West Indies.

In the year 1832 the *Speedwell* had her chance, and right well she took it.

On August the 31st, 1829, William Warren, the first lieutenant of the *Victor,* had been appointed to the command of the little schooner, as a reward for his share in the capture of the pirate *Las Damas Argentinas.* The captain of the *Victor* wrote of him as an officer 'thoroughly conversant with all the duties of his onerous office, in whom I had the most implicit confidence'.

Warren had to do nearly three years of cruising before he had an opportunity to distinguish himself, and all this time the *Speedwell,* after much hard service and many bumps on coral reefs, was not any too seaworthy; for, as far back as August 1827 I find that she was making sixteen inches of water an hour, however she was still able to sail, and on the 6th of April, 1832, overhauled the Spanish schooner, *Planeta,* with a cargo of slaves.

At daylight on the 3rd of June, 1832, she sighted a large brig, which after a short chase in which the *Speedwell* had much the best of it, shortened sail and hove to, ashamed apparently to run from a vessel only a third of her size.

The action that ensued was fought within pistol shot and lasted for an hour, at the end of which the slaver struck her colours.

She turned out to be one of the largest and most successful slavers out of Havana, the *Aquila,* a brig with a modern round stern, mounting eight thirty two-pounders and two twelve pounders of three hundred and thirty tons with a picked crew of seventy men.

That such a vessel should have been forced to yield after an hour's action points not only to very superior gun-drill on the part of the *Speedwell's* crew, but to masterly handling by her commander.

It was an even a greater victory than that of the *Pickle* over the *Bolodora.* unfortunately the logbook of the *Speedwell* for the summer of 1832 is missing, and contemporary accounts in the newspapers give no details of killed and wounded.

The men-of-war's men had the usual difficulty aboard the prize, which besides a crew of seventy had six hundred and sixteen slaves in her hold.

Lieutenant Warren, warned by the *Pickle's* difficulty, had a sufficient number of leg irons on board, and after the crew of the *Aquila* had been ironed, there were divided between the two vessels.

In the *Jamaica Courant* of August the 2nd, we are told that the brig was safely navigated to Havana and 'on nearing that port, the excitement on shore was very great, to see a 'cock-boat' escorting one of the finest vessels belonging to Cuba into port as a prize; and so annoyed was the Spanish Governor, at a circumstance which, he said, reflected discredit upon the national character, that the captain has been sentenced to prison for ten years'.

Hardly had the *Aquila* been condemned and the *Speedwell* regained her cruising ground than a third slaver fell a victim to her. This was the *Indagadera.*

Thus in less than three months the *Speedwell* had captured over one thousand slaves, and in the following August Lieutenant Warren was promoted to the rank of Commander.

He afterwards distinguished himself in command of the *Harlequin* in the first Chinese war and was rewarded with a C.B.

Thus the little *Speedwell* gave a worthy sailor his first chance in the service, for Warren, after passing his examination for Lieutenant had served ten more years before he received his commission.

A Ship of Babies

The only other capture worthy of note that took place in the West Indies in 1832 was that of a little Spanish schooner of only seventy-five tons by the eighteen-gun sloop *Dispatch,* Commander George Daniell, to the windward of Barbadoes.

This schooner, named the *Ross,* had two hundred and ninety two slaves, one hundred and seventy six males and one hundred and sixteen females, *most of whom were under twelve years of age!* These poor little mites were close packed on a deck with only three feet two inches under the beams. The capture took place on Christmas day, when the *Dispatch* was on her passage out to her station, and we may bet that the great-hearted British bluejackets made it up to the poor little black piccaninnies for their terrible experience.

In the year 1833 it was the turn of the *Nimble* to distinguish herself. On the 24th of February Lieutenant Charles Bolton was appointed to command her. This officer was a nephew of Nelson's eldest sister and a first cousin of the second Earl.

As far back as October 1824 we find him pirate hunting in command of the *Speedwell,* and he had been serving on the West Indian station ever since, being in fact one of those schooner sailors, who knew the Caribbean so well that they never needed to take a pilot.

Log of the *Nimble*

I do not think that a better idea of the life aboard a slave chasing war schooner than can be obtained them from the old official logbook:—

The following are extracts from the *Nimble*'s logbook:—

Log of H.M. Schooner *Nimble*

30 October.

4.00 a.m.	Saw strange sail—chased.
5.20 a.m.	Out cutter and boarded her: found her to be an armed schooner, but nothing on board to condemn her, having landed the slaves. Espended in bringing her to one musket ball cartridge.
7.00 a.m.	Standing in for Barracas.
7.40 a.m.	Fired eighteen-pounder long gun to bring a vessel to—found her to be a brig from St. Andero to St. Iago.
12 noon.	Hove to.
1.00 p.m.	In chase; lowered the topsail: hove to, boarded a Spanish schooner from Curacoa to St. Iago.
6.00 p.m.	Mustered at quarters.
8.00 p.m.	Calm.

10 November.

4.00 a.m.	Daylight observed strange sail—made sail in chase—set studding sails, ringtail and flying jib.
8.30 a.m.	Stranger hoisted Spanish colours and fired a gun to leeward.
9.00 a.m.	Closed stranger—fired two muskets at him, which he returned with a long gun—commenced the action.
10.00 a.m.	Stranger ceased firing and struck his colours, found him to be Spanish schooner, *Joaquina* with three hundred and twenty nine slaves.
p.m.	Found her sinking from shot holes between wind and water,—employed plugging them.

Expended during the action—powder

Long Gun	48 lb.
Fore gun	5 lb.
Shot round	14
Gun grape	6
Carronade grape	8
Tubes Quill	14
Cartridges musket	120
Lost overboard	Head sponge No. I. Rammer 1.
Tompions.	Eighteen-pounder 4
Swords.	SS. 2
Belts.	SS. 2
Scabbards.	2
Pistols pair.	1
Pikes	2

p.m.	In chase of a schooner standing in for the land fired eighteen-pounder long gun to bring him to—found to be an American.
4.00 p.m.	BC employed on board the prize. Found two slaves killed by a round shot.
6.00 p.m.	Filled.
12 November.	Bahia Honda S79E/85 miles—Tacked, down staysail and communicated with prize.
4.00 p.m.	BC found Captain of *Joaquina* had died of his wounds.
16 November	Came to in Havana Harbour.

(The *Joaquina* was condemned and *Nimble* returned to her station. In the log of the action it is amusing to note that it was taken as an opportunity to get rid of deficiencies—a method which still obtained in the last war.)

7 December.

a.m.	Light winds. Daylight obvserved strange sail to Eastward. Made all sail in chase. Water Hills NE 20 miles.
9.00 a.m.	Observed stranger sweeping. Out sweeps. Tried 8 guns to bring stranger to—split the bulwark by ditto.
Noon.	Employed sweeping—stranger ahead 2 miles Cape Corrientes N 72 W 123 Miles. Light wind—fired another gun at stranger. Observed him shorten sail and round to. Ran alongside and boarded him. Found her to be the Spanish schooner, *Manuelita,* 485 slaves and 34 men. Sent Mr. Armitage (Whaley Armitage—Master's mate, appointed to *Nimble* from *Columbine*) and prize crew on board.
17 December.	Arrived Havana.

Lieutenant Bolton had also destroyed a slaver named the *Amistad Havanera* whilst on the same cruise, thus he had equalled Warren's record in *Speedwell.*

This latter schooner, the oldest of the war schooners, proved to be so leaky and worn out that she was condemned at Jamaica in 1834 and sold out of the Service for the sum of three hundred and forty pounds ten shillings.

The *Nimble* also disappeared from the navy list in 1834, but in a more tragic way than the *Speedwell.*

Lieutenant Bolton's next cruise was upon the Bahama Bank, and he spent his Christmas and new year at Nassau.

Vice-Admiral Sir George Cockburn, who had been appointed to command the North American and West Indian Station in 1833, seems to have liked to have one of the schooners always acting in attendance upon him. The *Nimble* arrived at Jamaica on January the 18th, 1834, from Nassau, and Lieutenant Bolton found himself told off to attend the Admiral to Halifax.

Cockburn who was a martinet, had each schooner in turn under his eagle eye, and *Nimble* was followed first by *Pincher* and then by *Pickle.*

Meanwhile August found the *Nimble* back in the Bahama Channel and on August the 27th she arrived at Nassau with another capture—the Portuguese schooner *Felicidade* with one hundred and sixty four slaves. This vessel had been taken off the East end of Cuba. Her captain, two mates and boatswain, who were the only white men aboard, the rest of the crew being all negroes, had made their escape in a boat before the *Nimble* could overtake her.

The Wreck of the *Nimble*

On December the 4th, 1834 the *Nimble* was wrecked between Cay Verde just north of Caya Romano and the Old Bahama Channel, when in charge of a pilot. This was a most dangerous spot owing to shifting and rapid currents and dangerous overfalls, but both Bolton and his pilot, being out of soundings in six hundred fathoms of water, knew that they would receive ample warning of the reefs by the noise of the current rushing over them.

As it happened the decks of the *Nimble* were crowded with no less than two hundred and seventy two liberated slaves, from a slaver which she had just chased ashore.

The noise made by the chattering of the excited negroes was so great that Bolton and his pilot failed to hear the warning ripples of the current rushing over the reef, with the result that the little schooner ran hard and fast on a rock, called in the report Quay Island. The *Nimble,* it was at once seen was too badly bilged to be got off, and the difficulty was how to save the slaves, who were in such a panic that no less than seventy were drowned before they could be quietened. The remainder were taken off the wreck and with Lieutenant Bolton and the *Nimble's* crew reached Havana on November the 17th, 1834.

The fleet of West Indian war-schooners was still further reduced in 1834 by the sale of the *Kangaroo II.* This eighty-four ton schooner, which had been purchased in 1829 was sold by Sir George Cockburn for one hundred and sixty two pounds. She was evidently of no great value and I can find no evidence of her being concerned in any capture.

Besides the success of the *Nimble,* I can only find one other slave ship captured in the West Indies, in 1834, that was the Portuguese schooner, *Despiche* with two hundred and fifteen slaves by the *Firefly,* Lieutenant J. McDonnel, after a long chase of forty-eight hours.

The prize was sent into Havana under Henry M. Lockyer, master's mate of the *Firefly.*

Being Portuguese the Havana commissioners refused to deal with her and the unfortunate Lockyer was ordered to proceed to Nassau, land his negroes and then sail away to Sierra Leone for condemnation.

Columbine Salves a Merchantman

The saucy *Columbine,* Commander Love, sailed for England to pay off in the spring of 1834. During her commission of just under four years, she did not lose a man through sickness. She had had a happy and eventful commission, during which she had ranged the seas from Halifax to Cartagena and wherever she went, she received the admiration of sailormen.

As showing the useful work done by the only barque in the Royal Navy, here is an extract from one of her officer's letters and dated Carlisle Bay, Barbadoes, January the 28th, 1833.

> "On the morning of the 22nd, a signal was made for a ship on shore to windward; ours was instantly made by the *Pallas* frigate, Captain William Walpole, to render assistance, and off we started, and worked up and found her with her head in the breakers and her waterline two feet out of the water. As there was no time to be lost, and no effectual assistance could be afforded but by anchoring the *Columbine* within a cable's length, Commander Love got into the gig, leaving directions for the first lieutenant to stand in boldly, and to let go the anchor whenever he should hold up his hat.
>
> This was promptly done, and the distance was so fortunately judged, that after throwing all the sails flat aback, in order to lay the chain cable as taut as possible, and veering out to the clinch, we just reached the ship on the rocks, with the stream cable passed out of our stern port into her cabin window, and then hove as great a strain as it was possible to bear. We then commenced removing part of her cargo to schooners sent round for the purpose, assisted by the boats of the *Pallas* and *Arachne,* and had the satisfaction of getting her afloat after forty eight hours of incessant labour.
>
> She is now in the Carenage, ready for heaving down. During the whole time we had not a hammock down, or a watch below: there was not an experienced man in the whole island but considered it as impossible, and nothing but the instant-determination and exertion, joined with the most fortunate circumstances could have accomplished it. We are to sail tomorrow with troops for Antiqua and to carry others to Demerara".

Before sailing for home the *Columbine* called at most of the ports on the Spanish Main in hopes of a specie freight to England, but as she was not bound direct, we are told that the merchants preferred the packets, *Pigeon* and *Lady Mary Pelham,* as proceeding straight home.

Columbine sailed from Havana on January the 26th and had such bad weather that in one gale she was compelled to jettison two of her guns.

She arrived at Portsmouth on February the 26th and before being put out of commission at Sheerness, her officers gave Love a parting dinner as a token of their respect and esteem.

She was at once dismantled and rerigged as a brig. Under her new rig she proved even more successful and speedy than as a barque.

The first part of her fourth commission when she was captained by Commander Tom Henderson, was spent in the Mediterranean in sailing trials with the fleet before proceeding to the coast of Africa for the last two years of her time.

Loss of the *Firefly*

Of the few R.N. schooners two more came to grief in 1835—these were the little centre-boarder *Firefly* and the surveying schooner *Jackdaw* (a Seppings design built at Chatham in 1830, of one hundred and eight tons).

The former was on a passage from Belize to Jamaica with a few passengers.

Shortly after 9 p.m. on February the 27th, 1835, when the schooner had barely steerage way in a very light air, but was being hove along by a heavy swell, the mate in charge of the watch called his commander, Lieutenant John Julian McDonell, with the news that there was a dark loom ahead.

Scarcely had McDonell reached the deck before his ear recognised the deep booming sound of distant surf. He at once ordered the helm to be put down, but the shoal little schooner refused to come round against the run of the sea* and though the port sweeps were quickly manned, she got stern way on her and crashed stern on to the reef, which was the Northern Triangles in the Bay of Honduras.

The first shock drove in her stern frame, and as she was banged on the reef by the heavy rollers, it was at once recognised that the matter was critical. The night was very dark, and hardly had the *Firefly* struck before the wind shifted into the Norrard and began to blow in heavy gusts.

Nevertheless McDonell did all that a good seaman could do. The best bower was let go; the boats were hoisted out, soundings were taken round the schooner and the stream anchor laid out by the cutter.

But as soon as the cable was hove taut the jerk of the swell bumping the schooner upon the reef snapped the chain; at the same time the bower came home. The small bower was at once let go but this also came home. With the keel bolts and stern post started and the quarter deck torn up, McDonell realised that he could not save his vessel; and, as soon as it was light enough, began the work of making rafts, for the cutter and gig, the only boats, could not hold all the people.

By 7 a.m. a raft was completed, on which fifteen men took their places; whilst Nobbs, the assistant master, took a passenger, Captain West R.E. and his son, and another fifteen men into the cutter.

And now occurred the first of those accidents, which in a wreck mean the difference between life and death. The raft, which was lashed to the port side of the schooner, broke adrift and was swept away to the Southward by the strong wind and current. Nobbs in the cutter immediately went after the raft and caught it; but, with only four oars, found it quite impossible to pull back to the wreck against wind and current. He then with the raft in tow ran along the reef before the wind until an hour later he came up on a sand-bore at the South end of reef. With the cutter leaking so badly that she could hardly be kept afloat and the raft even less seaworthy he determined to land everybody upon the spit of sand; but unable to reach it with the raft, he cast the raft adrift and then landed his people in detachments.

Here he remained until daylight the following morning; the 1st of March. Then, leaving twenty-seven people upon the sand-bank, he set out in the cutter with five men in an attempt to regain the wreck. But with the wind blowing strongly from the North, with his mast and sprit both sprung, and no jib or mizen in the boat, he could not work to windward. With only a little salt pork and two beakers of water he decided to turn tail and run before the wind in the hope of reaching Belize. But the wind was too strong, and for two days the cutter could only scud under bare poles and she passed forty miles to the South of Belize. By this time all in the boat were suffering badly from thirst. However the wind dropped under the land and by noon on Tuesday, the 3rd of March, they were able to make Belize Roads, where they were received aboard his Majesty's eighteen-gun sloop *Fly*.

Meanwhile McDonell had put his sick men aboard the gig and sent her to Belize in charge of a midshipman, named Lockyer. Shortly after leaving the wreck the gig fell in with the cutter and raft and after giving Nobbs his commander's order to return to the wreck, Lockyer transhipped Captain West and his son into the gig. Nothing more was heard of this boat until some days afterwards when she was found washed up on the beach and broken in two some miles South of Belize.

No doubt all her occupants had been drowned in the surf.

---

* Nothing was said in the evidence as to the position of her centre boards. It is probable that if they were up, there was no time or, perhaps, thought to let them go, and thus the shoal schooner had no grip to hold her up to the wind.

With both cutter, raft and gig gone, Lieutenant McDonell set about constructing another raft.

This was finished during the day and made fast to the rocks within the reef; but on the 3rd the weather beginning to moderate, a stronger raft was made from the broken up quarter-deck; and on the 4th it was determined to leave the wreck, all hands being considerably weakened by exposure and want of food, and the lieutenant being in ill-health was specially exhausted.

Just as they were about to push off, their only food, a barrel of bread (hard-tack) was washed away and lost, leaving a beaker, about a third full of rum, as their only sustenance.

The raft was first of all steered towards a small cay, but the current carried it passed.

A sail was then hoisted, and every endeavour was made to reach the sandbore, on which people could be seen walking about.

McDonell was so done up that he had to be held on the raft. After consulting with Malcolm, the clerk, and a passenger named Price, a Honduras merchant, it was determined to steer West.

With nothing to eat and only a small quantity of rum to drink, which was served out at stated intervals, two days passed. At daybreak on the 6th of March, land was sighted ahead, and the following morning at between four and five a.m., the raft was hove up on the beach by the surf.

All hands were dead-beat and they immediately lay down on the sand and went to sleep.

Some hours later, when they awoke, to their amazement Lieutenant McDonell was discovered to be missing. It was supposed that they were upon Ambergris Cay, to the North of Belize. A search was made for their missing commander as well as for food and water; the merchant also declared that there was a plantation on the cay, belonging to one of his friends.

After a hunt in the woods, where they were able to ease their hunger and thirst by coconuts, a return was made to the beach, where everyone lay down exhausted.

Then one of the men declared he could see someone running in the surf about half a mile away. The gunner's mate, Ritchie, went to see and found his Commander quite off his head with delirium, and tried to entice him back, but in vain. Whilst Ritchie went for help, the delirious man disappeared, and he was not found until the following morning, asleep under a parmetta tree. He was fed on coconuts and though very feeble, became clearer in the head directly he was given the coconut milk.

All hands now set out in search of the plantation, Malcolm and Price helping McDonell along.

But in a short while the Lieutenant sank to the ground, being too weak to go any further.

Thereupon they left him, hoping to find the plantation a short way off.

But after walking some distance, they discoverd that they were upon the mainland.

This was Saturday night. Living solely on coconuts the march was continued until Tuesday when Malcolm dropped out, unable to go further.

He was afterwards found by natives and taken to Ambergris Cay; which the men had reached the evening before.

Meanwhile Nobbs with Rogers, the master of the *Fly,* had sailed in the Governor's schooner to pick the men off the sand-bore. These were rescued on Friday the 6th of March, and two seaman were found to be still aboard the wreck.

Pilot boats and exploring parties were next sent along the coast, and in two days one of the boats returned to Belize with the eight men, who had been with McDonell, these reported that they had left their officer, almost dead, in the woods.

Nobbs at once set off in a pilot boat in search of his commander. Beating up outside the breakers of Ambergris Cay, it blew so hard through the night that he could not land. Then with the wind and sea moderating, he landed and for three days searched the coast until he had the happiness of finding his commander, still alive, lying in a hut and being tended by Indians.

The Court Martial fully acquitted McDonell for the loss of the *Firefly,* noon and evening sights having put the schooner twenty-four miles from the reef at 4 p.m. But Malcolm, the clerk, and the men with him were strongly censured for deserting their sick commander.

Nobbs was deservedly commended for his behaviour, but for his resolute action the tragedy might have been far worse. One has to remember that in those days men before the mast considered themselves released from all discipline directly their vessel was abandoned and quite free to take what action they chose, even to disobeying their officers.

Wreck of the *Jackdaw*

The surveying schooner, *Jackdaw,* commanded by Lieutenant Edward Barnett had sailed from Port Royal on March the 8th, 1835 and anchored at the south Cay of the Serrana on the morning of the 10th in order to determine its longitude by observation.

Having taken his sights, Barnett sailed for Old Providence for the same purpose.

During the night the *Jackdaw* was set to the S.W. by a current with the result that at 4.30 the following morning she struck on the reef which extended more than ten miles to the Northward from the island, its length not being allowed for on the Admiralty chart.

A strong wind was blowing, a very heavy surf was breaking on the reef and the weather was hazy. Though the schooner was only five years old and very strongly built like all Sepping's vessels, it was soon seen that there was no chance of salving her.

The weather anchor was let go, the guns thrown overboard, the water started and the masts cut away, then a raft was constructed and with the boats dropped clear of the breakers.

But as the *Jackdaw* continued to hold together inspite of the heavy swell which was boiling in over the reef, Barnett managed to construct another larger raft on which he saved all his astronomical instruments and provisions.

Hardly had this been done before one of the Nassau wrecking sloops arrived on the scene, which landed the *Jackdaw's* crew.

The following morning the eighteen-gun sloop *Gannet* arrived and took the shipwrecked people back to Jamaica.

Skipjack* Captures *Martha

So far the year had been most unpropitious to the schooners, but on Wednesday the 8th of April, 1835 a large Spanish slaver was captured by the *Skipjack,* Lieutenant S.H. Ussher (oldest son of that very distinguished officer, Rear-Admiral Sir Thomas Ussher, K.C.B.)

At 7 a.m. when about thirty miles from the Little Cayman the *Skipjack* sighted a vessel a point on the weather bow, standing to the Westward under stunsails and heading directly for the schooner. However in a little while the stunsails came fluttering down, the stranger hauled to the wind and the chase was on.

By ten o'clock the little *Skipjack* had neared the slaver considerably. An hour later the latter hoisted a very large Spanish ensign and fired two guns to leeward, evidently hoping to intimidate the tiny schooner, not only by her size, but by the weight of her metal.

At 2 p.m. *Skipjack* sent a round from her Long Tom skipping after the chase and this was at once replied to by a broadside of both round shot and grape.

From two until five thirty a running engagement was carried on, then after firing two rounds from her stern chasers, the slaver decided to try and escape, and setting every sail possible, ran for it.

Still firing steadily, the *Skipjack* did not get up until half past ten at night, when running under the slaver's stern, Lieutenant Ussher hailed to know if she had struck.

A sulky reply in the affirmative came back.

This was a relief to the *Skipjack's* crew for they were almost out of powder, having fired away one hundred and forty rounds of shot and no less than four hundred rounds of powder. This must be very nearly a record for a slaver action.

On boarding the prize, she turned out to be the brig *Martha,* an ex coast-guard ship of the Spanish Navy, three times the size of the *Skipjack,* pierced for eighteen guns and mounting six congreve eighteen-pounders and two long twelve-pounders.

She had a crew consisting of captain, three mates, supercargo, doctor and fifty-six men, of whom one man was killed and eight wounded.

As usual in these slaver actions the war schooner had the best of the exchange with only one man slightly wounded and some of her rigging shot away.

The *Martha,* which was one hundred and sixteen feet long and thirty feet in breadth, had taken on board seven hundred and ninety negroes, out of which number one hundred and twenty three had died before she sailed, two hundred and seven had succumbed to dysentery during the forty-three days that she had been on her passage from Loango, leaving four hundred and sixty remaining. These poor wretches, when the firing began, stowed themselves away in the hold amongst the fire-wood, where unfortunately a shot came in and played havoc, one man having his head taken clean off, and a woman her left thigh as well as all one side of her head and face. Indeed a terrible sight met the victors, the slaves were lying about in every direction, thirteen killed in the action, numbers dead besides from dysentery, and a great many miserably mauled by shot with broken bones and torn flesh.

At the beginning of the action the captain of the slaver offered his crew one hundred dollars a man if they fought the *Skipjack* off, and his first intention was to run alongside and pour in a devastating broadside from his eight guns.

The Spaniard was baulked at the outset by the quicker movements of the schooner, but his men fought well until their best gunner was killed in the act of priming his gun, the ship's Long Tom; after which they ran below, leaving the captain, mate and boatswain's mate to secure the guns.

Arachne's Camouflage

Although the R.N. schooners were able to overtake the Cuban slavers, which were almost always the product of Baltimore and therefore excessively hard to catch, hardly a sloop or frigate on the station was capable of this feat, unless it was blowing very hard.

The *Arachne,* which until the advent of the *Columbine,* considered herself the fastest sloop on the station, was forced to adopt guile and camouflage in order to make a capture.

Right at the end of her commission when she was actually homeward bound she captured a slaver in this way. At the beginning of April, 1835, she sailed from Vera Cruz with one hundred thousand dollars in specie on merchants' account. On her way she touched at Havana, but a day or two before reaching that port a sail was sighted.

Suspecting the stranger to be a slaver, Commander Burney, at once started to camouflage his vessel. Her topgallantmasts were sent down, sail shortened, the guns hidden and a large Spanish ensign hoisted at the peak. Under the impression that the *Arachne* was a Spanish packet the slaver, a Spanish polacre schooner, called the *Joven Reyna,* came boldly on until she was under the warships's guns and was thus easily captured.

She proved to have two hundred and fifty six slaves on board, ninety-eight men, ninety-eight boys, thirty women and thirty children.

Having waited six days at Havana in order to see her condemned by the Mixed Commission, Commander Burney sailed for home in triumph.

Serpent and *Sita*

In saying that the slavers could outsail the R.N. sloops, I should perhaps have said the pre-Symondite sloops, for it took a very fast slaver indeed to get away from a Symondite corvette or sixteen-gun brig-sloop. For instance the Symondite sixteen-gun brig *Serpent,* when on a passage from Jamaica to Nassau, overtook and captured off the East end of Cuba an exceedingly fast Spanish slave-schooner, named *Sita,* which was only thirty-nine days out from the coast of Africa and had only lost six out of four hundred slaves.

Racer in a Hurricane

The *Racer,* another Symondite sixteen-gun brig, which had recently arrived on the station, was also successful in capturing a slaver off San Domingo, as indeed was the old eighteen-gun brig, *Cruiser,* this ship, however, had long had a reputation for exceptional speed.

The *Racer,* commanded by Commander James Hope, who afterwards distinguished himself by cutting the chain of the boom, blocking the river Parana, at the battle of Punta Obligado, had the misfortune to be dismasted in a hurricane when on a passage from Belize to Havana between the twenty-first and the twenty-ninth of September 1837.

Here is a terse relation of the experience:—

> "Gale for three days: sail shortened gradually to bare poles. On the 28th near the Grand Cayman gale at E.N.E. increased to a full hurricane.
>
> Noon of 29th Lat. 19°44′ Long. 83°23′. At 7 p.m. hove on beam ends, main mast went; righted with 5½ feet of water in the hold. At 9.30 p.m. again hove on beam ends, foremast went, righted immediately. James Martin and Henry Longmead drowned: C. Gainbridge, boy, and a soldier's child killed. Hold fetched away to leeward. Wreck cleared away. Seven feet of water pumped out. Midnight hurricane at its full height. At 2.30 a.m. of 30th wind veered to E.S.E., still at full force. Noon Lat. 20° 12′ Long. 84° 42′ wind E.S.E. but abated.
>
> October 1, noon Lat. 22° 22′ Long. 85° 36′, in Gulf of Mexico near Cuba: gale abating. Jury masts rigged. Bread spoiled, water lost, supplied from a vessel".

The *Racer* was fitted with *Romney's* main and foremasts and sailed for home, after a terrible finish to a very successful commission.

This was a notable hurricane: at Kingston all vessels were driven from their moorings, whilst on the Gulf coast and at Galveston, vessels were hurled ashore and left high and dry.

Ringdove in the Same Storm

Curiously enough the *Racer's* sister ship the *Ringdove** was not far away from her in this hurricane.

The *Ringdove,* Commander H. S. Nixon, was on the South side of Cuba, to Eastward of Trinidad, when the gale struck her from the Eastward early on the 28th of September. On the 29th wind increasing from East, *Ringdove* scudding to the Westward.

Noon Lat. 21°21′ Long. 82°56′. 30th, hard gale from the East, Lat. 23° 13′ Long. 86° 32′ in Gulf of Mexico.

7.30 p.m. Shipped heavy sea, stove weather ports, washed away the binnacles. Oct. 1st. strong gales, 10 a.m. moderating, set close-reefed main topsail.

Noon, Lat. 23′ 16″ Long. 87′ 34″, wind E.S.E. under main topsail, trysails and fore staysail.

---

* *Ringdove* was launched at Plymouth on June the 18th and *Racer* at Portsmouth on July the 18th. They differed slightly in their dimensions and tonnage as follows:—

	Tons.	Length. Gundeck	Length. Keel	Beam.	Depth.
Ringdove	429	100′ 5″	78′ 9″	32′ 4″	15′ 2″
Racer	431	100′ 8″	78′ 9″	32′ 4¾″	14′ 10″

This was *Ringdove's* second hurricane in one season. Her previous experience is thus described in her commander's letter to Sir Wm. Symonds.

Ringdove at sea. 1837.

Dear Sir,

We sailed from England June 26, to convey the news of the King's death to Barbadoes, which we did by arriving at Barbadoes July 23. Sailed again the 25th. Caught in a hurricane the 26th, which did great mischief at Barbadoes, St. Lucia etc. During it we were battened down, had topgallant yards and masts, jibboom, etc., on deck and scudding eight or nine knots, without a stitch of sail set. We had a small boat astern, which I felt so convinced we should lose, that I was on the point of cutting her away, but thought I would give her a chance, and most beautifully and safely she carried her.

We had a heavy, cross, chopping sea. After blowing in heavy squalls from all points, the gale settled from the Southward. I was glad to scud N. by E. to draw off from the islands.

The bowsprit worked a good deal, but otherwise she never strained a yarn, perfectly delighting me, as well as several old brig sailors on board.

After this we had a long series of light weather: in any other vessel I would have said, a dead calm, but she always kept her head the right way and though the log would have given nothing, we always found she had slipped from twenty to thirty or forty miles in the twenty-four hours.

In six weeks I may say we have been in Europe, Africa (St. Palmas) West Indies and North America (Bermuda).

Believe me, etc.,
H. Stopford Nixon.

Though the West Indian was such a popular station it must be confessed that it had two very serious drawbacks—drawbacks indeed is hardly the word—nightmares would be nearer the truth. The first was the hurricane such as the *Racer* and the *Ringdove* experienced, which might be expected in accordance with the well-known rhyme:—

June too soon
July stand by
August look out you must
September remember
October all over.

The Ravages of Yellow Jack.

The second was yellow jack, the cause of which was far from being suspected in the eighteen-thirties. Yet many captains realised that the best way to combat yellow jack was to get away to sea.

In 1835 the *Forte,* forty-four guns, whilst lying at Vera Cruz was attacked, a large proportion of her ship's company being laid low—As soon as possible she sailed away for Halifax.

The twenty-six-gun corvette, *Vestal,* left Jamaica for Bermuda on April the 28th, having had Captain Jones and nearly every officer and man attacked by the dreaded scourge, so that she had to be manned by supernumeraries in order to get away.

Captain Jones was sixteen days confined to his cabin, but managed to struggle up on deck and do duty when she sailed; and she had lost her surgeon and twenty ranks and ratings before leaving Port Royal.

The Crack *Comus*

In contrast to this sad state of things, the eighteen-gun sloop *Comus,* Commander W. P. Hamilton, arrived home in June 1836 after a four years' commission on the West India station, during which she had been at Jamaica through two sickly seasons without losing a man or indeed having any sickness of any sort aboard. And it was remarked that her crew not only had a most healthy appearance but looked the picture of real happiness when inspected on her arrival at Plymouth.

Perhaps a contemporary newspaper report will give the present seaman some idea of the delight taken in a smart ship by all and sundry during the days of our Wooden Walls.

The following is taken from the Hants. *Telegraph*:—

> "On Wednesday 3rd inst. H.M.S. *Comus* came into Hamoaze. We scarcely remember having seen a more beautiful sight of a British man-of-war under way.
>
> The ship sailed in under her topsails and courses, the topgallant and royal yards being manned; and the sailors, being dressed in white straw hats and duck trousers and shoes, had a very novel and pleasing effect. The Hoe and Mount Wise were crowded with spectators, among whom were a number of old officers expressing their admiration at the general appearance of the *Comus* and the excellent discipline of her ship's company.
>
> She had been anchored five days in the Sound waiting for orders, during which time she was visited daily by numerous parties of ladies and gentlemen, from whom the Captain received the most flattering compliments on the superior arrangements of all on board.
>
> On her passing Mount Wise, Lord Amelius Beauclerk and other naval officers remarked:—
>
> 'What a beautiful specimen of a man-of-war!'
>
> On Thursday his lordship, as port admiral, accompanied by his nephews, inspected the *Comus,* when the yards were manned and his lordship's reception on board was conducted in a manner which exhibited the perfect discipline of the ship.
>
> After the men had gone through the gun exercise and a number of manoeuvres on the yards and masts, his lordship expressed his entire approbation in the following words:—
>
> Captain Hamilton, I have not for many a year seen a ship more efficient or in higher order and discipline than yours, a circumstance which reflects the greatest credit on you and your officers, who, as well as the crew, appear to have their duty and business at their fingers ends. I shall take care (as is my duty) to represent the high state of discipline to the Lords Commissioners of the Admiralty: and I have no doubt that every person will receive from the Admiralty that encouragement, which is so highly merited and which ever will be the greatest advantage to our King and country".

The state of the *Comus* was wholly due to her commander: for he had had no lieutenant since February and had been carrying on duty with an acting master and one mate.

By the year 1837 there were no less than six of the sixteen-gun Symondite brig-sloops on the West Indian station, namely *Racer* (Commander J. Hope) *Ringdove* (Commander H.S. Nixon) *Serpent* (Commander R.L. Warren) *Sappho* (Commander T. Fraser) *Snake* (Commander A. Milne) and *Wanderer* (Commander T. Bushby).

The *Pickle, Pincher* and *Skipjack* had also been reinforced by the six-gun schooner, *Hornet,* one of the four Sepping designed schooners, which were built in 1831-1832.

Slavers Wrecked in the Bahamas

In spite of so many really fast cruisers, the captures of slavers in the West Indies during 1837 were far from satisfactory.

On the other hand the Bahama wreckers had a very busy and prosperous time owing to the unusual number of slavers, which were wrecked in the Bahamas during the year.

The first of these was a tiny schooner of under fifty tons, named the *Piombeter,* which had one hundred and eighty slaves on board, 'mostly fine young lads of under fifteen years of age'.

In July the Spanish schooner, the *Esperanza,* with three hundred and twenty negroes was wrecked, only two hundred and twenty being saved. This was a bad case, reported to the African Institution, for the most callous murdering of the miserable Africans—'when any of the slaves refused their food or became sick, the boatswain's mate, with a weighty club, struck them on the back of the neck, when they fell and were thrown overboard'.

On the 27th of October a Portuguese schooner was wrecked on the shore of Harbour Island, with over two hundred slaves on board—only fifty-three were saved, the greater number being drowned in their chains in the hold, whilst sixty bodies were washed ashore and twenty which were all fettered together were picked up dead floating in the harbour mouth.

But in some cases not a negro was saved.

The Spanish schooner, *Estella,* stranded on the Pedro Shoals; her crew escaped ashore leaving the three hundred Africans on the wreck.

On the news reaching Port Royal, the twenty-gun sloop, *Nimrod,* (Commander J. Fraser) and the schooner *Hornet* (Lieutenant H. Baillie) were sent post haste to the rescue. They found that the schooner had gone to pieces and every negro had perished.

There was also a very terrible case of a pirate slaver in 1837. This was the *Esplorador,* which sailed from Havana on June the 13th, 1837.

After failing to find a cargo in the Mozambique, this vessel, by pirating other slavers, made up a cargo of five hundred negroes. But off the Cape she encountered a two day gale during which hatches had to be battened down.

When the hatches were opened there were three hundred dead in the hold, suffocated!

American-Built Slavers at Havana

In order to be able to outsail the new Symondite cruisers the Havana merchants about the middle of the thirties began asking the Baltimore builders for clippers with still finer lines than any previously sent afloat.

The American flag was also used by Cuban slavers as a protection against the British sloops.

Here are a few extracts from the reports of the Havana Commissioners:—

"During the months of August and September (1836) there arrived here for sale from the United States several new schooners, some of which were already expressly fitted for the slave trade.

The *Emanuel* and *Dolores* were purchased, and have since left the port (we believe with other names) on slaving expeditions, under the Spanish flag. But, to our astonishment and regret, we have ascertained that the *Anaconda* and *Viper,* the one on the 6th and the other on the 10th current (October) cleared out and sailed from hence for the Cape de Verde Islands under the American flag. These two vessels arrived in the Havana, fitted in every particular for the Slave Trade; and took on board a cargo which would at once have condemned, as a slaver, any vessel belonging to the nations that are parties to the equipment article".

"Two American vessels, the *Fanny Butler* and *Rosanna,* have proceeded to the Cape de Verde Islands and the Coast of Africa, under the American flag upon the same inhuman speculation".

Consul Tolmé, also, wrote from Havana on the 11th of April, 1839:—

> "There appears more than ever I knew it before, an eagerness on the part of the Slave Traders to purchase fast-sailing American-built vessels and to send them out to Africa under the flag of the United States".

Not only was the flag being used, but captains and crews were being obtained from the United States.

On the 28th of October, 1837, a slaver schooner named the *Invincible* was wrecked in the Bahamas which had fitted out at Baltimore, whose captain was a native of Florida named Potts, and three-fourths of whose crew were Americans.

Naval Officers Visit Havana Slavers

Captain Sir Richard Grant of H.M.S. *Cornwallis* wrote the following interesting account of the slavers and slave barracoons at Havana to the *Nautical Magazine* in 1839.

"The slave vessels are intersperced among the shipping on the Cabana shore and are easily distinguished by their very neat and rakish appearance.

At the time I write there are upwards of twenty ships, brigs, brigantines and a fanciful variety of schooners; scarcely a day passes but some of them slip out always under the Spanish flag, and others having run their cargo, hoist the Portuguese colours, and boldly come in. The two largest and finest are the ships, *Venus* and *Socorro,* each about three hundred and fifty tons. They are much masted, in fact all legs and wings: I was surprised at their immense topsails. They are two beautiful corvettes, pierced for twenty guns, fitted in most costly style and well found.

The *Venus* is as sharp as our river steamers, and looks rather ticklish: her first voyage she made in three months and fourteen days, landing close to the Havana eight hundred and thirty slaves: it was considered the best speculation that had been for a considerable time and well rewarded the proprietors, who made the captain a present of twenty thousand dollars.

(Buxton, quoting a private letter, wrote:—

> 'The *Venus,* said to be the sharpest clipper-built vessel ever constructed at Baltimore, left that place in July, 1838, and arrived at Havana on the 4th of August the following. She sailed from thence, in September, for Mozambique: there she took in a cargo of slaves, being all this time under the flag of the United States. On the 7th of January, 1839, she landed eight hundred and sixty negroes near Havana, under Portuguese colours: and on the 9th these blacks with twelve hundred more, were seen at one of the Barracoons, within two miles of that city 'exposed for sale, and presenting a most humiliating and melancholy spectacle').

The *Socorro* arrived, having landed near Port Mariel, five hundred and seventy slaves, upwards of two hundred having died on the passage.

I went on board just as she anchored, she was very filthy, had thrown her guns overboard or landed them. The captain, who was a Frenchman, said they had had very bad weather. He was chuckling at having eluded the *Nimrod,* which vessel came in about an hour after him; she had two chronometers by Barraud and Arnold, excellent compasses, indeed, no expense is spared to ensure speed and safety.

An ex-lieutenant of our service is said to have made several very successful voyages.

The number of slave vessels have much increased within the last three years, and each vessel is required to make more voyages. What with insurances and the small number captured as compared with the great number fitted out, the loss and check is trifling; on an average I was informed by a Spanish merchant, whose authority may be relied on, our captures do not amount to more than three per cent".

In 1836 whilst the *Champion,* eighteen guns, Commander G.V.S. King, was lying at the Havana awaiting the condemnation of a schooner she had captured, ten slavers arrived in the port, having discharged their negroes at different places round the coast, and the slave traders openly admitted that twenty more were expected.

One of her officers and an American quaker actually visited the slavers in Havana and an account of this was given by the member of the Society of Friends to the *Colonization Herald*, Philadelphia.

This was in July, 1836, and he wrote:—

> "In company with an English Naval officer, I made a vist across the bay to several of these slave-vessels. We were permitted to walk over them, but no particular attention was paid to us; on the contrary, we were looked upon with suspicion and received short and unsatisfactory answers to our questions in general; all attempts to enter into conversation with those on board appeared useless.
>
> With one, however, we were more successful: an old weather-beaten Spaniard was walking the deck; although an old pirate, his expression of countenance was fine: taking a seat under the awning on the quarter-deck, offering him a bundle of cigaritas, and lighting one ourselves, by

> degrees we induced him to enter into conversation, and, in the course of one hour or more, I learned from him some horrid truths.
>
> He told us that, in four voyages, he had brought, in the vessel in which we were, sixteen hundred human beings: his was a fortunate vessel, and seldom lost more than half a dozen voyage: once, however, he told us he was not so lucky; a malignant disease broke out on board soon after leaving the coast: and out of three hundred taken on in Africa, but ninety-five were landed, more dead than alive, on the island.
>
> The material, such as handcuffs, chains and even the lower decks, are taken out and are fitted up on the coast of Africa. We saw the apertures in the decks to admit the air, and, as we were leaving the brig in our boat alongside, the captain exultingly told us that he knew we were officers of the British sloop of war, pointing to the *Champion,* which was riding at anchor at a little distance from us: 'but' added he 'you are welcome. I yesterday showed your captain (meaning of the *Champion*) all over my trim vessel. I have nothing to conceal—you dare not touch me here; and outside (with an expressive shrug of the shoulders) you may catch me if you can".

With regard to the new use of the American flag by Cuban slavers, this was due to the new equipment treaty concluded between Spain and Great Britain in 1835. The juggling with flags and papers, which at one time was the other way about, was started by Trist, the American consul at Havana.

But the success of the *Venus* under American papers aroused such indignation in the Down East anti-slavery states that in December, 1839, President Van Buren announced in Congress that foreign slavers were trading under the protection of the American flag and papers, and he even sent two U.S. cruisers out to the coast to check the practice.

The *Venus* was described as 'a splendid frigate' and 'one of the fastest sailing vessels ever built'. Nevertheless the old eighteen-gun brig, *Pelican,* built as far back as 1812, gave her such a run for her money that in order to escape she had to throw her deck cargo and spare spars overboard.

If the slave trade of Cuba flourished through the eighteen-thirties, it was not through any lack of effort on the part of the Royal Navy.

As a single successfully run cargo meant a fortune to the lucky owner, it was not surprising that gambling in negroes became almost a craze in Havana.

It was a paradoxical anomaly that the greater the success of the R.N. cruisers, the greater the profits of the slave trader; for as captures increased so the price of slaves increased—indeed the ratio between the two was so marked that many a Brazilian and Cuban merchant in black ivory blessed the Royal Navy.

Naturally many easily discourage Britons declared that the Royal Navy was doing more harm than good and that the amount of money spent in maintaining anti-slavery squadrons could be better used in bringing diplomatic and economic pressures to bear.

This argument was easily countered by the answer that every legitimate means, whether it was diplomatic, economic or simply armed force, should be used to stop the abominable traffic.

To return to the West Indian station. Every year the Service made greater and greater efforts with more and more ships, but it was only on the coast of Africa that slave catching was the sole duty of a cruiser.

On the W.I. and N.A. station there was a great deal of troop carrying to do; and, at a time when the controversy between the supporters of the new surveyor, Sir William Symonds, and his detractors raged high, every opportunity was taken for sailing trials.

Reports of commanding officers on the sailing capabilities of their commands poured into the Admiralty whilst every post brought letters to the surveyor containing voluminous statements in favour of his ships with log notes which were often so one sided that the truth was generally hard to come by.

Work of the *Vestal*

Nevertheless these service reports and letters are of tremendous value from an historical point of view for anyone interested in the last days of the Wooden Walls. Let me give an example.

After recruiting the health of her men at Bermuda, the *Vestal* raced the flagship *President* to Halifax, and from there returned home. Here are extracts from the letter of Captain W. Jones to Sir William Symonds, dated the 31st of December, 1836.

> "It is with a view of showing the utility of this ship as a vessel of war, that the following abstract of her service, during the year 1836, is respectfully submitted:—
>
> After being docked and refitted at Sheerness, in January, the *Vestal* returned to her station in the West Indies, arriving at Barbadoes the 4th of March.
>
> April 14th. Conveyed the Governor-General, Sir Lionel Smith, and his family from Barbadoes to Grenada.
>
> April 26th. Embarked at Barbadoes the 14th Regiment, consisting of four hundred and twelve officers, men and followers with their heavy baggage and landed them at St. Christopher's on the 28th.
>
> May 1st. Embarked at St. Kitt's the 67th regiment, consisting of four hundred and twenty one officers, men and followers, with their heavy baggage and landed them at Demerara on the 10th.
>
> May 14th. Embarked at Demerara the 86th regiment, consisting of four hundred and seventy two officers, men and followers with their baggage, and landed them on the 17th at Barbadoes.
>
> By these removals of troops, much valuable time and a heavy expense in transports was saved to the Crown. In the beginning of June, the *Vestal* was employed on a mission to St. Thomas's and Porto Rico, by which thirty-five negro British subjects were redeemed from slavery.
>
> 28th July to 3rd August—conveyed Commodore Superintendent Sir Thomas Ussher and his family from Bermuda to Halifax. 20th August—Left Halifax to cruise off Grenada, when, on 20th September, captured the *Negrinha,* Portuguese schooner, with a cargo of three hundred and thirty six slaves.
>
> 28th September—Captured the *Emprisa,* Spanish brigantine, with a cargo of four hundred and thirty four slaves.
>
> Same Date—Captured the *Phoenix,* Portuguese brigantine with a cargo of four hundred and eighty four slaves. Being a total, within eight days, of three fast sailing vessels and one thousand two hundred and fifty four slaves".

When Portuguese slavers were captured in the West Indies, the slaves were landed in the islands, but the vessels had to be taken to Sierra Leone to be adjudicated.

The *Negrinha* and the *Phoenix,* after their slaves had been landed at Grenada, were sent to the coast, each in the charge of a midshipman.

The difference of outlook between a Portuguese slave trader and a British naval officer is well shown by the following anecdote.

Anecdote of the *Negrinha*

The *Negrinha* was a small schooner of less than one hundred tons. Crammed with negroes to her utmost capacity, illness was rife and the stench, which rose from her 'tween decks was indescribable. Many of the dying blacks were brought on deck after the capture. One of these in the last stages of dysentery lay on the after locker by the taffrail. It was a night of heavy dew with the moon in her last quarter, shedding a cold light upon the deck of the slaver.

Shivering with the cold, the naked negro drew the Portuguese flag, which was lying upon the locker, over his emaciated body.

The Portuguese mate, noticing this use of his national flag, at once gave the dying negro a kick and dragged the bunting from him.

The midshipman immediately had the English ensign unbent from the signal halliards and placed over the poor creature—and 'instead of dying a slave under the flag of Portugal, he died a free man sheltered by the glorious banner of old England'.

Until the slaves were landed, owing to want of space, the prize crew had to follow the regulations of the Portuguese in managing the negroes.

Method of Feeding Negroes Aboard a Slaver

The following account will give a vivid idea of meal time aboard a slaver:—

"The negroes were fed three times a day on rice and palm oil. On these occasions they came on deck and were placed in groups of ten: then the cooks went round and emptied a bucket of rice on the deck in the middle of each group and another cook poured a cupful of oil on the top of it. If one of these hungry creatures dared to touch a grain of rice before the signal was given, the boatswain (Portuguese) flew at him and nearly flayed him.

When all was ready the captain gave a signal, and then the slaves uttered a cry that had a most unearthly sound. The deep bass of the men together with the shrill treble of the women's and children's voices, produced such a discordant cry of misery that must have reached to heaven! What it was for I could not make out, unless it was meant for grace! However, upon another signal being given, these half-starved wretches began to feed by stuffing handfuls of rice into their mouths, to the great danger of choking themselves, and as the heap of rice became less, so their motions became accelerated, until this extraordinary repast ended in a regular scramble (Note. [*Nautical Magazine* July 1862]).

A Perilous Passage

The midshipman in charge of *Negrinha* succeeded in navigating the schooner safely to Sierra Leone in spite of the fact that his navigation was very hazy. (The day's work which every midshipman had to send in daily to his captain, was usually fudged or copied from the second master).

The First Lieutenant lent him a sextant, in place of his own ancient quadrant and the surgeon lent him an old silver watch, which after it had had a fall on the deck would only go for five hours. The log line carried away on the 2nd day out; the schooner was so rotten that chain plate bolts, could be drawn out by hand; her water casks leaked; her sails split in every squall; her seams opened as she pitched, and let the water in; the pump was, of course, out of order, the fore trestle-trees broke off and let the topmast down with a run; the tiller broke short off in the rudder head; but after two months out of sight of land, the mid made a good landfall in the Cape de Verds; and having kept the rotten ship together with only such tools as a seaming needle and a small axe, he deserved much credit for safely making his port.

Sailing Performances of *Vestal, Snake* and *Ringdove*

That the *Vestal* could catch a slaver without much trouble is not surprising, for she certainly could sail.

Here is an extract from the letter of her captain referring to a passage from Rio to Montevideo, when she beat the *Racer* by eleven hours, the *Curacoa* by two days and a half and the Seppings schooner, *Spider* by more than a week:—

> "She walks along to the astonishment of everyone, twelve point seven knots under royals, wind two points abaft the beam; forty-eight and a half in four hours, under the same circumstances; two hundred and seventy two in twenty four hours, without a struggle, under royals, wind the same: four hundred and forty four in thirty-nine hours, wind the same; under topgallant sails, double-reefed fore and mizen and single-reefed main topsails and fore topmast studding sail, wind a-beam thirteen point six and thirteen for six successive hours; and yet I am told here the *Vestal* class can't sail!"

At the end of her commission under Captain Jones the *Vestal* came home from Halifax to Spithead in thirteen days, arriving October the 10th, 1837.

The Bishop of Nova Scotia, Sir Thomas Ussher, and their families were passengers aboard and it was a fine weather passage all the way.

Amongst Captain's letters in 1837, here are extracts from those of Commander A. W. Milne, H.M. brig-sloop, *Snake,* and of Commander H. Stopford Nixon, H.M. brig-sloop *Ringdove.*

Milne wrote from Port Royal on the 16th of December 1837:—

> "I have the satisfaction in, now, not only praising her good qualities in every way, but can adduce ample proof, from our having captured two slavers. One was the *Arrogante,* Portuguese brigantine, of about two hundred tons, American-built: and the other the *Matilda,* a Spanish two-topsail schooner, one hundred and ninety eight tons, and also of American construction. The former we caught running free, with a fresh breeze in squalls from the north: and falling calm, we had recourse to sweeps to finish the business, with the aid of the long gun.
>
> The *Matilda,* we cut off, running on shore, and hauled his wind, when we rapidly closed with him.
>
> We also chased, last June, a two-topsail schooner, and beat two days in succession when on a wind, closing with him at dark; but the wind changing brought him right ahead, and both of us before the wind. We ran this way for twenty hours, during which time he gained about two miles, and we lost him in the dark, after a thirty hours' chase and run of three hundred and sixty miles.
>
> We have found *Snake* answer beyond our expectation in every way,—her best point, about one point free; and maintaining her sailing with the wind. Her best trim is when having about six weeks to a month's provisions on board; then her draught is about eighteen inches by the stern."

Nixon also wrote from Jamaica in December, on the 24th to be exact:—

> "I have lately had an interesting chase after a Spanish man-of-war and a slaver brigantine, *La Vigilante,* claiming to be under the other's convoy; but whom I detained.
>
> *Ringdove* never pleased me so much, going free, before. We came in here a few days after, without grog for the day and but four day's provision and a little water: so she was flying light, and two feet ten inches by the stern.
>
> We have had great chasing and been beat by nothing but one light brigantine dead before it: yet the two vessels we have detained are only worry and annoyance. I enclose you a copy of my correspondance about the last, and a blood-thirsty attempt to assassinate my boat's crew. I am off to Carthagena tomorrow and expect to meet the Admiral and all the squadron here in February".

Pearl Captures Two Slavers

The lucky cruiser in 1838 was the corvette *Pearl,* which, it will be remembered, had been built by Sainty on the enlarged lines of Lord Anglesea's famous yacht, and was noted for her unusual speed when off the wind.

She was commanded on this, her third commission, by Lord Clarence Paget, a son of the famous Marquis.

When off Havana the *Pearl* overtook and captured the Spanish brig, *Opposicao,* with six hundred slaves on board, and this led to the capture of a second slaver, named the *Vengador.*

Paget put a new stratagem in.o operation. Let me quote his own words:—

> "Having some knowledge of the language, I persuaded the Captain (of the *Opposicao)* to give me information of another large slaver not far off, and I also obtained their private signals from him; so I put a prize crew on board and gave orders that if they saw a suspicous vessel they were to make the private signal:—'wish to communicate'.
>
> The next day I observed them make the preconcerted signal, whereupon the vessel bore down to them, and they summoned her to surrender.
>
> Unfortunately, however, she had landed five hundred slaves in the night. I took her along with the brig into Havana, where they were condemned and my share of the prizes was six hundred pounds".

The slaves were no longer landed in Cuba as the British Government were far from satisfied with the so-called Spanish indenture system; and so the liberated negroes had to be taken to Nassau, New Providence.

On his way to Nassau, Paget sailed in company with the French line-of-battle ship, *Hercule,* which had the Prince de Joinville on board, and the new corvette, *La Favorite*, considered a very fast sailer.

The opportunity was taken to try rate of sailing between the *Pearl* and *La Favorite* for two days in the Bahama Channel.

In this the *Pearl* had much the best of it. On the second day out, Paget was invited to dine with the Prince. Whilst they were smoking after dinner in the stern gallery the officer of the watch came down and reported the Bahama lights showing ahead. Paget at once advised standing off the land on the port tack, but the old captain, Cazy, of the *Hercule* decided to stand on. This decision soon had Paget uneasy and jumping into his boat, he hurried aboard the *Pearl,* where he found his master anxiously awaiting his return before going about.

The lights of the Frenchmen were soon lost to sight; but all through the night the *Pearl* was kept standing off and on in the same place making due allowance for the Northerly current.

When day broke there were the Frenchmen hull down with sails furled and topgallant mast on deck, evidently aground on the reef.

Paget at once made sail to their assistance. Through the maze of coral the corvette was conned from the foreyard. She found the *Hercule* on the ground with the *Favorite* standing by.

The *Pearl* let go both anchors as close as she could get to the stranded battleship and prepared to take her stream cables through the stern ports to the latter's aid. However, luckily, it was quite calm and at high water the *Hercule* floated off. Years after the Queen of the French thanked Lord Clarence Paget for coming to the assistance of her son.

Pincher Capsizes off the Owers

On the 6th of March, 1838, a sad tragedy reduced the West Indian Bermuda-built schooners by one. The *Pincher* had been sent home to pay off and incidentally to have her lines taken off.

She had just been recommissioned by Lieutenant-Commander T. Hope, and was working round to Portsmouth from Sheerness, which she left on Sunday the 4th of March.

Between six and seven on the evening of the 6th when working to windward off the Owers in company with the *Volage,* twenty-eight guns, she was overtaken by a violent squall. The *Volage,* which had her head to the Northward on the port tack, was caught aback; but the *Pincher,* under a press of sail on the starboard tack, lay down, filled and sank, with all on board. The *Volage,* as soon as she noticed that the schooner had disappeared, proceeded to the spot, but by this time it was dark and all she did was to fire a gun and burn a blue-light, and she did not even lower a boat before resuming her course to Spithead.

It was not until Monday, the 12th instant, that anything further was done. On that date the Cowes pilot boat *Neptune,* discovered the main-boom of the *Pincher* sticking, jaws upward, out of the water about five miles S.S.W. of the Owers Lightship. The jaw-rope had evidently broken allowing the jaws to rise though the boom was still held by the main sheet and topping-lifts.

The pilots at once reported their discovery to the port admiral. The second master attendant of the Dockyard was sent to the scene with a diver, and the *Pincher* was discovered lying on her port side in fourteen fathoms of water, with her sails set, sheets belayed, hatches open and nine corpses—one still in his hammock, below decks. Her hold was, of course, half full of mud, but her hull and spars were uninjured. She was successfully lifted and towed into Portsmouth harbour. She was never recommissioned but put in the sale list.

Last Days of *Skipjack*

Let us now turn to the *Skipjack.* On the promotion of Lieutenant Ussher in March, 1836, Lieutenant-Commander John James Robinson was given the command. This officer had already had considerable experience in hunting slavers. It will be remembered that he had served as mate aboard the *Dryad,* Commodore Hayes and in the *Fair Rosamond* at the capture of the *Regulo* and *Rapido,* being made acting-commander of that schooner for the remainder of her commission. In the West Indies he had already served in the *Vernon,* Cockburn's first flagship, the *Despatch,* sixteen guns, and the *Forte,* forty-four guns.

He did not, however, have many opportunities of catching slavers in the *Skipjack,* as the little schooner was used as a tender by the Admiral, and attended him to Bermuda and Halifax.

In August, 1838, we find *Skipjack* doing fishery patrol. On the 21st of that month she brought an American schooner, found trespassing in Canadian waters, into St. Andrew's

Robinson was succeeded in September, 1839, by Lieutenant Henry Wright, another experienced officer, who had served since 1831 on the West Indian station in the *Fly, Gannet, Racehorse* and *Vestal.*

Wright distinguished himself by capturing the Portuguese brigantine, *Ulysses,* in August, 1839.

The slaver had on board a crew of one hundred and fifty men and five hundred and thirty five slaves, a big opponent for a one hundred ton schooner.

In March 1841 Wright, having been nearly nine years in the West Indies, asked to be relieved on account of ill health. He was succeeded by Lieutenant A.C. May from the *Pilot.* This officer had not had such a long experience of the station as his predecessors and he was new to slave catching.

In June 1841, when the *Skipjack* was cruising on the North Coast of Cuba, May was informed by the master of a Scottish brig that he had been boarded by a pirate on the previous day. The Scot had evidently been bribed by the merchants of Havana to give false information. This was a common trick when slavers were due.

May fell into the trap and bore away in search of the pirate; and within twenty-four hours of *Skipjack's* departure two large slave brigs ran in and landed their cargoes.

May returned to Jamaica to reprovision in disgust. *Skipjack* sailed again with passengers for the Spanish Main. The weather was bad, the sky overcast and May got twelve miles out in his reckoning, with the result that, after grazing the rocks on Point Pedro, the *Skipjack* stranded on June the 31st on the S.W. point of the Grand Cayman.

Though her passengers and crew were saved, the little schooner became a total loss.

The Saucy *Pickle*

Of the three beautiful schooners, built at Bermuda in 1826, there now remained only the *Pickle.* She continued to weather out the squalls of the Caribbean and the wild gusts of the North Atlantic until 1848, when she disappeared from the Navy List. In all probablility she was sold out of the Service at Jamaica, being by that time pretty loose in her frame and leaky in her seams.

The *Pickle* seems to have been generally lucky in her commanders and in the West Indies had the reputation of being a happy ship. The life, indeed, aboard a tiny war schooner in such a paradise for cruising as the West Indies with the ever present excitement of the hunt after slavers and pirates, was much to be envied.

Seamen were allowed to volunteer for service in the West Indian schooners, and at the end of three years could take their discharge. There were men in the *Pickle* who served on and on like her clerk, J. Findlay.

A long and typical man-of-war's man's stave was composed in honour of the little schooner, and as this gives the true tang of the old Wooden Wall days, and reflects the usual outlook of the old time bluejacket, I give it in full.

The Saucy *Pickle*

Come all ye seamen stout and bold,
And listen to my story,
Of a little 'mudian craft, I'm told,
Port Royal's pride and glory.
About her hull she's tight and strong,
Though pretty, she's not fickle
The little craft t'which I belong
I calls the Saucy *Pickle*

Oh! we've a cook and a gunner too,
Likewise a boatswain's mate, sir!
And officers besides the crew
But they're among the great, sir!
But as for me and many more
To whom Fortune has been sad, sir,
We must clap a stopper on our jaw,
Or we'll catch the cat, by gad, sir.

Oh, we've as fine a gun on board
As ever hove a shot, sir;
And if a pirate we should board,
We'll show them British sport, sir.
We'll sink, burn or destroy them, boys,
On any tack, we vow, lads;
Long Tom he will annoy them, boys,
Abaft, abeam, or bow, lads!

Small arms we have in store besides,
The Dons for to amuse, sir;
If not content with our broadsides,
We'll show them we can use, sir,
Our cutlasses and bayonets bright
May vie with any crystals;
And if you wish to strike a light,
There's some muskets, boys, and pistols.

You'd laugh to see us rank and file
Like 'sodgers' on the deck, sir!
While officers, without a smile
Report that 'all's correct,' sir.
'Attention' first, then 'bayonets fix,'
Then 'shoulder arms' and 'slope them',
'Examine arms', 'right face', my bricks,
'Lodge arms' and then 'dismiss them'.

What'er you do or say, you'll mind
You're watched like any dog, sir;
they're glad if any fault they find,
To say, 'I'll stop your grog, sir'.
But after this I'll say no more
What punishment's awaiting;
Stand clear, my lads, of the cat's claw
And damn me, 'ware the grating.

Now three years full I've been and more
In this ere blessed bark, sir
Now I've a right to go on shore
And have a jolly lark, sir.
And now my time it is run out
I'll lay hold of the tiller:
My helm's a lee, I stand about
So goodbye to Andrew Miller.*

Her Commanders Since 1830

The following is a list of *Pickle's* commanders after her recommissioning in England in 1830.

1831	Thomas Taplin
1832	E. Stopford
1833	C. Bagot
1834-7	A.G. Bulman
1837-9	Philip Hast
1839-40	H. Holland
1841-3	J.B. Montresor
1843-6	J.A. Bainbridge
1846-7	H. Bernard

Most of these officers were old experienced lieutenants. One of them, Christopher Bagot, came to grief whilst commanding the *Pickle,* being dismissed the Service 'for occasioning the death of a marine by negligently firing a carronade before the deceased had time to get from before the muzzle of it,'. Here is a tragedy in three lines!

Bulman left the *Pickle* to command the *Fair Rosamond.* Hast retired from the R.N. and joined the Royal Mail Steam Packet Company, commanding one of their early steamers for years.

Copper Key First Lieutenant

For the commands of Holland and Montresor, I am able to draw on the latter's memoirs and the letters of Admiral Sir Astley Cooper Key, and am thus able to give a clear picture of the life aboard an R.N. schooner in the West Indies, with all its excitements and hardships—such a life as any naval officer would give much to experience in these days of science and mechanics.

When Cooper Key, a midshipman of the *Cleopatra,* arrived at Port Royal as one of the prize crew of the Portuguese slaver schooner, *Louisa,* caught outside St. Jago de Cuba with two hundred and eighty slaves by the frigate, in January 1840, he was so delighted by the novel experience, that he determined to try and get into a tender for a cruise.
Then, on February the 5th, 1840, the *Pickle* arrived and the Admiral gave Holland leave to fill the place of his second in command from the mates or midshipmen of the ships in port.

By the good offices of Frank Denison, the junior lieutenant of the *Cleopatra,* Holland was persuaded to select young Cooper Key. Captain Stephen Lushington of the *Cleopatra* also agreed to the midshipman going to the *Pickle* for a three months' cruise until May. The youngster must have been a favourite with his captain, for we read in a letter home of the mid's—"He gave me a champagne dinner, plenty of good advice, and duff".

And here is an extract from Cooper Key's first letter after joining the *Pickle*:—

"If you knew what an excellent man Holand is, you would not mind my going with him. In the first place, he is a perfect gentleman, and has two thousand pounds a year: then he is

* 'Andrew Miller' was the old Bluejacket's term for a man-of-war.

> a strictly religious and steady man, and a very good officer and sailor: he behaves to me as if I was his son. I am the only mid on board, therefore I am regular first-lieutenant, and carry on all the duty, which he does not interfere with.
>
> .... Holland has introduced me to all the captains and commanders in the harbour, and they asked me to every party. Meanwhile I am hard at work all day, from 5 a.m. to sunset, rigging the schooner, which I am doing all myself—and pretty hard work it is, I can assure you. We are refitting our rigging and we sail in a fortnight in search of vessels, engaged in the unlawful traffic of human beings".

On the 9th of March Key wrote:—

> "Here we are now, all ready for sea in the schooner, and we sail tomorrow morning at daylight for a three months' cruise. Lots of slavers knocking about now, and some larger than ourselves, so we stand in chance of an action. Would that not be splendid?"

The *Pickle's* cruising ground was the S.W. coast of Cuba. We are told that her rakish, piratical look frightened many a ship into headlong flight, but she had no luck with slavers during the cruise. The chief relaxation of a naval officer has always been a sport of some sort, and the Isle of Pines provided Holland and Cooper Key with the chance of a nice mixed bag of game consisting of wild oxen, pig, pigeons and parrots.

Holland was well provided with a shot gun and a Westley Richards double-barrelled rifle, and Key learnt that wild pig is a quarry worthy of any hunter.

He only had one chance of capturing a slaver. On the evening of the 23rd of April, whilst the *Pickle* lay at anchor in the track of the slaver's usual course, the dark shadow of a ship approaching before the wind was sighted.

Then, as she came nearer, the 'racial effluvium' of the negro assailed the nostrils of the *Pickle's* crew, and put them on the qui vive.

A musket was fired, but the slaver held her course. The long six-pounder was next fired and there was just light enough to distinguish the tumbling down of the stranger's topsail yard.

There was no time to get the *Pickle* under way, but the breeze was light, so into the schooner's gig jumped Holland, Key and ten bluejackets.

Though the gig pulled after the chase until daylight, it was no use, the slippery slaver managed to sneak out of sight during the darkness and there only remained Key's boyish letter in memory of the incident. This, I think, is worth quoting as showing the spirit which animated the Service in the days of our Wooden Walls.

> "If we had come up with her that night what a glorious fight we should have had! Holland would have been sure to have been promoted and so would I directly I had passed. It would have been a glorious cutting out expedition—only our ten men against at least thirty or forty on board the slaver. I can answer for it, they would not have beat us off. How glorious! Seeing one's name in the papers for something of that sort! Should not you like it, dearest mama?
>
> I was sharpening my sword in the most butcher-like manner all the chase. It was delightful to see how eager our men were to get up with her....
>
> The morning after the chase, after I came on board, I just laid my head down in the commander's cabin, and I can assure you I slept for ten hours without waking: fine constitution I have for sleep!"

His next letter, on April the 29th, he wrote:—

> "We have had a very amusing chase after a Spanish schooner. She sailed very fast, but we came up with her and found her to be an innocent merchantman. Sail Ho! again: I must go up and see what she is. She is only a small fore and aft schooner working to windward. Oh! how I long to take a slaver, to have command of her! I expect we shall take one before we get in".

On the 20th of May the *Pickle* arrived back in Port Royal harbour and Cooper Key found his own ship, the *Cleopatra,* awaiting him.

> "I left the *Pickle"*, he wrote, "with great credit, I can assure you. The men came aft for leave to give me three cheers as I left. Of course it was not allowed. Mr. Holland has given me an excellent certificate. After the usual form written by the clerk he has written in his own hand: 'Mr Key has had charge of a watch during this period, and I cannot speak too highly of the seaman-like and officer-like manner in which he has performed that, as well as any other duty I have entrusted him with".

A Narrow Escape

Holland did not always have such an effficient second-in-command as young Cooper Key and he used to relate how he made a practice of sleeping with his head on a coil of rope—probably the mainsheet is meant—which could not be moved without his being aware of it. This was owing to a narrow escape which the *Pickle* had had amongst the coral reefs. One night Holland awoke with a strange feeling of uneasiness. It was four bells, 2 a.m., in the dead of a dark night and blowing fresh. He at once went on deck, and there to his horror, showing grey against the blackness of the night, were line upon line of breakers—the schooner was running dead onto a reef.

It was too late to 'bout ship for she was regularly embayed, and, turning to the mate of the watch, he said: "We can do nothing, she must go".

Even as he was speaking, he made out a gap in the long line of surf, just a narrow opening, but wide enough to give the *Pickle* a chance for her life. The helm was put down, the schooner came up to the wind with a clatter of shaking canvas, and, handling like a top, shot head to wind through a narrow pass in the reef. The next moment she was in calm water, with the roar of the breakers beyond her stern. The head sails came down with a run, the anchor was let go and the *Pickle* swung clear of the jagged coral heads.

Lieutenant Holland had a painting done of the incident, of which the illustration is a copy.

Montresor's Delight in the *Pickle*

December 1841 found the *Pickle* at Bermuda, where Holland, being called home on family affairs, handed over the command to his old friend, Lieutenant Frederick Byng Montresor, who at the end of his first week aboard the *Pickle,* wrote in his private journal:—

"Hitherto she is all my fancy painted her.

Almost everybody seems to think that as I have never been in command of so small a craft before I shall soon repent my bargain: I hope not, with all my heart, as in that case it will be a dear one, since, although assisted in every way by her late commander, it has cost me one hundred and twenty pounds to join her".

January the 2nd, 1841, found the *Pickle* under her new commander, on her way from Bermuda to Jamaica.

His lively log gives us a glimpse of the little war schooner in rough weather:—

"I find I have a skittish little lassie to deal with: by Jove, she has been kicking her heels up, and such a quiet little creature as she showed out in harbour too!

It blew hard towards morning yesterday, and I became as sick as if I had never been at sea before!

At seven in the evening I took a glass of hot rum in the gun-room, and, in spite of my responsibility, slept pretty sound. I was awake, however, the whole of the middle watch, and on deck while shortening sail. The wind has shifted to about W.N.W. and the weather, which has been thick and squally, is clearing away into a strong breeze: she is knocking about a good deal and I am far from feeling well".

Three days later Montresor had found his sea legs again, and wrote;—

"January 5th, 1841. My barque in her beauty is bounding before me! Dear little girl! So she is! Eight knots an hour! Only fancy. We have now run into the trade and she has been slapping along with the wind right aft this twenty-four hours.

It certainly makes her 'rather' uneasy, and at one fell swoop this morning she broke all my washing apparatus: but I no longer feel any inconvenience from the motion".

A schooner in the West Indies without her modicum of cockroaches would be an anomaly

Here is a reference to them in Montresor's Journal:—

> "We are overrun with cockroaches: they are almost as big as mice.
>
> I was annoyed yesterday when I saw the rum being measured off for the evening's allowance: it was near the bottom of the cask, and the strainer was soon full of these horrible creatures. After allowing the rum to drip, drip, drip till it would drip no longer, the corporal, who had several times pulled a cockroach from the lower end of the strainer, limb by limb, now put his mouth to it and gave a desperate blow; out flew three or four well-saturated bodies, and the process of measuring recommenced".

On January the 10th, 1841, the *Pickle* anchored off Crooked Island with the object of buying a pig for the ship's company. The chief trader in the island, and old jew, of the name of Moss, was away, so things were to be had at a reasonable price, six dollars for the pig. When the purser asked for a receipt, two small ragged boys, the grandsons of old Moss, were the only persons on the island who were able to sign their names.

The day had passed when the war schooners were kept cruising round Cuba, and under Montresor, the *Pickle* was here, there and everywhere.

At one moment we hear of her arriving at Port Royal in five days from Carthagena with a freight of doubloons. The next she is off to Savanilla.

Santa Martha was another place much frequented by the *Pickle*. Here, Montresor picked up a specie freight worth thirty pounds in his own pocket.

Whilst the *Pickle* was lying at Santa Martha on July the 18th, 1841, the three-gun brigantine, *Charybdis,* arrived with despatches for the SNO at Santa Martha to proceed at once to Carthagena for the protection of British life and property. The Captain of the *Tweed* was SNO but he was away, so off went Montresor, with *Charybdis* under his orders for Carthagena, which was being attacked by General Carmona.

Pickle and *Charybdis* at Carthagena

At Carthagena the *Pickle* remained for the rest of the year with the *Charybdis,* Lieutenant M de Courcy, as her sole consort, in the important work of 'showing the flag' and protecting British lives and property.

Yet the five-gun schooner of one hundred and eighteen tons and the three-gun brigantine of two hundred and thirty seven tons were easily a match for all Carmona's gun-boats and armed schooners.

There were eight gun-boats belonging to the blockading squadron, and in August 1841 they attempted to take possession of an English merchantman, which had run into the port without realising that she was running into a hornet's nest.

Montresor at once acted with vigour; after sending a strongly worded letter of protest to the Federal General, he steered the *Pickle* in with guns loaded and tompions out, rounded to under the stern of the English trader and ordered her to get under way, and follow him out of the port. As the merchantman slowly sailed out, the nimble *Pickle* sailed round and round her with everyone of her popguns trained on the gun-boats, which wisely made no effort to stop her.

Montresor, when all was over, received a reply from the General, who compared himself to the 'unfortunate Napoleon' in having to yield to English injustice!

The next excitement came on November the 20th. At 3.30 a.m. Carmona made an assault on the town. For a time Montresor and his crew watched the proceedings whilst shot flew over their heads; but when cannon ball struck the *Little William,* which was anchored 'a biscuit's throw away', it was thought advisable to take the *Pickle* further off, and as soon as it was daylight, the war schooner escorted the *Little William,* to the Boca Grande anchorage.

But before this occurred a Colonel Rash, commandant of one of the surprised forts, paddled off to the *Pickle* in a canoe. His escape had been a narrow one. Knocked down, cut over the head and stunned on resisting the assault, he had come to, to find the fort in the possession of the enemy.

Springing up, he leaped over the parapet into the sea, swam to a canoe and paddled off to the *Pickle.*

Montresor called him 'the bravest man in Carthagena'.

All day the fighting went on and though Carmona won the suburbs, the citadel held out.

In the afternoon the *Pickle's* gig was sent in under the mate, with the corporal and a guard of marines, five bluejackets and the captain's coxswain, to provide a guard for the house of the British consul.

The undefeatable Colonel Rash insisted on going with them.

There were no more excitements for the *Pickle,* which sailed for Santa Martha on December the 23rd, 1841, leaving the *Charybdis* loaded down with English and American refugees to the number of forty-six men, women and children, whom her unfortunate commander, had to entertain and feed as best he could.

The *Pickle* turned up again on the 29th, having failed to reach Santa Martha. Let me allow Montresor to describe his experience:—

> "Fancy our little schooner beating against half a gale of wind, a sea running mountains high, and a lee current of forty-six miles in twenty four hours.
> Poor little creature! She tried and tried for five days, at the end of which time I found myself twenty-five miles from Carthagena, with my forerigging carried away, and the cap of my bowsprit gone, jib guys, back ropes and martingales, topmast and topgallant staysails adrift, and was obliged to up helm and return.
>
> During this really awful passage our men for five days were never dry, and even my cabin and the gun-room were obliged to be bailed out about twice a day. I slept all the time, when I dared sleep, on a wet bed; but as we had left our marines behind to guard the Consul, and were, besides, short of men, the hands were continually on deck . . . I sail as soon as I am repaired for Jamaica".

No sooner had the *Pickle* left Carthagena than trouble occurred. On February the 6th, 1842, the British brig, *Jane and Sarah,* and sloop, *Little William,* were seized by General Carmona's gun-boats and their passengers, of whom the most important was Colonel Gregg, imprisoned.

On the British Consul failing to obtain their release, young de Courcy wrote a letter to Carmona, but this was not even answered, in fact Colonel Gregg had already been shot.

Unable to obtain any satisfaction, de Courcy acted with vigour. Getting under way he proceeded in his three-gun brigantine to attack Carmona's squadron, which lay at anchor in the port. This consisted of a corvette, a brig and three schooners, which made the mistake of despising the little *Charybdis* and did not even trouble to weigh their anchors. Thus the English vessel was able to pick her way through the flotilla, raking them fore and aft.

The drawing by Lieutenant Warre shows the *Charybdis* being fired upon by all five vessels as she runs in under their sterns.

The first shot cut away the forestay, but otherwise the shooting seems to have been wild and ill-aimed: the brigantine received little damage and did not lose a man.

De Courcy concentrated his fire upon the Carmona flagship; in an incredibly short time the British fire had killed the Commodore and twenty-five men and down came the corvette's flag.

He next turned his attention to the brig, which he sank in five minutes—and it only needed two or three more broadsides to make the schooners surrender; thus in less than half an hour's action de Courcy had accounted for the whole squadron with little harm to himself.

Such a victory immensely increased British prestige, and de Courcy received immediate promotion.

In an affair of this sort where the vanquished greatly out-numbered the victors, it was not easy to take possession.

De Courcy anchored his vessel in the midst of the flotilla until he received instruction from the Admiral.

In the meanwhile he busied himself in refitting and patching up his prizes, and kept them from sinking by covering up their shotholes with sheet lead.

Heaving Down at Port Royal

January 1842 found the *Pickle* back at Port Royal. Here she was hove down in order that her bottom might be examined. This operation, always considered a fine test of seamanship in the old sailing days, did not go with a swing in the little schooner's case.

The boatswain of the yard, who, as a rule, played the leading part in such a ticklish job, held aloof for some reason or other and did not supply his best tackle with the result that the strop of the upper purchase block gave way, there was a surge on the capstan, the schooner fell over, slipped off the wharf, and, to the horror and consternation of her commander and crew, sank to the bottom of the harbour!

However, with the help of hands from the *Comus* and *Magnificent on the following day, she was successfully lifted and lashed alongside the old Galatea.*

At the second attempt to heave her down all went without a hitch. She was next surveyed by the superintendent carpenter, who wrote such a bad report on her condition, that a Board of three carpenters and a master was instructed to pronounce upon her. Their verdict was that she was unseaworthy and rotten almost everywhere.

The order then went forth that the little schooner was to await the new Commander-in-chief before being condemned to be sold.

Whilst awaiting the admiral, the *Pickle* lost the oldest members of her crew. This was the ship's dog, which had been four years in the schooner.

The dog used to swim ashore daily and, after a pasear and visit to his old haunts in Port Royal, would quietly swim off again. It was feared that one day a shark must have caught him.

At the beginning of March, the new Commander-in-chief, Vice-Admiral Sir C. Adam K.C.B. arrived.

He at once poo-poo-ed the survey report and ordered a fresh one. The *Pickle* having been hauled out of the water for the past two months, had dried out nicely and her bottom no longer appeared water-soaked, so the Admiral sent her off to Bermuda for a thorough repair and refit.

The second week in April found her under way again. On April the 19th, 1842, she anchored for the night on her way North under the lee of Castle Island.

Here she found two wrecking schooners from Halifax. Montresor evidently had no use for wreckers, witness the following entry in his journal:—

> "They tell me that these blackguards often allure vessels on shore purposely, in order that they may be the gainers of salvage money, and I believe they sometimes go so far as to take possession of ships and run them aground. A boat with six hands boarded us and the men were much disappointed, I expect, to find thirty fellows on the deck: another boat, which was lurking near, sheered off on hearing the boatswain's pipe—rare rogues all!".

A Launching Luncheon at Bermuda

Towards the end of July 1842, a renovated *Pickle* resplendant in fresh guilding, new paint and varnish lay already for launching. Alongside her was pitched a large tent, in which one hundred 'mudians were gathered to see the Governor's daughter break a bottle of red wine on the sharp stern of the little war schooner.

With the shores knocked away at a sign from the master shipwright, the *Pickle* glided into the water to the sound of hearty cheering.

Then all hands to the number of fifty-six sat down to a typical old time launching lunch, with its toasts, speeches and winding up rollicking dance.

Surrounded by a bevy of the Island's beauties, the happy Commander sang amidst thunderous applause the following touching composition to the Irish air of "Norah Kistal":—

The Saucy *Pickle*

Fill high the glass
The prettiest lass
That ever yet was toasted
Demands my lay;
Then fill, I say,
I'll prove all I have boasted.
In every limb
She's tight and trim
And truth is not less fickle:
All tongues proclaim
Her beauty's fame,
Dear, Saucy little *Pickle*.

To love her too,
Is but to woo
The love of fame and glory:
And slavery's chain
Shall ring again
To hear my darling's story:
And when my tale
The pirate pale
Shall hear—his ear shall tickle
Old ocean's boast
Shall be my toast,
Our heroine—the *Pickle*.

She's loyal, true,
And zealous, too,
And oh, My love's kind-hearted
in danger tried,
A sailor's bride
Ne'er, ne'er may we be parted
Though woman's eyes
We sailors prize,
Yet never would I stickle
To own, above
E'en woman's love
I prize my bonnie *Pickle*.

CHAPTER XV

THE COAST OF AFRICA 1834-1838

My gallant little hooker-my pride — my heart's delight
We've weather'd many a gale of wind — we've fought in many a fight:
No craft upon the ocean e'er behav'd so very well,
As when we topp'd the mountain sea, or climb'd the rolling swell.

Firm hearts of oak were all her crew — her officers were brave;
Her timbers stout — her bows well form'd to breast the dashing wave;
Her sticks were staunch — her sails, well bent — her shrouds taut as a bar;
Proudly she rode — 'the beautiful' — ready for peace or war.

Rear-Admiral Patrick Campbell

ON the 10th of October, 1834, Rear-Admiral Patrick Campbell in the *Thalia*, forty-six guns, arrived in the Gambia from England and relieved Rear-Admiral Warren, who had been waiting there impatiently for his arrival for the past three weeks.

Like his predecessors in this important command, Patrick Campbell was a very distinguished officer.

James, the naval historian, puts his cutting out of the *Desiree* from Dunkirk harbour as one of the most gallant feats in the Napoleonic wars, on a par with Cochrane's capture of the *Gamo*, Jerry Coglan's capture of *La Cerbere*, Keith Maxwell's cutting out of the *Chevritte* and Edward Hamilton's cutting out of the *Hermione*.

Campbell, when on duty, was a strick disciplinarian, but off duty he was a very different being-full of hospitality and kindliness.

Cooks Of The *Thalia* Gets The Cat

The *Thalia* seems to have had a very bad crew for a flagship; and they were almost mutinous when put on short allowance, and showed their displeasure by the cooks of the messes pouring the grog issues into the lee scuppers.

The Admiral promptly ordered twenty-four lashes of the cat to be given to each of the seventeen guilty cooks.

The punishment began at two bells, 9 a.m. At noon, just when the fifteenth cook had been flogged, Guthrie, the master, reported twelve o'clock.

"Make it so," acknowledged the Admiral, then he added:-

"Leave off flogging and pipe to dinner."

So two lucky men out of the seventeen, escaped the lash.

Campbell had no opportunity of doing more than pass down the coast on his way to the Cape where the Kaffir war absorbed most of his attention.

Trotter's Mosquito Squadron

Thus it was that we found Commander Trotter acting in charge of the fleet of slave-catchers in the Bights and along the windward coast. Whilst Trotter was busy pirate-hunting, his lieutenants—W. H. Quin in the *Britomart*, Huntley in the *Lynx*, Miall in the *Forester*, Parlby in the *Griffon*, McNamara in the *Buzzard*, Stevens and Thomson in the *Brisk*, Mercer in the *Charybdis*, and Rose in the *Fair Rosamond* were all doing excellent work.

It is said to have been due to Lord Auckland, who succeeded Earl de Grey in April, 1835, as First Lord of the Admiralty, that corvettes and large sloops were no longer appointed to the West coast of Africa, the work of catching slavers being entirely entrusted to such mosquito craft as the newly cut-down ten-gun brigs and their like.

Britomart was stationed in the North. Quin navigated the little brig fifty miles up the Gambia and was presented with a piece of plate, valued at one hundred guineas, by the merchants for the splendid way in which he had protected their trade.

An Early Rising First Lieutenant

This was not the man of whom so many quaint stories were told in the Service. That was Michael Quin. The latter desired the appointment of First Lieutenant of the *Madagascar*, about to be commissioned by Sir Robert Spencer, the late private secretary of the First Lord.

Quin started to knock up Spencer House at the unearthly hour of 3.30 a.m.

When at eleven o'clock Sir Robert at last consented to see the inportunate Quin, he asked the latter why he hed come at such an unreasonable time. Quin replied that he had not thought the hour unreasonable, for when acting as first lieutenant of a frigate, he was always at work by 3.30 a.m.

Needless to say Spencer could not resist this and Quin got his appointment.

W. H. Quin of the *Britomart*, had first of all commissioned the new brigantine, *Forester*.

The two new slave catchers *Griffon* and *Forester* sailed for the coast on January the 5th, 1833, at the commencement of a S.W. gale, which caused every ship in the channel to run for shelter.

***Forester* Ashore In Crow's Sound**

The *Griffon* put back, but the *Forester* took refuge in Crow's Sound, Isles of Scilly.

On both her anchors parting, she drove ashore on Crow bar, and all hands would probably have been lost had not a very gallant midshipman, Balwin Arden Wake, swum ashore with a line.

The *Forester* was refloated and towed back to Plymouth, where it was found she had lost most of her keel. Quin then went to the *Britomart* and G. G. Miall, who had previously commanded the schooner *Minx* on the Jamaica station, took out the *Forester*. In the course of a three and a half years commission the *Fortester* took five slavers and one thousand one hundred and fifteen slaves besides two slavers fully equipped.

J. E. Parlby of the *Griffon* captured the very beautiful Spanish brigantine, *Indagador* with three hundred and seventy slaves in the Bight of Benin on the 31st of October, 1834.

This vessel was afterwards very well known in the China Seas as the opium clipper, *Psyche*.

A few days later the *Griffon* captured the *Clemente* with four hundred and fifteen slaves. This vessel had been taken by the *Pylades* some months before on suspicion of being a pirate, but liberated again for want of proof.

The *Lynx* Overtakes A Decoy

Though slavers employed every sort of trick to escape from the British cruisers, most of these were commanded by officers, who had had long experience of the coast and were not easily hoodwinked.

As an example of this battle of wits we have the capture of the *Atrevide* by the little *Lynx* in December 1834. On the 20th of that month the brigantine ran into the roads of Whydah, and as usual Commander Huntley sent a boarding officer round the fifteen slavers lying there, in order to see how far advanced they were in their preparations for taking slaves.

The most advanced proved to be a most beautiful brig, called the *Atrevide*, which had her wood and water, the farina for the slaves, and even her live stock for the cabin table on board. She only needed to bend her sails and take her slaves aboard. Another brig, called the *Fortuna*, looking like a sister-ship, was not so quite advanced.

As soon as her examination officer was back aboard and the boat hoisted up, Huntly put to sea again. Then, directly he had put the horizon between himself and the Whydah roadstead, he proceeded to stand off and on in the expected track of the slavers.

At 7 a.m. on the 22nd two brigs were sighted. One was on the weather bow and the other on the weather quarter. Chase was immediately given to the one which was furthest out to sea.

The wind was fluky and light, and all day the *Lynx*, which was by no means a flyer on the wind, though quite fast off it, slowly gained on the chase, which, for a slaver, seemed to sail very badly with her tacks boarded.

Nevertheless it was evident that she had a good chance of escaping in the dark night, as the moon did not rise till 2 a.m. At dusk the chase was about four points on the cruiser's weather bow and could be seen down to her courses from the deck.

Fearful of passing her in the dark, at four bells (10 p.m.) Huntley took in his royal and flying jib, and with his night-glass took his seat in a deck chair at the gangway.

At two o'clock the small cabin-bell announced the rising of the moon. The usual deck bells were not allowed to be struck, as the loud strokes of the bell had before this been known to betray the presence of a cruiser to a slaver.

As the officer of the watch came up to his commander to report, the latter got the slaver in his lense.

"Set the flying jib and royal quickly," came the order. "Train the pivot-gun to fire just clear of the weather topmast backstays."

Then as the chase showed up at point blank range in the moonlight, Huntley went on to the captain of the gun:-

"Aim at her courses, Gould, or boom mainsail. We don't want to kill anyone."

One shot was enough! Down came her topsails and up went her courses. The shot, which had passed through her boom mainsail head had been the first indication of the presence of the *Lynx*.

But, alas, the prize turned out to be without slaves. It was the *Fortuna* acting as a decoy!

As a punishment the savage Huntley compelled the *Fortuna* to keep in his wake for a whole twenty-four hours, whilst he headed back in search of the *Atrivide*. The former had been on her way to Prince's Island, and when, at length, the commander of the *Lynx* allowed the empty slaver to resume her course, he told her captain that he might expect to see the man-of-war brigantine with the *Atrivide* in her wake at Prince's Island in a fortnight's time.

Huntley Wins The Trick

By daylight on the 24th, the *Lynx* had reached her usual station, just out of sight of the Whydah anchorage. All sails were furled except her fore and aft foresail and fore staysail, which were needed to steady her in the long rolling sea.

Then at ten o'clock the masthead man sung out:-

"Sail Ho! A brig standing directly for us-topgallantsails just showing."

For some time the stranger came on with all sail set, until down from aloft came the news that she had tacked.

In a moment the boatswain's pipe was sounding

"Hands make sail!"

All day the chase continued, close-hauled to the Nor-Westward with the wind fresh and squally.

At sunset the chase could be seen down to the foot of her topsails, then with dark she was lost to sight. It was now all a question of correctly guessing the slaver's tactics.

Huntly, after plotting out some calculations on the chart, gave the following order to young Johns, his second in command.

"Take in everything but topsails and foretopmast staysail, bear up and steer E.S.E. and let me know when you have run thirteen miles."

This meant that the *Lynx* was sailing at the rate of about three miles an hour, in exactly the opposite direction to that in which the chase was going. By midnight the distance had been run, and Huntley in his usual place at the gangway with his night-glass then ordered the brigantine to be brought on a wind on the starboard tack, heading S.S.W. under the same sail.

When Johns came on deck to take charge at 4 a.m., his commander said:-

"Take the glass, Johns; I expect a hard day before us and shall lie down here in my cloak: it will be good daylight about half past five: at five wear round, make all sail by the wind to the North West and have all studding sails ready for setting. Then call me. I am satisfied that the *Atrevide* is heading for us now under all sail."

At daylight Huntley was called. The morning was hazy and nothing was in sight, but a slaver's white cotton sails were not easy to distinguish in that white-grey atmosphere. Then as the sun rose and sent a golden beam of light through the mist, half the watch on deck called out:-

"Sail ho!"

There was the brig, just as Huntley had prophesied, standing directly for the *Lynx* on her lee bow.

She held on for so long before tacking that some doubt was expressed as to her identity, then round she came and the chase was on.

By 8 a.m. she could be seen down to her deck: by eleven her water-line was visible—the *Lynx*, in spite of her commander's assertion that she was "no use on a wind, being the true Seppings ten-gun brig breed, whose model might have been taken from a haystack", continued to gain slowly on the much vaunted Baltimore clipper until the latter, finding that she was being overtaken on a wind, at length bore away and set all her port stunsails.

But still the *Lynx* came on, until, just as the slaver was almost within range of the brigantine's long gun, a heavy tornado came raging up out of the N.E. The wind died out as the tornado approached. The *Atrivide*, which it reached first, was seen to clew up and haul down everything; then, the rain fell upon her like a waterspout, but just before it hid her from sight altogether, Huntley noticed that she was making sail again to whole topsails, courses, top-gallant sails, boom-mainsail and jib.

This was a thoughtless and unfortunate move on the part of the chase, as it gave away the strength of the tornado. The next moment she was hidden and the *Lynx* had it—first a flat calm, then a burst of wind, followed by deluging rain, dazzling flashes of lightning and long reverberating rolls of thunder.

Next with the electric fluid fizzing all about her and the thunder crackling and echoing like a giant falling down stairs, the *Lynx*, under her four lowers, as a Banks fisherman would call it, lay down to the strong wind, heading up about East.

However Huntley was convinced that the *Atrevide* would not hold to that course for fear of meeting other cruisers, and he put the brigantine round onto the starboard tack, heading almost Nor-west. Though the wind slowly took off, the rain continued to blot out the chase for over two hours and it was one o'clock before the sky began to clear. The *Lynx* had now been chasing blind for over two hours and every eye aboard was straining round the compass for a sight of the *Atrevide*.

Suddenly someone called 'Sail Ho!' and pointed on the lee beam.

"A mistake, I'm sure of it!" cried the knowing Huntley, "man the long gun and train it over the weather beam! That's where we shall see her, and well within range."

The wind grew lighter and lighter. The rain cleared away. The dazzling sun lit up the horizon. And there lay the chase becalmed, her wet sails hanging against the masts as she rolled.

She was just where Huntley said she would be! A shot was fired over her. Up went the blue and white bunting of Portugal, and then was slowly lowered. The *Atrevide*, with a crew of thirty-two and four hundred and ninety six slaves was Huntley's prize. And to increase his satisfaction the two ships arrived in West Bay, Prince's Island, on the exact day mentioned by the *Lynx's* commander when he said goodbye to the *Fortuna's* captain.

The slave trading *Madame Ferreira* could not with-hold a grimace when she greeted the victorious commander, for there were four slaves aboard the *Atrevide* which has been destined for her household.

As for the Portuguese captain of the *Fortuna*, his imprecations against the English, against the little *Lynx*, and against her commander in particular, were a fine effort of the imagination and a wonderful example of the wealth and beauty of the Portuguese language, when powerful expression was needed.

Meredith Oversteps The Law

Meredith, the anti-flogging commander of the *Pelorus*, was not so successful in matching his wits against the Guinea captains as Huntley.

The *Pelorus* and the *Pelican*, commander Brunswick Popham, were watching for a fine Spanish slaver to come out of the New Calabar.

A night came when the latter, having shipped her six hundred slaves, made sail to sea. But, on sighting the *Pelorus* at daylight, heading in under a cloud of sail, back she ran and landed her slaves again. Again this happened, and yet again. At last Meredith lost patience. He sent his boats into the river. When they arrived opposite the barracoons, the slaves, as usual, had all been landed and the Spanish crew were jeering and making obscene remarks from their emptied craft, which still had her sails hanging in the bunt and leach lines.

But, to the amazement of Spaniard and nigger alike, the boats quietly pulled ashore, marched an armed force up to the barracoons, and proceeded to round up the newly landed slaves. These were then herded into the canoes, which were lying drawn up on beach; paddlers were obtained from the shore to take the canoes off to the slaver; and as soon as both slaves and slavers had been bundled under hatches, the vessels anchor was lifted, her topsails sheeted home, and she was slowly worked down the river and out to the waiting *Pelorus*.

This action was, of course, quite illegal; and at Sierra Leone the slaver was promptly released and sailed away triumphant for Havana, whilst the infuriated Meredith was fined to the tune of eighteen thousand pounds.

Buzzard* And *Formidable

The capture which caused most stir in 1834 was that of the Spanish slaver *Formidable*, by the little *Buzzard*.

When the *Thalia* arrived in the Gambia on her passage out, she found the two-topsail schooner, *Buzzard*, lying there with her commander, Jeremiah McNamara, so broken down in health that he was being invalided home in the *Isis*.

The command of the *Buzzard* was first offered to Lieutenant Puget, first of the *Thalia*, but he refused. It was then offered to his brother, who was first of the *Isis*, but he shook his head. The Admiral thereupon offered it to every lieutenant in the two flagships, but not one of them showed any desire to leave his comfortable frigate for the tiny schooner.

Lieutenant Clement Milward, third of the *Thalia*, was, at last, ordered into the *Buzzard*.

The result taught all those lieutenants a lesson-namely that one should never refuse the opportunity of a command or other post of responsibility. It was by taking or even making such opportunities that officers like Nelson first gained a reputation in the Royal Navy.

Within two months Milward had fought a gallant action with a slaver three times his weight and been made a commander over the heads of everyone of those lieutenants.

Whilst up the Old Calabar the first lieutenant of the *Pelorus* visited a slaver, called the *Formidable*, which was in every way armed and equipped in accordance with her name. She was considered the finest slaver on the coast, and had been an old Guarda Costa, whose tonnage was greater than that of the sloop herself.

Her captain somewhat boastfully let it be known that he was not going to be taken by any of the new English Tom-tit cruisers; in which contemptuous way he alluded to the cut down 'tennies', such as the *Brisk, Charybdis, Lynx* and *Buzzard.*

But when on December the 17th, 1834, the *Formidable* sailed out of the river with seven hundred slaves on board, there was the *Buzzard* waiting for her.

The wind was light and fluky and it took the *Buzzard* seven hours to overhaul her big opponent.

This was chiefly done by means of the sweeps, which were kept going from 9.30 a.m. until 4.15 in the afternoon.

The *Formidable*, which was pierced for eighteen guns, had two long sixteen pounders and six Govers eighteen-pounders mounted so that in a game of long bowls, the cruiser was absolutely out-matched, Milward realised that his only chance of capturing his big adversary was by boarding.

As the *Buzzard* ranged up the slaver opened fire, and before the former could get alongside, her flying jibboom and fore and main topmast stays were shot away, her running rigging cut to pieces, and her sails holed and torn. The action was stated to have lasted three quarters of an hour, but this was evidently from the moment of opening fire, for the struggle on the brig's deck was short and sharp. The boarders had first to slash their way through high boarding netting before getting a footing on the slaver's deck, which was crowded with men, including numbers of armed negroes, dressed in red jackets.

It was a real old fashioned cut-and-thrust affair, with the heavy navy pistols hurled in the face of the foe after being discharged.

But however much Spaniards, Portugese and South Americans out-numbered British tars, when it came to cold steel they were beaten.

That the *Formidable's* crew fought with the utmost bravery is proved by their casualties: viz-six killed including the mate and carpenter; five severely wounded including the captain, eight others wounded, besides three of the armed slaves.

The losses of the *Buzzard* were astonishingly small. She had none killed and only six wounded, one man and a boy dangerously.

After Milward had been deservedly promoted, poor old McNamara, one of those worn out lieutenants of long service with little hopes of promotion, came out to take charge again.

But this time the climate finished him off, and on July the 27th, 1835, young Pat Campbell, the nephew of the Admiral, took command of the *Buzzard.*

When this despised Tom-tit cruiser arrived at Plymouth on April the 24th, 1838, she had freed no less than three thousand eight hundred and seventy slaves, during a commission in which she had had seven commanders.

The prize money of her gunner, who was the only officer who went out and came home in her, amounted to close on one thousand pounds.

One of the *Buzzard's* captures was the *Joven Carolina*, of two guns, thirty-three men, and four hundred and twenty two slaves.

This was a case of taking one's opportunity without an instant's hesitation.

On July the 22nd,. 1836, the *Buzzard's* boat, in charge of mate, Samuel Otway Wooldridge, was towing up the Old Calabar behind a steamer.

Suddenly, on rounding a bend, Wooldridge found himself close alongside a slaver, tiding down.

Casting off the tow rope he dashed alongside her, and before her crew could resist, had carried her. Then, when the crew showed signs of breaking out, he lowered a boat, put sixteen of them into it, and towed them astern till he reached the bar.

This he managed to negotiate without disaster, although he was new to the river, thus earning his promotion.

Success Of Mercer In The *Charybdis*

On her second commission, which dated from January the 11th, 1834, the *Charybdis*, which was even more successful than the *Buzzard*, was commanded throughout by a very experienced officer in Samuel Mercer, who started his naval life surveying the coasts of Africa under Commodore Owen in the *Leven*

Then, after two months in the Experimental Squadron with Captain John Hayes in the *Challenger*, he was again with Owen in the *Eden*, when that officer took possession of Fernando Po.

After close on eight years on the coast of Africa, he went surveying in the West Indies in the *Blossom*, Captain Richard Owen. Here he commanded the *Monkey* till October 1832.

Mercer did not have the luck to come across a fighting slaver, though in 5°21' N. 3°20' E. in April 1834 after a chase from daylight till 4 p.m. he had to fire fourteen rounds of grape and canister into a Portuguese brig, named *Tamega*, before she would surrender.

She had four hundred and forty four slaves on board. No slaves had been thrown overboard during this chase, but two years later, in February 1836, the *Charybdis* was chasing a Spanish slaver, called the *Argus*, when her Captain threw no less than ninety-seven slaves overboard.

Her last capture before sailing for home was a slaver with four hundred and seventy slaves, which had the very unusual rig for a slaver of three-masted schooner. This made the fourteenth vessel with slaves captured by the little *Charybdis*, which arrived at Portsmouth on October the 10th, 1837.

Trinculo Bumped Over The Bonny Bar

When the *Pelorus* sailed for England, Commander R. Meredith was succeeded as Senior Naval Officer on the coast by Acting Commander Henry Puget of the *Trinculo*.

For the first half of her commission, this brig had been on the East coast as well as the West; when Booth invalided at the Cape, Puget joined her from the flagship, and found her in a high state of discipline. Her first lieutenant was Roberts, known as 'Old Four Eyes'—he was believed to sleep in his spectacles, certainly he missed seeing very little that went on aboard the *Trinculo*.

He was later for a short time one of the many commanders of the *Buzzard*.

As second lieutenant, Bob Tryon joined from the flagship with Puget, taking the place of the Irishman of lunar fame.

The *Trinculo* was spoilt as a slave catcher because, instead of copper, she was sheathed with zinc, which it was found impossible to keep clean.

In spite of a steady diet of ship's provisions, salt junk, pork, peas and hard tack, which was scarcely the food for the tropics, besides being overrun by cockroaches, the *Trinculo* was extraordinarily healthy in the Bights.

This was attributed to the Captain's insistance that the lower deck be kept dry. Also the men, following Commodore Collier's rule, dressed in flannel, were never allowed to be about the decks in the heavy dew, and were ordered to change whenever they got wet.

In September 1835 the news of the Spanish treaty, which allowed vessels found equipped for slaves to be siezed, reached the coast.

The *Trinculo* learnt of this in rather a curious way. On September the 16th, 1835, she chased and overtook a sixteen-gun slaver, named the *Alerto.* When Tryon went alongside in the boarding cutter, he found no slaves on board, but was offered a glass of champagne by her captain, who turned out to be an officer in the French Navy.

The latter sent the following message to Puget:-

"Tell your captain I would have fought him had I been liable to capture, but I have no slaves on board. Tell him that he will find at Prince's Island the new treaty with Spain by which empty vessels may be taken."

Whilst the *Trinculo* was seeking these new orders in West Bay, the *Alerto* shipped six hundred slaves in the Bonny and got safely away for Cuba.

Towards the end of December, 1835, the boats of the *Trinculo* captured the Spanish brigantine, *Isabella Secunda*, with three hundred and forty seven slaves in the Bonny.

On January the 22nd, 1836, Lieutenant Tryon was again sent into the Bonny with the pinnace and two gigs. Off the town he found four empty Spaniards, whom he boarded and captured with the loss of one man wounded. Hardly, however, were the red and gold flags of Spain hauled down before the King of Bonny took action.

He sent off four large canoe loads of warriors, who overwhelmed all defence and locked up Tryon and his boat's crews in the slave barracoons. Luckily for all concerned, the second lieutenant of the *Trinculo* kept his head in the midst of a most ignominious and difficult situation. He managed to pencil the story of his misfortunes on a piece of paper and promised a canoe man a large 'dash' if he got it to Captain Puget. This the canoe-man succeeded in doing.

Puget at once determined to take the brig up the river. The difficulty in this was the bar.

The Eastern or Portuguese channel into the Bonny, though deep, was too narrow to navigate except with a leading wind, whilst the South channel had only fifteen feet of water on it at the top of the tide and the *Trinculo* was drawing close on eighteen feet. As luck would have it the *Lynx* arrived off the Bonny that very night; upon which Puget at once proceeded to lighten his brig by transferring spare spars, sails, provisions, cables and even shot, with the exception of four rounds; and by this means he got the *Trinculo's* draught of water down to sixteen feet. Though there was a heavy, breaking surf on the bar of the South channel, the indomitable Puget determined to run his ship at it and try and bump over.

The sturdy *Trinculo* stuck hard, then a huge comber boiled all round her and lifted her on a few feet before letting her down with a bump which almost shook the masts out of her.

Three times this happened before the brig found herself in deep water inside.

On the 26th of January, Puget anchored the *Trinculo* within point blank range of Bonny town, and just to show that he meant business, fired off four blank rounds.

The King gave in at once. Tyron and his men together with some British merchant seamen were released, and the *Trinculo* sailed in triumph down the Bonny and out by the Portuguese channel with the four captured Spanish slavers in her wake. This piece of resolute work brought promotion at last to that worthy old lieutenant, Henry Puget.

After being upwards of four years in commission, the *Trinculo* was relieved by the *Pylades*, and leaving Sierra Leone on March 28th, 1836, with a freight of four thousand three hundred ounces of gold and four tons of ivory, not to speak of three turtle and two hundred and forty parrots, most of which, we are told, reached home with a fair smattering of fo'c'sle English, she arrived at Spithead on the 14 of May.

The only turtle still alive was at once sent off to the First Lord of the Admiralty, a delicate attention that, it was hoped, would put him in a good humour when promotions came to be considered.

The Famous Slave-Catcher *Waterwitch*

The most famous cruiser that ever worked the windward coast, the Bights or the Southern station, and the one most dreaded and considered to be the fastest sailer that ever flew the pendant by experienced Guinea captains, made her first appearence on the coast of Africa in 1836.

This was the beautiful ex-yacht, *Waterwitch.*

Shortly after her exciting race round the Eddystone, Lord Belfast sold her to the Admiralty, and in November 1834 she was towed across from Cowes and docked at Portsmouth for the necessary internal alterations in order to fit her as a man-of-war.

At Portsmouth her model, when seen out of water, was tremendously admired and numbers of senior lieutenants applying for her, there was much discussion at the Admiralty as to whom she should be given; at last, at the beginning of December, Lieutenant John Adams, an officer of twenty-five years experience, who had served on the coast as first of the *Atholl* in 1829, and as commander of the *Plumper* in 1830, was appointed.

The only flaw that the critics could find in the design of *Waterwitch* was her stern with its short overhang and rounded up lines, which I believe, had been Lord Belfast's idea with a view to being able to fire out of the stern ports.

However this cut off stern offended the eye and spoilt the perfection of her proportions, so at Portsmouth her stern was rebuilt and she was given a beautiful tapering counter like a modern yacht; and this, everyone agreed, suited her to perfection.

Once, however, in the dockyard's hands and the ex-yacht was not likely to get afloat again in a hurry: but it must be admitted that a heated general election with Charlie Napier invading the political field and Admiral Sir Charles Rowley of the new Admiralty Board canvassing Pompey from house to house did a good deal to hinder work in the dockyards. Then in February 1835 came the death of James Peake, master-shipwright of Portsmouth, Richard Blake being appointed in his place.

However towards the end of March, 1835, *Waterwitch* was turned over to her commander, who soon advanced her equipment.

It was not thought advisable at first to send the *Waterwitch* to the coast; instead she was appointed to the Lisbon station; where she had an opportunity of sailing against her great rival, the *Pantaloon*, the beautiful *Magicienne* (one of the fastest ships in the Royal Navy, being a cut down forty-four-gun frigate converted to a twenty-six-gun corvette) the little Sainty-designed sloop, *Pearl*, the Symondite brig *Ringdove*, some of the ten-gun brigs and, of course, the Falmouth packets.

On the 27th of March 1835 Adams weighed from Spithead and gave his clipper brig her first testing under man-of-war conditions.

On Sunday the 19th of April the *Waterwitch* anchored in the Tagus; and for the rest of the year she remained on the Portuguese coast doing tender, dodging backwards and forwards between Lisbon, Corunna, Santander and the fleet. She arrived back at Plymouth on November the 12th, 1835, and was given a thorough refit, before being sent out to the coast of Africa.

Waterwitch And *Pantaloon*

On the first few days of her passage out it was agreed that her sailing should be well tested by a trial with the *Pantaloon.*

This trial took place from December the 24th to the 27th, 1836. The *Pantaloon* was commanded by Lieutenant Nicholas Cory, a very experienced officer who had lately come from the *Royal George* yacht. The two brigs were so closely matched that there was very little in it, though *Waterwitch* was undoubtedly the fastest in light weather. I have given the log of the *Waterwitch*, Admiral Sir Robert Stopford's interesting letter, and the two commanders' reports in an appendix

But it would be as well here to utter a word of warning against believing every statement made by a naval officer anent the sailing of his ship. Their letters seem to be impartial and full of careful statements, but too much reliance could never be placed upon them owing to the fact that in the days of sail both officers and men became so enamoured of their ships, so tremendously partisan, so blind to any defects and so unwittingly exaggerators of their good qualities that their witness became of very little account.

Even officers who did not belong to a ship, were often unduly biassed in her favour, and when there was no doubt about her being well beaten in a sailing trial every kind of excuse was made-she was out of trim, her copper was rough, etc., etc: and even in the case of an acknowledged slow-coach, her crew were wont to laud her as a superior man-of-war, whose port sills were higher out of the water, her gun platform more steady, or her stowage much superior to those of her faster rivals.

However, inspite of their undoubted partisanship these deceptive letters are very interesting, not only for their intimate glimpses of the superb seamanship and sea sense of their day, but as showing the tremendous interest taken by all naval officers in ship design.

After seeing the last of the *Pantaloon*, the *Waterwitch* hurried out to the coast of Africa and it was not long after her arrival in the Bights before she began to make captures.

On February the 8th, 1836 she overtook the *Seis Hermanos*, on March the 4th the *Joven Maria* fell a victim to her, and a week later she captured the *Galava Josifa*. This was good work for a few days over a month's cruising, and the slavers of crack Baltimore model soon found that a cruiser had arrived on the station that they could not get away from in light or fresh winds.

In December 1837 Lieutenant-Commander W. Dickey succeeded Adams, who as far back as the previous January had been promoted. The latter was lucky to get home before the arrival of a very unhealthy season.

Columbine As A Brig

It was only as it should be that the peerless *Columbine*, Sir William Symond's first man-of-war, should be the first Symondite to be seen upon the coast of Africa, though she was within a few months of being ten years old when she arrived in the Bights, under Commander Tom Henderson.

After Love had paid her off from the West India Station in 1834, the Admiralty had decided to refit her as a brig. This was done at Sheerness and cost four thousand eight hundred and twenty two pounds.

Tom Henderson who commissioned her for her fourth commission on the 2nd of June, 1834 was an officer of long experience in Revenue cruisers.

After a short service in the *Snapper*, cutter, he joined that famous revenue brig, the *Prince of Wales*, commanded for so long by Benjamin Oliver, and remained in her until he received his promotion in December 1829. He was then appointed to the coastguard and on the 22nd of February, 1832, greatly distinguished himself in an affray with armed smugglers, in which he was severely wounded.

For the next two years we find him in command of the revenue cutters *Victorine*, *Sylvia* and *Speedy*.

Though most cutter officers were looked down upon in the Service, this was far from being the case with Tom Henderson, who had a very high reputation as not only a magnificent seaman but a smart disciplinarian.

"No man understood better how to fit a sail than Henderson," wrote Harry Keppel, who had good cause to know, for his command, the sixteen-gun brig-sloop, *Childers*, made many a vain effort to beat the *Columbine*, both in the Mediterranean and on the coast of Africa.

The *Columbine* soon showed herself to be even faster as a brig than she had been as a three-master; and many naval authorities considered her to be the prettiest of all Symonds' designs, not excepting even the favourite *Pantaloon*.

By 1836 the West Indies had lost much of their importance, and the Mediterranean had become the crack station of the Service: but it was becoming a practice of the Admiralty to move ships from station to station, thus we find both *Columbine* and *Childers* after a couple of years in the Mediterranean, ending up their commissions on the West coast of Africa.

Tom Henderson's Letters And Reports

We are now entering upon the last few decades before the eclipse of oak and hemp, when the Wooden Walls had pretty nearly reached their zenith and the competition, not only in sailing, but in sail drill, had arrived at a pitch, that dwarfed every other feature of the Service, without even excepting gunnery, or tactical exercises.

Henderson's letters from the Mediterranean show this tremendous keeness regarding the sailing capabilities of the various ships in the fleet very clearly.

On his way out he relates, in a letter to Captain J. Wemyss, how after passing within hail, he ran an Austrian twenty-gun corvette hull down when off Majorca and then had an 'extraordinary advantage' over three 'fast-looking' Americans, two brigs and a clipper schooner.

At first he was kept on the move, dashing in every direction at the Admiral's beck and call, and this experience caused him to wax more and more enthusiastic regarding his command:-

"She steers and works like a boat . . . I am well manned and from having had so much knocking about, the men begin to work her smartly . . . She is, without exception, the most perfect beauty of a brig you ever beheld, and at a distance she is generally taken for a ten-gun sloop, she looks so small and well proportioned."

When he wrote to her designer, Henderson was even more enthusiastic:-

"*Columbine* has done more than I ever promised or predicted, and has more than answered my most sanguine expectations in every respect . . . Great efforts are making in *Barham*, and considerable bets are made: I have no fear of the result. The Commander-in-chief is very partial to the brig. We have been exceedingly fortunate in executing all his orders with great dispatch . . . She is at this moment the most beautiful thing I ever saw."

These eulogies must not be considered in any way exceptional. Henderson was a calm, shrewd Scotsman, a man used to writing a concise report, and not given to exaggeration. But in these days of machinery it is hard for people to realise with what devotion the sailor of the sail looked upon his ship.

On his return to England from the Mediterranean for a refit before proceeding to the coast of Africa, Henderson sent the following official report to the Admiralty, which I quote in full as it gives such an excellent idea of this last sailing phase in the Royal Navy:-

H.M.S. "Columbine", Hamoaze,
14th June, 1836.

My Lord,

In compliance with your memorandum of yesterday's date, calling upon me to furnish your Lordship, for the information of the Lords Commissioners of the Admiralty, with a detailed report of the qualities of the sloop under my command and of any trials that may have taken place between her and other ships,—I beg to acquaint your Lordship that on weighing from the Downs, on the 2nd of September, 1834, at 5.15 a.m. H.M.S. *Thalia* was seven miles directly to windward, and under sail before *Columbine*; that both vessels worked through the

Channel the whole day under double-reefed topsails, setting and taking in topgallant sails occasionally, and at 7.30 p.m. we anchored under Dungeness, three miles to windward of *Thalia*, having beaten her ten miles out of twenty-five. On the following day, under similar sail, both vessels weighed together about a mile distant, working through the Channel as before, when *Thalia* was lost sight of from the masthead in eleven hours; and ever since that period *Columbine* has had an advantage over every ship of war she has yet sailed with, of from one mile to one and a half miles an hour to the wind: excepting on one occasion only, beating between the islands of Cerigo and Servi with unsteady winds, when *Childers* for three hours following crossed on opposite tacks about the same distance, or rather less to windward than she was at starting, (viz., three cables length): but this was a singular exception only, as the very first opportunity after, of sailing with her in open sea room off Malta, on the 7th of August, 1835, under the observation of the Commander-in-chief, she beat *Endymion*, *Sapphire*, and *Childers*, at the rate of a mile and a mile and a half an hour to the wind: and, although *Childers* is the fastest vessel, excepting *Vernon*, she has sailed with, the advantage over her may be estimated at a mile an hour to the wind and sparing topgallant and topmast studding-sails off the wind.

On the first trial with *Scout* and *Childers*, by the order of the Commander-in-chief, on the 5th of November, 1834, our superiority over *Scout* was one and a half to two miles, and over *Childers* one mile to the wind, both in moderate winds and in strong winds: after *Scout* parted company we spared *Childers* topgallant sails and weathered on her nearly half a mile without them.

On the 7th of March, 1834, running with the wind abaft the beam, in a considerable sea, under treble-reefed topsails, double-reefed boom-mainsail and fore topmast staysail, lowering main topsail occasionally to keep on the Admiral's beam, from 8 p.m. till 4 a.m. of the 8th, we spared *Caledonia*, *Edinburgh*, *Revenge* and *Canopus*, courses and jib, *Thunderer* and *Portland* hauling up and setting square mainsail as necessary to keep station: and on the 9th, in working round the Island of St George with *Vernon* and *Portland*, whilst making the last tack to weather the island, the foreyard gave way in the slings, which compelled us to pass to leeward of it again: at fifty-four minutes past Noon *Vernon* spoke us abreast of the island, standing for Salamis carrying all sail. *Portland* was then hull down ahead, steering for Salamis also; and not withstanding the want of our foresail, we came up and anchored at the same time with *Portland* and only fifteen minutes after *Vernon*, each vessel carrying all possible sail.

3rd September 1835. At 2.30 p.m. commenced sailing with *Favorite* under royals and all sail to the wind, against a heavy head sea, *Favorite* three cables' length to windward, two points abaft our beam: continued on the wind, taking in royals and a reef in the topsails, following the motions of *Favorite*. At four *Favorite* from one and a half to two miles in our wake: at 4.10 tacked per signal: at 4.40 tacked again per signal, *Favorite* three and a half miles, two points abaft the lee beam. At five observed *Favorite* carry away her jib, and finding our superiority so great, took in topgallant sails and double-reefed the topsails, still gaining upon her. To the wind, with light winds, there was no comparison. During the sailing with *Favorite* the wind increased gradually to strong gales, with a heavy cross sea, and *Columbine* was extremely light, having supplied *Volage*, three days previously with all her provisions, excepting ten days to carry her to the squadron.

On the 14th of November, 1835, in a trial of twelve hours to the wind with *Revenge*, *Vernon*, and *Barham*: *Revenge* and *Barham* were half topsails down and *Vernon* half courses down, immediately to leeward,—*Revenge* and *Barham* fourteen or fifteen miles, *Vernon* nine or ten distant: and in running dead before the wind with those ships she took the lead until they went about nine knots, when they had the advantage.

At 6 a.m. 27th January, 1836, a French brig of war was discovered six or seven miles ahead. At seven both vessels were under topmast and topgallant studding sails. At eight *Columbine* was abreast of her. At nine both vessels came to the wind, with light winds. At ten they were under royals and all sail, French brig half a mile on the lee quarter. At 5 p.m. her royals were only to be seen from the deck, on the same bearing, we having left her immediately in the wind's eye ten or twelve miles, without ever going more than three and a half knots during the day. She was a brig of twenty guns, and appeared a powerful vessel.

On our passage to England we came up with, to the Southward of Ushant, and passed as if at anchor, the *Eclipse* and *Scorpion* packets: the first having sailed from Malta eight days before us, and although two days were lost at Gibraltar and Tangier, we arrived at Plymouth two days before them.

I have also to state that she is extremely easy in every description of sea, that she carries her sail with uncommon stability, being able to bear her lee ports open under double-reefed topsails and course, going nine knots close-hauled: steers and works well: and on a recent occasion ran twenty minutes under all sail before the wind, going eleven knots, without veering the tenth part of a point, with the tiller untouched by the helmsman. And I would humbly but safely assert she is, of the many vessels I have been in, the easiest in a head sea, and the most correct in steerage (inasmuch that our reckoning has scarcely been out a mile since I have commanded her): she also accommodates her crew with great comfort, stows foreign stores and provisions for four months, well, drawing about thirteen feet eleven inches forward and fifteen feet aft.

I have the honour to be, etc.,
Thos. Henderson, Commander.

To Admiral Lord A. Beauclerk.

Columbine Cuts Off The *Volex*.

The *Columbine* had scarcely arrived on her new station before she was given a chance of showing what she could do. The first of the mosquito squadron that she encountered was the little *Charybdis*. The latter's commander, Sam Mercer, was full of his fruitless chase of a slaver two days previously. Apparently four vessels of the squadron had chased this craft for forty-eight hours.

Henderson at once determined to see what his swift *Columbine* could do and here is his own account of his clever capture:-

"Knowing it to be the interest of the slaver to cross the Equator with all possible speed, and having perfect confidence in the superior sailing of the *Columbine*, I at once determined on going in quest of her: and allowing "Columbine" to sail one-third faster than any slaver, I gave an imaginary course to the chase, and shaped one to cut her before she could cross the Equator.

I succeeded in getting sight of her the third evening after receiving the information, and captured her the following morning,—a beautiful brig (the *Volex*) with five hundred and eight slaves on board;—thus showing the truth of my statement of her serviceable qualities. What would Nelson have given to have had a cruiser to trace up the enemy's squadron in such a manner in the days of Aboukir?".

The Symondite Brigantines

The *Columbine* was followed out to the coast by the new Symondite brigantines, *Bonetta* and *Dolphin*, of three hundred and nineteen tons.

These two little ships had been specially designed as slave catchers and their armament was the very latest thing in pivoting guns.

It is thus described in the United Service Journal.

"Her armament is the most perfect we have witnessed. She has one long thirty-two-pounder, eight feet long, and forty-nine hundredweight, mounted amidships as a pivot gun with five other shifting pivots, which enable the gun to fight a broadside, right ahead or astern.

She has likewise two thirty-two-pounders, six feet long and thirty-two hundredweight, mounted on the plan of Mr Fearnell of Poplar. Those guns will train within two points of the line of the heel, either forward or aft and are intended to be fought on the bow, amidships or the quarter. These guns are easily transported by shifting the trucks and a lever to any part of the deck, so that should it be required the three guns can be fought on one side. They are mounted on a slide and to prevent the recoil, have a compressing breeching which passes round a pivot at the side round which the slide revolves and over a pully attached to the carriage, so that the recoil is gradually stopped by a means the most simple and without the least fear of derangement."

In this arrangement we see the death knell of the old broadside carriage gun.

Griffon, which had arrived home from the coast during the summer of 1836, was ordered to be rearmed in the same way but with eighteen-pounders.

The *Bonetta* sailed from Sheerness with twenty thousand pounds of specie for the Cape on

July the 14th, 1836, under Lieutenant-commander P. Bisson, late commander of the *Quail* cutter; and *Dolphin* followed her in the autumn under T. L. Roberts with another twenty thousand pounds.

Both vessels turned out to be very fast and at the first opportunity they were tried out against *Columbine* and *Waterwitch*, the two fastest cruisers on the station.

The following letter to Sir William Symonds from Tom Henderson must be read with the usual allowance for undue bias in favour of his own ship:-

H.M.S. *Columbine*,
10th November 1836

My dear Sir William,

The accompanying diagram and copy of log will show you the result of a trial of sailing between *Columbine*, *Waterwitch* and *Bonetta*, under very unfavourable circumstances for your vessels; *Columbine* having on board four months provisions for one hundred and thirty nine men (i.e. more than five months for her complement) and a considerable quantity of stores for the squadron in the Bights of Benin and Biafra. *Bonetta* had nearly five months for her crew; whilst *Waterwitch* was in the best of trim imaginable, for the light winds which prevailed during the trial.

She was on her way to Sierra Leone to fill up with provisions and stores: we on our way to the coast, full as an egg, complying with the standing orders of the Commander-in-chief, directing vessels going there to carry as much provisions as they can possibly stow.

But not with standing the very great disadvantage we were under, out of the four points sailed on—and those the choice of the commander of the *Waterwitch-Columbine* and *Bonetta* being governed by signals made by him—we beat her on two points very much, were equal to her on the third and were beaten by her on the fourth, one-eighth of a mile.

Bonetta had an advantage over her on the two first points, but dropped on the two last.

Bonetta is a most powerful vessel and improves every day. She is the finest lieutenant's command on the coast... We only wanted wind.

Whenever the breeze freshened we headed instantly, but *Waterwitch*, being so much lighter was influenced by every flaw more immediately, but did not keep so good a wind as we did generally.

I was compelled to go to the Cape and was glad of it. The Admiral was much pleased with the brig and desired me to express his approbation of all he saw during his inspection, to the officers and crew. The same day our account for refit was handed on board, and after three months constantly under sail in all kinds of sea it only amounted to twenty-three pounds sterling, much less than my cabin expenses. She is a splendid craft.

After making an immense circuit of the coasts of Africa, we arrived at the Cape the day after *Bonetta*, and have had her in company ever since. She has improved wonderfully and threatens to push us hard on some points. *Waterwitch* was astonished at our sailing, and they are not anxious to meet us again. Adams says she (*Columbine*) sails much faster than *Pantaloon*.

Since leaving this quarter for the Cape, several good prizes have been made. We are now commencing an uninterrupted cruise, I hope; and as nothing can possibly get from us, we may be successful. Will you make my kind remembrances to Lady Symonds, and believe me.

Ever very sincerely yours
Thos Henderson

"Henderson's hope was fulfilled for writing again to Sir William from the Bight of Benin on April the 15th, 1837, he says:— Columbine has been very successful since her return from the Cape, having taken three clippers with one thousand one hundred and eighty three slaves on board, all by superior sailing; none of them being nearer than fifteen miles at starting".

Turning to the *Dolphin*, she had her first encounter with *Waterwitch*, in November 1836, when on her say to the Cape.

After five days sailing together, Roberts wrote to Symonds:—

"that vessel was left without a leg to stand on... *Waterwitch*... is reported to be the fastest vessel on the station, having sailed with and beat all of them..."

More details of this trial of sailing were given by John Sibbald, a mate of the *Dolphin* as follows:—

"We fell in with the *Waterwitch* off Cape coast on the morning of Sunday, 27th November (1836) and kept company until Wednesday 30th, when we tried rate of sailing with a fine breeze on the quarter, going six or seven knots.

At daylight the *Waterwitch* was about half a mile on the weather quarter and at sunset she was astern five or seven miles. The following day and Friday in sight: and on Saturday, our commander wishing to go to Ascension, we ran back and communicated, giving her all the provisions she wanted, and proceeded.

The whole of *Waterwitch's* officers agree that we beat them at the rate of half a mile an hour, and are more surprised at being beaten than we are.

Now we are the clipper of the Navy! . . ."

I will now quote from letters of Tom Henderson and Tom Roberts regarding a trial of sailing between *Dolphin, Columbine* and *Waterwitch* in the spring of 1837.

"The first time we met *Dolphin*," wrote Henderson, "we had rather an advantage over her: but on the 31st ult. (March 31) she beat *Waterwitch* and *Columbine* better than a mile to the wind in four hours. The winds were unsteady and she started on our weather bow, by which she gained at least a quarter of a mile: she is in very fine order and does her commander much credit. The same afternoon *Waterwitch* and *Columbine* made sail within speech of each other at two o'clock. And at four she was three quarters of a mile at a point before the lee beam and I daresay does not want to sail with us again.

Both she and *Dolphin* should sail round us: neither of them have a stick, anchor or hammock-netting above the gunwale.

If our upper works were clear, nothing could sail with us to the wind. Off the wind we are very superior".

Roberts wrote to Sir William Symonds:—

"On my first arrival at Prince's Island, in February, a short trial took place with *Columbine* without any advantage on either side. I was then swamped with provisions, having nine mouths on board, and every breaker of water filled up. The present trial took place in the Bight of Benin yesterday (March 31) all hands making sure of a victory and, I believe, all pretty well satisfied with their stowage.

Great preparations were made to beat the *Dolphin*. The race commenced shortly after seven o'clock in the morning and was continued until seven bells in the forenoon, making three tacks to windward, *Columbine* and *Waterwitch* sailing nearly alike: the *Dolphin* stepping out most gallantly in the wind's eye, keeping them nearly in the same line of bearing, and going steadily from them for the whole time, till the distance was increased to two miles, when the recall was made; average rate of sailing, five knots . . . after this I may be pardoned for offering my congratulation on your solid constructions, beating that shell of a thing, that skiff on the water *Waterwitch*, at all points, with her anchors from her bows and four guns below . . ."

Roberts enclosed the following:—

Notes taken on board *Dolphin* on a trial of sailing in three boards to windward between H.M. brigs, *Columbine* and *Waterwitch* and brigantine *Dolphin*, from 8 a.m. to 11.15 a.m. 31st March, 1837.

"7 a.m., tacked her signal, in company with *Columbine* and *Waterwitch* and made all sail by the wind on larboard tack.

7.10, *Columbine* E.N.E. distant three cables, *Waterwitch* N. by W. ½W. The further particulars of the trial are shown in the following table. The times taken by chronometer; angles by sextant. *Columbine's* main royal yard to water-line estimated one hundred and twenty five feet; *Waterwitch's* hundred feet: rate of sailing averaging five knots.

Times.		Bearings	Angles	Distance in feet
8.00	*Columbine*	E. by N.	1° 40'	4,470
	Waterwitch	N. by E.	1° 32'	3,737
9.00	*Columbine*	E.¼N.	0° 58'	
	Waterwitch	N.N.E.¾E.	1° 17'	
9.30	*Columbine*	E.S.E.	0° 47'	Tacked
	Waterwitch	E.N.E.	1° 15'	"
10.00	*Columbine*	East	0° 45'	
	Waterwitch	N.E.¼N.	0° 43'	
11.15	*Columbine*	East	0° 34'	Tacked 13,140
	Waterwitch	N.N.E.	0° 33'	" 10,420

Keeping both on nearly same bearing as they started *Dolphin* gained one and a quarter miles on *Columbine* and one and one-tenth of a mile on *Waterwitch*.

1837 A Sickly Season.

Though every precaution was taken to ward off the attacks of fever, dysentry, etc., on the deadly coast, every two or three years a season would come along, which took severe toll.

Without any knowledge of enteric or of the evil effects of the mosquito, the doctors had little chance of combating an epidemic.

In 1837 so severe was the sickness in the squadron that Admiral Campbell had to take his cruisers off the coast and send them to Ascension and St Helena to recover. But even Ascension succumbed to the prevailing fever, the whole garrison being affected at one time and twenty-six dying.

The *Forester* lost her commander and ten men: *Astra*, whilst surveying, lost three officers and twenty-two men: *Raven*, her assistant, lost surgeon, master, mate and ten men. *Harpy*, which came across to Sierra Leone from the West Indies with a captured slaver for adjudication, lost her commander, the Honourable G. R. Clements, her surgeon and eighteen men: *Bonetta* lost her commander, surgeon, clerk and twenty-two men: *Columbine* lost a considerable number of her fine crew whilst the poor little *Waterwitch* lost her new commander and suffered almost more than any other ship.

Curlew arrived home on September the 1st, 1838, having lost nearly all her officers and crew, only one officer, Sturdie, and eighteen men arriving home out of those who sailed out in her three years before.

Pelican, Commander B. Popham, was an extraordinary exception to the general ill-health.

She was out over four years on East and West coasts and never lost a man from fever or other illnesses.

Harry Keppel On The Coast

On the 24th of September, the brig, *Childers*, Commander Henry Keppel arrived at Sierra Leone from the Mediterranean. True to his character, Harry Keppel was as keen as mustard, and, as he says in his entertaining log, could think and dream of nothing but slavers. Unfortunately he had not much chance of catching any but the slowest, for, unknown to her crew, the *Childers* had seven feet of her false keel adrift and partly athwartships; and this accounted for her sailing better on one tack than the other.

Keppel, of course, had been on the ground. He was one of those officers who were never afraid of the 'putty', and he was accustomed to proclaim that he did not give a damn for the sailor who was.

In order to escape the consequences of the new Spanish treaty, Spanish slavers were now masquerading under American and Portuguese papers and colours and Keppel's first two captures he had to release for this reason.

They were both Spaniards, but the first showed American papers, flew the stars and stripes and called herself the *Peri* of Baltimore. This was off a place called New Cess near Cape Mount.

The second produced Portuguese papers obtained at Porto Praya, St Jago, but from the smell Keppel argued that slaves must have been on board very lately. He had the same experience when examining the slavers lying in the Trade Town anchorage. He sent his boats in with his first lieutenant, Goldsmith, under cover of a dark rainy night. The first slaver examined was the schooner, *Vigilante*, which had every preparation made for taking slaves on board and was evidently intending to sail before daylight. Her foretopsail yard was at the masthead, her cat-fall overhauled, and luff tackle stretched along the deck; but she produced Portuguese papers and could not be touched because she had no slaves on board.

The next vessel was a brig, the *Golenthokika*, which Keppel knew to be Spanish, as she had lain for some weeks close to the *Childers* in Barcelona. Her captain, however, produced Russian and Greek papers. The third vessel boarded produced Portuguese papers.

This was very dispiriting for a keen cruiser. Leaving Trade Town in disgust Keppel proceeded down the coast calling in at the various European forts and settlements in his course.

It was all new to the most lively officer in the Royal Navy, and he took the keenest interest in everything: at one moment he was enquiring concerning the various fetishes,—the crocodiles at Dix cove, who came to the call of a repulsive witch doctor, or the hyenas at Accra: next he was intrigued by their cotton coffee and tobacco growing: then he gathered statistics about palm oil, gold dust or elephants teeth: finally he never neglected an opportunity for sport in that mysterious jungle, which lay at the back of the white surf-bounded beaches of the ivory and gold coasts.

It was not until the Bight of Benin was reached that the *Childers* fell in with any of her fellow cruisers, but here she found the *Saracen*, *Viper* and *Waterwitch*.

Like everyone else Keppel was eager to try the paces of his command against the peerles *Waterwitch*, but a half-hour's trial to windward was sufficient to show him what the *Waterwitch* could do with the *Childers*.

Failing to find the senior officer on the coast or in the Bights, he put into Clarence Cove, where he remained for a week before sailing for West Bay, Prince's Island, where he made the acquaintance of the notorious Dona Ferreira, whom he describes as a kind and hospitable lady of rather dark complexion.

After a couple of days as the guest of Madame—the title by which Dona Ferreira was known to all English officers, for whom, by the way, she had a great partiality—Keppel sailed for that famous spot, the entrance to the Bonny river.

Here on December the fourth, 1837, after three months on the coast, he at length fell in with the *Pelican* and received orders from Popham to cruise between 4° and 2° North and 3° 30′ and 6° East: that is to say from Cape Formosa and the Nun entrance to the Niger as far West as Lagos, where he was to look out for the little *Buzzard* with provisions.

On his way to his station, Keppel had his first chase, but on his quarry rounding to in reply to a shot under her quarter, she proved to be an English palm-oil brig, the *Pink* of Liverpool. At daylight the following morning a Havana schooner was brought to, but she had no slaves on board and flew Portuguese colours.

Keppel next sighted a very rakish-looking craft, but she turned out to be the *Waterwitch*, which was looking after the section of the coast from Cape Fermosa to Old Calabar. At the same moment a strange sail was sighted, off went both men-of-war in chase, heading in shore. Just before dark it was noticed that the chase had another ship in company. It was a bright night and the cruisers ran right into the mouth of the St Barbara river, where they found the two slavers at anchor. They were both from Havana—the *Fecilidades*, brig, of two guns, two hundred and twenty eight tons and forty-two men and the *Maria Segunda*, schooner, of one gun, one hundred and seven tons and twenty-eight men. Both, having only just arrived, still had their trade on board, and Keppel remarks that they looked more like yachts than merchantmen.

A third slaver was all ready to take her black ivory aboard.

Three days later the *Maria Segunda* succeeded in getting away from the boats of the *Waterwitch* after a most unpleasant experience.

The pinnace and cutter failed to overtake her; but the gig, in charge of a midshipman, named Bowles, with a crew of only four men, managed to get up to her. Young Bowles calmly proceeded to pick off the slaver's crew, one by one with a fowling-piece; for all the world, described his coxswain, as if he had been shooting larks. In all the slaver had eight men killed by Bowles, and it was not until he had had one of his four men killed and another wounded that he reluctantly let her go.

Cruising During The Hamattans

For three weeks Keppel cruised to and fro in the Bight of Benin-three of the dullest weeks, he declared, that he had ever spent.

The Hamattan was blowing, so that the *Childers* was navigated in a thick haze, which narrowed the view of the mast head lookout to a bare cable's lengh.

The air was hot and dry and a steady irritant to the nerves, as is always the case with that wind. The brig was covered from her trucks to her deck with a fine, white dusty sand, which made all hands look like so many millers. The *Childers* was entirely out of fresh provisions, so that shark or dolphin were highly prized luxuries:

"During the Hamattans," wrote Keppel, "slavers generally escaped."

He was not very happy about the progress the suppression of the slave trade was making, and declared that in spite of the vigilance of thirteen cruisers, nine out of ten slavers got away.

False papers were a great contributing cause. Keppel came upon a beautiful Spanish brig, which had fitted out alongside him in Barcelona, but he could not touch her as she was under Russian colours.

One Spaniard, however, overreached himself. He was boarded by Lieutenant Hill of the *Saracen*. He was under Portuguese colours, and his papers stated that he was manned by two-thirds Portuguese. As this was not the case, this brigantine became a prize and her captain lamented his fate.

"I am the most unfortunate fellow in the world!" he exclaimed, "this is the third vessel I have lost in two years. That blackguard at Porto Praya told me the papers were all correct and I paid him a thousand dollars."

However in the end he had to be released.

After seeing nothing except a drifting palm tree for twenty-one days, Keppel was glad to proceed on the first Monday in January to the rendezvous appointed by the S.N.O. in 4° N. 4° E. Here Popham inspected his Mosquito fleet with as much style as the haughtiest of admirals. There was no manoeuvring, sail drill or firing exercises, of course: the little cruisers, what with sick men and hands away in prizes were too short-handed for that. For instance *Forester*, which had come out to relieve the *Columbine*, had lost six of her crew on the way down from Sierra Leone.

Fair Rosamond, which had recently sent a prize North, had lost her whole prize crew except the officer: *Bonetta* had only four men living out of two prize crews; *Curlew* was nearly unmanned, whilst the surveying cutter *Raven* was lying at Accra unable to put to sea for want of men.

Keppel's Account Of The Squadron

Keppel's remarks on this, his first encounter with the whole of the coast of Africa Squadron, are of interest from a Service point of view.

Most of the cruisers had skysails aloft and none of them had any points in their topsails below the second reef. The *Pelican*, Popham's little flagship, was 'in good discipline, beautifully clean and neat about the rigging.'

Scout 'loomed large in the Mosquito fleet: she was clean and very nice inside.'

Columbine 'looked, as she always did—beautiful. I think her by far the most perfect of Symonds' craft.'

'*Saracen's* commander, Hill, is an active fellow, but his vessel is a brute and nothing could make her sail or look decent.' Wrote Keppel.

He does not mention *Waterwitch*. No doubt she was left to watch the coast, as being the fastest of the lot.

After the inspection was over, a very good dinner was given by Popham aboard the *Pelican* to all his commanders: after which, each Mosquito cruiser returned to her station.

This time the *Childers* was given the *Columbine's* cruising ground, from 4° N. to the coast and thence to the Meridian of Greenwich at Accra.

Whilst heading in for the land in a thick Hamattan with both leads going, Keppel tumbled upon a slaver at anchor.

"Man and arm boats", was the cry; and they were alongside the stranger in a trice.

She turned out to be the *Camoen*, a lovely brig of one hundred and eighty tons under Portuguese colours—the first slaver Keppel had seen that was painted with a white stripe. As she had no slaves on board she could not be touched.

On the afternoon of the same day, the wind being very light, the boats were sent after another sail. When the *Childers* at length got up, she found the slaver had two large canoes, such as were used for embarking slaves, towing astern and the slave dealer was actually on board busy bargaining.

On being sent to the *Childers* to be examined, this man was immediately recognised by some liberated Africans, who had been put aboard from the *Columbine*, and they had to be held back from attacking him.

One native boy told how this ruffian had stolen him from his kraal and buried him in the sand on the beach for a whole day with a calabash over his head to hide him and with the threat that he would be killed at once if he cried out. Another boy had been bought by the slave dealer for a keg of rum.

This vessel was a brig of one hundred and fifty tons and twenty-five men, named the *Amigos*.

Aristocratic Guinea Captains

Keppel, who was the most friendly soul alive and ready to be civil to the devil himself, after remarking that the captain of the *Amigos* was an obliging, civil fellow, makes the following rather surprising statement:-

"Most of the captains of these slavers are superior men: some belong to good Spanish and Portuguese families: generally young, I believe many of them take command of these vessels for the excitement of the service."

A fortnight later as the *Childers* was standing in towards Quitta to pick up her boats, she encountered the slaver *Fortuna* coming to an anchor at Owye in man-of-war style.

This was a very handsome brig and well-known for the beautiful order in which she was kept up by her captain, whom Keppel made a point of interviewing, for he was the late commander of the *Veloz Passagera*—'a handsome, intelligent-looking man, a Biscayan', wrote Keppel, 'He bore the marks of the action about him, having but one arm.'

Another Guinea Captain, whom Keppel made the acquaintance of, was Don De Souza, a son of the famous Whydah trader. Keppel found him a young, well-educated seaman, commanding the largest slaver on the çoast, the brig, *Enterprise*.

Anothér captain proved to have been a guest of the *Childers* commander, when he gave a dance aboard the brig at Barcelona some three years before.

Whilst at Quitta the captain of the *Dos Amigos* lent his canoes for the taking off of fresh provisions to the *Childers*. He also accommodated Keppel's officers and stewards with beds. "The only return we could make for his courtesy", wrote Keppel, "would be to capture him when he had embarked his slaves".

As showing the difficulty of catching loaded slavers, between January the 11th and February the 3rd, the energetic Keppel boarded the following slavers without finding a slave:—

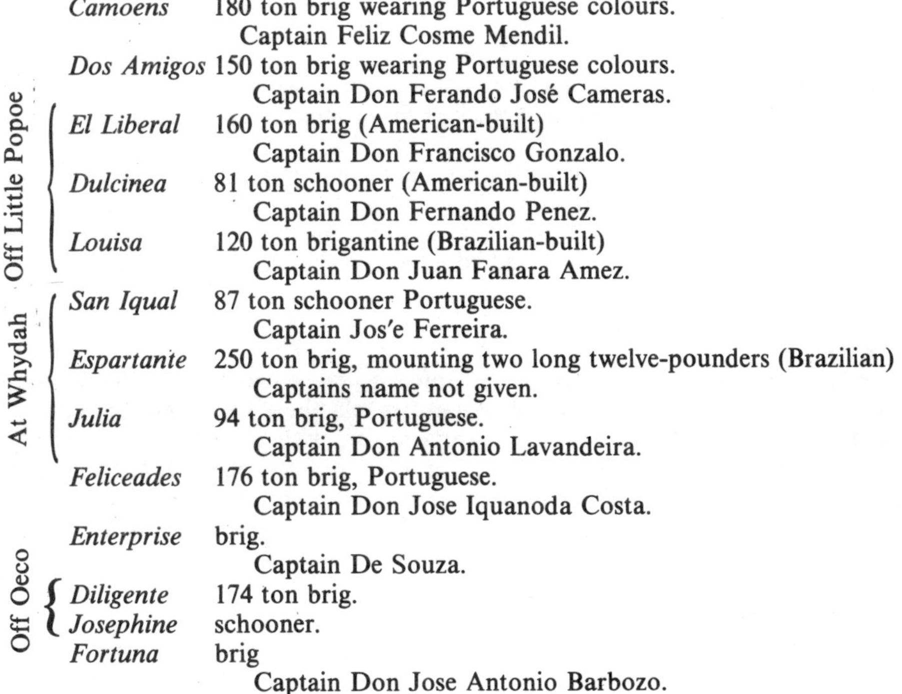

	Camoens	180 ton brig wearing Portuguese colours. Captain Feliz Cosme Mendil.
	Dos Amigos	150 ton brig wearing Portuguese colours. Captain Don Ferando José Cameras.
Off Little Popoe	*El Liberal*	160 ton brig (American-built) Captain Don Francisco Gonzalo.
Off Little Popoe	*Dulcinea*	81 ton schooner (American-built) Captain Don Fernando Penez.
Off Little Popoe	*Louisa*	120 ton brigantine (Brazilian-built) Captain Don Juan Fanara Amez.
At Whydah	*San Iqual*	87 ton schooner Portuguese. Captain Jos'e Ferreira.
At Whydah	*Espartante*	250 ton brig, mounting two long twelve-pounders (Brazilian) Captains name not given.
At Whydah	*Julia*	94 ton brig, Portuguese. Captain Don Antonio Lavandeira.
	Feliceades	176 ton brig, Portuguese. Captain Don Jose Iquanoda Costa.
	Enterprise	brig. Captain De Souza.
Off Oeco	*Diligente*	174 ton brig.
Off Oeco	*Josephine*	schooner.
	Fortuna	brig Captain Don Jose Antonio Barbozo.

On January the 18th, 1838, during the Hamattan, Keppel pitched a shot under the forefoot of a brigantine, which was looming indistinctly through the haze. She turned out to be the *Dolphin*, 'the nicest-looking vessel we have seen and appears in very good order,' declared Harry Keppel.

The *Dolphin* had been eighteen months in commission and captured one thousand six hundred slaves in nine different vessels, every one of which had been fallen upon accidentally. But all her officers, with the exception of the clerk and most of her crew had fallen victims to the climate.

A Smart Signalman

Keppel followed the usual coast practice of having two lookouts aloft, one a Krooman, with a doubloon for the man who sighted a prize.

His best lookout was a very smart signalman—in fact the smartest in the whole of Keppel's long experience.

A sail to the norrard being reported, this man went aloft and reported a square-rigged vessel before the wind. Then he announced that she was a man-of war, though none were expected from that direction—this he could tell from the squareness of her yards.

His next statement was that she was an 18-gun sloop—he had counted the cloths in her main topgallantsail! As soon as he could see her foreyard above the horizon he declared she was just out from home.

"How the deuce can you tell?" roared Keppel. "The three midship cloths of her foretopsail are discoloured", returned the signalman calmly.

"What the deuce has that to do with it?" roared Keppel again.

The signalman then explained that the lookout men were young hands, whose stomachs had not had time to grow accustomed to the coast swell. He proved to be right in every conclusion. The stranger turned out to be the *Modeste*, eighteen-guns, Commander Harry Eyres.

On February the 20th, 1838, off Lagos, Keppel fell in with his senior officer and received orders to sail for home. These orders, which had come through the Admiral at the Cape, were some six months late and Harry Keppel had received his promotion as far back as December the 5th, 1837.

When *Childers* sailed into Portsmouth Harbour at the end of April, 1838, her crew were astonished by the crowds of people that assembled on South sea beach to watch the gallant little brig sail by. This, however, was due to a rumour which had been spread in naval circles.

This was to the effect that the *Childers* had been lost with all on board, having capsized in a squall off the Gambia.

"I See The Keel"

That she had had one narrow escape from foundering when caught in a Mediterranean squall was well-known, as one of the characteristic stories told about her popular commander.

On January the 5th, 1835, Keppel was carrying on with topgallant sails set over double-reefed topsails in order to weather Cape Karabonn out of Vourla Bay. The brig was battened down, sheets of spray were flying over her, and both wind and sea were rising. Then an extra hard puff threw her on her beam ends, until her mainyard was dragging in the water.

Her crack first lieutenant, Goldsmith, who was up on the hammock-netting, holding on to a back-stay, sang out:—

"Hard up the helm!"

But little Keppel, as he hung on to the weather quarter like a limpet, to use his own words, was able to see the whole weather side of the brig showing out of water, and, without thinking, he roared in his impetuous way:—

"The helm be dammed! I see the keel!"

The rudder was, of course, useless, being out of water. For a few long seconds the *Childers* lay like a log; then as the squall took off, she brought her spars to windward and righted with the loss of everything moveable on deck, her hammock-nettings, port watch hammocks, half-ports (torn off their hinges) and harness-cask.

***Waterwitch* Short-handed.**

The next African cruiser to reach Spithead was the *Waterwitch*, on July the 20th, 1838. The famous slaver catcher had suffered a most sickly time ever since Adams had left her.

William Dickey, who had succeeded to the command had died on the 29th of May, 1838, off Prince's Island. About the same time she lost her assistant-surgeon and thirteen members of her crew. William Austen, mate, having given himself an acting order to take over the command of the brig, wisely decided to go straight away to Ascension in order to recruit the health of his crew. The *Waterwitch* arrived there on the 9th of June and found the inhabitants of the island slowly recovering from a severe epidemic, which had carried off nearly thirty people including Captain Bate, the popular Commandant.

As soon as twenty-five of her white crew were fit for duty, the brig was headed for home, but Austen was obliged to take nineteen Kroomen with him in order to help in working the ship.

The mate was deservedly promoted to lieutenant soon after her arrival, and the Kroomen were taken back to the coast in the *Columbine*, which had just been commissioned by Commander G. Elliot.

CHAPTER XVI

COAST OF AFRICA 1838-1841

"Think of undergoing eternal rancid butter, bad biscuit, tainted water, and milkless tea and coffee. For ever to hear no sounds but the rattling of sails and straining of ropes; whilst all around is sea and sky interminable: the distant line of the horizon being at times broken by blue, misty clouds, mocking the straining eye with the hope of a mountain coast, and to hear from the shadowy spectre of a captain in answer to the question, 'When shall we reach the shore?' the dead eternal:—'Never!!!' ".

(Four years in South Africa)

Rear-Admiral The Honourable George Elliot

ON the 7th of March, 1838, Rear-Admiral the Honourable George Elliot in his flagship, the *Melville,* seventy-two guns, arrived in Simons Bay, and relieved Rear-Admiral Sir Patrick Campbell of the arduous Cape command, comprising as it did both coasts of Africa from the Gambia right round to Zanzibar.

During Campbell's regime, that is to say between October 1834 and March 1838, the West coast squadron had taken fifty-seven slavers with one hundred and ninety thousand slaves on board. Besides which, in spite of false papers and colours, over thirty Spanish vessels had been condemned under the Equipment article in the Spanish treaty of June 1835.

A Prize Money Return

The following return of these, which was laid on the table in the House of Commons, is specially interesting, as showing how much prize money was paid.

The new Admiral at the Cape not only had a long and distinguished war record, but, like Hayes, was a designer of note.

The second son of the first Earl of Minto, he had served under many distinguished captains, including Nelson, Foley, Hyde Parker, Charles Thomson, Morice Pole and Masterman Hardy. He was a veteran of Hotham's actions, St. Vincent, the 1st of August 1798, and Copenhagen.

His two most successful designs were the *Modeste,* eighteen-gun sloop, and the most beautiful but ill-fated *Eurydice,* twenty-six-gun corvette.

He took up his difficult task just at the time when the slave trade was at its zenith and its prosperity causing a great deal of heart burning in England.

Name of capturing ship.	Name of Spanish slave vessel.	Net proceeds paid into the Registry			Amount paid to Captors being one moiety in each case.			Grand total received by cruiser.		
		£.	s.	d.	£.	s.	d.	£.	s.	d.
Brisk	*Constitucao*	178	4	0	89	2	9			
	O Veterano	2826	19	3	1413	9	7			
	Diligente	410	0	7	205	0	3			
	Eliza	417	8	11	208	14	5			
	Josephina	82	5	8	41	2	10			
	Ligeira	81	10	10	40	15	5			
	Veloz	165	12	2	82	16	1			
	Maria	177	12	2	58	16	1	2139	17	5
Britomart	*Dos Herma Nos*	44	1	7	22	0	9			
	General Mina	577	17	4	288	18	8	310	19	5
Buzzard	*Felicia*	14	6	0	7	3	0			
	Famosa Primeira	436	13	8	218	6	10			
	Atalaya	31	17	8	15	18	10			
	Sirse	175	11	7	87	15	5	329	4	1
Bonetta	*Cinco Amigos*	45	6	5	22	13	3	22	13	3
Charybdis	*Matilde*	488	3	10	244	1	11			
	Tridente	849	5	4	424	12	8			
	El Mismo	30	1	0	15	0	6			
	General Rica Fort	2941	15	3	1470	17	7			
	Cantrabra	30	4	5	15	2	2	2169	14	10
Curlew	*Rosario*	231	7	8	115	13	10	115	13	10
Dolphin	*Dolores*	108	18	11	54	9	5	54	9	5
Forester	*Golondrina*	198	2	10	99	1	5			
	Luisa	141	15	8	70	17	10	169	19	3
*Fair Rosamond**	*Constitucao*	1461	13	8	730	16	4	730	16	4
Pylades	*Gaceta*	11	2	9	5	11	4	5	11	4
Rolla	*Luisita*	232	2	3	116	1	1			
	Lechuguine	14	9	0	7	4	6			
	San Nicolos	10	17	8	5	8	10	178	14	5
Scout	*Descubierta*	72	9	2	36	9	7	36	9	7

Keppel's Review of the Slave Trade

There were many people, who agreed with the following review of the position by Harry Keppel:—

"It appears to me that while cruisers were not allowed by treaties with Spain and Portugal to capture vessels fitted for the slave trade without slaves on board, we did more harm than good.

Along the coast negroes are brought from the interior and confined in pens and, when closely watched by our cruisers, are frequently starved to death.

If a slaver is captured with slaves on board, the price rises on the other side of the Atlantic, which is immediately followed by the increase in the number of vessels that come out.

Some of these vessels are owned by the sons of wealthy Spaniards, who purchase American clippers, easily fitted as slavers who come to the coast of Africa as much on pleasure as business. The little Spanish I picked up at Barcelona enabled me to converse freely with these agreeable young roués, who, if they did not carry slaves, easily kept our cruisers employed by drawing their attention form the coast to chase these yachtlike slavers.

The found matches in our fifteen cruisers!"

Many cavelled at the cost of the squadron which at the end of Campbell's time consisted of one forty-six-gun frigate, carrying the flag (*Thalia*) three sloops of war (*Pelican, Scout* and

* The Government retained the seven hundred and thirty pounds sixteen shillings and four pence due to the *Fair Rosamond,* because they had to pay an award of one thousand seven hundred and thirty four pound fourteen shillings on the *Camoes,* which had been unlawfully made a prize by *Fair Rosamond.*

Columbine), seven brigs and brigantines (*Waterwitch, Forester, Buzzard, Curlew, Saracen, Bonetta* and *Dolphin*) and one schooner (*Fair Rosamond*).

The cost in wear and tear, victuals and wages came roughly to twenty two thousand pounds. Allowing a bounty for three hundred slaves per annum for each vessel would add another sixteen thousand five hundred pounds. Then there were the mixed court salaries, coming to about seven thousand pounds per annum.

The whole cost to the Exchequer of the West African squadron was in the neighbourhood of fifty thousand pounds per annum.

But if the slavers were the finest and fastest clippers that Baltimore could produce, the Royal Navy now had vessels, such as *Columbine, Waterwitch* and the new Symondite brigs and brigantines, which were capale of overtaking the fastest clipper under any conditions of weather.

Rattle Snake's Record Passage

In these days of great scientific progress few recognise how efficient all round our sailing navy was in its last days. For instance in the year 1839 the old twenty-eight-gun *Rattlesnake,* sailed from Madras on August the 24th, left Trincomalee on September the 3rd and anchored in Simon's Bay on Ocotber the 4th, having been only thirty days from Trincomalee to Cape Hanglip, considered the quickest passage for years.

On October the 6th she left Simon's Bay for Ascension, which she reached on October the 26th. Finally she sailed into Plymouth Sound on November the 27th, having been under sail between Madras and Plymouth for just eighty-one days.

It was in 1839 that a new scale of armament was instituted; as well as a new peace establishment for the R.N.

This will be found in the Appendix, along with a further change of 1847, in which I have only included the smaller classes.

Service on Coast of Africa Unpopular With Officers

With the advent of the Symondite brigs and brigantines on the coast of Africa, slavers, could no longer depend on being able to outsail their opponents, and during the eighteen-thirties the British squadron on the West coast was gradually increased both in numbers and efficiency. Yet many of the smartest officers in the Service did their very best to avoid being sent to the coast. Its opportunities of distinction, if they led to promotion, as often led to ill-health and half-pay.

It has been argued that many a naval officer made a fortune in prize money. But this is not true. The officers and men of a cruiser were entitled to four pounds per ton for every captured slaver without slaves on board. For slaves captured they received five pounds a head on all those delivered alive and two pounds ten shillings for each slave which died aboard after capture.

This, when divided up amongst a ship's company, did not amount to a vast sum and only too often years of ill-health had to be set against such pecuniary gains, for when the proper treatment of malaria was quite unknown to the medical profession, many an officer and man never really recovered from his slave hunting days.

A Deadly Monotony

Nor can the monotony of this service be exaggerated. This, added to the climatic conditions, not only aggravated ill-health, but caused depression and even nervous and mental breakdown.

Lord Clarence Paget, speaking in the House of Commons, thus described the life of a West coast man-of-war:—

"She cruised for six long months up and down within sight of a sandy beach with a heavy surf rolling and never seeing a living mortal".

It will be remembered that Keppel mentioned a drifting palm tree as the only object of interest seen from the *Childers* in a three weeks cruise.

Continuing Paget's eloquent description:—

"The monotony of the blockade is killing to officers and men. You can form no conception of what they have to undergo. I cannot speak too highly of their conduct under such trying circumstances—for months at anchor, rolling terribly, thermometer eighty-six degrees, no change of companions: no supplies of fresh stock except at long intervals.

We have not sufficient vessels to ensure certain reliefs".

Six Months Without a Prize

Whilst public opinion, as it became more informed, had gradually mounted in England against the slave trader, until the Act of 1839 at last gave the cruisers a fair deal, opinion against the iniquitous traffic was very slow in gaining headway abroad.

Foreign Governments would not enforce their own laws or carry out their treaty obligations. When cruisers were allowed to capture Spanish vessels under the Equipment clauses, Spanish slavers speedily took out Portuguese papers. The first effect of the Portuguese treaty was very encouraging.

For sometime not a single slaver showed up in the Bights. Several cruisers did not make a single capture and the smart little Symondite brig, *Cygnet,* after catching some of the fastest slavers on the coast, cruised for six months, just as Lord Clarence Paget had said, without seeing a sail.

The Portuguese, when they became liable to the Equipment clauses, like the Spanish, very quickly found a way through the clauses of the treaty by putting their slave ships under the stars and stripes and taking out American papers.

Naval Officers as Treaty Makers

When Naval officers had the chance of Making International agreements, the results have very often been more effective than those made by Politicians.

For instance, on May the 29th, 1839, Commander William Tucker of the *Wolverine,* senior officer on the West coast of Africa, who had first made his name in the *Hope* tender back in 1826, signed an agreement with the Governor-General of Angola, in which these two important clauses were included:—

3. 'If any English man-of-war under the order of the senior officer commanding Her Britannic Majesty's ships and vessels of war on the Western coast of Africa meets in any part of the ocean South of the Equator any vessel with a Portuguese passport, having a cargo of slaves on board, she shall be empowered to take her and send her to St. Paul de Loando to be adjudged according to the preceding article*.

4. Neither the senior officer commanding Her Britannic Majesty's ships or vessels of war on the Western coast of Africa, nor any officer under his orders, shall be responsible for any damage or expenses for the vessels captured in that manner with slaves on board and sent to St. Paul de Loanda to be adjudged'.

These clauses, it will be noticed, delivered over the slave trade South of the Line to the West coast squadron.

Denham Destroys the Gallinas Barracoons

The next hit at the slave trader by a Naval officer was made by Commander the Honourable Joseph Denham† of *Wanderer*, S.N.O. on the windward coast in 1840-1841.

* i.e. 'Punished with all the rigour of the Portuguese laws and especially according to the Portuguese decree of the 10th of December 1836.

† Son of the Right Honourable Lord Denham, Chief Justice of the Court of the Queen's Bench, and brother-in-law of Captain R. L. Baynes, C.B. and Lieutenant Fred Holland (commanding the R.N. schooner *Pickle*).

Denham was one of those commanders, who, like the old stalwarts of the Napolonic wars, believed in the effectiveness of a close blockade.

The year 1840 found him blockading the mouth of the Gallinas river, at that time the chief market on the coast for the Cuban trade.

With him he had the brigs *Rolla* (Lieutenant C. Hall) and *Saracen* (Lieutenant H. W. Hill).

Whilst on this duty he received orders from the Governor of Sierra Leone, Sir Richard Doherty, to procure the liberty of a lady of colour, a Freetown subject, named Try Nelson, who had been forcibly detained with her child at Dombocorro in King Siacca's territory (He was the head chief of the river) by a Mr. Manna on the pretext that one hundred and fifty Spanish dollars were owed to him by her mistress.

The powerful slave traders threatened to use force if Denham attempted to communicate with King Siacca and this gave Denham his opportunity.

Nine boats manned by one hundred seamen and marines were sent in and landed at Dombocorro without opposition. Manna, a scion apparently of Siacca's royal house, was ordered to produce the woman and child, but at once began to blacken the character of her mistress, Mrs. Gray. But the pair were handed over, and the kidnapping was only looked upon by Mr. Manna in the light of a joke.

However, before returning to his ships, Denham seized the chance of the owners of the slave barracoons having 'acted in defiance of the King Siacca's law'.

There were eight barracoons in all, containing gun-powder, gin, cottons and wollens with which to purchase slaves, and defended by guns. On the 21st. of November 1840 Denham concluded a treaty with King Siacca, by which nine hundred slaves were emancipated, the goods handed over to the king, the barracoons destroyed and their cannon spiked. Whilst the bluejackets put a torch to the slave factories, the king's deputies looked on, but the white slave traders were forced to take refuge aboard the *Wanderer*.

The legality of the whole transaction would have been doubted by anyone but the son of a great lawyer. Denham reported his proceedings to both Sir R. Doherty and Captain Tucker; the first forwarded his account to Lord John Russell at the Colonial office and the latter to the Admiralty.

Lord Palmerston Upholds Denham

The Government at once approved Denham's action, and in April 1841, Lord Palmerston voiced the general opinion that 'no better plan could be pursued for the suppression of the slave trade than a system of blockade combined with the destruction of the factories on shore upon the plan pursued by Captain Denham on the destruction of the slave factories at the Gallinas'.

It was just was well that the British Government backed up the enterprising Denham, for, when he arrived home in 1842, he was served with three writs for £180,000, £150,000 and £40,000 at the suit of the Gallinas slave traders, Senors Tomas Buron, Angel Jimessez and Pedro Martinez—their claims being damages for trespass.

The case of Buron verses Denham was tried on February the 14th, 1848, the attorney-general defending Denham. After three days, in which there was more than one exciting moment, the jury found the British Government and not Captain Denham responsible.

The case caused great excitement at the time, and Denham's name for an enterprising and stick-at-nothing officer was made.

The Blockade System

He also gained many advocates for his system of blockade at anchor. That this was most inconvenient was admitted by Theodore Canot at his station at New Cestros, when it was blockaded by the *Bonetta* in 1839.

'*Bonito* (*Bonetta*) held on with provoking pertinacity in front of my factory, so that I was troubled but little with company from Cuba for several months'. Wrote the slave trader.

Canot Exhibits His Slaves at Dinner

He also related how he showed off his well-fed slaves, his rice granary, his stores of merchandize, in fact his whole station, hut by hut, to the captain and surgeon of the war brigantine. They were even shown the slaves at dinner, where 'the washing, singing, distribution of food, beating time and all the prandial et ceteras of comfort were performed with the utmost precision and cleanliness'.

Canot specially remarked how the dapper little sawbones pried into every nook and corner until he reached the slave kitchen, where a caldron full and bubbling with the most delicious rice, and a pot simmering with meat and soup, supplied the final proof that Canot kept a humane, well-run station.

Canot Escapes From The *Galouptchick*

The sailors naturally contended that the whole show was got up for their benefit, upon which Canot produced his daily journal and account books. However the *Bonetta* remained a fixture; and in time the bubbling rice and smoking stew pots began to be considerably less full. This is in the end compelled Canot to go seeking for supplies aboard the slaver *Galouptchick*.

This vessel was a very fast, one-hundred-and-eighty-ton brig, which had shown her stern to many of the cruisers on the windward coast, but she fell a victim to the *Saracen,* the slowest of the lot, owing to being caught embayed close in shore.

Though manned by Spaniards, the *Galouptchick* had foreign papers in order to circumvent the new Spanish treaty. These were Russian papers of some years standing from the port of Odessa, but Lieutenant Hill finding that her slave deck was laid, her water casks were aboard, her crew Spanish and in addition that the notorious slave trader, Theodore Canot, was aboard decided to make a prize of her.

As there was no mixed court of Russians and English, she had to be sent to England for adjudication. It is often difficult to separate true from false in Canot's narrative. On this occasion he described how on the slaver's arrival at Sierra Leone, he made the after guard of the prize crew drunk and then swam ashore.

The *Galouptchick* caused something of a sensation when she arrived at Portsmouth in June 1839.

Success of *Bonetta* and *Dolphin*

The little *Bonetta* sailed for home in the spring of 1840, after a long commission on the coast of over four years, during which she had captured thirteen slavers and freed one thousand six hundred slaves.

During the last twenty-six months of her service she was commanded by Lieutenant-Commander J. L. R. Stoll, a very experienced and capable officer, who captured nine of her prizes, three of them fifty miles up the Congo and one cut out of the river Pongas after a smart resistance.

Her sister ship, the *Dolphin,* Lieutenant-Commander Holland, had arrived home in January 1840, with only about a dozen of her original complement left, but they had the consolation of a good fist full of prize money, one of her petty officers receiving upwards of seven hundred pounds.

The *Dolphin* reported the great success of the *Waterwitch,* Lieutenant H. J. Matson, which only arrived at Sierra Leone from England on May the 22nd, 1839. She had already caught four slavers.

Matson had a specially fine crew.

Manning Bills

In the thirties the manning of a ship often took weeks and months, her officers being sent to every sea port all round the Kingdom for men.

Some ships were popular for their own sakes, but as a rule it entirely depended on the reputation of the captain whether a man-of-war, battle ship or cruiser, filled up quickly with men.

As a rule small fry, especially slave catchers, were manned very quickly.

Matson posted the following bill for *Waterwitch* at Portsmouth.

WATERWITCH.
Fine Clipper Brig
Commanded by Lieutenant J. Matson
(late first-lieutenant of the *Pearl*)
LOTS OF PRIZE MONEY.

Like her rival, the *Pantalooon,* the *Waterwitch* was considered a sort of pet in the Royal Navy in the thirties and forties, and men boasted of having served in her.

Naturally no sooner were her bills posted than a crowd of seamen offered themselves and her Commanders could always pick and choose.

Matson's old ship, the *Curlew* was also commissioning at Portsmouth at this time.

Curlew's bill ran as follows:—

LOOK JACK
HERE'S A CHANCE

The lucky *Curlew,* that made lots of prize money on the Coast last commission is now fitting out under
Lieutenant George Rose
who knows the coast well and has vacancies for petty officers and seamen. Go to the sheer-hulk *Rendezvous,* Portsea and get a berth before it is too late.

In spite of this alluring bill *Curlew* did not man so quickly as the *Waterwitch.*

The *Winchester,* described as 'that beautiful frigate' found still greater difficulty in filling in spite of the following:—

'Any man volunteering for the *Winchester* will be received aboard the *Britannia,* and a tender sent round to bring them to the ship, bag and baggage. The landlord of the ship *Anson* will pay the waterage of any men to the flagship and Mrs. Capon and Mrs. Smart (two well-known bum-boat women) at the Point will do the same'.

Other ships fitting out at the same time, were the *Curacoa, Hydra* and *Childers.*

Curacoa's Bill had the following enticement:—

'Her masts and yards have been reduced since last commission
and an addition made to the crew of twenty men'.

The *Hydra,* described as a 'splendid steam frigate', would only receive men producing good certificates.

The *Childers* with a wealth of alliteration was advertised as:—

'The fine fast-sailing flying *Childers*'.

The Southern Squadron

The first British men-of-war to cruise against slavers to the South of the Equator on the West coast of Africa were the new brig-sloop, *Fantome,* Commander E. H. Butterfield, the *Waterwitch,* commanded by Lieutenant H. J. Matson and the *Brisk,* which on the promotion of Lieutenant A. Kellett (a cousin of Henry Kellett of surveying and Arctic renown) in the autumn of 1839, was taken over by Lieutenant George Sprigg from the *Melville,* Admiral Elliot's flagship. Sprigg like Butterfield and Matson was an officer of proved worth and experience.

With Butterfield senior officer the cruise of these three vessels in what were entirely new waters was extremely successful.

I will first of all quote three letters written home by the commander of the *Brisk, Fantome,* and *Waterwitch.*

The first in order of date is the following:—

Rivalry of *Fantome, Brisk* and *Waterwitch*

H.M.S. *Brisk*, St. Helena,
Oct. 21, 1840.

We have been sometime cruising off the Angola coast, where the slave trade is still going on to a great extent by Portuguese, Brazilians and, I regret to say, Americans: the latter not only bringing over the equipment for other slave vessels, but actually buying and selling themselves, and affording every assistance, as spies, etc., on the British cruisers, which they can do with so much felicity under protection of their own flag. A very glaring case has just occurred: the *Waterwitch* has captured an American brig deeply engaged in it with a valuable cargo. She found slaves on board purchased by the Captain and, in evidence before the Portuguese authorities at Angola, discoverd much to the great discredit of the Americans for allowing their flag to be so prostituted.

This is the fifth American vessel taken within the twelve months and yet the Yankee President refuses to enter into any treaty, as they are not engaged or likely to be, in it.

The Portuguese authorities have lately been much stricter within the limits of the colony in suppressing the traffic: but they are not to be trusted, as the captain of a Portuguese man-of-war was lately bribed to allow a barque to sail with eight hundred odd slaves on board, which she actually did, as it were, under his protection.

Fantome, the surveyor's new beautiful brig, captured a Brazilian brigantine fully equipped for the trade and sent her to Sierra Leone.

She was lately been trying rate of sailing with the *Waterwitch,* but cannot hold a candle to her.

In two different trials the *Waterwitch* beat her most decidedly, particularly in going to windward.

The last trial the *Fantome* tried her utmost, had her hammocks down and hung up, all weight removed from the extremes by clearing of storerooms, bread room, foremost and after guns shifted in amidships etc., etc., but to no purpose; the *Waterwitch* beat her as much or more than she did *Columbine* and I think now it can be safely pronounced the vessel superior or equal to her in sailing has not yet been launched.

We are now going to the Cape and expect our relief. All the squadron to the South of the Bights are quite healthy.

Yours etc., George Sprigg.

Next I will quote a short letter written by Matson six months later:—

H.M.B. *Waterwitch*, Off Ambriz,
April 16, 1841.

We have been to the Cape and have been hove down to have our copper repaired. We have been just four days back on the coast and this morning fell in with and captured after a three hours chase a Portuguese brigantine with three hundred and fourteen slaves on board and have sent her to be condemned.

The last we took was in December last and she had two hundred and eight slaves.

Yours etc., H. J. Matson

The third is a long one to Sir William Symonds from Captain Butterfield:—

H.M.S. *Fantome*,
Nov. 26, 1841.

My dear Sir William,

The *Fantome* arriving here to refit, after several months cruise off the coast off Angola, it is with pleasure I can inform you she has proved herself everything one can wish; and I think we are very fortunate in having captured sixteen slavers and one thousand three hundred and forty slaves.

On the 1st of May, 1841, I captured the *Josephine*, with two hundred and ninety slaves on board, after twenty-four hours chase and a run of two hundred and forty one miles. She was a brigantine with a maintopsail, of one hundred and fifty tons, and said to be the fastest vessel out of the Havannah. She had been cleared out of Whydah by *Lynx* and *Dolphin,* and subsequently by *Wolverine* and *Cygnet,* but very much outsailed them.

I was on my way from Ascension to the Congo. After having left the former place two days, we saw the vessel at half past seven a.m. three points on the weather bow, hauling her wind from us. The *Fantome* had on board six months' provisions and I feared trying on a wind.

The slaver, manoeuvring to find on what point I wished to chase, bore up three points, which I immediately did also. He then hauled up to two points free; we could see his foreyard from the quarter-boat, and were under double-reefed topsails. I immediately shook out all reefs, set fore and main-topmast studding sails, main royal and flying jib and went eleven knots.

I had only a second jib bent, as I split my jib, the day previous, into ribbands: and had only canvas on board to make another in lieu of the one I returned at Ascension, there being none in store: so I may say I had no jib during the chase. At 4 p.m. the slaver cut away his anchors, threw overboard his long gun, chain-cables, boat, took his wedges out, and sawed through the gunwale. At sunset we could just see his main-boom. At dark I luckily caught him in my large day-glass (there being fortunately a moon) fancying we were not near him. At 8 p.m. I knocked down my cabin bulkhead and cleared the after bread-room, putting all the bread into the fore part of the gun-room, and cleared out all the store-room and side bins. The guns were all squared and run in as soon as we saw him.

At 1 a.m. took in studding-sails and main-royal, and carried through a tremendous squall of wind and rain,—a thing I should never have attempted in any other built vessel; and gallantly she went through it. The slaver lost all his studding-sails, booms, and flying-jibboom, and was very nearly lost: had to let fly everything. We lost sight of him for about half an hour.

I set all studding-sails again in half an hour, and found we had neared him very much.

At 3 a.m. the moon went down. At 3.30 he bore up two points more, which I very fortunately saw him do, and continued in this course till daylight, when we were within gun shot.

He lost sight of us when the moon went down, and steered for a dark bank: did not see us again until I sent a shot through his foresail. He stood nine or ten before he hove to.

I was rounding to, to give him a broadside, when they all ran below. He was saying all day it was the *Waterwitch,* as he had fancied nothing could take him but her. I doubt very much, under the circumstances, that she could do so: although I believe she cannot be better sailed than under her present commander, Lieutenant Matson. I thought we overpowered him, and it would have taken us forty-eight hours to have taken him in light airs.

We have not had a fair trial with *Waterwitch:* unfortunately when in company, we have never had any wind, and I have been always full of provisions, or nothing in. The case mentioned in the paper of her having boarded a vessel first, is nothing to boast of. The chase began at 8 a.m. the vessel on our weather beam. I towed my pinnace until 10.30: and when we tacked, the *Waterwitch* was about a mile astern, or rather on the weather quarter. We came up from E.S.E. to S. by W., therefore giving the *Waterwitch* a great advantage: and by chronometer, at 4 p.m. she boarded the vessel fourteen minutes before us. The *Frisk* was lower yards down, before we came up, upwards of an hour going four knots, *Waterwitch* having held her own.

I firmly believe *Fantome* is fully equal to *Waterwitch* on a wind, and certainly superior off.

On one occasion we chased together with lower studding sails, and neared the *Waterwitch* a couple of miles in four miles: and on another occasion, going two knots dead before it, under all plain sail, from 9 a.m. until 3 p.m. we beat four miles. The *Waterwitch* has the *Lily's* topsail yard: the topsails are quite square: her topgallant sails longer than mine and her royals in proportion, giving her a great advantage on this station. She has no hammocks or nettings: her spare anchors are ashore; no quarter-boats.

Could the two vessels be sailed on equal terms I am quite certain *Fantome* would be found quite her equal, if not superior.

I sail today, for a six months' cruise, again off Angola, when I very much fear *Fantome* will have to go home, for her copper is in such a state that I have been obliged to put on twenty-four sheets as low as I could reach.

Yours etc.,

To Sir Wm. Symonds E. H. Butterfield

It will be seen that Butterfield did his best to champion his own vessel.

Looked at from the designer's point of view, the *Waterwitch* was undoubtedly superior to any of the Symondites.

A Tall Ship

As regards sails, commanders on the coast of Africa were allowed every latitude in this respect and skysails and flying kites of every description were set by enterprising officers, who were able to bear the cost out of their private purse of the additional canvas.

In the wonderful book *By Way of Cape Horn* by Paul Eve Stevenson, there is this testimony to the loftiness of a British man-of-war on the West coast.

"Mr. Rarx (second mate) told me the other day that he spent two years on the West African coast between Sierra Leone and Lagos aboard an English supply steamer: and that while there he saw what, in his estimation, was the loftiest rigged vessel that ever floated. "You can talk about your talk abouts," said he, "but that English man-of-war had four yards above her main royal. I'm telling you a fact," he added.

Evidence Before the Select Committee

Between the 2nd of May 1840 and the 25th of March, 1842 the squadron under Butterfield's command actually captured forty prizes and liberated five thousand three hundred and sixty slaves.

In his evidence before the Select Committee on the Slave Trade, of 1848, Matson gave still more remarkable figures, as follows:—

"From April 1840 to April 1843 one hundred and twenty slavers were captured South of the Equator by a squadron of scarcely ever more than three or four brigs.

During the same period sixty-five were captured North of the Line by a squadron of ten or fifteen vessels".

This success, in which *Waterwitch* played a great part, was so remarkable that both Butterfield and Matson were very closely questioned as to their methods by the Select Committee.

Here are a few points of interest in their evidence:—

Whilst the ships cruised from one end of the station to the other, from 3 South to 17 South, two or three boats from each cruiser were kept working close inshore.

"After the new regulations", said Butterfield, "implicit confidence was placed in the Portuguese authorities, and Loando and Ambriz were left in their charge: but there can be no doubt in my opinion that they all engage in the Trade.

When a slaver is going to sail, the Governor generally goes to his country house, and when he comes back he finds the slaver gone and makes a great fuss and offers a reward to catch them.

We always closed in whenever we had information he had gone to the country and I do not think we missed once taking a vessel coming out".

On the vexed question of searching American ships, Butterfield remarked:—

"We do not acknowledge the flag as the only thing to go by. We claimed the right to visit to ascertain if a ship is American, and, as soon as I saw that the papers were really American, we never searched further. We took several vessels without any flag at all, the Portuguese flag was always hoisted in vessels with slaves, the Brazilian with cargo".

Speaking of the size of slavers, Butterfield gave it as his opinion that in size slavers differed little between 1825 and 1845. If anything they were smaller. He saw one particularly fine slaver of three hundred tons from the East coast which had been condemned at the Cape and which Admiral Elliot wished to purchase for the R.N.

The smallest slaver taken by Butterfield was only about eighteen tons, an ex-merchant-vessel's launch, which had a crew of five and one hundred and five slaves, all children aged from eight down to three or four, of both sexes, with one girl of eighteen. They were lying on water casks, holding ten or twelve gallons; the bulwark was only three or four inches high and a rail of stanchions and bamboos was put round the side to prevent the children falling overboard.

The Southern station was far healthier than the windward coast or the Bights. Especially was this the case with the boat's crews, which were told to keep the slave ports in sight, occasionally landing for water.

Between 1840 and 1842 the *Fantome* lost a lieutenant, a master, a surgeon and a mate, besides five of a crew of one hundred and thirty five. These got their illnesses at Sierra Leone through taking prizes up.

As St. Helena was only eight or nine days sail from the South-West coast, Butterfield found it more advantageous to send his prizes there, but one of these was unlucky, having about seventy deaths on the passage including the officer in charge.

Feeding Liberated Slaves

Butterfield's account of the method of feeding liberated slaves is interesting:—

> "Many of the superior slaves are made head men, marked sometimes with a small rope or row of beeds round their necks. You feed the slaves by placing ten or twelve in a circle: rice and a little palm oil mixed with it, to soften it, is put into a wooden kid in the centre by the head man: then they generally make all the slaves sing while the rice is getting cool. Generally a handful of peppers is put into each kid and they eat it as soon as it is cool enough—none of the slaves begin to eat till the head men give the signal.
>
> Half the slaves are brought on deck and half left below. Half an hour after they done their dinner, my regulation used to be to send all to one end of the vessel; and as we gave them their water, to let them pass, or else many would have gone without and many got double. Grown-up slaves get about a pint each, children about two-thirds.
>
> On slavers they have regulation pots holding about a pint."

As regards the slave ports on the S.W. coast and their pilotage, Lieutenant Matson wrote a very interesting paper for the *Nautical Magazine*.

The Southern Station

The station extended from Cape Lopez to the Nourse or Cunene River, the boundary of Portuguese East Africa on the South. The snug little harbour of Luash was the furthest South of the slave ports; here the Benguela slavers generally embarked their cargoes. A little further South lay Elephant Bay, which Matson considered the best place on the coast for refitting and refreshing the ship's company after an arduous cruise. The rollers or calema, which made landing a danger, were not felt here, and it was an ideal place for a run ashore.

There were no natives to fear; wild game of every kind, big and little, for the sportsman: fish in abundance for the seine haulers; safe bathing in a healthy climate; and lastly excellent oysters could be gathered from the rocks. The only drawback except during the rainy season was lack of water, and for provisions it was necessary to go to Little Fish Bay where cheap vegetables and bullocks could be procured. The danger in this part of the coast was the long low-lying Salinas Point, where many a vessel piled up on the beach on a clear night, as the glittering white sand could not be distinguished from the sea until one was right upon it.

Benguela, a tumble-down mud town without any trade but slaves, was soon blockaded out of existence by the British cruisers. In a snug little cove to the Westward of St. Phillip's Bonnet a boat from the *Waterwitch* lay concealed for nine days watching a slaver in Benguela Roads, which it captured with three hundred and ninety slaves on board before the astonished Portuguese had cleared the anchorage.

Lobito, one of the best harbours on the coast, was only known to slave traders until *Waterwitch* found it in 1840. Even the Portuguese cruisers and Government authorities near by were ignorant of its existence.

Logito, twenty-five miles further North, had a factory for slaves and orchella. It was valued by the cruisers as a place where you could get good, wholesome water—not such an easy matter on the West African coast.

This was mountain water. As the ships could not get closer to the beach than a mile and a quarter, the water casks had first to be hauled off to boats anchored outside the surf and then rafted to the ships.

From Logito the cruiser could run N.N.E. for thirty-nine miles, to Quicombo Bay within a mile of high chalk cliff like the Sussex coast, yet without having soundings with the handlead

Quicombo and Nova Redonda with its delapidated fort, though handicapped by a heavy surf, which made surf boats a necessity, were both slaving centres; but the slave ships usually embarked their slaves in a small bay, a little South of Old Benguela Head.

The Rio Longo was the usual rendezvous for slavers taking their cargoes from Benguela and St. Paul de Loanda, the slaves being marched over land to the river. Matson remarks that there were no natives to be seen but great numbers of 'lions, tigers, deer and other animals'.

The nearest river to St. Paul de Loanda was the Coanzo, but this had an almost uncrossable bar.

The boats of the *Waterwitch* made several fruitless attempts to cross it, and the barge of the *Madagascar* was lost on the bar and its crew drowned within sight of the ship.

The sole attraction of St. Paul de Loanda was its excellent oranges, which could be bought at half a dollar the hundred between May and September.

The great river Congo was a good test of the handiness of a sailing ship. With a tide running six to seven knots and even more on the ebb, it was impossible to tackle the great stream unless the sea breeze was blowing strong, and even then it was not easy. The *Fantome,* sailing five knots, was swept round in a circle by the current, two or three times running and a shoal on the left bank, between five and six miles below Scotchman's head, picked up every stranger, including men-of-war, that entered the river, as the hand-lead gave no warning, the water shoaling suddenly from seven to two fathoms.

But the most dangerous place at the mouth of the Congo was the Mona Mazea Bank, upon which the furious current, in the grip of which a ship soon became unmanageable, always set so that the cautious captain anchored directly he had soundings. The clever *Waterwitch* used to steal into the river by working in the eddy within twenty yards of the shore round Shark's Point, when the sea breeze was too light to stem the current.

However the slaves from the Congo district were mostly shipped aboard slavers in Kabinda Bay.

I must not forget to mention Ambriz, an important slave mart as well as a great place for ivory and copal. About once a fortnight a caravan or 'tabooka' arrived at Ambriz consisting of slaves carrying tusks upon their heads.

There was a curious interruption to the slave trade at Ambriz whilst Butterfield was S.N.O. on the coast. An English ship named the *Rocket* arrived there with a cargo of soldiers' old red tunics, which had been done up by the East end Jew tailors. Whilst the English factor had these red jackets for sale, he could buy ivory at almost any price, nor would the natives sell a single slave as long as there was a red coat to be bought.

After Butterfield had left for the Brazil coast, Captain Foote of the *Madagascar,* forty-four guns, took over the station; and acting under his orders Matson destroyed three slave barracoons at Ambriz and five at Kabinda, releasing eleven hundred slaves.

A Fight up the Congo

The year 1841 was notable for the resistance to capture put up by several slavers.

The *Fantome's* sister ship *Persian,* commissioned in May 1840, by that well-known officer, Commander W. H. Quin, was sent to cruise off the Congo.

Quin died at St. Helena in November and was succeeded by Commander T. R. Eden.

In June 1841 Eden sent his pinnace and gig up the Congo under his first lieutenant, P. H. Somerville.

It so happened that the Cuban slaver, *Astrea,* was awaiting her slave cargo in the river, and she was manned by a crew of desperate men, who swore they would never surrender to any British mosquito cruiser or her boats.

The two boats dashed alongside and a most stubborn fight began. The *Astrea* was not carried until eighteen out of her crew of fifty had been killed outright, the losses of the boats being two killed and two wounded.

The *Persian* also made a prize of a Bremen barque the *Julius* and *Edward* which was lying off Kabinda with a cargo of 'Articles employed in the slave trade'. This ship had to be sent to the Hanseatic courts for adjudication.

Dolphin* And *Firme

A few days previous to the *Astrea's* desperate resistance in the Congo, the boats of the *Dolphin* captured the *Firme*, a beautiful brigantine of one hundred and seventy nine tons, a brand-new Baltimore clipper inward bound to Whydah from Bahia.

At daylight on Sunday, the 30th of May, the *Firme* was discovered on the cruiser's lee bow, heading in for Whydah Roads.

As soon as the *Dolphin* made sail in chase, the stranger headed away to the S.W. under every sail she could spread. The man-of-war being in shore had the stronger breeze and she raised the chase until her hull was in sight from the deck, but as the ships drew off shore the breeze lightened until by half-past six both were nearly becalmed.

Lieutenant Edward Littlehales, commanding the *Dolphin*, immediately sent away his cutter and gig, in charge of Mr Murray, mate and Mr Rees, second-master, in the hopes that they would be able to reach the chase before the making sea breeze reached her.

It was a hard pull of two hours and a half in the hot sun without their breakfasts for the nine men in the cutter and six in the gig. Both boats, well water-soaked after constant blockading work, pulled very heavy and the men had already had a hard time trimming and making sail in squally, rainy weather since daybreak.

As they pulled up to board, the crew of the *Firme*, taking care to keep behind the bulwarks, opened a steady fire, which pierced the planking of the boats and fell in a shower all round them. There were ten so-called passengers aboard the Brazilian, who not only helped to pass up powder from the magazine, but kept up a hot fire of musketry through the stern scuttles in the cabin. The *Firme* had her sweeps rigged out so that it was impossible to board from the chains, and she was so high-sided, being in ballast, that it was difficult to clamber over her bulwark rail.

As the boats pulled up on each quarter, the bowman of the gig, William Allen, was shot dead through the heart; the next moment the same fate over-took William Jacobs, bowman of the cutter.

14. The Capture of the Slave Brig *Gabriel*, by H.M. Brig *Acorn*, July 6th, 1841.

From an coloured lithograph after a drawing by N. M. Condy, in the National Maritime Museum.

[Facing page 336.

15. The Capture of the Slave Brig *Borboleta*, May 26th, 1845, by the boats of H.M. Brig, *Pantaloon*.

From an coloured lithograph by T. G. Dutton, after a drawing by H. John Vernon.

[Facing page 337.

Murray, a mate of six years standing, was knocked back into the gig by the butt end of a musket and his collar-bone broken, but he sprang up again and clutching the rail with his left hand, almost had it severed at the wrist by a blow of a cutlass.

Another slash at his head he was able to parry, and thus gained a footing in the face of the enemy,, quickly cutting down his first opponent.

He was well supported by a gallant old seaman, named John Smith, who had previously served on the coast in the *Ariadne*, *Brisk*, and *Atholl.*

A skillful swordsman, Smith found himself engaged by three men, a blow broke his right arm, but he immediately shifted his cutlass to his left hand, And he held them off until Rees, boarding from the other quarter, rushed to his assistance and cut down one of his assailants.

As soon as three or four blue jackets had succeeded in following their officers aboard, the crew of the *Firme* began to give away and finally made a rush for the hatchway. It was a hot affair for twenty minutes.

The slaver lost two killed and seven wounded, whilst the boats had two killed, (as usual two of the best men in the ship) Murray and Smith severely wounded, and two others slightly wounded.

Littlehales, incensed at the loss of two fine seamen, secured the crew and passengers of the slaver hand and foot kept them on bread and water for eight days until he was able to land them at Accra.

The Admiralty for this gallant affair at once promoted Augustus Charle Murray to lieutenant and John Fletcher Rees to the rank of master; John Smith being given a boatswains warrant directly he had passed the required examination.

A Dreadful Passage.

Perhaps the most unpleasant of all duties that fell to the lot of officers and men on the coast of Africa was taking prizes to their port of adjudication.

One of the worst experiences of this sort befell Murray as soon as he had recovered from his wounds.

Towards the end of June, 1840, the *Dolphin* captured a small schooner at Quitta and sent her off to Sierra Leone in the charge of her gunner.

About six weeks later, when running along the coast, the *Dolphin* sighted a schooner in shore about twenty miles below Accra, which from the number of canoes surrounding her appeared to be taking slaves aboard. The *Dolphin* at once steered for her, dropped a shot under her bows, which scattered the canoes, and then sent a boat aboard her. The boat returned with the news that the schooner was none other than their prize, the *Dores*, which in six weeks had only made thirty miles, and had buried the gunner and most of her prize crew from fever. The *Dolphin* was on her way to Accra for reprovisioning; and leaving the ill-fated schooner at anchor, she took in her provisions and then returned.

Murray was then placed in charge of the prize, with a new prize crew of two men and two boys, his complement being completed by a prisoner, a youth, who was the only survivor out of her original crew.

It was August the 12th, 1840, when Murray got under way for the run up the coast to Sierra Leone.

His first task was to overhaul the schooner, a small vessel some sixty feet long by fifteen in breadth, with a cargo consisting of tobacco and molasses. There was a tiny cabin aft, which could only be entered through a small skylight, this horrible hole, which was only eight feet long, five feet high under the skylight, three feet high on either side and narrowing from its forward bulkhead of eleven feet to only two and a half aft, was the only place of refuge not only for Murray, but for his four hands, for no less than one hundred and forty six days.

It swarmed with cockroaches and vermin of every description, it smelt horribly of bilge water and rotting tobacco, and it had not a chair or a table or a stick of furniture of any sort.

On deck there was the usual dogs-hole, but this proved to be still less habitable.

After three days scorching in the tropical sun, Murray searched the hold to find something to make an awning. A few monkey skins were found and the next three days were spent by all hands in sewing these together.

On the evening that the awning was finished, the weather broke, and all through the night the little schooner was steered before a furious wind under bare poles, the seas making a clean sweep of her deck. With sunrise next morning came a calm, and, noticing that the *Dores* was floating deeper in the water, Murray took a sounding of the well and found three feet of water in the hold.

The pump, which had been repaired aboard the *Dolphin* broke again almost at once, but after about and hour's search, a new box was found, and the pump was able to clear the vessel in about a couple of hours—but the tobacco had been soaked through and completely spoilt.

From this date, the schooner could just lay her course until when thirty days out, on a day when two large sharks were caught, the colour of the water changed, a sign that they were nearing land.

At daybreak on September the 14th the coast was made just below the river Sestos. Finding that he had only three days' provisions left, Murray, in hopes of weathering Cape Palmas, put his crew on half rations. But there was a strong current running along the shore, and when the *Dores* was tacked in again four days later, Murray found himself about forty miles below the river Sestos (or Sesters) and he was obliged to run back to Cape Coast Castle for provisions. He arrived there on September the 20th, the ship's company having eaten up the last of their food the day before.

The Governor supplied Murray with forty day's provisions and the *Dores* refilled her water casks; she was also laid ashore and about a ton of barnacles scraped off her bottom.

A tree nail was also found missing forward, which accounted partly for her leak.

Soon after making sail again from Cape Coast Castle a hot wind freshened into a three days gale, during which time no cooking could be done and the tough salt junk had to be eaten raw.

On the day after the gale had moderated, a strange sail approached the schooner—a rakish-looking brigantine of the slaver persuasion. Muskets were loaded and cutlasses sharpened, but at half past four a strong breeze got up when the slaver was only two and a half miles away. This wind placed the *Dores* to windward and by the following morning the stranger was out of sight.

For the next eight days Murray, whose only navigating instrument was an antique quadrant, which was sometimes ten, sometimes twenty miles, out of adjustment, reckoned that he was making about thirty miles a day. On the 9th day, the schooner was allowed to drift all day whilst her worn out sails were being repaired.

On the tenth morning the colour of the water changed and Murray once more stood off the land. At the end of another ten days Murray reckoned that he was within thirty miles of the Equator, but a good strong breeze springing up, he tacked and headed for Sierra Leone.

At this time his docile, well-behaved crew passed their time in cleaning their arms, making clothes and fishing. On the day the schooner was put round, three large sharks and a dolphin were caught; and on the next, seventeen bonitas, which were great treat in the food line: the following day thirty to forty bonitas and two large albacore rewarded the fishermen. During the dog watches Murray usually took the helm whilst his men had a sing-song. At other times he read and reread his Shakespeare. For several days it rained torrents and then on October the 4th, the day closed in with every appearance of a storm.

The thin, worn sails were lowered down and made well fast with the exception of the fore staysail, which Murray kept set in order to get the schooner's head before the wind.

By five o'clock the *Dores* rolled in a dead calm, the atmosphere being heavy, dark and gloomy. Then thunder began to roll along the horizon.

Murray, peering through the darkness caught sight of a wall of foam approaching from aft.

"Down forestaysail!" He roared, and hardly was the sail fast before the schooner was buried in a hill of water, whilst the wind shrieked through her rigging.

For five minutes Murray thought they were gone, but the schooner survived and at the end of half an hour the wind lulled. The young officer then battened his crew down below, and lashed himself to the helm: and hardly had he made these preparations before the wind came again with redoubled fury amidst flashing lightening, crashing thunder and torrents of rain. The storm eased up and dropped right away at about 2 a.m. when the exhausted Murray fell asleep.

He awoke at daylight to hear his crew hammering on the sky-light in their efforts to get out.

As he had not replied to their knocking, they feared that he had been washed overboard.

This blow evidently strained the schooner, for henceforward she made about two feet of water a day; and what was even more important most of the bread had been spoilt by salt water.

On October the 10th, one of Murray's small crew fell ill and very nearly died, but in about a fortnight he recovered, and for the rest of the dreary passage there was no more illness aboard.

From the 10th till November the 4th, the schooner was tacked three or four times a day. It was the height of the wet season and rained and rained. For days together Murray was unable to change his clothes.

It was rarely possible to cook, the food was mostly eaten raw, the bread was soaked through into pulp, and Murray wrote that at breakfast he was obliged to protect his cold cocoa from the rain with his own body.

For six weeks there was hardly a let up in the light head wind, the adverse current and the pelting rain, but all this time immense quantities of fish were caught. In fifty-five days Murray recorded in his log the capture of fifty-five skipjacks, forty-seven dolphins, one hundred and seventy sharks and seven hundred and seventy two bonitas. On November the 4th the land was made and to his horror Murray recognised Cape Lahon—in forty-one days the *Dores* had only made good one hundred and eighty miles. He was forced to recognise that the schooner could not stem the current.

There were only ten more days provisions, Murray now headed in shore and, taking bearings, he remained at the helm all night, only to discover at daylight that the schooner had only made three miles. However he determined to go on working along the shore. At the end of the second evening the *Dores* had made good seven miles, but by 10 p.m. the wind fell light, and with about two and a half miles an hour of contrary current, the schooner began to lose ground. The night fell upon a fresh anxiety, natives armed with pikes, spears and clubs could be seen outlined against the fires they had lit on the beach. Murray was convinced that they meant to attack him, especially as the schooner was being drifted further and further in shore without being able to find soundings.

Every preparation to fight off the natives was being made, when the first puff of the land breeze filled the sails and the schooner, regaining steerage way, was able to draw off, a hellish shout of disappointment being raised ashore.

Once more Murray put back to Cape Coast Castle for provisions. This time the Governor did his best to pursuade him to give up his voyage, the schooner being, by now, quite unseaworthy, and her sails rotten. But Murray held out against all arguments and anchoring within half a mile of the shore, proceeded to take in another fifty days provisions. These were all aboard but for one canoe load, which was actually alongside, when the current changed, and a huge swell began to run in and break outside the schooner, which with two anchors down was drifted for a quarter of a mile.

Murray now feared his charge would be lost in the surf, and he gave his crew orders to jump into the canoe alongside directly the schooner touched. Then three great hills of water rolled in, but after the third had passed over the *Dores*, an off-shore breeze made, her anchors were hurriedly weighed, and to the surprise of everyone, the little vessel was presently anchored safely outside the line of breaking surf.

With his vessel once more out of danger, Murray landed to dine with the Governor, leaving orders for a signal to be hoisted directly all the provisions were aboard. But hardly had be finished dinner, when a message was brought to him saying that one of his men, a black, had been killed by a shark. Apparently all hands had gone overboard to have a good wash after the job of provisioning, and all were on board dressing again except this man, who was swimming about.

Suddenly they heard him shriek, and he disappeared in a pool of blood. The others at once jumped into a canoe alongside which had been used to scrub the schooner's bottom, and paddled towards where he had gone down. He rose after a few seconds only to be dragged down again. The second time he came to the surface they were able to haul him into the canoe, but he died before they could get him aboard the schooner.

He had been bitten twice and most of one leg was gone including the thigh.

With this tragedy making his small crew still more short-handed, the Governor once more tried to get Murray to give up his voyage, but both officer and men refused to give in. The crew were given a chance to refuse to go on, but they all swore to stand by their officer to the last.

So about 7 p.m. on November the 16th, the *Dores* once more resumed her voyage. After standing up the land all night with a light fair wind, at breakfast the new bread was broken out and found to be completely rotten. Once more it was a case of putting back. This time the Governor sent off some good American bread, and at 3.30 p.m. the schooner set sail from the Cape Coast Castle for the third time. She only made nine miles in the night and all next day was calm. At 8 p.m., though out of sight of land, Murray recognised the noise of the sunset gun at Elmina, which was only about four miles from Cape Coast Castle; he dared not discourage his men by such information, and when the helmsman remarked upon it he passed it off as distant thunder

On the 24th of November the *Dores* was well off shore and amongst the fish again. Four large sharks and six bonitas were taken that day, and a tremendous dolphin, four feet seven inches long by one foot eleven inches, was captured though it had taken four days of angling before he would take the bait. As soon as he was hooked, the dolphin had ten sharks after him. It is always a difficulty to preserve one's catch from voracious sharks in the tropics. The dolphin could only outdistance his pursuers by making the most terrific leaps into the air at the end of the whole scope of line, and it took an hour to haul him in and land him on the deck of the schooner.

Other big fish caught were albacores five feet inches and five feet four inches in lengh and a huge barracouta.

The largest albacore followed the schooner for a week, refusing every kind of bait. Then when a shark had carried off the last of the hooks, a bent nail, well loaded with bait, did the trick.

With all their hooks expended, the keen crew of the *Dores* were forced to make a hook out of the curved handle of the kettle.

This made a hook with a shank two feet long, to which was bent six parts of fishing line about four fathoms long, bent onto a rope.

With this contrivance Murray declared that over two hundred sharks were caught and so many other fish, that in three weeks even the keenest of the fishermen had grown tired. At this time the rain fell steadily; the cabin smelt so horribly, that all hands preferred to sleep in the wet on deck and again for days together no one could change their clothes.

A pig had been shipped at Cape Coast Castle, which from extreme fatness was unable to walk.

The crew amused themselves by fitting him with a coat, trousers and a cocked hat, in which guise he was eventually landed at Sierra Leone and wheeled up to a friend's house in state.

Murray also had two parrots, which would follow him about like a couple of dogs, and race in their waddling way along the deck for food, directly he rapped with his cane.

So the time passed until December the 9th when Murray was nearly lost by getting caught by the legs in the coil of the rope, when a shark fourteen feet in lengh was being played. However before he was dragged overboard with the bight half hitched round his knee and shin-bone, his devoted men caught hold of him. For weeks afterwards he was unable to use his leg, but eventually completely recovered.

At last the *Dores* began to make better progress with the current beginning to run favourably.

The rotten sails had to be repaired with monkey skins, of which there seem to have been any number aboard. The schooner became more and more leaky. The cargo of tobacco was so rotten that no one could stand the stench below; and Murray dared not heave it overboard or the *Dores* would have capsized without ballast.

On the 14th of December the schooner survived another tornado. Two days later she was overtaken by an electric storm. As usual Murray took the helm and sent his men below.

The lightning played all about the schooner so that quite reckless by this time, Murray never expected to escape. The steely brightness of the forks lit up the scene and Murray wrote in his log:-

"I felt the heat from each flash as warm as if close to a fire." All the time it rained in torrents, and the rain leaked in through the deck.

But this storm too ceased as suddenly as it had begun, and as soon as the schooner was pumped out Murray bore up East, reckoning that he had made sufficient northing. For the next fortnight the schooner jogged along, her crew killing ten or twelve sharks a day, then on the 30th of December came their last and best day's sport, forty-five sharks being killed. The very next day the colour of the water changed and with three cheers, the main brace was spliced and a belated Christmas day was celebrated. On January the 4th, 1841, about sunset the land was sighted and Murray recognised the land-marks of Sierra Leone. By six o'clock the next morning the schooner was off the entrance and finally anchored off the town, one hundred and forty six days out and with just two days' provisions left.

Upon calling on the proctor, Murray found that he had a long ago been given up for lost, but also that he had been promoted for his capture of the *Firme*, and was thus able to sail for home at the first opportunity. Two days later the *Dores* was surveyed, and her condition and the sight of the miserable cabin caused still further amazement.

Fever was not too long in fastening upon the unfortunate Murray: the surgeon advised him to sail for home at the first opportunity and he at once took a passage in a ship bound to Madeira. He was handed despatches by Captain Foote of the *Madagascar*, bade goodbye to his faithful crew, and sailed within a week of getting ashore. Three weeks later he was landed half-dead at Madeira, where for a month he never left his bed; then he continued his passage in a wine ship; finally he handed Captain Foote's despatches to the Admiralty, all ready and eager for his next commission.

CHAPTER XVII

COAST OF AFRICA 1841-1845

"Whether tacking, talking, writing, wearing
Preserve your statiôn and the line of Bearing".

Command Changes

WHEN Rear-Admiral the Honourable George Elliot was hurried off to China at the outbreak of the First Chinese War, the Commander-in-Chief in Brazil, Vice-Admiral Sir Edward Durnford King, had for sometime to take charge of both stations; then in December, 1841, Rear-Admiral the Honourable Josceline Percy sailed in the *Winchester*, fifty guns, to take over the Cape.

During his command which extended to the spring of 1846, the Senior Officers on the West Coast were Captain Hugh Nurse of the new twenty-six-gun corvette *Iris*, who was succeeded by Captain William Tucker in the same ship. On this veteran of the coast being compelled to invalid in the autumn of 1842, Captain John Foote of the *Madagascar*, forty guns, was S.N.O. until he handed over to Captain W. Jones of the steam frigate *Penelope*, in June 1843.

It should be noted that these four officers were post-captains, whereas the previous S.N.O.'s, since the Swallow-tail had been struck, had only been commanders.

The Admiralty were again being forced to admit the importance of the station.

The Fighting *Gabriel*

About a month after the capture of the *Firme*, another fighting slaver, the notorious Baltimore-built clipper-brig, *Gabriel*, was taken by the *Acorn*, on her way to the Cape.

For some months every cruiser had been on the lookout for her, as her beating off of the *Termagant*'s boats off Cape Mount had made something of a sensation on the coast.

When the *Bonetta* sailed for home, the blockade of Theodore Canot's factory at New Cestros was taken up by the brigantine, *Termagant*, commanded by Lieutenant H. Seagram.

The destruction of the slave barracoons at Gallinas by Denham encouraged the local chief round New Cestros to loot Canot's factory and the slave trader was only just saved by an armed force from the *Termagant* from sharing the fate of his factory. Lieutenant Seagram offered his late antagonist a passage to Cape Mount, and it was when the *Termagant* lay becalmed off the hills of Cape Mount at sunset on February the 23rd that the raking masts and cotton sails of the *Gabriel* were revealed, cut out, as if in jet, against the glowing sky in the West.

All through the night the calm continued and at 9 a.m. the following morning, as soon as the cabin breakfast was over, Seagram led his boats to the attack. According to the commanding officer's report the force consisted of Seagram himself with twelve men in the cutter and Mr. Anthony Samwell, the second master, with eight men and two boys in the dinghy.

Canot's account is slightly different, he enumerates the force as six sailors and two marines under a supernumerary mate in the yawl: five seamen and four marines under

Seagram in the gig, 'a mere fancy craft', and the boatswain armed with musket and cutlass, paddled by two Kroomen in Canot's nutshell of a canoe.

The *Gabriel* opened fire on the boats at the extreme limit of range. This was at 10.20 a.m. At eleven she hoisted a large Spanish ensign, hauled her courses up and maintained a steady fire with her long guns. The dinghy, not being able to keep up, was taken in tow by the cutter.

Directly the boats arrived within musket shot, they received it hot and sharp, but beyond firing two Congreve rockets, made no reply.

As they dashed up on either quarter, the dinghy to starboard, in one fierce discharge of grape, lost three men killed and four wounded. Then with the injured men falling over one side, the boat turned bottom upward and drifted away, leaving its wounded men struggling in the water.

The cutter also failed to gain a footing on the slaver's deck; and at last, seeing that he was likely to be overpowered by sheer force of numbers, Seagram gave up the fight and dropped astern to pick up the wounded men in the water. The lieutenant himself was bleeding from a nasty wound on the head received from a handspike, and when he gained the deck of the *Termagant*, he and his men were in no condition for further hard service in the broiling sun, so the *Gabriel* slipped away directly the sea breeze reached her; being to windward, or rather to seaward, of the *Termagant*, she, of course, got it first.

Canot gives the following incidents, which receive no mention in Seagram's report:—

"The Kroo canoe dashed alongside with the velocity of her class and, as a petty officer on the Spaniard bent over to sink the skiff with a ponderous top-block, our boatswain cleft his skull with a musket-ball, and brought home the block as a trophy! . . . Seagram confessed that the Spaniard behaved magnanimously: for the moment our yawl was sunk, Olivares (the *Gabriel*'s captain), cut adrift his boat, and bade the struggling swimmers return in it to their vessel".

This, it was said, was the second occasion on which men-of-war boats had been beaten off by the *Gabriel*. It was known that the slaver had made two succesful trips from the Gallinas river, and it being evident that she intended to make that river for another cargo, the *Wanderer* was sent to blockade it.

However it was not the *Wanderer*, but the outwardbound *Acorn*, that captured her.

At 2.30 a.m. on July the 6th in 5° 16′ N. 17° 51′ W. Captain Adams discovered a suspicious-looking brig, 'hovering' on his weather quarter, and at once made sail in chase.

The two brigs were evenly matched and did not change their bearings for the next twelve hours, but at 2 p.m. on July 7th, the wind having freshened considerably, the chase carried away both topgallant masts. He at once bore away setting all his starboard stunsails.

At 3 p.m. the *Acorn* also kept away, setting starboard stunsails, royals and flying jib.

At 3.30 p.m. Captain Adams hoisted his ensign and fired a round shot, following it up with a shell, to both of which the *Gabriel* replied with his Long Tom, and at the same time showed Portuguese colours. Adams was careful to keep his brig right in the wake of the chase, so as to avoid having his spars shot away by her long gun.

At the same time he kept up a brisk fire from a long thirty-two pounder through the bridle-port and also burst two of the new shells over the *Gabriel*.

Things now began to look desperate for the slaver. Holes from shot were showing in her boom mainsail and main topsail, and a sure sign that she was losing ground, she proceeded to cut away all weight on deck, such as anchors, boats, spare spars, etc.

At 4.30 p.m. the wind came more aft, so *Acorn* hoisted a blue ensign in her main rigging as shown in the Condy lithograph. She then let fly a heavy fire of grape, which cut away the *Gabriel*'s boom sheet, lee main sheet, lower inner and fore topsail halliards, and the slaver's crew could be seen leaving their guns. A few seconds later down came her ensign, but she continued to carry on under every sail she could set.

At 5.30 with the chase within half a mile, Adams set his marines to work; their fire was so well-aimed that again the *Gabriel*'s crew began to seek refuge below, and then a lucky bullet parted her jib-sheet and she broached to. In another minute the *Acorn* ranged up alongside, the chase was over and both ships were hove to. Lieutenant Hankey, first of the *Acorn*, on boarding the chase, discovered to his delight that she was the notorious *Gabriel*, which in the two years that she had been out of the hands of her Baltimore builders, had proved so successful and so fatal to the cruisers on the station.

This time she was apparently bound from Havana to Kabinda. She was found to be armed with a long twenty-four-pounder pivot gun and two eighteen-pounder medium broadside guns, and she was manned by a crew of sixty-two men.

The *Acorn* was lucky to get off with one man wounded, for the *Gabriel*'s guns were well served, many of her shot passing over the *Acorn*'s quarterdeck and through her boom mainsail.

The crew of the Spaniard, for Spanish she was in spite of hoisting Portuguese colours, were taken aboard the *Acorn*, but Olivares, the captain, was missing. The prize was sent to St. Helena, and thus ended the career of one of the most determined slavers on the coast.

Pantaloon Goes to the Coast

It was not until 1842 that the beautiful little *Pantaloon* had a chance to show what she could do with slavers. As tender to the Royal Yacht, she seems to have been at the beck and call of everyone, with very little rest: for instance, in 1839, she was sent out to the river Gambia, with presents for well-behaved chiefs. We next hear of her crossing to Quebec on some errand or other, and no sooner had she returned to Portsmouth, than she was sent off to the North Sea on a fishery protection job.

However when her new sister ship, the *Rapid*, was sent afloat, the *Pantaloon*'s commander, Lieutenant Tryon , and her crew were turned over to the former, which took her place as tender to the *Royal George*. *Pantaloon* then fitted for a commission on the West coast of Africa under Lieutenant-Commander Charles Horace Lapidge.

Her first adventure was not a pleasant one, for she got ashore on the Arcas Shoal, Bassau Channel, river Gambia. The natives attempted to board and loot her, but were beaten off by her boats.

It was not a happy commission and ended in a crop of court martials, her commander being severely reprimanded.

A Piratical Felucca

At the beginning of the forties two feluccas appeared on the coast of Africa from Spain.

They were single-masted with a short stump of a mast and a tremendous lateen sail, bent on a yard one hundred and eighty feet long: they drew very little water and were specially adapted for sneaking up rivers, where, in smooth water, nothing could catch them if there was the slightest breath of wind. It was rumoured that they had been built at Barcelona and each was manned with between sixty and seventy of the most desperate, stick-at-nothing seamen, that could be picked up in the grog shanties of the Western Mediterranean ports.

For some time these feluccas were very successful and it was soon realised that the only vessel in the British Navy that had any hopes of catching them was the *Waterwitch*.

As it happened the famous gun brig fell in with one of these Spanish feluccas on her way out to Sierra Leone from home on her second commission.

The *Si*, for such was her name, was not keeping a very bright lookout and presently a round shot from the cruiser cut through the slings of her ponderous many-pieced yard and brought it tumbling down, so that her ferocious crew found themselves enveloped and half suffocated in the folds of the great lateen sail and without being able to fire a shot, fell easy victims to the *Waterwitch.* So enraged was the piratical captain of the felucca at this absurd denouement that he picked up a musket and put a bullet through his inattentive lookout at the masthead. The *Si* proved to be of seventy-one British tons and had three hundred and sixty slaves on board.

The second felucca soon showed that she was not going to be taken so easily and she several times fought off the men-of-war boats, that caught her up African slave rivers.

And the *Waterwitch* was the first cruiser to come near catching her. The rivers most favoured by this midget slaver were those of the Grain coast.

Into one of these Matson sent a beautiful little prize, well suited for river work, which he had named the *Pretty Polly*.

The commander of the *Pretty Polly* was instructed to lie in wait up the river and pounce out upon any unsuspecting slaver that showed herself. The first to appear was the notorious felucca, which so closely resembled the *Midge* in Michael Scott's masterpiece. Taking the *Pretty Polly* for a slaver she came on until she was within a quarter of a mile, when to the delight of the man-of-war's men she began lowering her immense yard. Aboard the *Pretty Polly* they waited, quivering with excitement, whilst the ponderous yard slowly descended its sturdy mast with much creaking of the great four-fold halliard blocks. But, alas, when the sail was half way down, the felucca's captain realised that the *Pretty Polly* was not what she pretended to be and immediately he gave orders for his sail to be rehoisted.

The *Pretty Polly* at once got under sail and opened fire. But soon the wind dropped away and the felucca's large crew, manning her sweeps soon outdistanced the few toiling men available for the *Pretty Polly*'s oars.

Then seeing that he had the advantage, the Captain of the felucca, who was rumoured to be an Englishman badly wanted for piracy, began to play with his opponent.

As the wind flickered and faltered his wonderful craft responded to the least breath. An more than once he bore down on the *Pretty Polly*, plumped a shot into her, then hove round and ran out of range again. After this irritating manoeuvre had been carried out several times, the toiling bluejackets, whose single popgun was easily outranged, were almost apoplectic in their heat and fury.

All this time the *Waterwitch* lay in the offing some fifteen miles away. During the night the *Pretty Polly* arrived alongside and told of her agonising experience. The beautiful gun-brig with *Pretty Polly* in company at once made sail for the river, Matson being convinced that his daring opponent would not leave without a cargo of slaves. And sure enough he was right; when the *Waterwitch* and her tender anchored off the barracoons the following morning, it was learnt that their mosquito-like opponent had been in during the night, seized a cargo of slaves by force of arms, and made her escape before daylight.

After her adventure with the *Pretty Polly*, the felucca twice escaped from the *Iris*, now (1842) commanded by our old friend William Tucker, who had been posted from the *Wolverine*,

Gallant End of Captain Tucker

Whilst in command of the *Wolverine* and the *Iris*, Captain Tucker captured no less than thirty-four slavers, fourteen in the brig and twenty in the corvette.

Unfortunately after his long experience of the unhealthy coast, he was so worn out with constant malaria that he was obliged to invalid in the autumn of 1842, and he sailed from the Cape for India in the East Indiaman, *Reliance*, which on the 12th of November, was wrecked off Boulogne. Captain Tucker was last seen by one of the survivors, supporting in his arms a young midshipman named Ford, whose leg had been broken by the fall of the mainmast.

When the poop was torn up by the fall of the mizen mast, both Captain and midshipman were hurled into the water. Tucker was known to be an excellent swimmer—in fact he had already twice jumped overboard to save men—but in accordance with his well-known character for unselfish gallantry, it was considered certain that he had perished in a valiant attempt to bring the helpless midshipman ashore.

Thus died one of the most successful of all slaver catchers.

The Felucca Captured

To return to the felucca, her next escape was from the two-gun paddle-wheeler, *Kite*, Lieutenant W. M. I. G. Pasco.

No more was heard of her until January the 13th, 1844. The pinnace of the six-gun steam sloop *Growler*, under command of her first lieutenant, Lieutenant Lodwick, was up the Junk river, when the notorious felucca appeared round a bend.

Instead of 'bouting ship' and running for it, the confident skipper of the felucca hove to and awaited the approach of the pinnace with a row of levelled muskets poking over the low rail of the slaver. With a cheer the pinnace gave way at a racing stroke.

This brought a high-aimed volley from the felucca, which at the same time filled her huge sail and set off down the river at a speed that was just about as fast as the pinnace could pull. The man-of-war boat had the usual boat's carronade perched in her bows. This was loaded with a round shot and a bag of one hundred and eighty musket balls crammed on top of it.

The firing of this gun brought a second volley from the felucca. This volley was better aimed, for two bluejackets fell over dead and Lieutenant Lodwick had the rim of his hat shot away and a couple of slugs in his left knee and thigh. The engagement now grew hot. Groans and screams from the felucca told of the boat-gun's success; but the pinnace was soon in a hopeless condition with half her men killed or wounded, her planking riddled through and through, and all her oars on one side shot away.

In going out over the bar, the felucca bumped heavily and carried away her rudder; but by this time, the boat was helpless, and when she was at length picked up by the *Growler*, could only report that the felucca was somewhere on the other side of the horizon.

No more was heard or seen of this elusive little slaver until January, 1848, when in the lightest of airs she escaped from the yawl of the *Rapid*. A few days later she was sighted by the *Philomel* and *Dart*, lying becalmed at daylight. The *Dart*'s boats were the first to get to her, but were beaten off by her long eighteen pounder. Then Lieutenant Wharton, first of the *Philomel* carefully pulled up in the wake of the felucca, which had lately shipped a mizen mast. This he was careful to keep in line with her main, so that her death-dealing Long Tom could not be trained upon him.

However, notwithstanding this caution on his part, the eighteen-pounder, being loaded with every kind of combustible, scattered missiles far and wide, and in one discharge put seven of his men hors de combat. He would have found the felucca a still harder nut to crack if he had not managed to pick off her captain before arriving alongside. This desperate ruffian, like his comrade in the *Si*, on the men-of-war being reported, had called his two lookouts from aloft and shot them dead for their negligence in not reporting the cruisers sooner.

With her captain laid low, the felucca did not make much resistance and Lieutenant Wharton had the satisfaction of taking possession of a vessel which had caused more casualties amongst the West African Squadron than any other two slavers put together.

Success of the *Albatross*

One of the most successful of slavers, the *Constancio*, a beautiful brigantine, of one hundred and seventy tons, was captured on July the 10th, 1844, by the brig *Albatross*, Commander Reginald Yorke, after a chase of ten hours.

The *Constancio* had made twenty-one successful voyages, carrying an average of six hundred slaves a voyage. She had beaten off men-of-war boats several times and had boasted that there was not a vessel in the squadron that could catch her.

The *Albatross* had arrived out in June, 1844, to take the place of *Waterwitch* on the Southern station, the latter having sailed for home in order to take part in the Experimental brig trials.

She quickly followed up the capture of the *Constancio*, by that of Brazilian brigantine, *Piedade*, and her good fortune continued, her fourth capture, that of the Brazilian brig *Albanez* of two hundred and fifty tons with seven hundred and forty three slaves on board being particularly lucky.

After chasing the brig in shore until it fell calm, her lookout reported that the chase, which could be seen down to the heads of her topsails, seemed to be on fire. On this Lieutenant James A. Dunbar was sent off in the pinnace with orders to bring back the figurehead or some evidential portion of the supposed wreck. It was a long pull of about twenty-five miles, and when the pinnace had got within five miles, a light breeze enabled the brig, which was not on fire—the smoke, etc., proceeding from fires on the shore—to out-distance the pinnace.

Dunbar, not knowing the coast, anchored for the night. The following morning at daybreak he pulled in again, and found that the brig was anchored off the dangerous bar of the Coanza river, and was busy taking aboard slaves from rafts, along with water and provisions.

The *Albatross*, which had also anchored under the land for the night, but a few miles further south, also made up towards the Coanza entrance, but the pinnace had captured both slaver and slaves by the time the *Albatross* arrived; and Dunbar daringly pushed on and crossed the bar in chase of a boat of fugitives with about a dozen children of under twelve on board. Musketry was then opened upon the pinnace from the bush on either side, and the boat containing the slave children was hurled on the beach by the surf. However with the aid of his Kroomen, Dunbar hauled the slaver's boat off safely, after which he recrossed the bar and secured the brig, which was adrift. This bare account does not give any idea of the difficulties attending this capture. In a heavy rolling sea and throughout a very dark night, the jabbering terrified negroes were transferred from the rafts to the slaver. This operation in a 'confusion too horrible to be depicted' took twenty hours of strenuous seamanship and tactful handling. The next day the *Albatross* and her prize proceeded to Loando, where provisions and water were bought for the *Albanez*, which was then sent off to Sierra Leone for adjudication.

Tottenham's Markmanship

One of the most gallant cutting out affairs in the history of the suppression of the slave trade took place in August 1845.

On August the 12th, when off Fish Bay, Commander Scott of the *Hyacinth*, sixteen-gun sloop, sent in his four-oared gig under John F. Tottenham, one of the ship's mates, with a message for the governor.

The weather being thick and Tottenham and his boat's crew quite unacquainted with the coast, he anchored for the night. The following morning, having been unable to find the port, he pulled away to the Southward in order to fall in with the *Hyacinth*, which he knew would be working down the coast. About noon a rakish-looking brig was seen, lying at anchor off the land; which, on spotting the man-of-war, slipped her anchor in a suspicious hurry and made sail. There being very little wind, and the brig being caught between Tottenham and the land, the gig was soon within musket shot of her.

The mate then fired a musket as a hint for the brig to show her colours and heave to. The only response was the opening of the brig's after port, through which a gun was run out.

Tottenham at once steered into the wake of the slaver, so that the gun could not be traversed sufficiently to lay on the gig. At this the brig's crew hauled the gun onto the poop, from which position it could be trained upon the boat, at the same time the slaver opened fire of musketry upon the daring gig.

There were only five hands in the boat and whilst four bluejackets pulled along steadily in the wake of the brig, Tottenham, seizing a musket, replied to the slaver's fire as fast as his spare hand could load. The mate fired with the greatest coolness and precision, picking off the crew of the gun, one by one—in fact when the poop of the slaver was examined afterwards, every bullet he had fired was traced to the gun carriage or its close vicinity.

Finding that he could not get away from the boat, or tack without being boarded, and, with four men wounded and one dying, the captain of the slaver ran his ship ashore. As the brig's crew, carrying three wounded men, splashed their way to the beach, eighteen men were counted by the jubilant bluejackets. Tottenham then took possession of the slaver, which proved to be a brig of two hundred tons, with equipment for a cargo of close on one thousand slaves. Her decks were littered with weapons of offence—muskets, a barrel of gunpowder, any quantity of ball cartridges, swords and bayonets lay scattered around the poop, whilst her two broadside four-pounders were loaded, with a heap of langrage shot piled ready beside them.

No papers could be found, but there was a Brazilian ensign in the cabin.

Tottenham had not long taken possession, when the *Hyacinth* hove in sight and with her aid it was not long before the brig was hove off into deep water.

For this cool piece of work, Tottenham received his commission.

War Steamers on the Coast

One of the first war steamers on the African coast seems to have been the *Pluto* of three hundred and sixty five tons, one hundred Horse power and three guns—an eighteen-pounder long run and two eighteen-pounder carronades, commanded by Lieutenant-Commander Blount. She arrived in 1841.

In 1842 when Captain Foote of the *Madagascar* was S.N.O. on the coast, he appointed mate, McLeod Baynes Cockraft, acting lieutenant-commander of the little paddle wheeler *Albert* of one hundred and fifty six tons and seventy horse power. Cockraft had only recently distinguished himself, when senior mate of the *Dolphin*, when he risked his life to save three Kroomen, left aboard a wrecked slaver, which had been chased ashore by the brigantine.

Cockraft had to handle his boat with the greatest care and skill in the high, dangerous surf and all the time he was under heavy fire from the beach.

Whilst in command of the *Albert* which was little more than a tug, Lieutenant Cockraft spent two months up the river Nunez, defending the British factories from hoards of hostile natives.

A paragraph cannot do justice to a brave little campaign which resulted in the destruction of the stockaded town of Casakabouli, which was defended by cannons of eighteen, twenty-four and thirty-two pounder calibre.

In this affray, Cockraft himself was within an ace of being captured at one moment, but so skillful were his tactics that he only lost four killed and eight wounded in the struggle. The appreciation of the white merchants was shown by the presentation of a hundred guinea' sword, whilst the Admiralty confirmed his lieutenant's commission.

The early paddle-steamer was hated and despised in the Royal Navy, both by officers and men, and it was only the most open-minded and enterprising officers who were willing to take command of these 'craft of the devil'.

Serving on the West coast of Africa in one of these paddle-wheelers was absolutely demoralizing for the true seaman, who was proud of his ship.

Below the heat of the fires and the poor ventilation made a steamer no fit habitation for anything but cockroaches, which insects, in size often as large as young mice, so swarmed aboard that no food could even be served up ungarnished by cockroach bodies. On deck and aloft these steamers were the despair of their first lieutenants for the filthy smoke blackened sails and spars and covered the decks with a layer of soot. And if this was not enough, the sorely-tried crew of a paddle-wheel gun-boat, their whites smudged and greased like modern boiler suits, had to put up with the jeers of their ultra smart confreres in the spotlessly clean sailing men-of-war.

One of the most trying results of the introduction of the steam engine was the conversion of the peaceful silence with that soothing gurgle and hiss of passing water, so characteristic of a ship under sail, to the noisy chug-chug and clash-bang of the iron piston rods, stokers slice and other new weapons.

"I never hears one of these varmint steamers a-spluttering and fizzing and hissing and screeching, but I thinks I hears Old Nick a-saying:—

'Ah, Jack, I've done for you at last!' For the Devil, d'ye see doesn't like sailors more nor he does Holy-water".

Was the comment of a Nelsonian seaman.

Steamers would no doubt have appeared on the West coast earlier but for the very strong feeling against them. The blue-jacket could hardly be brought to serve aboard a steamer on a foreign station—then there was the difficulty of coaling, whilst the engine room and stoke-hole of an early paddle-wheeler was a real fore-taste of Hell when in the tropics.

Following the *Pluto* and the *Albert* came the two-gun paddle-wheeler, *Kite*, Lieutenant-Commander W. M. I. G. Pasco, in 1842. She was of three hundred tons and one hundred and seventy H.P. and like the *Pluto* classed as a first-class steam-gun-vessel.

Then in 1843 arrived the six-gun, one thousand and fifty five ton, three hundred H.P. first-class steam-sloop, *Thunderbolt*, Commander G. N. Broke, afterwards wrecked in Alagoa Bay.

By 1844 the reign of the smoke-stack had become definitely established on the coast of Africa, the new arrivals being:—

Ardent—third Class steam-packet, 801 tons 200 H.P. 3 32-prs on pivots.
Growler—first-class steam-sloop, 1059 tons 280 H.P.
Hydra—second-class steam-sloop, 818 tons 220 H.P. 6 guns.
Penelope—first-class steam frigate 1616 tons 650 H.P. 16 guns.
Prometheus—third-class steam-sloop, 796 tons 200 H.P. 3 guns.
Eclair—first-class steam gun-vessel, 387 tons 180 H.P. 3 guns.

Conversion of the *Penelope*

Of these the *Penelope* deserves a more detailed description. She was one of the old forty-six gun frigates, built at Chatham in 1830 on the lines of the French *Hebe*. She was converted to a steam frigate at Chatham. First of all she was cut in half and sixty-five feet added amidships making her length two hundred and fifteen feet. Her engines, two in number had direct drive. She had bunkers for six hundred tons of coal, which was only sufficient to give her fifteen days steaming. Her new armament consisted of two ten inch eighty-four hundredweight pivot guns, fourteen thirty-two-pounder carronades on the quarter-deck and forecastle and eight sixty-eight-pounder sixty-five hundredweight shell guns on the main deck. This armament was altered in 1847 to:—

On main-deck—eight eight-inch, 65 cwt., 9 feet, slide and carriage, two 68-pounders, 36 cwt., 5 feet, 4 inches on Hardy's compressed carriages.

On quarter-deck and forecastle—two 68-pounders, 95 cwt., 10 feet on pivots, slides and carriages—4 eight inch 65 cwt., 9 feet on slides and carriages.

She was ship-rigged with the same amount of canvas as her original sail plan, but was given the new wire-standing rigging.

The paddle-boxes and floats were on Captain Smith's principle. She was fitted to carry a whole regiment of troops and was expected to run to the Cape in thirty days. It was reckoned that this conversion was forty thousand pounds cheaper than building a steamer of her size. She was fitted for the West coast and commissioned for the broad pendant of Commodore William Jones.

As she was converted and sent afloat only a short time after the launch in July 1843 of the new, giant merchant steamer, *Great Britain*, the two ships were naturally compared by shipping experts; and the comparison went much against the Admiralty and their technical staff, for, when the *Penelope* put to sea, she was found to be a long way below her marks and she showed herself so wet in a sea way, and so ready to dive into the smallest head sea, that she became known in the Service as the *Porpoise*.

Coaling the *Penelope* was also a slow process—whether at Kingston, Jamaica, Sierra Leone, or in West Bay, Prince's Island, taking from three to four days. The coal was sometimes taken aboard in her own boats, each of which was designed to carry ten tons.

Her best run under sail and steam for the twenty-four hours was just under two hundred miles, and in spite of all her drawbacks she did good work on the West coast. Indeed she had not been out long before she overtook and captured the largest steam slaver on the coast with one thousand slaves on board. This was an American-built steamer, named *Cacique*, which had been bought by a Brazilian, M. Leixas, in 1846 for twenty five thousand dollars, and equipped at Pernambuco for a cargo of fifteen hundred slaves.

She was caught waiting outside Kabinda for the remaining five hundred slaves to complete her cargo in March 1846.

Steam Slavers

As far back as 1838, steam slavers had begun to appear on the coast. In April of that year a steamer was chased away from the Gallinas river and was forced to return to Brazil for want of fuel. Another Brazilian steamer, after capture, was bought into the Service under the name of *Snap* by Commodore Hotham.

This vessel had her engines on deck!

The most notorious case in the forties was that of the British-built steamer, *Maid of Islay*, which was owned by a Bremen merchant at Sierra Leone. She actually came into the Gallinas under the British flag with a supply of rice for the barracoons. Mistaking her for a Brazilian steamer, *Don Luiz* of Gallinas sent off six boat-loads of slaves to her. Each of these boats was rowed by forty men and held two hundred slaves.

She then put to sea and was chased for eight hours by H.M.S. *Alert*. She showed no colours and after being hailed five times, was fired into and would have sunk but for the efforts of the seamen from the *Alert*. At Sierra Leone her master and crew managed to escape before her case came up for adjudication. Owing to the fact that the British member of the Court was home on leave the *Maid of Islay* was returned to her owners!

Though the paddle-wheel gun-boats were despised by all seamen they soon proved their worth against slavers.

The *Hydra*, Commander Young, captured the *Pepita* with three hundred slaves. This was one of the mosts successful slavers of the coast, which had again and again outsailed our cruisers.

The *Alert*, Lieutenant-Commander A. R. Dunlap, captured three slavers off Sea bar in eight days.

The *Styx*, first-class steam-sloop of one thousand and fifty seven tons, two hundred and eighty H.P. whilst cruising off Ambriz, took a vessel a week for eleven weeks, all being Brazilians.

The *Prometheus* arrived home in August 1847 having captured sixteen slavers during her commission and only lost four of her crew from sickness.

Black Water Aboard the *Eclair*

This freedom from fever was a great contrast to the terrible experience of the little *Eclair*.

The *Eclair* left Devonport for the coast of Africa in November, 1844, with a complement of one hundred and forty six officers and men under Commander Estcourt. Up to July, 1845, she lost nine men by what her surgeon termed 'common coast fever'. But four days after leaving Sierra Leone on July the 23rd, a bluejacket died of that particularly fatal type of fever, where the black vomit preceded death. On August the 21st, the *Eclair* arrived in the Gambia with eighteen cases, having already buried thirteen. From Gorre, Captain Estcourt hurried away to Bona Vista, Cape Verd Islands, where, on August the 31st, the Portuguese Governor allowed him to land his whole crew with the exception of the Kroomen and two officers.

When the steam-sloop *Growler*, Commander C. H. M. Buckle arrived at Bona Vista on September the 6th on her way home she found the *Eclair*'s people in a terrible state in spite of every known remedy and precaution taken by the latter's commander and surgeon. Four to five deaths had been occurring daily. The assistant surgeon, C. Hurtman, succumbed on the 7th of September, and Doctor G. M. McClure, who was a passenger aboard the *Growler*, on his way home on promotion from the *Actaeon*, twenty-six guns, at once volunteeered his services and attacked the disease with great vigour, but no success. Whereupon after a consultation between all the medical officers, it was decided that the *Eclair*'s people should be re-embarked and that she should proceed to Madeira, and if the salubrious climate of that island had no effect upon the epidemic that she should then sail for home.

On the 13th of September the *Eclair* sailed from Bona Vista, arriving at Madeira on the 19th. During that six day passage there were seventeen fresh cases, and five deaths, Captain Estcourt and the gallant Doctor McClure being amongst the number of the later. On the 16th, the devoted surgeon of the *Eclair*, Doctor Maconchy, was taken ill and died on the 21st.

The *Growler* arrived at Madeira on the 20th, to find that her own surgeon, Mr. Coffey, was the only medical officer left alive. Doctor W. F. Carter was the next medical officer to take up the fight, another gallant volunteer, and the day that he commenced his duties, Doctor Maconchy and two seamen died. The *Eclair* left Madeira on the 22nd, as the Portuguese authorities refused to allow any communication with the shore.

She arrived at Spithead on September the 28th having had five deaths and seven fresh cases during the passage. Out of her complement, she had had sixty-five deaths since April 1845 and only twenty-two men had escaped attack. Her surviving officers were First-Lieutenant Hartson, Third-Lieutenant Isaacson, Lieutenant H. Bullock and the master Henry D. Burney. Not one of the Kroomen aboard were attacked.

The ship was at once ordered to the Motherbank, but the epidemic continuing, on the 30th, she was ordered to Standgate Creek; here forty-one men who had either escaped or recovered were transferred to the *Revenge*—lying in ordinary, after they had been disinfected by a thorough bath, whilst recent convalescents—only two survived out of every three attacked—were transferred to the hulk *Benbow*. Only a few devoted officers and the Kroomen remained aboard the *Eclair*, and it was not until cold weather set in that the fever was at length conquered. The last victims being the master-at-arms, the blacksmith and a marine on October the 3rd; a sergeant of marines on the 6th; Doctor Bernard, on the 9th; Mr. James Saunders, the pilot on the 10th and the last death of all was that of Lieutenant Isaacson on the 12th.

Assistant-Surgeon Charles Coffey, was the only one to recover out of ten cases which occurred after the ship's arrival home.

The various methods of treating West African fever at this date are given at length in the *Nautical Magazine*. In the twenties the gun-brig *Plumper*, which had been for sometime up one of the rivers, sent thirty-five cases to Sierra Leone hospital. With the aid of the lancet and tremendous doses of calomel twenty-nine of these men were very quickly finished off. But in the forties surgeons had realised the fallacy of bleeding, which in the old days was the cause of half the mortality in the Service, and quinine was being more and more used.

American Cruisers on the Coast

In fulfilment of the Ashburton treaty, American men-of-war began to show themselves on the coast in the forties, making St. Iago, Cape Verd Islands, their headquarters. The American system of stations was a rotation one, their ships working from the Mediterranean to the West Coast of Africa and from there to the Brazils.

Slave catching was by no means popular in the U.S. Navy, for most of the officers came from the Southern, slave-running states: and the *St. Helena Gazette* reported that between April the 1st 1844 and July the 6th, 1845, whilst British cruisers captures seventy-five slavers, the Americans only captured one.

One of the first ships to be sent to the coast by the U.S. Admiralty was the brig *Porpoise*, of two hundred and twenty four tons (American) and armed with two long nines and twelve twenty-four-pounder carronades. She was commanded by Lieutenant Arthur Lewis, an old officer of seventeen years seniority, having under him three lieutenants and a crew of one hundred and twenty men. She was not a very popular craft, for her accommodation was very bad, her guns too heavy for her, and she was overhatted with tremendously raking masts, her mainmast from deck to truck measuring one hundred and thirty feet six inches. From taffrail to knightheads she was one hundred and five feet in length, her keel being eighty-five feet three inches, her beam extreme twenty-five feet seven inches, and depth of hold eleven feet. The *Porpoise* and her sister-ship the *Dolphin* were considered two of the fastest sloops in the U.S. Navy. they were built in the Boston Navy Yard in 1836, from the designs of Samuel Humphreys—to replace the 1821 schooners, which shared the delights of pirate hunting in the West Indies with the cruisers of the Royal Navy. They came out as what the Americans called hermaphrodites with the big boom mainsail and three small square sails on the main, but *Porpoise* when she appeared on the African coast was wholly brig-rigged.

She went missing in the China Seas in September 1854.

The *Felicidade* Tragedies

The slave trade was brought prominently before the British man in the street in 1845 through the publicity given to the tragedy of the *Felicidade*. On February the 27th, 1845, the Brazilian two-topsail slave schooner, *Felicidade*, was captured off Lagos by a boat from the *Wasp*, sixteen-gun brig-sloop, commanded by Commander Sydney Henry Ussher, late of the *Skipjack* schooner.

Having taken all but her master and one other man out of the slaver, Ussher sent

16. Commodore Sir Charles Hotham.

From a painting.

[*Facing page 352.*

17.

H.M.S. *Flying Fish* shortening sail in a tornado.
From a pen and ink drawing by the author.

From a sketch in the Illustrated London News, April 1846.

[*Facing page 353.*

Lieutenant Robert Douglas Stupart, midshipman Palmer and fifteen seamen to take the *Felicidade* to Sirra Leone.

On March the 1st, on her way up the coast, the *Felicidade* fell in with the slaver *Echo* with four hundred and thirty slaves on board, which Stupart promptly captured. Stupart then shifted over to the *Echo* leaving Palmer and eight hands in the *Felicidade*. He had meant to keep company up to Sierra Leone, but the two prizes losing sight of each other, the Spaniards overpowered the small prize crew of the *Felicidade* and murdered every single one of them. Then on March the 6th, the *Felicidade* was recaptured by the *Star*, six guns, Commander Robert John Wallace Dunlop, who quickly discovered something very suspicious in the story told by the Spaniards. He, thereupon, transferred them all to the *Star* and sailed off to Ascension with them, sending the *Felicidade* on to Sierra Leone in charge of Lieutenant John Wilson with four bluejackets, three Kroomen and two Brazilians.

On the 16th of March when the *Felicidade* was in 1° 18′ N. 3° 30′ W. and steering W.N.W. before a Southerly breeze, a black squall was noticed coming up astern about three p.m. The squall though of short duration, was a vicious one. Wilson's orders to the helmsman were to keep dead before it, but the man allowed the schooner to broach to and in a moment she was laid flat with her spars in the water. The prize crew managed to clamber out on to her side, but as she was full of water, Lieutenant Wilson feared that she would sink before long, and, as he had no boat, he at once set about constructing a raft. With their knives the seamen were soon able to cut away sails, rigging and small spars, whilst the Kroomen, being expert swimmers, by diving under water managed to free the main boom—this, with the mainyard, fore and main topsail and topgallant yards, stunsail booms, and gaffs made a raft which would just carry ten men. All night long they sat huddled together upon the lashed spars.

But at daybreak, the schooner being still held up by the air in her hold, the foreyard was added to the raft and a great effort was made to get at the provisions, but it was found impossible for even swimmers like the Kroomen to get into the hold, and only the beef kid with some putrid pork and a small one and a half gallon cask of rum could be salved from the wreck. Planks were torn from the bulwarks to serve as paddles, a light spar was stepped for a mast and a topgallant stunsail set, and at 9 p.m. on the 17th, finding the wreck settling down and showing signs of sinking, Wilson cast off and headed in for the land, Cape Three Points being distant about two hundred and thirty miles to the N.N.E. They had, of course, no compass, but it was easy to steer by the sun and stars.

For the first four days the sun was scorching by day but at night it was very cold. The raft floated so deep that every sea washed over it, yet in spite of being constantly soaked through, thirst began to be the main trouble.

On the fifth and seventh days welcome showers relieved the terrible torture of thirst, but on the ninth day Wilson found that the quartermaster and two of the Kroomen were off their heads through secretly drinking salt water against his orders.

All the time sharks in ever greater numbers swarmed round the raft. At last an eight foot shark was successfully lassoed and quickly killed, its flesh and blood greatly reviving the men, then on the tenth day a heavy rain squall filled the empty rum cask. It was too late, however, to save the two Kroomen and the quartermaster, who had been babbling in delirium for the past two days. On the following morning one of the Kroomen was found lying dead and both the other Krooman and the quartermaster died that day without recovering their senses.

Of the new stock of water, Lieutenant Wilson would not serve out more than would fill the heel of a shoe to each man three times a day, and this was not sufficient to relieve their parched throats.

Three more sharks were caught and eaten, also several flying fish; but, in spite of these, by the end of March things were looking very desperate.

Even though there were occasional rainshowers, the raft was so washed by the seas that any water caught was soon rendered brackish and unfit to drink. The raft, too, threatened to go to pieces and spare rope for lashings was becoming fast used up. The constant wetting not only caused stiffness, but swollen and even ulcerated limbs. Then when the mast carried away and could not be up ended again, this seemed the last fatality.

On April the 3rd, one of the Brazilians died.

However on the evening of the 4th, land was sighted, though after a squally night it could not be seen. A sail to leeward raised the spirits of the survivors, and they did all they knew to signal it.

When the stranger was seen to bear up and run away from them, all would have despaired had not another sail appeared in sight heading straight for the raft.

This turned out to be H.M. brig *Cygnet*, which duly rescued them after twenty days of suffering. Four days after the rescue the second Brazilian died, but Lieutenant Wilson and the three bluejackets recovered.

Meanwhile the murdering crew of the *Echo* were sent to England for trial.

Three of them, who turned Queen's Evidence, a Frenchman, a Portuguese, and an African native, were sent home in the *Heroine*.

The remainder—many of them badly hacked about, thus showing the desperate struggle for life put up by the prize crew—were sent in the *Rapid*.

To round up the gruesome story, in November the *Echo* arrived in St. Catherine's Dock, where she was an object of great interest. She very soon found a purchaser and was renamed the *Elizabeth*, though how the Act of Parliament forbidding the sale of slave prizes was got round I do not know.

Sale of Slavers Forbidden

The last slaver sold by auction at Lloyds was the brig *Cazador*. This was in July, 1836.

From this date the Act of Parliament came into force, and henceforth all slavers had to be destroyed.

At the time there were no less than twenty-four condemned slavers lying at Sierra Leone.

The only one of these to be sold was the schooner *Gazita*, which had been captured by the *Pylades*. She was hauled up, cut in two, and sold for one hundred and thirty two pounds.

Slavers As Opium Clippers

Previous to 1836 many an enterprising sea captain bought a condemned slaver cheap and made a rare lot of money out of her in some trade that required a fast ship.

For instance here is a list of slavers, which became celebrated opium clippers :—

Syed Khan—schooner, 191 tons condemned at Sierra Leone 19th January 1831. Bought by Messrs. David Clark, Samuel Brasier, John Fairlie, George Hartwell and John Turner, merchants of London.

San Antonio—schooner, 227 tons, condemned at Sierra Leone 1831. Bought by the Right Honourable Robert Earl of Harborough and converted to a yacht under the name of *Nymph*. In 1845 she was resold to Thomas Horsburgh, master mariner, for the opium trade.

Tangador—brig, 252 tons, condemned at Sierra Leone in 1834. Bought by Elias Deeper, master mariner, and George Hodgson and William Air, merchants of Freetown. In 1836 She was bought by Henry Pybus, master mariner and Gow and Brightmas, merchants of Calcutta, and renamed *Ann*, for the Opium Trade.

Indagador—schooner, 153 tons, condemned at Sierra Leone 1834. Sold to James Gardner of

Austin Friars, merchant in 1835, renamed *Psyche*, and became an opium clipper sailing under the flag of Dent and Co.

Isabella Estrella—brigantine, 182 tons, condemned at Sierra Leone in February 1836, sold to John Hamilton of Sierra Leone, merchant, resold in 1837 to Henry W. Schneider of London and again resold to Alexander Grant of London, ship owner, renamed *Kelpie*, and became an opium clipper.

Esperance—brig, 219 tons, condemned at Sierra Leone in 1836, sold to John Hamilton of Sierra Leone, merchant, resold to John Miller master mariner of Launceston, Tasmania, and renamed *Black Joke*, employed in opium trade.

Besides these vessels, which became noted in the opium trade, there were numbers of condemned slavers bought for the Ionian currant trade, and the Mediterranean and Azores orange and lemon trade, where quick passages were a necessity.

When Portuguese and Brazilian slavers became liable to capture South of the Equator, the cruisers on that station were allowed to send their prizes to St. Helena for adjudication, being only eight or nine days sail away.

Thus in the forties it was customary to see a score or more of condemned, or about to be condemned, slavers rolling off Jamestown.

After ajudication they were sold under the condition that they were broken up as speedily as possible.

The Rollers at St. Helena

On one occasion—February the 17th, 1846, that phenomenon of the South Atlantic, the "Rollers", most effectively did the breaking up before many of the vessels had been adjudicated upon.

The Rollers which come in upon the S.W. coast of Africa and the shores of St. Helena and even as far North as Ascension, are generally considered to be caused by pamperos, though it is possible that submarine earthquakes also may be their origin.

Here is a very vivid account of the Rollers, which came into the Jamestown anchorage a few days after the death of Napoleon, the experience of a midshipman of H.M.S. *Vigo*, the Guardship.

"... I was engaged in conversation with an officer of the Honourable company's ship, *Ganges* surrounded by native women, some children and Lascars, when I felt myself forcibly pulled by the arm and heard a person exclaim:—

'Look at the horizon, run, save yourself, we shall all be lost!'

I did look, and the sight I shall never cease to remember, it was so frightfully grand.

On the horizon from the North-West appeared an immense undulation, or swell, resembling a bank of water rolling majestically in, directly in the wind's eye. Whether it was my anxiety for the boats or that astonishment had paralysed me, I cannot tell, but I felt riveted to the spot alone, and before I could attempt to save myself, as others did by climbing the rocks, I was whirled along with the rapidity of lightning in the midst of this dark wave. Almost in an instant I experienced a violent shock, which stunned me for a few moments: on recovering the prefect use of my senses, I found myself in the Armourer's cave with the forge lying across my thigh. To this circumstance I must draw attention, as, by its weight keeping me from going into the sea as the water receded, and from being dashed against the rocks, to it I owe my preservation.

Near me were lying two Lascars, one split up the middle, the other's skull beat to pieces—both were dead. Fearing a return of the surf, as the sea usually rolls in quickly twice and then comes with redoubled violence, I made the best use of my lungs; the carpenter fortunately heard my cries and rescued me. My clothes were torn to shreds, my ears, eyes and nose filled with ashes and blood: but, with the exception of a few contusions and lacerated hands I was otherwise unhurt. One woman was drowned, and several men and women were picked up by the boats. This first swell that I have mentioned was the prelude to a gigantic surf, which lasted three days.

This phenomenon (as nothing like it had ever taken place in the memory of the oldest inhabitant), was attributed to an earthquake. We had only telegraphic communication with the ship while it lasted. The fortifications were much injured in front of Jamestown: huge rocks were torn up and tossed into our little bathing-place to the left of the landing: the Guardhouse was abandoned, the sea reaching the upper windows: the ships rode with sails aback to keep them astern of their anchors; and, while it lasted, to see the mass of water burst upon the cliffs, as if to shake the island from its foundation was the grandest sight I ever remember".

(*United Service Journal,* 1832).

The Rollers on February the 17th, 1846, were equally terrific, beginning on the night of Monday the 16th, they gradually increased "to an awful height, like so many rolling mountains one after another, driving everything before them".

The first vessel to come in on the beach and be smashed to splinters was the condemned slaver, *Cornelia.* The man in charge of her was only rescued five minutes before she was overwhelmed.

The next was the Brazilian brig *Des Cobrador* (127 tons), which had been captured by the *Star* and brought to the island by Lieutenant Meynell, a month before. She was torn from her anchors and hurled ashore "between the draw-bridge and the upper crane". Two of the people aboard managed to swim ashore, leaving the ship keeper and his wife hanging by the lee rail. The town major tried to get a rope aboard by means of a rocket, but it failed. Then Mr. Chatfield, master's assistant of H.M. brig *Flying Fish*, swam off with a rope. He was knocked senseless under the brig's counter and finally thrown back on the beach. Then an attempt was made to launch a whaleboat, but she was hardly in the water before she was dashed to pieces.

Next an American seaman, named Roach, succeeded in swimming off with a rope, and both the ship keeper and his wife were saved with the help of Dr. Tweedale of H.M.S. *Prometheus* and Lieutenant Grant, R.A.

This gallant rescue work was carried out within ten minutes of the *Des Cobrador* coming ashore. Five minutes later she went to pieces along with a prize schooner of the *Prometheus*, which had been hurled in alongside of her.

At noon the Brazilian schooner, *Acquilla*, a prize of H.M. brig *Cygnet*, broke adrift with the Brazilian brigantine *St. Domingo*, prize of the *Prometheus*, and both were hurled on the beach in front of the town. At one o'clock the hulk, *Rocket*, was turned end over end by an extra heavy roller and disappeared. At the same time the Brazilian schooner, *Entrazia*, prize of the *Prometheus*, sank at her anchors; whilst the Brazilian brigantine *Esperanza*, prize of the *Actaeon,* drifted out to sea, after her masts had gone by the board. At half past five the condemned Brazilian brigantine, *Julia*, prize of the *Star*, was thrown up on the West Rocks and disappeared in an instant; whilst the brig *Quatro de Marco*, which had been brought in on the 26th of December by the purser of the *Cygnet* with five hundred and forty slaves, was torn from four anchors and hurled ashore under Patten's Battery.

Besides these, three other slavers, which were being broken up, were washed ashore.

The damage ashore was estimated at twenty thousand pounds.

The wharf was totally destroyed and with it the water tanks for supplying shipping. The coal yard was gutted, the fortifications at Lemon Valley injured and the seas even rolled up as far as Ruperts, where the liberated slaves were located.

The merchant shipping escaped owing to the fact that it lay outside the breakers, but all communication with the shore was interrupted for some time.

Pantaloon* Captures *Barboleta

On January the 15th, 1845, the two Experimental brigs, *Mutine* and *Osprey*, sailed in company with *Pantaloon* and *Waterwitch* from Plymouth, *Mutine* being bound to the Cape, *Osprey* to the East Indies, and *Pantaloon* and *Waterwitch* to the West coast of Africa. It was hoped that they would make a grand race of it in continued sailing trials on the passage out, but on the 16th in a heavy swell both *Waterwitch* and *Pantaloon* carried away their main topgallant masts, and the four brigs lost sight of each other in the Bay of Biscay, and did not meet again.

The *Pantaloon*, commanded by Edmund Wilson, who had been very successful when in charge of the *Cygnet* between 1840 and 1843, had not been long on the coast before she distinguished herself by capturing the *Barboleta*, described as "a remarkably fine vessel of about four hundred and fifty tons, polacca rigged with immense sails—of great celebrity on the coast, armed with four twelve-pounders, with a mixed crew, composed chiefly of Spaniards, amounting to about fifty and equipped for any villainous service, whether slave dealing or piracy".

The *Pantaloon* first discovered the slaver off St. Thomas and a long chase ensued in which the *Barboleta* gradually ran the *Pantaloon* out of sight; then, as soon as the gun brig was below the horizon, she altered her course and doubled back to Lagos. But Edmund Wilson was well versed in the tricks of slavers and at daybreak on May the 26th, 1845, three days after the chase had commenced, the polacca, lying becalmed off Lagos, discovered to her dismay that the *Pantaloon* was only about a couple of miles away.

The two whale boats and cutter of the sloop were immediately piped away under the command of her first lieutenant, Lewis de T. Prevost, with the master, J. T. Croat, boatswain Pasco, and marines and seamen to the number of thirty all told.

Directly the boats arrived within range, the brig opened on them with roundshot, grape and canister; but the boats came on steadily, the marines replying to the fire from the slaver and the bluejackets pulling doggedly in the hot sun.

It was half an hour before they could get up to the *Barboleta*, and all the time a shower of every kind of missile from slugs to nails was poured upon them.

When the boats ran alongside, Prevost and the boatswain on the starboard side and the master on the port bow, it was by no means easy to gain a footing on the slaver's deck; but the gallantry of British seamen in cutting out affairs has always been very hard to withstand. Croat, the master, and a bluejacket gave a typical instance of this unbeatable courage, by actually climbing in through a port as the broadside gun was being fired out of it. The bluejacket was knocked overboard by the discharge, but nothing daunted, he clambered aboard again like a cat and was just in time to help his officer who was holding the fore-deck in a ring of Spanish knives.

Aft, Prevost, the boatswain and their men had to use their cutlasses with all their skill before they could clear the deck.

The resistance was desperate; and it was not until seven of their number lay dead and as many were severely wounded that the crew of the slaver turned their backs and made a bolt for the 'tween decks. In these affrays it was always noticeable how the very daring of the onslaught seemed to preserve the attackers. In this instance a seaman was killed and a marine died of wounds. The master was severely and the boatswain slightly wounded, the captain's coxswain, a quartermaster, an able seaman and a marine being also wounded.

Prevost was at once promoted and the little *Pantaloon* was the envy of every cruiser on the coast. It was always the hope and prayer of every young officer that he would some day come across a fighting slaver.

Flying Fish on the Coast

Whilst the *Pantaloon* was distinguishing herself in the Bights, the experimental brig, *Flying Fish*, was finding it very dull further North on her first commission against the slave trade, as witness the following letter to Sir William Symonds from her commander:—

Flying Fish, Cape Mount (Near Sierra Leone)
August 12, 1845

My dear Sir,

I wrote to Captain Symonds by *Growler*, as we have not had an opportunity of sending letters for two months. There is nothing doing on the northern part of the coast, but they seem more active in the Bights, where, I am happy to say, *Flying Fish* is now ordered. We have just taken in six and a half months' provisions, preparatory to a long cruise. I have dried my empty tanks and put the bread in, and we shall soon eat all that is above board. Nothing that we have ever met has the slightest chance with us, and a vessel seen from the royal-yard, in the wind's eye, is under our guns in three hours.

*Actaeon** is described as the most uneasy beast that ever was built: she rolls her main-deck guns in. It is a mistake to call this a smooth-water station: there is a heavy sea along the whole north coast. The *Fish* rides beautifully: for instance, we anchored in twenty-one fathoms of water, with stream-chain, and kedge-anchor (three and a half hundred weights) and veered to sixty fathoms: she rode out a fresh breeze with very heavy swell with royal-yards across.

I tried it as an experiment, lying seven miles off the land. I cannot say too much in her praise, and I am sure she has been well tried.

The American brig of war *Truxton*, whose Captain maintained she could beat everything on the coast, after being beaten six miles in three hours, acknowledged that we sailed 'pretty handsomely'. We were in chase of him and he tried his best to get away.†

Believe me, my dear sir,
Yours faithfully,
R. Harris

To Sir Wm. Symonds

In his letter Commander Harris omits to mention any details, whether of wind or sails.

According to sketches sent home, which were reproduced in the *Illustrated London News*, the *Flying Fish* not only crossed two skysail yards but spread full suits of stunsails, to royal stunsails, at both fore and main.

Whilst cruising off the Gold Coast, Harris fitted up his twelve oared pinnace with topsails over her standing lugs and sent her away under the first lieutenant with the cutter in company for cruises of a week or more's duration.

On the 14th of December, 1845, whilst these boats were away the *Flying Fish* discovered a sail under the land at daybreak. At 9 a.m. the wind fell and for the next hour, the heavy work of sweeping the brig was resorted to in order to keep the chase in sight.

At ten, there being no appearance of wind, Lieutenant St. Leger was sent away with the two whale boats and eighteen men. It was a long hard pull in the broiling sun, and when within three quarters of a mile of the slaver, St. Leger wisely gave his men a breather. However the chase was no *Barboleta* and before the boats reached her, she lowered her ensign and surrendered.

She turned out to be a beautiful brig, the *Eliza*, barely a year old, having cost eight thousand dollars. She was bound in to load her first slave cargo.

---

* *Actaeon* twenty-six guns, built 1831 by Superior shipwright Apprentices.

† The U.S. brig of war, *Truxton* was launched from the Gosport Navy Yard in 1842. She was designed by Francis Grice and was undoubtedly a very fast brig with her fine lines and great dead rise.

She cost forty thousand eight hundred and sixty seven dollars to build, and registered three hundred and twenty nine American tons, her main measurements being:—

Length between perpendiculars, one hundred feet: beam extreme, twenty-eight feet two inches: depth of hold, thirteen feet: mean draft, twelve feet three inches.

She mounted ten thirty-two-pounder carronades and two long thirty-two-pounder guns. Her sail plan was high and narrow, with the same measurements at both fore and main: masts from deck to track, one hundred and forty feet without allowing for the doublings: lower yards fifty-five feet: topsail yards, forty-two feet: topgallant yards twenty-eight feet and royal yards twenty feet.

She had a short life being wrecked on Tuxpan Bar, Mexico, on August the 15th, 1846.

Commodore Jones Succumbs to the Climate

Ever since Admiral Hayes had finished his term on the West coast in 1832 no Commodore had been appointed until Captain Jones of the *Penelope* was instructed to hoist the broad pendant in the spring of 1844. For ten years the Admiral at the Cape had been responsible for the coast of Africa from the Gambia to Zanzibar, and at last the Admiralty were made to understand that the station of such wide extent and of such importance was too much for an officer, who was obliged to take a strong part in guiding the destinies of the South African Colonies, and to lend his aid against the turbulent kaffirs.

Commodore Jones arrived home in the spring of 1846, having been very ill for some time with African fever. He died at Haslar Hospital on May the 24th, 1846.

CHAPTER XVIII

HOTHAM'S COMMAND

Set every stitch of canvas to woo the fresh'ning wind;
Our bowsprit points to Cuba, the coast lies far behind.
Filled to the hatches full, my boys, across the seas we go;
There's twice five hundred niggers in the stifling hold below.
'A sail! what say you, boys? Well-let him give us a chase
A British man-of-war you say-well, let him try the race;
There's not a swifter vessel ever floated on the waves
Than out tidy little schooner well ballasted with slaves'.

Now stronger yet and stronger still came down the fiery breeze,
And ever fast and faster sped the strange ship on the seas,
Flinging each rude and bursting surge in glittering halves back,
And bearing high to heaven aloft the English Union Jack!
'Now curses on that ensign' the slaving captain said;
'There's little luck for slavers when the English bunting's spread.
But pack on sail and trim the ship: before we'll captured be
We'll have the niggers up, my boys, and heave them in the sea'.

Hoarse was the slaving captain's voice and deep the oath he swore:
'Haul down the flag; that's shot enough, we don't want any more.'
Alongside dashed the cruiser's boat to board and sieze the prize.
Hark to that rattling British cheer that's ringing to the skies!
'Up, up with the negroes speedily; up, up and give them breath;
Clear out the hold from stem to stern: that noisome den is death;
And run aloft St George's Cross, all wanton let it wave
The token proud that under it there never treads a slave'.

The Slave Chase

THIS ballad, in imitation of Macaulay's Lays, was called the "The Slave Chase". C. H. Firth in his Introduction to "Naval Songs and Ballads" says that it was a great favourite with Captain Montagu Burrows, who served in the *Winchester*, flagship, and the sixteen-gun brig, *Sappho*, on the Cape Station as a lieutenant in the forties.

Firth also says it was a popular favourite, often reprinted by Fortey, Such and later publishers of street ballads.

Commodore Sir Charles Hotham

The Admiralty had wanted to appoint Captain Charles Hotham Commodore on the West coast in the spring of 1844, but Hotham in the steam frigate, *Gorgon*, was serving on the South East coast of America, and when the British ministers at Buenos Aires and Montevideo, as well as the merchants of those places, heard that Hotham was to be sent away from their station, they made such strong representations to the Admiralty that the latter reluctantly agreed to let Hotham remain in the River Plate, and promoted Jones.

This well shows the light in which Charles Hotham was regarded, not only in his own service, but by all those with whom he had to do.

He was, in fact, one of the outstanding Naval Officers of his time.

Entering the R.N. in 1818, he first distinguished himself as a mid in a cutting out affair, in which the boats of the *Naiad*, forty-six guns, destroyed a sixteen-gun brig anchored under the fortress of Bona in the face of a tremendous fire from its canons and the muskets of four hundred soldiers. This gallant action gave proof of his personal courage.

The Salvage Of The *Terror* Bomb.

In January 1828 he was appointed first lieutenant of the *Terror*, bomb, which sailed with stores for the Mediterranean fleet. On February the 19th, the *Terror* was wrecked on the coast of Portugal near Villa Nova de Millefuentes.

On the previous day the land had been made about Cape St Vincent bearing S.E. By 3 p.m. it was blowing a hurricane, and the brig under maintopsail and fore topmast staysail, her topgallant masts and yards being struck, lay down with her lee rail in the water.

To save the *Terror*, the main topsail was handed; but with the wind veering to West at dark, the ship was caught on a dead lee shore. Then the heavy sea began to take toll-boats, lee bulwarks, quarter and everything moveable were all washed away and the deadlights stove in. At 2 a.m. when the order had been given:-

'Hands, wear ship.' the breakers showed up so close, that it was immediately changed to 'Let go the anchors.' The best bower brought her up in seventy fathoms, then snapped: the small bower with its cable out to the clinch, dragged.

Captain Hope then determined to slip the anchor and try and work off clear of the rocks under his lee: but the shackle holding the cable round the mainmast had so much strain on it, that the bolts could not be drawn. In this dilemma, the master, up to his waist in water on the main-deck attempted to cut a link with a cold chisel, whilst the hands went aloft to loose the fore-topsail and courses.

With the breakers sweeping the ship from stem to stern; on the cable parting, her head was forced round in-shore, and her keel began to strike heavily on the ground.

The situation now appeared desperate. The darkness of the night increased the confusion. The fury of the surf which raged over the wreck, actually washed the barge, which was stowed between the masts, over the side. It was extremely cold, and when the order went out:—'Everyone look out for himself!' many of the hands were so benumbed that they could not lash themselves, so as to prevent being washed overboard. Yet there was no lapse from discipline, everyone aboard behaving calmly and coolly, though death stared them in the face. Whilst the fury of the storm was at its worst, shortly after the *Terror* had struck, the hulk of a dismasted vessel was swept by.

But soon after this the force of the seas diminished. When day dawned it was found that the bomb had picked upon the only piece of sandy beach to strand upon, with rocks to either side of her.

She had come ashore at the top of the flood, a mile to the Northward of the river of Villa Nova and as the tide ebbed had docked herself in the sand.

Nearby lay the wreck of the merchant brig, *Jane of Liverpool* in two halves and half buried in the sand. This was the vessel that had swept by in the night. A mile away lay the barge, with the dead body of the carpenter's mate beside it, but two sheep which had been in it, were found grazing on the shore unhurt. To either side lay wreckage of every kind—masts, yards, hatches, hen coops etc.

Whilst the tide was away from the bomb-vessel, her crew worked valiantly to get everything ashore; and a freight of twenty thousand pounds, provisions, ammunition, small-arms and spars and sails were all carried above the high water mark. Meanwhile natives with bullocks, mules and asses appeared on the scene, intent on wrecking; and only musket shots fired over their heads kept their plundering hands away from the King's stores. One fellow, indeed, had to be made a prisoner, and after being kept in irons all night, was brought out with a rope round his neck, as if for hanging, before being allowed to rejoin his countrymen.

With darkness and high water the gale blew up again and about 2 a.m. a gun was heard. At daybreak a schooner was seen on the rocks within half a mile of the other two wrecks. This turned out to be the *Fancy* of Arbroath, which along with the *Jane* had been in sight of the *Terror* on the afternoon of the 18th. Hotham with four volunteers using the *Jane's* boat, managed to make two dangerous trips through the surf and rescue the seven men composing the schooner's crew.

For the next forty-eight hours it continued to blow hard: and when, at last, the wind went down and a careful examination of the wrecked bomb-vessel could be made, it was found that she was bilged on both sides, her back broken, fore-foot, keel and stern-post knocked away and bulwarks levelled. Few seamen would have suggested salving such a wreck, yet Hotham urged it, and Captain Hope agreed to make a try at it.

The second lieutenant was thereupon despatched to Lisbon with a full report for the Britsh Admiral, who at once sent the *Pyramus* round to the scene with orders to ship the *Terror's* supernumeraries and twenty thousand pounds. Fearful of sharing the fate of the *Terror,* the *Pyramus* sailed as soon as her freight was aboard.

Then with the help of shipwrights and caulkers sent by the Portuguese Government, the shell of the *Terror,* which had been stripped to her kelson, was in the end floated successfully.

It would take a whole chapter to describe the methods employed, but immense casks, used in the Tagus for lifting ships, when hove down, were lashed to the hull only to be broken up by the violence of the surf. At the pump brakes and purchases, Portuguese soldiers urged on by a stout Colonel, who had been seven years with Wellington, aided the British bluejackets in their final effort when, at the top of the tide, after much strenous heaving, the *Terror* became once more water-born. After temporary repairs at Lisbon, she sailed for home with the pumps going without ceasing. Captain Hope was at once given another command, Hotham and his senior midshipman, Robert Cleugh, being promoted. The Lord High Admiral H.R.H. the Duke of Clarence (afterwards William IV) voiced the feeling in the Service, when he said 'No one but a seaman could have saved the ship', and directed that no Court martial should take place.

The Salavage of the *Gorgon*

Hotham's first command was the ten-gun brig *Cordelia,* on the Mediterranean station, where his uncle, Vice-Admiral the honourable Sir Henry Hotham, was Commander-in-Chief.

That his services in the Mediterranean were not colourless is proved by the fact that he was presented with a jewelled sword by the Grand Seigneur of the Turks. He received his promotion to post captain on June the 28th, 1832.

After the usual period on half-pay he commissioned the celebrated steam frigate, *Gorgon,* on November the 25th, 1842, and was sent to the River Plate, where General Rosas was causing trouble and arousing anxiety in the chancelleries of the great powers.

The *Gorgon* had a long and varied career in the Royal Navy; but, at first, illiterate Jack was not greatly enamoured of her name and rather fought shy of her.

The story goes that two seaman were overhauling the ships in the docks at Portsmouth with a view to shipping.

On coming alongside the new *Gorgon,* they proceeded to slowly spell out her name—but unfortunately they read it backwards:—

"N O G R O G!! Come away, Bill, that ain't no ship for us.

No grog h'indeed. We ain't shippin' in you an' you may lay to that—no, not if you was the finest frigate in the sarvice, 'stead of a stinkin' puffin' Billy".

And they passed on with a great air of disgust.

It was now that Hotham not only increased his reputation as a magnificent seaman, but made his name as a commander who could handle a difficult situation with rare diplomatic genius and carry a difficult campaign to a successful conclusion, besides fighting a victorious battle, where want of absolute success would have been fatal.

On the 11th of May, 1844, the *Gorgon* was blown ashore in Montevideo Bay by a pampero.

When the fury of the storm was over, the great eleven hundred ton paddle-wheel frigate was high and dry, two miles from where there was water enough to float her; in a situation where the ordinary rise of tide was only four feet, and imbedded in sand to a mean depth of eleven feet. Until Captain Hotham began his preparations for floating her, no one amongst the many British or foreign sailors on the station dreamt that her salvage was possible, and even his own officers and crew were taken by surprise by his determination and confidence.

A long book has been written by the famous Admiral Sir Astley Cooper Key, on the recovery of the *Gorgon*—he was her third lieutenant.

This book describes how a mud machine dug a channel in the sand and mud: how anchors were laid out; and how camels, caissons, tanks and casks were built and how complicated purchases were rigged. Again and again gales of wind undid the work of weeks—again and again the sailors set to it again. There came a day when every expert considered it necessary to take her heavy engines out, but Hotham held firm against any such proceeding, he saw clearly how necessary their help was going to be. At last after weeks of heaving the ship through the mud, on the morning of October the 29th Hotham made the proud signal '*Gorgon* is moored'. H.M.S. *Curacoa* immediately fired a gun and in every ship in Montevideo Bay the crew sprang into the rigging and gave three hearty cheers, which were returned with equal spirit from the *Gorgon*.

(Note: Extract from a letter written by Captain Sir Thomas Pasley Bart of the H.M.S. *Curacoa,* dated October the 18th, 1844.

> "I was much pleased to be present and was infected with the singular state of excitement and enthusiasm which pervaded everyone. Hotham alone contrived to appear outwardly calm and he was feeling more internally of course than any of us.
>
> It is impossible to give him too much credit for the untiring energy, the patient, determined perserverance and the fertility in expedient and contrivances that he has displayed and it has been wonderful to see the elasticity with which he has risen after seeing repeatedly all his plans and labours overthrown by some gale of wind or deluge of rain which has in a few hours destroyed the work of weeks and caused labour for weeks more to restore things to what they were.
>
> Often I have feared his health would break down, and more than once I have seen him quite prostrated by positive bodily illness brought on by excessive fatigue and exertion. Few men would have shown such unflinching constancy as he has done and it is not to detract from the merit of the officers and men, who have behaved admirably that I say their conduct has been what it is mainly from having Hotham for their captain.
>
> No one can know what he has gone through better than I, for with the exception of eighteen days I have been living with him for three whole months.
>
> I went to him on the 13th of July and left him on the 14th of October, so that I have had good opportunities of witnessing what he his made of".
>
> Pasley adds "The *Gorgon* was more than two miles and a half from water deep enough to float her".)

The Battle of Obligado

If Hotham's refloating of the *Gorgon* was quoted in every nautical service as an example of what scientific seamanship, accompanied by unconquerable determination, could do; his victory at Obligado up the Parana river a year later was hailed by the British nation as a proof that we still had officers of Nelsonian quality in the Royal Navy. The battle of Obligado showed him to be a commander of unusual stature and the British Government signified their approval by an immediate award of the K.C.B.

At this psychological moment when, a man of forty, he was at the height of his reputation, he was asked to go to the West coast of Africa as Commodore.

Hotham was far from being physically strong, and very much doubted whether his constitution would stand the coast, but he considered it his duty to accept the post, though he knew that the Admiralty half expected him to refuse.

It will perhaps be of interest to gain a glimpse of his character through the eyes of his brother officers.

In a letter home, on joining the *Gorgon,* Lieutenant Astley Cooper Key wrote:—

> "I admire Captain Hotham more every day: he is a reserved man, but a first rate officer, and in every sense of the word a gentleman . . . .
>
> Captain Hotham is not a scientific man, but is decidedly a clever man, a good linguist, very well informed in history and politics, and I imagine, for a naval man, a good diplomatist".

In his next letter Cooper Key wrote:—

> "We are with a captain peculiarly careful about the health of his men".

In his report on the Battle of Obligado, Rear-Admiral S. H. Inglefield, Commander-in-Chief, South America, was almost enthusiastic in his praise:—

> "Captain Hotham's letters bring the merit of the contest so fully to the mind that I feel it now only remains for me to express to their lordships the high sense I entertain of the gallantry, zeal and ability, which animate that excellent officer, who has on every occasion given me perfect satisfaction in the performance of his various duties and I beg to recommend his services most highly to their lordships' favourable consideration".

For some reason or other Hotham was told to exchange into the *Devastation,* and leave the *Gorgon* and his devoted ship's company behind.

He tried his best to get Cooper Key as his commander, but the latter's service was too short and the regulation forbade it.

The *Devastation* was a paddle-wheel sloop of one thousand and fifty eight tons, and four hundred H.P. built at Woolwich in 1841 from Sir William Symonds' designs, an improved *Gorgon.*

Hotham and the French and American Admirals

The new commodore soon made his presence felt on the coast. A very practical, logical and far-sighted man, his first action on reaching his station was to hunt up the American and French admirals and gain an insight into their methods of working, seek their friendship, and arrange a cooperative system of cruising.

By the Convention of 1845 the two governments had agreed to keep squadrons of twenty-six ships on the coast, but the French being only allowed by their instructions to stop their own slavers were of little use and in August 1848 Hotham reported that in two years they had not made a capture.

They were even suspected by our cruisers of playing a double game.

The Americans likewise could only deal with vessels flying their own flag with slaves aboard, and as the stars and stripes were downed directly the slave deck was laid, the most zealous of American naval officers had to spend their time looking on.

Treaty Making with the Chiefs

Hotham's next proceeding was to open negotiations with the various chiefs along the coast, those of the Manna country being the first to fall in with his suggestions.

Captain George Mansel of the *Actaeon,* twenty-six guns, and Commander Alexander Murray of the *Favourite,* eighteen guns, were the chief officers entrusted with the important duty of treaty making, the former in the Cape Mount district and the latter at Bimbia.

It was this method of encouraging legitimate trade and even subsidizing the traders, which really broke the back of the slave trade on the windward coast, so that Hotham was able to report that slavers had been effectually checked on either side of the Sierra Leone colony.

For instance we find the following report from Commander Edward Dixon of H.M.S. *Rapid,* senior officer of the Sierra Leone Division.

> Sir,
> "I have the honour to inform you that to the best of my belief no vessel has escaped with slaves from the Gallinas or Shebar from 1st November, 1847 to 12th May, 1848".

Matters were not so satisfactory to the Southward—in the Bights and South of the Equator.

Hotham's First Report

In his first report, after, six months on the coast, Hotham wrote on the 7th of April, 1847.

> "I heartily wish it were in my power to make a favourable report of the suppression of the slave trade in these districts (Bight of Benin and Kabenda) but difficulties are here accumulated greater than our cruisers have been able to overcome.
>
> The greater part of the slaves are sent to Bahia and Pernambuco. The vessels are employed are of the best construction and in many class outsail our men-of-war. The *Dos Amigos* has beaten two of our finest brigs in a fair chase.
>
> She is well handled and carries over eight hundred slaves each trip".

Hotham's New Station Methods

Hotham was the first commanding officer to report on the internal water communication round the Bights of Benin and Biafra, which made it easy for slaves to be run from fifty miles inland to any point on the coast, where it was known a cruiser had recently left her station in order to wood and water.

Hotham, however, instituted a second line of cruisers. Besides his in-shore squadron, he kept a ring of his fastest sloops, such as the *Waterwitch, Pantaloon, Contest, Rapid,* etc., well out to sea on the usual tracks of slavers bound both to Brazil and Cuba.

Of these outside ships, the *Waterwitch* was specially successful and actually caught the slavers passing between St. Helena and Ascension as far to the Westward as ten to fifteen degrees West Longitude.

Mansfield Preserves the *Romeo Primero*

On July the 22nd, 1847, the *Waterwitch* captured the Brazilian brigantine *Romeo Primero.*

Commander Thomas Francis Birch sent his prize off to St. Helena for adjudication under Lieutenant Walter George Mansfield with only four bluejackets. After experiencing some very unfavourable winds, Mansfield at length bore up for Sierra Leone.

On August the 11th, the four most determined men of the slaver's crew made a very dashing attempt to recapture their vessel.

Mansfield received nine wounds and one of his men was killed, nevertheless he managed to preserve his command and sailed into Sierra Leone on September the 1st. He recovered from his wounds and for his gallantry was promoted.

The *Sealark* was lucky enough to capture a schooner with one hundred and eighty nine slaves on board when fourteen days out on her way home.

It was only in the Bights that Hotham kept most of his cruisers off shore; on the Northern division they were often instructed to maintain a close blockade.

Though at home some criticized the commodore for keeping cruisers far away from the coast, the scheme proved successful in two ways.

Health of the West Coast Squadron

No officer took greater care of the health of his squadron than Hotham, and this distant cruising was very healthy, whereas river work certainly was not.

Hotham was very much against boat service up rivers as being a great cause of fever epidemics—an officer sending his boats up a river in the Bights, had to show cause in writing.

As a result of his care Hotham was able to report:—

> "The general state of health of the squadron is excellent, the percentage of the whole squadron, including the hospital is only four and three quarters per cent, a marvellously low average for any part of the world, It will by my study to change the stations of the cruisers periodically and remove any vessel where symptoms of disease may be developed."

The deaths in the Squadron since 1842 are therefore of interest—allowance must be made for the gradual increase in the number of ships.

In 1842 when the West coast squadron consisted of *Madagascar,* forty-four, *Iris,* twenty-six and a dozen brigs and brigantines the deaths were sixty. In 1843, a healthy year, twenty-five; in 1844, forty-nine; in 1845, one hundred and twenty nine: in 1846 eighty-eight, and in 1847 when the squadron reached thirty ships, sloops, brigs and steamers, the deaths up to June the 30th dropped to twenty-six.

As regards the much criticized expense of the Squadron, two heavy new items had to be allowed for—the up-keep of machinery and the cost of coal.

The Accountant General's Return

The accountant-general's return for 1846-1847 dated 13th December, 1847 was a follows:—

	£
Wages and Victuals	220,233
Wear and tear of hulls, gear, stores	49,313
Wear and tear of machinery	17,790
Value of coal provided	14,287
	301,623

And here are the expenses incurred by the British Government in suppressing the slave trade for four years.

	1844 £	1845 £	1846 £	1847 £	Total. £
Wages of Seamen, victuals, etc.	217,527	291,501	301,623	306,336	1,116,987
Grants for Civil Establishments in Africa.	12,800	11,639	16,401	12,553	53,393
Charges on liberated Africans.	29,552	6,591	19,516	18,442	74,101
Salaries, Expenses and Commissions under treaty engagements.	26,730	20,924	20,400	20,490	88,544
Bounties in slaves and slave vessels captured and destroyed	37,483	55,553	31,287	54,289	178,612
Total	324,092	386,208	389,227	412,110	1,511,637

When sundry expenses directly or indirectly connected with the West coast squadron were added, these totals were brought up to:—

1844 £389,097, 1845 £452,612, 1846 £454,861, 1847 £495,630. Thus, by 1848, it was reckoned that the suppression of the slave trade was costing the British Government half a million sterling per annum.

But Hotham's success was undoubted, for instance in twenty two months Commodore Jones took one hundred slavers in the same time between October the 14th 1846 and August the 13th 1848, Commodore Hotham captured one hundred and forty three slavers.

Hotham's Inspections

Hotham was a strict disciplinarian, and his inspections and exercising of ships were exceedingly thorough. This was a period in the history of the Royal Navy when smartness in evolution and sail drill were thought more of by commanding officers than any other training and consequently had been raised to an almost incredible pitch of perfection.

In spite of the advent of the paddle-wheel, quickly followed by the screw, the burning subjects of sailing speed and ship design were considered to be still of the first importance. Sail drill became one of the last efforts of the old seamen to combat the invasion of machinery.

Hotham, though a taut hand was a just one, and gave praise when it was earned. In the old days cruisers were often allowed to get pretty slack and there were few commodore's inspections; but Hotham not only inspected every ship of his command in sail drill, sending down masts, shifting topsails, etc; but at small arms and cutlass exercises and even firing at a target. When possible two or three ships were exercised together.

For instance here is the testimony of Commander Montresor of the *Wanderer*.

. . . he made the signal for the three brigs (*Wanderer, Cygnet* and *Star*) to shift topmasts: the men were nervous: they were dreadfully afraid of the Commodore, and we thought we were very long about it, but were greatly relieved to find we had beaten both brigs. The *Wanderer* was then ordered, by signal, to fire three rounds, quick firing: at the close of our probation we were much gratified at seeing the signal:—

"Well done, *Wanderer, Cygnet* wants exercise".

In the summer of 1847 the *Penelope* arrived out, commanded by Captain L. T. Jones, who had been Hotham's first Lieutenant in the *Cordelia*.

The Commodore thereupon shifted his broad pendant to the frigate, and the *Devastation* went off to the Cape station.

Slavers Use American Flag

Hotham's chief handicap in his work was that he was not allowed to search vessels flying the American flag and thus many a bona-fide slaver went free. The Baltimore schooners and brigs now sailed direct for the coast with dollars in specie to pay for a cargo of slaves, as well as holds full of tobacco, coarse clothes, powder and arms, in which articles of trade American merchants were always able to undersell the British. As a rule the slaver did not change her flag until she had her slave deck laid, her water and farina on board, and was ready to ship her slaves. The American squadron was often accused of being luke warm and even pro the slave trader*, but Hotham bore testimony in its favour in these words:—

> "The officers of the U.S. Navy are extremely active and zealous in the cause and no fault can be attributed to them".

At Angola too, Hotham recorded a change of heart. Where before the whole Portuguese and native population had been accustomed to live on the slave trade, the new Governor, we

* Lieutenant A. H. Foote, commanding the U.S. brig, *Perry*, captured two slavers, though this was said to risk his advancement in the U.S. Service.

are told 'looking neither to the right or to the left, has strictly obeyed his orders and the traffic has in consequence received the severest check'. (Hotham's report.)

Warning Signals

On the Northern Division in 1848 the slave trade at Cape Mount and the Gallinas had revived after King Cain had been killed, and the treaties entered in to with King Fano-Toro were thus brought to nought. At the beginning of the year there were said to be six hundred slaves in the barracoons at the Gallinas and the traders had instituted a system to notify slavers of the presence of cruisers.

All along the coast a line of signals were maintained every night. A single light shown on any portion of the coast meant that there were no cruisers about and that it was safe to run in and ship a cargo.

Two lights together inferred that the whereabouts of the cruisers was uncertain, and three lights were a sign of great dangers—this was still further accentuated when a cruiser was at anchor off the barracoons by a large bonfire, into which gun powder was thrown at constant intervals, which showed up in sudden flashes and could be seen twenty miles away. At this date large canoes, holding two hundred slaves or more, were sent out to sea to look for slavers, and were sometimes found forty miles off shore in fine weather.

The Northern Division

The cruisers of the Northern Division were given forty miles of coast to watch a piece; and in the rainy season, when visibility was reduced to a few miles, it was easy for slaves to be moved up and down the coast for shipment, once the cruiser was definitely located.

The job of watching Cape Mount and the Gallinas had been assigned to the *Rapid,* Commander E. Dixon; the *Sealark,* Commander W. B. Monypenny; and the *Bonetta,* Lieutenant-Commander F. E. Forbes.

***Bonetta's* Captures**

Between March and October 1848 the *Bonetta,* which was probably the fastest of the three, captured the following slavers:—

15 March.	*Dos Amigos.*	Brazilian	brig	408 slaves.
31 May.	*Phoco-foo*	"	schooner	equipped.
12 June.	*Tragas Millas.*	"	Brigantine	equipped.
28 June.	*Andarinha.*	"	schooner	"
10 August.	*Alert.*	No flag.	"	"

Besides these it was supposed that she had sunk a slaver during the night.

It happend to be Lieutenant Forbes's first chase after reaching his station. On March the 6th, 1848, a schooner was sighted off Cape Mensurada standing in for the land. During the chase the usual calm between the land and the sea breezes had to be crossed and the slaver, as usual with her kind, did everything to lighten herself in order to get across the calm belt, throwing overboard boats, spare spars, casks, coops, etc.

She got across and so did the *Bonetta* and the chase grew very exciting as the two vessels approached the land, Then, of a sudden, the stunsails of the chase, which gleamed white in the sunlight, melted away, her masts took a heavy list, and it was at once realised the she had hauled to the wind. A few minutes later two sails were noticed in-shore—these turned out to be the *Rapid* and her Yawl.

The slaver heading out to sea, managed to get across the *Bonetta's* bow, and when she had run both cruisers well abaft the beam, she slowly bore away until once more she was right before the wind under stunsails.

18. The Capture of the American Slave barque *Orion* by H.M. Steamer *Pluto*, November 30th, 1849.

From a watercolour by J. Taylor in the National Maritime Museum.

[*Facing page 368.*

19. Freetown, Sierra Leone.

From a coloured Aquatint after the painting by W. J. Huggins, in the National Maritime Museum.

[*Facing page 369.*

By sunset the *Bonetta* had closed until she was almost within range of the chase. But about 8 p.m. down came a tornado and the slaver was lost to sight. An hour and a half later the watch below aboard the *Bonetta* were almost thrown out of their hammocks by a shock as if the brigantine had struck a rock, but at the time the ship was at least fifteen miles off the land. The night was thick and nothing could be seen, but Lieutenant Forbes felt sure that he had run over the chase, for no more was seen or heard of her.

In the chase of the *Dos Amigos,* which began at 3 p.m. and lasted through the night, there was a bright moon and the slaver tested the *Bonetta's* sailing on every point of the compass—however the two vessels were within range at daylight and three rounds brought the Brazilian up into the wind in surrender.

On the 16th of May, the *Bonetta* was becalmed within four miles of a brigantine, named *San Francisco.*

The latter got away and shipped slaves at the Gallinas in August, but was captured on her return to the coast by the *Sealark.*

When the *Bonetta* took possession of the *Phoco-foo,* the latter had been so damaged by her crew, rigging cut to pieces, masts sprung, etc., that it was decided to destroy her. A train of gunpowder laid, a slow match lighted and the schooner headed for the shore without a soul on board. As she hit the beach, she blew up and all night burnt furiously, lighting up the sky for miles around and serving as a warning to slavers.

The *Tragas Millas* was caught in a calm, the *Bonetta's* boat under midshipman. Smallpage, having a fifteen mile pull in the broiling sun.

***Andarinha's* Adventures**

As a proof that the cruisers were not so ineffective as their critics declared, the slaver *Andarinha* in May, 1848, attempted to get into a southern port, but, on the 5th of May, was chased to sea by one of the steam cruisers. On the 3rd of June, she ventured in-shore again and attempted to reach Ambriz, but had to flee before another cruiser. Failing to the Southward she then sailed for the Pongos, a run of fifteen hundred miles. Again she was chased off. Then on the 28th of June, with Cape Mount Bay under her lee, she found herself cut off by the *Bonetta.* In trying to cross the latter's bows, and thus get to sea, when, being the fastest sailer, she would probably once more have got clear, she came within range. A lucky shot between wind and water caused such a leak, that she was forced to surrender. Her adventures clearly show that the Guinea Captain's life had become far from easy.

In September 1848, while in chase of a brig, the *Bonetta* was obliged to heave to in order to pick up a man who had fallen overboard. Luckily the *Sealark* was at hand and during the afternoon both cruisers were able to open fire on the chase, which at 7 p.m. rounded to and surrendered.

This brig proved to be the *Achilles.* Her master had cleared four thousand dollars in the successful voyage of the *San Francisco,* which he had invested in this vessel, thus losing it all again.

It was this money gamble which made the slave trade so attractive to Cuban and Brazilian seamen. Without the risk of capture, the profits would have been reduced to an ordinary trading figure. As the slave captains expressed it:—

"No hae contrabanda, no hae contrabandista!"

During the last few months of his command, Commodore Hotham came north to bring the chiefs of the Gallinas to submission.

But before commencing operations he sent the following letter to Commodore Bolton, commanding the American squadron and a letter in like terms to the French Commodore.

H.M.S. *Penelope,* Gallinas,
4th February, 1849.

Sir,

I do myself the honour to inform you that in consequence of the continued violation of the treaty concluded with the chief's of Gallinas by Captain Denman in 1840 for the suppression of the slave trade, I have declared war with that country and established a blockade with a sufficient and effective force between Solyman Point on the South and Cazel on the North.

I request you will be pleased to give public notice to American citizens trading on the West coast of Africa.

I have, etc.,
Charles Hotham.
Commodore and Commander-in-Chief.

Slave Settlements Destroyed

Hotham was not content with simply blockading, he sent Captain Jones of the *Penelope* into the Gallinas with the boats of the squadron to destroy the slave barracoons; and the *Sealark's* boats were instructed to destroy the slaving towns at Cape Mount and Manna river.

The result of Hotham's operations were the surrender of three thousand slaves to Captain Dunlop of the *Alert* and the promise of the chiefs to relinquish all traffic in slaves.

The Southern Station

On the Southern station the following captures were made by cruisers and condemned between the 1st of January and the 8th of June, 1848:—

By the *Styx,*	Commander H. Chads.	11 slavers.
By the *Devastation,*	Commander R. C. Mitchell.	4 "
By the *Hound,*	Commander G. H. Wood.	2 "
By the *Albatross,*	Commander A. Farquhar	2 "
By the *Contest,*	Commander A. McMurdo	4 "
By the *Cygnet,*	Commander G. Kenyon.	1 "
By the *Heroine,*	Commander C. Edmunds.	2 "
By the *Siren,*	Commander T. Chaloner.	2 "
By the *Firefly,*	Captain John Tudor.	1 "
By the *Grappler,*	Lt. Commander T. H. Lysaght.	1 "

One thousand one hundred and seventy two slaves were liberated and one hundred and sixty three died before adjudication.

In April 1849 Commodore Sir Charles Hotham arrived home with the reputation of having been the most successful of all the Admirals and Commodores that had struggled with the slave trade.

Nevertheless neither he nor his country were at all satisfied with the condition of the trade, though, as a matter of fact, the traffic on the West coast was nearer its collapse than anyone had any idea of. Dissatisfaction with its efforts in any direction, is always a healthy sign with the British nation; and after forty years of chasing and blockading, the Royal Navy was really beginning to gain results on the West Coast.

The Select Committee

Since the spring of 1848 a carefully chosen select committee had been enquiring into the condition of the slave trade and into the methods adopted for suppressing it.

Already the following officers had given evidence:—

Captain Denham (*Wanderer),* Captain Birch (*Waterwitch*), Captain Butterfield (*Fantome*), Captain Allen (*Wilberforce*), Commander Matson (*Waterwitch*), Commander Riley (*Star*), Commander Montresor (*Cygnet* and *Wanderer*).

Admiral Dacres, Commander-in-Chief at the Cape, had been examined on the East coast trade, Mr. Hudson, the British representative, wrote explaining conditions in Brazil, the Commissary judges, Mr. Hook from Sierra Leone and Mr. Kennedy from Havana had sent in reports, Mr. Waddell, a missionary of two and a half years residence on the Old Calabar had given his evidence, and lastly Lord Plamerston and the Right Honourable Stephen Lushington had explained the aims and endeavours of British statesmen.

But no sooner had Sir Charles Hotham arrived in England than the Committee pounced upon him and plied him with close upon five hundred questions.

During his two and a half years in command of the West African Squadron Hotham had captured one hundred and seventy six slavers and freed fifteen thousand four hundred and sixty two slaves, and his success is well seen in the following return presented to the House of Commons.

Captures in the Forties

Date	Slavers Captured	Slavers Condemned.	Slaves Captured.
1840	79	76	3192
1841	78	66	4519
1842	58	53	3177
1843	44	38	3612
1844	52	46	3472
1845	95	84	4443
1846	47	45	2200
1847	81	80	6706
1848	91	90	6712

The legal trade was at least two hundred sail, mostly British. This trade was freed from the fear of Piracy or attack by natives through the presence of the British squadron.

When Hotham was called to give evidence there was a strong political party in England, who were for withdrawing the cruisers and trusting entirely to trade and legislation.

This party, headed by Cobden, had their eyes blinded to everything except the trade of Great Britain. They cared not whether coffee, cocoa, or sugar were slave grown so long as the English working man had a cheap breakfast table. But luckily for the prestige of the Old Country such men were still in the minority.

Evidence of Officers

The evidence of many of the witnesses stressed the value of the R.N. squadron, and a few of the most significant points are worth quoting:—

Mr. Hudson, writing from Rio, stated:—

> "That great preparations were making there for slave trading adventures, but that the enterprises of those slave traders were going to be directed chiefly to the Eastern coast of Africa, because the effectual vigilance of our cruisers on the Western coast rendered enterprises on that part of Africa exceedingly hazardous and attended with much loss".

As against this we have Admiral Dacres (late in command at the Cape) declaring that "for upwards of a year the slave trade has been almost entirely extinguished on the East coast of Africa, and that the Portuguese authorities had co-operated cordially with the British cruisers". He is referring, of course, to the Portuguese and not to the Arab slave trade.

Mr. Hook, after his experience of thirty years in Africa was very strong in condemning any withdrawal of the British squadron.

> "It is my firm belief" he declared, "that in nine or twelve months after the withdrawal of our squadron the whole of Western Africa from Cape Verd to Benguela would present a scene of cruelty and devastation too fearful to contemplate: all the progress of Christianity,

civilization and commerce would be annihilated—in a word, Western Africa would, in the course of a year or two, be rolled back to its worst pristine savage condition: the coast would become the resort of the most degraded renegades and pirates of Brazil and other nations. If your merchants entertain a hope that the trade of palm-oil, gold, ivory, ground nuts, hides, wax etc., will continue to exist after the withdrawal of our squadron, I fear they will be woefully disappointed.

The thousands of palm-oil carriers and agricultural labourers would instantly be kidnapped and carried aboard slave vessels: after a time the remaining natives would avoid the coast, as they would the locality of the plague.

I would venture to remark that hardly any squadron, however, vigilant—and none could be more so than the present—could alone effect the total abolition of the slave trade on the coast unless it be supported by a zealous, honest cooperation of the Brazilian and Spanish Governments."

Other witnesses, who were not naval officers, paid a like tribute to the efforts of the British cruisers, Mr. Kennedy expatiated upon "the depressed state of the slave market at Havana, consequent on the very high prices slaves have been raised to by the untiring exertions and successful efforts of our cruisers".

His other points were equally encouraging:—

(1) The price of a slave necessary to cover the risk of capture and a profit to the dealer was so high that the cultivator in Cuba could not afford to pay it.

(2) For the past ten years insurance houses had refused to take out policies on slaves in consequence of their heavy losses by them.

(3) The high price is and must be a check to the trade and the high price is owing to the blockade of the coast.

Commander Riley of the *Star,* during the nine months in the Bight of Benin declared that the squadron on that station took seventeen slavers, ten empty, seven with slaves, of which he took two only, but he gave it as his opinion that only five vessels escaped from the Bight whilst he was stationed there.

He went on to state his considered opinion that "five steamers would have suppressed the slave trade entirely along the Bight of Benin".

Commander Montresor also supported the employment of steamers; estimating the length of coast to be blockaded to be from 15° N to 15° S., he suggested substituting eighteen screw steamers for sailing ships, each to cover one hundred and twenty miles of coast, with small paddle steamers at intervals of forty miles.

Mr. Waddell, the old Calabar missionary, considered that the cruisers had succeeded in extinguishing the Bight of Biafra trade, but that if they were withdrawn, the slave trade would be in full swing again in the Calabar river in less than twelve months.

But the most important evidence under the consideration of the Select Committee was that of the late Commodore on the West coast.

Hotham, whose exertions had gained the high approval of the Admiralty, and whose reputation in the Service was as great as that of any other serving officer, both for his acknowledged abilities and high professional character as well as for his active and enlightened mind, was examined for three whole days.

He reckoned his captures to be about a third of the slavers engaged in the trade: in his opinion the blockade of the whole line of coast, extending two thousand one hundred and ninety five miles, was not practicable at all seasons of the year, and at all periods of the twenty-four hours, because, given twenty-four cruisers, ninety-one miles would have to be watched by each cruiser.

He produced a chart of the coast which aroused a great deal of interest and discussion, for upon it he had marked a blue line, extending from Quitta at Cape St. Paulo to Loango Bay, just North of Kabenda; and a red line from Kabenda to Logito, just North of Lobito and Benguela.

These lines showed the inland waterways by means of which slaves could be quickly transported from place to place in order to dodge the cruisers.

Though Hotham was obliged to admit that the British squadron could never hope to destroy the slave trade without the help of other factors, such as the honest cooperation of other nations in controlling their own nationals and the encouragement of legitimate trade in Africa, he ended his testimony with great emphasis in the following words:—

> "I anxiously hope that the slave trade may never be allowed: if you were to remove all restrictions and take your squadron entirely away, small speculators would spring up and under sell those who are now in the market: the slave trade would be greatly increased in its horrors and it would be impossible to calculate the calamities which would ensue: besides this, pirates would abound and in my opinion it would be impossible for a legitimate trader to conduct his operations upon the coast".

At the end of Sir Charles Hotham's evidence, Lord John Hay, one of the members of the Select Committee, rose and informed his fellow members that the Admiralty had testified their high approval of Sir Charles' conduct whilst in command of the African squadron and gave it as his opinion that it had been possible to have stopped the trade, Hotham would have done so.

The Committee's Finding

In their final report the Select Committee considered:—"that a long and large experience of attempts to suppress the slave trade by a naval force leads to the conclusion that to put down that trade by such means is impracticable".

Upon this finding after a most exhaustive enquiry many people believed that the British Government would cut expense on their anti-slavery ships and perhaps remove the squadron from the West coast of Africa altogether. But it is not in the nature of the Britsh nation to give up a fight in such a fashion, and the strength of the anti-slavery squadrons were maintained in spite of the opposition of the free-traders, headed by Gladstone, Cobden and Bright.

Lord Palmerston, who had long been the main driving force in England against the slave trade, was perhaps the first to realise that the tide was at last turning against the inhuman traffic. He it was who backed the Admiralty in their plan of building small swift screw steamers for the coast of Africa.

In June 1850 the British Admiral at Rio received orders from Lord Palmerston that slavers were to be seized not only upon the High Seas but in Brazilian waters. He was encouraged to take this very decided step by the rise of a young anti-slavery party in Brazil, which was strong enough in July 1850 to get a law passed through the Brazilian chamber of Deputies declaring the slave trade to be piracy.

CHAPTER XIX

THE COAST OF BRAZIL

I have wrenched it free from the halliard to hang for a wisp on the Horn,
I have chased it north to the Lizard—ribboned and rolled and torn.
I have spread its fold o'er the dying, adrift in a hopeless sea:
I have hurled it swift on the slaver, and seen the slave set free.
(The English Flag)

Brazilian Government Unable to Enforce Anti-Slavery Laws.

IT was not until 1839 that any real progress was made in combating the slave trade on the Brazilian coast.

Before that date captures were rare.

When in 1825 the treaty that gave Brazil her independence and made Don Pedro, Emperor of all the Brazils, was concluded in London, the British Government seized the moment as opportune for making a treaty, which outlawed the slave trade, put all Portuguese or Brazilian slavers on a par with pirates and established mixed commission courts of Adjudication.

But a Govermnent that makes laws contrary to the will of its people is never able to enforce such laws, and that, in the main, was the history of the Brazilian slave trade.

Though in 1831 an act decreed that save traders should be punished and their vessels forfeited, little came of it. Again in 1834, the Brazilian Government declared all slavers entering Brazilian ports liable to capture, and it was even believed that the next step would be the Manumission of all the slaves in Brazil. But the wealth of the country was all in the hands of the big slave owners and slave dealers, and the sole result of the Government's action was a few captures of slaves by British cruisers on the South American station. For instance in 1833 the Symondite brig, *Snake*, Captain W. Robertson, captured the *Maria da Gloria* with four hundred and twenty five slaves, and on June the 16th, 1834, the eighteen-gun sloop *Satellite*, Captain R. Smart, captured the *Duqueza di Braganza* with five hundred and seventy seven slaves near St. Sebastians.

No doubt the captures would have been more numerous had not the South American squadron had such a tremendous mileage to cover.

Sir Michael Seymour, the Commander-in-Chief of the South American station and his successor Sir G. E. Hammond, only had a dozen cruisers on a station, which extended from Pernambuco round to Callao; and it was only possible to spare a couple of the fastest sloops to cruise against the slavers. Occasionally a slaver was picked up by chance, such as was the case of the piratical slaver, *Clemente*, which the *Pylades* captured on her way home from Bahia.

The *Clemente* was a Spanish schooner, armed with a long gun and five hundred barrels of gun powder, with a large crew and all fittings and boilers for slaves.

She had left the Havana with the Mexican post-office packet, and the latter so distrusted her piratical appearance that she returned to port.

Lord Palmerston's Bill of 1839

It was not until Lord Palmerston brought out his Slave Trade Suppression Bill in 1839 with its equipment clauses; and Portugal's surrender of her rights to the slave trade South of the Equator that the Brazil coast became as vulnerable as the coast of Africa to the Brazilian slaver.

And it was about time that energetic steps were taken, for the trade was rampant.

Where Slavers Fitted Out

Slavers fitted out in ever increasing numbers at Pernambuco, Bahia, Campos, Rio, Santos, Paranagua, St. Catherine's and in many little-known Bays and Creeks. For instance in one month in 1839 thirty-six slavers fitted out at Rio, into which port one thousand and forty two slaves were brought in January 1839, and one thousand six hundred and thirty seven in ten ships in February 1839.

Horrible Treatment

Brazilain slave owners contended that their slaves had much better treatment than those on the Cuban sugar estates. Yet suicides of slaves by drowning themselves in the sea were so common that it was no unusual thing to see the bodies of negroes floating off the most fashionable bathing beaches of Rio; whilst a police officer, known as 'the captain of the Woods' was specially employed to search the jungle for escaped slaves. The iron collar, too, upon a negro, signifying that he had escaped and been recaptured, was a very common sight on every coffee plantation.

The Slave Market

But what made British Naval officers return to their ships, burning with zeal against the cruel traffic, was a sight of the Vallongo or slave market on the Northern outskirts of the city of Rio de Janeiro. This consisted of a long alley of filthy sheds and benches, upon which were ranged for sale the piteous lots of negro men, women and children from the different slave ships.

With their limbs branded and covered with bruises and putrifying sores, the result of heavy fetters, with their ribs almost breaking through the skin from long starvation, with tragic, mournful, half-scared eyes, these human cattle, all naked but for a single ragged clout, would at stated intervals break out into a low plaintive chant. This told of their hopeless and forlorn condition in a way which went straight to the hearts of the British sailors, though it had not the slightest effect upon the callous dealers. These ruffians would crack their well-blooded raw-hide whips in order to set a whole new row of half-dead Africans hopping from leg to leg in an effort to show their activity and so escape the whistling thong.

As a hint that the British Government were in real earnest the forty-two gun, *Crescent* was fitted out as a slave depot for captured negroes and sent out to Rio with a surgeon and assistant surgeon in the winter of 1839-1840.

Success of Cruisers

Then cruisers began to capture the equipped slavers as soon as they left the Brazilian ports for the African coast. Commodore T. B. Sullivan, C.B. commanding the *Stag*, forty-six guns, took the slave brig, *Pompeio*; Captain W. Smyth of the brig-sloop, *Grecian*, rounded up the notorious brig *Recuperador*, and detained the *Castro*, which had boilers, etc., on board for the well-known slave barque, *Constante*; whilst Captain Christie of the *Rose* detained the *Nova Aurora* and captured the *Convencao* after a long chase.

In spite of the fact that the British Commissioner voted for the condemnation of all these ships, the Brazilians released every one of them on different quibbles and returned them to their owners, who in every case were notorious slave traders such as Manoel Pinto de Fonseca, Jose Bernardino de Sa, Pedro Blanco, Manoel Martius Machado, Amancio Nunes, etc.

But in vain did the Brazilian Commissioner fight for his slave trading countrymen; during the years 1839 and 1840 many of the slave traders were brought to the verge of bankruptcy, the price of newly landed African slaves rose from forty to sixty and seventy milreis, and the import of negroes fell from thirty thousand in 1840 to fourteen thousand in 1842.

This favourable result must in great part be credited to Commander Butterfield's famous little squadron, operating upon the S.W. coast of Africa, but the South American station also had its successful cruisers.

H.M. Brigantine *Fawn*

Perhaps the chief of these was a beautiful little brigantine, the *Fawn*, which had been purchased at Rio in 1839. She had been the slaver *Caroline*, and it is probable that she was Baltimore-built. She had a burthen of one hundred and sixty-nine tons and her dimensions were:-

Length 74 feet 10 inches, breadth extreme 23, depth of hold 8 feet.

She mounted six guns and with a crew of forty men was sent to cruise on her old trade, in charge of Lieutenant-Commander John Foote.

The *Fawn* was not long in making a name for herself. On March the 20th, 1840, she captured the *Roza*; on June the 23rd 1840 the *Venus*; on August the 3rd, 1840 the *Sandade*, and on December the 31st, 1840, when cruising in company with the ten-gun brig, *Partridge*, Lieutenant W. Morris, about twenty-five miles to the eastward of the island of St. Sabastian, she fell in with the Portuguese slave brig *Acceicera*. There was hardly any wind and at 6 p.m. both cruisers sent their boats after the slaver had captured her. She proved to be from Quillimane to Ilha Grande with three hundred and thirty-two slaves on board, having lost twenty-four on the passage. This was, of course, far below the usual percentage, but the slaves were at their last gasp for want of water.

The *Fawn*'s next capture was the Brazilian slave brig, *Denas Fevereira* on the 19th of February 1841. This was a large brig and as she ran in for the land, about eighteen miles off Cacupos on the Brazilian coast, she paid not the least attention to the little *Fawn*. The slaver evidently failed to recognise the brigantine as being an English man-of-war, and when Lieutenant-Commander Foote dropped a couple of rounds from his thiry-two-pounder Long Tom under her forefoot, great confusion was observed aboard her, as she bore up and made a run for it. The *Fawn*'s Long Tom was aimed first ahead and then astern of her, in order to avoid hurting the slaves: but when Foote perceived that the brig began to draw away from him he sent two rounds close under her stern and a third, aimed for her deck, was about to be fired when she rounded to and gave in.

I will now quote from the *Fawn*'s log in order to show the terrible state in which the greater number of Brazilian slavers arrived on the coast.

Her is the extract from the cruiser's log book:-

> "In about twenty minutes we came up and boarded her. The slaves were all below, with the hatches on. On turning them up a scene presented itself enough to sicken the heart even of a Portuguese—the living, the dying and the dead huddled together in one mass. Some unfortunates in the most disgusting state of smallpox in the confluent state, covered from head to foot, some distressingly ill with opthalmia, a few perfectly blind: others, living skeletons, with difficulty crawled from below, unable to bear the weight of their miserable bodies: mothers with young infants hanging at their breasts, unable to give them a drop of nourishment—how they had brought them thus far appeared astonishing. All were perfectly naked, and their limbs much excoriated from lying on the hard plank for so long a period.

> On going below, the stench was insupportable. How beings could breathe such an atmosphere and live, appeared incredible. Several were under the loose planks, which were called the deck, dying, and one dead".

The brig was only thirteen days out from Bahai Fort near Benguela, yet in that time she had lost one hundred and thirty out of five hundred and ten negroes from scurvy and smallpox. Thirteen more died on the passage to Rio; twelve died aboard the brig in Rio Harbour, and a number more aboard the receiving ship, *Crescent*.

After the brig's hold had been well fumigated, the British minister determined to send the prize to the nearest Court of Vice-Admiralty for adjudication which was at Georgetown.

The brig, sailed in charge of G. Johnstone, mate of the *Fawn*, on March the 19th with one hundred and eighty of the negroes.

Every necessary medicine had been placed on board along with fresh provisions, including tapioca and lime juice. The passage took fifty-three days, during which twenty more of the slaves died, from general debility. Four more died after being landed, and twenty-nine were sent straight to hospital.

Two hundred slaves had been left behind aboard the *Crescent*, which were later also transported to British Guiana.

The *Fawn* did not last long as a slave catcher. In June, 1842, she left St. Helena for the coast of Africa. A few months later we find Lieutenant-Commander Foote on his way to to Natal from the Cape. In 1842 the little brigantine was back at the Cape in charge of Lieutenant-Commander J. Nourse.

Here, like the ten-gun brig, *Badger*, she ended her days at the inglorious occupation of a tank-vessel. Foote was promoted and in the Crimean War was in command of the screw sloop, *Conflict*, in the Baltic. In May, 1853, he was drowned in the surf on the bar at Memel.

Curiously enough, he was succeeded in the command of the *Conflict* by Captain Arthur Cumming, who had also distinguished himself slave catching on the Brazilian coast in the forties.

H.M. Brig-Sloop *Frolic*

Cumming was a lieutenant aboard the brig-sloop *Frolic*, which between 1843 and 1845 was most successful in hunting down slavers on the coast of Brazil.

The *Frolic* was not a Symondite, being designed by Captain William Hendry, R.N. a former senior student at the Naval College.

She was a large brig with the same armament of sixteen guns as the larger Symondite brig-sloops, her burthern in tons being five hundred and ten and forty-two ninety-fourths (old measurement) and three hundred and thirty-four (new measurement).

Her chief dimensions were:-

	feet	inches
Length between perpendiculars	107	4
Length of Keel	84	$3^1/_8$
Length of water line	105	
Breadth Extreme	34	
Depth of Hold	15	6

It will thus be noticed that she was just a bit bigger all round than the *Grecian* class of Symondites. After a trial against the ten-gun brig *Nautilus*, she had her sail plan altered, her masts being replaced and shifted further aft; and she was given spars and sails of the same size as the *Grecian* class. She then proved herself to be very fast in light winds, being superior both on and off the wind in light weather to the Symondites, though in strong winds they had the best of her, as was proved by a trial with the *Pilot* in September 1848, at the beginning of her second commission. It will thus be seen that she was an exceedingly fine specimen of the brig-sloop.

Her first commander was William Alexander Willis, who was a first-rate officer, having been first lieutenant of the *Vernon* in 1831-1832, when she was Sir George Cockburn's flagship in the West Indies.

From June 1833 to September 1834 Willis commanded the schooner, *Skipjack*, on that station; and afterwards was Cockburn's flag-lieutenant in the *President*. He was promoted in October, 1835, and previous to having the *Frolic*, had commanded the *Jaseur*, sixteen guns, in the Mediterranean. *Frolic*'s complement consisted of one hundred and six officers and seamen, twenty marines and twenty-four boys.

Her great success on the Brazilian coast was illustrated by the very spirited drawing by Vernon, which shows Willis hanging onto his stunsails to the very last moment and only luffing up when the chase was in the breakers and the *Frolic* herself on their very edge.

Arthur Cumming Captures *Vincedora*

One of the brig's most notable captures was that of the *Vincedora*. After the usual chase the slaver was becalmed just out of gun shot.

Thereupon Willis sent Lieutenant Arthur Cumming after her in the cutter.

Just as Cumming was springing aboard over the slaver's counter, a draught of air filled her sails and she drew ahead. One of her crew slashed off the head of the boat-hook, by which the bowman was holding on, the latter fell back, and, before anything could be done, the cutter dropped astern, leaving Cumming alone on the deck of the *Vincedora*.

His first action was to shoot down the captain of the slaver. Next, with desperate sword-play he fought his way to the tiller, cut down the helmsman, and shoving the helm hard down, threw the *Vincedora* all aback so that her way was stopped. Then with his back against the tiller, thus keeping it hard over, he managed to defend himself until the boat was able to pull up alongside once more, when the *Vincedora* was soon overcome by the eager bluejackets.

Though she only measured fifty-five tons, the prize proved to have three hundred and thirty-eight slaves on board, whose condition was truly terrible. When the *Vincedora* arrived at Rio, Sir Thomas Pasley, captain of the *Curacoa*, went aboard her, and the following extract from one of his letters gives one a vivid idea of a typical Brazilain slaver's state at the end of her run from the African coast:—

> "I went this morning (September 10th, 1843) the first thing after breakfast, to see the negroes taken from the slaver and down to the *Crescent* (hulk), and in my life I have never witnessed anything so shocking. About four hundred and fifty were packed into that small vessel, as you would pack bales of goods; and disease of all sorts became rife among them. Some were carried up the side in a state of emaciation, such as I would not have imagined possible to exist with life; others with raw sores, their bones all but through them, and some dreadful cases of smallpox, covered from head to foot. These were all sent back to the schooner, being contagious, none such being allowed in the *Crescent*.
>
> Some children were in the last stage of emaciation and sores. It was dreadful; and so distressing, I could have cried. The patience, or rather the apathy, with which it was all borne was astonishing.
>
> Happily for them, they have not the same feelings we have. They were fed immediately they came on board, and soon recovered their spirits. Those who were not ill were ready to sing and dance the next day. Some of the women had infants; but of the other children, whose ages were from five to nine there were no parents, or none to be discovered among the adults. After all these miserable creatures were brought on board, several women came, tolerably well dressed, and fat and sleek—to my great astonishment, till I was told that these were the harem of the prize's crew, and were fed well and taken care of.
>
> Ill looking rascals these crew were, twenty-seven of them, mostly Portuguese. They were all confined in the *Crescent*'s prison by night, and left at large in the day-time for the present.

> The officers and men of the *Frolic* were not a little to be pitied, who had to live on board such a disgusting vessel, first with the Africans, and afterwards when they were removed; for the shocking state of filth, and the stench was not to be endured, and yet, tracing the smallpox among them, I would not let them communicate with the ship".

Sir Thomas Pasley was wise to take precautions. Arthur Cumming himself fell a victim to the smallpox a few days after rejoining the *Frolic* and had to be invalided home. This officer became one of the most distinguished in the Service, dying in 1893 when Admiral Sir Arthur Cumming, K.C.B.

Capture of a Battery at Sidon

He gained his first commission by a fine piece of spectacular heroism in the 1840 Syrian Campaign. The yarn is well told in Admiral Sir J. C. Dalrymple Hay's "Lines from my Logbooks":—

"The castle, which stands on an island, is united to Sidon by a long, low bridge without parapets, which crosses the sea to the shore.

The fire of the *Thunderer*, the Turkish flagship, on which Sir Baldwin Walker's flag flew, had driven the Egyptians out of the Castle. It and the island were occupied by Turkish troops.

A battery of six guns enfiladed the bridge on the side of Sidon, and the troops hesitated to cross.

Thereupon was seen a very well-dressed midshipman stepping coolly out into the middle of the bridge. The six guns were fired, and the midshipman was seen taking out his white handkerchief and dusting his boots, sticking his glass in his eye, drawing his sword, and waving to the troops to come on. The action was electric and the troops charged. The battery was carried, and Arthur Cumming was deservedly promoted as soon as he had passed his final examination".

Cumming cultivated a cool daring and never lost an opportunity of displaying it. He had the Humane Societies medal for saving several lives by jumping overboard after drowning men. But, not long after the Sidon affair, he rather over did his eagerness in this direction. His ship, the *Benbow*, was running into Suda Bay. It was a Sunday forenoon and everyone was spruced up for divisions, when the straw hat of an unfortunate bluejacket blew overboard.

Cumming was sitting in the ward room at the stern port. On seeing the hat drifting by, imagining that its owner was underneath it, and without waiting a second, overboard he went through the port without even doffing his best uniform coat. And when, after being picked up, he came aboard like a drowned rat, he had to submit to a deal of chaff from his messmates.

Captain Willis Attacked

So great was the success of the *Frolic* that the Brazilian slave-traders determined to try and make an end of her enterprising captain.

The story is well told in one of Astley Cooper Key's letters, quoted by Admiral Colomb in his Memoirs of Sir Astley Cooper Key.

The *Curacoa*, Key's ship, had just been convoying a merchant barque, chartered to take three hundred liberated slaves to Demerara; and on her arrival back at Rio on January the 12th, 1844 Key wrote:-

> "On our arrival we heard that Captain Willis of *Frolic*, and one of his officers, had been attacked on shore at Santos Bay (a celebrated slave port about two hundred miles South-west of Rio) and were lying in a dangerous state on board.
>
> The surgeon of the *Frolic* would not allow them to proceed to sea, and, as they were short of provisions, we sailed for Santos to supply her.

On our arrival there we found that what we had heard was too true. The facts are these.

The *Frolic* had been stationed off Santos for some time to aid in the suppression of the slave trade, and had annoyed the Brazilians very much by the captures she had made, and also by having blockaded for three weeks two slave brigs in the port of Santos.

One afternoon Captain Willis, his master (May) and the captain's steward, landed to walk to the town; the nearest way to which was by a narrow lane about three miles in length. It being broad daylight, they probably went on shore without their swords; and although May had a brace of pistols in his pocket, he did not load them.

On their return, a little after sunset, the Commander and May were walking together, and the steward a little behind them, when they heard the steward call out. They ran towards him and just had time to see that there were seven Brazilians, armed with bludgeons, when they were knocked down, and remembered nothing further.

These ruffians had beaten them most unmercifully, thrown them into a ditch, and left them for dead. A Brazilian gentleman passed by about an hour after, picked them up, and with the assistance of some others sent them on board. Captain Willis had his skull fractured, his head severely cut in two places, his arm and two fingers badly broken. May escaped much better, having sustained no serious injury beyond a broken head and being most awfully bruised all over. The steward had his thigh broken and some other minor injuries.

We immediately sent on shore to the police to make them find out the offenders, and they have seven men in custody, but only one of them can be sworn to: they are the crew of one of the brigs in Santos".

Poor Willis was never fit for service again. He had to invalid, was granted a pension for his wounds in 1848, and, after being Captain of Greenwich Hospital for seven years, died in 1863.

He was succeeded in the command of the *Frolic* by Cospatrick Baillie Hamilton on April the 8th, 1844, and not long after the *Frolic*'s career as a slave hunter ceased for she was sent round the Horn to the Pacific. Her second commission was in the Mediterranean pirate hunting under that noted officer, N. Vansittart.

Then, in 1854-1856 we shall find her once more hunting slavers, but this time on the East coast of Africa.

Success of the *Spy*

Between 1843 and 1845 the slavers on the coast of Brazil were being harried by several fast cruisers. These were the brigs *Grecian* and *Philomel*, the brigantine *Dolphin* and the *Arrow* ketch.

Of these the *Dolphin*, commanded by Lieutenant W. O'Bryen Hoare was perhaps the most successful. On January the 2nd, 1844, off the Isle of Porcus, one hundred and sixty miles South of Rio de Janeiro, she captured three slavers. She was almost as successful on the Brazilian coast as her new sister-ship the *Spy* was on the African. The *Spy* certainly took toll of the Brazilian slavers during 1843.

On January the 24th, she captured the *Bom Fim* and *Clio*, on May the 29th the *Esperanza*, and on August the 9th the finest Brazilian slave brig in the trade. This was the *Furia* of upwards of two hundred tons with five hundred and thirty-nine slaves on board, which was taken by the *Spy* in 5° 3′ N. 2° 56′ E. after a chase of twelve hours. The brigantine's next captures were the *Egria* on September the 5th and *Linda* on November the 20th.

The Parana Campaign Helps Slavers.

Slave catching on the Brazil coast was severely interfered with in 1845 owing to the operations up the Parama river.

Both *Dolphin* and *Philomel* played a very gallant part when the British and French force under Charles Hotham opened the Parana to trade by that most dashing little battle of Obligado.

Whilst the cruisers were withdrawn the slave traders once more regained their courage; in fact they gave many instances in the next year or two of their boldness and enterprise.

Wasey Tricked by Brigands

At the beginning of 1846 Brazilian brigands played a very clever trick upon a prize of the *Alert*'s. The little Symondite paddle-wheeler, commanded by Charles John Bosanquet, had sent a prize, captured off Kebanda to Sierra Leone for adjudication.

Almost overwhelmed by a succession of fierce winds, the mate in charge of the prize, Edward Frodsham Noel K. Wasey, found himself blown across the Atlantic, and after a hair-raising time at length succeeded in anchoring his water-logged craft—she had seven feet of water in her hold—at Maranhao.

Whilst he was ashore trying to hire a vessel, as the prize seemed likely to sink under his feet, a band of brigands, disguised as Brazilian soldiers went aboard the prize and offered refuge to both the crew and the seventy to eighty negroes, who formed the slaver's cargo.

Having no orders, the prize crew refused to leave their ship, but seeing that by this time the slaver's deck was level with the water so that the smallest wave slopped aboard, they allowed the sham soldiery to take the slaves ashore, in order to save them from drowning which otherwise seemed likely to be their fate. Needless to say these unhappy negroes were never seen again by Wasey and his prize crew. However the Admiralty recognised the former's skill and seamanship in saving his unseaworthy craft by at once promoting him to Lieutenant.

Lieutenant D'Aguilar Beats Off Brigands

This was not the only instance of its kind on the coast of Brazil.

In 1848 the *Grecian*, Commander Louis Symonds Tindal, sent a prize into Bahia under Lieutenant Francis James d'Aguilar.

A most determined attempt was made to recapture this slaver by another lot of so-called brigands from the shore.

But though his crew of ten men were only armed with muskets, the prize having no guns, d'Aguilar managed to hold off the Brazilians after a most desperate affray in which he and most of his men were wounded and, it was reported, no less than ten of the attackers killed and thirty wounded.

It was not until the summer of 1850 when Rear-Admiral Reynolds, C.B., received Lord Palmerston's orders not only to seize Brazilian slavers on the high seas and in territorial waters but even up the South American rivers, whether full or empty, that the knell of the Brazil traffic in African slaves was sounded.

The British Squadron

At this date the British Squadron on the station consisted of:—

Southampton, fifty, Captain N. Cory. Flagship of Rear-Admiral Reynolds, C.B.

Tweed, eighteen, Commander Lord F. Russell.

Cormorant, six, steam sloop, Commander H. Schomberg. (This was a paddle-wheeler of the *Gorgon* type, built at Sheerness, 1842, of one thousand and fifty-seven tons and three hundred H.P.).

Sharpshooter, eight, iron screw sloop. Lieutenant-Commander John Crawshaw Bailey. (Built at Blackwall 1847 from Fincham's designs, of five hundred and three tons and two hundred and two H.P.).

Rifleman, eight screw steamer (four hundred and eighty-six tons, one hundred H.P., built Portsmouth 1846, designer Fincham). Lieutenant-Commander S. S. L. Crofton.

Griffon, three, brigantine, Lieutenant-Commander Thorburn.

Kestrel, brigantine, two hundred and two tons, keel sixty-two feet six inches, beam twenty-three feet seven inches, depth eleven feet three inches. Lieutenant-Commander H. Baker.

The Brigantine *Kestrel*

This was not a large force especially as *Griffon* and *Kestrel* were kept busy running up and down the coast with the mails, but it has to be remembered that the squadron on the West coast of Africa was very strong.

The brigantine *Kestrel* was an interesting craft, having lately been a flagship of the Royal Yacht Squadron, belonging to the late Lord Yarborough. She was a beautiful little vessel built in 1837 and no doubt served her purpose well; but with steam rapidly ousting sail where speed was required, she only served this one commission.

***Sharpshooter*'s Prizes**

The first cruiser to ignore the Brazilian coast forts was the *Sharpshooter*, which on June the 23rd, 1849, cut out the slaver *Polka* from under the guns of *Macahe*, the fort fired on her but without effect. When Commander Bailey paid off the *Sharpshooter* at Portsmouth in December 1851, he had made the following captures:-

A brigantine with slave equipment off Rio.

A brigantine with slave equipment off Cape Frio.

The two-top-sail schooner *Polka* at Macahe.

A topsail schooner with slave equipment off Campos.

This vessel which was heavily armed, had managed to get away from the *Sharpshooter* four days previously and landed a cargo of slaves in the meanwhile.

A cutter with seventy-four slaves off Manquinas (twenty-six had died on the passage across).

The schooner *Valaroso* with slave equipment off Rio.

A brig off Busios with one hundred and two slaves.

A schooner cut out of the Tigucas River by *Sharpshooter*'s four boats and thirty-six men aided by one boat and six men of the paddle-wheeler *Locust*. (two hundred and eighty-four tons, one hundred and eighty H.P., built Woolwich 1840, designer Symonds).

A brig fully equipped off St. Paulo, Bahia.

A Gallant Rescue from the Surf

The little *Rifleman* distinguished herself by a most gallant piece of life saving in 1849.

No war had been fuller of deeds of brave self-sacrifice than the Royal Navy's century-long war against the slave trader.

Again and again British seamen risked and even sacrificed their lives for the sake of the negro, who was regarded by all other nations solely from a market point of view.

One of the bravest of all these rescues of the unfortunate black was that carried out by the officers and crew of the *Rifleman*.

When cruising under sail to the North of Cape Frio on the afternoon of June the 28th, 1849, the *Rifleman* sighted and gave chase to a slaver that was trying to work along the shore.

Darkness did not put an end to the chase, for directly the moon rose, the slaver could be clearly seen. As soon as she saw that the cruiser was still on her trail, the chase bore away before the wind with all stunsails set and headed right into the breakers.

In a very few minutes, without attempting to shorten sail or even haul down her kites, she took the beach, showing up as a black gap in the long white line of surf.

The *Rifleman* steamed in as close as she dared and then sent her boats alongside.

The wreck was found to be deserted by her crew, but they had made no attempt to get their cargo of negroes ashore and these in a state of terror crowded the deck of the slaver.

After furling the sails, the boats returned to the *Rifleman*, two midshipmen, Pocock and Beckett, being left aboard in charge of the slaves.

But as the night advanced, both wind and sea increased, until the surf began to make a clean break over the vessel and wash the slaves overboard.

On recognising what was happening, Commander Crofton sent his second master, Hitchings with a fresh boat's crew to take charge of the wreck. Then as soon as it was light enough he worked his ship inshore until she was near enough to get a hawser aboard the wreck.

The only chance of saving the slaves and even his boats' crews in the terrific surf that was running by this time, was to haul them through the surf by means of a cradle travelling along the hawser by the ordinary life saving method used on the English coast.

The slaver lay with her stern to the breakers. The hawser was apparently made fast so that the cradle came in over the counter.

In the pause between the advent of each roller, a slave had to be lashed in the cradle; then the signal was given and the unfortunate negro was hauled through the surf to the *Rifleman*'s boats, which lay outside the outermost breakers. Hitchings himself took the post of danger. He lashed himself to the stern bitts and received the slaves as they were passed along the deck by the two midshipmen and the bluejackets. Every roller, as it came thundering in, washed clean over the second-master, yet he stuck to his difficult and dangerous job throughout the entire day and by the time the last negro had been hauled out to the boats, both he and his men were pretty near deadbeat. Again and again Hitchings, Pocock, Beckett and the boats' crews risked their lives for the drowning blacks.

Crofton himself had his gig stove and was with difficulty hauled out the surf by one of his men. Nor did a single member of the *Rifleman*'s crew eat, drink or change their drenched clothing until they had done what they could for the wretched negroes.

Many of these in their weakened state had to be masssaged and rubbed back to life after their passage through the surf.

Each slave was taken charge of by a member of the *Rifleman*'s crew, who with perfect unselfishness clothed them in their own clothes and nursed them as if they were their own children.

In this way one hundred and twenty-seven men, women and children were saved from the wrecked slaver.

The *Cormorant* up the Paranagua

In the summer of 1850 full advantage of Lord Palmerston's orders was taken by Captain Schomberg of the *Cormorant*.

First of all he adventured up the Rio Frio and ferreted out the notorious slaver, *Rival*.

Lieutenant Charles Maxwell Luckraft in command of the cruiser's boats, successfully captured and burnt the *Rival* to the fury of the local slave traders, who opened a hot musketry fire upon the *Cormorant* from the banks of the river, as she ran out to sea again.

On June the 29th, Captain Schomberg put into the Bay of Paranagua and after saluting the fourteen-gun fort at the entrance of the river, Paranagua, steamed fifteen miles up to an island, which was reported to be the headquarters of a nest of slavers.

On his approach two bona fide merchantmen were noticed shifting their anchorage, leaving four evident slavers lying off the island.

The *Cormorant* anchored with a spring on her cable so as to be able to open fire, if necessary, in any direction. Her boats, two cutters and gig, under Lieutenant Luckraft were then sent to take possession of the slavers. One vessel, a brigantine, was scuttled and sunk by her people to avoid being taken, but the other three were brought off and anchored under the guns of the sloop. These were the ship *Campadora*, ex American *Lucy Ann*, and the brigs *Donna Anna* and *Serea*, both notorious slavers.

On July the 1st, the *Cormorant* with her prizes in tow, set off down the river. On passing the fort, she came under a heavy fire from the battery to which she quickly replied.

The range was almost point-blank, the passage being very narrow. In the exchange of shot the *Cormorant* had one man killed and two wounded besides receiving five balls in her hull whilst the fort was almost demolished.

When she arrived at the bar, there was not enough water to cross so Schomberg was obliged to anchor inside, and before proceeding he burnt the two brigs.

When the *Cormorant* arrived at Rio, the opulent slave traders started a riot, British sailor's boarding houses were attacked by the mob and several Englishmen roughly handled.

Nevertheless the Brazilian as well as the British Government approved Schomberg's action. The insurance of slave ships thereupon became prohibitive, rising to over twenty-five per cent, at the same time the price of slaves ran so high that it became cheaper to employ free labour on the coffee plantations.

At long last the steady perseverance of the British Navy was having its reward.

The Squadron in 1852

The following little table tells a tale.

Imports of slaves into Brazil.	
1850	23,000 negroes
1851	3,000 negroes
1852	700 negroes

In 1852 the following cruisers patrolled the coast:-

Rifleman, Lieutenant-Commander R. H. Dalton, off Victoria.

Bonetta, Lieutenant-Commander Wake, off Rio.

Plumber, twelve-gun screw sloop, Commander Nolloth, off the Rio Grande.

Express, six, Commander Fead, off Bahai.

Locust, paddle-wheel, two hundred and eighty-four tons, (built at Woolwich, 1840, from Symond's design) Lieutenant-Commander G. F. Day, off Bahia.

Centaur, six, steam-frigate, one thousand two hundred and sixty-nine tons, five hundred and forty H.P. (Built at Portsmouth 1845 from Symonds' design). Captain E. St. L. Cannon, flagship of Rear-Admiral W. W. Henderson, at Rio.

Sharpshooter, Lieutenant-Commander John E. Parish, cruising.

Trident, six, iron screw, eight hundred and fifty tons, three hundred and fifty H.P. (Built Blackwall 1846 by Ditchburn and Mare). Lieutenant-Commander Robert B. Harvey, cruising.

Vixen, six, paddle-wheel sloop, one thousand and fifty-four tons, H.P. two hundred and eighty. (Built at Pembroke 1840, Symonds' design) Commander Fred L. Bernard, cruising.

This squadron was more than ample and the Royal Navy's long fight against the Brazilian slave traffic seemed to be practically over.

The Last Trick

Then in 1855 an epidemic of cholera and yellow fever amongst the slaves on the coffee plantations led to a number of clippers being fitted out in the United States for the purpose of trying to run slaves into Brazil.

Only one or two of these got through the cruisers' blockade. Excitement in Brazil was at fever heat when a small schooner with two hundred and fifty negroes was ordered to be arrested by the local police near Pernambuco. The police absented themselves, but an ex-magistrate with the English name of Drummond managed to get one hundred and sixty of

20. The Honourable Sir Henry Keppel as a Rear-Admiral.

From an Engraving by Henry Robinson after the painting by Henry Weigall in the National Maritime Museum. [*Facing page 384.*

21. H.M.S. *London*, Guardship at Zanzibar.

Lent by the Nautical Photo Agency.

[*Facing page 385.*

the slaves secured for liberation, but the slave dealers quickly kidnapped one hundred of these.

The President's enquiry into the case was unsatisfactory. The British Government remonstrated. Englishmen in Rio were hardly safe from attack and there was a great outcry in the Brazilian press. But English pressure prevailed, the President was dismissed, and the Brazilian slavers finally lost heart.

CHAPTER XX

THE LAST OF THE WEST COAST TRAFFIC

High on the masts sits the Reefer Bold,
He fears not the heat, and he laughs at the cold;
No home loves he, like the deep blue sea;
Oh! the life of a Reefer's the life for me.

The West Coast Squadron Under Commodores Fanshawe and Bruce.

COMMODORE Arthur Fanshawe, C.B. in the steam frigate *Cantaur* succeeded Hotham on the West coast of Africa. He took over a squadron of thirteen sail and seven steam cruisers.

In July 1852 his successor, Commodore Henry W. Bruce, with his flag in the old *Penelope* had fourteen sail and fourteen steam under his command.

These figures show that the anti-force party in Great Britain were very far from getting their own way.

Both Fanshawe and Bruce were newcomers to the West coast, but they were officers of long service, Fanshawe being an old *Amazon* and *Endymion* man, whilst Bruce had been a midshipman aboard the *Euryalus* at Trafalgar. Most of their officers were old West coasters. Captain Lyster of the *Penelope* had been on the coast for two and a half years under Sir James Lucas Yeo in *Inconstant* and *Semiramis. Waterwitch's* old commander, John Adams had the steam frigate *Sampson,* the dashing Arthur Cumming was in command of the *Rattler.* Tom Etheridge, who had the old packet brig, *Penguin,* had been first lieutenant of the *Larne* and the *Star* on the coast.

George Alexander Seymour, commanding the steamer *Firefly,* had been first of the *Lily.* John Barling Marsh, commanding *Heroine,* had been first of the *Pelican* under Popham. Henry Temple, commanding *Dolphin,* had been senior of *Actaeon* under Mansel, and also of *Ferret.*

R. D. White, commanding *Cygnet,* had paid off *Sealark* from the coast in 1847. George Lavie of *Alecto,* had been Number One of the *Isis* from 1842 to 1845. Commander Henry Richard Foote of the *Prometheus,* after gaining his commission in the *Madagascar,* had commanded the *Heroine* and been up the Niger under Trotter, as had James Newburgh Strange, who had the steam sloop, *Archer.* W. A. Rumbaıow Pearse of the *Athol* had served in *Penelope* under Commodore Jones.

Of the sailing ships serving on the coast at the beginning of the fifties, the oldest and by far the most famous was the beautiful and much beloved *Waterwitch.*

Each time she arrived home it was rumoured that she would be sold out of the Service or broken up, but always after having had her defects made good, she had been once more recommissioned for the West coast.

Tornados and Thunderstorms

How many tornados she had weathered out it would be difficult to say—running at any rate to many each year. Twice in her existence she was struck by lightning and only saved from destruction by her Snow Harris lightning conductors.

The first occasion was under Commander Quin at 2 a.m. on June the 20th, 1849. The electric fluid passed overboard by the main conductor without doing any harm. Then on the 8th of June, 1852 her mainmast was again struck, but the conductors carried the charge over the side without any damage to the brig, though several of her men were slightly affected by shock.

Few will realise what a danger a thunder-storm at sea was in the old days of oak and hemp—to be struck by lightning was indeed one of the most common accidents of the sea.

Shipping columns were always full of instances—of decks ripped up, sails and rigging set on fire, holes torn in the side, dismastings, magazines exploded and ships sunk.

In 1798 H.M.S. *Resistance* was blown up by a flash of lightning in the Straits of Malacca.

In 1805 on the coast of Africa, the *Squirrel,* sloop, was nearly sunk, her planking was stove in, and the caulking stripped out of the seams.

The terrifying effect of being struck by lightning in the days before the Harris conductor has been very well described by Sir Henry Huntley.

His command, the brigantine *Lynx,* was lying in West Bay, Prince's Island. At 4 in the morning he was awakened by the officer of the watch with the news that a heavy tornado was approaching over the mountains. He gave orders for the cable to be veered to ninety fathoms and for a leadsman to go into the chains with the lead—a precaution to see that the vessel did not drag her anchor when the full force of the storm struck her. He also gave orders for the men to be piped down out of the wet, an important health precaution.

Now let me quote from his descriptions:—

> "The lightning began to stream over the forest, showing for an instant its dark masses crowded together at the foot of the craggy mountains, which prolonged and sent back the roar of the thunder that followed each flash: a gust of wind passed over the vessel, and a few heavy drops of rain fell, the fore-runners of the terrific powers which were in wildest fury acting behind: suddenly, in its direct strength, the tornado burst upon the *Lynx*—lightning, thunder, rain and wind, seemed to contend for individual mastery—the fiery stream glancing upon the rugged face of the mountains, appeared to seek some object upon which to wreak its desperate vengeance, vanished as quickly as it came, and left only a dense impenetrable darkness: the thunder followed, each peal resounding as if those granite masses were each time freshly crashed; at last the *Lynx* herself seemed an instant to be brilliantly illuminated, every mast and rope was a separate line of fire, an unusual crackling noise was heard, and the rigging of the foremast appeared to be lying in confusion—again intense darkness prevailed—and a terrific peal apparently exulted in the savage character of the hour. The foremast had been struck . . . "

The well was sounded, but no damage had been done below. Huntley sung out to the helmsman to know if the brigantine was driving.

There was no answer. The lighting had struck down the leadsman. Quickly the tornado passed away. With daylight the damage was revealed.

The fore topmast, topgallant and royal masts had been shivered into laths, a large chunk, six feet long, had been neatly cut out of the lower mast and the forecastle was a tangled mass of scorched rigging.

To show the smartness of the old time seaman, by two o'clock that afternoon the brigantine sailed out of West Bay under all sail with rigging repaired, new spars aloft and her foremast cleverly scarfed.

Attack on Lagos

The last active service of the *Waterwitch* was in the attack on Lagos. Her last commander was Alan Henry Gardner, son of General the Honourable William Henry Gardner, and grandson of Admiral the first Lord Gardner and nephew of Admiral the second Lord Gardner. He had never served on the African coast before, having mostly been in crack sloops such as the *Dido* under Captain Lewis Davies and *Aigle,* Captain Lord Clarence Paget, on the smart Mediterranean station.

Lagos had always been one of worst centres of the West African slave trade and since the usurper, Kosoko, had obtained power, the place had become the plague spot of the whole coast. The countryside for leagues around was terrorised by his roving warriors, who burnt the kraals, committed every sort of cruelty and atrocity in their frenzied raiding, and drove the wretched survivors of their fury into the Lagos barracoons.

In the autumn of 1851, Beecroft, the British Consul at Fernando Po, and one of the most experienced and oldest traders in the Bights, backed up by Wilmot of the *Harlequin,* Gardner of the *Waterwitch* and Patey of the steam-tender *Bloodhound,* had an interview with King Kosoko, but the slave trade was too profitable for the savage king to forego it, even in return for the most munificent 'dash' and promises of large increases in legitimate trading. Though the interview came to nought, Beecroft was not discouraged and backed by the little squadron of cruisers, consisting of *Harlequin, Waterwitch, Philomel* and the steamers *Niger, Volcano* and *Bloodhound,* he determined to teach the blood-thirsty Kosoko a lesson.

First of all the bar was carefully sounded and the channel marked by the masters of the *Waterwitch* and the *Bloodhound.* This was a most necessary preliminary, for this bar had ever been a hinderance to the trade of Lagos, the Channel shifted almost daily, the surf was often terrific, and the depth of water rarely exceeded fifteen feet.

At daybreak on November the 25th, 1851, twenty-three boats holding two hundred and fifty officers, seamen and marines, led by the *Bloodhound,* flying a white flag of truce, crossed the bar. The senior officer commanding the expedition was Commander Forbes of the *Philomel* in his whale boat. The consul, Beecroft, was in Commader Wilmot's gig, which with the pinnace, cutter and two whale-boats formed the *Harlequin's* contingent. *Philomel's* pinnace with a twelve-pounder carronade in her bow under Lieutenant Williams along with her cutter and second whale-boats; *Volcano's* whale-boat, carrying her commander Coote, with her cutter and paddle-box boats under Lieutenants Reeves and Robson; Commander Heath of the *Niger* in his gig with three cutters, a whale-boat and the pinnace under Lieutenant Dunn; Commander Gardner of the *Waterwitch* in his whale-boat, Lieutenant Graham in the brig's pinnace, her second whale-boat and cutter, completed the force.

The bar was crossed under a heavy fire of musketry from the distant shore, but it did no harm and the flag of truce was kept flying.

When within a mile and a half of the town the *Bloodhound* grounded and could not be got off. Thereupon after a short delay the boats formed into line and pulled on without her, Beecroft with a flag of truce in the *Harlequin's* gig leading the way. As the expedition neared the town, a heavy fire of guns and musketry was opened upon it, the beach for over a mile being crowded with armed warriors. Seeing that there was no hope of a peaceful reception, the flag of truce was hauled down and the boat carronades opened fire upon the yelling mob ashore with both shrapnel and round shot. This was the signal for the *Niger,* lying just outside the bar, to throw a few shells onto the point at the mouth of the river. The boats made a landing on a filthy beach, where nowadays English ladies may be seen promenading on horseback or in motors along an up to date esplandade.

Leaving a strong guard over the boats, the little force of about one hundred and sixty officers and men then charged into the town in the face of a most determined resistance.

The streets of Lagos at that date were narrow and intersecting. Foes who were beaten back in heavy hand-to-hand fighting, dashed down side alleys and reappeared again in other positions of defence. After firing a number of the thatched huts Forbes prepared to retreat, being greatly outnumbered by the enemy, who at the least estimate amounted to five hundred spears with reinforcements pouring in from all sides.

In such a fight against odds, with wildly excited warriors firing every kind of strange "bundook" and "elephant gun" at any range and any elevation, it was surprising that there were not more casualties amongst the bold invaders. *Niger* was the unlucky ship, she lost two mates (Dyer and Hall) killed, and three marines and four seamen severely wounded. The only other dangerous casualties were a quartermaster of the *Philomel* and two seaman of the *Volcano*.

Slight wounds from spear thrusts and many hurts from spent bullets were not even reported.

Considering that every hut in Lagos was held like a fort and that the town was defended by half a dozen large cannons and any number of swivels ably served by trained gunners, it is amazing that the small British force was able to do what it did.

Every man was safely re-embarked, and the boats tied onto the *Bloodhound* for the night, during which she was refloated.

The bar was safely crossed at daybreak the following morning. Then the *Niger* was hurried off in search of Commodore Bruce, she also took the wounded to Sierra Leone hospital. *Harlequin* remained on guard outside the bar whilst the remainder of the squadron returned to their cruising stations.

Commodore Bruce, on hearing of the action, at once made plans for finishing the punishment of Kosoko.

Akitoye, the legitimate king of Lagos had taken refuge with the missionary at Badagry.

Promising to reinstate him, the Commodore arranged that Akitoye with all the followers he could raise, estimated at about five hundred, should be at hand when the next attack on Lagos took place. On December the 23rd, 1851, the following ships arrived off the bar:—the brigs, *Waterwitch* and *Sealark,* and steamers, *Sampson, Penelope, Volcano, Teazer* and *Bloodhound.*

Captain Lewis Tobias Jones of the *Sampson* was given the command of this new expedition, with Captain Henry Lyster of the *Penelope* as his second. In spite of the known lack of water, the little *Bloodhound* and the screw steamer *Teazer* were ordered to lead the way into the river, the boats under Commanders Coote, Gardner, and Charles Farrel Hillyar following.

On December the 24th Captain Jones landed below the town with Beecroft and joined forces with Akitoye. Christmas day was spent aboard ship in the usual Naval fashion, whilst Kosoko's gunners amused themselves by trying to drop rounds upon the nearest ships.

Then on December the 26th, the expeditionary force moved up the river under a brisk fire from the banks. But once again half its effectives were put out of action by the grounding—first of the *Teazer* and then of the *Bloodhound.*

Opposite the latter was a battery of guns, which exchanged a hot fire with the *Bloodhound's* eighteen-pounder gun and howitzer, but luckily the gunboat was almost out of range of the musketry from the shore. The situation was an unpleasant one, so Lieutenant Thomas Saumarez with the *Sampson's* boats and marines under Lieutenant Edward McArthur, was ordered to land and spike the guns. This was no easy task. The only way to reach them was by a narrow creek, which was blocked by stakes, and, as the boats entered the creek, they came under very heavy rifle fire.

The carpenter of the *Sampson,* axe in hand, standing up to his neck in water, made a vain attempt to cut away the obstruction. But it was no use, in less than no time Saumerez himself was wounded in three places, Midshipman Thomas Richards was killed and ten men badly wounded. Enfiladed from all sides and under heavy fire from the bush Saumarez was obliged to retire to the *Bloodhound.*

The *Teazer* found herself in an even worse situation, being under fire from a battery of guns behind a stockade, which were admirably served, and threatened to destroy the gun-boat before the tide floated her. Captain Lyster thereupon determined to land from the boats, rush the stockade and spike the guns. The boats were formed in line abreast and pulled for the shore in the face of a force reckoned at one thousand five hundred muskets, besides the guns.

Corbett's Gallantry

Led by Lieutenant John Corbett, the bluejackets and marines dashed yelling at the stockade: the black warriors astounded at such boldness, retired precipitately into the bush, from whence they fired at pistol range upon the attackers.

Corbett succeeded in spiking the guns, with the loss of Midshipmans F. R. Fletcher and a number of men killed and wounded. At this moment Captain Lyster ordered an immediate retreat for the boats, the enemy having worked round to the beach again and cut off one of them. These were shoved afloat under a hot fire at point blank range.

Next Lyster and Corbett had to go to the rescue of the *Victoria,* Consul Beecroft's launch, which her kroomen had anchored right in the line of the hottest fire. They found the boat, which was described as a rocket boat, straining on a chain cable, which was shackled into the bottom of her stern. There was not sufficient weight of muscle to weigh the anchor and when they wanted to slip the cable, the shackle pin was found to be rusted into the shackle.

The gallant Corbett at once went overboard and after struggling for some time under a tremendous fire, managed at last to cut the chain adrift with a cold chisel, just as Lyster dived into his assistance. As Corbett poked his head above the stern board, he gasped out:—

"I have done it and am alive!" He had already been severely wounded in the attack on the stockade and in cutting the *Victoria* adrift he received five more wounds, whilst Lyster got hit in the back. The boat was then successfully taken alongside the *Teazer.*

In the fight at the landing place, the natives had managed to carry off the boats captured.

Loath to leave her in the hands of the enemy and still more loath to waste lives in recapturing her, Lyster gave leave to mate James Bower Balfour and gunner H. A. Dewar to try and destroy her with a rocket. They made a wonderful shot with their very first rocket and blew up her magazine.

It was not until sunset that the *Teazer* was refloated, and her salvation had cost fifteen officers and men killed and sixty-three wounded. At 7 a.m. on the 27th the *Teazer* was able to proceed on the tide to the aid of the *Bloodhound,* aboard of which was Captain Jones.

The former anchored within range of the town at 8.10 a.m. and shortly afterwards a general bombardment of Lagos began, the rockets boats under Lieutenant Edward Marshall being specially successful, firing many houses and blowing up a magazine.

The boat's under Coote and Gardner were late in getting upon the scene, but soon after 10.30 Coote with some gun-boats and a rocket boat was ordered to pull in and fire a few rounds at Kozoko's kraal. By the afternoon half Lagos was on fire and the rest laid flat. Captain Jones sent a message, giving Kozoko till the Monday morning to surrender. This was a mistake, for on Sunday the chief and two thousand of his supporters retreated into the depths of the bush, and as soon as the punitive force had retired, made his headquarters at Appi, forty-five miles further up the lagoon. Here in July, 1854, he made an agreement with the British Consul and Commander Miller of the *Crane,* whereby he gave up the slave trade.

On Monday morning Gardner and Coote brought off or destroyed no less than fifty-two cannons of all calibres. Finally Akitoye was reinstalled as king. This little action cost the Service fifteen killed and seventy-five wounded, but it was one of the prime causes of the quick decay of the slave traffic in the Bights.

Akitoye, a decadent chief, committed suicide in 1853, and his son Docemo reigned in his stead under the protection and strictly obedient to the British consul. Whenever he showed signs of making up to the slave traders, a British gun-boat appeared on the scene, finally in August, 1861, he ceded his country to Great Britain, lock, stock, and barrel, in return for a life annuity of one thousand five hundred pounds. From that date Lagos and the surrounding territory came into the British Empire and eventually, under Sir John Glover, became one of the most successful of our crown colonies. Indeed by 1865 the Lagos trade in palm oil had become so brisk that there was not sufficient tonnage to cope with it.

By this time in all the oil rivers the cold-blooded traffickers in human flesh were discontentedly trying to subsist upon the growing, but less profitable, trade in ground nuts and palm oil.

All the senior officers in this successful Lagos expediton received their promotion, whilst the gallant Corbett was specially rewared with a commander's epaulettes, and master's-assistant B. F. B. Clarke, who had helped him to spike the guns of the troublesome battery, also received a step up the ladder.

The British Squadron Makes Headway

In August 1852 the state of the slave trade on the West coast of Africa was a proof that the squadron was not the useless expense that our political cranks and theorists contended it was.

Taking the coast from North to South:—

At the Portuguese settlement of Bissao only a very occasional slaver managed to slip away, and this certainly not with the open countenance of the local Government.

The Rio Pongas, which until lately had been shipping two thousand slaves a year from several factories, was considered clear of the trade.

The Shebar factories were also closed to black ivory. Hotham had destroyed the large barracoons in the Gallanis in 1849 and here also, instead of supplying eight thousand negroes a year, the trade was said to be dead.

The Pennsylvania Colonization Society demanded some credit for their efforts in Liberia.

They claimed that there was no longer any slaving in the Sugry river nor at Cape Mount, at Cape Mesurado and in the mouth of the Junk river. The factory in the St. John's river was in ruins. Bassa Cove, which in the twenties, shipped five hundred a month, was deserted.

Theodore Canot Retires

The notorious Theodore Canot had retired from New Cess, and when he appeared off the coast in the American barque, *Chancellor,* he found that his legitimate factory, containing only trade goods had been burnt by the neighbouring chiefs. He was a ruined man and retired to South America, the *Chancellor* having been seized by the U.S. schooner, *Dolphin,* because of her slave deck and water casks.

In 1853 Canot was introduced to Brantz Mayer of the Maryland Historical Society, and the latter was responsible for the notorious slave traders entertaining if hardly elevating memoirs.

The Rascally King of Dahomey

In the Bight of Benin there was still one blot on the landscape and that was the rascally King of Dahomey, who supplied Whydah.

Both naval officers and consuls tried their powers of negotiation on him without success.

His message to the Queen of England showed his mentality. He begged the Queen to put a stop to the slave trade everywhere else and allow him to continue it. He also begged her to allow no ships to trade at any place South of Whydah in his dominions, as by means of such trade his people were getting rich and resisting his authority.

He ended up by asking for plenty of good Tower muskets and blunderbusses to enable him to make war!

He was credited with receiving over fifty thousand pounds a year in head money, some eight thousand slaves being supplied annually from Whydah.

This was the one plague spot in the Bights, now Lagos was finished with, for the Bonny, which, in the early forties was exporting fifteen thousand negroes a year, was now given up to legitimate trading, and the Cameroons and Calabar rivers were said to be equally free of all traffic in black ivory.

To the South of the Line the trade in negroes was still in full swing, for if cruisers were known to be blockading the chief slave marts, the caravans proceeded elsewhere, even on occasion crossing the continent to the Mozambique.

To the South of the Gaboon, Lopez, Mayumba, Loango, Kabenda, the Congo, Ambriz, Loando, Quicombo, Benguela, and in fact the whole one thousand miles of Portuguese coast line had to be closely watched by the R.N. cruisers, for owing to the internal waterways, shown by Hotham in his famous chart, as well as by caravan further South, it was possible to ship negroes from a particular district at a port perhaps one thousand miles away.

In Cuba and Brazil, the slaves shipped at Lagos and Whydah had always been preferred as the best agriculturalists. Domestic servants usually came from the Bonny and Calbar rivers, whilst the negroes of the Congo were considerd the most amenable and the best tempered.

Cuban Slave Statistics

The latest reports of slaves safely landed in Cuba gave the following statistics:—

In 1849 twenty slavers landed six thousand five hundred and seventy five African negroes.

In 1850 seven slavers landed two thousand three hundred and twenty five African negroes.

In 1851 seven slavers landed three thousand six hundred and eighty seven African negroes.

American Slavers

The slave ships still came almost entirely from American ship-building yards, but since the boom in clipper ships, larger vessels were entering the trade with the hall-mark of the New York shipwrights upon them.

Of such was the brig *Hanover,* which in February, 1852, landed six hundred and fifty slaves at Sierra Morena in Cuba. Another notorious American slaver was the barque, *Lady Suffolk,* which in April, 1853, landed six hundred slaves in Cuba.

Owing to the law not allowing British cruisers to capture vessels under the American flag two other Americans got safely away from the Southern station at this time—these were the schooner, *Sarah Hope,* with six hundred and the barque, *Republic,* with seven hundred slaves.

The American Commodore, Isaac Mayo, in the *Constitution* was fully informed of these Yankee slavers by Commander Miller of H.M.S. *Crane,* and as a consequence the *H.N. Gambril,* which had long been watched and repeatedly boarded by the Britisher, was captured by the *Constitution* some sixty-seven miles South of the Congo.

In 1852 the *Pennsylvania Colonization Herald* published the following account:—

> "The slavers are all sharp-built vessels, intended expressly for fast sailers. They mount commonly one gun, sometimes as many as eighteen. The one gun is a long thirty-two pounder: and where there are more, some are always of this description. They are almost all of Baltimore build. The way of procuring them is said the following:—

Mercantile houses in the Havana, and other ports in Cuba and Brazil, send orders for fast sailing vessels to their correspondents in the United States, of course saying nothing about their being designed for slavers. Even the shackles for securing the slaves, and the gratings to cover the hatches, not infrequently go from this country; (U.S.A.) though a part of the latter are sometimes prepared on board. The shackles are put up in barrels and shipped as merchandise. The crews are principally Spanish and Portuguese, French and Dutch Creoles and a sort of Lingua Franca men, of no nation, or rather of all nations, belonging nowhere, or everywhere, and speaking all the Atlantic languages.

Some of the crew are frequently Americans, who sometimes do not know the nature of the voyage until they arrive on the coast of Africa.

The slaver sails from our ports as an American vessel, under the American flag, with American papers, and appears like a regular trader. She goes to the Havana or Rio Janeiro, is denationalized, receives a new name, and takes Spanish colours and papers or Brazilian colours and papers.

Sometimes, but rarely, this is done at the Cape de Verde Islands. These vessels frequently put into Sierra Leone: and as all appears fair and smooth and strictly regular, it is impossible to prove that they are slavers, although not a man in the place has the least doubt of it. Here they procure provisions and water as lawful traders. The captains always have plenty of money, and pay well for everything, and take care to give no offence. They are generally men of polished manners and gentlemanly appearance".

Though slave trading was practically squashed on the Northern Division by 1853, the cruisers had to be as vigilant as ever, for at the very first opportunity both slave traders and native chiefs began the old game again.

The Chief Moodah Punished

The sore even opened on the Sierra Leone river at Medina, where the chief, Keleh Moodah, proved to be in league with a slaver though openly professing to fulfil the conditions of the treaty.

When Governor Kennedy was unable to obtain any satisfactory explanation from the truculent chief, who had even dared to make a prisoner of a British subject, the little *Teazer,* Lieutenant Rich, towed up the armed boats of the brig *Linnet;* the expedition being under Commander Need of the war-brig. At a palaver at Medina commander Need read out the Governor's despatch; but the chief, surrounded as he was by his warriors armed with spears, cutlasses and muskets, would only give insolent answers. Whereupon the naval officer and his escort made a quiet and dignified retreat to his boats. His departure was the signal for a grotesque war dance on the beach before the town. A bare twenty minutes passed before this was rudely interrupted by a rain of shot and shell from the *Teazer* and a cross fire from the boat guns. The bombardment lasted for a quarter of an hour of rapid fire, then Commander Need landed again to be received by a very contrite and chastened chief.

Slaverly in the Pongas

Shortly after this punishment of Keleh Moodah, the Governor learnt that there were two vessels loading slaves in the Pongas. He at once sent information by the steamer *Pluto* to the senior officer of the Northern Division, Captain Seymour of the *Firefly.* The latter sent word to Commander Need, who on the 30th of April once more manned and armed his boats.

After pulling about twenty miles up the Pongas the boats came upon a handsome brigantine of two hundred and fifty tons with her sails loosed. She was quickly captured, but all her crew, except two men, escaped by leaping overboard and hiding in the bush.

Further up hidden in amongst the mangroves the other slaver, a schooner of about one hundred tons, was discovered, but her crew also fled into the bush. The two slavers were brought out and sent off to Sierra Leone for adjudication.

Trouble with the Ashanti

In the same year a ticklish situation developed at Cape Coast Castle where Major Hill was glad to have the support of the steamer *Polyphemus,* the brig *Britimart* and the 'brigantine' *Spy.* After the previous Ashanti war two tribes of Assins had crossed the boundary river, Pratt, and put themselves under British protection. The king of the Ashanti, after many vain attempts to get the Assins back into his fold, at last sent a bribe of three hundred ounces of gold to two of the Assin chiefs, Gabriel and Chiboo; but the chiefs spent the money in riotous living instead of taking their people back to the Ashanti fold; and when the King sent a small party of Ashanti warriors to bring the two chiefs to their agreement, the Assins not only refused to go, but, made prisoners of the Ashanti, and at the same time they sent their two delinquents to Major Hill.

At once twenty thousand Ashanti poured into the Assin territory to the rescue. But Hill acted with resolution and without hesitation.

At a grand palaver in a clearing outside the town of Dunquah the two chiefs were tried and beheaded; then the party of Ashanti, who had been made prisoners, were sent back to their king with Hill's ultimatum that if he did not immediately recall his warriors from the war path, the white man would attack with shot and shell. The king of the Ashanti lacked the nerve to bring the dispute to such a conclusion; and he saved his face by disowning the whole affair, and calling off his warriors.

Up the Congo the trader, who was taking the place of the slaver, had to proceed warily. As Hotham had told the Slave Trade commission, the West African Squadron had a secondary duty and that was to act as a protection to the legitimate trader, both against pirates and treacherous natives.

The Navy in the Congo

A case in point was that of the American brig, *Mary Adeline,* which when working into the Congo on June the 19th, 1853, touched the ground off Sharks Point, and was speedily hard and fast, being silted up by the strong current.

Luckily H.M. brigantine, *Dolphin,* Lieutenant-Commander Webber, was anchored within sight; and in less than half an hour her boats were alongside the American with anchors and hawsers.

These were laid out on the falling tide and every preparation made for heaving off the next day. But at daybreak the following morning a fleet of canoes were seen approaching.

Each canoe held about forty natives, most of whom were armed with muskets—their aim was evidently to loot the stranded brig.

Webber acted promptly; a boat's gun and ammunition were sent aboard the *Mary Adeline,* and the *Dolphin* was shifted so as to be in a position to protect the brig.

Whereupon the canoes landed their warriors, and presently a force of some three thousand natives opened fire from the shore upon the stranded brig. But a rapid fire of shot and shell from the *Dolphin* soon cleared the beach of marksmen, every native retreating into the shelter of the thick bush. The first efforts to float the *Mary Adeline* on the top of the tide were unsuccessful.

That evening the paddle-wheel sloop, *Firefly,* arrived in the river, and at once sent her boats to help in floating the brig.

During that night (the 20th) the natives collected on the beach and fired a few wildly aimed rounds at the brig; and at daybreak they again seemed to be meditating attack, but a shell from the *Dolphin* drove them into the bush again. During the 21st, the surf was so heavy that the *Dolphin's* cutter was capsized by the rollers, one man being badly injured, whilst an attempt to float the brig was being made.

On the following day the cargo of the American was all transferred to the war brigantine, and, after a great deal of what sailors call 'dry pulling', the *Mary Adeline* was hove off into deep water.

Her fate, but for the Royal Navy, would have been far from pleasant.

During the year 1854 not more than three or four slavers made their appearance in the Bights Division whilst English palm oil traders were everywhere.

The Last of the Trade in the Bights

In May, 1854, Lieutenant Young of the *Antelope* handed over the division to Commander Miller of the brig *Crane,* who in his turn handed over to Commander McDowall Skene of the *Philomel* in 1855. The other cruisers on the station were the brigantine, *Dolphin,* brig, *Arab,* and three-gun screw gun-boat *Minx,* which had been built at Blackwall in 1846 from designs of Sir William Symonds (tonnage three hundred and one. H.P. one hundred).

Two slavers only succeeded in getting away from Whydah; the American brig *Spread Eagle,* which had long been under suspicion, managed to get clear on May the 16th with seven hundred slaves on board; and the French brig, *Cesar,* which had been condemned as unseaworthy by a recent survey, slipped off under Spanish colours on July the 26th.

The American brig *Carrier Pigeon,* failing to get a cargo of slaves at Little Popo, contented herself with one of palm oil.

The only slaver attempting the Bonny was the Spanish schooner, *Merecerdita* (ex *Oregon*), and her fate was a curious one. Her Captain finding himself a black sheep amongst a host of British palm oilers, gave up his ship to Captain Birkett of the English merchantman, *Bell:* but another palm oiler, Captain Hemingway of the English ship, *Roderick Dhu,* proceeded to take forcible possession of the slave schooner, intending to use her 'for his own private purposes'; then the *Crane* came up the river and the fat was in the fire. Hemingway was forced to make a written defence, hand over the thirteen members of the Spanish crew, and eat humble pie, whilst Lieutenant Foster, senior of the *Crane,* was sent after the slaver, which had been turned into a trader. In the end the *Merecerdita* had to discharge Captain Hemingway's cargo at Bonny, the Court of Adjudication refusing to confiscate it.

In 1854 Commodore Adams, a very old hand on the coast, took over the squadron from Bruce and he found his time mostly taken up by what was becoming of greater and greater importance, namely, negotiations and treaties with the native chiefs.

Even at Whydah the slave traders were becoming discouraged, and two of them, Domingo Moastique and Baieta, retired to Cuba in disgust.

The palm oil traders, however, could not stand the exactions of the king of Dahomey and settled themselves at Ahgwey and other places, that were out of his reach.

So quiet was the slave trade through 1854 that the *Arab,* the smartest sailer on the station, which had run from Prince's Island to Lagos in three days, was ordered by the Admiralty to proceed to the West Indian station.

Despondency in Cuba

At Cuba, too, slaving was not the financial success it had long been. Most of the old slave merchants had retired with handsome fortunes, their places being taken by pure speculators.

Nor was it easy to obtain crews for slavers at even forty dollars a week. Great respect was held for the Royal Navy, 'its efficiency and the honourable demeanour of its officers'.

A Cuban seaman told Kennedy, the British Consul, that he had been captured seven times in eight voyages; another said he had only made three slaving voyages but had been captured each time.

However heavy mortality of slaves from a cholera epidemic in Brazil and the enterprise of American speculators caused the dying trade to flare up again in 1856.

American Speculators Enter the Trade

Here is a quotation from the *New York Times*:—

"We have over and over again called public attention to the fact that the slave trade, in spite of all the laws against it, is actively carried on from the ports of New York and Baltimore.

Scores of vessels fitted out here, ostensibly for some of the obscure ports of Cuba or South America, start for the coast of Africa, take in cargoes of slaves and in spite of laws, cruisers and Government officials, land them in Cuba, where the market is always open".

In the *Falmouth Post*, Jamaica, of December the 9th, 1856, was published the following:—

"We have been informed by a gentleman, attached to the schooner, *Emily,* now in this port from the Grand Caymanas, that an American brigantine, named, *Nehemiah Hans,* arrived at that island about a month ago, after having landed five hundred and eighty four slaves at Cuba.

She bought at the Caymanas one hundred and seventy tons of guano at ten dollars per ton and employed eleven men at the rate of fifty dollars a month for the chief mate, thirty dollars each for second mate and boatswain, and twenty-five dollars each per common seaman.

It was evident that the *Nehemiah Hans* was about returning to the coast of Africa for another cargo of human beings, as the Captain purchased a large quantity of provisions, poultry, etc., and a lot of turtle. Truly the slave traders are becoming more and more emboldened when they fearlessly enter a British port and employ British subjects to assist them.

We trust therefore that the authorities at headquarters in Spanish town will adopt measures that will render nugatory any further attempt to hire seamen at the Caymanas for the prosecution of this infamous traffic".

The *Arab*'s Pinnace Makes a Capture

Early in the year the pinnace of the *Arab* made a capture off the South coast of Cuba owing to information given by Captain McLanchlan of the Caymanas schooner, *Star.*

The pinnace under Lieutenant Edward Stubbs had left the *Arab* off Trinidad de Cuba on April the 2nd, 1857. Two days later Stubbs anchored in the Boca Grande where he found the *Star,* which was a wrecker. Her captain was full of local information, all invaluable to a cruiser.

He informed Stubbs that for about two months three slavers had been lying wrecked on Man-of-war Cay. Another wrecked slaver he had sighted on Cotten Cays, with the lifeless bodies of twenty Africans floating around it.

On the West point of Cay Grande, he declared there were eight Spanish pilots on the lookout for slavers, who had told him they were expecting a vessel daily. On the 9th Lieutenant Stubbs, after a cruise off Cay Grande determined to keep out of sight of these vigilant pilots on the Cape, so he went in round the point and hid himself.

On the 12th, at 9.30 a.m. his patience was rewarded by the sight of a schooner running down under square sails. The pinnace immediately weighed and stood across the passage. As the sun approached the zenith the wind dropped, the pinnace got her oars out and the slaver cut the boat towing astern adrift and stood out to sea. The pinnace then hoisted her colours and fired a shot or two across the schooners forefoot. At 3 p.m. the bluejackets were still at the oars, whilst a marine, named Baird, maintained a steady fire on the schooner, which now lowered a boat.

A lucky shot at the boat shattered her rudder and she at once tossed her oars in token of surrender.

Aboard her Lieutenant Stubbs found the Captain of the slaver, her cook, and the captain's private slave, besides several fully loaded Colt's revolvers.

On leaving the schooner the slave captain had lashed her helm and with all sail set she was running straight for the reef. He had also loosed the slaves, one of whom luckily knew enough to put the helm down when she was within one hundred and fifty yards of the rocks. When Stubbs boarded her he found the unfortunate negroes tearing everything to pieces in their vain search for food. Only two days' provisions were found to be on board and the slaves were dying of starvation. The schooner had left Kabenda forty-six days previously with five hundred slaves and had lost one hundred and twenty on the passage. The captain refuse to give his name or that of his vessel, but admitted that the capture would cost him thirty thousand dollars.

The interpreter was more communicative, and he declared that two vessels weekly were to be expected from the coast of Africa with from five hundred to seven hundred slaves apiece. He also explained that when slavers were unable to escape cruisers they were run ashore and the slaves allowed to perish, so that on this particular portion of the Cuban coast, the shore was white with human bones. On Thursday, the 16th, the slaver was anchored in St. Ann's Bay, Jamaica, where Messrs. Bravo and other local landowners sent a steer, yams and bread aboard for the famished slaves, thirty of whom were in a dying condition.

The negroes, on the prize's arrival at Kingston, were landed at Fort Augusta where everything possible was done for their comfort.

At Port Royal the Spanish captain openly boasted that he had made twenty-seven trips across the Atlantic with slaves and only been captured three times.

He was very impatient to get back to Havana, where he declared a new vessel was waiting for him.

Capture of the Barque *Emilia*

The year 1857 was notable for the number of American slavers captured. Between June 1857 and June 1858. British cruisers took twenty-two slavers, all of which with one exception were Americans, hailing from New York, Boston or New Orleans.

The year was also remarkable for the size of the slavers, many of them being barques of six to eight hundred tons.

On March the 22nd, a French-built barque, named *Emilia,* was captured in the Florida Channel by the British cruisers *Styx* and *Jasper.*

This vessel, of close on eight hundred tons, had been bought for seven thousand pounds and fitted for carrying slaves at a cost of one thousand two hundred pounds. She cleared from Havana for Marseilles with a crew of forty Dagoes of every degree, each of whom had been promised nine hundred dollars should the voyage turn out successful. Her cargo was eight hundred casks of rum.

Unfortunately for this well-camouflaged and highly superior slave ship, the British cruisers had learnt all about her from an English merchantman that had left Cuba, a few days ahead of her.

After a chase of twenty miles and a few rounds dropped round her, she hauled down her colours; on being searched, the rum casks were found to contain nothing but water, the top tier being coloured so as to deceive the authorities.

A more successful enterprise was that of an American barque, which managed to land six hundred negroes at La Punta de Teja near the Rio de Palma. It was rumoured that General Concha received three ounces of gold (fifty-seven dollars) and his deputies one and a half ounces, hush money, for each negro landed.

A Big Cargo of Slaves

The largest cargo of slaves ever stowed up to that date was captured by the *Pluto* in 4° 15′ S. 9° 30′ E. on November the 30th, 1857. This was eight hundred and seventy four negroes in the barque, *Orion,* which after being sighted at daybreak under a press of sail was speedily overhauled with the aid of steam.

Alecto's Success

The *Firefly* also captured a clipper barque reckoned to be worth eight thousand pounds, but the *Alecto* seems to have been the most successful of the steam cruisers, capturing no less than seven prizes in two months, her last being the very fast brigantine, *Windward,* with six hundred slaves on board.

The most successful of the cruisers showed considerable cunning in outwitting the slavers.

In this instance the commander of the *Alecto* gave out that she was out of coal and was off to St. Paul de Loanda to replenish her bunkers.

The slave traders calculated upon this necessity, and immediately her smoke was noticed disappearing under the horizon to the Southward, the brigantine slipped into the Congo and took her live cargo on board.

But as soon as she was clear of the coast the *Alecto* had doubled back, and at 2.50 p.m. on November the 3rd, as the *Windward* raced off the land on the port tack, there lay the *Alecto* waiting for her with sails furled and fires banked.

The chase started with the cruiser under steam alone, but she soon found that the brigantine was leaving her in the fresh breeze, and she was obliged to set every rag: even then as the wind freshened the slaver continued to gain, and it was only in the lulls that the *Alecto* with flames spouting from her funnel could shorten the distance between them.

All through the night the chase went on. When the moon was obscured by cloud the brigantine was lost sight of, but directly it reappeared, there she was right ahead leaning under the heavy press of sail. Several rounds were fired at her, but they all fell short.

Towards morning the wind began to drop and the *Alecto* was soon within range, when a couple of rounds caused the slaver to heave to and surrender.

The *Windward* was taken to St. Helena; she was only one hundred and seventy seven tons, American measurement, and in that short passage she lost one hundred and forty nine of her slaves in spite of everything that the prize crew could do.

American Cruisers

When, after years of unavailing struggle, the Royal Navy with the aid of the paddle and the screw was at last succeeding in checkmating the wily Portuguese and the callous Spaniard, it must have been very discouraging to find a sudden activity springing up amongst the slave merchants of the Southern States of America. Throughout the last half dozen years of the fifties, feeling between North and South on the slave question was rapidly being fanned to fighting heat. It was unfortunate, too, that the U.S. Navy should have had such a preponderance of Southerners amongst its officers.

Slavers captured by U.S. men-of-war were not easily condemned in the American courts, nor was the gallantry and enterprise often shown in hunting slavers considered any help to promotion in the U.S. Service. Yet there was good work done in spite of the strong under-current of animosity against officers, who dared to show zeal in hunting the slaver.

In 1845 the U.S. brig-of-war, *Truxton,* put an end to the successful career of the New Orleans schooner, *Spitfire,* by catching her in the Rio Pongas with three hundred and forty six negroes under hatches.

Though she measured little more than one hundred tons, the year before, this slaver had landed three hundred and thirty nine negroes near Matanzas in Cuba.

In June 1850, Commander Foote of the U.S. brig *Perry,* which he had disguised to look like a palm-oiler, captured the large full-rigged slaver, *Martha,* which actually showed two tiers of painted ports. The *Martha* was running into Ambriz and was very taken aback when the innocent-looking merchantman turned out to be a national ship. The slaver proved to be all ready for her cargo, with material for her slave deck, water tanks, farina and beans, not to speak of four hundred wooden spoons and leg irons for one thousand eight hundred slaves.

As the cutter from the *Perry* was rowing aboard the *Martha,* her captain threw his desk of papers overboard. But this desk was promptly picked up. It contained proof of the ship's American nationality—she had exchanged her American ensign for a Brazilian on realising that the *Perry* was a man-of-war.

This two-decker slaver was condemned at New York and her captain, who was admitted to bail for three thousand dollars, wisely forfeited the money and disappeared. Commander Foote's zeal was far from being appreciated and he was very shortly after moved to a station, where any chance of distinguishing himself was nil.

Commander Andrew Hull Foote was the son of Governor S. A. Foote, and had earned his lieutenant's commission for his gallantry against the West Indian pirates in the twenties and especially for his part in the capture of the pirate Cofrecina, in 1825. He afterwards greatly distinguished himself in the North and South war.

The Slave Dealer Lamar of Savannah

In the years just before the outbreak of this civil war, the Southern slave dealers were very active in smuggling West African negroes into America. The most notorious and enterprising of these American slave speculators was Charles A. L. Lamar of Savannah, Georgia, who owned the schooners *E. A. Rawlins, Richard Cobdens* and *Wanderer.*

He was a gruff-voiced, blustering, fat man with a red tooth-brush of a moustache and a cocksure manner—not at all the usual type of polite, slow-speaking Southerner.

His name for slaves was:—'African apprentices to be bound for the term of their natural lives'.

In his dispute with the authorities his language was picturesque and free, with a Mark Twain twang and a Bret Harte twist.

When the customs detained the *E. A. Rawlins* under suspicion, he wrote to the Secretary of the Treasury complaining of 'his damned saphead of a collector'.

It is doubtful whether his interest in the notorious yacht-slaver *Wanderer* dated from her first or her second voyage, but it seems most probable that he owned shares in her from the start.

The Schooner *Wanderer* Slaver-Yacht

This schooner was designed by W. J. Rowland and built at Port Jefferson, Long Island, by James G. Baylis, for M. D. Johnson, a well-known member of the New York Yacht Club.

At her launch in June, 1857, she was considered one of the finest yachts ever built in America and as regards her sailing powers, a 'world beater', to quote a common expression of that date.

In her lines, appearance and sail plan she was an enlarged *America;* the following comparisons may therefore be of interest:—

	Tons	Length overall	Length Keel	Beam	Draught	Main lowermast	Main boom	Main gaff	Main topmast
		ft.	ft.	ft.	ft.	ft.	ft.	ft.	
America	170	95	80	22½	11	81	58	26	
Wanderer	250	104	95	26½	10½	84	65	35	35

Wanderer had a standing bowsprit, measuring twenty-three feet outboard, whilst *America* had a running bowsprit thirty-two feet long.

There can be no doubt that the *Wanderer* was exceedingly fast. On one of her first trips she is said to have sailed from New Orleans to New York in nine days.

It was early in 1858 that she was bought by W. C. Corrie of South Carolina, described as a "gentleman of leisure, of aquatic taste, who moved in the first circles of his native state".

As a rich Southerner with excellent credentials, he was elected a member of the New York Club on May the 29th, 1858.

A few days later he took his new acquisition out for a cruise and on June the 25th came into Charleston. Here for ten days the Wanderer was refitting, and it was whispered along the water front that tanks for one thousand two hundred gallons of water had been placed under her cabin floors.

Wanderer's First Run with Slaves

Though she still flew the N.Y.Y.C. burgee, contrary to all yacht club rules and etiquette, she had shipped a supercargo—Captain Egbert Farnham, later notorious as one of Walker's fillibusters. Her commander was a brother of Raphael Semmes of Alabama fame. The *Wanderer* cleared for Trinidad and the West Indies. Corrie kept up his pose of a wealthy yachtsmen cruising for pleasure; and after calling in at Trinidad, appeared next at St. Helena, where the *Wanderer* was the centre of much gaiety.

After leaving St. Helena, Corrie was next heard of off the mouth of the Congo, where H.M. paddle-wheel sloop, *Medusa,* Commander William Bowden, had her station.

The two ships fraternised. Corrie entertained the English sailors sumptuously. His champagne flowed day and night and the strongest heads in the cruiser's wardroom could hardly stand against it; thus, when the jovial yachtsman suggested that they search his yacht in case he intended to ship a cargo of slaves, his humour was received with roars of laughter.

As soon as Corrie had found out just what the cruiser's future movements were to be, the two ships parted; the *Wanderer* at the very first opportunity slipped into the Congo and took on a cargo of seven hundred and fifty prime young negroes of between thirteen and eighteen years of age.

On the 1st of December the bogus yacht arrived off the coast of Georgia, and, as soon as it was night, crept into the Great Ogeechee.

She anchored in an excellent hiding place behind a large overgrown swamp.

That experienced slave-smuggler Lamar was then communicated with. It was necessary that the *Wanderer* should be able to run by the fort at the entrance to the Savannah river without being challenged. Lamar invited the officers of the garrison and all the local officials to a grand ball, at the same time he provided a banquet with plenty of strong drink for the soldiers. When the festivities were at their height and the sentries and lookouts at the fort were seeing double, the *Wanderer* ran in and brought up off Jekyl Island, where the slaves were put ashore after a landing fee of fifteen thousand dollars had been paid. The negroes were then scattered on Lamar's cotton plantations and sold as opportunity offered. The whole business was cleverly handled and proved a great financial success, the slaves selling for six and seven hundred dollars apiece. Corrie, Lamar, Captain A. C. McGhee, and others who were in the swim, cleared upwards of ten thousand dollars apiece and Captain Semmes was paid a bonus of three thousand five hundred dollars.

It was impossible to keep a smuggling run of this magnitude secret, and soon the whole story was out; the United States District Attorney at Savannah seized the *Wanderer,* and Lamar in his usual style wrote that "there was hell to pay". Corrie, Lamar and as many of the *Wanderer's* crew as could be rounded up were arrested and brought to trial.

But as usual in such cases in the Southern States, all were acquitted and no one punished.

The yacht, however, was forfeited and sold by auction; whilst at the New York Yacht Club meeting of February the 3rd, 1859, Corrie was expelled from the club and the *Wanderer's* name deleted from the list of club yachts.

Lamar, having spread some fearsome threats against anyone who dared bid against him, bought the *Wanderer* at the auction for four thousand dollars. The only man who dared to make a bid against the slave dealer was the keeper of the gaol, whose head was promptly punched by the irate Lamar.

Further Adventures of the *Wanderer*

No sooner was the *Wanderer* clear of the courts, than she was sent off again on another slaving trip to the Congo. This time, though she successfully loaded six hundred slaves, she had no chance of hoodwinking any British Cruiser, and she was chased off the coast, but she was so fast that she got away and made a very fast run across the Atlantic to Georgia.

Unfortunately she got ashore between Jekyl and Cumberland Islands in a gale of wind, and some of her negroes were washed overboard and drowned. The remainder were shipped to New Orleans and sold.

Whilst the *Wanderer* lay off Lamar's Cotton Press in the Savannah river, fitting out for her next voyage, many rumours were spread about her destination. Some said that she was off to China for a load of Canton coolies, others declared that she was only bound to Matanzas, Cuba, for a cargo of fruit.

Lamar had been rash enough to give the command of his schooner and to sell a share in her to a seaman of many aliases, who called himself Martin, though he had been previously known as Potter, Dresser and Walker.

In October, 1859, the *Wanderer,* was once more ready for sea, but Lamar, finding that he was quite unable to get Martin to pay for his share, and with a very shrewd suspicion that the 'gol-darned rapscallion' intended to run away with his ship, went to the collector of the Port and asked him to seize the schooner.

Whilst he was away after the collector, the *Wanderer's* new captain acted in real Bully Hayes style. That night whilst the stevedores were rushing the last of his stores aboard, he calmly announced:—

"Not a man puts his foot over the rail tonight".

Immediately a chorus of protests broke out.

Martin with an unsheathed cutlass in one hand and a horse-pistol in the other then went from man to man and with a low-toned, cold-blooded ferocity and the pistol poked hard against the man's ear, he enquired:—

"Do you want to go over the side? No? Then get down into the cabin".

In this way he soon had every man aboard sitting uncomfortably in the *Wanderer's* elegant saloon. Each in turn under the compulsion of a flourished revolver was obliged to sign articles for a voyage to St. Helena. Directly these formalities were over, Martin lowered his pistol and soon had his shanghaied crew in a good temper by opening a dozen of champagne.

The *Wanderer's* reputation for good drink and plenty of it still held.

The following morning when the disgruntled Lamar and the grumbling Collector appeared, there was no ship.

Outside of Tybee, Martin let the shipping-master and his runner, who under some compulsion had filled up his crew at the last moment, leave in their boat with many sarcastic messages for Lamar and the good people of Savannah.

"I'm off to Africa for a load of niggers", yelled Martin, as he let draw his fore-staysail sheet.

But he never got near the Congo.

His first port of call was to be the Western Isles. There were no charts or chronometer aboard, and not much in the way of provisions, but drink of all sorts was plentiful, and the steward's chief duty was opening bottles.

Though Martin was never dead drunk he was never quite sober; and in his reckless state he did his best to drive the gallant schooner under, sailing her without mercy. She made a very fast run to the Azores, but recognising two men-of-war lying off, he slipped away again without touching.

The *Wanderer's* next port was Madeira. Here the carpenter deserted and Martin had to get away in a hurry to avoid being seized.

A few days later, being almost out of provisions, he left the schooner to board a French barque.

Directly the boat had got well away from the ship's side, her mate, Weston, who had little use for his drunken skipper, made sail and set a course for America.

Lamer's first news of his lost schooner came from Boston, where he learnt she was in the hands of the U.S. Marshal. She was appraised at five thousand nine hundred and forty dollars, and another one thousand dollars to cover the costs was required before Lamar could obtain possession of his stolen *Wanderer*.

Apparently his father, Gazaway B. Lamar now came upon the scene, and, it was said, bought the schooner from his son.

We next hear of her lying for sale at Havana where she had been sent by the Lamars.

At this moment, hostilities between North and South began and the *Wanderer* was at once bought by New Orleans speculators to be fitted out as a Confederate privateer.

In May 1861, she put into Key West and was seized by Lieutenant Tunis A. M. Craven—the man who afterwards went down in the *Tecumseh,* his last words being:—

"After you, pilot".

She was thereupon confiscated for some irregularity in her papers—anyway she had a long twenty-four-pounder on board, and with a crew of twenty-five men, was considered valuable as a cruiser. She was given the duty of patrolling the Gulf with a headquarters at Pensacola. After the war her history became shrouded in mystery—mystery always seems to have been the métier of this beautiful vessel—but it is generally supposed that she ran in the cocoanut trade between the West Indies and America until she one day stranded on Cape Henry and became a total loss.

The old slaver-dealer, Charles Lamar, was killed on April the 16th, 1865 in the last battle of the war at Columbus, Ga.

The Notorious Guinea Captain Francis Bowen

Most of the Guinea Captains and slave traffickers of American nationality did their best to keep out of the limelight of publicity, but there were two of these captains in the years just before the North and South war, who failed very signally to hide their tracks from the public gaze. These were Captain Francis Bowen of *Nightingale* fame and Captain Nathaniel Gordon of the *Erie,* the only man ever executed for slave trading.

Of the two, Captain Bowen was the more deserving of such an end. He was one of those peculiar beings, who seemed to be a mass of contradictions.

Of a rock-like nature with an icy nerve and an absolute lack of any human feeling for either man or woman, he yet possessed a keen sense of humour and showed an unmoved and utterly fearless bearing in the face of even the most sudden and catastrophic reversal of fortune.

He was a small man, clean shaven, grey haired, quiet mannered and always very well dressed. If the sea had left its mark upon him in his tanned features, firm lips and shrewd far-seeing eyes, there was no hint in his appearance of the cruel, sardonic, stick-at-nothing devil, which his acts revealed him to be.

He spoke French, Spanish and Portuguese perfectly. He was very well read and with his cultivated intelligence and cynical wit was an unusually entertaining raconteur.

He had apparently sailed into every nook and corner of the world and experienced every comedy and tragedy possible on the high seas.

He was the son of a well-to-do New York merchant, and as a boy ran away to sea. His family referred to him sadly as the 'black sheep', but 'big bad wolf' might have been a better description, for amongst bad men, he stood out as a born leader. Though number one always was his chief concern, he could be generous and kind on occasions. Nor was his depravity ever that of a libertine, for he possessed an iron self control and despised all forms of self indulgence.

Nothing is known of his early days at sea, but before he became a Guinea captain, if we are to believe his own words, he commanded one of those American clippers, which were engaged in the Chinese Coolie trade.

The name of his ship is not certainly known, but he told the following gruesome story to his last captor, Lieutenant Robert Jukes Hughes of H.M.S. *Zebra*. His cargo of Chinamen, after setting the ship on fire, made a determined effort to break out. They were driven back from the hatch gratings by rifle fire, but instead of venturing below to put out the flames, Bowen battened down the hatches over his wildly screaming coolies and in the end they managed themselves to extinguish the fire, though many were suffocated by the smoke or perished in the flames.

According to Bowen when he eventually arrived at New York, there was an enquiry and he was arrested and refused bail. He would certainly have been hanged, he declared, had he not made a spectacular escape.

After this he decided that as live cargoes went, African blacks were far preferable to Cantonese coolies, and henceforth he engaged so whole-heartedly in the slave trade and his success was so great that he became known as 'the Prince of Slavers'. Yet he managed to keep out of the limelight until as sole owner and commander of the American slaving barque, *Sultana,* he was found preparing to ship negroes fifteen miles up the Congo by the U.S.S. *Sumpter*. Fortunately for Bowen the *Sumpter's* commander happened to be a Southerner, who after detaining the *Sultana* for three days, allowed her to go free 'declaring against every proof that there was nothing in the ship but was in her manifest'.

The quotation is from a letter published in the life of George Hamilton Perkins, that gallant officer who in the battle of Mobile Bay commanded the monitor *Chickasaw* in her fight with the Confederate armour-clad, *Tennessee*. Perkins was then acting master of the *Sumpter*. In the same letter, he wrote:—

> "When I saw Bowen in command of the *Sultana,* he was living very luxuriously: everything in his cabin had elegance and everything about his career was as nearly as possible like that of the romantic pirate and slave captains, who are introduced into novels".

Bowen, as soon as the *Sumpter* had left the river, loaded his live cargo and got successfully away. With the money made by this voyage he bought the *Nightingale,* one of the most famous of American clipper ships.

The Slave Ship *Nightingale*

It was something of a come-down for the peerless *Nightingale* to become a slaver, for she was built in 1857 as the very latest thing in luxury liners, intended to carry American millionaires across the Atlantic to the World Fair.

She was designed and built at Portsmouth, New Hampshire, by Samuel Hanscomb Junior with accommodation for two hundred and fifty passengers of all classes.

Finished like a yacht, her interior decoration was spoken of as 'lavish'. In her staterooms were brass bedsteads instead of the usual standing bunks.

Called after the famous singer, her figurehead represented a bust of Jenny Lind whilst on her stern was an elaborate carving of the singer, reclining at full length with a Nightingale in full song upon her finger.

In size the *Nightingale* could not compare with the *Black Ball* packets of her date. With the same beam, thirty-six feet, as the *Cutty Sark,* she was twenty-five feet shorter in her length on deck, and her tonnage by modern measurement was only a little over six hundred and fifty seven tons, though it was reckoned as one thousand and sixty at her launch on June the 16th, 1851.

She was, of course, an out and out clipper, with very fine ends and an unusual amount of dead rise at half-floor, namely thirty-six inches. She had a tall sail plan without much width, her main yard being seventy-one feet long, topsail yard fifty-seven, topgallant forty-two, royal thirty-two and skysail twenty-five.

After a checkered start to her career, in which the financing of her building broke down, and the trip to the World's Fair of 1851 never eventuated, she was sold to Sampson and Tappan and was put into the Australian passenger trade and the Chinese tea trade.

On these runs perhaps her best passage was from Shanghai to New York in 1856—eighty-eight days.

The best run of which there is record, was three hundred and sixty five miles in the short twenty-four hour day when running the Easting down to Melbourne in 1854.

She was able to log over sixteen knots.

When Captain Bowen took her over, he loaded her in New York with grain and left for Liverpool on September the 18th, 1860. At Liverpool he refitted her throughout for carrying slaves, and on November the 24th left the Mersey with a cargo of guns, powder and cotton prints valued at twenty-one thousand dollars.

On January the 14th, 1861, she was boarded at St. Thomas by H.M.S. *Archer* and U.S.S. *Mystic,* but apparently her papers were found to be in order.

Bowen had cleared from Liverpool for Bombay, and his crew believed that was his destination.

A week later found the *Nightingale* in the Congo. At the end of March, he was just about to load his cargo of negroes when the U.S.S. *Saratoga* appeared in sight. It was a wild, overcast night, and very dark, when not lit up by lightning, but the flashes enabled the *Saratoga* to make out the suspicious clipper and Commander Alfred Taylor ran down and boarded her. But Bowen's papers were so cunningly prepared that without slaves on board no naval officer dared make the *Nightingale* a prize. Even though it was evident that she had everything ready for a live cargo.

Bowen then gave out that he was bound to Benguela and ordered his slaves to be taken overland to Kabenda. For the next three weeks the *Nightingale* stood off and on under topsails, awaiting an opportunity to load, and communicating with the shore by means of a Frenchman of unprepossessing appearance.

During this time he was boarded more than once by men-of-war. On these occasion he used to send half his crew to their hammocks to play sick, the lack of sufficient fit men being his excuse for failing to proceed on his voyage.

Having found out that all the American cruisers, who had been left to look after this super-slaver by the British cruisers, were going down to Loando to replenish their bunkers, Bowen at last ventured to stand in shore.

But Taylor of the *Saratoga* was too wide-awake; hardly had Bowen dropped his anchor before he was boarded by a boat from the man-of-war.

But they were too soon, the *Nightingale,* as before, was found to be empty with the bogus sick men in their hammocks.

Then the *Saratoga* stood away to the Southward, bound apparently to Loando. Directly her smoke was no more visible to the South, Bowen ran into Kabenda Bay, and anchored.

This was on April the 19th. As soon as it was dark the *Saratoga* doubled back under sail alone and anchored about three miles from the *Nightingale.*

At 10.30 p.m. two boats were lowered and under Lieutenant Guthrie pulled away for the slaver under muffled oars. When they boarded the *Nightingale* at ten o'clock in the morning it was a complete surprise. The clipper had nine hundred and sixty one slaves on board, her capstan had been muffled so that she could weigh her anchor as quietly as possible and she would have been away to sea in another hour.

Bowen was found in his cabin, entertaining friends from the shore. He took his reverse with his usual sang froid:—

"Gentlemen, I have played a bold game and lost, as you have played a better".

He remarked coolly, and he declared that he was about to take on six hundred more negroes, or they would not have found him there.

The famous slaver was confined to his luxurious cabin, where his lurid yarns kept Guthrie and the officers in command of the prize crew spell-bound.

Within twenty-four hours, according to his own story, he had so worked upon Lieutenant Guthrie* who happened to be a Southerner and a slave owner, that he connived at Bowen's escape.

Bowen and a Spaniard, who was masquerading as the captain of the *Nightingale,* slipped through the stern port, lowered themselves into a boat, which was hanging astern, and quietly pulled ashore and disappeared.

Lieutenant Guthrie on his arrival at New York reported the escape as follows:—

> "... I regret to say that an American named Francis Bowen and a Spaniard named Valentino Cortina affected their escape during my watch on deck on the night of the 22nd of April ... the first person named was known to be the commander of the *Nightingale* prior to her capture, and the latter was represented as such at the time ... "

Guthrie had a hard task before him.

African fever and other diseases were raging already amongst the negroes, and both Guthrie, Lieutenant Tyler and many of his prize crew became infected, two of the men dying. Out of the nine hundred and sixty one slaves, only eight hundred and one survived when the ship was anchored off Monrovia on May the 7th, and many more died from actual starvation after being landed.

On Monday, May the 13th, the voyage to New York was continued, but so sickly were the crew that at one time there were only four men fit for duty in one watch and three in the other.

The *Nightingale* was duly condemned and was bought into the U.S. Navy for thirteen thousand dollars.

Throughout the North and South war she served in the Gulf of Florida as one of the blockading squadron. After which she returned to trade, and after having passed through the hands of several American owners, was bought by the Norwegians and put into the timber trade with the yards stripped from her mizzen and a wind-mill over her after hatch.

On April the 17th, 1893, she was abandoned at sea when on a voyage from Liverpool to Halifax. This was in 43° N. 47° W. and her master, Captain Englebrilsen, and all the hands were taken off by a passing ship.

Bowen, was, of course ruined. At the end of 1861 he appeared in Boston disguised as a common sailor, but finding that a reward had been offered for his capture, he slipped away again and presently appeared at Havana, where he had money owing to him.

---

* Of the officers in charge of the prize, John Guthrie was from South Carolina, Charles W. Hayes came from Alabama and H. B. Tyler from Virginia.

Bowen's Last Slaver *Mariquita,* ex Mackerel-Fisherman

No more was heard of him until April, 1863, when H.M.S. *Zebra* captured a little fore and aft schooner of one hundred and sixty tons in the Congo with over four hundred slaves on board.

This, one of the last of the West coast slavers, had been a Boston mackerel fisherman.

She was of beautiful model and very fast, 'we got fourteen knots out of her during a squall on the way across', wrote Lieutenant Robert Jukes Hughes, the prize master in charge of her.

She was also very handy, her main sail, foresail and fore staysail all working on horses, so that the helmsman could put her about without calling the watch.

She was named the *Mariquita,* and her captain was none other that Francis Bowen, who had sailed her out from London to the Congo with a crew consisting of two men and a boy—a bit of a come-down for the prince of slavers; yet, when he was captured and once more had lost his all, he was not a wit cast down and entertained his captors in his usual irrepressible style.

He seemed equally callous, whether of his own fate or that of his human cattle.

The *Mariquita* was so packed that even with her handiness it was difficult to work her.

"Going across to St. Helena we had to work her, using the bulwark for a deck with life lines from the fore and main rigging on both sides, as there was not a bare square foot on the upper deck, on which the male slaves were packed like sardines (lying down, of course, for it was dangerous for them all to stand up at once), women and children were all below on a deck of about three feet nine inches to four feet in height".

When the *Mariquita* arrived at St. Helena, Bowen and his crew were landed; at parting Bowen told Hughes that he had fully intended recapturing the schooner, but could never catch the latter asleep.

Hughes, in his letter to me, wrote:—

> "Bowen had been very carelessly searched on board our craft (H.M.S. *Zebra*) and had managed to secrete a revolver, which I did not find until we arrived in St. Helena Road," and he added:—
>
> "Bowen, from what I saw of him, would stick at nothing".

At St. Helena, Captain John Moresby of the gun boat *Snake* paid a visit to the *Mariquita.* In his book *Two Admirals* he thus described this visit:—

> "A sight which modern eyes can happily never witness (but common enough then) awaited us at St. Helena. H.M.S. *Zebra* had sent in a slaver prize, a little graceful schooner of only one hundred tons, with raking spars and a mainmast of ninety-two feet in length.
>
> On board this fairy-like craft were stowed no less than four hundred and twenty seven slaves, and probably many more had died before she was captured. They were stowed horribly in three tiers, one above the other, allowing just head room for a crouching position, the lower and middle tiers receiving the filth and abominations of those above them. The officers and crew had ample quarters, therefore the space in which these poor creatures were fettered to endure the horrors of the Middle passage was about forty feet by fifteen feet, and twelve feet in depth. Nothing more terrible can be conceived of any Inferno, and though they had been released and cleansed, the foetid smell still overpowered all else. It is a merciful characteristic that the buoyancy of this unhappy race brings speedy forgetfulness of past trouble. Once set free they were chattering and laughing like a parcel of schoolboys, awaiting their removal to the confortable barracks on shore: and the schooner was sold by the Prize Courts".

Again Captain Bowen's trail is lost until 1872 when he gained command of the American paddle-wheel steamer *Virginius* which had the reputation of being a Cuban filibuster. It was his last adventure on the high seas; for on obtaining the agency of the P.M.S.S. Co. at Colon, he turned over a new leaf, became religious and took to writing sermons. For a while at Colon he managed the Howard House for Mrs. Susan H. Smith, then he retired and after living in a sanctimonious atmosphere throughout a long-drawn-out old age, the Prince of Slavers is reported to have died about 1893.

Nathaniel Gordon, Guinea Captain, Hanged in U.S.A.

Captain Nathaniel Gordon was making his fourth slaving voyage, when his ship, the *Erie* was captured off the Congo river by the U.S. steam sloop *Mohican.*

The *Erie* had been fitted out for slaving at Havana under the superintendence of her captain.

Gordon was a native of Portland, Maine and was thirty-five years of age when captured, a slender, dark-complexioned sailor of medium height with penetrating eyes and dark whiskers.

He had worked his way to command from the usual American beginning of ship's boy.

The trial, as may be imagined, caused tremendous excitement and fierce partisanship in the United States, and the newspapers were filled with the usual harrowing details, sentiment being worked up to fever heat through the person of Gordon's young and beautiful wife and six year old son.

During the night before his execution, he managed to take poison, but after giving him convulsions for some hours, the effect wore off, and on February the 22nd, 1862, he was hanged in the presence of over one hundred witnesses in the courtyard of the Tombs Prison.

At the time of his capture he was said to have made over one hundred thousand dollars in the slave trade, but the whole of these ill-gotten gains were used up in the expenses of his defence.

The Royal Navy Vanquishes the Slave Trade on the West Coast

In 1865, the year that Lord Palmerston, that greatest of all political opponents of the slave trade, died, Commodore Wilmot in command on the West coast reported that the slave trade in the Atlantic ocean was practically extinct and the report of the Mixed Court at Sierra Leone showed not a single capture.

At long last the ceaseless efforts of the Royal Navy had overcome the most inhuman, yet most profitable trade, the world has ever known.

CHAPTER XXI

AGAINST THE MOZAMBIQUE TRADE

'Oh who can tell, save he whose heart hath tried,
And danced in triumph o'er the waters wide,
The exulting sense, the pulse's maddening play,
That thrills the wanderer of that trackless way?'
—The Corsair—

The Dark Continent

AFRICA has been well named the Dark continent—throughout the nineteenth century, it was a dark continent indeed. From the Sahara to the Cape, from the white Atlantic beaches and jungle-clad river banks of the bights to the malarial harbours of the Zambesi delta and the wild desert coasts of the Azanian sea, man has massacred man, tribe has preyed upon tribe, and slavery has ever been the natural result of want of bravery in fight or skill in arms.

Into this seething cauldron of rapine and death came the slave caravans of the rapacious Arab and the cunning Portuguee half-caste, raiding where they could not trade, destroying with their modern weapons those who dared to resist them.

At one time it was reckoned that they took two children out of every three. What wonder that slaves were cheap in the Mozambique and in the Zanzibar slave market. Throughout the first half of the century Portuguese slavers thronged the ports of South East Africa; and Arab dhows ran up the coast to Zanzibar with their holds full of 'black ivory' and crossed to Arabia, Persia and even India; whilst the French slave trade from the coasts opposite Madagascar to Reunion was still going strong in the sixties.

As evidence of the numbers of slaves exported in the early days from the two great Portuguese slave ports of Quillimane and Mozambique, here is the British Consul's report from Rio de Janeiro in 1823 of the arrivals of slave ships in two months:—

Arrivals of Slavers at Rio, 1823

January 16th.	Ship *Flor de Sintra*, from Mozambique, 429 slaves, 52 deaths, 55 days' passage.
January 16.	Brig *Zephiro*, from Quillimane, 416 slaves, 9 deaths, 48 days passage.
January 20th.	Ship *Principe Regente*, from Mozambique, 733 slaves, 44 days' passage.
January 22nd.	Brig, *Trajano*, from Quillimane, 517 slaves, 24 deaths.
February 9th.	Brig *Amazona*,66 days from Mozambique, 465 slaves, 8 deaths.
February 13th.	Ship *Mariana*, 65 days from Mozambique, 520 slaves, 79 deaths.
February 13th.	Ship *Nove de Janeiro*, 108 days from Mozambique 594 slaves, 68 deaths.
March 5th.	Brig *Conde dos Arcos*, 63 days from Quillimane, 402 slaves, 57 deaths.
March 6th.	Ship *Leopoldina*, 65 days from Quillimane, 481 slaves, 201 deaths.
March 6th.	Brig *Minerva*, 64 days from Quillimane, 440 slaves, 45 deaths.
March 7th.	Brig *Sua da Gina*, 66 days from Quillimane, 338 slaves, 98 deaths.
March 18th.	Brig *Sua de Baluarte*, 96 days from Quillimane, 335 slaves, 48 deaths.

Dhow Slave Cargoes, in the Twenties

The mortality figures in this return will be noticed. In the dhow coasting voyage such a percentage of deaths would have caused a loss on the speculation.

A dhow of from eighty to one hundred tons carried from one hundred to one hundred and fifty slaves. The trade was mostly in the hands of the virile, semi-piratical Northern Arabs—fine seamen, who bore incredible hardship as all in the day's work, and to whom starvation on a diet of a few dates or a mess of mealies was their usual state of existence.

Their live cargoes received all there was to be had, and, if already weakened by the long tramp to the coast, many of the negroes failed to survive the rigours of the dhow's scanty regime, the nakoda or captain could only shrug his shoulders and murmur piously 'Allah is good'.

A Heavy Task

At a date when the efforts of the Royal Navy had at last succeeded in stamping out the slave trade in the Bights of Biafra and Benin, it was reckoned that one hundred and eighty thousand negroes per annum were being marched to the chief slave marts on the East coast. On a trek of perhaps three hundred or four hundred miles, quite two-thirds of this number succumbed to disease or want of stamina, nevertheless the Sultan of Zanzibar's income in 1867-1868 from head money was given before the Select Committee by the Honourable C. Vivian as at about fifty six thousand pounds or two hundred and seventy thousand dollars.

It will thus be seen that the task of the Royal Navy in suppressing the slave trade on the East coast of Africa was even a greater one than that on the West coast.

If the squadron on the West coast was starved in its early days, the British squadron operating against slavers in the Mozambique Channel seldom numbered more than three or four cruisers, whilst further North little effort was made to combat the Arab slave trade until the home Government took over from the Indian Navy.

Indian Hostility

So great was the hostility to any suppression of the slave trade to India in the early days, that it was as much as his life was worth for an officer of the Indian Navy to make a capture, and thus that fine service played practically very little part in the arduous task of stopping the trade in 'black cattle', as the Arabs termed it.

Early Mauritius Trade

During the Napoleonic Wars when Mauritius was better known as the 'Ile de France' and 'Reunion' as 'Bourbon', the French bought numbers of slaves to work on the sugar plantations of these islands. In 1815 H.M. schooner *Magnet* captured a French slave schooner, which had already run five cargoes successfully from Madagascar to Mauritius.

This time it had one hundred and seventy Madagascan natives on board, which it had intended to smuggle ashore on an unfrequented part of the island of Mauritius.

The Zanzibar Slave Market in 1814

In the *Naval Chronicle*, of 1814, there is the following account of the slave market at Zanzibar.

> "The slaves are brought to market early in the day, but the principal show commences about three or four o'clock in the evening, where they are set off to the best advantage, by having their skins cleaned and burnished with oil, their faces painted with red and white stripes and sometimes their woolly hair plaited and ornamented with a yellow powder, which are esteemed marks of beauty and elegance among them: their hands and feet are decorated with rings and bracelets and a new wrapper of striped or plain coloured cloth, placed on their bodies. They are ranged in line commencing with the youngest, increasing to the rear according to their age: at the head of the file, which is composed of both sexes and of all ages from six to sixty years, walks the miscreant who owns them.
>
> Behind and on each side are stationed two or three of his domestic slaves armed, who serve as a guard.

> When a slave dies, the corpse is often permitted to putrify on the beach, not a rag of cloth or a handful of earth being laid over it, in consequence, the stench about the town is intolerable".

In the same article the annual export of slaves from Zanzibar to Mauritius, Muscat and India was reckoned at ten thousand of all ages and both sexes. At that date Zanzibar belonged to the Imaum of Muscat.

Purvis of the *Magicienne*

Between 1817 and 1819 Captain John Brett Purvis, commanding the *Magicienne*, forty-two guns, (afterwards cut down and famed for her speed and beauty as a twenty-four-gun corvette), was S.N.O. in the Indian Ocean with his headquarters at Port Louis, Mauritius.

His efforts were seriously interfered with by a cyclone, which on the 1st of March, 1818, drove his frigate, along with forty sail of European merchantmen and country wallahs, as well as innumerable smaller craft, ashore in Grand Port and Port Louis.

Again in July, 1818, he was called away to the Cargados Garragos Reef to rescue the crew of the stranded East Indiaman *Cabalva*, for which he received the thanks of the Court of Directors along with two hundred guineas for the purchase of a piece of plate.

Previous to this he had saved the passengers and crew of the free-trader *Albion*, wrecked on Foul Point near Trincomalee, for which he received a piece of plate valued at one hundred guineas.

Captain Fairfax Moresby

With such a large area to cover. Captain Purvis could hope to make little impression on the iniquitous trade, and it was not until Captain Fairfax Moresby, commanding the *Menai*, twenty-six guns, became S.N.O. at Mauritius that any headway was made. This most energetic and determined officer not only made treaties with the King of Madagscar and Imaum of Muscat, but had such successes against French slavers that he had his command on the coast extended to June 1823.

Capture of the *Camilla*

The most renowned slaver on the coast was the schooner *Camilla*, commanded by a Frenchman named Leroux, who swore that he would blow his vessel out of the water, crew, slaves and all, rather than submit to an English cruiser. On hearing of this threat, Moresby at once went in search of the *Camilla*.

One evening towards sunset the topmasts of the *Camilla* were seen by the lookout of the *Menai* showing over the low land of Imbat.

She was lying under the guns of the fort in the harbour of Zanzibar.

The following night was a very dark one. Moresby sent his boats in to cut her out under his first lieutenant, George James Hay.

Unable to see his way through the Channel between the islands at the entrance, Hay lay on his oars until the glinting lights of the false dawn showed him his prey. But it was still quite dark when the boats dashed alongside the *Camilla*, the pinnace on the starboard bow, and the yawl and gig on either quarter. No one could be distinguished upon the deck of the slaver, but as Hay and his second-in-command advanced across the forecastle, first one then the other was laid prostrate by being knocked over by a terrible bearded monster, which suddenly emerged out of the darkness.

This, the only lookout on the deck of the *Camilla*, proved to be a huge black ram.

The noise going on above awoke one of the sleeping crew, who called out:—

"Qui diable va là? Vous vous amusez, donc, mes brebis? C'est Grégoire que vous arrangera, joliment, les affairs. Ha! Qui vive?".

As the speaker came up the forecastle ladder he was sent sprawling head over heels, and the hatch secured.

Leroux, himself, was also caught napping, being found fast asleep in his berth.

However, being under the guns of the fort, Leroux was not unduly alarmed and pointed smilingly at their forty muzzles, depressed down onto the decks of the slaver. And sure enough ten minutes later a boat put off with a message from the Governor that if any attempt was made to move the *Camilla* out of the harbour, he would open fire.

Hay's reply was characteristic of the Royal Navy: he told the Governor to blow away and be damned, for the British fleet, then off Pembas, would speedily blow him and his fort into the water.

He then held his pistol in line with Captain Leroux's head, and ordered him to pilot the *Camilla* out of the harbour; though the Frenchman nearly had an apopletic fit in suppressing his fury, he was forced to obey.

Later in the day the *Menai* with her prize came to an anchor opposite the fort, and the now thoroughly crestfallen Governor at once sent off his apologies, saying that he had mistaken the men-of-war boats for pirates—a stock and convenient excuse in those stirring times.

The *Camilla* proved to be a most valuable prize, for, besides one hundred and forty slaves, ten thousand Spanish dollars were found on board.

The schooner turned out to be well worthy of her fame as a clipper. She was renamed *Wizard* and converted into a tender, Hay taking command and doing excellent work cruising in the Mozambique Channel.

Bad Crowding of Dhows

In those early days Captain Moresby found the dhow slave traffic to Zanzibar in a terrible condition. He thus described it to that great enemy of slavery, Thomas Fowell Buxton:—

"The Arab dhows, or vessels, are large unwieldy, open boats, without a deck.

In these vessels temporary platforms of bamboos are erected, leaving a narrow passage in the centre. The negroes are then stowed, in the literal sense of the word, in bulk: the first along the floor of the vessel, two adults, side by side, with a boy or a girl resting between or on them, until the tier is complete. Over them the first platform is laid, supported an inch or two clear of their bodies, when a second tier is stowed, and so on until they reach the gunwale of the vessel.

The voyage, they expect, will not exceed twenty-four or forty-eight hours: it often happens that a calm, or unexpected land breeze, delays their progress: in this case a few hours are sufficient to decide the fate of the cargo: those of the lower portion of the cargo, that die, cannot be removed. They remain until the upper part are dead, and thrown over, and from a cargo of from two hundred to four hundred stowed in this way, it has been known, that not a dozen, at the expiration of ten days, have reached Zanzibar.

On the arrival of the vessels at Zanzibar the cargo is landed: those that can walk up the beach are arranged for the inspection of the Imaum's officer and the payment of duties—those that are weak or maimed by the voyage are left for the coming tide to relieve their miseries. An examination then takes place, which for brutality has never been exceeded in Smithfield".

The Black Pirate

In his reference to pirates the Governor of Zanzibar meant, of course, European pirates.

At this distance of time it it practically impossible to disentangle truth from fiction regarding European pirates cruising in the Indian Ocean during the first half of the nineteenth century,

Ever since the days of Avery and Kidd the waters around Madagascar bore a bad reputation for harbouring the European corsair, whereas it was mostly in the Red Sea and Persian Gulf and around the Kathiawar Peninsular that robbery on the high seas was resorted to by the native seamen. The truculent Arab preyed upon the Indian budgerows and patimars when he was not running a cargo of slaves or arms.

But in the thirties of the last century, there was a typical long, low, rakish-looking schooner lurking in the Mozambique Channel and under the high land of Madagascar in the path of the homeward bound trade from China and India.

This sinister craft, which was commanded by a red-haired giant of, I fear, British nationality, became, for a short while, the scourge of the Indian Ocean and raised quite a panic among timid voyagers.

She was known as the *Black Pirate* because not only her topsides, but her spars, yards and even blocks were painted black. The credit of destroying her was given to the East Indiaman *Simoon*, Captain John Ponsonby (Commander R.N. retired).

The action was fought with exceeding skill by the ex-naval officer and has been recorded in detail, in a scarce little book of sea memories, published by her fourth officer, and named the *Log of the Fortuna*.

The *Simoon*, a little over two months out from Gravesend with twenty-five passengers—mostly ladies going out to join their husbands in India, was running along the wild East coast of Madagascar with the land in plain sight ten or fifteen miles to leeward, when a sail was sighted standing off shore towards the Indiaman.

The fourth mate was sent up to the mizen cross-trees to report upon the stranger, and when he called down that she was a schooner under an immense spread of canvas and of very doubtful honesty as regards her appearance, Captain Ponsonby, himself, went aloft with his chief officer and turned his own private telescope upon the sail—this was a very powerful glass which had been presented to him by the great Duke of Wellington in recognition of his part in the bombardment of the castle of Scylla in the Peninsular war.

One look was sufficient to convince the captain of the *Simoon* of the schooner's identity, and, on reaching his quarterdeck, he had the hands turned up and made them a short speech, telling them that he feared that the approaching vessel was none other than the *Black Pirate* and that he proposed to bear away before the wind on the Indiaman's best point of sailing in order to avoid the rover if possible, conceiving 'Defence not Defiance' to be his duty.

The *Simoon* had an armament of ten carronades, four of which were thirty-two-pounders, the rest being eighteen-pounders; but amongst her freight she had some long thirty-two's destined for the fort of Calcutta: one of these the Captain ordered to be brought up out of the hold and rigged amidships on the spindle of the after-deck capstan. Luckily the guns were stowed in the main hatchway and easy to get at.

Captain Ponsonby's short sailor-like speech concluded with these words:—

"The motto of those scoundrels chasing us is 'Dead men tell no tales'. They are no doubt a mixed scum of all nations. Now, men, will you let a horde like that capture our ship or will you stand by me like true British seamen?".

The answer came in the form of three cheers led by the old silver-haired boatswain. Then the steward appeared with the grogcan and the mainbrace was spliced before the *Simoon* was prepared for battle.

Besides a crew of fifty, there were half a dozen military officers aboard the Indiaman who, whilst the decks were being cleared, guns cast loose, shot and shell handed up, and armsracks filled, eagerly overhauled pet rifles and elephant guns in readiness for the fray.

The East Indiaman had been bowling along seven knots on a taut bowline, but the schooner soon showed that Captain Ponsonby had correctly judged her character, by hauling up and heading directly for the *Simoon* under her fore and aft canvas alone.

Let me quote the fourth mate of the Indiaman:—

"No peaceful trader, and few men-of-war ever spread such sails: for she carried immense staysails on every stay, besides taunt-rigged gaff-topsails above her huge mainsail and fore and aft foresail, with a large ringtail projecting beyond her mainsail and a great jib-topsail bellying above her head sails".

The *Simoon* let go her bowlines, eased off tacks and sheets and trimmed her yards till the wind was a point or two abaft the beam: and with all weather to royal stunsails and her three skysails set, the Indiaman began to increase her speed, changing the jerky straining motion of an apple-cheeked wooden vessel when close-hauled for the easy, slow rolling of running free.

The pirate held on in order to gain the weather-gauge and when within about five miles bore away into the wake of the Indiaman, resetting her square sails again.

Then as the sun rose it began to scorch up the wind, and after a hasty glance at his flogging topsails, Captain Ponsonby gave orders to prepare for action and have everything ready for shortening sail directly the enemy were within range. Again I will quote the fourth officer:—

"The order was promptly executed. The guns were all loaded with solid shot, the gunner, who had served in the same capacity in a King's ship with our captain, taking particular care with the loading of the long thirty-two we had rigged amidships, himself fitting a rope grammet over the shot, and ramming it home with extra force. The sailmaker and his mates placed in convenient places stoppers for splicing temporarily an important rope that might be shot away, whilst the carpenter's crew got ready plugs for stopping shot-holes as well as spars for fishing any mast that might get seriously injured.

Cutlasses and pistols were buckled on by the seamen, a select party of marksmen being armed with musket and bayonet and placed under the orders of Colonel O'Brien, who volunteered his services. The surgeon took up his quarters, and made his preparations for the wounded in our ward-room, being, moreover assisted by a clerical passenger, as also by Lady Murray and a strong-minded gentlewoman.

The rest of the ladies were made as comfortable as possible in the after-hold, where they were below the water-line and safely out of range of the enemy's fire. All the remaining gentlemen, to the number of six, including the Colonel, preferred to join in the defence of the ship. As they were mostly military men and had rifles of their own, they formed a valuable addition to the Colonel's small marine force.

The ropes of the running-gear, connected with the stunsails and other light canvas, were carefully coiled on deck in 'Flemish coils', all ready for letting go and so that no hitch might take place through a kink in a rope whilst shortening sail.

The crew were then told off into two parts—one division to work the big guns: the other, to work the ship and act as small-arm men, as boarders or however necessary. The party of marines belonged to this latter body, and those of them, who were seamen were stationed in the mizen, main and fore-tops with a plentiful supply of ammunition".

Hardly were these preparations completed before the pirate schooner gave a taste of her quality.

Luffing up, she fired a round from her Long Tom amidships and at the same time hoisted her colours, a white skull and crossbones on a black ground. The round fell short.

Then up went the red ensign to the peak of the Indiaman, being greeted by three thunderous cheers by her crew.

Those of us, who have experienced 'zero hour', can well imagine the heartening effect of those cheers upon the tension of that moment before battle with that tiger of the seas.

Before the pirate was in range, the breeze completely faded out, leaving both vessels motionless upon a glassy sea.

But this was not for long—presently a strange splashing showed on either side of the pirate. She was using her sweeps. This put the heavy Indiaman at a great disadvantage, but Captain Ponsonby was equal to the emergency. A couple of boats were lowered, a drag consisting of a topsail, with its foot weighted, and its head bent to a spare yard, was taken a good distance ahead of the *Simoon* and dropped into the water. Then two lines were bent to the yard and led to either quarter to act as springs, by which to slew the Indiaman in any direction needful.

Within another hour the pirate was close enough for the wild whooping and shouting of her men and the creaking of the sweeps to be heard aboard the Indiaman.

She had been well named the *Black Pirate*.

As the sun set , 'unusually red in a crimson tinted sky', it was right behind her in her wake, so that not only her hull and spars, but her sails, appeared of an inky hue, whilst the sweeps projecting from her ports showed like the black legs of some monstrous insect.

"As she came on thus, thrown out black, huge and sinister against the blood-red background of the crimson sunset, she seemed to present a perfectly diabolical appearance, and this was made still more terrible when the fierce, fiend-like yelling of her pirate crew rang echoing through the surrounding silence of the still night air".

The pirates, pulling furiously at their sweeps, were evidently working themselves up into a state of frenzy. Yet there was need for hurry. Night was falling and the weather showed every sign of a storm brewing. All day the barometer had been falling. They were well within the Mauritius cyclone zone and at the worst season of the year. The very redness of the sunset was a warning, as was the peculiar seaweedy smell of the glassy sea.

The black, weird-looking schooner kept the Indiaman's stern dead on end as she pulled up: then, when within fifty yards, she brought her port guns to bear by backing her starboard sweeps and fired her broadside into the Indiaman's stern. But Captain Ponsonby had previously ordered his crew to lie down, and the iron shower passed harmlessly through the rigging, except for a couple of round shot which lodged in the stern frame. A second shower of grape and canister either bespattered the stern, to the consternation of the women below, or flew over head, though two of the *Simoon*'s crew were hit by ricocheting shrapnel and wounded, one, it was feared, mortally.

Then came the Indiaman's chance.

"Haul away on your starboard guy! Stamp and go! Stamp and go! run away with it!" Cried Captain Ponsonby.

And as the line of men on the rope walked forward with the drag rope, round came the *Simoon*'s bow until her port broadside could be trained down on the pirate's crowded decks.

"Are you ready at the guns?" roared Ponsonby through his speaking trumpet.

"All ready, sir", came from each gunner, as he stood, lighted match in hand.

"Fire!"

Every gun was double-shotted with grape and canister rammed down on top of round shot.

The Indiaman's small-arm men also opened a steady fusilade. Though casualties were heavy on the deck of the pirate schooner, a yelling horde of ruffians began to lay out along her bowsprit and jibboom, ready to board the *Simoon*, as the men at the sweeps pulled her alongside. Jostling each other on the foredeck, balancing themselves on the bulwark rail and out along the jibboom, standing in the folds of the head sails, which had all been hauled down, the pirates, some stripped to the waist others in striped calico shirts with silk sashes, from which peeped the butts of pistols, were brandishing their cutlasses and boarding pikes, in a fury of impatience to get to hand-grips. Screeching too, like lost fiends, they presented a truly terrifying spectacle, and a strange contrast to the silent, yet undaunted crew of the Indiaman.

Amidst the noisy gutturals of a dozen barbarous tongues, the hoarse, gruff commands of an English voice could be distinguished.

As the schooner pulled ahead in her endeavour to get alongside the *Simoon*, with her port drag rope strongly manned slowly turned her head away and brought her starboard broadside to bear. Then, as the pirates, some of whom had been leaping high in the air and running up the schooner's forerigging in their eagerness, prepared to jump onto the channels and the rail of the Indiaman, the latter's broadside, accompanied by a deep throated cheer, was fired point-blank into the surging mass of screeching wretches.

At this moment the sun sank below the horizon, leaving only a deep red glow which in the most lurid fashion outlined the rigging of both ships, edged the silhouetted figures of the pirates with red fire and so touched the folds of the schooner's canvas that her drooping sails seemed to be dripping blood.

In the rapidly fading tropical twilight the sheets of flame spouting from the muzzles of the guns and the leaping flashes from the small arms lit up the devilish faces of the corsair's crew; whilst sulphurous smelling clouds of smoke rose twisting and wreathing about the rigging of both ships and imparted an almost supernatural aspect to the scene.

It might well have been a conflict in hell, what with the eerie red light, the din and crash of musket and cannon, the roars, screams and groans of the combatants, and the enveloping wreaths of suffocating smoke.

The starboard broadside of the *Simoon* spread havoc on the teeming decks of the pirate: the yelling horde were mown down as one man lay quivering, moaning heaps, whilst rivulets of blood began to run out of her scupper holes. Then onto her rail sprang the huge, menacing figure of the pirate captain.

For a bare second he remained in plain view, shaking his fist in a fury of rage, then leaping back upon his own quarterdeck, he roared out to the men on the sweeps to back water. As the schooner was backed under the stern of the Indiaman, out of range of her deadly broadsides, heavy rain drops began to patter upon the latter's decks from a black, arch-shaped cloud overhead.

Then came the first hissing breath of the approaching storm, Crack! crack! crack! went the *Simoon*'s stunsail booms!

"Let go your skysail halliards!" bellowed Captain Ponsonby to his sail trimmers.

"Let go your royal and topgallant halliards!" He went on in the same breath.

Luckily the wind had come up from astern, and both vessels ran away before it, their yards black with men shortening sail. But as soon as both had been snugged down, the action was continued until darkness and the increasing gale separated the combatants.

Some of the long-sighted tars of the Indiaman declared that they had seen the pirate schooner go down head first after firing her last broadside. The gunner, too, declared that he had slapped fourteen rounds from the long thirty-two into her between wind and water, and that with her whole side broken in she could not possibly have lived through the gale that followed the action. And this was probably the case, for no more was ever heard of the *Black Pirate*, which had caused so much terror in Madagascan Seas.

An English Pirate

The following account of an English pirate, which is contained in an article by Captain L. O'Connor, of the first West India regiment, published in the *United Service Journal*, of October 1845, may possibly refer to the *Black Pirate*:—

> "There is one singularly degraded and solitary character on the coast, said to have belonged to our Navy, but dismissed for improper conduct from the Service. This modern *Blackbeard*, commands a large, swift and powerful schooner, fully armed and well manned, and he hovers without the limits of our cruising ground. Should any slaver fall within his course he takes her cargo nolens volens and proceeds direct to the nearest slavemarket. If this disgrace to the name of Englishmen is once captured by any power, a strong rope, a brief shrift and the yardarm, will be his reward.

> The idea of pirates and buccaneers is treated in England as traveller's tales, marvellous adventures or apocryphal accounts, but such is not the case. When once on the West coast of Africa the old and experienced captains proceed with caution and circumspection; they look well to the trim of their sails: see that their arms are in good order; and although they may not fear, still they don't despise danger from a pirate.
>
> When the *General Palmer*, transport, an old East Indiaman, which conveyed the detachment of the West India Regiment under my command, to Sierra Leone in May, 1843, neared the Cape de Verd Islands, the well-known haunt and depot for slavers and pirates, the agent in charge, a lieutenant of the Royal Navy, was not satisfied with four eighteen-pound carronades on deck: but employed the ship's company in fishing up several ancient pieces of ordnance from the hold . . .
>
> These ante diluvian cannon were greased, blackened, and mounted on carriages and poked through the ports . . ."

The Aldabra Muskets

In those days the coral atoll of Aldabra was reputed to be a favourite piratical resort.

Here in a clearing in the scrub under the shade of a clump of screw pines and casuarina trees, a cache of over one thousand muskets was discovered by a landing party from the *Jaseur*, eighteen guns, led by her first lieutenant, that experienced pirate-hunter Francis Liardet. In this domain of the giant tortoise (Testudo elephantina), a search was made for buried treasure, but the eager bluejackets only succeeded in disturbing a few sacred egrets and stately ibises.

Whilst brilliant scarlet, yellow and green weaver birds flighted over their heads, the *Jaseur*'s sportsmen had easy targets presented to them by green pigeons, jet-black shrikes, and bright-hued sun birds, but dense flocks of crab-plover and other shore birds left the coral beaches and took refuge in the lagoon from the ever-popping guns.

No treasure was found, but the island was over-grown with scrub and they might as well have looked for rupees and pice in the Forest d'Ambre of Madagascar.

Bosanquet at Mozambique

Througout the 1830's the Portuguese slave trade from Mozambique and Quillimane was at its height, but in September 1836, the ten-gun brig *Leveret*, Lieutenant-Commander Charles John Bosanquet, on pulling into Mozambique, found the place in a state of insurrection, all the authorities having been thrown into prison, and riot and disorder reigning supreme.

Bosanquet acted at once with characteristic vigour, and by a bold coup de main succeeded in restoring order.

Landing after dark with the greater part of his ship's company, aided by those who were still at large of the Queen of Portugal's officers, he took the insurgents by surprise, occupied the Custom and Government houses, captured the eighty-four-gun battery, and rescued the leading people of the place from the horrors of their own prison.

After holding the town for three days, he was able to re-embark after a most meritorious piece of service, for which he received a most handsome letter of thanks from the Governor and was made a commander of the Portuguese order of Christo.

Three months later he chased the Portuguese slaver, *Diogenese*, of five twenty-four-pounders and seventy men, for eight hundred miles, and finally captured her by boarding, when she had arrived within musket shot of the Mozambique battery and a Portuguese frigate lying off the town. When the *Leveret* was paid off at the end of July, 1839, Bosanquet found that he had been promoted commander in previous May, for his excellent work on the East coast.

22. H.M. Schooner *Pickle* running through a pass in the reef.

From a pen and ink drawing by the author, after an oil painting.

[*Facing page 416.*

23. H.M.S. *Pilot* — Built 1879.

[*Facing page 417.*

Slave Trade Booming in 1837

In spite of his energy and that of W. L. Castle commanding the sloop *Pylades*, Commander Harry Eyres of the new ship-sloop *Modeste*, Commander J. Reeve of the sixteen-gun brig *Lily*, Captain Cook of an English trader reported that only one slaver out of twenty-one sailing from the Mozambique and eighteen from the Quillimane was caught by the cruisers in 1837.

The passage to Rio and Havana from the East coast ports being much longer than from the Atlantic ports was much more costly in negro life.

For instance in 1837 the brig *Adamastor*, embarked eight hundred slaves at Quillimane and lost three hundred and four on the run to Rio, the brig *Leao*, on the same passage lost two hundred and eighty three out of eight hundred and fifty five, and the brig, *Flor de Quilimane*, one hundred and sixty three out of eight hundred and fifty. In the following year *Cintra* lost two hundred and fourteen out of nine hundred and seventy, *Brillante* two hundred and fourteen out of six hundred and twenty one, and *Commodore* three hundred out of six hundred and eighty five. Slavers rounding the Cape thought themselves lucky if they only lost one third of their cargo, but they were able to make a profitable voyage if they landed only half of their slaves.

Profits of *General Espartero* and *Venus*

It was at this date that such superior Baltimore clippers as the *General Espartero* and *Venus* began running cargoes of slaves from East Africa to Cuba.

According to the report of the Havana Commissioners, dated 18th of September, 1838, to Lord Palmerston, the *General Esperarto*'s owner made a profit of seventy thousand dollars on her voyage that year.

Their report of January the 19th, 1839, on the *Venus* was equally disheartening. They wrote:—

> "With regard to the ship *Venus*, otherwise *Duquesa di Braganza*, we should state that the original cost, we understand, was thirty thousand dollars: and that the fitting-out and expenses of every kind for the voyage, including the value of the return cargo, was estimated at sixty thousand more, say altogether one hundred thousand dollars. The number of negroes brought back was eight hundred and sixty, and they are said to have been sold at three hundred and forty dollars per head, producing the sum of nearly three hundred thousand dollars, of which, therefore, two-thirds was net profit. So long as such returns can be effected, we fear that no efforts whatever will be effectual in suppressing the traffic, and certainly not while the dealers have only to meet such a system of corruption as prevades every department of the Government of the Island".
>
> Class A (Further Series) 1838-1839.

A Masquerading Frenchman

It was just about this date that the notorious Theodore Canot made his remarkable voyage as sailing master of the Brazil-built, three hundred ton brig, *San Pablo*. He found this vessel fitting out at St. Thomas, her captain being a very wily Frenchman.

Whilst she was fitting out, a rumour reached the harbour that a Danish cruiser was outside the port. This caused an instant bustle aboard the brig. During the night stores and provisions were tumbled aboard; sixteen twenty-four-pounder carronades were lowered into the hold; her kelson was lined, fore and aft, with round shot and grape; her magazine stocked with powder barrels: her tanks filled with water; and before dawn she was to sea with a crew of fifty five scoundrels of every caste, colour and nationality.

By six bells, 7 a.m., she was two miles away, waiting with her main topsail aback and a 'coasting flag at the peak'. A lugger shortly came off to her with six kegs of specie and several chests, which turned out to be full of uniforms: 'Gold-laced caps, blue coats with anchor buttons, single epaulettes and side arms', were distributed to the officers. Then the French captain made a speech to all hands, offering a bounty of one hundred dollars to each member of the crew if his enterprise turned out well. That night he discussed his plans with Canot. Except in the presence of a French cruiser, he intended to masquerade as a French-man-of-war, hoisting the Bourbon lilies and wearing the Bourbon uniform. Officers were to have double pay.

During the first few days at sea the *San Pablo* was painted and rigged to look like a cruiser, her guns were mounted, and her men well drilled both at big guns and small arms.

When twenty-seven days out the provisions were replenished at the Cape de Verds and a course set for the Cape.

Here a French transport was encountered, whereupon the royal ensign of Portugal was hoisted to the peak of the brig, and in case of accident guns were double-shotted, matches lighted, and the small arms chest unlocked. However after an 'amiable chat' in Portuguese, the Frenchman asked leave to send his letters aboard for delivery at Mauritius.

As it would have been risky to allow the naval officers aboard, several imaginary cases of small-pox were invented on the spur of the moment, and this information caused the transport to fill away on her voyage without further delay.

Ten days later the *San Pablo* anchored at Quillimane amongst a lot of slavers, which appeared to have been lying there for some time.

The French masquerade was now carried out in the most thorough manner. After a salute of twenty guns, the captain in full uniform called upon the Governor. Canot had orders to maintain naval discipline and routine aboard, even to striking yards and firing a gun at sunset. Next morning early the specie was landed in the Governor's barge. On the fourth day after his arrival Canot saw the expected signal flying from the fort, and during the following three days eight hundred negroes were embarked from a small beach, and nine days after anchoring, the *San Pablo* got under way again with a full cargo of slaves.

Now it was the recognised practice for each arrival to await her turn to load, and of the fourteen vessels lying at Quillimane, some had been over fifteen months waiting. The astute French captain had roused no suspicion of his real object owing to his man-of-war ruse; and his well-placed largesse soon won over the authorities and the slave factors.

All had gone according to plan, but now the tide turned with a vengence.

The French captain had contracted fever ashore and was soon out of his mind. After nine days head gale off the Cape, it was found that smallpox had broken out in the hold. Only the bravest members of the crew would enter the 'tween decks to haul out the dead negroes. They handled the bodies with tarred mits on their hands, but the contagion soon spread till twelve of the hands were down. Then the doctor and Canot decided to make a quick end of the infected negroes by the liberal use of laudanum. When the *San Pablo* reached the Equator, only four hundred and ninety seven skeletons remained out of the cargo of eight hundred slaves.

Soon after this Canot forcibly took calomel from the ill-furnished medicine chest of a Belfast brig.

Canot's next adventure was an encounter with a man-of-war schooner which overhauled him. Again, he showed his infinite recourse.

Whilst the schooner was speaking him from a position across his hawse, Canot put his helm up, rammed the little cruiser near her bow, and carried away her bowsprit and foremast. Then with the aid of his stunsails, managed to get away with only the loss of his jibboom.

How true this account of his encounter with a British war schooner may be, it is impossible to say—as there were no reports of such an affair taking place, and the cruiser seems to have behaved with a singular lack of seamanship and prudence in allowing herself to be caught so simply.

The following night the French captain died, and according to Canot was buried under a choice selection of the flags he had honoured with his various nationalities. He had, by the way, provided himself not only with Portuguese papers, but Spanish and Danish.

The remains of the *San Pablo*'s cargo was landed and housed in a hacienda nine miles East of St. Iago de Cuba, the brig herself being set on fire, scuttled and sent adrift.

Crazy Slavers

It must not be supposed that all the slavers in the Mozambique channel were of the Baltimore clipper type. Most of the Brazilian slave ships were typical merchantmen, ships and barques of from three hundred to four hundred and fifty tons, some American-built, others from the Baltic; these were better fitted for slaves than the fine-lined clippers.

The smaller Brazilian slavers were miserable craft, 'crazy old coasters' of every form and rig, but mostly brigs.

Portuguese slavers were to be found in every river and port between Cape Corrientes and Zanzibar, but Quillimane was the main slave mart South of Zanzibar.

Most of the rivers had dangerous bars.

In 1843 the American twenty-gun corvette *Concord* stuck on the bar of a river to the Northward of Quillimane. After being lightened as much as possible, she eventually beat over into deep water inside, but both her captain and purser were drowned.

The *Lily* Colony at Mauritius

In order to combat such superior vessels as the *Venus*, the *Columbine*, the new ship-sloop, *Modeste*, and the new brig sloops, *Lily* and *Acorn*, were sent to cruise in the Mozambique channel in 1838-1839.

Before leaving Spithead, *Modeste* and *Lily* had a trial together in smooth water, in which it was found that the former was best off the wind and the latter to windward.

It is possible that the *Lily*'s name may still be remembered at Mauritius, where she landed a number of released slaves, who all took the name of *Lily* and formed a little colony.

The brig served two commissions on the East coast. 1837-1839 under Commander J. Reeve and from May 1839 to January 1844 when she had three different commanders, Charles Deare, J. J. Allen, and George Baker—with but one first lieutenant throughout, George Alexander Seymour, a very smart officer.

***Acorn* in the Mozambique**

The *Acorn* was commanded by John Adams, late of the *Waterwitch*.

Adams after his first cruise in the Mozambique Channel wrote the following interesting letter to Sir William Symonds:—

> H.M.S. *Acorn*, Simon's Bay, 10th June, 1840
>
> Sir,
>
> I have been delaying from time to time writing you, until I could with safety report the qualities of the brig. The only vessel we met on our passage from England was a French twenty-gun brig, which we sailed round and round, much to his annoyance. We left this place for Isle of France, with a very heavy gale aft, and a tremendous sea; and ran ten days, during which time she never shipped a single drop of water, except the little from the ports.
>
> She was all this time under close-reefed main-topsail and double-reefed foresail. She has beat *Lily*, by their own account, two and a half miles in three hours and a half, dead to windward. On chasing a slaver, only courses up to windward, we made but one tack, going bodily to windward in three hours.
>
> The first shot cut away her jib-stay and head of the sail. The prisoners then on board told us she was considered the fastest vessel out of Rio.
>
> We beat her, under tipsails, going eight, with a nice breeze: she under a press of sail.
>
> Our trial with *Modeste* was short, but we had the advantage on all points.
>
> I experienced the heaviest gale I have ever been in a short time since in Mozambique: I may say, a perfect hurricane.

We were only fifteen miles from the shore when it commenced: our sails were blown to pieces. I never met a finer sea boat, and her working is quite perfect: she will stay as fast as the men can go from brace to brace. I consider her, as far as I may be allowed to judge, perfect.

She carries her long guns well: and only I wish we had four more.

If allowed, there is but one alteration I would make; that is, her main-topmast, either by putting in stools in the chains for more spread to the backstays, or taking off two feet of the mast, and giving it to the yard.

Going eleven knots, coming into this place under topsails and topgallantsails, in company with a fast American barque, (which we passed as if at anchor) to see the result, I furled the topgallantsails, double-reefed the topsails and found her go just the same.

On this point I have made repeated trials and find she likes low sail, which gives us the opportunity of keeping way with other ships with little sail, when they are under all.

We stow now six months' of everything, and fifty tons of water: not a thing on either deck. I have such confidence in her, I would sail, or work, against any vessel of her tonnage on the sea.

I have the honour to remain, Sir William
Your obedient servant
John Adams, Commander.

A Long and Successful Commission

In a long commission of four years and eight months, the *Acorn* proved very successful, capturing three thousand three hundred tons of shipping and liberating one thousand five hundred slaves.

For some time Adams was in charge of the Mozambique station and his enterprise and energy very nearly brought the slave traffic of those parts to a standstill. The *Acorn* herself captured the following slavers:—

The *Jehovah* on February the 14th, 1840; *Pancao* on June the 12th, 1840; *Quarto de Marco* on November the 24th, 1840; *Amelia* on December the 8th, 1840 and *Rahamana* on February the 2nd, 1841. Two of these were large ships, capable of stowing one thousand slaves apiece, and in one of them Adams found a very valuable cargo and upwards of forty thousand dollars in specie.

Three Arab dhows were also taken. Adams had two very capable and experienced lieutenants on F. T. B. Hankey, who proved very useful as a Portuguese interpreter in interviews and negotiations with the Governor of Mozambique, and William Austen, who, it will be remembered, brought the *Waterwitch* home in 1838.

The commission was split in two owing to the intervention of a coral reef, which knocked away four feet of the false keel and in January 1841 *Acorn* sailed from the Cape for Plymouth in order to be repaired.

On the 4th April, 1841, in 40° 52′ N. 18° 16′ W. the sloop fell in with the abandoned, seventy tons fruit schooner, *Mary Ann*, of Weymouth, and in spite of the heavy sea running Lieutenant Hankey managed to get aboard her. The schooner still had her sails set, but her rudder had been carried away.

By fine seamanship Hankey managed to get her hawser aboard the *Acorn*, which towed the lame duck for five hundred miles, whilst Hankey was fitting a jury rudder; he then sailed her home.

It was on her return passage to her station that the *Acorn* took the notorious slaver, *Gabriel*, in 5° 16′ N. 17° 51′ W. which capture I have described in another chapter.

On September the 28th, 1843, the brig arrived in Plymouth to pay off after her long and successful commission.

That it had been a happy commission was in great part due to her surgeon, T. Jewell, who for his kindness and attention to the sick was presented by the grateful crew of the *Acorn* with a handsome silver snuff-box, valued at twenty-five pounds.

Adams was deservedly posted.

In 1849 he was acting as slave commissioner at Loango, then in January, 1850, he was appointed to the command of the *Gladiator*, six guns, on the African coast; four years later he was commodore of the station in the *Scourge*, six guns.

In February, 1863, he was made a rear-admiral of the Blue.

He died on December the 17th, 1866, having entered the Service as a first-class volunteer in June, 1808.

Though he constantly distinguished himself as a midshipman in cutting out affairs during the Napoleonic wars, he made his name in the Service for the great part which he played in the suppression of the slave trade.

Besides the Naval silver medal with nine clasps, Adams had several medals from the Royal Humane Society, having saved no less than eleven persons from drowning at different times.

Bully Wyvill

Another very noted commander on the East coast was Captain Christoper Wyvill, known in the service as Bully Wyvill. He commissioned the twenty-six-gun Symondite, *Cleopatra*, in April 1842.

This his first commission in the treacherous Mozambique Channel was marred by an unhappy tragedy in a small bay to the North of St. Augustine's Bay on the West coast of Madagascar, which had the sinister name of Murderers' Bay.

Murderers' Bay

It was during 1824 when Admiral Owen was surveying the East coast of Africa that he lost two midshipmen, Bowie and Parsons of H.M.S. *Barracouta*, who were killed by natives on Murder Island in this bay, and afterwards buried by their shipmates on another island, which Owen named Grave Island.

In spite of Owen's efforts, the survey of much of the West side of the Indian Ocean was still very imperfect in the forties and British men-of-war were always reporting new reefs and shoals, which in many instances they discovered with their keels.

Whilst Rear-Admiral the Honourable Josceline Percy was fully occupied at the Cape, Wyvill was S.N.O. in the Mozambique Channel.

The Channel with its many uncharted reefs, its swift currents and terrific storms was a dangerous cruising ground and the river bars were even more hazardous to cross than those in the Bights. Then on the Madagascar shore the natives were not to be trusted, being very wild and treacherous. The *Cleopatra* was unlucky enough to get ashore in Murderers' Bay, but was kedged off successfully, but when Wyvill sent his pinnace under Lieutenant Milesworth with thirteen men to retrieve the kedge, the boat was attacked in plain sight of the frigate.

Lieutenant Milesworth was killed, and every man in the boat either killed or wounded.

The *Cleopatra*'s best capture was the Brazilian barque *Improviso*.

Mutine* Overtakes *Diana

Besides the little frigate there were several smart brigs slave hunting in the Mozambique Channel during the early forties such as the *Sappho*, Commander the Honourable G. Hope, *Bittern*, Commander G. Peel, *Helena*, Commander Sir C. Ricketts, and *Mutine*, Commander R. B. Crawford, *Snake*, Commander Thomas Bourmaster Brown, and *Arab*, Commander William Morris.

Mutine, lately arrived from the Experimental brig trials, soon proved her speed by outsailing both *Cleopatra* and *Helena*, and Crawford was still more elated when he overtook and captured the slaver *Diana*, which had previously shown her stern to every British cruiser on the station.

Wreck of the *Snake*

It says much for the navigation and seamanship of the cruisers that so few of them came to grief in these dangerous waters.

A notable exception was the *Snake*.

On her way down the coast from Zanzibar, having touched at Johanna, the *Snake* ran on an uncharted reef to the South of Mozambique on October the 29th, 1847.

The brig unfortunately got ashore on the top of the tide which was aided by the strong current.

As the water receded, she fell over on her side and started her butt-ends, soon filled with water and was in a hopeless case.

Up to this date she had had a most successful commission, having been out twenty months without a death.

Luckily the weather kept fine, the crew were soon safe ashore and bivouacking under tents made of sails and it was possible to save most of her stores.

But the brig herself was soon broken up by the heavy surf, which was pounding the reef.

Eventually the shipwrecked men were taken to the port of Mozambique and housed in the San Domingo barracks.

Besides the brigs, in the latter part of the forties two very beautiful little corvettes were sent to the East coast. These were the *Eurydice*, Captain Talavera Vernon Anson, and the *Brilliant*, twenty-two (razeed forty-two) Captain Rundle B. Watson.

The first steam sloops on the station were the *Rosamond*, commanded by Captain John Foote (late of brigantine *Fawn*), *Thunderbolt*, six, Commander G. N. Broke, *Geyser*, Captain Francis T. Brown and the little flagship steam tender, *Dee* under various lieutenants.

Expeditions Against Angoxa

Next to Quillimane and Mozambique, one of the biggest slave depots on the East coast was the fortified Arab town of Angoxa, which supplied the dhows carrying slaves to Zanzibar.

Though in Portuguese territory, the inhabitants of Angoxa would brook no interference from white men and towards the end of the forties, more than one attempt was made by the Portuguese, aided by landing parties from the British men-of-war, to subdue the place.

The port of Angoxa was defended by six large cannon and a force of some two thousand Arabs and negroes. The first combined attack upon it was repulsed with heavy losses although it consisted of two Portuguese regiments assisted by a large detachment from the Cape Commander-in-Chief's flagship *President* and the *Eurydice*.

The second attempt made in November, 1849, by the British alone had better results.

In May 1849 Bully Wyvill, in the thirty-six-gun frigate *Castor*, was appointed Commodore at the Cape and on the East coast of Africa.

As Wyvill was detained at the Cape by colonial affairs, he sent the *Castor*'s boats along with the little paddle-wheeler, *Dee*, to cruise in the Mozambique Channel in search of slavers.

The boats, consisting of the pinnace and barge, the latter a boat presented to Wyvill by the Imaum of Muscat during the *Cleopatra*'s commission, were hoisted aboard the *Dee* which was commanded by Lieutenant R. J. F. Crowther.

The first place to wood and water when bound to the Mozambique from the south was St. Augustine's Bay, South of Murderers' Bay on the West coast of Madagascar.

But a guard always had to be mounted on the beach as the natives were a most warlike and treacherous race and expert spear throwers.

After touching at St. Augustine's, the *Dee* made straight for Angoxa, and anchored at the mouth of the river on November the fifteenth, 1849.

The boats of the *Dee* and the *Castor* were then lowered, manned and armed and under

Lieutenant Crowther set off up the river with the intention of finding out whether the barracoons were full of slaves, the fort manned and on the lookout, and any slavers at the anchorage.

At this date it was the usual ruse of the Brazilian slavers to disguise themselves as American South Sea whalers, which were very numerous round Madagascar at certain seasons of the year. Then when they saw the coast was clear of cruisers they would anchor at the mouth of a river, and be supplied with slaves by dhows, which at other times took black ivory up to Zanzibar and even on to the Persian Gulf.

At one p.m. on November the 17th, the men-of-war boats, six in number, on rounding a bend of the river suddenly came into view of the fort.

Crowther noted with satisfaction that an Arab slave dhow of about one hundred tons was hauled close in under the walls.

The tide was rising and the boats pulled steadily in line abreast. Suddenly a red flag fluttered up the flag pole of the fort and a second later a tremendous tom-tom-ing commenced.

The boats managed to get within two hundred yards of the stockade before they grounded.

The fort opened upon them with round and grape to which the *Castor*'s pinnace replied with spherical case shot and the other boats with grape and canister. The shells of the pinnace bursting within the stockade, drove the Arabs into the woods on either side, from which they maintained a galling fire of musketry.

The fort itself was completely silenced within a quarter of an hour. The dhow was hard and fast aground but the gallant master's-assistant, Dyer*, in one of the *Dee*'s paddle-box boats succeeded in getting alongside, and clambering over her high stern set her on fire. Thus the dhow was destroyed, though the brave boat's crew had two men badly wounded.

By 5.30 p.m. the Arab slave-dealers had received a severe lesson—not a single defender remained, the dhow was burnt out, and the red flag on the fort lowered, but it was impossible to do more, for both Arab and negro had taken refuge in the thick bush, and Crowther wisely retired on the falling tide.

Boat Work in the Mozambique Channel

It was determined, however, to blockade the river and try and prevent the slave traffic which went on between the islands of the Premiera Group and the mainland.

At the mouth of the Angoxa lay the small island of Mafamale of some four or five acres in extent and protected to seaward by a coral reef.

The two *Castor* boats were detailed for this service; tents, two four-ton water tanks and two months' provisions, not forgetting the men's rum rations and several cases of bottled beer for the officers, were landed from the *Dee*, which then went off cruising.

This was the first example of a practice, which became very common in later years on the East coast—I mean that of provisioning open ship's boats for lengthy cruises on their own along the dhow infested shores where honest traders were rare to find all the way from the Persian Gulf and Suez right down to the Zululand border.

At first it was slave smuggling, then gun running was added, finally hashish, and anything contraband of value was shipped into the dark holds of the Arab dhows.

This first boating experiment with its camp on Mafamale and its lookout mounted at the top of the highest tree on the island, was a regular picnic for the young officers, bluejackets and marines. The days began and ended with a bathe. After the usual morning parade, cleaning and inspection of arms, etc., the time was passed in hauling the seine, salting fish for ship's use and collecting oysters from the rocks.

---

* Only a few months later Dyer was drowned through his boat being capsized on Quillimane Bar.

The cooks were always plentifully supplied with extras, but the favourite dish for officers and men alike was a sort of hot-pot or Scotch hodge-podge, known in the Service as a 'kettler', which consisted of a stew of everything available except fish, dished up in a large willow-pattern basin.

In order to watch the whole group of islands, the pinnace, armed with her twelve-pounder shell-firing gun and manned by a mid and twenty men under Lieutenants Campbell and Sullivan, cruised as far south as Casuarena Island.

On this island a cache of provisions was carefully buried, but a careless spark from a pipe set fire to the bush on the island and gave away the pinnace's presence to the natives on the mainland, who as soon as Campbell continued his cruise, came off and removed everything in the cache.

When the pinnace, returning in expectation of finding something to replenish her depleted stock, not a tin or the stave of a cask remained, and things would have gone hard with Campbell and his merry men had not the barge most opportunely arrived under Lieutenants Albert and Patterson.

Both boats then returned to Mafamale. Here also provisions, except for the inexhaustible seine fish of every hue and kind, were running low when on January the 5th, 1850, the famous brig *Pantaloon*, commanded by Lieutenant Hyde Parker, dropped anchor off the encampment.

The meeting was celebrated in truly British fashion. A sporting contest was got up whilst a grand banquet was being prepared.

It is interesting to note that the game was 'rounders'. Next the seine was hauled, by which means the brig's company received a most welcome supply of fish.

The day ended with the usual sing-song, in which the drinking of a pint of salt water was the punishment for not responding with a song when called upon.

The boats were seven months away from the *Castor* and for nearly three months their crews kept their health. This was considered to be entirely owing to the strict observation of the following rules:—

1. The boats were never allowed to remain in the rivers at night.
2. The men were never allowed to sleep on the mainland.
3. Every man, in spite of the heat, had to sleep in his blanket suit under a rain awning.
4. An extra rum ration with a stiff dose of quinine in it was served out daily.

Two men only, succumbed to fever, and after some very crude amateur doctoring had to be taken a hundred miles up the coast to the hospital at Mozambique.

Though the hardships of an open boat battling against wind and current could not kill a tough bluejacket, the deadly atmosphere of a Portuguese hospital soon proved fatal.

Second Cruise of *Castor*'s Boats

The next cruising ground of the *Castor*'s boats was the ninety to a hundred miles of coast between the Querimba Islands and Cape Delgado.

This was by no means a picnic like Mafamale as the crews were not allowed to sleep out of the boats, the islands being considered unhealthy—at the same time the rainy season was beginning to make itself felt.

Though it was very well commanded by, first, Lieutenant Campbell and, then Jones, second master of the *Dee*, this boat cruise did not have much success.

It was the first attempt to interfere seriously with the Arab dhow slave trade. Several dhows were boarded, but without an interpreter or definite instructions, the boats were unable to differentiate between the so-called legal trade and the illegal trade, and in the end no dhows were detained.

Hyde Parker of the *Pantaloon* and the Portuguese Governor

There were only three cruisers stationed on the coast to the South of Zanzibar at the beginning of 1850, and uncertain how to act with regard to the Arab traffic, the extent of which was hardly realised at this time, the captains of the British men-of-war still concentrated upon the hunting of Portuguese and Spanish Slavers.

The little *Pantaloon* under Hyde Parker, who four years later was killed at Soulina in the Crimean war, was the most successful cruiser. She captured the Spanish slaver *Philanthropy* with four hundred slaves and Lieutenant Campbell gave up his charge of the boats in order to go prize-master.

As showing Hyde Parker's wide-awake enterprise the following story is told of how he made one of his captures.

Hearing that there was a slaver about to load in Mozambique, Hyde Parker sailed into the port in order to keep a watch upon her.

After paying the usual ceremonial visit to the Portuguese Governor, Hyde Parker received an invitation to dine with that worthy. However he had managed to obtain secret information that no sooner was he comfortably at dinner than the slaver intended to ship her cargo and slip out of the port, thinking that the gun-brig would be doubtful how to act with her commander ashore.

So Parker pleaded important duty and declined the invitation. A few days later he was again invited to dine, again he refused. Finally a Portuguese official came aboard with a third invitation and an intimation that should he again decline it, his Excellency the Governor would consider the refusal an insult and report the matter to his government.

Whereupon Parker calmly replied that he would dine with pleasure if the Governor would promise that the brig would not be allowed to sail whilst they were at dinner.

The Governor having assented, the Commander of the *Pantaloon* sat down to a long ceremonial dinner.

Parker and the Governor were politely taking wine together, when an English voice was heard in altercation outside and a moment later an irrepressible midshipman burst into the dining room and with a curt bow to the Governor begged to be allowed to give his commander a message from his first lieutenant.

Then in a low voice, he murmured in Parker's ear:

"The slaver is under way".

His Commander immediately rose to his feet and still preserving his calm, asked politely to be excused on the plea of urgent business.

There were significant glances passed among the Portuguese at table—they well knew the cause of this sudden hurry.

As Parker pulled off to the *Pantaloon*, he saw that the slaver was making for the South Channel between St. Georges and St. Iago islets.

The tide was falling, sand banks and coral knolls lay in the slaver's path, but she had the benefit of a local pilot nor did she draw the water needed by the *Pantaloon*.

But Parker found that his first lieutenant had made every preparation. The brig was all ready to slip, all but the two forward broadside guns had been buoyed, so that they could be dropped overboard as the shallow water was approached; at the same time each bluejacket with a round shot on each arm had orders to run into the bows at the bosun's pipe, so as to bring the *Pantaloon*, which was trimmed well by the stern, onto an even keel.

By this means the war brig was enabled to follow the slaver in safety across the shoals.

Once outside, the *Pantaloon* was soon up to her quarry, which was captured and sent off to the Cape in charge of a prize crew.

The *Pantaloon* then ran back to the harbour of Mozambique and having recovered his guns, Hyde Parker called once more on the Governor and intimated that he feared he must report the case to his Admiral.

The Governor, who, in countenancing the slavers, had been trying by this means to increase his miserable salary, was recalled in disgrace whilst the Commander of the *Pantaloon* received his promotion.

Frigate or Farm Yard

The other two ships on the station, the *Orestes* and *Castor* were not as successful as the little *Pantaloon*. Between May, 1850 and February, 1851, Bully Wyvill in spite of all his keenness never made a capture.

After leaving the Cape, he ran up the coast to Zanzibar, where he anchored on April the 29th, 1850.

On sailing from Zanzibar for an extended cruise the maindeck of the *Castor*, which was only one hundred and sixty feet long, was as crowded with live stock as that of the contemporary Western Ocean Packet or Black-wall frigate, with fifty bullocks besides sheep and pigs penned between the guns.

The Imaum of Muscat had also given the captain a superb Arab horse, which after being nine months aboard the *Castor* would do everything but smoke a pipe. Though the crew had tried hard to teach the clever animal to smoke and chew tobacco, it was wise enough to remain a non-smoker.

An amusing story is told of Bully Wyvill.

One day on coming on deck he found a bluejacket stowing hay for the live stock under the spanker boom. After watching the man's efforts in that draughty spot to make the hay sit down, the Commodore held up his hands in astonishment, and calling to the Commander enquired:—

"What is that man doing, Captain Bunce?"

"Stowing the hay sir".

"Stowing hay? By God! Sir! What's his rating?".

"Able seaman, sir".

"A.B.?—not fit for it! send for the clerk, Captain Bunce, and disrate him, he can't make a haystack".

So the unfortunate bluejacket was disrated.

The Commodore kept his ship at sea till February, 1851, before putting into Mauritius to refit.

By this date all hands were on short allowance of both provisions and water, and in the midshipman's berth, recourse was had to cocoanut shells, both to eat and drink out of and, the unkind said, also to wash in.

Commander Bunce at Keonga

Though unsuccessful in his chase after slavers, Bully Wyvill relieved the boredom of the cruise by sending his boats in shore to attack barracoons or destroy dhows.

One of the first of these expeditions was to burn the barracoons of Keonga.

The boats were sent in under the fire-eating Bunce, whose valour was not to be measured by his inches—like the gallant Keppel he was a tiny little man.

In their eagerness the boats were too soon on the tide and through the lack of water were obliged to anchor and breakfast in full view of the town, thus the Arabs were given ample warning of their intentions.

After breakfast, the boats were pulled in until the grounded some distance out from the beach.

In order to avoid a wetting Commander Bunce ordered the tallest man in his boat's crew to carry him ashore. The result was scarcely dignified, for the huge bluejacket calmly tucked his commander under one arm whilst he held his rifle in the other.

Brandishing his sword so that it nearly took of his coxswain's nose and shouting out encouragingly:—

"Come on, my lads, come on! Advance skirmishers and fall in on the beach", the little commander kicked out astern as if he had been swimming.

The village of huts was defended by a trench and stockade. It stood on a slight eminence which could only be reached by a narrow track through the mangroves.

All hands were eagerly anticipating a hot little cut-and-thrust affair, but as the column of marines and bluejackets came doubling out into the open, headed by Bunce and his officers, the only defender that could be seen was the dignified figure of a solitary Arab.

The man held up his hand and the attacking force came to a halt. A palaver followed.

The barracoons were, of course, empty. The Arab leader had no objection to their burning the barracoons, but he declared that if they attacked the town itself, they would find themselves hotly resisted.

Of course all slaves had been spirited away into the bush; a vain search was made, the Arab himself led the force to the barracoons: these were fired, but Bunce agreed to spare the town to avoid useless bloodshed.

Castor and the War Schooner

Towards the end of her time in the Mozambique Channel the *Castor* became very sickly.

Out of her complement of three hundred and twenty men (less fifty attached to the little *Dart*, her tender), she had no less than one hundred and thirteen on the sick list, mostly with dysentry.

Though the doctor besought the Commodore to steer for the Cape, that keen old sea dog kept on making excuses, his last being that he had information of a large slave barque in the Mazemba river.

With all his boats away under lieutenants, his frigate must have been decidedly short-handed when the day came that a vessel with studding-sails set was reported coming out of the Mazemba river. The supposed slaver was heading straight for the *Castor* but it was eleven o'clock at night before she discovered the waiting frigate and by this time she was close aboard within hailing distance.

A rattle of blocks and clatter of voices were heard as she put her helm over and trimmed so as to avoid a collision.

Then above all the noise, rose the stentorian voice of the Commodore:

"What ship is that?".

A high squeaky voice replied:—

"De Portugae man war schooner, *Don Ramon*. What is dat sheep?".

With a mighty stamp of his foot the disappointed Commodore replied with a roar of smothered sea language, which must have sorely puzzled the Portuguee.

Then his anger began to rise and vent itself on his equally disappointed ship's company.

"Make sail and keep her away", he roared like an angry bull.

The *Castor* was too short-handed for this to be done smartly, certainly not smartly enough for Bully Wyvill.

"Shift topsails!" He screeched, but changing his mind before the men received the order, "Away aloft"; he countermanded his words and thundered:—"Beat to quarters, man the port guns, and fire four rounds of blank cartridge!".

At this moment the man-of-war schooner lay close aboard and almost becalmed on the frigates port quarter.

As the *Castor*'s guns began to go off in not quite such a perfectly timed salvo as the Commodore would have liked, screams came from the schooner, her halliards were let go and her sails came down with a run, and the squeaky voice in its halting English besought the frigate to have mercy.

But when the smoke had cleared away, there were no signs of the war schooner.

The captains of the guns were closely questioned. Could there have been a shotted gun fired? The most alarming rumours got about the station, for she was not heard of for ten months and then she was discovered five miles above the town in the Quillimane river, secured to a tree by a hawser and with not a soul on board but a half-daft negro.

Meanwhile Bully Wyvill had hurried off to the Cape where the Kaffir war took up all his attention, a naval brigade from the *Castor* being landed at Buffalo mouth.

The Capsizing of the *Dart*'s Cutter

In the middle fifties the cruisers reported no Portuguese slavers in the Mozambique Channel: but in March, 1856, great excitement was caused by the news that the famous missionary, Doctor David Livingstone, who had left Loanda on the South West coast as far back as September, 1854, had arrived at Tete and intended to make his own way down the river Quagga to Quillimane.

In April the little *Dart* arrived off the river mouth, and her commander, second master McClure, in his haste to get tidings, rashly attempted to cross the bar at nearly low water. The cutter capsized, two of the best swimmers managed to make the shore, but the rest clung to the over-turned boat.

McClure, in heavy blanket clothing, was the first to let go his hold from exhaustion, and when, twenty-four hours later, the boat drifted ashore twenty miles to the North East only three bluejackets remained alive. These men made the best of their way to Quillimane and reached the town on Saturday morning, four days after the swamping, and only an hour before the *Dart*'s gig under the gunner arrived to find out what had happened.

This tragedy, incurred on his account, was very much felt by the large-hearted Doctor Livingstone when he reached Quillimane on May the twentieth.

The doctor was eventually taken aboard the gun-brig, *Frolic*, and conveyed to Mauritius, whence he returned home via the Red Sea, Egypt and France.

Keppel Captures *Manuela*

Bully Wyvill was succeeded by that indefatigable pirate-hunter, H. D. Trotter, the old *Castor* still flying the broad pendant in the Mozambique, but Commodore Trotter had little opportunity for his well-known zeal, and the luck of capturing the finest and largest slaver on the East coast was reserved for that popular little Admiral, Harry Keppel, who, with his flag in the *Brisk*, Captain de Horsey, captured the fullrigged slaver *Manuela*, ex *Sunny South*, American clipper, on August the 10th, 1860.

Only the day before the steam-corvette had been into Mozambique, and Keppel had suspected one of the vessels lying there of being a slaver in disguise.

On the morning of Sunday the 10th, the *Brisk* was running North before a very light southerly wind under all sail. The eager Keppel proposed that the fires should be lighted and banked up, but De Horsey was one of those pious officers, more common in the R.N. in those days than they are now, who considered any unnecessary work as a desecration of the Sabbath.

In the afternoon a sail was reported.

"Take your glass aloft, Captain De Horsey, and have a look at her", advised Keppel cunningly, and before the *Brisk*'s commander was halfway up the fore-rigging, the little admiral had ordered the fires to be lighted.

The stranger could only just be seen about four points on the starboard bow.

As soon as the *Brisk*'s course was altered and the telltale smoke rose from her funnel, the lookout on the fore-top-gallant yard, sung out:—

"She's gone round without taking her studding sails in".

Sail aboard the *Brisk* was carefully trimmed amidst suppressed excitement; "and" remarked Keppel, "Hottentots and bandsmen, who on other occasions only looked at ropes, now laid hold of them with a will".

The captain at the masthead hailed the quarterdeck with the information that he feared the chase was too large for a slaver, being evidently an American clipper with a big sail plan and an unusual number of staysails, however the fact of her altering course was an encouraging point.

By 3 p.m. the *Brisk*, going eleven and a half knots in a fresh breeze, closed the chase sufficiently for her hull to be seen from the deck, the latter being almost becalmed. When the *Brisk* was near enough for her ensign to be distinguished by the stranger, the signalman aloft on the corvette reported that he noticed a man walk aft and bend a flag on the signal halliards of the chase's spanker-gaff; that another man then knocked him down, and substitued and hoisted American colours, only to have them quickly hauled down before they blew out properly by a third man. This fully confirmed the Admiral's suspicions and he ordered a blank round to be fired and the signal "Heave to" to be run up.

As the *Brisk* closed up under the slaver's lee with every telescope and eye fixed upon the latter's crowded decks, a white package was thrown from her taffrail into the sea.

"There go her papers!" roared an old West coast hand. "She's a slaver all right".

The *Brisk* ran through the stranger's lee within half a cable's length, but still the latter held on with her peak halliard's bare, and her sails full.

As soon as the corvette was under her lee bow, the quarter boats were launched and sent aboard her under Lieutenant Adeane, at the same time in answer to a blank gun, the slaver squared her main-yard, studding sails and all.

There were some anxious minutes aboard the *Brisk* until a small white ensign was seen blowing out from the ship's spanker gaff.

Then a voice hailed the corvette, with the news that there were eight hundred and fifty slaves under the stranger's hatches.

She proved to be an old Rio clipper packet, the *Sunny South*, of seven hundred and two tons, built at New York in 1854 and sold to Havana owners in 1859. She had sailed from Cuba on March the 5th, 1860, having cleared for Hong Kong under Chilean colours and the new name of *Manuela*.

As a slaver she was a most superior vessel, being valued at twenty thousand dollars and considered the fastest vessel belonging to the port of Havana. Her dimensions were:—

Length 154′ 8″, breadth 34′ 4″ and depth 16′ 6″.

On a slave deck seven feet high she had stowed eight hundred and forty six slaves without any of the usual over-crowding.

Besides captain and three mates she carried a pilot and a surgeon, her crew of all nations coming to forty all told.

She had taken weeks to gather her cargo together and was hovering about off the coast in hopes of stowing another fifty in her hold.

She was sent off to Mauritius under Lieutenant Burlton for adjudication, the Admiralty bought her, and for a short while under the new name of *Enchantress* she cruised against the slavers: finally she ended her days as a store ship for British cruisers at Johanna

Her capture may be said to have brought an end to the slaving by Portuguese and Spaniards on the East coast of Africa.

CHAPTER XXII

HUNTING THE ARAB SLAVE DHOW

Hoos! y'r jambiyah[1] is red! you have ze
ostreech fezzer![2] Aie! Aie! You are a man!

The Arab Sailor

AFTER many years of contending against the various 'dago' nationalities—the Frenchie, the Spaniard, the Portuguese and the many Latin and Indian mixtures of the South American republics, the Royal Navy found the Arab slaver to be a very different proposition.

Muscular long-limbed and lean, the Arab sailor was physically perfect, in spite of being badly nourished, often starved and always sun-baked. But above all things he was a man, a virile male, a great fighter, whose values were almost all primitive. Values like those of the American Red Indian and the African Zulu and Masai.

He excelled nearly all races in endurance of hardship and the stoical bearing of pain.

With the fatalistic outlook of a religious fanatic, he cared nought for death and he bore the most cruel blows of fate with an ever unflinching mien. In some ways he resembled the Pathan, especially in his cruelty and his cunning, but he was a more sober character than the tribesman of the Indian Northern frontier, more dignified, more unsmiling and with a very different kind of humour, though, like the Pathan, he keenly appreciated a good joke, and at suitable occasions was not averse to badmasti or rough horse-play.

Self-control was his supreme asset.

The true Arab always maintained his dignified calm and never raised his voice in dispute.

Nor can it be said that he was ever consciously cruel, though supremely indifferent to suffering, whether of himself, of his slaves or of his animals.

Though the wretched captives in an Arab caravan or Arab dhow had just as hard a time as those in a similar situation on the West side of Africa, and were treated with the same total lack of mercy and indifference to the sacredness of human life, yet there was just this difference—the Arab shared his food and water with his slaves, gave them of his own fare and when rations ran short, all shared alike, the man with the whip and the man in the neck-yoke and leg-irons.

But the Arab of the desert and of the sea was a very different being from the town Arab—the dirty, dissipated, sensual, apathetic degenerate of Zanzibar, whose only desire in life was to live in slothful ease, surrounded by his black concubines, with his stomach as his chief god, and his smallest wants supplied by his slaves.

But for the slave trade which even the most callous of Arab dealers admitted was a debasing and low business, the whole of Zanzibar's industry was in the hands of competent Indian banias in the worst days of the East coast slaving.

---

[1] The jambiyah is the crooked Arabian dagger.
[2] The wearing of the ostrich feather is the mark of one who has killed his man in fight.

These were the merchants, whose influence extended North to Bagdad and Muscat and South to the Portuguese towns along the Mozambique coast. They paid for Manchester and American cottons, Venetian beads and brass-ware, Sheffield cutlery, Birmingham hard-ware, Persian and Indian silks and dyed cloths, European wheat and East Indian rice with such products of the country as the ivory tusks of the African elephant, cloves, cinnamon and nutmegs from Zanzibar and Pemba, and gum copal, or shellac, dug up in immense quantities upon the islands and the coast.

The Arab Dhow

Being a nomad from prehistoric times, it is not surprising to find that the Arab's means of transport for the conditions of his life, whether for crossing the Arabian desert or the Indian ocean, were as nearly perfect as could be—I refer to the Bedouin camel, the Arab horse and the Bugala or coasting dhow.

The pure-bred "dalul" or riding camel would carry his rider one hundred miles a day for a week on end, besides supplying both the men and the horses in the caravan with—at times their only available sustenance, camel's milk.

The Arab horse, likewise, is the King of his race, excelling all other horses in brains, stamina and looks.

In the strength of the famous Kuhaylan strain, in the elegant deer-like beauty of the Saglawi, and the speed of the Mu'nigi, from which has come the English thoroughbred stock through the Darley Arabian, the desert wanderer was lucky in having an animal which was as useful a companion through life and as great a pet as an English bobtail sheepdog or a Scotch collie to the shepherd of the United Kingdom.

In the same way the better class of dhow was admirably adapted for the waters in which it operated, though it was built in the crudest fashion with no attempt at finish or polish.

Yet no less an authority than Admiral Colomb testified to its astonishing speed in the following words:—

"These vessels are enormously swift: they would tax the powers of our fastest yachts in light winds: the most speedy man-of-war, under steam and sail, has her hands full when she gives chase to them in a breeze. I have doubted of success, when rushing after them at ten and a half miles an hour. I have missed my quarry when I had not immediate means to go more than ten miles in the hour".

Though they were very lightly, not to say weakly built, and nearly always leaked, they were yet fine sea boats, and handled easily.

The largest of the true dhows were of the following dimensions more or less:—

Length 85′: beam 20′ 9″: depth 11′ 6″.

These carried poops with even stern windows, their decks were laid and they were, what was called grab-built, that is sharp-prowed with a long raking stem, the greatest draught of water being at the lower end of the cut-water, which was pretty well under the foremast.

These dhows were ballasted with sand or shingle, and sheathed with a composition of lime and shark's oil, which, hardening under water, made an anti-fouling as tight as new copper, according to Burton, and quite impervious to worm.

To the eyes of Northern seamen, the Arab dhow seeemed to be very much over-canvassed with their immensely long lateen yards and well bleached sails, which in the dazzling sunlight of the Arabian sea and Indian ocean showed like patches of snow upon the horizon.

These lateen sails were never reefed, a large and a small yard and sail being always carried. Nor was the dhow ever tacked, she always wore round before the wind and then hauled upon the other board.

Her ropes were mostly coir and her anchors of the creeper description.

In the early days the big one-hundred-ton Northern dhows, which were built in the Persian Gulf, or along the Arabian coast in the neighbourhood of Muscat, were generally armed with a small brass cannon of sorts, rarely larger than a three-pounder; this was supplemented by flint-lock muskets, though the foremost Arab preferred the two-handed sword and curved dagger of his ancestors, whilst the negro slaves, who always formed about a third part of the dhow's crew, often flourished assegais.

The big Northern craft, variously named Bateele, Badane, bagala or bugla (this last meaning 'mule', apparently because it carried cargo) had a very bad reputation along the African coast, for they were generally manned by the fiercest of the piratical gentry of Oman, called Soree pirates, who were as ready to prey upon their own countrymen as smuggle slaves, rifles or hashish, and were greatly feared by the more peaceful seamen of the Zanzibar district.

Yet they seldom put up any fight against the boarding bluejacket with his dreaded cutlass, though when chased they ignored rifle fire and never lowered their immense yards in token of surrender until a round shot had plumped into the sea near enough to splash their crowded decks.

They had a nasty habit, however, of throwing their slaves overboard when chased, especially when close in shore, when they hoped that the greater number of them would be picked up by canoes from the beach.

It must not be supposed that, when roused or put to it, the Arab was any gentler in his methods than the West coast slaver.

Early in the sixties the 'nakhoda' or captain of a large dhow with two hundred and forty slaves on board ordered each slave's throat to be cut, and the dying negro to be then dropped overboard in the path of the chasing man-of-war; luckily the boats got up alongside before more than thirty had been despatched.

Such men were dangerous customers to deal with, and the prize crew of a Northern dhow always had to keep their eyes open for squalls: for instance the prize crew put aboard a dhow by the steam sloop *Lyra* in 1861, were overpowered and thrown overboard, their officer being rendered helpless by being blinded and swaddled in a long turban cloth. Luckily the empty man-of-war cutter was towing astern, and though the Arabs tried to sink it with heavy stones, they failed to bilge it and the prize crew managed to scramble aboard and make their escape.

One of the neatest ways of capturing the Persian Gulf dhows from a chasing man-of-war boat was by cutting the yoke lines, which led from their very distinctive huge 'hurricane' rudders through outriggers on the quarters and so in board.

These, being fitted low down, could be easily cut by a sharp knife in the hands of the bowman.

Such a method of capture reminds one of the early West Indian buccaneer and his rudder-jamming trick.

The most numerous of the Southern dhows were the buglas, running from ten to one hundred tons, which were built all along the African coast and plied between the Mozambique and Zanzibar. Several hundreds of these worked up and down the coast, using the monsoons, so as to make favourable winds of them.

Horrors of the Northern Dhow Voyage

It is hard to imagine worse horrors than those of the Atlantic slave ship's middle passage, but they were at any rate equalled by the Northern dhow's one thousand five hundred mile voyage between Zanzibar and the Persian Gulf.

Throughout the long trip the slaves sat from daylight to dark, naked and exposed to the full rays of the tropical sun by day, and to the cold sprays and keen winds by night.

24. H.M.S. *London* — 1840.

[*Facing page 432.*

25.

The Opium Clipper *Psyche*, ex-slaver *Indagador*.
From a drawing by F. G. Hely.

In the National Maritime Museum.

[*Facing page 433.*

About sunset, the only meal of the day was served out—a mess of burnt, boiled millet seed—about a sailor's kid-full for a gang of thirty men, women and children, who squatting round on their haunches, dipped their eager fingers into the platter, rolled it into balls, and crammed these into their mouths.

Lucky was the slave—or strong—who managed to swallow three small balls; then the dish was empty, a wild scramble taking place for the last few mouthfuls, with little chance for the children or mothers with babes slung on their backs. Even the last grain or two, scattered on the dirty planks of the deck were fought for.

After this a drink of water apiece was served out. There were, of course, no sanitary arrangements whatever in an Arab dhow, which gave off a conglomeration of the vilest odours imaginable.

Boarding parties were often quite knocked out by the stench, which generally produced sickness and not seldom fever in hardened British seamen; nor could the dhows ever be washed out and purified sufficiently to get rid of the sickly smell, even loose articles of furniture being impregnated with it.

One would hardly believe it possible for human beings to survive such an existànce, but somehow or other about half the wretched negroes survived the long voyage to the Persian Gulf.

A Rough Slavery Time Table

The time of sailing depended greatly upon the monsoons. During March and April dhows carried slaves from Conducia and Angoxa to Mozambique, and from the Querimba isles during January and February.

From March to September the Southern dhows supplied the Zanzibar market.

The Northern dhows sailed for the Persian Gulf during March, April and May, putting in at Pangani and Brava for water, and generally running outside Pemba so as to avoid the customs.

Arabs attached much importance to propitious days in the calendar, and they prefer to start on a voyage at the full and change of the moon.

To show the extent of the Arab slave trade during the fifties, it was reckoned that close on fifty thousand slaves were bought and sold on the East coast yearly.

In 1859 at Zanzibar a tax was paid on 1900 slaves, about eight thousand were imported by the Sultan and his numerous relations, it was admitted that the duty was evaded on at least twenty thousand.

To supply fifty thousand slaves, five times that amount were slaughtered in the interior of Africa by the attacks upon kraals by the armed slave-traders, the adults being killed and the children stolen.

Arabs always preferred to catch their slaves young.

The piratical dhows from Arabia left the Persian Gulf with the last of the N.E. monsoon, towards the end of March.

They were laden with a cargo of what they were pleased to call slave food; besides millet, this consisted mostly of putrid shark, which was sold in the bazaar on their arrival at Zanzibar.

Then, when the S.W. monsoon set in, they began working the coast to the Northward, kidnapping men, women and children as far the Juba islands.

Their last watering place on the coast was Brava, they then headed for the slave marts of Soor and Muskat in the Gulf of Oman.

The Legal Slave Trade

Besides the legitimate traders, who carried ivory, gum, etc., there was the so-called 'legal traders' slave trade, which by the treaty of 1847 allowed all dhows, carrying the Sultan of

Zanzibar's pass and a Banian's custom's clearance paper, to carry slaves within the limits of 10° S. and 2° N. These were supposed to be domestic slaves for the Sultan's own use.

The Matapa Slave Barges

Very different to the dhows were the native-built river barges, which often ventured along the coast with the help of the monsoon. These 'matapas', as they were called, were most primitive craft, consisting of strips of bark, sown together with raw hide and roughly caulked with cotton and rags.

They were flat-bottomed and only drew a few inches of water, and like all flat-bottomed boats except the Thames barge, were driven by a plain, square sail or rather mat of straw, and hoisted by a straw halliard.

In the matapas one hand had to be kept bailing or they would sink. They were built, owned and run by negroes, who brought them from high up the rivers down to the coast, and ventured up to Zanzibar in the fine weather at the tail end of the S.W. monsoon.

Slave Catchers of the Indian Navy

It was not until the beginning of the eighteen-sixties that British cruisers began to attack the Arab slave trade with any real vigour.

Before this date the dhows and other craft of the Persian Gulf, Red Sea and Indian Ocean, which engaged in the slave trade, were left to the Indian Navy. This did its best in a service, which was most unpopular with all Indians.

The Indian Navy's fleet in the forties and fifties was a very meagre one, but it had a few small brigs and schooners, which, when they were not surveying or engaged in punitive expeditions, were sent up the Persian Gulf and Red Sea after the Arab slavers.

The smartest of these slave chasers were the following:-

Euphrates, brig,	255 tons, 10 guns, built at Bombay 1828.
Tigris, brig,	258 tons, 10 guns, built at Bombay 1829.
Mahi, schooner,	157 tons, 3 guns, built at Bombay 1834.
Constance, schooner	182 tons, 3 guns, built at Bombay 1838.

These vessels were commanded by a lieutenant, and officered by three midshipmen apiece, who kept all watches and did the duties of executive officers.

Though the Indian Navy was a fine service with lots of opportunities for the fire-eater, its officers were generally neglected and their many gallant actions were quite unknown to the British public; many of them, too, succumbed to the climate, before they had been able to rise in their profession.

Of these four small cruisers, the fore-topsail schooner, *Mahi*, was particularly successful in 1858 under Lieutenant J. G. Nixon.

On one occasion she sailed into Aden with three large bugalars as prizes.

Soon after this, Lieutenant Nixon sent his two armed boats' crews to the attack of an Arab fort, which lay three miles inland across the desert.

On the approach of the armed bluejackets under two midshipmen, Low and Dodd, the Arabs dragged a six-pounder out into the open and let them have a shot or two; but with a cheer the midshipmen led a charge upon the gun.

The Arabs did not wait to defend their gun, but retreated hurriedly into the fort, where, after the usual Eastern parley, they agreed to allow the boat party to search the fort for slaves.

The great iron-studded door was slowly opened, and in marched the bluejackets showing a bold front, though they had no idea what was in store for them. But the Arabs showed little spirit and allowed them to return to the beach in triumph with the thirty young female slaves.

The next adventure of the *Mahi*'s company was not so successful. One day as the sun set she found herself in chase of a suspicious-looking bugala in a strong breeze and under a press of sail.

Though the schooner occasionally yawed and let drive at the chase with her pivoting thirty-two-pounder, the latter held on, carrying her big lateen sail in the hard wind with the valour of desperation—it was evident that she was full of slaves.

The *Mahi* was also overpressed and as darkness fell, Lieutenant Nixon gave orders for a double reef to be taken in the fore topsail.

Hardly had the men laid out on the yard, before a sharp crack was heard and the foremast suddenly swayed aft, then down came both fore and main topmasts.

Luckily no one lost his hold—seamen were like cats in those days—and down to the deck slid the topmen by the backstays.

With a dirty night coming on, the *Mahi* was in a pretty mess, for the bowsprit had broken short off by the gammoning, and was lying alongside with the jibboom and all its gear.

The foremast was, also, found to be sprung in two places. The chase soon disappeared into the darkness. The war schooner, having salved the gear alongside, managed to make the lonely anchorage of Berbera Creek, where her crew speedily fished her foremast, sent out a jury bowsprit, and then proceeded to limp back to Bombay.

The Re-occupation of Perim

A year before this, the little *Mahi* had made history by hoisting the British flag on the island of Perim, thus claiming it as British territory, or rather, proving that we had re-occupied the island, which had been evacuated by its British garrison in 1799. The cause of the hurrying off of the schooner was the arrival at Aden of the French brig-of-war *Narcisse*, which had come from Zanzibar with orders to take possession of Perim.

A week or so later when the French brig dropped her anchor off the island, she found the British flag flying from a suspiciously new-looking flag-post, and the rakish-looking war schooner of the Indian Navy, commanded by Lieutenant C. B. Templer, lying at the anchorage, surrounded by bugalas; whilst ashore a row of tents indicated the presence on the island of fifty sappers under Lieutenant J. M. Greig of the Bombay engineers and a detachment of the Bombay Artillery under Lieutenant Billamore.

It was Brigadier (later Sir William) Coghlan, the political resident and commandant of Aden, who had acted so promptly.

The French also had providence against them, for the *Narcisse* had intended proceeding direct to Perim from Zanzibar, but having sprung her bowsprit and foremast in a squall, she put into Aden to get some new iron work forged.

The day, the 10th January, that the big French war brig anchored in Aden harbour, the *Mahi* slipped out with her orders, and on the 12th of January re-occupied Perim, whilst the British arsenal at Aden busied itself with forging iron bands for the Frenchman's damaged spars.

Another case of perfidious albion!!

The Cape Squadron in 1860-1861

The Squadron which that jovial little Admiral, Harry Keppel, had under his command for combating the East coast slave trade consisted of the beautiful screw frigate, *Forte*, of fifty-one guns and four hundred H.P. commanded by Captain E. W. Turnour, (Keppel's flagship); the *Brisk*, sixteen-gun screw corvette, two hundred and fifty H.P., Captain Algernon de Horsey; the *Wasp*, thirteen-gun screw sloop of one hundred H.P., Commander Charles Stirling; the *Sidon*, twenty-two gun, five-hundred-and-sixty H.P., paddle-wheel frigate, commanded by the gallant Captain R. B. Crawford, who, it will be remembered, in the middle forties had commanded the *Mutine*, chasing Portuguese slavers in the Mozambique Channel; and the twelve-gun brig, *Persian*, Commander Edward Hardinge.

All these vessels, with the possible exception of the *Sidon*, could sail much faster than they could steam, and rarely used their engines when there was any wind. As for the little *Persian*, she was the last sailing man-of-war on the Cape station.

"Pompo" Heneage

Keppel had as his flag lieutenant the greatest dandy in the Service, but an officer of great efficiency and gallantry; Algernon C. F. Heneage, always known as Pompo.

The story of his joining his first command is a good example of his gallantry.

The last few months of Keppel's time in command of the Cape Station was spent in visiting the West coast. Whilst the *Forte* lay at Sierra Leone, the screw sloop, *Falcon*, arrived in charge of her first lieutenant, her commander, Arthur G. Fitzroy, having succumbed to the climate.

Keppel, as was the custom, gave the vacant command to his flag-lieutenant, and he thus graphically described the joining of his first command by Lieutenant Heneage:—

"I appointed my flag lieutenant, Algernon C. F. Heneage, to poor Arthur Fitzroy's vacancy in the *Falcon*. She was lying in the river, where there was nothing above the surface to be seen moving but shark's fins. The new Commander was well got up, as was his wont, even to kid gloves. Just as his four oared-gig was getting alongside, one of the boys missed his footing and disappeared. In a moment Heneage unbuckled his sword, dived and saved the boy. He read his commission at the capstan in his muddy suit—a good beginning!".

Heneage, in command, was as particular about his vessel's appearance as his own; and he was wont to say in his peculiar staccato way of speaking:—

"I expect—my ship—to be—a burnished mass—of SPARKLING GOLD!!".

When he became an admiral in charge of a foreign station his lordly air of superiority amongst his compeers of other nationalities did more, perhaps, to maintain the prestige of the Royal Navy than even his daring and successful handling of difficult diplomatic situations.

Only once did he suffer a defeat of his 'amour propre'. When he was in command of the Pacific station, rooms were reserved for him in the best hotel in San Francisco, then a 'rip-roaring and wide-open' town. As the manager of the hotel was showing Heneage the rooms that had been reserved for him, the latter to his horror noticed a large spittoon in his sitting room.

"Take—that—beastly—thing—away!". He ordered, emphasizing each word in his usual precise fashion, which was so awe-inspiring.

To which the wholly unimpressed manager responded with true Western directness:—

"Wa-al, admiral, jest as yew wish; but, mind yew, if yew spits on the carpet yew'll hev' to pay for it!".

The Unfortunate *Wasp*

During the sixties there was never more than four cruisers between Cape Guardafui and Delagoa Bay; and, of these, one would sure to be wood and watering at the delightful island of Johanna and another, perhaps, repairing damages from the cruel fangs of coral reefs in the dock at Port Louis.

Admiral Sir Harry Keppel used to say that he did not give a damn for the officer who was afraid of getting ashore; and certainly the East coast cruiser who kept out in deep water was not going to catch many dhows.

Few ships, however, even in the Mozambique Channel, had such an unenviable experience in this respect as the *Wasp*.

She was the third ship of her name in the Service, the first being a fireship and the second one of the celebrated eighteen-gun brigs of the *Cruiser* class, which during her last commission in the middle forties had made a very good haul of West African slavers, when commanded by Sydney H. Ussher.

This *Wasp* under Keppel was her successor, a wooden screw sloop of very good sailing qualities but without much power under steam.

She was the first to give the name a bad reputation through her many standings.

She was followed by a gun boat of four hundred and fifty-five tons, which was wrecked on September the 22nd, 1884, on the North end of Tory Island, when only six lives were saved out of her complement of fifty-eight.

Her successor, another gun boat of six hundred and seventy tons, was lost in a typhoon with her whole ship's company of seventy-three officers and men, when bound from Singapore to Hong Kong. Several vessels were sent out to look out for her, but not a trace of the unfortunate vessel was ever found.

The third *Wasp* began her commission badly, for after leaving Sheerness on the 9th of June, 1860, she nearly got ashore at the back of the Isle of Wight, having over-shot the mark in the run to Spithead and found herself off Portland. This was due partly to fog and partly to bad navigation.

After beating back to Spithead she sailed for Plymouth, and when standing off and on abreast of the breakwater, very nearly went ashore on the rocks at Penlee Point. Commander Stirling then seized the opportunity and got rid of his inefficient master and also of a drunken lieutenant.

William Kennedy, afterwards Vice-Admiral Sir William Kennedy, K.C.B. was the ship's first lieutenant, and a propos of the incompetent navigator he told the following amusing story of an old ship mate, who, when, in command of a gun boat in the Baltic, had the ill-luck to get ashore when there was no leadsman in the chains.

The night before his court martial was due, he sent for a trusty old quarter-master, and, when the cabin door had been carefuly shut, he asked the man:—

"What soundings did you get immediately before the ship struck?".

"Me, sir", stuttered the astonished quarter-master, "why sir, I wasn't in the chains!".

"Silence, sir", returned the Captain in his severest tones as he proceeded to pour out a stiff nor'wester of grog, "remember, you are on oath! What soundings did you get?".

With one eye on the nor'wester, and just a little flicker of a smile in the curves about his clean-cut lips, the old seaman replied:- "ten fathoms, sir!".

Whereupon his captain maintaining his severest quarter-deck manner asked, as he handed over the nor'wester, "you are prepared to swear to that?".

Needless to say the following day the quarter-master's "ten fathoms" got his captain acquitted.

Beyond the gallant saving of a man overboard by Kennedy, the unluckly *Wasp* had no further adventures till she reached Madeira.

Like most officers at that date Stirling had a holy horror of steam, and when leaving Madeira he insisted on getting under sail in a flat calm, with the result that the *Wasp* drifted about until she ran foul of a Portuguese schooner at anchor.

The skipper of this craft roused out of a sound sleep by the crashing together of the two vessels, to the severe detriment of his own, expended the choicest oath in his vocabulary upon the culprit; but the *Wasp* soon drifted out of hearing on her way to smash up a second anchored vessel, which she remained foul of until two in the morning; and it was not until daybreak that she managed to crawl out of the Bay, leaving two vessels in a state of wreck behind her. Her own sides were also severely knocked about.

Luckily for the gun boat she was built of best British oak, and she needed to be, for in making Simon's Bay in the fog with the engine going for the first time since leaving England, she was run upon the rocks and began to bump so heavily in the long ground swell that large pieces of her keel began to float up alongside.

Nothing could be seen of the shore, though jagged rocks could plainly be distinguished a few feet underwater.

Luckily for the *Wasp* she was surrounded by a field of giant kelp which eased the force of the breakers.

In the midst of the hurly-burly, whilst the watch were busy hoisting out the pinnace and getting a kedge anchor ready, there came a piteous high-pitched shriek from below:—

"She's going to the bottom! She's going to the bottom!".

"For god's sake quieten the doctor", said the over-strained first lieutenant to the master, who was on the bridge beside him. At which the latter put his head down the hatchway and roared:—

"She's on the bottom, you old fool!".

Just as the captain was giving orders for the guns to be hove overboard, the *Wasp* slipped off into deep water. The next moment the fog lifted and disclosed cliffs towering high above the ship's mast heads.

There being then no dry dock at the Cape, the *Wasp* was ordered to Mauritius, where she was docked in the trou fanfaron at Port Louis.

As soon as she was repaired, the *Wasp* started slave hunting in the Mozambique Channel, whilst her first lieutenant went away in the pinnace with orders to seize all dhows with or without papers.

After a few weeks cruise during which neither the gun boat nor her pinnace made a capture, the *Wasp* headed for Zanzibar.

With the current setting over a hundred miles in the twenty-four hours to the Southward, and little wind, she found herself entangled amongst the coral reefs to the Northward of Ibo, and at six o'clock one evening she once more found herself ashore.

Though the chart gave five fathoms, at low water the ship was high and dry on the coral reef near a small island called Congo.

During the night she lay over on her beam ends and her crew were able to walk round her, but with a tidal rise and fall of thirteen feet, at the top of high water, she was hove afloat. However, in trying to thread his way through the reefs, Stirling put her ashore again in a far worse place.

This time she had a razor-back rock under her bilge, the engines were lifted from their bed so that they could not be used, and it was feared her back was broken.

With a list of seventeen degrees she strained so much that many of her beams were broken and water poured into her. Anchors were laid out, guns hove overboard, and provisions and water landed on the island which was little more than a patch of sand, a waste of scrub and a few odd cocoanut trees.

A Hard Boat Voyage

Whilst the ship's company continued to lighten the wreck—broiling work in the tropical sun—Kennedy, with an interpreter, set off in the cutter to get help from Zanzibar.

Leaving the ship on February the 3rd, 1861, he had the difficult task of beating his way four hundred miles dead to windward against the North-East monsoon in a twenty-five foot boat.

He was hardly out of sight of the wreck before the cutter nearly foundered in a heavy thunder squall, and he had to jettison all his water breakers but one and most of his provisions.

He soon found that he could only trust one of his crew to steer besides himself, and this was a man who had been shipped in Port Louis.

In those days a sailor's frock hanging out on the fore-deck of a merchantman was the recognised signal to all men-of-war that a man aboard wished to join the Service; and it was thus that the *Wasp* picked up a valuable seaman named John Sutton.

After thrashing to windward for two days and nights in a heavy sea during which the boat's crew were unable to cook anything and had to eat their pork raw. Tongy Bay was reached, where Kennedy and his worn-out men were glad to stretch their legs and dry their clothes, also a kindly Arab chief eased the commissariat problem by giving them a sheep.

Two days later Cape Delgado was weathered, and the boat worked into the Rovuma.

On the 9th of February in a storm of thunder, lightning and rain, Kennedy ran for shelter to the slaving port of Kiswara, where he was able to fill his water breakers and get a few cocoanuts.

Between Kiswara and Quiloa the cutter had a hard forty-eight hour fight to windward, during which time her crew again had to eat their food raw.

The next port of call was Kinvinge, as the cutter with her colours flying was run on the beach she was surrounded by a crowd of excited blacks.

Kennedy knew this was taking a risk, for the natives of this district had probably never seen white men before, but he was desperately in need of food and water.

However boldness paid. He marched his men up to the village and found a fine-looking, white-bearded chief enjoying his hookah in front of his house.

The chief was very friendly, gave Kennedy a bullock and offered him the loan of a dhow. The bullock was promptly shot and cut up, but, as the dhow was not ready for sea, Kennedy, after resting his men for thirty-six hours, preferred to go on without it.

The boat was next anchored under the lee of Tonga Island at noon on the 13th of February after a hard beat. By this time many of the crew were beginning to knock up from being constantly wet. Kennedy's sovereign remedy being rum and quinine.

After a night's rest the cutter set off again and ran into a flat calm. Her sorely-tried crew now had their worst experience; let me quote from Kennedy's journal:—

> "We were rapidly drifted by a strong tidal race towards a coral reef, upon which a fearful sea was breaking. The sails being useless, we took to the oars, but the broken water knocked them out of the men's hands.
>
> It was too deep to anchor, and we were helpless. The black rocks stood up like a wall, with the raging surf breaking against them. The sea was now going over both gun-whales, and our destruction seemed certain for the instant the boat touched the rocks she would have been dashed to pieces and every soul devoured by sharks, which crowded round us eager for their prey. Just as it seemed we were about to be dashed upon the rocks a breeze sprang up from off the land which soon, by God's mercy, carried us out of danger".

After this escape the cutter had a hard beat against the strong monsoon, until she was able to run in under the lee of the island of Monfia on the 16th. Here Kennedy decided to commandeer a dhow, which was lying at anchor in the bay, for the hardships were telling so severely on his boat's crew that he proposed to go on with only Sutton his coxswain and three other men in the cutter leaving the dhow to bring on the rest of the party.

The dhow's nakhoda was considerably astonished when the boat load of ragged, shoeless bluejackets, burnt almost black by the sun and bearded like Welsh bards, boarded his vessel.

Kennedy described his own attire as consisting of a flannel shirt, duck trousers and an old uniform cap. The nakoda had some reason for taking this disreputable gang for pirates, especially when he was threatened with a loaded rifle until he agreed to carry them to Zanzibar, although his dhow was really bound to the Southward.

After half a keg of dates, a little port and one of the cutter's two rifles had been passed on board he was induced to get under way, whilst Kennedy and his four remaining hands went ashore to fill their water breaker and to get some cocoanuts. The lieutenant also shot a monkey and a few pigeons to help out the commissariat.

The strength of the monsoon compelled the cutter to anchor amongst several dhows on February the 18th. Whilst they were getting under way the following morning, the enterprising Kennedy noted the following in his journal:—

> "While getting under way the dhow fell foul of us, carrying away our bowsprit; but during the confusion that ensued we boarded her and took a fine spar out of her to make a new one, then we sheered off and beat up between the mainland and Monfia".

That afternoon the cutter, heavily pressed and with two men bailing, passed the commandeered dhow, jogging northwards.

Anchoring under the mainland for night, Kennedy and his coxswain Sutton went foraging, their provisions being almost exhausted.

Knowing that the natives were hostile he left the boat stern on to the beach with an anchor out, ready to haul off at a moment's notice. Having no shot he loaded his only rifle with chopped up lead.

Whilst reconnoitreing the village about a mile inland he came upon a pair of fat geese, and getting them in line, knocked them over with one shot. This brought out a crowd of angry villagers, armed with spears, upon which Kennedy and his coxswain each seized a goose and made a run for it. Though Sutton fell into a bush of Wait-a-bit thorn and dropped his goose, besides getting his feet and legs full of thorns, the two maurauders succeeded in making the boat safely.

The cutter then sailed away with the goose being plucked over her stern and its furious owners brandishing their spears on the beach.

After the goose had been eaten, both water and provisions ran out, and when the Southern end of Zanzibar was sighted at daylight on February the 22nd, the cutter's crew had been without food for three days, and their water breaker was dry.

With a head wind, it took them all day working up to the island.

After a long chase and the firing of several shots to bring her to, a fishing boat was over-taken, which handed her over a large bread-fruit in exchange for a little gun powder.

At sunset, the famished crew of the cutter succeeded in making a landing on the island, and in procuring some cocoanuts.

On the following day at 4 p.m. the boat was beached abreast of the British Consulate after a passage of nineteen days. On measuring up his track on the chart, Lieutenant Kennedy found that he had sailed eight hundred miles. The dhow arrived twenty-four hours after the cutter, and her captain was handsomely rewarded. Kennedy admitted that he did fairly by the men. The lieutenant had left orders that at the least sign of treachery, the Arab was to be thrown overboard, so it was as well for him that he tried no tricks.

Colonel C. P. Rigby, The British Consul at Zanzibar

At Zanzibar the *Wasp*'s lieutenant and his boat's crew found themselves in the capable hands of that splendid officer, Colonel Rigby, the British Consul, who had done so much during his term of office to combat the Arab slave trade.

It was the case of the right man in the right place. He not only thoroughly understood the Arab, but could speak Arabic and many of the coast dialects fluently.

He was up to every trick and dodge of the slave traders, and was a perfect mine of information to the cruisers, who owed most of their captures to his help.

In this very year of 1861 it was due to him that such a blockade of the slave ports was kept up by the boats of the *Gorgon, Lyra* and *Ariel* that not a single slave dhow succeeded in getting to the Northward of Zanzibar.

It was said that he had emancipated a thousand slaves by his own personal efforts, and the Arab slave dealers were so incensed against him that his life was considered in danger, yet he did not hesitate to take his morning and evening walks through the poorest parts of the town.

High and low the respectable Arabs adored him; and where ever he went emancipated negroes, bowing to the ground, salaamed and blessed him.

He compelled the Sultan to respect the treaties and to restrain so far as was possible the inhumanity of his slave dealers.

When Colonel Rigby left for England at the end of 1861, there was an immediate brisk up of the dhow slave traffic with all its horrors, full advantage being taken of the inexperience of the new consul.

The Arab Jubran

Colonel Rigby's right hand man was an Arab named Jubran, whose job was to keep the Consul informed of all dhow movements, especially in the illegal slave traffic.

Jubran's life was in still greater danger than Colonel Rigby's, and one day he was kidnapped and carried off in a dhow to be hanged on the nearest uninhabited island.

The Consul on hearing of Jubran's capture at once hauled down the flag at the Consulate and told the Sultan that it would not be rehoisted until Jubran was delivered up alive.

The Sultan fearing the wrath of England had the man brought back, and ever after this Jubran redoubled his efforts against the slave traders.

He was a brave man and absolutely devoted to Colonel Rigby.

The Zanzibar Yacht to the Rescue of *Wasp*

Using his influence with the Sultan, Colonel Rigby arranged that the Royal yacht should be placed at Kennedy's disposal.

This was a beautiful little twenty-gun corvette of six hundred tons, named *Iskundah Shah*, and had been built of teak in Bombay at the cost of forty thousand pounds. She was commanded by an intelligent Arab named Mohamet bin Hames, who had been educated in England.

The old Sultan and Imaum of Muscat, Syud Said, had had quite a fleet, and he had even presented an Indian-built battleship, named *Imaum*, to King William the fourth, which was added to the British Navy and ended her days as guard ship at Jamaica.

In 1834 the Arab fleet at Zanzibar consisted of one seventy-four-gun ship, one fifty-gun ship, a twenty-six-gun frigate, a twenty-four-gun corvette, a ten-gun brig, and a schooner yacht.

When Syud Said died in 1855 this fine fleet was allowed to slowly disintegrate, and in 1872 a cyclone destroyed the last remnant, amongst which was a twenty-six-gun frigate named *Victoria*, a present to the Sultan from the Queen of England.

The idea of a cruise even as far as the Kerimba Islands came as such a shock to the ships company of the *Iskundah Shah* that her sailing date had to be delayed, Captain and crew being drunk and incapable for forty-eight hours; and, then, as soon as the crew had sobered up, they all went on strike for arrears of pay, which in the usual Arab fashion had gone into the captain's pocket.

By the time that the *Iskundah Shah* was ready to sail the *Wasp*'s lieutenant and his boat's crew were all more or less suffering from fever.

There was no doctor on board nor medicines, but Kennedy had bought a lump of opium, the size of a cocoanut, in the bazaar at Zanzibar for the use of the *Wasp*'s doctor. Bits of this weighed out on a pair of scales in the cabin were served out to his sick men, which, although it could not keep out the fever, relieved the pain and kept the fever victims in a state of semi-stupour.

To make matters worse, the North-East monsoon had given way to the calms and catspaws usual between monsoons. The Arabs too, were no handlers of a square-rigged ship, when they tried to tack her, they invariably missed stays and had to bear away and wear her like a dhow.

For ten miserable days the yacht knocked about in light airs, during which time Kennedy and his sick men subsisted upon opium and lemonade.

One night Kennedy was called to see one of his men, whom the coxswain declared was dying. He found him stretched out on the main-deck and apparently without life. As a last chance he put a lump of opium in his mouth, and the next morning to the astonishment of all hands this man was better and eventually recovered.

The Arab navigating officer was quite incompetent, and one night whilst the sick lieutenant was dozing in his chair, Sutton, the coxswain, who seems to have been the only fit man left of the cutter's crew, again came below and declared that he could hear the roar of the breakers ahead.

Kennedy thereupon took charge from the useless Mohamet, sent Sutton into the chains to get a cast of the lead, and another of his men to the wheel. By this time a line of breakers could be seen stretching across the corvette's bow:

The lead gave fifteen fathoms, whereupon Kennedy ordered the anchor to be let go and the sails furled. The next morning they found that they were off the mouth of the Rovuma river within ten minutes of the beach and sixty miles out of their reckoning.

It was not until March the 7th that the corvette came in sight of the *Wasp*. To the astonishment of Kennedy's fever-stricken crew the gun boat was observed to be lying at anchor evidently afloat and "all ataunto".

The Saving of the *Wasp*

It appears that a few days after the cutter had left, the cables were hove taut and the foresail, the only canvas still bent, was set to a strong breeze from aft.

The men were getting their suppers when the *Wasp* suddenly began to move, and after a series of bumps slipped off the reef into deep water, where she was anchored.

The next question was could they keep her afloat, for whilst on the reef she had leaked through every seam. However no sooner was she afloat than the seams took up.

The next thing to do was to get guns, shot, powder and stores on board again. By the time this had been done half the ship's company were on the sick list, the assistant surgeon and several of the men had died, and the senior surgeon was so broken down that he had to be invalided.

On the 20th of March the *Wasp* arrived at Johanna, here she remained until the 7th of May when H.M.S. *Ariel* arrived to escort her to Mauritius.

After being once more repaired in the Trou Fanfaron she was ordered to the Cape. Here a court martial acquitted her captain, officers and ship's company of all blame for the stranding, and gave them great credit for getting her afloat. She was then ordered home, and on her passage left St. Helena in company of the China clipper *Etheral* which she dropped astern and hull down by sunset, then proceeded to make a fast passage home under sail.

She did not reach Spithead without one last contretemps, for running up Channel before a sou'west gale she found herself one morning off Brighton and had to beat back.

CHAPTER XXIII

HUNTING THE ARAB SLAVE DHOW

(Continued)

"The English, one can discern withal, have been perhaps as brave a People as their neighbours: perhaps, for Valour of Action and true hard labour in this earth, since brave Peoples first were made in it, there has been none braver anywhere or anywhen".

(Carlyle)

The Success of the *Gorgon*'s Boats

IN June 1861, the old paddle-wheel frigate *Gorgon* arrived on the East coast to play a very successful part against the Arab's slaving dhow. At the time she was considered a very expensive vessel to employ in such work, as her sailing power was negligable and she consumed, what at that time was considered a tremendous amount, namely, twenty-six tons of coal in the twenty-four hours, which was reckoned to cost about twenty-five shillings for every mile under steam.

However, with the advent of the sixties, a cruiser was not nearly so important as her own boats. In this matter of boats the *Gorgon* had a great advantage, for besides a large pinnace and whaler, she had two flat-bottomed, shallow-draft boats, which in the days of paddle-wheel men-of-war, were known as paddle-box boats.

The usual cruiser's boat was a small gig or twenty-five foot cutter such as that in which Kennedy made his difficult passage to Zanzibar.

These boats were not nearly strong enough for such an arduous service on a stormy and dangerous coast, and though they generally managed to survive ship-wreck, returned to their ships in a quite unseaworthy condition.

Boats were generally sent out for a month at a time, and each boat was given its cruising area and place of rendezvous.

During the first few years of this arduous boat-service on the East coast, the boats' crews had a very rough time with little protection from the blazing sun of the tropics, the burning winds or the breaking seas. Indeed the interior of one of these cruiser's boats was compared to a floating midshipman's chest, being generally half full of dirty water.

Six weeks' provisions, stores, etc., had to be crammed into them somehow, and when they left their parent ship their gun-whales were often only a few inches above the water.

All sorts of rigs were tried by their enterprising officers and crews to improve their sailing, and the latten sail was usually found to be the most effective.

In spite of its many hardships, the life in the boats was very popular with bluejackets, for they delighted in the free, slack-disciplined, easy-going life with its chance, not only of prize money, but of loot.

Indeed the crew of a man-of-war boat after they had been out for some weeks resembled pirates rather than smart bluejackets with their red flannel caps and ragged shirts.

The looting when a dhow was captured, gradually became so bad that the Sultan of Zanzibar complained that our cruisers were plundering his subjects; so the order went forth amongst the anti-slavery squadron that every boat as well as her crew was to be searched for plunder at the end of her cruise.

Let me quote the *Gorgon's* assistant pay-master, W. Cope Devereux's account of such a search:—

> "Each boat is examined separately, the cutest corporals acting as searchers, beginning at a man's head and feeling to his toes.
>
> Jack's sacred stow-places are invaded by the hated hand of a Royal Marine; the little slit in his cap is pryed into, his jacket, clothes, bags, soap, shoes, etc., all examined. Then the boats undergo the ordeal. Rudder-heads are opened; the lining of the gun-whale separated; guns searched; keel-thwarts, bottom-boards etc., etc., are sounded by the aid of a carpenter's hammer and chisel.
>
> It is rather amusing to see Jack's spoil disgorged—the objects of his fancy disclosed to the eyes of Royal Marines, who laugh at and chaff him to his great annoyance.
>
> Silver chains, antedeluvian watches, dirty old rings, antique ear-rings and nose suspenders, and weighty anklets and bracelets, scimitars, daggers, dangerous flint guns and Birmingham pistols, necklaces and charms, silks and cottons, articles of Arab costume, from the concubine's silver-spangled skull-cap to her chemise; and from her lord's turban to his primitive sandals.
>
> Ivory, mats, bed-gear are all disgorged; and by the vast heap collected I should think that hundreds of Arabs had been divested of their finery.
>
> Having respectfully submitted to this ignominous examination, Jack rolls forward with his arms full of spoil, growling like a great bear.
>
> It is certainly rather a disgraceful ordeal to undergo by anyone, but Jack looks at it in a different light. Having undergone all the dangers and vicissitudes of boat-work, he thinks he should be allowed to keep all loot, whether money or jewellery, etc., collected during the cruise, honestly or dishonestly".

With the aid of Jubran, sailing on board the *Gorgon,* as interpreter, and the advice and information supplied by Colonel Rigby, the boats of the great paddle wheel frigate succeeded in very effectively blockading the coast, and in the course of three months, the old ship and her flotilla captured no less than eighteen dhows.

The first of these dhows fell to the *Gorgon* herself.

On the morning of the 19th of August, 1861, this dhow was seen to be ashore on the reef to the northward of Querimbo Island. Captain Wilson boarded her himself. She was found to be fitted for the slave trade with a crew of twenty-five Arabs, but with no colours or papers.

Her Nakoda declared that he had been chased ashore in the dark by a British cruiser, supposed to be the *Penguin.*

The dhow had been bound to Cormoro with one hundred slaves, which has been shipped at Conducia. These had been landed on the island.

When Captain Wilson boarded her, attempts were being made to refloat her, but the dhow which measured one hundred and seventy two tons was found to be badly injured by the reef and Wilson had her burnt.

The second dhow was a Persian Gulf vessel of one hundred and fifty six tons. She was found lying at anchor on the 3rd of August off Lindey river. This dhow was manned by twenty Joasme Arabs, and was fitted for slaves with slave food on board; she also was destroyed.

On the 9th of August, whilst cruising off Kiswara Harbour two of the *Gorgon's* boats gave chase to a couple of dhows.

After an hour's run the dhows lowered their sails and were boarded. Neither had papers nor colours, and both were fitted for the slave trade. The first with a crew of fifteen, well armed Arabs, and the second with twelve.

The first dhow was destroyed and the second abandoned in a sinking state.

On the 24th of August, G. Harris, the second master of the *Gorgon,* received information from Colonel Rigby that one of the Sooree piratical dhows was going to pick up a cargo of slaves from the coast about seven miles north of Zanzibar.

As soon at it was dark Harris sailed out of Zanzibar Harbour accompanied by one of the Consulate boats, which could identify the dhow.

About midnight a dhow running out to sea to the northward was hailed to heave to, and as she paid no attention Harris determined to board. Her crew, however, resisted with drawn swords and for two or three minutes the fighting was sharp. The Arabs were then driven overboard.

The dhow proved to be a Persian Gulf pirate, a vessel of one hundred and sixty nine tons. Seventeen slaves were found hidden away aboard, and it was known that boats were expected with another one hundred and fifty slaves. She also was destroyed.

The next dhow was captured by Lieutenant Harvey at Port Wangekee on Pecubu Island on the 8th of September. She was a big dhow of two hundred tons with a crew of twenty Sevoodi Arabs. She was all ready to take on slaves with their food aboard, but with no papers or colours. She was destroyed.

Dhow number seven was caught off Mombasa on the 14th of September, waiting for slaves. Her burden was sixty-six tons, and, being considered unfit for the voyage to the port of adjudication, she was scuttled.

On the 18th of September the *Gorgon's* pinnace under Lieutenant Ross and whale-boat under acting-sub-lieutenant Price stood into the Melinda anchorage about 3 p.m. to replenish their water breakers.

Lying in the roadstead were three dhows, and a fourth, a small one, was seen to shove off from the shore crowded with some forty or fifty men armed with muskets.

As the two boats sailed in between the anchored dhows and the dhow coming off from the shore, the crews of the former were seen to jump overboard and swim ashore.

As the boats approached the smaller dhow the Arabs aboard her opened fire, to which the howitzer of the pinnace replied with canister and grape, aided by musketry from the whale-boat.

After sustaining a running fight for quite a while those Arabs, who had escaped being killed and wounded, jumped overboard from the dhow and swam ashore. The boats then took possession of the four dhows in spite of a heavy fire from the shore.

A negro was found in the small dhow, who said that one hundred and eighty slaves had been landed so that the dhows, which were bound to the Persian Gulf, could be cleaned and watered.

Previous to this affair, on the 29th of August, Ross and Price captured the notorious Sultan of Angoxa who was suspected of having instigated the murder of the *Lyra's* boat's crew in the Angoxa river two years before.

When intercepted by the *Gorgon's* boats between Port Pangane and Mahatto Island this slaver and pirate was busy stealing negroes.

He had three dhows which during an hour's chase exchanged shots with the boats, but made no resistance on being boarded.

On the old Sultan laying claim to the dhows he was asked to show passports or papers, but he could only produce an envelope addressed to Queen Victoria.

Two revolvers marked with the broad arrow were found upon him. These probably belonged to the *Lyra's* murdered men.

When the three dhows were captured it was about 5 p.m. and with the wind increasing and a heavy sea running, Lieutenant Ross decided to anchor the boats and the captured dhows about two miles to the South of Mahatto Island.

As the wind increased the boats became surrounded by heavy breakers, and began to drag their anchors. The dhows with their indifferent creepers could not be brought up and, after drifting for nearly two miles, were in great danger of being driven upon a reef to leeward, upon which a tremendous surf was breaking.

As the only chance of saving their lives. Lieutenant Ross removed the slaves and crews from two of the dhows into the 3rd, whose nakoda declared that he knew a passage through the reef.

The other two dhows were then burnt at about 6 p.m., and whilst the pinnace and whale-boat passed an anxious night at anchor in a wild turmoil of broken water, the third dhow managed successfully to thread the reef and escape destruction.

The fourteenth dhow to be captured was intercepted on her way to Quiloa for a slave cargo on the 6th of September. She was a vessel of one hundred and nine tons with a crew of thirteen Arabs and plenty of slave food on board, but without papers or colours. She was burnt.

The fifteenth dhow was chased for six miles off the Wasseem reefs on the 11th of September. Finally her crew ran her ashore amongst the mangroves and managed to get away inland with about sixty slaves.

Four hours later, at 6 p.m., another dhow crowded with negroes was sighted and chased. She also ran ashore amongst the mangrove bushes, and before the *Gorgon's* boat could get up her crew and slaves had disappeared into the interior.

The seventeenth capture was a large matapa of seventy-five tons, which was sighted by the *Gorgon's* pinnace then in charge of Mr. Hanson, the bo'sun. This was on the 13th of September.

When summoned to heave to she opened fire upon the pinnace with slugs and jingal balls. She also succeeded in landing her slaves safely after running ashore amongst the mangroves. But the matapa was burnt.

At 8 p.m. on October the 3rd two of the *Gorgon's* boats were cruising off Shella Point when they saw a dhow heading in for the land.

The dhow managed to make the beach before the boats came up, and her Arab crew could plainly be seen with drawn swords driving their slaves overboard. The boats however, were in time to prevent thirty-two male slaves and twelve females from leaving the dhow, which was refloated and brought alongside the *Gorgon* in Kuryhoo Roads.

Luckily the slaves were removed into the cruiser for the dhow, being leaky and unattended, sank where she was anchored.

I have given this record with some detail, because it was perhaps the greatest success in such a short period that the Royal Navy ever had in its long years of strife with the Arab slaver.

A Hot Action

The *Gorgon's* boats were lucky in having no casualties, but it must not be supposed that the Arab could not be put up as stern a fight as the Spaniard or the Portuguee. Indeed from the beginning of the sixties the Zanzibar and Arabian coasts gave the young Naval officer and bluejacket many a chance to prove his gallantry and gain promotion.

Let me contrast the experiences of the gun-boats *Griffon* and *Wasp,* the first on the West coast and the latter on the east.

In 1865 the *Griffon,* Commander Perry, paid off from the West Coast having taken six large fully equipped slavers, including the clippers *Catilina* and *Venus,* which, having failed to run the blockade, surrendered without resistance.

At about the same date, the 12th of May to be exact, the pinnace and cutter of the *Wasp* which had returned to the East coast under Captain W. Bowden, chased a large Northern dhow some eight or nine miles from the port of Zanzibar. On the boats overtaking the slaver a desperate fight took place. The Arab crew of seventy men refused to surrender, and when the boats' crew had at last obtained possession of the dhow's deck, the greater number of the Arabs jumped into their stern boat and got safely away, leaving behind them three dead and thirteen prisoners, besides two hundred and eighty three slaves.

The following returns of the Naval casualties will show how fierce was the resistance.

John New, coxswain of the pinnace, the first man to board the dhow, spear wound in his chest, and large blood-vessel divided. Killed.

Charles C. Rising, lieutenant in command of the boats, sword wound in neck, very severe; All muscles left side of neck divided; sword wound of left hand, very severe; hand amputated, except little finger and thumb; sword wound of right, thigh severe and dangerous.

Charles B. Theobald, lieutenant, spear wound of left wrist very severe; spear went through joint.

William Wilson, midshipman, sword wound of back, severe; sword wound of right wrist, severe; some tendons and nerves divided.

Oliver Norville, second captain of the foretop, spear wound of abdomen, penetrated and very dangerous.

John Cramer, captain of the after-guard, spear wound through fore-arm very severe.

John Williams, A.B., sword wound of fore-arm, severe; spear wound of chest, slight.

Charles Treganna, ordinary seaman, spear wound of back, slight.

William Springall, sail-makers crew, spear wound of fore-arm, slight.

The Difficulties of the Cruisers

Whilst their boats worked the coast on either side of the great slave focal point, Zanzibar, the cruisers made many vain attempts in the early sixties to capture larger game: but a gun boat steaming eight knots had not much chance against the slave steamers, which came out from Cadiz and Marseilles and were able to steam fifteen knots.

In June, 1864, two of these racing steamers successfully got away from Mozambique with full cargoes of black ivory.

Another irritating factor in the life of the cruisers was the continued immunity of those ships and dhows which hoisted the French flag and pretended to carry indentured black labourers to the French Islands.

Though this French traffic in slaves known as the engagées system, practically ceased in 1862, as far as Reunion was concerned the French continued to ship large quantities of negroes to Mayotta and Nossi-Be under the cloak of the term *Free labour immigration*, the recruiting for which was in the same blood-stained hands as that for Zanzibar and the Arabian Gulf.

Even when the United States of America at length agreed to the system of mutual search, France alone of the nations held out against it. Though the French had more men-of-war based in the Mozambique Channel than Great Britain they allowed every illegal trader, even the most piratical of Northern dhows, to use the tri-colour for protection. And not only did they allow their own flag to be thus scandalously abused but their agents competed with the half-cast Portuguese and the Arab slave dealer, and played their part in de-populating thousands of miles of Africa.

The Cormoro Island were their headquarters and chief slave mart, and here British officers had to shut their eyes to the presence of French slavers lying immune from search within a few cable lengths of their own ships.

The French engagées system was no whit less cruel than the Arab slave trade, whether in its recruiting or in its conveyance of negroes.

One of those pioneer missionaries, who shared Livingstone's labours, the Reverend Horace Wallar, in giving evidence before the Select Committee of the House of Commons in 1871 testified as follows:—

> "I have seen a French ship lying at the Island of Johanna crammed with slaves, with one of our men-of-war within a cable's length of her, and the poor creatures jumping overboard and swimming to us to protect them; and the Arabs would say to us, "there is a French ship full of slaves, if it was one of our ships you would burn her directly; why do you not go and take her?"

Another scandal in the eyes of the British officers was the Zanzibar legal trade. The southern limit of this trade was Quiloa, but most of the legal-trade dhows obtained their cargoes at Quillimane, Angoxa, Mozambique, Ibo and other Southern ports belonging to the Portuguese, and only called at Quiloa to obtain the necessary pass and to make up their full cargo, the Custom House tax being only paid on the new additions.

Here is an experience of Captain Sulivan when in command of the eleven-gun, screw-sloop *Pantaloon* in 1866:—

One morning whilst the *Pantaloon* was lying at Zanzibar, Jumah, the ship's interpreter, knocked at the Captain's cabin door and, slipping off his sandals before entering, exclaimed:—

"My master, spose you come on deck me show you something".

"What, Jumah?"

"One big dhow commeen in full nigger".

"Well, what's the use, Jumah, we can't take her here".

"No, not now, but spose you met her yesterday you take her, for she got more slaves than licence".

Captain Sulivan going on deck with the interpreter was just in time to see a large dhow sail close by the *Pantaloon's* stern, with her upper bamboo deck so crowded with squatting negroes that not an inch of planking was visible.

As she sailed by every black face turned towards the man-of-war as if beseeching her aid, but aft on her poop a number of white-clad Arabs raised a derisive cheer, and a man, who was evidently her nakoda, called out amidst laughter:—

"Why you no come and take us, are you afraid?" At which Jumah roared back "We catch you another day". To this the Arab returned "I got lots of slaves on board, tell the captain to come and see". Which sally produced more laughter on the poop of the dhow.

The great yard of the slaver was than lowered as she rounded to and anchored within pistol shot of the *Pantaloon.* An hour later her slaves were being exhibited in the Zanzibar slaver market.

Some Statistics in the Sixties

It might be thought that with the advent of the faster cruisers the Arab dhow trade could no longer continue to survive, yet one has to admit that notwithstanding the large number of men-of-war boats patrolling every yard of the coast from the Mozambique Northwards and as many as seven screw corvettes and gun boats stationed at the most important trade centres, the Arabs contrived somehow, to keep up their imports of slaves into Arabia and Persia.

The trade tended to shift further and further North along the coast of Africa as the slave caravans, working the interior, emptied the villages further South.

By 1867, the task of combating the Arabian slave trade was entirely in the hands of the Commodore of the East India Squadron, The Cape command confining itself to the South and West coasts of Africa.

In July, 1867, Sir Leopold G. Heath, K.C.B. (Commodore second-class) was appointed to the East India Station with his broad pennant in the old "Forte" and the following ships under his command:—

Cossack, 16-gun screw corvettte, 1,296 tons, 250 H.P., Captain John E. Parrish.
Dryad, 4-gun screw sloop, 1,086 tons, 300 h.p., Commander P. H. Colomb.
Nymph, 4-gun screw sloop, 1,081 tons, 300 h.p., Commander John C. Wells.
Daphne, 4-gun screw sloop, 1,081 tons, 300 h.p., Commander G. L. Sulivan.
Star, 4-gun screw gun vessel, 695 tons, 200 h.p., Commander S. de Kantzow.
Bullfinch, 3-gun double screw gun vessel, 663 tons, 160 h.p., Commander E. F. Lodder.

In his evidence before the Select Committee Commodore Heath gives the following statistics:—

Total captures in 1867 18 dhows and 431 slaves emancipated.

This was a happy year for the slave traders as most of the squadron were employed in Annesley Bay in the expedition against Abyssinia.

Total captures for 1868 were 66 dhows of 7,233 tons from which 1,097 slaves were emancipated.

Total captures for 1869 were 32 dhows of 3,431 tons from which 1,117 slaves were emancipated.

Out of 400 dhows boarded by our cruisers and their boats in the spring of 1868 only 11 carrying 958 slaves could be detained.

The largest capture being 380 slaves in a dhow captured by the *Wasp.*

During their commissions the *Daphne* and the *Nymph* captured sixty slave dhows.

The *Star* was also very successful.

These figures may be compared with those of the ships in the early sixties. We have already mentioned the success of the *Gorgon.*

The *Ariel,* 9-gun screw sloop, between 1862 and 1864, captured eighteen slavers. The *Lyra,* 7-gun screw sloop of 488 tons, 60 h.p., Captain Robert Augustus Parr, paid off in April 1868, having captured eleven dhows in a fifty-two-month commission.

As some guide to the extent of the slave trade in the late sixties, the Sultan of Zanzibar received two hundred and seventy thousand dollars from slave taxes between 1867 and 1868.

The missionaries, Doctors Kirk and Livingstone, reckoned that for every slave delivered safe at Zanzibar, four or five slaves lost their lives on the journey.

From the Arab habit of running their dhows ashore through the surf, when chased, great numbers of slaves were also drowned in the breakers.

Rescue Work in the Surf

In chasing slaved dhows which were running up the coast to the Northward from Zanzibar, the cruisers had great difficulty in preventing the nakodas from running ashore and driving their slaves inland where they could not be got at.

This the nakodas of the Northern dhows never hesitated to do, in spite of the very heavy surf in which all weak and sick slaves were invariably drowned and the dhow itself reduced to match-wood in a very few hours.

As a kidnapped slave cost nothing and a bought one only cost a few yards of calico, the loss of a few slaves in the surf was a matter of indifference, whilst a dhow of between one hundred and thirty and one hundred and fifty tons, capable of carrying one hundred and fifty slaves, could be bought for less than a thousand dollars, thus the loss of the vessel was also a small item in a slave trader's budget.

Nevertheless to run one's ship ashore in a very heavy surf demanded considerable courage, especially as the slave crew generally had to remain to the last and drive the slaves overboard at the sword point, and thus had to brave the surf themselves and risk being drowned.

One of the tricks of the Arabs to frighten the slaves into leaving the hold of the dhow for the shore, was to point to the smoke coming from the funnel of the chasing cruiser and say:—

"White man is lighting a fire to cook nigger with". By this means the terror stricken negroes—the greater number of them mere children—were persuaded to risk their lives in the boiling surf rather than remain aboard the dhow.

The Cruise of the *Daphne* off the Somali Coast

On October the 21st, 1867, the *Daphne,* commanded by that very experienced officer, Commander G. L. Sulivan, steamed out of Zanzibar on her passage to Bombay. When thirty miles off the coast and outside the coasting route of the dhows, she steered North until she was opposite Brava, she was then run onto the coast and anchored in the path of the dhows on the 24th.

The first dhow to come along was a legal trader from Zanzibar, with the Sultan's sister on board and about a dozen domestic slaves.

She was, of course, exempt from capture.

On the following day another legal trader was intercepted, but aboard her two boys were discovered who had been kidnapped from Pemba Island. She was, therefore, detained and subsequently condemned.

Out of the two thousand dhows which sailed to the Northward from Zanzibar at the beginning and close of the monsoon, practically every dhow had children aboard who had been kidnapped and were afterwards sold in Arabia, Persia and even India. But it was very difficult for the cruisers to gain evidence of these kidnappings, so the greater number of these dhows had to be allowed to pass.

The true slave dhows had no means of escaping the waiting cruiser, owing to both wind and current setting them down towards her as she lay to the Northward in their course, with her boats spread out on either hand like a spider awaiting the flies.

On October the 28th, the first slave dhow was seen approaching from the Southward. As the cruiser steamed towards her, the dhow, which was close inshore put her helm up and ran for the beach.

Directly she took the ground, the heavy breakers made a clean sweep over her and she was a wreck in a few minutes.

From the *Daphne,* which ventured in until she was only just outside the first line of breakers, the black masses of the unfortunate slaves could be seen struggling in the surf, and finally in small groups crawling up the beach into the hilly country beyond.

As it was evident that numbers of blacks were drowning in the surf, Captain Sulivan ordered his life-boat to be manned and lowered. She was a beautiful five-oared boat, built by White of Cowes, and Sulivan took charge of her himself.

> "I intended", he wrote, "if the bar appeared too dangerous to cross; not to risk the lives of the crew; and I confess after my experience I never would allow a boat to attempt it again on this part of the coast; it did not look so bad outside. We gave way and at this time we could see many of the slaves on the beach and in the water.
>
> Suddenly we found ourselves amongst the breakers. The sea struck us abaft, and washed clean over the boat from stem to stern; and she must have broached-to if it had not been for the weight of two of us on the yoke line. (Sulivan had Breen, a mishipman, and Richards, the carpenter, in the stern sheets with him.)
>
> Then another sea struck us, and then another, washing over the whole length of the boat and everyone in it; but owing to her admirable constuction, the seas went out over the bows, leaving only a few inches of water in her. In a few minutes we were over the bar, and inside it was comparatively smooth. But how was it possible ever to get out again? was the first thought that struck me as I never saw worse-looking breakers, not even at Buffalo Mouth or Algoa Bay. They extended the whole length of the coast for many miles, and from the inside we saw what they really were".

Sulivan was too late to save many of the slaves, but he found seven children, of from five to eight years of age, lying on the edge of the surf, too weak to crawl away into the bush. One or two of them were still in the position in which they had had to crouch for so many days aboard the dhow, that is, with knees doubled up against their faces. It was a week before these poor mites could stretch out their legs.

Whilst Sulivan was getting these children aboard the boat about twenty Somalis came out of the bush waving spears and fire-locks, but a shot at their feet from Sulivan's rifle made them keep their distance.

The difficulty, as Sulivan had foreseen, was to get the boat out safely through the surf, and by this time it was nearly dark.

Twice her crew made an attempt and the boat was hurled back on to the beach. Sulivan then waited over a quarter of an hour for a lull in the weight of the surf, then he gave the word, and with the children stowed in the bottom of the boat, the breakers were successfully crossed, with only one heavy sea washing them from stem to stern.

On the 29th of October, another full dhow was chased ashore. This time the *Daphne's* boats were only able to retrieve one half dead male slave out of the one hundred and nineteen that were in the dhow.

On the 30th, a third dhow ran ashore to escape the cruiser. This time in attempting to come through the surf, having failed to cut off the escaping Arabs and negroes, the *Daphne's* boat was rolled over and over and everything washed off her.

The ship, which lay about half a mile off the beach, had no boat to go to her aid, as the other cutter was detached and out of sight along the coast, the whaler could just be seen boarding a dhow on the horizon. The gig was in the offing in chase of another dhow, and even the dinghy, was away hanging onto the stern of a newly captured slaver.

It was not until the gig answered her recall signal and came back that help could be given to the cutter.

A line was then floated through the surf to her and she was towed off by this means. Her crew arriving on board like drowned rats and utterly exhausted.

Three miles to the South of Brava a ledge of coral stretched out beyond the breakers for about twenty or thirty yards, behind this Captain Sulivan hid his two cutters in charge of sub-lieutenants Farr and Henn, where they could not be seen by dhows running up along the coast until they were abreast of them.

This ruse proved very successful, and by the 5th of November, the *Daphne* had captured fifteen dhows, and her deck was crowded with three hundred and twenty two rescued slaves.

On the previous day the *Star* had made her number on her way to Bombay.

Sulivan being senior officer ordered the *Star* to carry on his good work whilst he resumed his passage to Bombay. But with only ten tons of coal on board at a season of calms between monsoons, and with a mile an hour current to the Southward, he was forced to put into Zanzibar to coal.

The emancipated slaves were eventually landed at the Seychelles, Unfortunately, besides dysentery, and other diseases, small-pox broke out amongst the negroes and even infected some of the *Daphne's* crew.

Cruising on the Arabian Coast

During the sixties, the traffic along the Arabian coast from the Gulf of Aden round to the ports of the Persian Gulf was very heavy, but the cruisers had to board from fifty to sixty dhows before they came across one slaver.

Here dhows were taken to Aden for adjudication.

It was monotonous work for the most part, but there was one compensation, some of the white sandy beaches, especially around the Ras Madraka were splendid for hauling the seine, for fish of every description were very abundant.

On this coast the Great Ray (the giant Manta or Devil fish) can be seen in shaols, at times leaping out of the water and somersaulting in the air, at others swimming under the surface when they could be easily seen by the light green colour of the water above them.

At the end of the sixties, as many as five ships were sometimes stationed on this line of coast and the Somali shore to the South of it.

In a single month, that of May, 1869, thirteen dhows were destroyed and nine hundred and sixty seven negroes emancipated.

Two full ships, having four hundred and twenty slaves, were caught off Ras Assuad on the African coast.

Of Ras Haffun a dhow with two hundred and thirty six slaves was captured.

At Maculla three dhows were detained with fifty-seven slaves. Another slaver with seventy-nine slaves was taken between that port and Ras Madraka, and finally the *Dryad,* the sister ship of the *Daphne,* between Ras Madraka and Ras el Hed had captured three dhows, destroyed two in the surf and rescued one hundred and seventy five slaves.

Another sister ship of the *Daphne,* namely the *Nymphe* was cruising at the time on the North-West coast of Madagascar in order to stop the dhows, which were running slaves into Majunga.

In his evidence before the Select Committee, Admiral Sir Leopold Heath confessed himself puzzled as to how the enormous number of slaves were exported along the coast without being captured, for he reckoned that twenty thousand slaves had been exported from Zanzibar to the Persian Gulf and yet of four hundred dhows boarded during the season of 1868 only one thousand slaves were found, and he suggested that the East India squadron should be increased from seven to ten ships.

Toggle, Becket and Kid

It may be perhaps of interest to describe the procedure when a slave dhow with slaves on board was captured by one of our cruisers.

As soon as possible the slaves, men, women and children were fallen in on deck. After having been herded below in the dark they could hardly see in the glaring sunlight, and those who could stand were generally shaking all over with terror.

The first thing to do was to clean off the indescribable filth, and the hose was played on them until they satisfied a smart lieutenant's ideas of cleanliness. They were then numbered and listed under curious names of Toggle, for a man, Becket, for a woman, and plain Kid, for a child.

The bosun walked down their ranks singing out Toggle, Becket or Kid as the case might be. The ship's steward and his assistant next appeared, carrying a large tub, full of balls of dholl or mealies, each half-starved negro receiving a lump.

The stewards were followed by two seaman carrying buckets of water, a pannikin of which was next served out to each slave. Last of all came a seaman, attended by "Dusty" the steward's boy, carrying a kid of flour. The duty of this sailor was to sprinkle a handful of flour over the wolly head of each negro as soon as he had been fed and watered, the object being to prevent him from getting a second whack.

The Policeman of the Seas

It was during the last thirty years of the nineteenth century that the British Navy began to be recognised as the policeman of the seas.

Wherever there was trouble, whether it was a Pacific typhoon, a West Indian hurricane or that worst of all nature's cataclysms, an earthquake—whether it was a South American revolution, an outrage by pirates, a murder of missionaries by savages, or, possibly, just a stranded liner in distress, there the Royal Navy was to be found, its decks crowded with refugees, its cabin turned into sick berths and its holds stocked with comforts. When it was not saving lives it was kept busy in hunting the outlaw, whether he was a Chinese pirate, a New Hebridean black-birder, an Alaskan seal-poacher, a stealer of pearls from some tabooed atoll lagoon, a Red Sea hashish smuggler, a Persian Gulf gun-runner, or our friend, the Arab slave dhow.

Of all the lawless sea adventurers it is probable that the Arab gave the most trouble and offered the greatest resistance. Indeed it was recognised by our admirals that only a constant "showing of the flag" could keep the incorrigible Arab from his unlawful occasions.

The Affair at Kiunga

The coasts and seas of Arabia and the Dark Continent gave many a young lieutenant a chance to act on his own initiative, even to heading a punitive expedition into the unknown jungle or waterless desert.

At Kiunga, on the Somali coast, one of the *Daphne's* officers, sub-lieutenant Marcus McCausland was treacherously killed by natives.

On hearing what had happened, Sub-lieutenant Percy Hockin, who had been boat cruising in company with McCausland, promptly landed with his boat's crew and, in spite of the odds, both in men and weapons, being heavily against him, forced the murderers to give up the body; and not content with this he then sailed to the Southward until he came across the boats of the *Briton,* under Lieutenant Arthur Stevens Philpotts; with these he returned and, landing with this small reinforcement, proceeded to lay most of Kiunga flat with the ground.

The Zanzibar Protectorate

Zanzibar remained a thorn in the flesh of every Commander-in-chief on the East India Station, until Great Britain, in sheer desperation, declared a protectorate over it.

How often do we hear foreign politicians, and even our own, asserting that the British Empire has been gathered together by the sword and other unlawful means! but, in the case of Zanzibar and also that of Lagos, (and one could quote many other instances,) the reluctant British Cabinet was forced in the cause of humanity to take over and bring the miss-governed, backward races under the fold of the British flag.

This, in spite of the continued solicitations of the man on the spot, whether he was a missionary, a consul, or just a Naval officer, the home authorities, especially when a Liberal Government was in power, were extremely slow to do.

Though Zanzibar continued to be the centre of the Arab slave trade throughout the seventies and eighties, a protectorate was not declared until 1890.

In 1874, H.M.S. *London* was moored in the harbour as an earnest of our determination to suppress the slave traffic, as well as to act as a mother-ship for all the men-of-war boats and launches, which were needed to patrol the inner waters between Zanzibar, Pemba and the mainland.

It is interesting to note that a young lieutenant serving aboard the *London* afterwards became Sir Lloyd Wlliams Mathews, advisor through five troublous reigns to the Sultan of Zanzibar.

Brownrigg's Valiant Death

It might be thought that the command of a stationary guardship at Zanzibar would be a pretty dull job, but this was far from being the case.

On December the 3rd, 1881, Captain Charles James Brownrigg of the *London,* set off for Pemba with ten men in his steam pinnace with the intention of seeing how his cruising boats were getting along.

On his way to find these, he sighted a dhow full of slaves, which was flying French colours.

Wishing to verify her nationality, Brownrigg steamed up alongside, upon which, the dhow's crew fired a volley at point-blank range, killing or wounding more than half the occupants of the pinnace.

Taken by surprise, the boat's crew were unable to put up a fight; Brownrigg, alone, standing in the stern sheets with a clubbed rifle, fought like a Viking, as the Arabs swarmed on board the pinnace.

At last, after sustaining twenty wounds, he fell back shot through the heart. The Arabs then scrambled back aboard the dhow and cast the pinnace off.

Besides Brownrigg, three of her men were killed and three badly wounded, the other four having been driven overboard by the furious onslaught of the Arabs. These swimmers managed to regain the pinnace and ran her back to the *London.* The dhow was afterwards captured, but her slaves had been removed.

The Last Schooners in the Royal Navy.

In the autumn of 1880 the Admiralty bought two beautiful schooner-yachts, the *Undine* and *Harrier,* and after altering them internally and fitting them with a nine-pounder gun and one hundred and seventy rounds of ammunition, besides a machine-gun and armoury of rifles, pistols, swords, boarding-pikes and axes, sent them out to Zanzibar to see what they could do against the Arab slave dhow.

At this date there were still several men-of-war schooners in the Service. There were, for instance, five 120-tons schooners built at Sydney, N.S.W. at the beginning of the seventies to police the Solomons and New Hebrides and control the Kanaka labour traffic, which was closely akin to slavery.

These schooners, the *Alacrity, Beagle, Conflict, Renard* and *Sandfly*, were armed with one Armstrong gun and rocket-tube, and were manned by twenty-five bluejackets under a lieutenant and a sub-lieutenant.

One of their commanders, Lieutenant Thomas de Houghton of the *Beagle* wrote the following letter about them in volume II of the *Mariner's Mirror*:—

> "I commanded the *Beagle*, one of the five, from December 1877 to March 1881. They were good boats, but not built for sailing, and were very uncertain in stays.
>
> It may be of interest to know we carried sweeps and frequently used them, dodging amongst the coral reefs of the South Pacific.
>
> There were times when you must go round or go ashore, so when the helm was put down, we used to give way the lee sweep.
>
> We also carried boarding nettings as a defence against the natives.
>
> One ton of coal was all we carried and six weeks' water—no condenser, of course—so we had to "wood and water" just as they did one hundred years ago.
>
> It was a pleaant adventurous life and helped you to realise the old days".

I happen to have the log of the *Beagle* during 1882 and it confirms the pleasant life.

The *Sandfly* Tragedy

It also had its spice of danger, witness the death of the gallant young commander of the *Sandfly*, Lieutenant James St. Clair Bower.

On October the 13th, 1880, Bower, in his whale boat with five seamen, left the schooner anchored at Tezemboka in the Solomon Islands, in order to survey the East coast of Florida Island.

Bower had told his second-in-command, Sub-lieutenant Edward Eden Bradford that he would be back by the 17th.

When on the 20th there were no signs of the whale boat returning, Bradford sailed the *Sandfly* over to the East coast of Florida to look for the missing boat. Here she picked up one of the missing seamen, named Savage, who announced that the lieutenant and the rest of the whaler's crew had been massacred by natives.

It appeared that whilst the boat was hauled up on the beach at Nogu Island, Bower gave his crew permission to bathe.

Unfortunately the men were allowed to scatter away from the whale boat, then there came a sudden rush of natives who took possession of the boat and killed the men in the water.

Bower and Savage who happened to be some distance from the boat escaped by hiding in the bush.

The following morning the two men were discovered and chased, until Bower fell dead, being shot by one of his own rifes which had been found in the whale boat.

Savage, being a very active man, managed to outdistance his pursuers and finally swam across to an uninhabited islet. Here he contrived to make a raft on which he attempted to cross over to Florida, and he thought he was done for when he was overhauled by natives in their beautiful Solomon Island canoes. These, however, were a different tribe to those who had murdered Bower and they did not harm him.

Young Bradford immediately sailed to take vengeance on his commander's murderers.

At Raita Bay he landed with eight men, intending to burn the villages and the canoes of the offending tribe. However, he, in his turn, was ambushed in the bush and had one seaman killed and another wounded.

He managed to recover all the bodies except that of Lieutenant Bower. He then sailed for Sydney.

The corvette *Emerald*, Captain William Henry Maxwell, with Bradford on board, was sent back to execute justice, but though she succeeded in regaining the *Sandfly*'s whale boat at Baranago and destroyed their villages, she failed to capture the real culprits.

It was not until some time later that through the good offices of Bishop Selwyn the chief murderers were handed over to the *Renard*, Lieutenant Commander Walker S. King, and at once executed.

Years afterwards a white trader found the skull of poor Bower in a gamal house or Solomon Island temple. This skull was identified by its teeth.

The End of the Sydney Schooners

The *Beagle* had a romantic end, being sold to Messrs. W. F. Walker and Co., of Melbourne. She was employed under Captain C. W. Gallois taking passengers and cargo to Apollo Bay and Lorne. Thence she generally coasted to Waratah Bay returning to Melbourne loaded with lime. Then one day she was sold, to go, so it was rumoured, to the South Seas. She disappeared from Melbourne with a swindler aboard, who had defrauded a bank of ten thousand sovereigns; and nothing was heard of her for some years, then she reappeared on the West coast of South America.

The *Renard* was sold to private owners in 1893 and leaving the Solomons on the 21st of January, 1894, for Sydney was never heard of again.

The *Conflict*, after being sold about 1885, was wrecked on the Nasilai reef near the Gun Rock Passage, Fiji, and went to pieces. For many years her main mast served as a flag staff at Government House, Suva.

The Schooners *Lark* and *Dart*

The Sydney-built schooners were replaced first of all by two very much larger schooners.

The first of these was the *Lark* of 349·7 tons and the following dimensions:—

Length 101′ 6″, breadth 23′ 2½″, depth 11′ 3″.

This vessel, before being sent to Australia, had been tender to the *Egmont* at Malta under the name of *Cruiser*. She was replaced at Malta by a sailing sloop of 950 tons, which also took her name.

The *Dart* built at Barrow and purchased into the Navy in 1882 was a very large vessel for a two-master, having a displacement of 434·5 tons and these dimensions:—

Length 133′, breadth 25′ 2″, depth 13′ 5″.

Neither of these two schooners was a clipper, but their commands were much sought after, for their cruises amongst the islands of the South Seas were what Jack called "a picnic party".

Besides a little surveying, the chief work of their officers seems to have been pigeon shooting and curio collecting.

The Schooners *Sparrowhawk* and *Mermaid*

Whilst I am about it I may as well mention two other schooners which flew the white ensign in the eighties.

The first of these was the *Sparrowhawk*, which was originally a yacht, named the *Falcon*, built at Wyvenhoe in 1875 by John Harvey and Co. She was purchased by the Admiralty for surveying in 1877 and renamed the *Sparrowhawk*.

With a displacement of 86 tons her dimensions were:-

Length between perpendiculars 70′ 6″, breadth 16′ 4½″, depth 10′ 7″.

She was used for surveying on the Jamaica station, and in this work amongst coral reefs her draught of water was of importance. This was 9′ 2″ forward and 10′ 7″ aft.

The other vessel was a very old veteran in the coast-guard service, a fore-and-aft schooner of 165 tons, called the *Mermaid*, which was sold at the end of the eighties to British Columbia.

She was sailed out round the Horn to Vancouver, there she joined the British Columbian sealing trade and formed one of that adventurous fleet which had been immortalised in Kipling's "Rhyme of the Three Sealers" and Jack London's "Sea Wolf".

After an exciting career in what may be fairly described as a forbidden trade, for most of the best rookeries had been put out of bounds for Canadians by the Japanese and Americans, she ended up as the Sand Head light-ship at the mouth of the Fraser river.

The Schooner Yachts *Undine* and *Harrier* as Cruisers

Neither the Australian schooners nor the *Sparrowhawk* and *Mermaid* could be compared with the *Undine* and *Harrier*, which were two of the finest schooner yachts of their day, and both very fast.

The *Undine* was the larger of the two, a most beautiful schooner of 280 tons and the following dimensions:—

Length 106′ 8″, breadth 23′ 5″, depth 12′.

Her first name was, I believe, *Morna*. Her last owner was the Baroness Meyer de Rothschild, who renamed her *Tzarina* and lived aboard her for nearly a year.

The *Harrier* was built by Hansen andd Sons of Cowes in 1872 for Mr. John Pollock of Lismany, Ballinasloe, who made a number of long cruises in her.

Of 190 tons, she was 90′ 4″ in length between perpendiculars, with a breadth of 19′ 4″ and depth of 10′ 6″. She was bought by the Admiralty for the sum of £2,874. Both schooners were commissioned on January the 3rd, 1882. The *Undine*, by Lieutenant-Commander H. McA. Cutfield, and the *Harrier* by Lieutenant-Commander Scott J. B. Willcox. The latter was an officer of some weight, topping the scales at 19 stone. He commanded the *Harrier* for some years, and how he manoeuvred himself up and down the narrow yacht companion, was always a puzzle to his fellow officers.

Sailing in company on the 12th of March, 1882, the two schooners proceeded by the Suez Canal. The *Undine* being based at Zanzibar where she arrived on June the 15th, whilst the *Harrier*'s station was the Arabian coast. She started her first cruise on the day the *Undine* arrived at Zanzibar.

This experiment of using two fast schooner yachts against the slave dhows was soon given up, and on March the 20th, 1883, the *Undine* and the *Harrier* sailed for Australia in company with H.M.S. *Osprey**.

Harrier reached Fremantle on February the 11th, and *Undine* three days later. They were meant to replace the locally built schooners at the job of patrolling the Pacific Islands and watching over the Kanaka Labour Traffic.

These two fine-lined yachts were certainly better able to catch a fast black-birder than the bluff-bowed Sydney schooners.

On January the 14th, 1885, they were recommissioned, *Undine* by Lieutenant-Commander Charles H. Cross with a complement of thirty-four men, and the *Harrier* by Lieutenant-Commander F. O. Pike with a complement of twenty-eight men.

They remained in the Service until 1888, when the *Harrier* was sold to the London Missionary Society for £1,200 and employed in the New Guinea Missionary Service, whilst the *Undine* disappeared into oblivion amongst the host of South Sea Island schooners.

The *Harrier* was lost a few years later whilst making one of her customary passages from Port Moresby to Cooktown. She had got safely through the ticklish navigation of the outer barrier reef of the Lark Pass and was within twenty miles of her destination when she went hard aground on what was known as the F. reef, and became a total wreck. Luckily the Queensland Government schooner, *Governor Cairns*, happened to be in the neighbourhood and took off her captain and crew.

The Era of the Steam Pinnace

Before the year 1863 no man-of-war carried a boat propelled by a steam engine, but in that year some 42-foot launches were built for the Service. The Marine engineers, Messrs. Humphrey, being the first builders. But in this the French were at first ahead of us with their powerful steel towing launches.

With the help of Mr. G. S. White of Cowes and other builders of small craft, the Royal Navy was soon provided with a fleet of boats varying in length from 20′ to 56′, and in speed from 6½ to 15 knots.

These boats were built of wood,, not steel, like the French, and were supplied to every ship in the Service.

Up to 1878 the limit was a 42′ boat of 50 H.P. and a speed of 8½ knots.

Ten years later the Naval steam pinnace, 52′ long was capable of a speed of 15 knots, her H.P. being 134 and her steam pressure 120 pounds. She had compound engines, forced draught, and a locomotive, wet fire-box boiler. She was followed by one of 56′, 150 H.P. of the same speed. It was such a cruiser as this which, during the eighties, became the bug-bear of the Arab slaver.

These steam cutters and pinnaces, however, did not always have it their own way.

The Gallant Fight of Lieutenant Frederick Fogarty Fagen

In May 1887, Lieutenant F. F. Fagen of the *Turquoise*† was cruising in her pinnace (with a complement of five bluejackets, one Marine and an interpreter) off the island of Pemba.

At daybreak on May the 30th, whilst he was lying at anchor under the land, a dhow was sighted close to. Fagen thereupon sent the interpreter (rowed by two men) in the dinghy to find out what was her cargo.

As soon as he was near enough the interpreter hailed her. The reply was a volley of musketry. At which, Fagen promptly opened fire with the pinnace's nine-pounder.

---

* *Osprey*, composite sloop of 1,130 tons, H.P. 1,010, built at Sheerness in 1876, speed 11·5 knots, length 170′, beam 36′, draught of water 15′ 11″.

† *Turquoise* composite corvette of 2,120 tons displacement and 1,990 H.P. built at Hull in 1876, length 220′, beam 40′, armament 12 64-pounder, muzzle-loading, rifled guns, speed 12·3 knots.

The boldness of the Arab crew of this dhow, who were no more than thirteen in number, is scarcely believable. Instead of hauling down their red Arab flag, they steered the dhow alongside the pinnace and endeavoured to capture her by boarding.

In such a case the Irish Lieutenant was in his element.

"Stand to it, my lads", he yelled, and shooting the first two of the attackers with his revolver ran the third through with his sword. The fourth of these determined Arabs would certainly have put his spear through that excited officer had not the cutlass of an A.B., named Pearson, intervened.

The fight then became desperate. Three of the bluejackets were cut down, but Fagen, using his revolver in his left hand, his right arm being hors de combat with a bad wound, and one other man who was also wounded, succeeded in keeping the Arabs at bay.

Finally, the dhow, having lost nine of her men, gave up the struggle and ran for it. However the pinnace and dinghy hung on her heels as she skirted the edge of the surf.

At last a lucky rifle shot killed her helmsman; the dhow then ran ashore and fell over on her beam ends. Fagen, notwithstanding the fact that he only had two sound men besides the interpreter, at once ran the pinnace into the surf in order to rescue the unfortunate slaves in her hold.

With incredible difficulty, and in spite of a scattered rifle fire from the shore, 53 negroes were rescued. Twelve others being drowned in the surf.

As a result of this gallant action, Fagen received his promotion, but he had to be invalided home on account of his wounds. One bluejacket died and three others had to be sent to hospital.

The Death of Lieutenant Myles Cooper

A very similar affair with an equally heavy casualty list took place off Pemba a little over a year later.

This time the steam cutter of the *Griffon** under Lieutenant Myles. Harry Cooper came up with a dhow about 10 p.m. on October the 17th, 1888.

On the Lieutenant hailing the dhow to lower her sail and allow him to board her, a volley was fired which mortally wounded Cooper and severely wounded two out of his seven men.

The ship's corporal, John Bray, who was acting as the cutter's coxswain then took charge, and kept up a fire upon the dhow until both she and the cutter ran aground within a few yards of each other.

The Arabs, jumping overboard, succeeded in making their escape by swimming to the shore.

Bray managed to refloat the cutter and then towed the dhow off into deep water with her 79 slaves still aboard, but the wounded were in so serious a state, especially Lieutenant Cooper, that Bray, putting two men in charge of the anchored prize, raced back in the cutter to the *Griffon.*

Poor Cooper died before the ship was reached, but the other two, an armourer's mate and a sail-maker's mate, recovered.

For this resistance on the part of his subjects, the Sultan was made to pay 20,000 rupees, which sum was used to found the Cooper Institute for sailors at Zanzibar, the following year.

The Abyssinian Traffic

With the partitioning of the whole littoral of East Africa, from the Portuguese borders to beyond Cape Guardafui, amongst the great European powers the Arab slave trader found

* *Griffon*, composite gun vessel of 780 tons and 790 H.P. built by Laird at Birkenhead in 1876. length 13′ 2″, speed 10·87 knots, armament two five-inch 38 cwt breach loading rifled guns and two 64-pounder ditto.

himself obliged to seek further north for negroes—from the tribes of the Ethiopian plateau, and henceforward the Red Sea and the Gulf of Aden became the habitat of the slave dhow.

Most of the slaves were young men and girls from the half-starved tribes—the Chancallas, Wallamos and Garagays, living in the desert regions of Abyssinia. They were bought from their own parents with the usual "cum shaw" for the chief.

There was no cruelty about the transactions, and those chosen to go as slaves actually considered it an honour. It was, of course, a long march from the desert to the coast.

The first halt was made within the fortified stone walls of the Aragoubas, where the slaves were housed in specially-built underground rooms, whilst the caravan for the coast assembled.

In the caravan itself there was no need for neck yokes or fetters of any sort, though there was need of armed guards.

The head of the caravan had, of course, to pay toll to each tribe whose country he passed through, and he had to defend himself against marauders.

The route led through the country of the Danakils, the slave traders making for either Zeila, Eid, Roheita or Tajurrat.

At these ports the slaves were embarked for Arabia in the swiftest of the local dhows, known as "Zarougs".

Since the slaves were exchanging parched desert villages either for the comfortable and lazy life of the domestic Arab slave, with plenty to eat and little to fear, or else for the blacksmith's forge, the rope walk, the weaver's loom or the carpenter's bench, they were only too willing to be sold for their equivalent in printed cottons and copper leaf.

The nakods of the Zarougs were careful only to take a few slaves at a time, and these, mingled amongst their crew made it very difficult for the cruisers. Often the slaves were run across in genuine fishing boats, disguised as fishermen, and the profits of the dhows were still so attractive that the trade is not dead even at the present day, though it is probable that not more than a hundred or two of slaves for the Arabian market are run across the Straits of Bab-el-Mandeb and the Red Sea every year.

The last capture of a dhow with slaves on board was made by H.M.S. *Cornflower* in June 1922.

The Arab is as unchanging as the land in which he lives and there is a romance and fascination about his free, open-air life which many a British traveller and many a Naval officer has found hard to resist.

And now it is time to coil up and pipe down, in the confident hope that the present-day Naval officer has all the dash, swift initiative and leadership possessed by his fore-bears of the nineteenth century, whose exploits I have tried to describe. And if the bluejacket, with no longer any need to pull his arms out in propelling a heavy boat, or to race aloft and fist canvas in the life and death struggle of competitive sail drill, is less physically fit, I am sure that he has all his ancestors' courage and fortitude, as indeed he needs to have in these momentous days when the cutlass and the pike have given place to those horrors of modern science; the delay-action shell, the air bomb, the depth charge and poison gas.

The British Emir-el-Bahr is still Lord of the Sea although—

> "Beyond the path of the outmost sun through utter darkness hurled—
> Further than ever comet flared or vagrant star-dust swirled—
> Live such as fought and sailed and ruled and loved and made our world".

APPENDIX I

TRIAL OF SAILING BETWEEN *PANTALOON* AND *WATERWITCH*

December 24th—December 27th, 1835

Both brigs had just had a thorough refit at Plymouth. For some time past the *Pantaloon* had been used as an Admiral's packet, running between England and Sir William Parker, Commander-in-Chief of the channel fleet off Lisbon.

Lieutenant Cory had only lately taken her over from Lieutenant-Commander Dacres, who had had her for two years; and it was due to him that the *Pantaloon* was given an improved bow to stop her pitching so heavily when in a head sea.

Letter from Admiral Sir Robert Stopford to Sir William Symonds

37 Upper Harley Street,
1st January, 1836.

My dear Sir William,

Considering it desirable that the Admiralty should be in possession of all the information relative to the recent trial of sailing between *Pantaloon* and *Waterwitch*, I send you extracts from a letter, received today, from my son on board *Pantaloon*, dated 27th December, Lat. 47° 18′ N. Long. 14° 18′ W. (In the Atlantic) upon the accuracy of which I will venture to say you may perfectly rely.

The 25th of December was the first day of trial.

"We ran for seven hours off the wind, first on the quarter, then on the beam, going eight or nine knots, at the end of which *Waterwitch* was one and a half miles ahead. On the 26th we hauled to the wind together at nine o'clock, under double-reefed topsails and courses, jib, and reefed boom-mainsail-*Pantaloon* with main-topgallantsail.

We started ahead of her (*Waterwitch)* directly, and kept it up, when she shook a reef out of her boom-mainsail. Tacked at ten: she set her main-topgallantsail. Tacked at eleven, when she was one and a half miles to leeward. A little before twelve, out reef of our boom mainsail; both of us set four topgallantsail at once, and shook out second reefs, the *Waterwitch* being three miles to leeward at least.

The wind gradually fell after one, when our advantage was not so great. We bore up at a quarter past three, and were twenty-six minutes running down to her, going at the rate of seven and a half knots.

The day we sailed from Falmouth the wind was light and variable, and then she played with us; but give the *Pantaloon* a good steady breeze going to windward, and we will bang her till she can't see, to use an elegant expression. We gained on her today in stays very much, being round nearly a minute before her. We were a minute and a half in stays, and I think gained a cable's length on her then.

On the 27th we tried with the wind abeam, single reefed topsails and topgallantsails, and she beat us a little; but I don't think they sail her fairly.

She started just astern of us, and tried to jockey herself ahead; but finding we could jockey also, she made our signal to keep our course.

She than ran to leeward some way, and then luffed up under our lee bow,—making us luff up also to keep clear of her; and then shot ahead.

She has beat us today in three hours ahead, as much as we beat her yesterday in one hour in the wind's eye. When carrying studding-sails, she spreads three hundred yards of canvas more than we, and has a jib large enough for a frigate.

She cannot fight her guns properly, her ports being too small: and her own officers say that the work we go through in a year in the packet service would tear her to pieces.

Her courses have more drop than ours, owing to her bulwarks being much lower.

I leave people at home to judge which is the superior vessel althogether as a man-of-war. Give me the *Pantaloon*".

Log of *Waterwitch*

December 24

Hove shot-loosed sails. P.M. Light winds and fine, trimmed to light variable. 4 p.m. Black Head W. by S. ½ S. 5 45 p.m. in topgallantsails. 6 p.m. Lizard Light W. by N.

Falmouth Light N.E. by N. seven miles.

Pantaloon in company. 10.30 p.m. squally. Lizard Light N. by W. sleet. lowered topgallantsails and up mainsail. Hoisted a light for *Pantaloon.* 11 p.m. set topgallantsails and mainsail

12 midnight Lizard Light E. by N. *Pantaloon* W.S.W.

Friday December 25

Light breeze and cloudy.

3 a.m. trimmed—up mainsail.

7 a.m. St. Agnes Light N. by E. Made sail to topgallantsails. Wind variable *Pantaloon* in company. 9.20 trimmed, 10.30 a.m. trimmed, 11.8 a.m. *Pantaloon* made signal to trim ship.

Gained on her after trimming—smooth water, long swell. 3 p.m. Shortened sail to let *Pantaloon* come up. Judged to be nearly two miles astern.

8 p.m. fresh wind and cloudy, logging 8.4.

26 December

3.40 a.m. Trimmed. 8.45 a.m. *Pantaloon* passed to windward, made sail on larboard tack, double-reefed topsails, courses, jib and boom mainsail, *Pantaloon* had her main topgallant sail. *Waterwitch* fore reaching.

9.46 Tacked. Trimmed at 9.46 a.m.

Pantaloon gained continually by tacking.

10 a.m. going 6.6, a good headswell.

10.7 a.m. Set topgallantsail, carrying slack helm.

10.43 a.m. tacked 10.47 trimmed. *Pantaloon* gained 455 yards by tacking, our yards were hauled as quick as hers, but we had not strength to get tacks down and sheets aft quick enough.

11 a.m. Secured lee guns.

11.35 a.m. set fore topgallantsail, not so much sea. Found the want of an inner jib, ours being too large, bagged to leeward.

Noon fresh winds and cloudy. *Pantaloon* nearly hull down to windward. Between two and three we neared her, being able to see her white streak.

4.40 p.m. shortened sail, *Pantaloon* bearing S. by E. 3/4 E. nearly three miles. We were very dry all day.

Impossible to take heel of pendulum from the quick motion. *Pantaloon* bore up for us. hove to.

4.17 filled. 6 p.m. down jib, set staysail.

7 p.m. double-reefed boom mainsail.

27th December

Out second reef in topsails and set topgallantsails, courses and boom mainsail.

9 a.m. Both vessels under same sail. *Pantaloon* on our bow, got under her lee and dropped astern.

10.50 a.m. Going ahead of *Pantaloon.* She appeared to ship a great deal of water and heel over more than we (who) were very dry. Got anchor four feet further aft.

1.30 p.m. Shortened sail for *Pantaloon,* one and a quarter miles astern of us. Commander of *Pantaloon* came on board. 2.30 p.m. he left, fired a gun and parted company.

We had hammocks stowed in the nettings and lee guns squared.

Fresh breeze and cloudy.

Hours	Knots	Fathoms	Courses	Wind	Weather	Weather	Sea
26 Dec.							
9 a.m.			W. by S½S	S. by W.	Fresh	Rather Squally	Rough
9.40	4	2	W. by S.	S. by W.	”	Not Steady	Rough
10.00			S.E. by E½E	S. by W.	”	Steady	Rough
10.40	6	6	S.E. by E½E	S. by W.	”	Steady	Rough
11.00	2		W. by S.	S. by W.	”	Steady	Rough
11.30			W. by S.	S. by W.	”	Steady	Less sea
12.00	7		W. by S.	S. by W.	”	Not Steady	Rough
12.30			W. by N.	S. by W.	Not so Fresh	Variable	Rough
1.00	7	2	W. ½ N.	S. S. W.	Moderate	Variable	Rough
1.30			W. ½ N.	S. S. W.	Moderate	Variable	Rough
2.00	6	4	West	S. S. W.	Moderate	Steady	Rough
2.30			West	S. S. W.	Moderate	Steady	Rough
3.00	5	4	West	S. S. W.	Moderate	Steady	Rough

Direction of swell	What sails set	How carried helm	Bearing of *Pantaloon*	Distance by angle	Estimated Distance
From S.W. on weather bow.	Courses double-reefed	Amidships	S. W.	873 yrds.	3 cables
S.W.	Topsails Jib and boom Mainsail	Amidships	S. ½ W.	895 yrds.	—
S.W.	”	2 spokes a lee	—	1483 yrds.	½ mile
S.W.	Courses double-reefed topsails	Slack	S. by W.	1837 yrds.	—
S.W.	Main topgallant sail, jib, boom mainsail	Amidships	S.S.W.¼. W.	2427 yrds.	—
		Amidships	S. by W¼W.	2908 yrds.	1½ miles
S.W.	Courses Double-reefed Topsails	½ a spoke a-weather	S.3/4 W.	3411 yrds.	—
S.W.	Topgallant sails, jib and boom mainsail	S. ½ W. ”	4242 yrds. South	2 miles 5818 yrds.	—
S.W.	Courses Single-reefed topsails	”	—	—	—
S.W.	Topgallant sails jib and boom mainsail		S. ¼ E.	6876 trds.	3 miles
			”	”	—
S.W.			S. ¾ E.	5818 yrds.	nearly 3 miles

General Remarks by John Adams
Lieutenant commanding *Waterwitch*

8.45 a.m. *Pantaloon* passed to windward and made sail on a wind on larboard tack: she had her main topgallant sail set, we had not.

9.30 a.m. *Pantaloon* weathering. *Waterwitch* fore-reaching.

9.35 a.m. Made signal to tack; helm put down at 9.40.
Trimmed on starboard tack at 9.46 *Pantaloon* had her yards trimmed before us and gained by it considerably. We were not able to trim the yards quick enough.

10 a.m. Going 6.6 with a good head swell.

10.7 a.m. Set main topgallantsail, carrying a slack helm.

10.43 a.m. Tacked by signal; helm put down at 10.43. Trimmed at 10.49. *Pantaloon* gained between the time of putting helm down and being trimmed again 455 yards, owing to her being able to trim her sails so much quicker than us, but we had not strength enough to get the tacks down and sheets aft.

At 11 a.m. Stowed the hammocks amidships, and squared the lee guns. Helm amidships.

11.35 a.m. *Pantaloon* and us set fore topgallant sails. Not much sea. The whole of the day we felt the want of an inner jib, ours being so large, bagged us to leeward.

1.00 p.m. *Pantaloon* and us shook out our reef.
From 11 a.m. till 2 p.m. the *Pantaloon* was going bodily to windward, while we were forereaching. Wind getting lighter.

At 2 p.m. *Pantaloon* nearly hull down to windward. Between 2 and 3 p.m. we neared her, being able at 3 to see her white streak.

3.40 p.m. Shortened sail, *Pantaloon* then being S. ¼ E. nearly 3 miles. We were very dry the whole day—did not ship one drop of water. This day we had the hammocks stowed amidships on lower deck and the lee guns squared. Impossible to take the heel by pendulum from the quick motion.

John Adams, Lieutenant commanding
Waterwitch.

Hours	Knots	Fathoms	Courses	Winds	Weather Strength	Weather Variation	Inclination of pendulum
9.00	—	—	—	S. by W.	Strong	Steady	8°
9.30	—	—	—	S. by W.	"	Unsteady	8½°
10.00	6	4	W.S.W.	Variable	"	Variable	9°
10.30	—	—	W.S.W.	"	"	"	9°
11.00	7	—	E.S.E.	Sly.	Fresh	"	9°
11.30	7	—	E.S.E.	"	"	"	9°
12.00	8	—	W. by S.	S.S.W.	"	Unsteady	8½°
12.30	8	—	W. by S.	S.W. by S.	"	"	8½°
1.00	7	4	West.	S.W. by S.	Moderate	"	8°
1.30	7	4	West.	S.W. by S.	"	"	8°
2.00	6	—	West	S.W. by S.	"	"	7°
2.30	6	—	West	S.W. by S.	"	"	5°
3.00	3	4	W. ¼ N.	S.W. by S.	Light	"	4°
3.30	—	—	—	—	—	"	4°

Sea	Distance of Swell	Sail set	Helm how carried	Bearing of *Waterwitch*	Estimated Distance	Distance by angle
A head wind while on larboard tack	Westerly	Started under double-reefed topsails, courses, jib, single-reefed boom mainsail and main topgallant sail	2 spokes a weather	N.E. ½ N.	310 yds.	0.19
			"	N. 3/4 E.	938 yds.	0.24
			"	N. by W.	1504 yds.	0.31
			1 spoke a weather	N. by W.	1664 yds	0.34
			"	N. by E.	2401 yds.	0.52
			2 spokes a weather	N. N.E.	3673 yds	1.15
				N. by E½E.	4029 yds	1.23
				N. ½ E.	5204 yds	2.13
				North	6573 yds	6.41
				N. ¼ W.		
				N. ¼ W.		
				N. 3/4 W.		
				N. 3/4 W.		
				N. by W.		
				N. by W¼W.		

General Remarks by Nicholas Cory
Lieutenant commanding *Pantaloon*

Started a little before 9 a.m. under double-reefed topsails courses, jib, single-reefed boom mainsail and main topgallantsail. *Waterwitch* under double-reefed topsails, fore-topmast staysail and two reefs in her boom mainsail. At 9 *Waterwitch* down foretopmast staysail, set jib and whole boom mainsail.

At 9.50 answered signals to tack, tacked, one and a half minutes in stays. At 10.17 *Waterwitch* set her main topgallantsail. At 11 answered signal to tack, one and a half minutes in stays.

11.45 set fore-topgallantsail and out reef of boom mainsail. 11.50 *Waterwitch* set fore-topgallant sail.

At 1 out two reefs of topsails. At 1.5 *Waterwitch* did the same. At 1.30 *Waterwitch* too far to leeward to take a correct angle, supposed to be about three and a half miles.

At 2 supposed distance three and a half miles. At 2.30 wind more moderate—this half hour we have not increased the distance. At 3 less wind. *Waterwitch* appears to have neared us a little. At 3.30 *Waterwitch* shortened sail, distance about three miles on our lee beam. Bore up to close; the inclination of the pendulum could not be accurately ascertained, the motion of the brig being so quick.

It appears to me that the *Pantaloon* has a decided advantage over the *Waterwitch* close-hauled with a fresh breeze, but not so in light winds. I have remarked during this day's trial that the brig has been remarkably easy and dry, although going against a head sea.

Nicholas Cory, Lieutenant
Commanding *Pantaloon*

"My pet *Pantaloon*", as Admiral Sir William Parker called her, was given another antagonist in a sailing trial in 1836, this was the sixteen-gun brig *Scylla.*

The following quotation from a letter of the famous Admiral the Honourable Sir C. Paget shows how most of her opponents fared:—

"This morning . . . I made the signal for them both to weigh, with a fine breeze about North-West: and I attended in the *Emerald.*

I started them from the Breakwater to go round the Eddystone and back. *Pantaloon* had the lead about two or three cables' lengths. Wind abaft the beam, a little South-West swell, and with single-reefed topsails, courses, topgallantsails, royals, and foretopmast and topgallant studdingsails.

Pantaloon kept the lead, rounding the Eddystone four minutes and a half before *Scylla:* and, coming back on a wind, and having to make a couple of tacks, rounded the light-vessel forty-two minutes before her competitor".

APPENDIX II

New Armament and Peace Establishment For the British Navy, 1839.

Armament

First rates. 120 Guns *(Caledonia)*.

Where Carried	No. of Guns	Calibre	Weight	Length
Lower Deck	4	8 inch	65 cwt.	9 ft.
Lower Deck	28	32 prs.	56 cwt.	9 ft. 6 in.
Middle Deck	2	8 inch	65 cwt.	9 ft.
Middle Deck	32	32 prs.	50 cwt.	9 ft.
Main Deck	34	32 prs.	41 cwt.	8 ft.
Quarter Deck }	6	32 prs.	45 cwt.	8 ft. 6 in.
Forecastle }	14	32 prs.	17 cwt.	Carronades

Weight of each broadside 2028 lbs.

The ships in this class were:—

Caledonia, Britannia, Hibernia, Howe, Nelson, Neptune, Prince Regent, Royal George, Royal William, St. George, St. Vincent, Trafalgar, Waterloo.

110 Guns *(Royal Frederick)*.

Where Carried	No. of Guns	Calibre	Weight	Length
Lower Deck	6	8 inch	65 cwt.	9 ft.
Lower Deck	24	32 prs.	56 cwt.	9 ft. 6 in.
Middle Deck	4	8 inch	65 cwt.	9 ft.
Middle Deck	26	32 prs.	56 cwt.	9 ft. 6 in.
Main Deck	30	32 prs.	41 cwt.	8 ft.
Quarter Deck }	6	32 prs.	45 cwt.	8 ft. 6 in.
Forecastle }	14	32 prs.	25 cwt.	6 ft.

Weight of each broadside 1940 lbs.

The ships in this class were:—

Algiers, Royal Frederick, Royal Sovereign, Victoria.

104 Guns.

Where Carried	No. of Guns	Calibre	Weight	Length
Lower Deck	4	8 inch	65 cwt.	9 ft.
Lower Deck	24	32 prs.	56 cwt.	9 ft. 6 in.
Middle Deck	2	8 inch	65 cwt.	9 ft.
Middle Deck	28	32 prs.	48 cwt.	8 ft.
Main Deck	30	32 prs.	82 cwt.	6 ft. 6 in.
Quarter Deck }	6	32 prs.	45 cwt.	8 ft. 6 in.
Forecastle }	10	32 prs.	17 cwt.	Carronades

Weight of each broadside 1772 lbs.

The ships in this class were:—

Camperdown, Inpregnable, Princess Charlotte, Royal Adelaide, Queen Charlotte.

Second rates. 92 Guns *(Rodney).*

Where Carried	No. of Guns	Calibre	Weight	Length
Lower Deck	6	8 inch	65 cwt.	9 ft.
Lower Deck	26	32 prs.	56 cwt.	9 ft. 6 in.
Main Deck	4	8 inch	65 cwt.	9 ft.
Main Deck	30	32 prs.	56 cwt.	9 ft. 6 in.
Quarter Deck / Forecastle	26	32 prs.	41 cwt.	8 ft.

Weight of each broadside 1652 lbs.

The ships in this class were:—
London, Nile, Rodney.

84 Guns *(Asia).*

Where Carried	No. of Guns	Calibre	Weight	Length
Lower Deck	6	8 inch	65 cwt.	9 ft.
Lower Deck	24	32 prs.	56 cwt.	9 ft. 6 in.
Main Deck	2	8 inch	65 cwt.	9 ft.
Main Deck	30	32 prs.	48 cwt.	8 ft.
Quarter Deck / Forecastle	6	32 prs.	41 cwt.	8 ft.
	16	32 prs.	17 cwt.	Carronades

Weight of each broadside 1488 lbs.

The ships in this class were:—
Asia, Bombay, Calcutta, Canopus, Clarence, Formidable, Ganges, Monarch, Powerful, Thunderer, Vengeance.

80 Guns *(Superb).*

Where Carried	No. of Guns	Calibre	Weight	Length
Lower Deck	8	8 inch	65 cwt.	9 ft.
Lower Deck	20	32 prs.	56 cwt.	9 ft. 6 in.
Main Deck	4	8 inch	65 cwt.	9 ft.
Main Deck	24	32 prs.	50 cwt.	9 ft.
Quarter Deck / Forecastle	24	32 prs.	41 cwt.	8 ft.

Weight of each broadside 1496 lbs.

The ships in this class were:—
Collingwood, Goliah, Superb, Vanguard.

Third rates. 78 Guns *(Bellerophon).*

Where Carried	No. of Guns	Calibre	Weight	Length
Lower Deck	4	8 inch	65 cwt.	9 ft.
Lower Deck	26	32 prs.	56 cwt.	9 ft. 6 in.
Main Deck	2	8 inch	56 cwt.	9 ft.
Main Deck	30	32 prs.	45 cwt.	8 ft. 6 in.
Quarter Deck / Forecastle	6	32 prs.	41 cwt.	8 ft.
	10	32 prs.	17 cwt.	Carronades

Weight of each broadside 1356 lbs.

The ships in this class were:—
Achille, Bellerophon, Cambridge, Donegal, Foudroyant, Hindostan, Indus, Kent, Revenge.

72 Guns *(Edinburgh).*

Where Carried	No. of Guns	Calibre	Weight	Length
Lower Deck	4	8 inch	65 cwt.	9 ft.
Lower Deck	24	32 prs.	56 cwt.	9 ft.
Main Deck	28	32 prs.	41 cwt.	8 ft.
Quarter Deck }	4	32 prs.	41 cwt.	8 ft.
Forecastle }	12	32 prs.	17 cwt.	Carronades

Weight of each broadside 1224 lbs.

The ships in this class were:—
Agincourt, Ajax, Anson, Armada, Bellisle, Bellona, Benbow, Black Prince, Blenheim, Carnatic, Cornwallis, Defence, Devonshire, Edinburgh, Egmont, Hastings, Hawk, Hercules, Hogue, Illustrious, Imaum, Implacable, Invincible, Malabar, Medway, Melville, Minden, Minataur, Pitt, Pembroke, Redoutable, Russell, Stirling Castle, Sultan, Talavers, Tremendous, Wellesley, Wellington.

70 Guns *(Boscawen).*

Where Carried	No. of Guns	Calibre	Weight	Length
Lower Deck	4	8 inch	65 cwt.	9 ft.
Lower Deck	22	32 prs.	56 cwt.	9 ft. 6 in.
Main Deck	2	8 inch	65 cwt.	9 ft.
Main Deck	26	32 prs.	50 cwt.	9 ft.
Quarter Deck	16	32 prs.	39 cwt.	7 ft. 6 in.
Forecastle				

Weight of each broadside 1228 lbs.

The ships in this class were:—
Cumberland, Boscawen.

Fourth rates. 50 Guns *(Barham).*

Where Carried	No. of Guns	Calibre	Weight	Length
Main Deck	6	8 inch	65 cwt.	9 ft.
Main Deck	22	32 prs.	56 cwt.	9 ft. 6 in.
Quarter Deck }	22	32 prs.	45 cwt.	8 ft. 6 in.
Forecastle }				

Weight of each broadside 908 lbs.

The ships in this class were:—
Alfred, America, Barham, Conquestador, Cornwall, Dublin, Eagle, Gloucester, Vernon, Vindictive, Warspite.

50 Guns *(Portland).*

Where Carried	No. of Guns	Calibre	Weight	Length
Main Deck	4	8 inch	65 cwt.	8 ft.
Main Deck	26	32 prs.	50 cwt.	8 ft.
Quarter Deck }	4	32 prs.	50 cwt.	8 ft. 6 in.
Forecastle }	16	32 prs.	25 cwt.	6 ft.

Weight of each broadside 872 lbs.

The ships in this class were:—
Chichester, Java, Lancaster, Portland, President, Southampton, Winchester, Worcester.

Fifth rate. 44 Guns *(Madagascar).*

Where Carried	No. of Guns	Calibre	Weight	Length
Main Deck	2	8 inch	60 cwt.	8 ft. 10 in.
Main Deck	26	32 prs.	40 cwt.	7 ft. 6 in.*
Quarter Deck }	4	32 prs.	40 cwt.	7 ft. 6 in.*
Forecastle }	12	32 prs.	17 cwt.	Carronades

* *Congreve* or *Bloomfield.*

Weight of each broadside 740 lbs.

The ships in this class were:—

Africaine, Andromeda, Druid, Endymion, Eurotas, Forte, Forth, Horatio, Hotspur, Isis, Leda, Madagascar, Maeander, Nemesis, Seahorse, Stag.

Endymion to carry 24 32 prs. 40m cwt. on main deck, 14 32 prs. carronades on her quarter deck and forecastle.

42 Guns *(Resistance).*

Where Carried	No. of Guns	Calibre	Weight	Length
Main Deck	2	8 inch	50 cwt.	7 ft.
Main Deck	26	32 prs.	39 cwt.	7 ft. 6 in.*
Quarter Deck	4	32 prs.	39 cwt.	7 ft. 6 in.*
Forecastle	10	32 prs.	17 cwt.	Carronades

* *Bloomfield.*

Weight of each broadside 708 lbs.

The ships in this class were:—

Aeolus, Amazon, Amphitrite, Blonde, Boadicea, Briton, Cerberus, Circe, Clyde, Crescent, Daedalus, Diana, Fisgard, Fox, Hamadryad, Hebe, Latona, Laurel, Leonidas, Melampus, Mercury, Mermaid, Minerva, Naiad, Nereus, Penelope, Proserpine, Resistance, Seringapatem, Sirius, Tenedos, Thalia, Thames, Thisbe, Trincomalee, Undaunted, Unicorn, Venus.

38 Guns *(Belvidera).*

Where Carried	No. of Guns	Calibre	Weight	Length
Main Deck	2	8 inch	50 cwt.	7 ft.
Main Deck	24	32 prs.	39 cwt.	7 ft. 6 in.*
Quarter Deck }	6	32 prs.	39 cwt.	7 ft. 6 in.*
Forecastle }	8	32 prs.	17 cwt.	Carronades

* *Bloomfield.*

Weight of each broadside 644 lbs.

The ships in this class were:—

Belvidera, Brilliant, Havannah, Owen Glendower.

36 Guns *(Pique).*

Where Carried	No. of Guns	Calibre	Weight	Length
Main Deck	4	8 inch	60 cwt.	8 ft. 10 in.
Main Deck	18	32 prs.	56 cwt.	9 ft. 6 in.
Quarter Deck } Forecastle }	14	32 prs.	41 cwt.	8 ft.

Weight of each broadside 648 lbs.

In the *Amphion, Castor,* and *Inconstant* 32 pre25 cwt. 6 foot guns are to be substituted for those of 41 cwt.

The ships in this class were:—

Active, Amphion, Cambrian, Castor, Chesapeake, Constance, Flora, Inconstant, Pique, Sybelle.

Sixth Rate. First Class. 26 Guns *(Vestal).*

Where Carried	No. of Guns	Calibre	Weight	Length
Main Deck	2	8 inch	50 cwt.	7 ft.
Main Deck	16	32 prs.	40 cwt.	7 ft. 6 in.*
Quarter Deck / Forecastle	2	32 prs.	40 cwt.	7 ft. 6 in.*
	6	32 prs.	25 cwt.	6 ft.

* *Congreve* or *Bloomfield.*

Weight of each broadside 452 lbs.

The ships in this class were:—
Carysfort, Cleopatra, Creole, Iris, Juno, Spartan, Vestal.

24 Guns *(Curacoa).*

No. of Guns	Calibre	Weight	Length
24	32 prs.	40 cwt.	7 ft. 6 in.

Congreve or *Bloomfield.*

Weight of each broadside 384 lbs.

The ships in this class were:—
Aigle, Curacoa, Magicienne, Tribune.

20 Guns *(Calypso).*

No. of Guns	Calibre	Weight	Length
20	32 prs.	40 cwt.	7 ft. 6 in.

Congreve or *Bloomfield.*

Weight of each broadside 320 lbs.

Second Class. 26 Guns *(Andromache).*

Where Carried	No. of Guns	Calibre	Weight	Length
Main Deck	2	68 prs.	36 cwt.	5 ft. 4 in. Carronades
Main Deck	18	32 prs.	25 cwt.	6 ft.
Quarter Deck / Forecastle	6	32 prs.	25 cwt.	6 ft.

Weight of each broadside 452 lbs.

The guns in this class all on Hardy's Compressor Carriages, and the fore-most and after-most guns on each side of the quarter deck and forecastle fitted for transporting.

The ships in this class were:—
Actaeon, Andromache, Calliope, Conway, Imogene.

26 Guns *(Alligator).*

Where Carried	No. of Guns	Calibre	Weight	Length
Main Deck	2	32 prs.	52 cwt.	6 ft.
Main Deck	18	32 prs.	17 cwt.	Carronades
Quarter Deck / Forecastle	6	18 prs.	15 cwt.	5 ft. 6 in.

Weight of each broadside 376 lbs.

The guns all on Hardy's Compressor Carriages; fore-most and after-most guns on each side of the quarter-deck and forecastle fitted for transporting.

The ships in this class were:—
Alligator, Crocodile, Herald, North Star, Samarang, Talbot, Tyne, Volage.

18 Guns *(Daphne).*

No. of Guns	Calibre	Weight	Length
18	32 prs.	40 cwt.	7 ft. 6 in.

Congreve or *Bloomfield.*

Weight of each broadside 288 lbs.

The ships in this class were:—
Daphne, Dido.

SLOOPS

20 gun ship-sloops. *(Nimrod).*

No. of Guns	Calibre	Weight	Length
2	32 prs.	25 cwt.	6 ft. on
18	32 prs.	17 cwt.	transporting carriages carronades

Weight of each broadside 320 lbs.

The ships in this class were:—
Nimrod, Pearl and *Tweed.*

18 gun ship-sloops. *(Modeste).*

18	32 prs.	25 cwt.	6 ft.

Foremost and after most guns on transporting carriages.

Weight of each broadside 288 lbs.

The ships in this class were:—
Modeste, Rover.

18 gun ship-sloops. *(Harrier).*

No. of Guns	Calibre	Weight	Length
2	32 prs.	25 cwt.	6 ft. on
16	32 prs.	17 cwt.	transporting carriages carronades

Weight of each broadside 288 lbs.

The ships in this class were:—
Champion, Comus, Electra, Favourite, Fly, Harrier, Hazzard, Hyacinth, Larne, Orestes, Pylades, Racehorse, Satellite, Scout, Wolf.

16 gun ship-sloops. *(Columbine).*

No. of Guns	Calibre	Weight	Length
4	32 prs.	25 cwt.	6 ft. on
12	32 prs.	17 cwt.	transporting carriages carronades

Weight of each broadside 256 lbs.

The ships in this class were:—
Acorn, Albatross, Arab, Bittern, Columbine, Elk, Fantome, Grecian, Heron, Liberty, Persian, Pilot, Squirrel.

16 gun ship-sloops. *(Childers).*

No. of Guns	Calibre	Weight	Length
2	32 prs.	25 cwt.	5 ft. 4 in. on
14	32 prs.	17 cwt.	transporting carriages carronades

Weight of each broadside 256 lbs.

The ships in this class were:—
Childers, Clio, Cruizer, Harlequin, Jaseur, Lily, Pelican, Pelorus, Racer, Raleigh, Ringdove, Rose, Sappho, Scylla, Serpent, Snake, Sparrowhawk, Trinculo, Victor, Wanderer, Wasp, Wolverine, Zebra.

10 gun brigs. *(Algerine).*

No. of Guns	Calibre	Weight	Length
2	18 prs.	20 cwt.	6 ft.
8	18 prs.	10 cwt.	carronades

Weight of each broadside 90 lbs.

The ships in this class were:—
Algerine, Britomart, Camelion, Curlew, Espoir, Harpy, Leveret, Musquito, Nantilus, Pantaloon, Partridge, Rapid, Rolla, Saracen, Savage, Sealark, Scorpion, Waterwitch, Weazle, Wizard.

3 gun brigantines. *(Dolphin).*

No. of Guns	Calibre	Weight	Length
1	32 prs.	40 cwt.	7 ft. 6 in.
2	32 prs.	32 cwt.	

Weight of each broadside 64 lbs.

The ships in this class were:—
Bonetta, Dart, Dolphin, Spy.

3 gun brigantines. *(Brisk).*
(cut down 10-gun brigs).

No. of Guns	Calibre	Weight	Length
1	32 prs.	40 cwt.	7 ft. 6 in.
2	24 prs.	10 cwt.	carronades

Weight of each broadside 56 lbs.

The ships in this class were:—
Brisk, Buzzard, Charybdis, Forester, Griffon, Lynx, Termagant.

Carronades in all ships mounted on Sir Thomas Hardy's
Compressor Carriages

Peace Establishment

Ship	1834			1839		
First Rates						
Caledonia	1834	790	(58 boys)	1839	820	(66 boys)
Royal Frederick	1834	750	(58 boys)	1839	758	(66 boys)
Princess Charlotte	1834	670	(58 boys)	1839	725	(66 boys)
Second Rate						
Rodney	1834	720	(52 boys)	1839	695	(60 boys)
Asia and *Vanguard*	1834	630	(52 boys)	1839	645	(60 boys)
Third Rate						
Revenge	1834	570	(45 boys)	1839	590	(53 boys)
Edinburgh	1834	520	(45 boys)	1839	540	(53 boys)
Boscawen	1834	520	(45 boys)	1839	570	(53 boys)
Fourth Rate						
Barham	1834	420	(41 boys)	1839	445	(47 boys)
Portland	1834	380	(41 boys)	1839	395	(47 boys)
Fifth Rate						
Madagascar	1834	275	(34 boys)	1839	290	(39 boys)
Resistance	1834	275	(34 boys)	1839	280	(39 boys)
Belvidera	1834	260	(34 boys)	1839	265	(39 boys)
Pique				1839	305	(39 boys)
Sixth Rate						
Carysfort	1834	190	(26 boys)	1839	205	(33 boys)
Curacoa	1834	175	(26 boys)	1839	210	(33 boys)
Calypso (building)				1839	185	(33 boys)
Andromache	1834	160	(26 boys)	1839	165	(33 boys)
Dido and *Daphne*				1839	160	(33 boys)
SLOOPS						
Nimrod	1834	120	(22 boys)	1839	130	(24 boys)
Modeste				1839	125	(24 boys)
Rover				1839	125	(24 boys)
Harrier	1834	110	(22 boys)	1839	120	(24 boys)
Columbine	1834	110	(22 boys)	1839	115	(24 boys)
GUN BRIGS AND BRIGANTINES						
Algerine	1834	50	(9 boys)	1839	60	(10 boys)
Brisk	1834	50	(9 boys)	1839	55	(10 boys)
SCHOONERS AND CUTTERS						
	1834	40	(8 boys)	1839	40	(8 boys)

APPENDIX III

NEW ARMAMENT, SMALL CLASS. 1847

At the end of 1847 there was a further change in the Armament, and the number of guns in the brigs were reduced as follows:—

16 gun brig-sloops

2 32-pr. 39 cwt. 7 ft. 6 in. and 14 32-pr. 25 cwt. 6 ft.

Ships of this class were:—

Atlanta, Camilla, Frolic, Helena, Siren and *Zebra* (Complement 130 men).

14 gun brig-sloops

12 32-pr. 25 cwt. 6 ft. and 2 32-pr. 39 cwt. 7 ft. 6 in.

Ships of this class were:—

Champion, Comus, Electra, Favourite, Hazard, Hyacinth, Larn, Orestes, Racehorse, Rose, Satellite, Scout and Wolf (Complement 130 men).

12 gun brig-sloops

10 32-pr. 25 cwt. 6 ft. and 2 32-pr. 39 cwt. 7 ft. 6 in.

Ships of this class were:—

Acorn, Albatross, Arab, Bittern, Columbine, Contest, Daring, Despatch, Elk, Espiegle, Fantome, Flying Fish, Goshawk, Grecian, Heron, Kangaroo, Kingfisher, Mariner, Martin, Mutine, Persian, Pilot, Recruit (Complement 130 men).

12 gun brig-sloops

2 32-pr. 33 cwt. 6 ft. 6 in. and 10 32-pr. 25 cwt. 6 ft.

Ships of this class were:—

Childers, Cruizer, Harlequin, Liberty, Lily, Pelican, Racer, Ringdove, Sappho, Serpent, Snake, Sparrowhawk, Squirrel, Wasp and *Wolverine* (Complement 130 men).

8 gun brig-sloops

2 32-pr. 33 cwt. 6 ft. 6 in. and 6 32-pr. 25 cwt. 6 ft.

Ships of this class were:—

Cygnet, Ferret, Heroine, Hound and *Philomel* (Complement 80 men).

8 gun brig-sloops

2 32-pr. 32 cwt. 6 ft. 6 in. and 6 32-pr. Carronades.

Ships of this class were:—

Alert, Linnet, Ranger, Star (Complement 80 men).

8 gun brig-sloops

2 11-pr. 20 cwt. 6 ft. and 6 18-pr. 15 cwt. 6 ft. 6 in.

Ships of this class were:—

Britomart, Pantaloon, Rapid, Sealark and *Waterwitch* (Complement 80 men).

6 gun brigs

2 32-pr. 32 cwt. 6 ft. 6 in. and 4 18-pr. 10 cwt. carronades.

Ships of this class were:—
Chamelion, Curlew, Espoir, Nantilus, Rolla, Royalist, Saracen, Savage, Scorpion and *Wizard* (Complement 65 men).

3 gun brigantines

1 32-pr. 39 cwt. 7 ft. 6 in. and 2 32-pr. 22 cwt. 6 ft. 6 in.

Ships of this class were:—
Bonetta, Dart, Dolphin and *Spy* (Complement 60 men).

3 gun brigantines

1 32-pr. 39 cwt. 7 ft. 6 in. and 2 24-pr. carronades

Ships of this class were:—
Griffon and *Lynx* (Complement 60 men).

APPENDIX IV

SPAR DIMENSIONS
of the Gun Brig Classes

Masts and Yards	*Cruizer* 18 guns			*Snake* Class			*Grecian* Class			*Cygnet* Class		
	Length ft.	in.	Diam. in.	Length ft.	in.	Diam. in.	Length ft.	in.	Diam. in.	Length ft.	in.	Diam. in.
Mainmast from deck to lower side of trestle-trees	44	4	23	46	3	—	47	6	24	42	7	21
Head	12	0	—	12	0	—	12	0	—	11	0	—
Main-topmast (including head)	41	0	12½	42	6	14	44	6	14	41	0	12½
Head	5	6	—	5	9	—	6	0	—	5	6	—
Main-topgallantmast from lower side of fid-hole to hounds.	19	6	7½	20	0	8	21	0	8	19	6	7½
Pole	13	0	—	13	6	—	14	0	—	13	0	—
Mainyard (including yardarms)	55	0	13	58	0	13½	61	0	14½	55	0	13
Each yardarm	2	4	—	2	5	—	2	7	—	2	4	—
Main-topsail yard (whole length)	41	0	9	43	0	9½	45	0	10	41	0	9
Each yardarm	3	5	—	3	7	—	3	9	—	3	5	—
Main-topgallantyard (whole length)	27	0	6½	28	6	7	29	6	7½	27	0	6½
Each yardarm	1	2	—	1	2	—	1	3	—	1	2	—
Main-royal yard (whole length)	20	6	4	21	0	4½	22	0	—	20	6	4
Each yardarm		10	—		10	—		11	—		10	—
Foremast from deck to lower side of trestle trees	38	3	22	41	9	22	43	6	22½	39	6	19
Head	11	0	—	11	0	—	11	0	—	10	0	—
Fore-topmast (including head)	41	0	12½	39	6	14	39	6	14	36	0	12½
Head	5	6	—	5	4	—	5	4	—	4	10	—
Fore-topgallantmast from lower side of fid-hole to hounds	19	6	7½	18	6	7	18	6	7	17	0	6½
Pole	13	0	—	12	6	—	12	6	—	12	0	—
Fore-yard (whole length)	55	0	13	52	6	12½	52	6	12½	47	6	11½
Each yardarm	2	4	—	2	3	—	2	3	—	2	0	—
Fore-topsail-yard (whole length)	41	0	9	39	0	8½	39	0	8½	36	0	8
Each yardarm	3	5	—	3	3	—	3	3	—	3	0	—
Fore-topgallant-mast (whole length)	27	0	6½	26	0	6½	26	0	6½	24	0	6
Each yardarm	1	2	—	1	1	—	1	1	—	1	1	—
Fore-royal-yard (whole length)	20	6	4	19	6	4	19	6	4	18	0	3½
Each yardarm		10	—		10	—	19	10	—	18	9	—
Gaff	37	0	8½	37	0	8½	39	0	8½	34	0	8
Mainboom	57	0	13½	57	0	13½	59	0	13½	51	0	12
Bowsprit exclusive of housing	27	6	22	27	6	22	29	0	22½	23	0	18
Jib-boom	30	0	9½	30	0	9½	33	0	10½	28	0	9
Housing	—		—	15	4	—	14	9	—	13	1	—

APPENDIX IV

SPAR DIMENSIONS
of the Gun Brig Classes

Siren Class			Experimental Brigs 12-guns			*Fair Rosamond*			*Pantaloon*		*Waterwitch*	
Length ft.	in.	Diam. in.	Length ft.	in.	Diam. in.		Length ft.	in.	Length ft.	in.	Length ft.	in.
51	10	26	71	3	23		52	0	47	0	42	0
13	0	—	—		—		7	9	10	9	10	9
46	6	14½	42	6	14		32	3	35	6	35	6
6	3	—	—		—		3	6	5	0	6	0
21	6	8½	20	0	8		10	9	19	3	20	0
14	6	—	13	6	—		7	0	13	9	12	6
64	0	15½	58	0	13½		43	0	50	0	51	6
2	8	—	—		—		—		—		—	
47	0	10½	43	0	9½		28	0	41	0	44	0
3	11	—	—		—		—		—		—	
31	0	7½	28	6	7		18	9	27	6	27	0
1	4	—	—		—		—		—		—	
23	0	4½	—		—		—		19	6	19	0
	11	—	—		—		—		—		—	
47	8½	24	65	4	22		43	0	43	0	38	0
12	0	—	—		—		7	9	10	3	10	0
41	0	14½	39	6	14		26	9	36	9	35	0
5	6	—	—		—		4	9	5	3	5	9
19	6	7½	18	6	7		14	0	19	3	20	0
13	0	—	12	6	—		11	6	13	0	12	6
55	0	13	52	6	—		56	0	50	0	51	3
2	4	—	—		12½		—		—		—	
41	0	9	39	0	8½		40	6	41	0	42	0
3	5	—	—		—		—		—		—	
27	0	6½	26	0	6½		25	6	27	0	26	6
1	2	—	—		—				—		—	
20	6	4	19	6	4		19	0	19	0	19	0
20	10	—	—		—		25	0	35	0	38	0
39	0	8½	37	0	8½		56	0	50	0	51	0
59	0	13½	57	9	13½		17	6	28	0	27	9
31	0	24	27	6	22		26	0	28	0	30	9
34	6	11	30	0	9½		9	6	11	0	11	0
14	5	—	15	4	—	Flying jibboom	26	3	28	0	30	6

BIBLIOGRAPHY

Acton—Prize Causes.
Admiralty Reports—(Admiralty Library).
African Institution Reports.
Aimes—History of Slavery in Cuba.
Bandinel—Some Account of the Trade in Slaves from Africa (1842).
Bevan, A. Beckman and Wolryche-Whitmore, H.B.—A Sailor of King George (The Journals of Captain Frederick Hoffman, R.N.).
Bradlee, F. B.—Piracy in the West Indies.
Brenton, Captain Edward Pilham—Naval History of Great Britain 1783-1836.
Briggs, Sir John H.—Naval Administration 1827-1892.
Buxton, Sir Thomas Fowell—The African Slave Trade and its Remedy.
Canot, Theodore—Memoirs of a Slave Trader.
Cave—A few words on Slavery and the Slave Trade (1849).
Chapelle, Howard Irving—The Baltimore Clipper.
Clarkston, Thomas—History of the Abolition of the Slave Trade.
Clowes, Sir W. Laird—The Royal Navy.
Colomb, Admiral P. H.—Slave Catching in the Indian Ocean.—Memoirs of Sir Astley Cooper Key.
Cooper Key, Astley—Recovery of H.M.S. *Gorgon.*
Crueze, A. F. B.—Treatise on Naval Architecture.
Cupples, George—The Greenhand.
Devereux, W. Cope—A Cruise in the *Gorgon.*
Dow, G. F.—Slave Ships and Slaving. (Marine Research Society). Mass. U.S.A.
Drake, Captain Richard—Revelations of a Slave Smuggler 1807-1857 (New York 1860).
Edye, John—Calculations relating to the Equipment, Displacement, etc., of Ships and Vessels of War (1832).
Eliot, Sir Charles—The East African Protectorate.
Falconbridge, Alexander—Account of the Slave Trade on the Coast of Africa (London 1788).
Ferryman, Mockler—British West Africa.
Fincham, John—A History of Naval Architecture.
Fitzgerald, Admiral Penrose—Memories of the Sea.
Forbes, Lieutenant F. E.—Six Months Service in the African Blockade.
Fremantle, Admiral Sir Edmund R.—The Navy as I have known it.
Gates, W. G.—Ships of the British Navy
Gilly, William, O. S.—Shipwrecks of the Royal Navy.
Hall, Captain Basil,—Voyages and Travels.
—The Midshipman.
Hay, Admiral Sir J. C. Dalrymple—Leaves from my Log books.
Huntley, Sir Henry,—Seven Years Service on the Slave Coast (2 Vol.).
James, William—The Naval History of Great Britain.
Kennedy, Admiral Sir W. R.—Hurrah for the Life of a Sailor.
Keppel, Admiral Sir Henry—A Sailor's Life under Four Sovereigns.
Leardet, Captain F.—Professional; Recollections on Seamanship.
Leonard, Peter—Voyage to Western Africa.
Lever, Darcy—Young Sea Officers Sheet Anchor (1835 ed.).
Livingstone, David—Missionary Travels in South Africa.
Low, C. R.—History of the Indian Navy (2 Vol.).
Maclay, Edgar Stanton—A History of American Privateers.
Mariner's Mirror, The (The Journal of the Society for Nautical Research).

Marshall, Lieutenant John, R.N.—Royal Naval Biography.
Mathieson, W. L.—Great Britain and the Slave Trade.
Mends, B. S.—Admiral Sir W. R. Mends, G.C.B.
Montresor, Commodore F. B.—Leaves from *Memorie's* Log Book.
Moresby, Admiral John—Two Admirals.
Nautical Magazine, 1832 on.
Naval and Military Magazine (4 Vol.).
Naval Sketch Book (2 vol. 1826).
Naval Sketch Book (2 vol. 1835).
Navy Records Society Letters of Lord Barham (2 Vol.).
Navy Records Society Letters of Lord St. Vincent (3 Vol.).
Navy Records Society The Spencer Papers (4 Vol.).
Noble, Sam—'Tween decks in the Seventies.
O'Byrne, William—Naval Biography.
Otway, Sir Arthur—Autobiography and Journals of Admiral Lord Clarence Paget.
Ouseley, W. G.—Notes on the Slave Trade, 1850.
Parliamentary Papers.
Robinson, Rear-Admiral Hercules—Sea Drift.
Robinson, Commander C. N.—The British Fleet.
Scott, Michael—Tom Cringle's Log.
—Cruise of the *Midge*.
Select Committee Reports.
Sharpe, James A.—Memoirs of Rear-Admiral Sir William Symonds.
Southey, Captain, R. N.—Chronological History of the West Indies.
Sulivan, Captain G. L.—Dhow Chasing in Zanzibar Waters.
Turnbull, David—Cuba with notices of Porto Rico and the Slave Trade (1840).
United Service Journal (1829 onwards).
Walsh, Rev. Robert—Notices of Brazil (1830).
Williams, Gomer—The Liverpool Privateers.
Yule—The African Squadron vindicated.